SOVIET POLICY TOWARD THE MIDDLE EAST SINCE 1970

Third Edition

Robert O. Freedman

PRAEGER

PRAEGER SPECIAL STUDIES • PRAEGER SCIENTIFIC

Library of Congress Cataloging in Publication Data

Freedman, Robert Owen.
    Soviet policy toward the Middle East since 1970.

    Bibliography: p.
    Includes index.
    1. Near East—Foreign relations—Soviet Union.
2. Soviet Union—Foreign relations—Near East.
I. Title
DS63.2.S55F73 1982   327.47056   82-9014
ISBN 0-03-061362-0   AACR2
ISBN 0-03-061361-2 (pbk.)

To My Mother and
the Memory of My Father

Published in 1982 by Praeger Publishers
CBS Educational and Professional Publishing
Division of CBS Inc.
521 Fifth Avenue, New York, New York 10175 U.S.A.

© 1982 , 1978 ,1975 Praeger Publishers

23456789 052 987654321
Printed in the United States of America

PREFACE
To the First Edition

The four-year period between the death of Egyptian President Gamal Nasser and the sudden resignation of U.S. President Richard Nixon witnessed a number of major upheavals and changes in the always volatile Middle East. The Arab-Israeli conflict again erupted into full-scale war in October 1973, bringing the United States and the Soviet Union to the brink of nuclear confrontation. The war also brought on a five-month oil embargo against the United States and a quadrupling of oil prices. In addition, the period witnessed the failure of a Communist-supported coup d'etat in the Sudan and a major rearrangement of Middle Eastern alliances. Egypt, under its new President Anwar Sadat, moved from a position of hostility toward oil-rich Saudi Arabia to an alignment with it, while simultaneously moving from an alliance with the Soviet Union to a more neutral position between the superpowers following Sadat's expulsion of the Soviet military forces from their Egyptian bases in July 1972. Indeed, by the time of Nixon's resignation it appeared that Egypt was moving toward the United States—despite all the military aid given by the Soviet Union during the October war. Soviet policy makers struggled to deal with these developments. It will be the purpose of this book to demonstrate how the Soviet leadership sought to cope with Middle Eastern developments that it not only had not planned but also found most difficult to control.

A number of scholars and government officials were kind enough to comment on this manuscript at various stages of its preparation. Special thanks go to Professors Aaron Klieman of Tel-Aviv University, Abdul Said of American University, Melvin Croan of the University of Wisconsin-Madison, and Teresa Rakowska-Harmstone of Carleton University, as well as to David Albright of *Problems of Communism* and Norman Anderson of the State Department's Egyptian desk, whose criticisms helped improve the manuscript. In addition, I would like to thank the other members of the State Department's Near East/South Asia section and the diplomats representing Egypt, Jordan, and Israel who were kind enough to grant me interviews during my research. Finally, I would like to thank the large number of American, Israeli, Arab, and Soviet scholars with whom I had long discussions about the Middle East and my students at Marquette University from whom I learned so much. Needless to say, while I am indebted to all these individuals for their assistance, the views in this book are my own and I bear full responsibility for any errors.

I received research support for this study from Marquette University and from the National Endowment for the Humanities. This support enabled me to travel to the Middle East and to the Soviet Union. I would like to thank the personnel of the Zionist Archives in Jerusalem and the library of Radio Liberty in New York who afforded me every courtesy during my research. I would also like to offer my thanks to Karen Scibilia, who helped me maintain my files on the Middle East, Sandy Feuerabend, who typed the manuscript, and special thanks to Russ Eisenberg for his enthusiastic encouragement.

A final word of thanks to my wife, Sharon, without whose support this book never could have been written.

Portions of this study initially appeared in articles that I wrote for *Problems of Communism* and the *Naval War College Review*. I gratefully acknowledge permission to reprint the material.

PREFACE
To the Second Edition

In the period since the completion of the first edition of this book in November 1974, the drama of Middle Eastern politics has continued to unfold rapidly. A second disengagement agreement (Sinai II) was signed between Egypt and Israel, a bitter civil war erupted in Lebanon that ultimately precipitated a Syrian invasion of that country, and Egyptian President Anwar Sadat made a dramatic visit to Jerusalem to try to convince the Israelis to accept his version of a peace settlement. Throughout this period the Soviet leaders have encountered considerable difficulty as they have sought to pursue policies at variance with the desires of the leadership of the states in the region. The theme of the first edition of the book, that Soviet policy in the Middle East was primarily a reaction to a series of regional developments that the Soviet leaders not only had not caused but also found increasingly unable to shape to fit their goals in the region, would appear to be borne out in the second edition as well.

I am indebted to a number of scholars and government officials for their comments on the sections of the manuscript dealing with Soviet policy from 1974 through 1977 that have been added for this second edition of the book. Special thanks go to L. Dean Brown of the Middle East Institute; Yaacov Ro'i of Tel Aviv University; Arthur Klinghoffer of Rutgers University; John Damis of Portland State University; and Martha Mauntner and Jim Collins of the Department of State, whose comments helped improve the manuscript. Naturally, while I am beholden to all these individuals for their help, the views in this book are my own and I bear full responsibility for any errors.

Since the completion of the first edition of this book a number of studies have appeared that have dealt with the events preceding the 1973 Arab-Israeli war, with the war itself, and with the postwar shuttle diplomacy of U.S. Secretary of State Henry Kissinger. These works have included books by such "participant observers" as Mohammed Heikal, speeches and memoirs by Middle Eastern leaders such as Anwar Sadat, and "exposes" by such journalists as Edward Sheehan and Matti Golan, along with a number of excellent monographs on various facets of Soviet and American policy toward the Middle East during this period. These works have proved very useful to me in my revisions of Chapters 2 through 5 of this book, as have the kind comments and recommendations of the scholars who reviewed the first edition of the book.

In preparing the second edition of this book, I received a great deal of assistance from the director of the library of the Baltimore Hebrew College, Jesse Mashbaum, and his staff assistants, Betty Sachs, Sonia R. Kozlovsky, Dr. Rosy Bodenheimer, and Ina Rubin. A special word of thanks is due my secretary, Elise Baron, for her assistance in typing the manuscript (often deciphering almost undecipherable handwriting in the process), and to Elaine Hurwitz Malinow and Mimi Cohen for their help in maintaining my files on the Middle East. Special thanks also to Russ Eisenberg for his enthusiastic encouragement.

Finally, I would like to express my deepest appreciation to my wife Sharon, without whose continuing support neither the first nor the second edition of this book could have been written, and to my two children, Debbie and David, who showed great understanding while their father was working.

PREFACE
To the Third Edition

The increasingly rapid pace of Middle Eastern developments since the completion of the second edition of this book in March 1978, and Moscow's efforts to manipulate these developments for its own benefit, have prompted me to extend my analysis of Soviet policy in the region to February 1982. A number of incidents dominate this period: the Camp David agreements between Israel and Egypt and the subsequent Egyptian-Israeli peace agreement which led to Egypt's isolation in the Arab world; the fall of the Shah of Iran, once the pillar of U.S. policy in the Persian/Arab Gulf, and his replacement by a virulently anti-American Islamic fundamentalist regime which held American diplomats hostage for 444 days; a communist coup d'état in Afghanistan and the subsequent Soviet invasion of that country; the outbreak of war between Iran and Iraq; and the development of an increasingly military-based U.S. policy that sought to counter the Soviet threat to the Middle East by a combination of anti-Soviet alliances and the establishment of increased U.S. military power in the region in the forms both of naval flotillas and a rapid deployment force.

Nonetheless, despite the fact that many of the developments in the 1978-1982 period were negative ones as far as the United States was concerned, Moscow did not appear to be able measurably to improve its own position in the region other than by profiting from American losses. Thus, while Iran turned away from the United States, it did not turn toward the USSR, and when war broke out between Iran and Iraq, Moscow could only look on while its regional position deteriorated because of the war. Similarly, the Soviet invasion of Muslim Afghanistan cast a pall on Soviet efforts to improve relations with the conservative regimes of the Gulf, while the rise of Islamic fundamentalist feeling also threatened to infect the USSR. Thus the overall thesis of the first two editions of this book, that Soviet policy has been primarily a reaction to a series of regional developments that the Soviet leaders not only had not caused but also found increasingly unable to shape to fit their goals in the region, would also appear to be borne out in the third edition as well.

Once again I am indebted to a number of scholars and government officials for their help. Martha Mautner and Wayne Limberg of the Department of State have been very kind in frequently sharing their assessments of Middle Eastern events with me; Ambassador Philip Habiib, Ya'acov Ro'i of Tel Aviv University, Galia Golan of The Hebrew University of Jerusalem, John Campbell of the Council of Foreign Relations, Bard O'Neil of the U.S. National Defense University, and Robert Rand of Radio Liberty have provided me with a great deal of intellectual enrichment as I studied the twists and turns of Soviet policy and Middle East politics. The help of all of these fine people is deeply appreciated; naturally, I alone bear full responsibility for any errors in the analysis.

The preparation of the third edition of this book would not have been possible without a great deal of supporting assistance. The director of the Baltimore Hebrew College library, Dr. Jesse Mashbaum and his staff assistants, particularly Betty Sachs, Jeanette Katkoff, Dvora Finkelstein and Elaine Mael were most helpful in procuring the necessary research materials for me. Once again I must thank my supersecretary Elise Baron for so expertly preparing the manuscript while at the same time attending to the needs of our graduate students. Thanks are also due to Andrea Broumberg and Sammie Goldberg for helping me to maintain my newspaper files on the Middle East and the Soviet Union, and to Russ Eisenberg for his continuing inspiration.

Finally, I would like to express a special word of thanks to my wife Sharon, who, while pursuing a full-time career of her own, provided me with the special type of companionship that supported me during the writing of all three editions of this book, and to my children Debbie and David, who make it all worthwhile.

CONTENTS

1
Introduction

Since the death of Stalin in 1953, the Soviet Union has become increasingly active in Middle Eastern affairs, and by the time of Egyptian President Gamal Nasser's death in 1970, even Western statesmen had to acknowledge that the USSR had become one of the leading powers in the region. Yet while there has been general agreement that the Soviet Union now plays an important role in the Middle East, no such consensus exists regarding the USSR's goals in the region. Some observers have contended that the main Soviet goal is an offensive one—to dominate the Middle East in order to deny its oil, strategic communication routes, and other assets to the United States and her allies. An opposing view holds that the Soviet aim is primarily defensive, to prevent the region from being used as a base for an attack upon the USSR. Other hypotheses place Soviet objectives somewhere between these two extremes.[1]

The Soviet leaders themselves have justified their activity in the Middle East both in terms of its proximity to the southern border of the USSR and in terms of their responsibility as leaders of the "world revolutionary" and "national liberation" movements.[2] Whatever the ultimate goal of Soviet policy—and the author sees it basically as an offensive one—it is evident that since Stalin's death, the Soviet leadership has been making a determined effort to increase Soviet influence in the Middle East. To this end the USSR has extended large amounts of military assistance, as well as economic aid and diplomatic support, to a number of key Middle Eastern states, in an effort to influence their domestic and foreign policies, while also signing long-term "Friendship and Cooperation" treaties with them.

Influence, however, is very difficult for statesmen (and political scientists) to measure.[3] The leaders of all the great powers want their nations' interests to be considered very seriously by leaders of other nations when decisions are being made. Yet, as both the United States and the Soviet Union have learned over the last two decades, the mere provision of military and economic aid is no guarantee that a client state will do the superpower's bidding in either foreign or domestic policy, particularly when the client regime's leadership is making decisions of great importance. The spectrum of influence extending between normal and even good diplomatic relations, on the one hand, and "control" or dominant influence, on the other, is a very broad one, as the Russians have discovered in their dealings with the nations of the Middle East, particularly in the period since Nasser's death, when the region's complexity and volatility have increasingly hampered Soviet policy makers. Indeed, in order to understand fully the nature of the Soviet drive for influence in the Middle East and the regional obstacles to it, it is first necessary to analyze briefly the nature of and the interrelationships among the nations of the region. Far from being a "vacuum of power" as the ill-fated Eisenhower Doctrine of 1957 characterized it, the Middle East is a highly complex region with numerous power centers and power conflicts, and the region's complexities have provided both opportunities and problems for Soviet policy makers.

THE CONTEMPORARY MIDDLE EAST: A BRIEF OVERVIEW

From an ethnic, religious, political, and economic standpoint the Middle East is perhaps the most complex region on earth. Sunni and Shii Muslims; Greek Orthodox, Maronite, Coptic, Catholic, and Protestant Christians; Jews; Kurds; and Armenians coexist uneasily in an area characterized by unstable and frequently changing governments, and periodically convulsed by fighting between Arabs and Israelis, Iraqis and Kurds, Lebanese Christians and Muslims, Sudanese Arabs and blacks, Jordanians and Palestinians, North and South Yemenis, and Iranians and Iraqis. Western-style democracies, feudal monarchies, and "Arab Socialist" military dictatorships are all present, along with a number of other forms of government. Adding to the region's complexity is its broad spectrum of economic systems, which range from free-enterprise capitalism to state socialism.[4]

There are basically two forms of monarchy in the Middle East. Some nations, such as the Sultanate of Oman and the sheikhdoms of the Persian Gulf, can be called feudal monarchies. Others, such as Jordan and Morocco, whose rulers have initiated major economic development projects along with social reforms, can be termed "modernizing" monarchies. Saudi Arabia, whose leaders have embarked on a massive economic development plan while seeking to limit social reform, falls midway on this spectrum. The only democracy currently in existence in the region is Israel, as Lebanese democracy seems to have been aborted by the civil war of 1975 and the Syrian invasion of 1976, while a military coup in 1980 overthrew the democratic regime in Turkey.

The Arab military regimes of the Middle East—Egypt, Syria, Iraq, Libya, Algeria, South Yemen, and the Sudan—form another major class of Middle Eastern governments. Although all these nations call themselves republics, despite the fact that their leaders came to power through military coups d'état, they differ in the degree to which they tolerate Islam, foreign investment, and private ownership of land and industry, to mention only a few important categories. The most recent addition to the taxonomy of Middle Eastern governments has been the Islamic fundamentalist regime of Ayatollah Khomeini which came to power in Iran in 1979 after the Shah was ousted. While still in the process of final crystallization, the regime's fundamentalism has already had a major impact on its neighbors in the Persian/Arab Gulf.

Soviet leaders, in attempting to classify these varied nations according to the doctrines of Marxism-Leninism, have encountered serious difficulties. According to the Marxist-Leninist ideology, which serves to legitimize the rule of the Soviet Communist Party as well as to provide a *Weltanschauung* for its leadership, the nations of the Middle East must be somewhere on the long road to Communism. The fact that a nation may be a feudal monarchy one day and proclaim itself an "Arab Socialist Republic" the next, after a coup d'état, presents a number of difficulties for Soviet ideologists.[5] While usually accepting the anti-imperialist tenet of Marxism-Leninism, the new military leaders have usually rejected such other basic tenets of the Soviet doctrine as the supremacy of the working class, dialectical materialsm, and atheism—indeed, the identification of the Soviet Union with atheism has proved to be a major obstacle to the spread of Soviet influence through the predominantly Muslim Middle East, where religion plays a major role in everyday life, a role that has increased in importance since 1970.[6]

A more serious problem to the Soviet leaders is the fact that the Communist parties of some of these Arab military republics (which theoretically should be leading them down the path to Communism) remain as suppressed under the new regimes as they were under the old feudal monarchies. The Russians have had to decide whether or not to give military and economic support to non-Communist "bourgeois" nationalist leaders such as Saddam Hussein of Iraq, who, although they suppress the Communist parties of their countries, nevertheless pursue "anti-imperialist" foreign policies often favorable to the Soviet Union.[7]

Even in cases where the Communist Party of a Middle Eastern nation has been tolerated, the Soviet leaders have had great difficulty in determining the degree to which the Communist Party of that country should try to retain its independence while cooperating with the ruling nationalist party. In addition, some of the Middle Eastern Communist parties have proved uncomfortably independent of Soviet direction; this, too, has posed serious problems for the Russian leaders.[8]

The numerous conflicts in the Middle East present another major dilemma for the Russian leaders. While the Arab-Israeli conflict is perhaps the most familiar one to Americans, other conflicts of high intensity abound within the region. Iraq and Iran, whose leaders profess different variants of Islam, were on the verge of war over their Shatt Al-Arab River boundary before the

Iran-Iraq accord of March 1975, as each accused the other of aiding dissident movements within its borders. Yet another factor that embittered relations between the two countries was their struggle for power over the Persian/Arab Gulf, a struggle that sharpened in intensity as British forces were withdrawn from the area in 1971. Full-scale war finally did erupt in September 1980, as Iraqi leader Saddam Hussein sought to score a major defeat on the fundamentalist regime which, after taking power in 1979, was posing an increasing threat both to his domestic position and to his pretensions of leadership in the Gulf.

Another conflict in the Middle East involves the relations between Syria and her two smaller Arab neighbors, Jordan and Lebanon. Successive Syrian regimes have sought to dominate the two nations and even to incorporate them into a "greater Syria." The Syrians threatened to invade Lebanon during the Lebanese-Palestinian guerrilla conflict in 1969 and actually did invade Lebanon in 1976. Similarly, a Syrian force invaded Jordan during the Jordanian civil war of September 1970 and, after a brief period of reconciliation in the mid-1970s, Syrian-Jordanian relations were again very tense at the start of the 1980s. Syrian-Turkish relations have also been strained for a long time, for the Syrians remember with great bitterness Turkey's annexation of the Iskenderun region before World War II, when France had a mandate over Syria.

One of the major inter-Arab conflicts of the 1960s was the struggle between Egypt and Saudi Arabia over North Yemen. This conflict, which almost broke into full-scale war in 1963, cooled off following the Egyptian withdrawal from Yemen in 1967, after the Six Day War, and remained dormant in the early 1970s as the new Egyptian President, Anwar Sadat, sought to forge an alliance with Saudi Arabian King Faisal. Nevertheless, this conflict could erupt again if Egypt tried to restore its influence in southern Arabia. However, for the time being at least, it has been superseded by the intermittent conflict between North and South Yemen (both of whom border Saudi Arabia), which reached the stage of a border war in 1972, and by the guerrilla war that South Yemen has been intermittently supporting in the Dhofar region of neighboring Oman, which also borders Saudi Arabia.

Conflict also pervades the relations among the Arab "republics" in the center of the Middle East. The historical competition for power in the region between Egypt and Iraq goes back to biblical days, and differences over an Arab-Israeli peace settlement have soured relations between the two states throughout the 1970s. Egyptian-Syrian relations are also strained, despite Syrian-Egyptian cooperation in the 1973 Arab-Israeli war. An even greater hostility permeates relations between Iraq and Syria, currently ruled by rival wings of the Ba'ath Party, as each regime has sought to overthrow the other. Finally, Libya and Egypt, temporarily allies in the early 1970s, have been at loggerheads since 1973 and briefly went to war in 1977.

Other conflicts in the Middle East include the one between Algeria and Morocco (they fought a brief border war in 1963 and are currently fighting a proxy war over the former Spanish Sahara); between Iraq and Kuwait (Iraq tried unsuccessfully to annex Kuwait in 1961 and mounted minor invasions in 1973 and 1975); and between Ethiopia and Somalia, which went to war in 1977 over Somali territorial claims against Ethiopia, even though both states had self-proclaimed Marxist governments. In addition, since 1966 there has been a struggle for power in Jordan between the Palestinians and the regime of King Hussein, while at the same time the various Palestinian guerrilla organizations have been fighting among themselves for control of the Palestinian resistance movement.[9] Domestic conflicts with serious international implications include the hostility between Christian and Muslim Arabs in Lebanon, which erupted into civil war in 1958 and again in 1975-76, and which heavily overshadowed the Lebanese government's conflicts with the Palestinian guerrillas in 1969 and 1973; the strife between Arabs and blacks in the Sudan (the long and bloody civil war between the two groups came to an end in 1972); the endemic conflict between the Iraqi government and its Kurdish minority, which periodically erupts into full-scale war; and the struggles of the Kurdish, Azerbaizhani, and Arab minorities for autonomy in Iran.

These interstate and intrastate conflicts have been a major obstacle to the Soviet Union's efforts to extend its influence over the entire region. While siding with one party to a conflict has given the USSR entree to a regional state, the Soviet action has usually meant alienating the other party and driving it into the arms of the West, as well as enabling the state receiving Soviet aid to exploit Soviet assistance by undertaking actions not necessarily to the liking of the Soviet leadership. Indeed, there have been a number of cases where a regional client state's goals have differed sharply from Soviet global aims, and the Soviet leaders have therefore run the risk of being pulled into a Middle East war over an issue of only secondary or tertiary importance to the USSR. Consequently, the Russians have had a difficult time trying to follow an even-handed policy in such conflicts as the Ethiopian-Somali, Iranian-Iraqi, North Yemeni-South Yemeni, and Syrian-Iraqi, however much the Soviet leadership may have wished to spread the mantle of a "Pax Sovietica" over the region. Even in the case of the Arab-Israeli conflict, where the Soviet leaders sided with the Arabs, they had to limit their aid to the Arab states lest the USSR become involved in a serious confrontation with the United States. Such a development could, at worst, escalate into a war between the superpowers or, at the minimum, jeopardize the economic and strategic benefits flowing to the Soviet Union from the Soviet-American détente.

Another Middle Eastern problem with which the Russians have had to contend is the issue of Arab unity. Despite the numerous conflicts among the Arab states, there has also been a strong psychological drive for unity. Yet even here conflict is present, since the Arabs have been unable to agree on a political structure on which to build their unity or on which Arab leaders would lead a unified Arab world. The one serious attempt at a union of Arab states—the Syrian-Egyptian union—lasted only three years (1958-61), and the confederation of Egypt, Libya, Syria, and the Sudan, which came into being in 1970, and the Libyan-Egyptian union of 1972 soon collapsed because of personality and policy conflicts between the different nations' leaders. The Arab drive for unity has posed yet another dilemma for the Soviet leadership, and at one point it brought Khrushchev into an open confrontation with Nasser. Initially opposed to the idea of Arab unity because of its prewar German and postwar British sponsorship, the Soviet leadership vacillated in the 1950s and 1960s, before increasingly supporting the idea of Arab unity on an "anti-imperialist" basis in the 1970s, as the only way in which the mutually hostile Arab states could bury their hostilities (and their suspicions of Arab Communist parties) to join together against the West.

In addition to these regional obtacles to the extension of Soviet influence, the Soviet leadership has been beset with nonregional obstacles. First and foremost among these is competition from other powers, particularly the United States, which actively opposes Soviet efforts to secure dominant influence over the Middle East. Capitalizing on the Soviet debacle in the Sudan, where an abortive Communist-supported coup d'état in July 1971 led to a sharp deterioration in Soviet-Sudanese relations, both the United States and Communist China used the opportunity to improve relations with the once strongly pro-Soviet Nimeri regime. Similarly, as Soviet policy clearly began to tilt toward Iraq during the struggle with Iran, the United States moved to consolidate relations with the Shah and weaken Soviet influence in Iran, only to have this policy backfire when the Shah was overthrown. For the Soviet leadership, however, the most serious arena of Soviet-American competition for influence in the Middle East has been Egypt, the most populous and militarily powerful of the Arab states in the region. Indeed, the Soviet-American competition for influence in Egypt, which increased sharply after the death of Nasser, is one of the main themes of this book.

While the Soviet Union and the United States have been the main nonregional powers competing for influence in the Middle East, one cannot overlook the activities of a number of Western European powers, especially France, in the region. Although the Soviet leadership was no doubt pleased with the disarray in NATO caused by transatlantic differences in Middle Eastern strategy in the 1956 and 1973 wars, it must have been less happy with the fact that the Europeans were alternative sources of economic and military assistance to the Middle Eastern states, who were able to play off all the nonregional powers against each other, thus limiting the amount of influence any one power, including the USSR, could wield.

Another important factor affecting Soviet policy toward the Middle East is the Sino-Soviet conflict. While China is, as yet, only tangentially involved in the Middle East, its conflict with the Soviet Union erupted into a much-publicized series of border clashes in March 1969. These clashes underscored Chinese claims to large parts of Soviet Siberia and raised the possibility that, should the Soviet Union become involved in a major war in the Middle East, the Chinese might avail themselves of the opportunity to move into Siberia. In addition, the Soviet leadership has long been concerned over the establishment of a Sino-American axis aimed against the USSR, and the surprise visit to Peking of Henry Kissinger in July 1971, which was followed by President Nixon's visit in early 1972, must have made a number of Soviet leaders worry that the Sino-American axis was under way, a fear that may well have been rekindled following the formal Sino-American "normalization" in December 1978. These concerns with the Chinese challenge have forced Soviet leaders to exercise a certain degree of caution in their Middle Eastern policies, lest the United States, which occasionally seemed willing to provide long-term credits for the ailing Soviet economy, depart from its détente policy and align itself with the Chinese. For this reason, the Soviet leadership was unwilling to provide all the aid desired by the Arabs in their confrontation with Israel, but this, in turn, was to cause an exasperated Sadat to expel the Soviet military advisers from Egypt in July 1972 —two months after the first Nixon-Brezhnev summit.

Another factor affecting Soviet policy that stems from the triangular relationship with the United States and China is the issue of Jewish emigration from the Soviet Union to Israel. In an apparent move to gain support in the United States following Kissinger's visit to Peking, the Soviet leadership decided in late 1971 to increase the emigration quota from 300 to 3,000 per month. While popular in the United States, this decision was decidedly unpopular in the Arab world, which saw the Jewish immigrants to Israel, a number of whom were highly skilled, as increasing Israel's military power in its confrontation with the Arabs.[10]

Thus, the Soviet leadership has been confronted by a number of regional and extraregional obstacles in its efforts to increase Soviet influence in the Middle East. Interestingly enough, the Soviet leaders (and many Western leaders as well) tend to view the Middle East as what political scientists call a "zero-sum game" contest for influence in which, where one side wins, the other side must lose an equivalent amount. This is somewhat ironic, since in the absence of the sanction of armed force, the ability of a major power to influence a smaller state is marginal at best. Indeed, the mere provision of economic and military assistance is not enough, as the Soviet leadership discovered in its attempts to change Yugoslav, Albanian, and Chinese policy through manipulation of military and economic assistance.[11]

Given the complexity of the Middle East and the major obstacles facing the Soviet leaders in their attempts to increase Soviet influence in the region, Soviet policy in the period since Nasser's death can perhaps best be viewed as a highly opportunistic one in which the Soviet leaders have primarily reacted to and, on occasion, attempted to exploit regional developments and trends that they had not caused but that they nonetheless hoped to manipulate to weaken Western influence in the Middle East. Unfortunately for the Russians, however, Middle Eastern trends have not always gone in pro-Soviet directions, as Dmitry Volsky, associate editor of the Soviet foreign policy weekly *New Times*, somewhat ruefully acknowledged when commenting on the anti-Soviet and anti-Communist reaction in the Arab world to the Communist-supported coup d'état attempt in the Sudan in July 1971:

> It would be difficult indeed to find a spot in the world where the situation is as contradictory as it is in the Middle East. It is not surprising, therefore, that many observers are finding it difficult to establish what the dominant trend in this troubled area is.[12]

A decade later, Volsky was to make a similar lament following the collapse of the Arab summit at Fez:

> The Arab world is living through difficult, troubled times, full of contradictions . . . [thus] the internecine conflicts by which, alas, the entire Arab and indeed, the whole Muslim world is rent.[13]

Soviet policy toward the Middle East in the post-1970 period, therefore, will be seen primarily as a series of reactions to developments originating within that volatile region—developments that Soviet leaders discovered they often could neither control nor manipulate.

A NOTE ON SOURCES

The primary source for this study is the Soviet press, especially *Pravda* and *Izvestia*, which reflect the official viewpoint of the Soviet government, as does Radio Moscow, another source utilized extensively. In addition, the Soviet foreign affairs weekly, *New Times*, has been cited frequently because it usually reflects the opinion of the Soviet Foreign Ministry. Among other Soviet journals, only the *World Marxist Review* can be considered a major source for this study, not only because it reflects the thinking of Soviet party leaders but also because it provides a sounding board for the opinions of nonruling Communist party leaders. In the period since the 24th Congress of the Communist Party of the Soviet Union (CPSU) in 1971, Arab Communists have utilized the journal to voice their open disagreements with certain aspects of Soviet Middle Eastern policies. The more specialized Soviet journals, such as *Narodi Azii i Afriki*, *International Affairs*, and *Mirovaia ekonomika i mezhdunarodnye otnosheniia*, have been cited only occasionally since they tend to reflect the speculative attitudes of Soviet scholars and research institutes, rather than the official policy of the Soviet government.

On the Middle Eastern side, I have depended primarily on statements by national leaders as broadcast over their government radios or printed in the local press or in interviews with Western correspondents. Since my reading knowledge of Arabic is limited, I have depended on translations of the Arab press found in the *Record of the Arab World* and the *Foreign Broadcast Information Service*. The journal, *The Middle East* (London), is also a very useful source of information about the region. The *Journal of Palestine Studies* has also provided useful data on the Arab world, and the detailed chronology in the *Middle East Journal* has been of great benefit. For the Israeli point of view, I have relied on the *Jerusalem Post* and *Ha'aretz*. I have also had the opportunity to discuss my research with Egyptian, Jordanian, Palestinian, and Israeli officials, American State Department and intelligence officials, and a number of Arab, Israeli, American, and Soviet scholars working on Middle Eastern problems, all of whom have presented useful perspectives to help me understand the Middle East, a region that poses numerous obstacles not only for outside powers trying to influence developments there but also for scholars seeking to understand the area.

NOTES

1. For general surveys of Soviet involvement in the Middle East prior to 1970, see Walter Laqueur, *The Struggle for the Middle East* (New York: Macmillan, 1969); Aaron Klieman, *Soviet Russia and the Middle East* (Baltimore: Johns Hopkins, 1970); and M. S. Agwani, *Communism in the Arab East* (Bombay: Asia Publishing House, 1969). For a review of the three books, see Robert O. Freedman, "Soviet Dilemmas in the Middle East," *Problems of Communism* 23, no. 3 (May/June 1972), pp. 71-73. More recent studies include George Lenczowski, *Soviet Advances in the Middle East* (Washington, D.C.: American Enterprise Institute, 1971); Michael Confino and Shimon Shamir, ed., *The USSR and the Middle East* (Jerusalem: Israel Universities Press, 1973); Yaacov Ro'i, ed., *From Encroachment to Involvement: A Documentary Study of Soviet Policy in the Middle East 1945-1973* (Jerusalem: Israel Universities Press, 1974); Jon D. Glassman, *Arms for the Arabs: The Soviet Union and War in the Middle East* (Baltimore: Johns Hopkins, 1975); Baruch Hazan, *Soviet Propaganda: A Case Study of the Middle East Conflict* (Jerusalem: Israel Universities Press, 1976); Galia Golan, *Yom Kippur and After: The Soviet Union and the Middle East Crisis* (New York: Cambridge University Press, 1977); and Yaacov Ro'i, ed., *The Limits to Power: Soviet Policy in the Middle East* (London: Croom Helm, 1979). For a general discussion of possible Soviet objectives in the Middle East, see A. S. Becker and A. L. Horelick, *Soviet Policy in the Middle East*, Rand Publication R-504-FF (Santa Monica, California: Rand Corporation, 1970), pp. 63-64. For a recent Arab viewpoint, see Mohammed Heikal, *The Sphinx and the Commissar* (New York: Harper & Row, 1978).

2. For a Soviet view of the USSR's policies in the Middle East, see O. M. Gorbatov and L. I. Cherkasskii, *Sotrudnichestvo SSSR so stranami arabskogo vostoka i Afriki* (Moscow: Nauka, 1970) and E. M. Primakov, *Anatomiia Blizhnevostochnogo Konfliictu* (Moscow: Mysl', 1978). See also documents in *SSSR i arabskie strany 1917-1960* (The USSR and the Arab States) (Moscow: Government Printing Office of Political Literature, 1961); and *The Policy of the Soviet Union in the Arab World* (Moscow: Progress Publishers, 1975).

3. Political science models dealing with the exertion of influence in Soviet foreign policy in general and Soviet foreign policy toward the Middle East in particular are still relatively rare. For a general study of influence the interested reader is advised to consult J. David Singer, "Internation Influence: A Formal Model" in the influence theory section of *International Politics and Foreign Policy*, ed. James N. Rosenau (New York: Macmillan, 1969). Singer makes the useful distinction between influence leading to behavior modification in a target state and influence leading to behavior reinforcement. Another useful study, which examines the phenomenon of influence from the perspective of the target

state, is Marshall R. Singer, *Weak States in a World of Powers* (New York: Free Press, 1972), especially chapters 6-8. See also Richard W. Cottam, *Competitive Interference and Twentieth Century Diplomacy* (Pittsburgh: University of Pittsburgh Press, 1967). For an attempt to analyze Soviet influence in the Third World, see Alvin Z. Rubinstein, ed., *Soviet and Chinese Influence in the Third World* (New York: Praeger, 1975). For an effort to measure Soviet influence in Egypt, see Alvin Z. Rubinstein, *Red Star on the Nile: The Soviet-Egyptian Influence Relationship since the June War* (Princeton: Princeton University Press, 1977).

4. For a useful introduction to the varied nations of the Middle East, see Peter Mansfield, *The Middle East: A Political and Economic Survey*, 4th ed. (London: Oxford University Press, 1973); Paul Hammond and Sidney Alexander, eds., *Political Dynamics in the Middle East* (New York: Elsevier, 1972); Don Peretz, *The Middle East Today*, 3rd ed. (New York: Holt Rinehart and Winston, 1978); and David Long and Bernard Reich, eds., *The Government and Politics of the Middle East and North Africa* (Boulder, Colorado: Westview, 1980).

5. For Soviet efforts to deal with the military role in Third World states, see R. E. Sevortian, *Armiia v politicheskom rezhime stran sovremennogo vostoka* (The Army in the Political Regime of the Countries of the Contemporary East) (Moscow: Nauka, 1973); and G. L. Mirskii, *Tretii mir: Obshchestvo, vlast', armiia* (The Third World: society, authority, army) (Moscow: Nauka, 1976).

6. For a Soviet view of the role of religion in Third World states, with a special focus on Islam, see B. Gafurov, ed., *Religiia i obshchestvennaia misl' narodov vostoka* (Religion and Social Thought of the Peoples of the East) (Moscow: Nauka, 1971). For a more recent view, which takes into account the impact of the Iranian Revolution, see Leonid Medvenko, "Islam and Liberation Revolutions," *New Times* (Moscow) no. 43, 1979, pp. 18-23 and "Islam: Two Trends," *New Times* no. 13, 1980, pp. 23-25.

7. In the 1930s the Soviet leadership faced the same dilemma in its relations with Ataturk's regime in Turkey and Chiang Kai-shek's regime in China. In both instances Russian support was given to the "bourgeois" nationalist regime rather than to the Communists. For an analysis of these events, see Adam Ulam, *Expansion and Coexistence: The History of Soviet Foreign Policy 1917-1967* (New York: Praeger, 1968), pp. 167-81. For an overall analysis of the twists and turns in Soviet ideological formulations about the Third World, see Ishwer C. Ojha, "The Kremlin and Third World Leadership: Closing the Circle?" in *Soviet Policy in Developing Countries*, ed. W. Raymond Duncan (Waltham, Mass: Ginn-Blaisdell, 1970), pp. 9-28; and R. A. Yellon, "Shifts in Soviet Policies toward Developing Areas 1964-1968," in Duncan, op.cit., pp. 225-86. See also Jaan Pennar, *The USSR and the Arabs: The Ideological Dimension* (New York: Crane Russak, 1973). Evaluations of the overall success (or lack thereof) of Soviet policy in the Third World, are found in W. Raymond Duncan, ed., *Soviet Policy in the Third World* (New York: Pergamon, 1980); and Robert Donaldson, ed., *The Soviet Union in the Third World* (Boulder, Colorado: Westview, 1981). For Soviet views of the problem, see R. A. Ulianovsky, *Sotsialism i osvobodiv-shikhsia strany* (Socialism and Liberated States) (Moscow: Nauka, 1972); and R. M. Avakov et al., *Razvivaiushchiesia strany: Zakonomernosti, tendentsii, perspektivy* (Developing States: Regularities [of Development], Tendencies, Prospects) (Moscow: Mysl', 1974).

8. For a study of Soviet policy toward the Communist parties of the Arab world, see Robert O. Freedman, "The Soviet Union and the Communist Parties of the Arab World: An Uncertain Relationship," in *Soviet Economic and Political Relations with the Developing World*, ed. Rogert E. Kanet and Donna Bahry (New York: Praeger, 1975); and John K. Cooley, "The Shifting Sands of Arab Communism," *Problems of Communism* 24, no. 2 (1975), pp. 22-42.

9. For a study of conflicts within the Palestinian movement and its relations with the Arab states, see William B. Quandt, Fuad Jabbar, and Ann Lesch, *The Politics of*

Palestinian Nationalism (Berkeley: University of California Press, 1973). See also Bard E. O'Neil, *Armed Struggle in Palestine* (Boulder, Colorado: Westview, 1978).

10. For an examination of Soviet policy on the emigration issue, see Robert O. Freedman, "The Lingering Impact of the Soviet System on the Soviet Jewish Immigrant to the United States," in *The Soviet Jewish Emigre*, ed. Jerome M. Gilison (Baltimore: Baltimore Hebrew College, 1977).

11. On this point, see Robert O. Freedman, *Economic Warfare in the Communist Bloc: A Study of Soviet Economic Pressure against Yugoslavia, Albania and Communist China* (New York: Praeger, 1970).

12. *New Times* no. 44 (1971), p. 7.

13. *New Times* no. 49 (1981), p. 12. In my view, *Pravda* and *Izvestia* differ only insignificantly in expressing the official Soviet viewpoint. For a study that sees more important differences between the two papers as well as between them and *Trud*, *Krasnaia zvezda*, *Sovetskaia Rossiia*, and *Komosomolskaia Pravda*, see Dina Spechler, *Internal Influences on Soviet Foreign Policy: Elite Opinion and the Middle East* (Jerusalem: Soviet and East European Research Center, Hebrew University, 1976).

2

From World War II
to the Death of Nasser

In the period since World War II, the Soviet Union has tended to pursue one line of policy toward the two northernmost nations of the Middle East—Iran and Turkey (hereafter called the Northern Tier)—and another toward the other Middle Eastern states. The reasons for this may be traced to both geography and history. Iran and Turkey differ sharply from the other nations of the region in three important respects. Both nations have long borders with the Soviet Union, and both have fought numerous wars against invading Russian troops in the last 400 years. As a result, both Iran and Turkey have had a great deal of experience with Russian imperialism, and for this reason the Soviet leadership has had far greater difficulty in extending Soviet influence in these nations than in the other countries of the Middle East, which neither border on the USSR nor possess a long experience in dealing with Russian imperialism. Indeed, all the nations of what we shall call the Southern Tier have had bitter experience with *Western* imperialism—particularly that of Britain and France—which dominated the region from Morocco to the Persian Gulf in the interwar period. It is in this part of the Middle East that the Soviet Union has seen the greatest increase in its influence since the end of World War II, although the Russians have proven unable to expand their influence to the point of actual control in any nation of the area.[1]

THE STALINIST HERITAGE, 1945-53

Stalin's foreign policy toward the Middle East was a relatively uncomplicated one. Immediately after World War II, he demanded that the Turkish government cede to Russia parts of eastern Turkey and grant the Soviet Union a military base in the Turkish straits. In addition, Stalin claimed the right to a trusteeship over Libya and postponed the withdrawal of Soviet occupation forces

from Iran until well into 1946. These relatively crude attempts at territorial ag-
grandizement were counterproductive. Instead of increasing Russia's security
through the acquisition of territory (a similar motive governed Soviet policy in
Eastern Europe during this period), Stalin's actions served only to drive the nations of the Northern Tier into the arms of the West.[2]

Stalin's policies toward the Southern Tier were scarcely more productive.
Viewing the world in terms of two camps, Communist and anti-Communist, Stalin was either unable or unwilling to see that the leaders of the new nations of
what we now call the Third World wished to belong to neither camp, but desired
to remain neutral. The Soviet press called such leaders as Nasser, Shishakli, and
Nehru "lackeys of the imperialists," and described the newly formed Arab League
as an "instrument of British imperialism." The Soviet recognition of the state of
Israel in 1948 and its diplomatic and military support for it during the first Arab-
Israeli conflict (1947-49) seem to have been aimed at weakening Britain's position in the Middle East and depriving it of key military bases.[3] In any case it did
not improve the Russian position among the Arab states, while the period of
good relations between the USSR and Israel was of a very short duration.[4]

Thus, Soviet policy toward the Middle East under Stalin was unproductive,
if not counterproductive, and Russian influence was at a low ebb in both the
Northern and Southern Tiers of the region at the time of Stalin's death in March
1953.

THE KHRUSHCHEV ERA, 1953-64

The death of Stalin brought a fundamental change in Soviet policy toward
the Middle East. Although the Russians had begun to take the side of the Arabs
in the Arab-Israeli conflict as early as 1954, when Malenkov was still premier,
the real change in Soviet policy did not emerge until after Khrushchev ousted
Malenkov from the premiership in February 1955. Unlike Stalin, Khrushchev
was not afflicted with a two-camp view of the world. Instead, he saw the world
as being divided into three main zones or blocs—the socialist bloc, the capitalist
bloc, and the Third World, which he hoped to win over to Communism through
political support and large doses of economic and military aid.[5] An irony of this
development was that the new American Secretary of State, John Foster Dulles,
had a two-camp view of the world much like Stalin's and tended, therefore, to
have little patience with the neutralist aspirations of Third World leaders. Hence,
when Dulles tried to integrate a number of Arab states into a military alliance
aimed against the Soviet Union, he greatly offended their sensibilities, particularly since England, the former colonial overlord of much of the Middle East,
was to be a founding member of the alliance. Egypt's Nasser was particularly irri-
tated by this development, since his principal Arab rival, Nuri Said of Iraq, em-
braced the alliance (the Baghdad Pact)—and the military and economic assistance

that went with it. Nasser then turned to the Russians for arms, and the end result of the process was that Nasser, through the now famous arms deal of 1955, actually invited the Russians to participate in the politics of the Middle East.[6] By obtaining large amounts of sophisticated weaponry from the USSR, Nasser clearly demonstrated the Arabs' independence from their former colonial masters; for the Russians, on the other hand, it was a means of gaining influence in the Middle East.

Nonetheless, even in the process of gaining influence in the Middle East through the sale of weapons, the Russians got themselves involved in a dilemma that has persisted until today. Mere provision of weapons to a country, regardless of its need for the weapons, does not give the donor nation control over the policies of the recipient nation. To the contrary, the supply of advanced weaponry may enable the recipient nation to embark on a military adventure that the donor nation considers undesirable. Even worse, such a military adventure might threaten to drag the donor nation itself into a war it does not want. Although the supply of weapons to military regimes may be relatively inexpensive in terms of cost to the Soviet economy, in terms of the risk that the Russians might be involved in a war not of their choosing as a result of such military assistance, the cost of such aid can be very high indeed. The Russians became aware of this danger in 1956 with the outbreak of the Sinai campaign, and found themselves in an even more dangerous predicament with the outbreak of the Six-Day War in 1967 and the Yom Kippur War in 1973. Heavy arms shipments to Egypt preceded each conflict, and the Russians were in danger of involvement in each war.[7]

Besides running the risk of direct involvement in an Arab-Israeli war, the Russians faced yet another dilemma in their dealings with Nasser. While happily accepting large quantities of Soviet economic and military aid, as well as support against the West following the nationalization of the Suez Canal in 1956 and during the subsequent Suez crisis, Nasser declared the Egyptian Communist Party to be illegal and kept its leaders in prison. Indeed, he made it very clear that he differentiated between the Soviet Union as a "great friend" and the Egyptian Communist Party, which he considered a threat to his dictatorship. As early as August 16, 1955, Nasser had stated in an interview in the Lebanese newspaper *Al-Jarida* that "nothing prevents us from strengthening our economic ties with Russia even if we arrest the Communists at home and put them on trial."[8]

Such a situation posed a painful dilemma to Khrushchev, a dilemma that he never really resolved. Nasser was a useful ally in the cold war, regardless of his treatment of the Egyptian Communist Party. Nonetheless, since Khrushchev considered himself the head of the international Communist movement, he felt constrained to try to protect the Communist parties of the Middle East. On several occasions he complained to Nasser about the treatment of the Egyptian Communists, but Nasser denounced such "interference" in Egypt's "internal affairs," and relations between the Soviet Union and Egypt deteriorated as a result.[9]

The role of the Communist party was to prove a stumbling block in Khrushchev's policies toward Syria and Iraq as well. In 1957, Syria, of all the nations of the Southern Tier, seemed most ripe for a Communist seizure of power. The Syrian Communist Party had grown rapidly since the overthrow of the Shishakli dictatorship in 1954, and the Syrian government was very pro-Russian. The USSR sent a great deal of economic and military aid to Syria in 1957,[10] and Syrian leaders were frequent visitors to the Soviet Union in that year. Yet even as Syria appeared on the brink of "going Communist" (as some U.S. newspapers speculated), an event occurred that could only have shocked and disappointed the Soviet leadership—the union of Syria and Egypt into the United Arab Republic.[11] And just as the Egyptian Communist Party had been banned by Nasser, so too was the Syrian Communist Party, hitherto the strongest in the Arab world. While the official Soviet response to the announcement of the formation of the United Arab Republic was restrained in tone,[12] the event marked a victory for Arab nationalism, as espoused by Nasser, and a defeat for Arab Communism and, to a lesser degree, the USSR.

The conflict between Arab nationalism and Communism (and indirectly the USSR) became even more acute following the overthrow of the pro-Western regime of Nuri Said in Iraq in July 1958. While Nasser, who later flew to Moscow to discuss this event, had high hopes that Arab nationalists who backed him would take power and bring Iraq into the Egyptian-dominated United Arab Republic, it soon transpired that Kassem, who emerged as the leader of the new regime, was an independent Arab nationalist, one who was willing to utilize the Iraqi Communist Party to combat Nasser's followers in Iraq. Indeed, the Iraqi Communist Party was prominently represented in the new Iraqi regime, and the Soviet leaders soon began to give Iraq large amounts of economic and military aid, much as they had done with Egypt and Syria earlier.[13] In addition, however, the Soviet Union came out in support of Kassem in his efforts to keep Iraq independent of Nasser's unity movement.[14] *Pravda* pointedly stated on March 30, 1959:

> It has lately become apparent that some public figures in the Near East mean by Arab nationalism the immediate and mechanical unification of all Arab states by one of them, regardless of whether they want it or not. All who do not agree with this are denounced as Zionists, communists and enemies of the Arab people.[15]

Despite a brief rapprochement with Nasser in 1960, Khrushchev once again clashed with Egyptian leaders in May 1961 during a visit by an Egyptian parliamentary delegation headed by Anwar Sadat, who was then chairman of the United Arab Republic's National Assembly. Khrushchev attacked the Egyptian leaders for opposing Communism and told them, "If you want socialism, you should not oppose Communism," since the one automatically followed the other. He also told the Egyptians, "Arab nationalism is not the zenith of happiness," and "Life itself will impose Communism." The Egyptians retorted angrily and Soviet-Egyptian relations suffered another setback.[16]

Meanwhile, despite Soviet military, economic, and diplomatic support, Kassem had proven to be a difficult person for the Soviet leaders to work with. Although he pulled Iraq out of the Baghdad Pact (securing, in the process, a large Soviet loan), he also skillfully played the Communists off against the Nasserites, weakening both, and emerged himself as the dominant force in Iraq.[17] By 1961 the Communists had lost their last positions of power in his regime and Kassem ruled alone—although he tolerated the presence of Communists in Iraq to a limited extent. The Iraqi Communists lost even this tenuous degree of freedom, however, when an avowedly anti-Communist group of army officers overthrew Kassem in 1963 and proceeded to execute hundreds of Iraqi Communists and drive the remainder either underground or into exile. Although this regime was itself overthrown before its anti-Communist policies led to too severe a breach with the USSR, its successor was not much more hospitable toward the Iraqi Communist Party.

By this time, however, Khrushchev had switched his primary interest in the Arab world to yet another country, Algeria. Following the end of the Algerian war of independence with France in 1962, the USSR established close relations with the regime of Ahmed Ben-Bella. Soviet economic and military aid was provided to Ben-Bella, who allowed a number of Algerian Communists to participate, as individuals, in his regime (the party itself remained illegal) while also nationalizing a sizable portion of Algeria's agricultural land and industry. Relations between the two countries grew so warm that Ben-Bella was awarded the Lenin Peace Prize and decorated as a "hero of the Soviet Union" during his visit to Moscow in April 1964, and at the end of the visit the Algerian leader secured a major loan.[18]

These developments in Algeria, coupled with Nasser's nationalization of a large portion of Egyptian industry following the breakup of the union with Syria in the fall of 1961, encouraged Khrushchev to believe that the Arab nationalist leaders were turning toward socialism even without the help of the Communist parties. Indeed, it probably appeared to Khrushchev that his prediction made to Sadat in 1961 was now coming true. By 1963 Soviet ideologists were casting around for an explanation for this behavior, one that would justify increased Soviet support for such regimes. (The support most likely would have come anyway, but a new ideological concept would help justify it, both to suspicious Communists who were suppressed under the Arab nationalist regimes, and to those in Moscow who questioned the wisdom of aiding leaders such as Ben-Bella and Nasser.[19]) Consequently, the terms "noncapitalist path" and "Revolutionary Democracy" were born. By "noncapitalist path" Soviet ideologists meant an intermediate stage between capitalism (or the primitive capitalist economies the nationalist leaders had inherited from the colonial period) and socialism, and the highly optimistic Khrushchev often used the terms "noncapitalist path" and "socialism" synonymously in describing the progress of such regimes as Nasser's and Ben-Bella's. The term "Revolutionary Democracy" was used to describe those states moving along the noncapitalist path toward socialism without the help of a Communist party, which according to previous Marxist-Leninist theory was supposed to be the sine qua non of a transition to socialism.[20]

These semantics enabled Khrushchev to attempt to solve his dilemma of dealing with both nationalist leaders like Nasser and the Communist parties of their states, a dilemma that had caused problems for Soviet policy makers in the past. Arguing that the Egyptian Communist Party would be more effective working from within Nasser's regime to win the Egyptian leader to "scientific socialism," Khrushchev—and his successors—urged the Egyptian Communist Party (a weak and faction-ridden organization) to dissolve officially and join the Arab Socialist Union (ASU), which was Nasser's mass political organization and the only one permitted in Egypt. In another policy innovation, the Soviet leadership moved to establish direct party-to-party relations between the CPSU and the ASU, such as had already been done with Ben-Bella's Front de Liberation Nationale (FLN), in which Communists occupied key positions. In establishing direct party-to-party relations, the Soviet leaders claimed that this would enable the CPSU to directly transmit its revolutionary experience to the one-party regimes of the Arab states and thereby hasten the trip of Egypt and Algeria down the noncapitalist path toward Communism.

As might be expected, a number of Arab Communists took a rather dim view of these developments in Soviet strategy, which many of them saw as the effective end of their political existence. Writing in the *World Marxist Review*, a journal that serves as a sounding board for the world's nonruling Communist parties as well as for the CPSU, several Arab Communists voiced their unhappiness with these Soviet ideological innovations. Thus, Fuad Nasser, Secretary General of the Jordanian Communist Party and generally a strong supporter of Soviet foreign policy (particularly in the Sino-Soviet conflict), stated in the course of a 1964 symposium on Arab socialism and Arab unity:

> Latterly, there has been a great deal of talk about these ex-colonial countries taking the non-capitalist way, although *frankly speaking* we still are not sufficiently clear as to what this means.[21] [emphasis added]

Similarly, Khalid Bakdash, Secretary General of the Syrian Communist Party and perhaps the most prestigious Communist leader in the entire Middle East (and also a staunch supporter of Soviet policy), pointedly stated:

> *Some people say*, and this can be heard in Syria as well, that the communist parties no longer play the role they used to. This is a shortsighted view, to say the least, and to say it would be tantamount to denying the need for the continued existence of the party. . . . This is a shortsighted view because the role of the working class

in our countries is bound to grow with the development of the national-liberation movement. The stronger the communist parties and
the more ground the ideas of scientific socialism gain, the more certain our progress in the future.[22] [emphasis added]

A second area of disagreement that arose during the symposium dealt with
the degree of criticism to which the Revolutionary Democratic leaders should be
subjected by Arab Communists. Bakdash took the lead in urging that the short-
comings of these regimes should be clearly pointed out, while other Arab Communists argued that only the positive (that is, genuine socialist) aspects of Nasser's
and Ben-Bella's programs should be commented upon because the main role of
the Arab Communists was to disseminate "scientific socialism" among the
masses. Bakdash disagreed with their emphasis, arguing that while it was important for Arab Communists to teach "scientific socialism" and to promote friendship between their countries and the Soviet Union, it was also important to
point out the differences between the Communists and the Revolutionary
Democrats.[23]

While the Arab Communists debated the advantages and disadvantages of
assisting the Revolutionary Democratic leaders, Khrushchev paid a visit to Egypt
in May to examine the situation for himself. Although the visit was supposed to
demonstrate the rapprochement between the USSR and Egypt, as symbolized by
the Aswan Dam, it also illustrated Khrushchev's fundamental inability to understand the major currents in Arab politics. According to an Egyptian account of
his visit, the Soviet leader seemed amazed at the popular responses Iraqi President Aref got from the Egyptian crowds when he cited Koranic verses in his
speech. In addition, Khrushchev clashed with Ben-Bella, who reportedly told the
Soviet leader that he knew nothing about Arab unity or the Arabs. To this
Khrushchev is supposed to have replied, "I must admit I don't understand you,
for there is only one unity, the unity of the working class."[24] Nonetheless, the
visit ended on a positive note, at least for the Egyptians, who were the recipients
of a $277-million loan, and Nasser became the second Arab leader to be made a
"hero of the Soviet Union."[25]

In addition to their activities in Egypt, Syria, Iraq, and Algeria during the
Khrushchev period, the Russians also became active in other parts of the Arab
world, although to a much smaller degree. The USSR gave military and economic aid to Morocco and Yemen (and was caught in the middle of the Algerian-
Moroccan war of 1963) and granted economic assistance to Tunisia and the Sudan.[26] In addition, diplomatic relations were begun with Libya and Jordan, although repeated Soviet efforts to establish diplomatic relations with Saudi Arabia proved unsuccessful.

Khrushchev's policy toward the Northern Tier nations, Turkey and Iran,
was far more limited in scope. Since these two nations were military allies of the
United States, Khrushchev was not above rattling Soviet rockets at them, much

as he periodically did to Britain, France, and West Germany. This, as can be imagined, was not conducive to an improvement of relations. Nonetheless, toward the end of Khrushchev's reign, relations with both countries were moderated. In the case of Iran, this was primarily due to the Shah's announcement in 1962 that no foreign missiles would be permitted on Iranian soil. This led to a major improvement in Soviet-Iranian relations. Leonid Brezhnev made a state visit to Iran in 1963, and the USSR gave Iran a $38.9 million loan in the same year.[27] It should be pointed out, however, that Iran was sorely beset by internal difficulties at the time of the Shah's announcement. The major land reform campaign under way at the time had aroused a great deal of opposition to the Shah's government, and the improvement of relations with the USSR enabled the Shah to concentrate his attention on his internal opposition.[28]

Soviet-Turkish relations during the Khrushchev era were considerably cooler. While the Russians had renounced their territorial demands against Turkey soon after the death of Stalin, Khrushchev had threatened to go to war against Turkey in 1957 over an alleged Turkish plot to invade Syria. Although in the atmosphere of East-West detente following the Cuban missile crisis of October 1962 some Turks called for closer relations with the Soviet Union, Khrushchev's policy toward the Cyprus crisis, which involved support for the Greek position and military aid for the Cypriot regime of Archbishop Makarios, was a major stumbling block in the way of a rapprochement between the two countries.[29]

All in all, the Soviet Union's position in the Middle East at the time of Khrushchev's fall in October 1964 was considerably better than when Khrushchev came to power. Of perhaps greatest significance, the Baghdad Pact had been all but destroyed by the withdrawal of its one Arab member, Iraq. In addition, the Russians had succeeded in establishing diplomatic relations with almost all the states in the Middle East and had given many of them military and economic aid. The Middle East was clearly no longer the Western sphere of influence it had been at the time of Stalin's death, and the Russians could justifiably consider themselves to be an important factor in Middle Eastern affairs.

The Soviet position, however, was far from a dominant one in 1964. In the countries in which the USSR could be said to have had the most influence—and in which it had spent the most money (Egypt, Syria, Iraq, and Algeria)—the Communist parties remained illegal and many Communists languished in jail. Voices were already being raised in Moscow that too much had been spent with too little return. Although Arab leaders often joined the Russians in denouncing "imperialism," all had fairly good relations with the Western powers, and Russia was unable to control any of them. It was beginning to appear that, far from being exploited by the Russians, as many in the West had feared when the USSR had made its dramatic entrance into the Middle East in 1955, the Arab nations were actually exploiting the Russians. They had gained large amounts of military and economic aid, while sacrificing none of their sovereignty. A Soviet commentator stated several years later:

The existence of the world socialist system may be used to the advantage not only of Revolutionary Democrats or other representatives of the workers; certain judicious bourgeois circles in a number of countries are very successfully using this circumstance to strengthen the political sovereignty and economic development of their countries.[30]

Soviet gains were also limited in the realm of ideology. To be sure, the state sector had been enlarged and the private, or capitalist, sector reduced in many of the states of the region, particularly Egypt and Algeria. In addition, some foreign investments had been nationalized, and there had been a considerable amount of land reform. Nonetheless, these social reforms had been undertaken by nationalist regimes, operating independently of the Communist parties of their countries. Khrushchev hailed these reforms as demonstrating that a number of Middle Eastern nations had taken the noncapitalist way, and in his usual optimistic way went on to equate the noncapitalist way with the road to socialism on which the Communist nations of the world themselves had embarked. Khrushchev's successors, however, clearly differentiated between these two concepts. One Soviet commentator, in assessing the overthrow of such pro-Russian regimes as Nkrumah's in Ghana and Sukarno's in Indonesia, noted ruefully that the noncapitalist road was by no means irreversible.[31]

In sum, when Khrushchev fell in October 1964, the Soviet position in the Middle East was far better than it had been at the time of Stalin's death (it could hardly have been worse), yet it was far from a position of dominance or even preponderance of power. The nations of the Northern Tier, Iran and Turkey, remained firm allies of the United States, although both had improved relations—to a point—with the Soviet Union. Soviet influence had risen fastest among the Arab states, particularly Egypt, Algeria, Syria, and Iraq, but even in these states it was clearly limited. Each of these countries had maintained its independence of action both domestically and in foreign policy and, as argued above, tended to extract far more from the Soviet Union in the form of economic and military support than it paid in political obedience. To be fair to Khrushchev, it should be pointed out that the Middle East was not the primary area of Soviet concern during the period in which he ruled. Khrushchev's main concerns were the problems of Eastern and Western Europe and the rapidly escalating Sino-Soviet conflict. With the rise of the Brezhnev-Kosygin leadership to power, however, Soviet interest began to focus more closely on the Middle East.

THE BREZHNEV-KOSYGIN ERA, 1964-70

When the impulsive and energetic Khrushchev was replaced by the conservative and rather phlegmatic duo of Brezhnev and Kosygin, Western observers called the changeover in leadership "the triumph of the bureaucrats."[32] Like bureaucrats everywhere, they were tired of the constant administrative reorganizations of the Khrushchev era, along with his impulsive actions in foreign policy.[33] Unlike Khrushchev, who tried to spread Soviet influence everywhere in the world at a rapid pace, the new leaders appear to have decided to concentrate Soviet energies and resources on becoming the dominant power in the Middle East, while adopting a much more gradualist policy toward the growth of Soviet power in other parts of the non-Communist world. The Soviet drive for power and influence in the Middle East became increasingly evident in 1965 and 1966, both in the Northern Tier nations, which became the recipients of large amounts of Soviet economic aid, and in the Arab states of Egypt, Syria, Iraq, and Algeria. By early 1967 the new Soviet policy was in high gear, and at least part of the responsibility for the June 1967 Arab-Israeli war can be attributed to the USSR, which was exploiting the Arab-Israeli conflict to increase its influence among the Arab states.

While the Israeli victory in the Six-Day War was a temporary setback for the Russians, one consequence of the Arab defeat was a marked decline of American influence in the radical Arab states of the region.[34] As a result the Russians redoubled their efforts to oust Western influence from the Arab states, while cementing their newly improved relations with Iran and Turkey. Yet, by becoming more involved in the Middle East, the Soviet leaders encountered a number of serious problems, and although by the death of Nasser in September 1970, Soviet influence in the Middle East had reached its highest point since World War II, the Russians were still far from controlling the region. They instead found themselves paying a far higher price than ever before in terms of economic and military aid for their "influence," while running an increasingly serious risk of war with the United States—just at a time when the Sino-Soviet struggle was heating up.

In assessing the Brezhnev-Kosygin approach to the Middle East, it is first necessary to analyze the international situation that the new Soviet leadership faced when it took power in October 1964. Next, an examination will be made of the innovations and changes the new leadership made in Soviet policy toward the region. Finally, an assessment will be made of the Soviet position in the Middle East at the time of Nasser's death.

The New International Situation

In surveying the Soviet position in the world after they took power in 1964, Brezhnev and Kosygin seem to have reached the conclusion that the further expansion of Soviet influence in Western Europe and Latin America was out of the question, at least for the time being, since these areas were of vital importance to the United States, which had demonstrated its clear military superiority over the Soviet Union during the Cuban missile crisis. Similarly, the active hostility of the Chinese Communists had confronted the Russians with a clear danger as well as an obstacle to the spread of their influence in South and Southeast Asia. While the USSR still had several important footholds in Africa, the Soviet leaders evidently decided that, because of the serious problems facing the Soviet economy, they should begin to concentrate their military and economic assistance in the Middle East, an area contiguous to the USSR and one holding greater possibilities for Soviet gains.[35]

The growing influence of the Russian military, with its call for an expanded navy, probably was a contributing factor to this decision. The key naval communication routes that run through the Middle East, and the Russian need to cope with American missile-carrying Polaris submarines already cruising in the Mediterranean at the time of Khrushchev's fall, made the region a particularly important one for the Soviet military. In 1964 a special Mediterranean unit was formed as part of the Soviet Black Sea fleet.[36]

A second contributing factor to the Soviet decision was the increasing instability in the region itself. Nasser's prestige had begun to wane, as his regime was beset with increasing economic and political difficulties, not the least of which was the failure of Egyptian intervention in the Yemeni civil war. Egypt's relations with the United States also began to deteriorate badly in the 1965-66 period.[37] In addition, the endemic Arab-Israeli conflict had begun to worsen, the frequently changing Syrian and Iraqi regimes were unable to cope with internal difficulties, and the British were hard-pressed to maintain their position in riot-torn Aden. All these developments must have tempted the Russians into greater involvement.

The Soviet leaders' attempt to gain increased influence in the Middle East was also aided by a number of events occurring elsewhere in the world in the 1965-66 period. Perhaps the most important was the large American troop commitment to Vietnam in 1965. This was a major bonus to the Russians for a number of reasons. Not only did the Vietnam War cause increasing internal turmoil in the United States itself, but it also served another major Soviet goal—the containment of Communist China. For with a half-million American troops to its south, a hostile India (supported by both the United States and the Soviet Union) to its southwest, and thirty Russian divisions along its northern border, China was indeed "contained"—from the Russian point of view, that is. Another important consequence of U.S. policy in Vietnam was that it tended to divert American energy and attention from other parts of the world, including the Middle East, thus enabling the Russians to operate more freely there.[38]

A second major bonus for the Soviet Union was China's so-called cultural revolution, which occurred in 1966. This effectively removed China from competition with Russia in the Third World and greatly reduced Chinese influence in the international Communist movement. Not having to compete economically with China for influence throughout the Third World allowed the Russians to concentrate their resources in the Middle East.[39] It should be added that the cultural revolution, much like the U.S. involvement in Vietnam, tended to divert Chinese attention from the Middle East.[40]

Yet another bonus for the Russians came with the British decision to pull out of Aden (now the People's Democratic Republic of Yemen) in February 1966. This, together with increasing discussion in England about the necessity for pulling out of the Persian Gulf as well, must have given the Russians the impression that a major power vacuum was opening up along the southern and eastern periphery of the Arabian Peninsula—a power vacuum that the Russians could fill. The fact that Western unity also seemed to be breaking down, as evidenced by de Gaulle's 1966 decision to take French military forces out of NATO, also must have been encouraging to the Russians. This French move, coupled with the British decision to pull out of Aden, made it appear very unlikely that the Western powers would develop a joint policy to confront the Russians in the Middle East.

Soviet failures elsewhere in the Third World also must have sharpened the Russian drive into the Middle East. The fall of Sukarno's regime in Indonesia in October 1965, a regime in which the Russians had invested nearly $2 billion in military and economic aid, was a blow to the Russians. Four months later, in February 1966, came the fall of Nkrumah's regime in Ghana, and the Russians lost their investment of nearly $500 million in military and economic aid. Both pro-Russian regimes were replaced by pro-Western ones.[41]

These events must have made the Russians prize even more highly the good relations they still had with a number of Middle Eastern nations, particularly the regimes of the "radical" Arab states, in which they had similarly invested extensive economic and military assistance. This was particularly true of the Syrian regime, which took power after a coup d'etat in February 1966 and announced its intention to undertake a major "socialist transformation" in Syria as well as work for improved relations with the Soviet Union. The fact that this regime took power so soon after the overthrow of Nkrumah must have been heartening for the Russians; even more heartening was the new regime's decision to permit the Syrian Communist leader, Khalid Bakdash, to return from his eight-year exile in Europe.[42] Yet the Russians were to find that their initial enthusiasm for the new Syrian regime was to become a very costly one, for it was this regime, with its encouragement of the Palestinian guerrillas, that was to help precipitate the June 1967 Arab-Israeli war.

New Policy Initiatives

The decision of Brezhnev and Kosygin to make the Middle East a primary area of Soviet interest meant that the new Russian leaders would have to come to grips with some of the dilemmas left unsolved from the Khrushchev era. Most important of these was the role the Communist parties of the Middle East were to play in the political and economic life of the countries in which they operated. While Khrushchev had been generally ambivalent about this, the Brezhnev-Kosygin leadership adopted a clearer position. They no longer entertained much hope that any of the Communist parties of the region would seize power; indeed, confronted by a hostile Communist China, the Russian leaders must have wondered if it was to their benefit if any more countries were taken over by independent Communist parties. In any case the new Russian leaders began to emphasize the importance of good state relations with the nationalist leaders of the Middle East, and generally let the Communist parties of the region fend for themselves. In the case of the Northern Tier states, the Russians virtually disregarded the Communist parties; in the case of the Revolutionary Democratic Arab states, the parties were urged to disband and their members urged to join the large state parties of their countries, such as Egypt's Arab Socialist Union, with which the Russians, in a policy change begun in Khrushchev's last months in power, were trying to develop party-to-party relations.

Thus, in April 1965 the Egyptian Communist Party was officially dissolved; a communique later published in *Al-Nahar* (Beirut) announced the termination

> of the existence of the Egyptian Communist Party as an independent body and the instruction of its members to submit—as individuals—their applications for membership in the Arab Socialist Union, and to struggle for the formation of a single socialist party which would comprise all the revolutionary forces in the country.[43]

Unfortunately for the Soviet leaders, the new strategy met with serious difficulties only two months later as Ben-Bella was ousted from office by Hoauri Boumedienne, the Algerian military chief, who had earlier complained about the growth of Communist influence in the Ben-Bella government. Boumedienne purged the Algerian government and the FLN of its Communist members and publicly stated that Communists would have no part in his new government.[44] For reasons of international politics, the Soviet leadership did not break relations with the new regime, even when Algerian Communists were imprisoned by it. The CPSU even continued party-to-party relations with the now Communist-free FLN, perhaps hoping thereby to maintain socialist influence on the Boumedienne regime from above. Nonetheless, party relations with the FLN proved to be an embarrassment for the Soviet Union because the Algerian Communist Party, although now illegal, continued to operate. At the 23d CPSU Congress in March 1966, the Algerian FLN, which was invited as a friendly (albeit non-Communist) party, walked out rather than see the Algerian Communist Party seated as an official delegation.[45]

Thus, the new Russian leaders had run into a dilemma. In seeking to develop close party ties with the non-Communist state parties of the radical Arab states, they invited the Algerian FLN to the conference; yet, because of the Sino-Soviet conflict and for reasons of domestic legitimacy, they had to invite the Algerian Communist Party as well. The Soviet goal to remain the leaders of the international Communist movement had once again come into conflict with its Middle Eastern policies. Unfortunately for the Russian leaders, this particular conflict was to occur again.[46]

Meanwhile, in Egypt the decision to dissolve the Communist Party had not led to the hoped-for increase in Communist influence in the Nasser regime, although it did remove a major irritant in Soviet-Egyptian relations. While the former members of the party were given posts in the Egyptian mass media, the Youth Bureau, the Ministry of Education, and even the Central Committee of the Arab Socialist Union, power remained in the hands of Nasser and his entourage, and there was no noticeable increase in socialist legislation as a result of the Communist presence. While the Marxists may have hoped to form "vanguard cadres" in the Arab Socialist Union, they were unable to do so; indeed, the only vanguard organization within the ASU was a quasi-secret police cadre system controlled by Ali Sabry and Shaari Gomaa, which arrested and periodically imprisoned the former Communists.[47]

Perhaps because of the apparent failure of the Egyptian experiments in Communist Party dissolution, or because of the prestige of Khalid Bakdash, who had strongly opposed it, the Soviet leadership did not actively pressure the Syrian Communist Party to dissolve following the coming to power of the pro-Russian left-wing Ba'ath regime in Syria in February 1966. Instead, the CPSU established party-to-party relations with it, thus extending Soviet party relations to the third Arab state in the Middle East. The Soviet action was preceded by the decision by the new regime to permit Khalid Bakdash to return from exile, and the subsequent Soviet loan of $132 million to Syria for the construction of the Euphrates Dam. The timing of the loan, coming so soon after Bakdash's return, is clearly reminiscent of the $277 million loan to Egypt in 1964 following Nasser's decision to free imprisoned Egyptian Communists. It would thus appear that a demonstrative act by a nationalist Arab leadership toward its Communist Party, one of little or no political cost to the leadership, might well bring a reward well out of proportion to the cost involved.[48]

In addition to deemphasizing the importance of the Middle Eastern Communist parties and attempting to develop close party ties with the nationalist parties of the radical Arab states, there was another policy change under Brezhnev and Kosygin. This involved a revised estimate of the desirability of Arab unity. While Khrushchev was ambivalent on the issue of Arab unity and occasionally opposed it because he feared that it would be a barrier to the spread of Russian and Communist influence, the new Russian leadership gave it a strong endorsement. The reason for this change in policy lay in the fact that beginning in 1965 the Russians tried to forge a quasi-alliance of the "anti-imperialist" forces of the Middle East under Soviet leadership. The fact that perhaps the only issue on which all Arabs can agree is opposition to Israel had led the Russians to brand Israel as the "imperialist wedge" in the Middle East and to link closely the Arab struggle against Israel with the "struggle against imperialism." One of the Soviet goals in this process was to limit the internecine conflict among the Arab nations, particularly Egypt, Syria, and Iraq, which was as endemic to the Middle East as the Arab-Israeli conflict.[49] In addition, the Russians hoped that, by becoming the champion of the Arab states against Israel, they could line up the Arab states against the West as well. Yet this policy, while it paid some dividends to the Russians, also proved to be a very dangerous one, since it almost got the Russians involved in the June 1967 Arab-Israeli war and into an open conflict with Israel and the United States in July 1970.

Soviet Policy toward the Northern
Tier under Brezhnev and Kosygin

When the new Russian leadership began to step up the Soviet drive in the Middle East, attention was first turned to the nations of the Northern Tier. A deliberate effort was made to improve relations with Turkey, and the Russians shifted their position on the Cyprus issue to gain Turkish support. Kosygin visited Ankara in September 1966, and a $200-million Soviet loan was worked out in which the Russians were committed to construct a steel mill and several other industrial projects. Interestingly enough, the agreement stipulated that the Russian loan could be repaid by the shipment of certain types of Turkish products— products that had a difficult time finding markets in the West.[50]

Soviet relations improved even more rapidly with Iran. In July 1965 the Shah paid an official visit to the Soviet Union, and in January 1966 the Russians gave Iran a $288.9 million loan for a series of industrial projects.[51] Of greatest diplomatic importance was the Soviet-Iranian agreement reached at the same time, whereby the Russians would provide Iran with $110 million in military equipment, primarily small arms and transport equipment, in return for Iranian gas. While some Western commentators stated that the Russians were now making dangerous inroads in Iran, it appeared that the Shah was utilizing the Soviet arms for several purposes of his own. The first was to persuade the United States to sell Iran more sophisticated weapons, including antiaircraft equipment, under the implicit threat that Iran would otherwise turn to the USSR.[52] Perhaps more important, however, was that the USSR, in supplying arms to Iran, had implicitly strengthened the Shah in his dealings with Iraq, a nation with good relations with the Soviet Union and one with which Iran was continuously in conflict; the new Soviet-Iranian detente enabled the Shah to focus his attention on the power struggle in the Persian Gulf. In any case, the Russians evidently found their rapprochement with Iran to be a most satisfactory one, because in April 1968, in another visit to Iran, Kosygin offered still another loan, this time for up to $300 million.[53]

By the summer of 1970 the Brezhnev-Kosygin leadership had agreed to provide no less than $788.9 million in economic aid to the nations of the Northern Tier, along with $110 million in military aid. Yet what had the Russians obtained in return? Relations had improved considerably with both Turkey and Iran, but both remained within the Western alliance system, and any thoughts of a drift toward neutralism seemed to have been aborted by the Soviet invasion of Czechoslovakia in August 1968. Soviet ships now visited Iran's Persian Gulf ports (along with Iraq's), but this merely made the Russian choice more difficult in case of a clash between the Persian Gulf powers. Indeed, as the politics of the Persian Gulf grew hotter with the British withdrawal from the region in 1971, the Russians were to find that Iran had exploited her newly improved relations with the USSR to achieve her own objectives in the region.[54] Similarly, although the Russians enjoyed a larger degree of freedom of maneuver through the straits as a result of their improved relations with Turkey, the Turks remained quite independent, as evidenced by their refusal, despite a great deal of Soviet pressure, to return the Lithuanians who had hijacked a Russian plane to Turkey in September 1970.

Soviet Policy toward the Southern Tier under Brezhnev and Kosygin

The Russian leadership's policy toward the Arab nations and Israel from 1964 until the death of Nasser was considerably more complex than their policy toward Iran and Turkey. Mention has already been made of the changed Soviet position on the desirability of Arab unity and the Soviet effort to promote close party relations between the CPSU and the radical Arab socialist parties of the region. Economic and military aid continued to play an important role in the Soviet-Arab relations, as it had done under Khrushchev, but Soviet political support for the radical Arab regimes, primarily Syria's, was perhaps even more important. The Syrian regime that had taken power in February 1966 espoused not only the need for a socialist transformation in Syria and close cooperation with the Soviet Union, but also military and financial assistance for the Palestine Fatah guerrilla organization led by Yasir Arafat, which began a series of terrorist attacks against Israel. These attacks placed the narrowly based Ba'ath regime in danger of retaliatory attacks by Israel, which might cause its fall; in order to avoid such a possibility the Soviet leadership urged the other Arab states, especially Egypt, to join together with Syria against the "imperialists" and Israel. This was the theme of a visit by Soviet Premier Kosygin to Cairo in May 1966, in which the Soviet leader called for a united front of progressive Arab states "such as the United Arab Republic, Algeria, Iraq and Syria to confront imperialism and reaction."[55] Kosygin's visit to Cairo was followed by a trip by Iraqi Premier Bazzaz to Moscow in late July, in which the Soviet leadership publicly ended its rift with the Iraqi government over its persecution of the Kurds and the Iraqi Communist Party, and urged the Iraqis to join in the anti-imperialist front of the Arab states.[56] In November 1966 the Arab united front sought by the USSR began to take shape as Egypt and Syria signed a defensive alliance, and the Soviet leaders may have hoped that this would deter any major Israeli attack on Syria.[57] Nonetheless, the Syrian government seized on the alliance to step up its support for Palestinian guerrilla attacks on Israel, and by April 1967 the Syrian-Israeli and Jordanian-Israeli borders had become tinderboxes.

The Israelis had initially restricted themselves to retaliatory raids against the Jordanians, through whose territory the guerrillas had come from Syria. In early April they decided to retaliate directly against the Syrians. Following Syrian shelling of Israeli farmers from the Golan Heights, the Israeli air force took to the skies to silence the Syrian artillery and in the process shot down seven Syrian jets that had come to intercept them. This defeat was a major blow to the prestige of the Syrian government, and when coupled with anti-Ba'ath rioting led by Moslem religious leaders in early May, it appeared that the shaky Syrian Ba'athist government was about to fall. These developments led the Russians, who were concerned about the collapse of their main Arab ally in the Middle East and the center of anti-Western activity, to give false information to the Egyptians that Israel was planning a major attack on Syria. Nasser, then at the low point of his prestige in the Arab world, apparently seized this opportunity to regain his lost prestige and again appear as the champion of the Arabs by ordering the UN forces to leave their positions between Israel and Egypt, and by moving Egyptian troops to the borders of Israel. In addition, he blockaded the Straits of Tiran to Israeli shipping and at the end of May signed a military alliance with his erstwhile enemy, King Hussein of Jordan. Following the military encirclement of Israel, it appeared that war was but a few days away, and on the morning of June 5, 1967, the Israelis decided to strike before they were attacked. In the course of six days the Israelis succeeded in defeating the armies of Egypt, Syria, and Jordan and capturing the Sinai Peninsula, the Jordanian section of the West Bank of the Jordan River, and the Golan Heights in Syria.[58]

While Arab leaders may have hoped that the Soviet position of support for the Syrian regime, Soviet efforts to tie it to Egypt through a defense agreement, and Soviet efforts to rally an "anti-imperialist," anti-Israeli alliance among the Arab states would mean Soviet military support to the Arabs during the war with Israel, Soviet military aid was not forthcoming. The only substantive action the Russians took was to break diplomatic relations with Israel, an action also taken by the other Soviet bloc states in Eastern Europe (with the exception of Rumania) and Yugoslavia.

As might be imagined, the lack of Soviet support during the war and the Soviet efforts to achieve a cease-fire with Israeli troops still occupying Arab territory were bitter pills for the Arabs to swallow, and Soviet prestige dipped in the Arab world as a result. In an effort to compensate for their limited support of the Arabs during the war, the Soviet leaders moved immediately to rebuild the armies of Syria and Egypt and offered Soviet weapons to Jordan in an effort to attract King Hussein to the Soviet side. In addition, the Soviet leaders attempted to capitalize on the heightened military weakness of the Arab states and their diplomatic isolation (much of it self-imposed) to increase Soviet influence throughout the Arab world. Having broken diplomatic relations with the United States and Britain during the war, Egypt, Syria, Iraq, and the Sudan had nowhere else to turn for sophisticated military equipment, although French President Charles de Gaulle, in condemning Israel for attacking the Arabs, sought to spread French influence in the Arab states and at the same time to obtain new markets for France's battle-proven Mirage jet fighter-bombers. China was also not idle during this period. Immediately after the war, the Chinese diverted to Egypt four shiploads of Australian wheat destined for China and gave Egypt a $10-million loan.[59] The Chinese proved unwilling, however, to give the Egyptians what they really wanted—an atom bomb. As Mohammed Heikal relates in *The Cairo Documents*, the Chinese leaders refused the Egyptian request and told the Egyptian delegation that if they wanted atomic weaponry, they would have to develop it themselves, just as China had done.[60]

One consequence of the June war that the Soviet leaders welcomed was the oil embargo that the Arab states imposed on the United States, Britain, and West Germany. An article in the August 1967 issue of *International Affairs* stated:

> The oil weapon is a powerful weapon in the hands of the Arab countries. This is the first time in the history of the Middle East that the Western World has been made to feel who is the real owner of Arab oil. Let us add that the Western powers depend heavily on Arab oil.[61]

Despite Soviet urging, however, Arab solidarity on the oil embargo could not be maintained, particularly since the conservative Arab states—Saudi Arabia, Kuwait, and Libya—were demanding its termination.[62] In addition, both the United States (then possessing an oil surplus available for export) and Iran stepped up production to compensate for the Arab oil cutoff, and Western Europe was in no danger of running out of oil. Consequently, at the Arab summit conference in Khartoum in August 1967, the Arab states agreed to terminate the oil embargo. The rich oil states—Saudi Arabia, Kuwait, and Libya—agreed to provide Egypt and Jordan with an annual subsidy to compensate them for war losses. (Syria, which boycotted the conference, was not included in the subsidy arrangement.) In return, Nasser agreed to pull Egyptian troops out of Yemen, thus ending the threat to Saudi Arabia's southern border.

While not too pleased with the end of the Arab oil embargo and the end of "anti-imperialist" Arab unity created by the war, the Soviet leaders may have been relieved that the rich oil states were sharing with the USSR the expensive burden of supporting the chronically poor Egyptian economy. Writing in *New Times* after the conclusion of the Khartoum conference, Igor Belyayev and Yevgeny Primakov, two of the senior Soviet commentators on Middle Eastern affairs, seemed to agree with the Khartoum decision:

> It was a matter of sober calculation. Refusal to pump oil for the United States, Britain and the Federal Republic of Germany caused no actual shortage of oil and oil products in Western Europe.[63]

Nasser's agreement at the Khartoum conference to withdraw Egyptian troops from Yemen appeared to most observers at the time to mean that the Saudi-backed Royalist forces would emerge victorious from the long and bloody Yemeni civil war. To prevent this from happening, the USSR engaged in a massive airlift of military equipment to the Republican forces in late 1967, and this helped prevent a Royalist victory. Unfortunately for the Russians, however, squabbling among the Republican forces was eventually to result in a coalition government of Royalists and Republicans and a Westward turn in Yemeni foreign policy.

To the south in Aden, the Soviet leaders quickly recognized the nationalist regime, which came to power after the British withdrawal at the end of 1967, and which proclaimed Aden to be the People's Democratic Republic of South Yemen. Within two months the USSR had begun to send military equipment to the strategically located state at the entrance to the Red Sea, and it was not long before the South Yemeni Defense Minister journeyed to Moscow to ask for more aid. South Yemen, however, was plagued by a festering civil war between two radical nationalist groups who had fought each other as well as the British during the independence struggle. It was also beset by continuing tribal strife and an ill-defined border with North Yemen, which soon was the scene of military conflict. In this situation the Soviet Union tried to maintain as neutral a position as possible toward all groups while at the same time acquiring storage facilities and naval landing rights in the port city Aden.[64]

While the Soviet Union became active in southern Arabian affairs following the June war because of the exigencies of the political situation (North Yemen) and perceived opportunities (South Yemen), the main focus of Soviet activity in the 1967-70 period lay in its relations with the war-weakened regime of Egyptian President Gamal Nasser. Soviet-Egyptian cooperation manifested itself primarily in the diplomatic and military spheres, but the USSR also continued to lend money to Egypt for industrialization. In November 1967 the United States and the Soviet Union, together with Britain, worked out a vague formula, UN Resolution no. 242, which called for Israeli withdrawal "from occupied territories" (without stating how far the withdrawal should go) in return for Israel's right to live in peace within "secure and recognized boundaries" (without stating where these boundaries should be or defining the word "secure"). Resolution

no. 242 also created a UN mediator, Gunnar Jarring, who soon began a long, te-
dious, and ultimately unsuccessful series of meetings with Israel, Egypt, and Jordan, all of whom had accepted the resolution while interpreting it quite differently.[65]

The failure of Jarring's diplomatic efforts, as well as various Soviet-sponsored four-power and two-power conferences to obtain an Israeli withdrawal
from the Sinai Peninsula, prompted Nasser to begin a war of attrition with the
newly rebuilt army against Israel in April 1969. Hoping to use Egypt's superiority in artillery to cause unacceptable casualties to Israeli forces dug in along the
canal, Egyptian guns began a steady pounding of the Israeli positions. The Israelis, with only a twelfth the population of Egypt, and inferior in artillery
pieces, decided to use the one weapon in which they had almost absolute superiority, their air force, to silence the Egyptian artillery. Having accomplished this
with minimum losses in aircraft, the Israelis then embarked on a series of deep
penetration raids into the heartland of Egypt in an effort to persuade Nasser to
give up his war of attrition, and by January 1970 Israeli planes were flying at
will through eastern Egypt.

This situation was humiliating to Nasser. Having lost the 1967 war and the
Sinai Peninsula, he now seemed unable even to defend Egypt's heartland. Consequently, in an effort to remedy this politically intolerable situation, Nasser flew
to Moscow and asked the Soviet leaders to establish an air-defense system
manned by Soviet pilots and antiaircraft forces, and protected by Soviet troops.
The cost to Egypt, however, was a high one. To obtain Soviet aid, Nasser had to
grant to the Soviet Union exclusive control over a number of Egyptian airfields
as well as operational control over a large portion of the Egyptian army.[66]

In deciding to help the Egyptians, the Soviet leadership was faced with a
difficult decision. On the one hand, failure to help Nasser might mean the Egyptian president's ouster by elements in the Egyptian leadership less friendly toward the USSR at a time when the United States was trying to rebuild its position in the Arab world. In addition, the airbases that the USSR would control
could be used by Russian pilots not only to intercept the Israelis but also to fly
covering missions for the Soviet Mediterranean fleet. This would be of great tactical benefit to Soviet commanders because the USSR possessed no genuine aircraft carriers of its own at the time. A final argument in favor of the Soviet commitment to Egypt was that it would be a demonstration to the Arab world that
the USSR was an ally to be counted on.

Despite these clear advantages, there was one major disadvantage—the negative effect on the United States of the Soviet intervention. Up to this time, other
than supplying limited numbers of military advisers, both superpowers had refrained from a major commitment of combat troops to any nation in the Middle
East. Now, with between 10,000 and 15,000 Soviet troops to be stationed in
Egypt and with Soviet pilots flying combat missions, there was the serious possibility of a superpower confrontation. Given American troop commitments in

Vietnam and the harsh clamor in the United States not to commit any more Americans to combat duty, the Soviet leaders were probably safe in assuming that no American ground troops or pilots would be stationed in Israel. (In any case, the Israelis stated that they wanted only American materiel, not American troops.) Nonetheless, there was still the possibility that in the event of a confrontation between the Soviet Union and Israel, the United States would be drawn in on the side of the Israelis.

Finally, perhaps reasoning that their investment in Egypt, still the most powerful and most influential of all the Arab states, was too great to give up, or perhaps believing that a Vietnam-burdened Nixon administration would not act decisively in the Middle East despite its public statements to the contrary, the Soviet leaders decided to take the risk and commit pilots and combat troops to Egypt. Fortunately for the Soviet leaders, Israeli Defense Minister Moshe Dayan stated that the Israeli air force would cease its deep penetration raids of Egypt so as to avoid a confrontation with the Soviet pilots; this, initially at least, took some of the heat out of the situation. By the end of June, however, with Soviet forces engaged in establishing the air-defense system near the Suez Canal, Soviet-Israeli clashes did occur, and on one occasion the Israelis shot down five Soviet-piloted Migs. In addition, President Nixon publicly warned the Russians that the Middle East could drag the superpowers into a direct war, just as happened in 1914. Perhaps fearing such an eventuality, or perhaps wishing to consolidate their new military position in Egypt, the Soviet Union agreed to an American-sponsored 90-day cease-fire arrangement after lengthy and "frank" consultations with Nasser in Moscow.[67] The cease-fire was eventually to last for more than three years; but soon after it came into effect (August 8, 1970), and in large part because of it, Jordan was to erupt into civil war, a development to be discussed below.

While the USSR had enhanced its military position in the eastern Mediterranean through its acquisition of bases in Egypt, both Soviet and Communist influence in Nasser's regime still remained limited. Although Soviet commentator Georgi Mirsky had optimistically stated shortly after the June war in a *New Times* article, "It is not to be excluded that left socialist tendencies in the Arab world will gain as a result of the recent events,"[68] events were to prove otherwise. Perhaps emboldened by the results of the war, the Egyptian Marxists demanded the liquidation of the Nasser regime's right wing and the transfer of power to "revolutionary cadres."[69] These demands went unheeded. Nasser did purge some rightists, primarily to secure his own political base, although his action was widely interpreted at the time as a concession to the Russians. In an interview in *Jeune Afrique* on October 1, 1967, an Egyptian Communist testified to the weakness of his movement in Egypt:

> We have committed major errors, we have been "drooling" so much during the years because Nasser had permitted us to participate in

national life and had given us posts in editorial offices and the university, that we have let ourselves become embourgeoises. We have lost all contact with the masses and these, abandoned to themselves, are completely disorganized. The truth is that we are tired and not at all prepared to return to prison.[70]

Despite the aid he was receiving from the USSR, Nasser also tried to maintain some ties with the West. He continued to rely on American oil companies to search for oil in Egypt. He also reportedly advised the new Libyan leader Mu'ammar Kaddafi, who came to power in September 1969 after overthrowing King Idris, to turn to France and not to the USSR for arms.[71]

While Soviet influence had increased quite sharply in Egypt, it remained quite limited in Syria and Iraq, the other two major recipients of Soviet attention in the region. For example, the Soviet leaders were unable to persuade either the Syrians or the Iraqis to accept the Soviet-backed UN Resolution no. 242 or to cooperate with Egypt in seeking a political settlement to the Middle East crisis. Syria and Iraq also rejected the cease-fire agreement of August 1970, much to the chagrin of the Soviet Union. In Syria, Soviet efforts were hampered by the Syrian Communist Party, which actively campaigned against Defense Minister Hafiz Assad in his struggle for power with Salah Jedid, the ex-army officer who was head of the Ba'ath party. The Syrian Communists not only harmed their own fortunes in Syria (limited as they were) but Soviet-Syrian relations as well, as the Soviet Ambassador, Nuradin Mukhdinov, was drawn into the power struggle pitting the Communists and Jedid on one side against the ultimately victorious Assad on the other.[72]

In May 1969 Assad, who was angered both by Soviet meddling in Syrian politics and by the failure of the USSR to provide what he thought were sufficient weapons, dispatched his close friend, Syrian Chief of Staff Lt. Gen. Mustafa Tlass, on an arms procurement trip to China. There, perhaps acting on Assad's instructions, Tlass allowed himself to be photographed waving the famous little Red Book of Chairman Mao's sayings. Coming only two months after the bloody Sino-Soviet clashes along the Ussuri River, Tlass's action must have been particularly galling to the Russians after all the Soviet economic, military, and diplomatic support for Syria. According to the Jerusalem *Post*, Assad reportedly had said prior to Tlass's journey:

Why should we not boycott the Soviet Union and its supporters inside the country? If we do so, we can force them to review their stand. Either they give us what we want and what is necessary or they will lose our friendship.[73]

The Soviet leaders may have taken Assad's warning seriously, or they may have concluded that it was counterproductive to get too closely involved in internal Syrian politics. In any case, by the end of 1969 they had dissociated themselves from the power struggle in Syria, which Assad seemed certain to win. The Soviet leaders may have taken some consolation from the fact that Assad was more willing to cooperate with the other Arab states than Jedid was, although the Communist Party of Syria, which had opposed him, continued to be persecuted. The persecution was severe enough for the Soviet press to take public notice; on July 18, 1970, the Soviet newspaper *Trud*, in an article signed "Observer," protested against the arrest and murder of a number of Syrian Communists.[74]

The Soviet Union's relations with Iraq during the 1967-70 period were a bit warmer than with Syria, although the two states continued to disagree on such Middle Eastern political issues as Resolution no. 242, the Iraqi government's treatment of its Kurdish minority, and its persecution of the Iraqi Communists. Iraq had long been isolated both in the Middle East as a whole and in the Arab world, and successive Iraqi governments looked to their tie to the USSR as a means of balancing off Iraq's strained relations with its pro-Western neighbors, Iran, Saudi Arabia, Jordan, Turkey, and Kuwait. From the Soviet point of view, the weak Aref regime in Iraq was not only yet another base for Soviet influence in the region; it was also a potential source of oil. By 1967 Soviet planners had begun to change their earlier optimistic predictions that the USSR would have sufficient oil and natural gas to meet all its internal needs as well as increasing amounts available for export to the Soviet bloc states of Eastern Europe and to hard-currency customers in Western Europe and Japan. While the USSR had large reserves of oil and natural gas, most of these were located in the frozen wastes of eastern and western Siberia and would have required large infrastructure investments before they could be developed. Consequently, in December 1967 the USSR signed an agreement with Iraq to provide credits and equipment for the northern Rumelia oil field, with the USSR to be partially repaid in crude oil. In the same year the Soviet Union had also signed long-term agreements with Afghanistan to import natural gas and with Iran to import both oil and natural gas. Soviet thinking at the time seemed to revolve around the idea that the USSR could import oil and natural gas from the Middle East to serve industries in the southern part of the Soviet Union while selling Soviet oil and natural gas to Eastern and Western Europe. Such a plan would also enable the Soviet leaders to postpone, at least for a while, the huge infrastructure investments needed to develop Siberian oil and natural gas.[75]

The coming to power of the Al-Bakr regime in July 1968 had little effect on Soviet-Iraqi relations at the state level, which continued to be very good, despite the fact that Iraqi Communists continued to be persecuted. According to a reliable source, Al-Bakr even negotiated with the Communists to obtain their participation in his government; but by demanding too much (that is, the Defense Ministry) the Iraqi Communist Party wound up with nothing.[76] Nonetheless, the Soviet leadership evidently found its relations with the Al-Bakr regime to be more than satisfactory, since in July 1969 another long .erm oil agreement was signed between the two countries for the development of the oil fields of northern Rumelia. In this one the USSR was to be repaid for its credits and equipment exclusively in Iraqi crude oil.[77] A *Pravda* article by Yevgeny Primakov on September 21 had warm praise for the Al-Bakr regime, although it chided the regime for failing to agree with Resolution no. 242 and for failing to reach an agreement with the Kurds.[78]

While the USSR and Iraq were able to agree on oil development, and the Soviet government warmly hailed the agreement reached on March 11, 1970, between the Iraqi government and the Kurds, the two nations remained divided on policy toward the Arab-Israeli conflict. Iraq opposed the cease-fire agreement of August 1970, and a *Pravda* article of August 1, 1970 called the Iraqi opposition to the cease-fire "incomprehensible" and went on to note:

> the stand taken by the leadership of Iraq's Ba'ath party is surprising.
> . . . *Without warning*, Baghdad began saying that "attempts are being
> made to dispose of the Palestine question" and so forth . . . the nega-
> tive attitude of Iraq's Ba'ath Party leadership toward President Nas-
> ser's initiative and toward the position of the UAR government does
> not contribute to the actual struggle against the aggressor and the
> forces of Imperialism and Zionism that support aggression.[79] [em-
> phasis added]

The fact that the Russian leadership used the phrase "without warning" probably indicates that they were not even consulted by the Iraqi regime on this important policy statement. It is interesting to note that even after an Iraqi delegation went to Moscow for talks in early August, there was no change in Baghdad's position. Despite Iraqi opposition to this relatively important initiative backed by the USSR, the Russians not only did not exert any pressure on the Iraqi leadership (such as curtailing or even cutting off military or economic aid), they went ahead and signed a protocol on trade and economic cooperation with the Iraqis on August 13, 1970, which called for an increase in trade and Soviet assistance. The Russians then granted the Iraqis a $34 million loan on August 30.[80] These events indicate not only a limited degree of Soviet influence in Iraq but also a clear desire by the Russians to maintain good relations with the oil-rich and strategically located nation that had become Egypt's chief rival in the Arab world.

As the Soviets stepped up their efforts to oust Western influence from the Middle East following the June war, developments in the Arab states of North Africa appeared to fall nicely into place for them. In Libya, the pro-Western regime of King Idris was overthrown in September 1969 by a military junta headed by Mu'ammar Kaddafi, whose first major foreign policy demand was for the United States and Britain to leave their military bases in Libya—a demand both Western nations speedily complied with. In Algeria, Boumedienne's decision to nationalize the French-owned oil industry led to a withdrawal of French technicians, and the Soviet Union immediately sent its own technicians to replace them. It should be mentioned, however, that in the cases of both Libya and Algeria, the steps taken by the nationalist regimes to lessen Western influence in their countries did not mean they had opened the door to Soviet control. Both Boumedienne and Kaddafi pursued independent foreign and domestic policies, as their frequent clashes with both the USSR and the United States clearly indicated.

One country where the Soviet Union appeared to make deep inroads was the Sudan. Following a military coup d'etat in May 1969, Jaafar Nimeri came to power. He proclaimed the Sudan to be a democratic republic and defined the main foreign policy aims of his regime as the support of national liberation movements against imperialism, active support of the Palestinian struggle, and extension of the Sudan's ties to the Arab world and the socialist countries. Domestically, Nimeri proclaimed the formation of a single party of "workers, peasants, soldiers, national bourgeoisie and the progressive intelligentsia." Communists were prominently represented in Nimeri's first cabinet, although the Communist Party, like all other existing parties, was officially dissolved.[81]

The Soviet leadership wasted little time in consolidating its relations with Nimeri's regime. The Sudanese leader was invited to Moscow in November 1969, and agreements were signed for the expansion of trade and cultural and scientific cooperation.[82] State relations continued to improve in early January 1970, as Soviet navy warships paid a visit to Port Sudan and the USSR began to supply the Sudan with military equipment.[83] As Soviet-Sudanese relations improved, the Soviet leaders apparently decided that in order to solidify ties with the strategically located nation and to avoid possible future complications, the powerful Sudanese Communist Party should dissolve (as Nimeri had demanded), its members to join Nimeri's one-party regime as individuals, much as the Egyptian Communist Party had done earlier.[84] However, the Sudanese Communist Party was split, and the faction led by Secretary General Abdel Mahgoub apparently refused to comply with the Soviet requests. Nonetheless, Mahgoub was willing to support the Nimeri regime, and in an interview with the Soviet journal *Za rubezhom,* which was broadcast over Radio Moscow in Arabic on August 11, 1969, the Sudanese Communist leader stated:

> The communists believe that the present government is a progressive one and that the May 25th movement had created the best circumstances for continuing our people's struggle for realizing the tasks of the national democratic revolution. Therefore, the Communist Party sincerely supports the new government's policy.[85]

Yet, as the situation in the Sudan developed, it became clear that Nimeri was using the Sudanese Communists to weaken his right-wing enemies, the Mahdiists. Once the Mahdiists were eliminated as a political force, Nimeri arrested and then exiled Mahgoub, who had become increasingly critical of Nimeri's policies, including the entry of the Sudan into a projected confederation with Egypt and Libya. While the anti-Mahgoub faction remained allied to Nimeri and in the government, it appeared that the Sudanese leader had learned the lesson, taught by Kassem a decade earlier, of playing off the Communists against other political forces, and that the Communist Party's future in the Sudan was limited indeed.

If the postwar atmosphere in the Arab world was conducive to weakening Western influence, it also provided fertile ground for the growth of the Palestinian resistance movement, a multitude of guerrilla organizations, which launched attacks against Israel (most of them unsuccessful), capturing the imagination of an Arab public still shocked by Israel's defeat of the regular Arab armies. As the Palestinian guerrilla organizations increased in power, they began actively competing with each other for recruits, funds, and prestige while at the same time increasingly becoming a challenge to the established governments in the Arab world, particularly those in Jordan and Lebanon, where large numbers of Palestinian refugees were located.[86] While the Soviet leadership initially played down the significance of the guerrilla organizations because it preferred to work through the established Arab states, the Russians could not long overlook either the growing power of the Palestinian guerrilla movement as a factor in Middle Eastern politics or the growing involvement of the Chinese Communists in the movement. By providing military equipment and ideological training to a number of the guerrilla organizations, the Chinese were seeking to increase their influence in the Middle East via the guerrilla movement.[87] By mid-1969 the Soviet leadership evidently decided that it was time to get involved with the guerrillas. It did so in a cautious manner, however, and it was not until after the death of Nasser and the severe beating taken by the Palestinians in the Jordanian civil war that the Soviet Union began to court the guerrillas in a serious manner.

At the Seventh World Trade Union Congress in Budapest in October 1969, Politburo member Aleksandr Shelepin came out with the first public sign of Soviet support for the guerrillas:

> We consider the struggle of the Palestine patriots for the liquidation
> of the consequences of Israeli aggression a just anti-imperialist strug-
> gle of national liberation and we support it.[88]

By stressing the term "liquidation of the consequences of Israeli aggression," however, Shelepin was manipulating the meaning of the guerrilla organizations' fight to coincide with the Soviet-backed UN Resolution no. 242. Indeed, in 1969 the guerrilla organizations were virtually unanimous in proclaiming their intention to liquidate Israel itself, rather than to aid the Arab states in recovering the land lost to Israel in 1967. By the end of 1969, however, after observing how clashes with the guerrillas had shaken both the Lebanese and Jordanian governments, Soviet leadership may have begun to envision the Palestinian movement as a useful tool for weakening or even overthrowing the two pro-Western regimes and replacing them with governments more friendly to the USSR.[89]

In February 1970, Yasir Arafat, who had replaced Ahmed Shukeiry as head of the Palestine Liberation Organization (PLO), the loose federation of the guerrilla organizations, after the 1967 war, was invited to Moscow (he had gone to Moscow in July 1968 as part of an Egyptian delegation), but the visit was kept in low key, as the invitation came from the Soviet Afro-Asian Solidarity Organization rather than from a higher-ranking organ of the Soviet government. The very next month, however, Arafat was given a high-level reception in Peking, and the Palestinian guerrilla leader warmly praised the Chinese for their assistance. As Sino-Soviet competition for the allegiance of the guerrillas grew, the Soviet leadership decided that its position would be improved if the Communist parties of the Middle East formed their own guerrilla organization, which would be able to participate in, and hopefully influence, the PLO from the inside. Consequently, the Communist parties of Lebanon, Syria, Jordan, and Iraq formed the Ansar guerrilla organization in March 1970, but as a Jordanian Communist Party member was to complain two years later, Ansar had very little influence in the guerrilla movement.[90]

One of the main problems plaguing the PLO was the very sharp competition among its constituent organizations for power. Some guerrilla groups were avowedly Marxist, such as the Popular Front for the Liberation of Palestine (PFLP) and the Popular Democratic Front for the Liberation of Palestine (PDFLP). Others were the instruments of Arab governments, such as Asiqa (Syria) and the Arab Liberation Front (Iraq). Still others, such as Fatah, the largest, proclaimed themselves ideologically neutral and were willing to accept aid from all sides. By June 1970 the intra-Palestinian struggle for power had reached a peak, with the PFLP openly challenging Fatah's leadership and seeking to bring down the regime of King Hussein in Jordan as well. By this time the guerrillas had established a virtual state-within-a-state in Jordan, and the compromise agreement worked out in June between Hussein and the guerrillas testified to their growing power. The acceptance by King Hussein of the American-sponsored cease-fire agreement (Egypt and Israel also agreed) in August set the stage for the final showdown. Fearing that the Palestinian cause would be overlooked in a direct settlement between Israel and Jordan and Egypt, and feeling that the time had come to topple the Hussein regime, the PFLP embarked on a skyjacking spree that resulted in the flying of three skyjacked passenger planes to a guerrilla-controlled airstrip in northern Jordan and their demolition, while the troops of King Hussein, which had surrounded the guerrilla airstrip, looked helplessly on.[91]

Hussein seized this opportunity to end the guerrilla threat to his regime and began military attacks on the guerrillas. While his army was attacking the guerrilla positions, the Syrian government, then headed by Salah Jedid, dispatched an armored brigade to help the guerrillas. At this juncture the United States moved the Sixth Fleet toward the battle area and, acting jointly with Israel, threatened to intervene if the Syrian forces were not withdrawn, as both Kissinger and Nixon clearly indicated that they would not permit the pro-Western regime of Hussein to be ousted by the invasion of a client state of the Soviet Union.[92] The Soviet leadership, during this period, after initially appearing to support the Syrian move, became conspicuous by its inaction.[93] For this reason, or because of the strong American-Israeli stand, or, most probably, because he saw a chance to embarrass Jedid, General Assad, who controlled the Syrian air force, refused to dispatch Syrian jets to fly covering missions for the Syrian tanks. The result of Assad's decision was that the Jordanian air force and tank units badly mauled the invading Syrian army, which was forced to retreat in disarray to Syria. The emboldened Hussein then turned to finish off the guerrillas and had almost completed the job when an Arab League cease-fire arranged by Nasser came into effect.[94] It was to be the Egyptian president's last act as an Arab leader, however, because on the very next day he died of a heart attack, an event that was to lead to a transformation of the Soviet position in the Middle East. Before this transformation is discussed, however, it is necessary to evaluate the Soviet Middle Eastern position at the time of Nasser's death.

THE SOVIET POSITION IN THE MIDDLE EAST AT THE TIME OF NASSER'S DEATH: A BALANCE SHEET

In assessing the Soviet position in the Middle East at the time of Nasser's death, it is clear that the primary Soviet gain since Khrushchev's ouster had been an improvement in the Soviet military position in the region, although this was not an unmixed blessing for the Soviet leaders. The USSR had acquired air and naval bases in Egypt, and port rights in Syria, the Sudan, North Yemen, South Yemen, and Iraq. These bases in Egypt gave air cover to the Soviet fleet sailing in the eastern Mediterranean and thus were substitutes for aircraft carriers, which the Soviet navy did not then possess. Yet the large military presence of the Soviet Union in the Middle East also contained a major risk for the Soviet leadership. There were a number of Arabs who wanted to involve the USSR in a war against Israel, regardless of the international consequences of such an action. One of the reasons that the Soviet Union accepted the American cease-fire initiative in the summer of 1970 appears to have been a desire to cool down its rapidly escalating conflict with Israel, which might soon have involved the United States as well. Thus, while the Soviet military position in the Middle East had improved by the time of Nasser's death, so too had the chances of a military confrontation between the United States and the Soviet Union—a development the Soviet leaders probably wished to avoid at almost any cost, given the increasingly hostile relations between the USSR and China.

Other than improving their military position in the Middle East, there were few other concrete gains the Russians could point to from their expensive involvement in the region at the time of Nasser's death. The Russians seemed to have assumed the role of military supplier and financier of the economically weak radical Arab regimes of the area, and they appeared to be attempting to buy influence in the Northern Tier nations as well. Nonetheless, as Aaron Klieman pointed out in his 1970 study of the Soviet involvement in the Middle East, "In return for enabling the Soviets to claim influence, the Arabs expect Moscow to supply loans, weapons, technical advice, diplomatic support, and favorable terms of trade."[95] The obvious question is, Who was exploiting whom in this relationship? In addition, Soviet "influence" was far from reaching a position of control over the policies of any of the regimes in the region. The continued opposition of Syria and Iraq to such Soviet-supported peace initiatives as UN Resolution no. 242 and the 1970 cease-fire agreement presented serious difficulties to Soviet policy makers, who sought to create a unified Arab stand on a Middle Eastern settlement that would be favorable to both the USSR and its Arab allies.

An even more serious problem for the Soviet Union at the time of Nasser's death was the reemergence of the United States as an active factor in Middle Eastern politics. While the U.S. position in the Arab world reached a low point following the Six-Day War, it appeared to have made a substantial recovery by September 1970. The Rogers Plan, formally announced on December 9, 1969, called for an almost total Israeli withdrawal from territories occupied in the 1967 war, and seemed to be a demonstration of the Nixon administration's "evenhandedness" in the Arab-Israeli conflict.[96] The cease-fire between Israel, Egypt, and Jordan that began in August 1970 was an American initiative, and although it was violated by Egypt (Israel received compensation for this by increased delivery of American weapons), it nonetheless seemed to set the climate for substantive peace negotiations. The strong American support for King Hussein's regime when Syrian tanks invaded Jordan in September 1970, during Hussein's crackdown on the guerrillas, helped restore a great deal of American influence in Jordan and in the region as a whole. The Soviet Union's disinclination to get involved in support of one of its erstwhile clients, Syria, against a client of the United States, Jordan, was also not lost on the Arab world.

Perhaps even more important, however, was the impression, spread in the Arab world by American declarations of an evenhanded policy in the Middle East, that the United States might be willing to assist the Arab states in regaining at least part, if not all, of the land lost to Israel in 1967—something the Soviet Union had been unable to do by diplomacy and was still unwilling to do by force.

Thus, the specter of rising American influence in the Arab world and the disunity among the Soviet Union's Arab clients were the major problems confronting the Soviet leadership when Gamal Nasser, the man who had been the linchpin of Soviet strategy in the Middle East, departed from the scene.[97]

NOTES

1. For an analysis of Soviet policy toward the Middle East between 1917 and 1945, see Ivan Spector, *The Soviet Union and the Muslim World* (Seattle: University of Washington Press, 1956). This book also contains a useful survey of czarist foreign policy toward the Middle East from 1552 to 1914. For an analysis of Soviet policy toward the Communist parties and radical movements of the Middle East in the interwar period, see Walter Laqueur, *The Soviet Union and the Middle East* (New York: Praeger, 1959), pp. 1-134. For an excellent treatment of Western involvement in the Middle East, see William R. Polk, *The United States and the Arab World*, 3d rev. ed. (Cambridge, Mass.: Harvard University Press, 1975).

2. For a detailed examination of Soviet pressure against Iran and Turkey, see Howard M. Sachar, *Europe Leaves the Middle East 1936-1954* (New York: Alfred A. Knopf, 1972), chap. 9.

3. According to Khrushchev's memoirs, Stalin considered the Near East part of Britain's sphere of influence and felt that Russia did not have the power to challenge Britain there directly. See Strobe Talbott, ed., *Khrushchev Remembers* (Boston: Little, Brown, 1970), p. 431. Soviet support for the ouster of British and French troops from Lebanon and Syria in 1946 seems to have been motivated by the same considerations as its early support for Israel. A collection of Soviet documents pertaining to its relations with the Arab world from 1917 to 1960 is found in *SSSR i arabskie strany* [The USSR and the Arab states] (Moscow: Government Printing Office of Political Literature, 1960). The documents pertaining to Soviet support of Lebanon and Syria are found on pages 87-96 of that volume.

4. For a detailed analysis of the USSR's relations with Israel, see Avigdor Dagan, *Moscow and Jerusalem* (New York: Abelard-Schuman, 1970). For an analysis of Soviet behavior during the Israeli struggle for independence, see Robert O. Freedman, "The Partition of Palestine: Conflicting Nationalism and Power Politics," in *Partition: Peril to World Peace*, ed. Thomas Hachey (New York: Rand McNally, 1972).

5. In the 1955-56 period, while there were already some strains in Sino-Soviet relations, Russia was still the unquestioned leader of the socialist bloc. In addition, the rapprochement between Yugoslavia and the USSR that took place at the time seemed to many observers to bring Yugoslavia back into the Soviet sphere of influence. (Yugoslavia had been ousted from the socialist bloc by Stalin in 1948 and had subsequently turned to the West for aid.) Thus, Khrushchev apparently considered that any state that became Communist would automatically come under Soviet leadership. This situation was to change radically with the onset of the Sino-Soviet conflict several years later. For an excellent survey of Soviet policy toward the Middle East under Khrushchev, see Oles M. Smolansky, *The Soviet Union and the Arab East under Khrushchev* (Lewisburg, Pa.: Bucknell University Press, 1974).

6. Two useful analyses of the background to the arms deal are Uri Ra'anan, *The USSR Arms the Third World* (Cambridge, Mass.: M.I.T. Press, 1969); and Amos Perlmutter, "Big Power Games, Small Power Wars," *Transaction* 7, nos. 9-10 (July-August 1970): 79-83.

7. For an analysis of the Middle East arms race as a cause of the Arab-Israeli wars, see Nadav Safran, *From War to War* (New York: Pegasus, 1969). For a description of Soviet efforts to avoid participation in the 1956 conflict, see J. M. Mackintosh, *Strategy and Tactics of Soviet Foreign Policy* (London: Oxford University Press, 1963), pp. 185-87. The Soviet threats against Britain, France, and Israel were not issued until after the crisis had abated, and seemed primarily directed toward a propaganda advantage with respect to the United States, which had also opposed the attack on Egypt. In 1967 Nasser's claim that American and British planes were involved in the attack on Egypt seemed to be a ploy to get the Russians to intervene on his behalf. For a discussion of Soviet behavior in the 1973 war, see chap. 5. For an analysis of Soviet arms shipments to Egypt prior to each conflict, see Jon

D. Glassman, *Arms for the Arabs: The Soviet Union and War in the Middle East* (Baltimore: Johns Hopkins, 1975).

8. *Al-Jarida* (Beirut), August 16, 1955, cited in Laqueur, *The Soviet Union and the Middle East,* pp. 219-20.

9. Press Release 50/59 (March 20, 1959), UAR Information Department, Cairo. Document found in Walter Laqueur, *The Struggle for the Middle East* (New York: Macmillan, 1969), p. 235.

10. Data are available only on the economic aid, which consisted of an $87.5-million loan for a dam and power plant on the Euphrates River, and other projects. Kurt Mueller, *The Foreign Aid Programs of the Soviet Bloc and Communist China* (New York: Walker, 1967), p. 225.

11. For a detailed discussion of the events leading up to the union, see Patrick Seale, *The Struggle for Syria* (London: Oxford University Press, 1965); and Malcolm Kerr, *The Arab Cold War* (New York: Oxford University Press, 1970).

12. *New Times,* the Soviet foreign affairs weekly, stated on February 21, 1958: "The Soviet people rejoice in the progress achieved by the friendly Arab nations. *The USSR has never interfered in the internal affairs of any country, Arab or otherwise"* [emphasis added]. *New Times,* no. 7 (1958): 6.

13. On March 16, 1959, the Soviet Union gave Iraq a $137.5-million loan for 35 industrial and agricultural facilities, and on August 18, 1960, a $45-million loan for construction and equipment for the Baghdad-Basra railroad. Data from Mueller, op. cit., p. 223.

14. Nasser was incensed at Soviet support for Kassem, whom he considered a dangerous rival. The Egyptian leader was even more angry at the Russians for opposing the efforts of the Nasserites in Iraq who wished to have their country join the UAR. The Russians apparently felt that their influence would grow faster in an independent Iraq. In a reception for a visiting Iraqi delegation in March 1959, Khrushchev pointedly remarked in a general attack on Nasser: "Untimely unification ultimately undermines the unity of the people, rather than strengthens it. . . . What ensues is not greater unity but a division of forces. Who profits from this . . . only the Imperialists." *Pravda,* March 17, 1959), translated in *Current Digest of the Soviet Press* 11, no. 11 (April 15, 1959): 8.

15. Cited in Aryeh Yodfat, *Arab Politics in the Soviet Mirror* (Jerusalem: Israel Universities Press, 1973), p. 211.

16. For an Egyptian perspective on these events, see Mohammed Heikal, *The Cairo Documents* (New York: Doubleday, 1973), pp. 152-53.

17. For an examination of Kassem's activities, see Majid Khadduri, *Republican Iraq* (New York: Oxford University Press, 1969); and Uriel Dann, *Iraq under Kassem* (New York: Praeger, 1969). Chapter 11 in M. S. Agwani, *Communism in the Arab East* (Bombay: Asia Publishing House, 1969), is also worthy of examination, as it deals in detail with Kassem's manipulation of the Iraqi Communist Party.

18. The Russians got a late start in developing relations with the FLN because Khrushchev did not wish to antagonize French President Charles de Gaulle, whom he hoped to wean away from NATO. The loans that the USSR promised Algeria ($100 million in 1963 and $128 million in 1964—Mueller, op. cit., p. 226) seem also to have been aimed at gaining the USSR admission to the second Bandung Conference of Afro-Asian states, which was scheduled to be held in Algeria in 1965. For an overall discussion of Soviet-Algerian relations, see David and Marina Ottaway, *Algeria: The Politics of a Socialist Revolution* (Berkeley: University of California Press, 1970).

19. In the first installment of his memoirs, Nikita Khrushchev referred to those members of the Soviet leadership who opposed his policy toward Egypt as "those skunks, those narrow-minded skunks who raised such a stink and tried to poison the waters of our relationship with Egypt." See Talbott, op. cit., p. 450.

20. For analyses of the Soviet ideological convolutions, see Richard Lowenthal, "Russia, the One-Party System and the Third World," *Survey,* no. 58 (January 1966): 43-58;

Yodfat, op. cit., chap. 1; and Phillip Mosley, "The Kremlin and the Third World," *Foreign Affairs* 46, no. 1 (October 1967): 64-77. See also Jaan Pennar, *The USSR and the Arabs: The Ideological Dimension* (New York: Crane Russak, 1973).

21. "Socio-Economic Changes in the Arab Countries and 'Arab Socialism' Concepts," *World Marxist Review* 7, no. 9 (1964): 60.

22. Ibid., p. 63.

23. Ibid., p. 62.

24. Heikal, op. cit., pp. 155-57.

25. This sizable loan, like similar loans to Algeria, may have been related to Soviet efforts to gain entry into the second Bandung Conference of Afro-Asian states. The Chinese Communists strongly opposed the admission of the USSR to the conference and offered loans of their own in an effort to prevent it. A very useful chart comparing Chinese and Soviet loans to Afro-Asian countries in the 1963-65 period is found in Marshall Goldman, *Soviet Foreign Aid* (New York: Praeger, 1967), p. 190. The loan may also have been related to Nasser's decision to free a large number of imprisoned Egyptian Communists (an action taken before Khrushchev's visit) and may have served as an incentive for the Egyptian leader to allow some of them to serve in his regime.

26. The Russians justified their assistance to the feudal regime of the Imam of Yemen on the basis of his "anti-imperialist" policy toward British-controlled Aden. Following the death of the Imam in 1962, a civil war broke out in which the Egyptians intervened with large numbers of troops. The USSR supported the Egyptian intervention, although it maintained a number of military advisers there as well.

27. The loan was for a number of projects, the most important of which was a dam. Data from Mueller, op. cit., p. 224.

28. For a more detailed description of the Shah's problems, see Laqueur, *The Struggle for the Middle East*, pp. 30-35.

29. Ibid., p. 17.

30. Nodari Alexandrovich Simoniya, "On the Character of the National Liberation Revolution," *Narodi Azii i Afriki*, no. 6 (1966), translated in *Mizan* 9, no. 2 (March-April 1967): 48.

31. Ibid., p.. 45. A Soviet evaluation of the role of the national bourgeois in the "noncapitalist way" that appeared soon after Nasser's death is found in R. Ulianovsky, "Nekotorie voprosy nikapitalisticheskogo razvitiia" [Some problems of noncapitalist development], *Kommunist*, no. 4 (1971): 103-12.

32. For a detailed description of the new Soviet leadership and its policies, see Sydney Ploss, "Politics in the Kremlin," *Problems of Communism* 19, no. 3 (May-June 1970): 1-14.

33. For an excellent analysis of the factors, both domestic and foreign, that led to Khrushchev's fall, see Carl Linden, *Khrushchev and the Soviet Leadership 1957-1964* (Baltimore: Johns Hopkins Press, 1966).

34. For a description of the U.S. position in the Middle East at this time, see Polk, op. cit., chap. 19. Another useful source for examining the post-1967 situation is John Badeau, *An American Approach to the Arab World* (New York: Harper & Row, 1968).

35. An examination of Soviet policy toward sub-Saharan Africa during the early years of the Brezhnev-Kosygin leadership is found in Robert Levgold, "The Soviet Union's Changing View of Sub-Saharan Africa," in *Soviet Policy in Developing Countries*, ed. W. Raymond Duncan (Waltham, Mass.: Ginn-Blaisdell, 1970), pp. 62-82.

36. For an analysis of Soviet military strategy during the 1965-69 period, see Thomas W. Wolfe, *Soviet Power and Europe* (Baltimore: Johns Hopkins Press, 1970). For an examination of Soviet policy in the Mediterranean, see Kurt Gasteyger, "Moscow and the Mediterranean," *Foreign Affairs* 46, no. 4 (July 1968): 676-87.

37. Badeau, op. cit., p. 158.

38. See William B. Quandt, *Decade of Decisions: American Policy toward the Arab-Is-raeli Conflict 1967-1976* (Berkeley: University of California Press, 1977), p. 38.

39. The competition was becoming very expensive, as indicated by a large number of Soviet loans to Afro-Asian countries in the 1963-65 period. These loans appear to have been motivated, at least in part, by the Soviet effort to gain admission to the second Bandung Conference of Afro-Asian states, which was scheduled to be held in Algeria in 1965.

There is some indication that Nasser was able to secure a Soviet promise to accelerate the construction of the Aswan Dam in return for supporting Soviet admission to the confer-ence. On this point, see Sevinc Carlson, "China, the Soviet Union and the Middle East," *New Middle East*, no. 27 (December 1970): 34. In addition the Soviet decision to give $250 million in loans to Algeria during the 1963-64 period may have been motivated by the same considerations.

40. Interestingly enough, the only Chinese ambassador not to be called home during the cultural revolution was Huang Hua, China's ambassador to Egypt.

For a useful survey of Communist China's policies toward the Middle East until 1964, see Malcolm Kerr, "The Middle East and China," in *Policies toward China: Views from Six Continents*, ed. A. M. Halpern (New York: McGraw-Hill, 1965), pp. 437-56. For a more re-cent analysis, see Carlson, op. cit., pp. 32-40.

41. A detailed analysis of Soviet policy toward Sukarno's regime is found in Ra'anan, op. cit., pt. 2. For a case study of the Soviet experience with Nkrumah, see W. Scott Thompson, "Parameters on Soviet Policy in Africa: Personal Diplomacy and Economic In-terests in Ghana," in Duncan, op. cit., pp. 83-106.

42. It appears that this decision was a ploy to get Soviet support for the narrowly based regime. Whatever the reason, the Russians pledged in April 1966 to help build the large Euphrates Dam and extend the Syrian railroad network (Laqueur, *The Struggle for the Middle East*, pp. 89-90). For an excellent study of the rise of the Ba'ath to power in Syria, see Itamar Rabinowich, *Syria under the Ba'ath 1963-1966* (Jerusalem: Israel Universities Press, 1972).

43. Cited in Shimon Shamir, "The Marxists in Egypt: The 'Licensed Infiltration' Doc-trine in Practice," in *The USSR and the Middle East*, ed. Michael Confino and Shimon Sha-mir (Jerusalem: Israel Universities Press, 1973), p. 295.

44. For a description of these events, see Ottaway, op. cit., chap. 9.

45. For a description of the effect of this incident on Soviet-Algerian relations, see Ottaway, op. cit., p. 234; and the report by John Cooley in the *Christian Science Monitor*, April 2, 1966.

46. It was the Syrian Communist Party's turn to embarrass the Russians in 1968. Dur-ing the Budapest Consultative Conference of Communist Parties, the Syrian delegate, Khalid Bakdash, attacked Rumania's position on the Arab-Israeli conflict, calling the Rumanians "tools of the Zionists," and even went so far as to claim that the Rumanians were "putting themselves outside the Communist movement." It is doubtful that the Russians, who had convened the conference in an effort to garner support for the expulsion of the Chinese Communists from the international Communist movement, wished to provoke the Rumani-ans to such an extent, and Bakdash was compelled to retract his remarks. The Rumanians walked out anyway. A detailed description of the conference is found in *World Communism 1967-1969: Soviet Efforts to Reestablish Control* (Washington, D.C.: U.S. Government Printing Office, 1970), pp. 63-91. For an excellent study of the effect of the Arab-Israeli conflict on Soviet relations with Eastern Europe, see Andrew Gyorgy, "Eastern European Viewpoints on the Middle East Conflict," paper delivered to the National Meeting of the American Association for the Advancement of Slavic Studies, Denver, Colorado, March 25, 1971.

47. Shamir, op. cit., pp. 298-310.

48. For a different view of these events, see George Lenczowski, *Soviet Advances in the Middle East* (Washington, D.C.: American Enterprise Institute, 1971), pp. 113-14.

49. For an excellent study of relations between the Arab states at this time, see Kerr, op. cit., chaps. 5 and 6.

50. Laqueur, *The Struggle for the Middle East*, p. 36. For the importance of this type of agreement for a developing country, see Robert O. Freedman, *Economic Warfare in the Communist Bloc* (New York: Praeger, 1970), pp. 5-6.

51. Mueller, op. cit., p. 224.

52. For a description of Western speculation on this point, see Laqueur, *The Struggle for the Middle East*, p. 40. There is also evidence that both Morocco and Jordan used the same ploy to acquire more military equipment from the United States.

53. Aaron S. Klieman, *Soviet Russia and the Middle East* (Baltimore: Johns Hopkins Press, 1970), p. 51.

54. See Chapter 3, pp. 72-74.

55. See the report by Hedrick Smith in the New York *Times*, May 18, 1966.

56. For a useful description of the triangular relations between the USSR, the Kurds, and the Iraqi government at this time, see R. S. Rauch, "Moscow, the Kurds and the Iraqi Communist Party," *Radio Free Europe Research Report* (September 1, 1966).

57. *Pravda*, November 22, 1966, had the following comment about the treaty: "The defense treaty signed by the UAR and Syria is called upon to play an especially important role in rebuffing the intrigues in Imperialism and Arab reaction."

58. Perhaps the best study of the events leading up to the war is found in Walter Laqueur, *The Road to Jerusalem* (New York: Macmillan, 1968). See also Charles Yost, "The Arab-Israeli War: How It Began," *Foreign Affairs*, 46, no. 2 (January 1968): 304-20. For a collection of Arab viewpoints on the June war, which tends to minimize the role of the USSR in the outbreak of the conflict, see Ibrahim Abu-Lughod, ed., *The Arab-Israeli Confrontation of June 1967: An Arab Perspective* (Evanston, Ill.: Northwestern University Press, 1970). For a description of the military preparations and tactics of the opposing armies, see David Kimhe and Dan Bawly, *The Six-Day War: Prologue and Aftermath* (New York: Stein and Day, 1971).

59. See the report by Paul Wohl in the *Christian Science Monitor*, August 1, 1967, for a description of Chinese activity in the Middle East at this time.

60. Heikal, op. cit., p. 313.

61. L. Sedin, "The Arab Peoples' Just Cause," *International Affairs* 13, no. 8 (August 1967): 28, cited in Lincoln Landis, *Politics and Oil: Moscow in the Middle East* (New York: Dunellen, 1973), p. 64.

62. For an analysis of Soviet policy toward the Arab oil "weapon" during the 1967 war and its aftermath, see Landis, op. cit.; Abraham S. Becker, "Oil and the Persian Gulf," in Confino and Shamir, op. cit., pp. 191-94.

63. Igor Belyayev and Yevgeny Primakov, "The Situation in the Arab World," *New Times* (September 27, 1967): 10, cited in Landis, op. cit., p. 64.

64. For an analysis of the highly complicated situation in Aden (South Yemen) at the time of the British withdrawal, see Humphrey Trevelyan, *The Middle East in Revolution* (Boston: Gambit, 1970), pt. 3. Trevelyan was in charge of the British withdrawal from Aden.

65. For an account of the diplomatic attempts to fashion a peace settlement after the 1967 war, see Yair Evron, *The Middle East* (New York: Praeger, 1973), chap. 3.

66. For a description of Nasser's visit to Moscow, and of Brezhnev's decision to send troops to Egypt, see Mohammed Heikal, *The Road to Ramadan* (New York: Quadrangle, 1975), pp. 83-88.

67. According to Heikal, Nasser wanted the cease-fire so that he could finish building the missile wall that would not only protect Egyptian armed forces on the West Bank

but also give protection over a strip 15-20 kilometers wide on the East Bank and thus cover an Egyptian crossing—as indeed happened in the 1973 Arab-Israeli war. See Heikal, *The Road to Ramadan*, p. 93. For a detailed study of the war of attrition, see Lawrence L. Whetten, *The Canal War* (Cambridge, Mass.: M.I.T. Press, 1974). For examinations of the Soviet role during the war of attrition and the violation of the cease-fire, see Robert O. Freedman, "Detente and Soviet-American Relations in the Middle East during the Nixon Years," in *Dimensions of Detente*, ed. Della W. Sheldon (New York: Praeger, 1977); and Alvin Z. Rubinstein, *Red Star on the Nile* (Princeton: Princeton University Press, 1977).

68. Georgi Mirsky, "Israeli Aggression and Arab Unity," *New Times*, no. 28 (1967): 6.

69. Shamir, op. cit., p. 302.

70. Cited in Jaan Pennar, "The Arabs, Marxism and Moscow: A Historical Survey," *Middle East Journal* 22, no. 3 (September 1968): 446.

71. For sympathetic treatments of Nasser's attempts to keep some freedom of maneuver during the post-1967 period, see Anthony Nutting, *Nasser* (New York: Dutton, 1972), chap. 21; and Robert Stephens, *Nasser: A Political Biography* (New York: Simon and Schuster, 1971), chap. 19.

72. For an excellent study of these events, see Avigdor Levy, "The Syrian Communists and the Ba'ath Power Struggle 1966-1970," in Confino and Shamir, op. cit., pp. 395-417.

73. *Jerusalem Post*, April 11, 1969, cited in Lawrence J. Whetten, "Changing Soviet Attitudes toward Arab Radical Movements," *New Middle East*, no. 18 (March 1970): 25.

74. *Trud*, July 18, 1970.

75. For studies of the Soviet need for Middle Eastern oil and natural gas, see Landis, op. cit.; Becker, op. cit.; and Robert W. Campbell, "Some Issues in Soviet Energy Policy for the Seventies," *Middle East Information Series*, no. 26-27 (Spring-Summer 1974): 92-100. See also Arthur J. Klinghoffer, *The Soviet Union and International Oil Politics* (New York: Columbia University Press, 1977).

76. On this point, see Uriel Dann, "The Communist Movement in Iraq since 1963," in Confino and Shamir, op. cit., pp. 377-91.

77. For a general examination of Soviet-Iraqi relations during this period, see Y. A. Yodfat, "Unpredictable Iraq Poses a Russian Problem," *New Middle East*, no. 13 (October 1969): 17-20. A detailed listing of the oil agreement between Iraq and the USSR is found in "The Broad Soviet Interest in Iraqi Oil," *Radio Liberty Report* (April 17, 1972), p. 2.

78. *Pravda*, September 21, 1969. The agreement between the Kurds and the Iraqi government in 1966 never materialized.

79. Translated in *Current Digest of the Soviet Press* 22, no. 31: 10.

80. For an analysis of these aid agreements, see Y. A. Yodfat, "Russia's Other Middle East Pasture—Iraq," *New Middle East*, no. 38 (November 1971): 26-29.

81. For studies of the highly complex situation in the Sudan, see Haim Shaked, Esther Souery, and Gabriel Warburg, "The Communist Party in the Sudan 1946-1971," in Confino and Shamir, op. cit., pp. 335-74; and Anthony Sylvester, "Mohammed vs. Lenin in the Revolutionary Sudan," *New Middle East*, no. 34 (July 1971): 26-28.

82. *Sudan News*, January 13, 1970, cited in *Record of the Arab World*, 1970, p. 419.

83. *TASS*, January 2, 1970, cited in *Record of the Arab World*, 1970, p. 418.

84. According to Aryeh Yodfat, "The USSR and the Arab Communist Parties," *New Middle East*, no. 32 (May 1971): 33, the USSR advised the Sudanese Communist Party to dissolve as early as May 1969. Shaked et al. argue that the party was urged to dissolve in 1970, after Nimeri had shown the first signs of turning against it.

85. Cited in Shaked et al., op. cit., p. 354.

86. For an excellent study of the activities and problems of the Palestinian guerrilla organizations, see William B. Quandt, Fuad Jabbar, and Ann Lesch, *The Politics of Palestinian Nationalism* (Berkeley: University of California Press, 1973), especially pts. 2 and 3.

87. For an analysis of the relations between China and the Palestinian guerrillas, see Carlson, op. cit.; and "Peking and the Palestinian Guerrilla Movement," *Radio Free Europe Research Report* (September 1, 1970). Another useful source is R. Medzini, "China and the Palestinians," *New Middle East,* no. 32 (May 1971): 34-40.

88. Cited in Paul Wohl, "New Soviet Revolutionary Stance in the Middle East," *Radio Liberty Dispatch* (May 25, 1970), p.. 2. For a study of Soviet policy toward the PLO during this period, see Galia Golan, *The Soviet Union and the PLO* (Jerusalem: Soviet and East European Research Center, Hebrew University, 1976), pp. 1-3.

89. For analyses of the Soviet dilemmas in dealing with the Palestinian guerrillas, see Y. A. Yodfat, "Moscow Reconsiders Fatah," *New Middle East,* no. 13 (October 1969): 15-18; and John Cooley, "Moscow Faces a Palestinian Dilemma," *Mid East* 11, no. 3 (June 1970): 32-35.

90. Naim Ashhab, "To Overcome the Crisis of the Palestinian Resistance Movement," *World Marxist Review* 15, no. 5 (May 1972): 75.

91. For a description of these events, see Kerr, op. cit., chap. 7, especially pp. 144-48.

92. For an analysis of American policy during the Jordanian civil war, see Evron, op. cit.; and Robert J. Pranger, *American Policy for Peace in the Middle East, 1969-1971* (Washington, D.C.: American Enterprise Institute, 1971), pp. 39-48.

93. For an analysis of Soviet policy during this crisis, see Freedman, "Detente and Soviet-American Relations in the Middle East during the Nixon Years."

94. For a description of the atmosphere during the cease-fire talks, see Heikal, *The Cairo Documents*, p. 4.

95. Klieman, op. cit., p. 78.

96. An official description of the Rogers Plan, which basically calls for the withdrawal of Israeli forces from all but "insubstantial" portions of the territory captured in 1967 in return for a binding peace settlement, is found in United States Department of State, *United States Foreign Policy 1969-1970: A Report of the Secretary of State* (Washington, D.C.: U.S. Government Printing Office, 1971). For an analysis of American attempts to implement the Rogers Plan, see Pranger, op. cit.; and Quandt, op. cit., chap. 3.

97. For an analysis of Nasser's role as a "broker" of Soviet interests in the Arab world, see Malcolm Kerr, *Regional Arab Politics and the Conflict with Israel* (Santa Monica, Calif.: Rand Publication RM-5966-FF, 1969).

3

From Nasser's Death
to the Soviet Exodus
from Egypt

SOVIET POLICY UP TO THE 24TH CONGRESS OF
THE COMMUNIST PARTY OF THE SOVIET UNION

From the Soviet point of view, the most serious aspect of Nasser's death was that it removed the one man in Egypt so obsessed by his humiliation at the hands of the Israelis that he was willing to give up a considerable amount of Egyptian sovereignty in an effort to get revenge for his humiliation. The Russians were clearly concerned that Nasser's successor, who would not be bridled with his mistakes, might prove to be a considerably more independent person, one who even might turn to the United States for assistance. Consequently, Premier Kosygin led a large Soviet delegation to Nasser's funeral and remained in Cairo for several days of meetings with Egypt's new leadership, which was headed by acting President Anwar Sadat. The communique released at the end of the visit pledged continued Soviet-Egyptian cooperation and appealed for the "unity of action of all Arab states on an anti-imperialist basis" as the way for the Arabs to achieve success in their "just struggle for national independence, progress and a rapid solution of the Middle East conflict."[1]

Nonetheless, the presence at Nasser's funeral of a senior American official, Elliot Richardson, was a matter of concern for the Soviet leadership, as it seemed to be a signal from the Nixon administration of the desire for improved Egyptian-American relations. *Pravda* correspondent Yuri Glukhov wrote on October 17:

> The period following the death of Nasser has witnessed the development of bitter psychological warfare by Western propaganda which hopes to revitalize the forces of domestic reaction, smash the United Front in the UAR, foment internal crisis and *drive a wedge between*

> the UAR and its friends. Once again the alleged inconsistency of the UAR's policy of non-alignment with the particular nature of its friendship with the Soviet Union has been raised. Rumors have been spread about Nasser's "behests" and his "last words" concerning the choice of a successor—words spoken literally on his deathbed. As might be expected, the persons named as successors are those in whom the West has a material stake.[2] [emphasis added]

Writing a week later in *New Times,* after Sadat's succession to the presidency had been legitimized by a nationwide referendum, Viktor Kudryavtsev stated:

> The political consolidation in the UAR has smashed the hopes of those who thought that after Nasser's death Cairo would not be able to play the active and important role in the Middle East as it has played so far. . . .
> The results of the referendum are therefore a big success not only for the Egyptian people, but for all the Arab peoples who see in the UAR a state making an important contribution to their common struggle against imperialist aggression.[3]

Unfortunately for the Russians, however, Sadat was later to prove far more difficult to deal with than Nasser had been.

In addition to the succession crisis in Egypt, the Russians were also confronted with government shakeups in Iraq and Syria following Nasser's death. In Iraq, Hardan Al-Takriti, one of the vice-presidents, was ousted, apparently for his role in the failure of the Iraqi troops stationed in Jordan to come to the aid of the Palestinian guerrillas during their war with Hussein's troops.[4] A far more serious shakeup occurred in Syria, where the pro-Russian group of Ba'athist leaders led by Salah Jedid was finally ousted by the Syrian defense minister Hafiz Assad—the man who had clashed with the Russians in the past.[5] Writing in *Pravda* on November 28, 1970, two weeks after Assad took power, Aleksei Vasilyev commented:

> Imperialist propaganda and certain press organs in Arab countries connected with Western interests have gone out of their way to raise a fuss over the events in Syria and have tried to picture the situation as if the Syrian Arab Republic had almost repudiated its former anti-Imperialist policy. . . . Imperialist propaganda has been speculating on the discrepancies [within the Syrian leadership] and has been striving in every way possible to exaggerate their significance and scale, provoke crisis and skepticism in Syria, and activate the forces of reaction in Syria, and splinter the A.S.R.P. [Ba'ath Party] and other progressive patriotic forces, including the communist party.[6]

While Vasilyev praised the new Syrian regime for "maintenance and extension" of the reforms of its predecessor, and its plan to develop relations with the USSR and to join the proposed Arab federation of Egypt, Libya, and the Sudan, he nevertheless warned the Syrian leadership:

> Imperialist circles and reactionary elements in Syria have not forsaken their plans. Stability in Syria and the success of the program of action outlined can be assured only if the new leadership will count on the cooperation of all patriotic and progressive forces within the country and a lasting union with the progressive regimes, and on friendship and fruitful cooperation with the socialist countries.[7]

Faced by these important domestic changes within their major Arab clients, the Soviet leaders adopted a policy of "watchful waiting" in the Middle East in the five months following Nasser's death. Unwilling to see a resumption of the Arab-Israeli conflict while the Arab world was in such a disarray, and with new regimes in office in Syria and Egypt, the Soviet Union continued to support the principle of an Arab-Israeli settlement along the lines of UN Resolution no. 242. The USSR also supported the mission of Gunnar Jarring, which had been reactivated in December, although the Swedish diplomat's trips to Cairo and Jerusalem were to be no more successful in 1971 than they were in 1968. Soviet policy during this period appeared to focus on consolidating relations with the new regimes rather than embarking on any new policy initiatives. There were frequent trips between Moscow and Cairo, highlighted by Egyptian Vice-President Ali Sabry's long visit to the USSR in December 1970, Soviet President Nikolai Podgorny's visit to Egypt the following month to celebrate the opening of the Aswan Dam, and Sadat's flight to Moscow at the beginning of March, following a breakdown in the Jarring talks. Indeed, Podgorny, according to an Egyptian account of his visit, "sounded such a cautious note that he profoundly shocked" his hosts, while Sadat, during his visit to Moscow, got promises of arms—but it was to be a long time before the promises were realized.[8] The new Syrian leader, Hafiz Assad, was also a guest of the Russians as he made a state visit to Moscow at the beginning of February. The Soviet leaders seem to have gone out of their way to establish a good working relationship with their erstwhile opponent, who also seemed to realize the advantages of maintaining Syria's economic and military ties to the USSR, although the visit was not without its strains. Thus, although Kosygin in his welcoming address to Assad mentioned Resolution no. 242, Assad did not; the final communique, which described the talks as taking place in an atmosphere of "frankness and friendship," also failed to mention the UN Resolution.[9] During this period visits between Soviet and Iraqi delegations were also exchanged, as the Russians worked to further improve relations with the Al-Bakr regime. In addition, a Soviet delegation visited Khartoum in an attempt (which proved unsuccessful) to settle the rift between

Nimeri and the Sudanese Communist Party. During this period the Russians also began to publish their monthly military journal, the *Soviet Military Review*, in Arabic, in an effort to instruct Arab officers and noncommissioned officers in Soviet tactics and ideology. Finally, at the request of the once strongly pro-Western Lebanese government, the USSR entered into negotiations for the sale of Soviet arms.

As stability returned to the Arab world, the Soviet Union once again began to urge that the Arab nations unify to combat the "imperialists." A new drive for Arab unity was already under way in the proposed federation of Egypt, Libya, and the Sudan, which was launched in December 1969 and which Syria joined on November 27, 1970.[10] The Russians moved quickly to throw their support behind the federation as an "anti-imperialist force in the Arab world" when it began to take definite shape in November 1970. An article in *Pravda* on November 11 described a meeting in which the leaders of Libya, the Sudan, and Egypt were working out the plans for the federation, commenting:

> This event is concrete evidence of the Arab people's will toward unity, so that they can oppose *imperialist* plans to divide, fragment and weaken the national liberation movement in the Near and Middle East.
>
> What serves as the true foundation for rapprochement . . . is the similar progressive social and economic measures within each of the three countries, these countries' *anti-imperialist course in foreign policy, and their policy of strengthening cooperation with the Soviet Union and the other socialist countries.*
>
> This conference of leaders from the UAR, Libya, and the Sudan has dealt a blow to the calculations of the aggressive circles in Israel and that country's protectors to weaken the will of the Arabs in the *struggle against imperialism.*[11] [emphasis added]

The following day *Izvestia* correspondent L. Koryavin emphasized that this was only the first step in a broader Arab unity:

> The creation of a federation of these three Arab states is also important because it builds a firm foundation for the subsequent strengthening of inter-Arab unity. The leaders of the UAR, Libya and the Sudan have repeatedly emphasized that cooperation among these three countries is not some isolated occurrence; on the contrary, these leaders intend to strengthen ties with other Arab countries in the future as well, and they are confident that the present federation will serve as the nucleus of broader Arab unity in the time to come.[12]

Syria's decision to join the federation was heartily approved by the Russians, since conflict between Syria and Egypt in the past had been one of the main obstacles to the "anti-imperialist" Arab unity that the Russians so strongly supported. Indeed, the federation received its highest degree of official Soviet support during Assad's trip to Moscow when Soviet Premier Kosygin stated:

> We believe that the Arab countries will unite their efforts more closely in the anti-Imperialist struggle, in the struggle for the elimination of the consequences of the Israeli aggression. During all these years, at all stages of the Near East crisis, Imperialism has placed its stakes on the lack of unity in the Arab world. Counting on this disunity, it unleashed aggression and again counting significantly on this, it is trying at present to prolong the elimination of the consequences of aggression. The Soviet Union hails the efforts of the United Arab Republic, the Syrian Arab Republic, the Democratic Republic of the Sudan. and the Libyan Arab Republic aimed at strengthening the unity of their actions in the anti-imperialist struggle and it *has no doubt that all the other countries of the Arab East will also make a contribution to the strengthening of this unity.*[13] [emphasis added]

While Egypt, Syria, Libya, and the Sudan moved toward a Soviet-approved federation, the Soviet leaders were careful to maintain good relations with Egypt's main Arab opponent, Iraq, which was highly critical of the proposed federation, and which characterized Sadat's meetings with Gunnar Jarring as "discussions of solutions of surrender."[14] Thus, while the Russians agreed on March 16, 1971, to give Egypt a $415 million loan to be used for rural electrification, desert reclamation, and a number of industrial projects, on April 8, 1971, the Iraqis were the recipients of a $224 million loan for the construction of an oil refinery and two oil pipelines. This Iraqi loan, just like the one in 1969, was to be repaid by oil—a commodity that the Russians were beginning to find more and more expensive to produce at home. The Soviet loan also served to strengthen the hand of the Iraqi leaders in their bargaining with the Western oil companies, which had become very heated. Interestingly enough, the large Soviet loan was offered despite the Ba'ath regime's severe persecution of the Iraqi Communist Party, persecution serious enough to draw public criticism from *Trud* on February 11, 1971, in an article protesting the murder of two Iraqi Communists in a Baghdad prison. The article asked pointedly:

> How much longer will the criminal reactionary elements in Iraq enjoy the freedom to carry out their black deeds and thus besmirch the name of their country in the eyes of progressive and democratic people?[15]

All in all, by the beginning of April it appeared as if the USSR had succeeded in rebuilding its position in the Arab world. Despite major governmental changes in Syria and Egypt, both Arab states were closely cooperating with the Soviet Union, and the Russians seemed to have established good working relationships with the new leaderships. As an added bonus for the Russians, the Syrians and Egyptians were cooperating closely for the first time since 1961 and, together with Libya and the Sudan, they were beginning to implement the Arab Federation that appeared to be closely aligned with the Soviet Union. Russian ties with Iraq remained strong (despite the persecution of the Iraqi Communist Party), and the Soviet leaders may even have begun to hope that it might not be too long before Iraq too joined the Arab Federation. Thus, at the time of the 24th CPSU Congress, it appeared as if the USSR had not merely successfully weathered the changes in the Arab regimes, but had actually improved state-to-state relations with them. Consequently, the Soviet leadership saw little need to alter its policies toward the nationalist regimes—and the Arab Communist parties—despite the continued persecution of the Arab Communists, which in the case of Iraq and the Sudan had become increasingly severe. Speaking at the Congress, Brezhnev described developments in the Third World in a very optimistic light, although he was far more realistic than his predecessor, Khrushchev, in estimating the time span involved in the transition of the ex-colonial nations of the Third World to socialism:

> Today, there are already quite a few countries in Asia and Africa which have taken the *non-capitalist way of development, that is the path of building a socialist society in the long-term.* Many states have now taken this path. Deep-going social changes, which are in the interests of the masses of people and which lead to a strengthening of national independence are being implemented in these countries, and the number of these changes has been growing as time goes on. . . .
>
> In the countries oriented towards socialism, the property of the imperialist monopolies is being nationalized. This makes it possible to strengthen and develop the state sector, which is essential as an economic basis for a revolutionary-democratic policy. In a country like the United Arab Republic, the state sector now accounts for 85 per cent of national production. . . . New serious steps in nationalizing imperialist property have been taken in Algeria. Many foreign enterprises, banks and trading companies have been handed over to the state of Guinea, the Sudan, Somali and Tanzania. . . . Important agrarian transformations have been carried out in the UAR and Syria and have started in the Sudan and Somalia. . . .
>
> Comrades, in the struggle against imperialism an ever greater role is being played by the revolutionary-democratic parties, many of which have proclaimed socialism as their program goal. The CPSU

has been actively developing its ties with them. We are sure that co-operation between such parties and the Communist Parties, includ-ing those in their own countries, fully meets the interests of the anti-imperialist movement, the strengthening of national independence and the cause of social progress.[16] [emphasis added]

In a feature article discussing the 24th CPSU Congress in the June 1971 is-sue of the *World Marxist Review*, Boris Ponamarev, head of the CPSU Central Committee Department for International Communist Affairs, further empha-sized the Soviet leadership's commitment to improving relations with the so-called revolutionary democracies:

> The CPSU will continue to extend and deepen friendly ties with rev-olutionary-democratic regimes, *our comrades-in-arms* against imperi-alism.
>
> The participation of national-democratic parties in the work of the 24th Congress reflects the growth of our mutual ties. In recent years this has been one of the specific directions in the alliance between the CPSU and the national-liberation forces. Ties of this kind, estab-lished these days by many fraternal parties, *actually represent a fun-damentally new form of solidarity between the world communist movement and the forces of national liberation.* [emphasis added]

As a sop to the Third World's Communist parties, however, Ponamarev added:

> The participation of revolutionary democracies in the CPSU Con-gresses, our Party hopes, will not only stimulate their greater cooper-ation with our Party and the world communist movement, but will also facilitate allied relations between them and the communists in their own countries.[17]

Despite the reduced importance given to the Arab Communists at the 24th CPSU Congress, however, an Arab Communist party managed to be an irritant in Soviet relations with a "revolutionary democracy," just as happened at the 23rd CPSU Congress when the FLN delegation walked out rather than see the Alge-rian Communist Party seated as an official delegation. In this case the Iraqi Com-munist Party leader, Aziz Mohammed, used his opportunity to speak (an Iraqi Ba'ath delegation had also been invited) to denounce the Ba'athist government for its persecution of the Iraqi Communists and for arrogating all power in Iraq to itself.[18]

This was to be only a minor problem for the Soviet leadership, however, when compared to the events that took place soon after the 24th CPSU Con-gress—events that were to shake severely the Middle Eastern position of the Soviet Union and lead to the decimation of one of the most important Communist parties of the region.

THE COUP D'ETAT IN THE SUDAN

As the Soviet-supported Arab Federation reached its final stages with a Cairo meeting of the heads of state of the member nations on April 12, 1971, difficulties arose that were to cause serious problems for the Soviet Union. In the Sudan, Mahgoub's faction of the Sudanese Communist Party came out strongly against the federation. Sudanese Premier Jaafar Nimeri was forced to leave the unity talks in Cairo to fly to Moscow in an effort to get Soviet support in pressuring the Sudanese Communists, whose members occupied important posts in the government and trade unions, into giving up their opposition to the Sudan's participation in the federation. The Russians, however, were either unwilling or unable to bring effective pressure to bear on the Sudanese Communists, and the report of Nimeri's visit in *New Times* (April 28, 1971) said nothing about the Sudanese Communists or the proposed federation. The end result was that the Sudan pulled out of the talks in Cairo and was not a signatory to the preliminary agreement, which was signed in the Egyptian capital on April 17, 1971.[19]

Despite the opposition of the Sudanese Communists to the federation, the Soviet leadership greeted the signing of the preliminary agreement with enthusiasm and *Pravda* hailed it as

> a new step towards the unity of the Arab states, and a further strengthening of the battle front against the forces of Zionism and neo-colonialism in the Middle East. . . . The main feature of the Federation is its progressive, anti-imperialist character. The consolidation of unity between the progressive Arab regimes leads to the strengthening of their common anti-imperialist front, the consolidation of the position of each of the three states and their inevitable victory over the forces of aggression, Zionism and neo-colonialism.[20]

On April 25 *Pravda* made it even more clear that the Soviet leadership hoped to use the federation as a device to weaken Western influence. *Pravda* stated: "The creation of the Federation has been received with alarm in Washington and Tel-Aviv because it strengthened the anti-imperialist front in the Middle East."[21] Less than four months later, however, the Russians were to take a very different position on the federation, which suddenly demonstrated anti-Communist and anti-Soviet instead of anti-Western tendencies.

While the Sudanese Communists opposed the federation, there was also strong opposition in Egypt. Seizing on Egypt's participation in the federation as an issue to challenge Sadat, Ali Sabry, in an apparent bid for power, moved to oust the Egyptian president. Sadat proved too skillful a politician, however, and succeeded in removing Sabry from his post as vice-president.[22] What made this more than another Arab power struggle was that Sabry was fired on May 2, 1971 —three days before the arrival of U.S. Secretary of State William Rogers in Cairo, in the first official visit of an American secretary of state to the Egyptian capital since 1953. Consequently, the removal of Sabry, perhaps the man closest to the Soviet Union of all the top Egyptian leaders, was interpreted in the West— and not only in the West—as a gesture to Rogers (who had come to Cairo to follow up Sadat's plan for an interim peace settlement)[23] and a signal that the Egyptians might be willing to move closer to the United States and away from the USSR—if the United States were to bring the necessary pressure on Israel. Indeed, *New Times* commented in early May:

> The American government clearly wants to use it [Rogers' tour] to reaffirm its support for the forces in the Arab countries that are opposed to cooperation with the Soviet Union and to progressive social reforms, and at the same time to strengthen the position of the conservative elements whom Washington regards as its potential mainstay in that quarter. . . . American diplomatic efforts to set Arab countries against one another and *to drive a wedge between them and the Soviet Union* can only aggravate the situation in the Middle East and hamper the political settlement of the Arab-Israeli conflict.[24] [emphasis added]

Reinforcing such speculation were a series of events several months earlier. Mohammed Heikal, editor of *Al-Ahram* and often (but not always) a spokesman for the Egyptian government, had come out in his weekly column for an improvement of relations with the United States in order to limit U.S. support for Israel. Sadat himself had warmly greeted the chairman of New York's Chase Manhattan Bank, David Rockefeller, during the American banker's visit to Cairo.[25]

Whether the speculations on an Egyptian gesture to the United States were true or not, they were believed to be true. When Sadat followed up the removal of Sabry by a wholesale purge of all his major opponents on May 14, 1971, including Shaari Gomaa, who as head of the Egyptian secret police was another individual widely rumored to be close to the USSR, and Diaddin Daoud, who had publicly criticized Heikal for looking to the United States and for attempting to "vilify and discredit the very substance of our relations with the USSR," the speculations grew in intensity.[26]

In addition to possibly signaling to the United States for an improvement of relations, the purges enabled Sadat to strengthen his own position with respect to the Soviet Union by making it far more difficult than before for the

Soviet leaders to factionalize against him in the Egyptian leadership. It is clear that the Russians were more than a little unhappy about the governmental changes in Egypt, although they proved powerless to do anything about them. Their true feelings may be understood by a *New Times* editorial citing the Beirut daily *Al-Anwar:*

> As the Beirut paper *Al-Anwar* wrote on May 14, 1971, the recent developments in Egypt "had disturbed the Arab nation and had aroused anxiety among the masses at a time when the decisive clash with the enemy requires the mobilization of the forces and the unity of the revolutionary leadership in the face of the American-Israeli plot."[27]

The Russians themselves were disturbed and anxious. One week after the second purge, Podgorny made a trip to Egypt that resulted in the signing of the Soviet-Egyptian treaty, a document that had been under discussion for several years. There was a great deal of speculation about this treaty at the time. Some commentators alleged that the Russians had spread the mantle of the "Brezhnev Doctrine" over Egypt and had thus irreparably limited Egypt's freedom of action in the international arena. The impact of the treaty was, however, far less significant. At least from the published articles (there have been as yet no "leaks" of any secret articles), the impression obtained is that the treaty was merely a codification of the existing Soviet-Egyptian relationship. The Egyptians did not commit themselves beyond agreeing to consult regularly with the Russians, something they were doing already, and agreeing not to join any alliance hostile to the Soviet Union, something they were then unlikely to do in any case. For their part, the Russians were also very careful to limit their military involvement by article eight of the treaty, which stated that military cooperation would be limited to "assistance in the training of UAR military personnel and in mastering the armaments and equipment supplied to the United Arab Republic with a view of strengthening its capacity to eliminate the consequences of aggression."[28]

Perhaps the greatest importance of the treaty to the Russians was as a demonstration that the United States had failed in its attempts to "drive a wedge between Egypt and the USSR." In a dinner speech in Cairo following conclusion of the treaty, Podgorny stated:

> The treaty between the Soviet Union and the United Arab Republic signifies a new blow to the plans of international imperialism which is trying in every possible way to *drive a wedge* into the relations between our countries, to undermine our friendship, and to divide the progressive forces.[29] [emphasis added]

Sadat's speech in reply had a very different content and tone:

The most important thing is that you have displayed true understanding in *all* conditions. We appreciate this above all. We feel that it is true understanding that must be the criterion in evaluating anyone's position. . . . *When each of us understands the meaning and tasks of the other's struggle, when each of us understands the nature and principles, values and rights defended by the other . . . when each of us understands this, the rest will come by itself.*[30] [emphasis added]

What Sadat seemed to be saying was that he very much appreciated the fact that the Russians did not interfere during his ouster of Sabry, and that they acknowledged his freedom of action. Indeed, the signing of the treaty was itself an implicit endorsement of the Sadat regime.

The Soviet leadership, however, was not yet satisfied with the progress of events of Egypt or the reliability of Sadat. While a front-page editorial in *Pravda* on June 2 stated that the Soviet-Egyptian treaty "signifies a new blow at the plans of international imperialism which is trying in every way to drive a wedge in the relations between the two countries,"[31] three days later *Pravda* published an article by Yevgeny Primakov strongly criticizing Arab politicians who advocated improving relations with the United States as a way of increasing pressure on Washington to cease its support of Israel. Significantly, Primakov stated that the purpose of Rogers' trip was to revitalize pro-American sentiment, which was still "rather rife in a number of Arab countries," and that "American maneuvers" in the Middle East were aimed at driving a wedge between the USSR and Egypt.[32]

One week later came the trip to Israel of Victor Louis, the famous Soviet correspondent long rumored in the West to have ties to the Soviet secret police. Louis' previous major international trip was to Taiwan in October 1968, at the height of the Sino-Soviet conflict. That trip had aroused a great deal of speculation in the West that the USSR was about to establish diplomatic relations with the Chinese Nationalist regime of Chiang Kai-shek, the bitter enemy of the Chinese Communists. This clearly had been a move to bring pressure on the Chinese Communists; and the same tactic, sending an "unofficial envoy" to Egypt's enemy and arousing speculation that the USSR was about to reestablish diplomatic relations with Israel, can be seen as a similar attempt to bring pressure on Sadat.

Sadat, however, did not appear to be moved by these pressures. To be sure, he appointed a former Egyptian Communist, Ismail Sabri Abdullah, as Minister of Planning. In addition, another former Egyptian Communist, Lufti Al-Kholi, now free of persecution by Sabry and Gomaa, could state that "for the first time since 1952 there exists in Egypt a national front in which Marxists participated as such and were recognized as a Marxist trend and not only as individuals."[33] However, these gestures were only sops to the Soviet Union, and the Egyptian president took a far more important step in the latter part of June when he invited Saudi Arabia's King Faisal to Egypt for consultations. The visit, which lasted a week, signaled both the end of a long period of Egyptian-Saudi hostility and a new entente between the two Arab powers that was to reach its highest point several years later in their cooperation in the October 1973 Arab-Israeli war. In June 1971, however, Sadat's rapprochement with the pro-Western king must have appeared to the Soviet leaders as yet another step by Sadat toward the United States.

The Soviet Union was to receive an even sharper blow to its Middle Eastern position in July, following the abortive coup d'etat in the Sudan. As mentioned above, the Mahgoub faction of the Sudanese Communist Party had resisted Nimeri's demands to dissolve the party and had opposed the Sudanese leader's plans to join the Arab Federation. Faced by these challenges to his power, on May 25, 1971, Nimeri cracked down hard on the Communists. He arrested 70 Communist leaders, including nearly all the Central Committee, and dissolved the unions that served as the Communists' bases of power.[34] While Nimeri was careful during this process to pledge that such actions would not harm Soviet-Sudanese friendship, it is clear that the Russians were not at all unhappy when Nimeri was ousted less than two months later, on July 19, by a group of army officers opposed to many of his policies. Soviet correspondent Dmitry Volsky, in reporting the goals of the new regime, which, while not Communist, was supported by Mahgoub's wing of the party and which pledged close cooperation with the Soviet Union, took the opportunity to comment negatively on Nimeri. In a *New Times* article, Volsky complained that some of the factories that had been nationalized in 1970 had been turned back to private ownership by Nimeri and that the ousted Sudanese leader had begun to include businessmen in his government as well.[35]

The Russians thus received a severe shock only three days later when, with the aid of Libya and Egypt, Nimeri was able to return to power. One of the Sudanese leader's first actions was to order the execution of the leading Communists in the Sudan, including the General Secretary of the party, Abdel Mahgoub, and Lenin Prize winner Ahmed El-Sheikh, who were blamed for instigating the abortive coup d'etat. Here again the Soviet leadership was faced with an old dilemma: Should it sacrifice hitherto good relations with a Middle Eastern government for the sake of a Communist party?

The Russians at first adopted a relatively moderate stance to the events in the Sudan, condemning the crackdown on the Communists and the announced plans to execute the two key Communist leaders, but still holding out the hope for an improvement in Soviet-Sudanese relations. A TASS statement of July 28, 1971, commented:

> All Soviet people, profoundly sympathizing with the friendly Sudanese people, are anxiously following the development of events in the Sudan. Together with the world's progressive public, they express the hope that the Sudanese leadership will realize the danger of the

path onto which it is pushing the country and the danger the present situation poses for the very destiny of the Sudanese national democratic revolution, and will find the strength to return to the path of strengthening the unity of all the national patriotic forces, thereby ensuring success in the struggle against imperialism and reaction, for the consolidation of their national independence and for the social progress of the Democratic Republic of the Sudan.[36]

When the TASS statement failed to elicit any change in Nimeri's anti-Communist campaign (Mahgoub was executed despite Soviet protest on July 28), the Soviet tone became harsher. A *Pravda* comment by "Observer" on July 30 stated:

> The wire services are bringing more and more new reports about the unbridled arbitrary rule and the mass arrests and executions of patriots in the Sudan. To all intents and purposes an atmosphere of the cruelest terror against the country's progressive forces, first of all against the communists, has been established in the country.
>
> All this gives ground for drawing the conclusion that the Sudan is taking a course aimed at the complete liquidation of the Sudanese communist party and the physical extermination of its leaders, activists and rank and file communists. . . .
>
> The Soviet Union, and this is well known to all the Arab peoples, strictly adheres to a policy of non-interference in the internal affairs of other states. . . . However, the Soviet people are not indifferent to the fate of fighters against imperialism, and for democracy and social progress. No one should have illusions on this score. For this reason, the words of certain Sudanese leaders to the effect that the repression against the communists will not affect the close relations between the Sudan and the Soviet Union sound strange, to say the least.[37]

The Russians also complained about "unfriendly actions" against Soviet representatives in the Sudan, damage to Soviet property, and threats and "acts of violence" against Russian personnel in Khartoum.

Nimeri, meanwhile, bitterly rebuked the Soviet leaders for their support of the Communists, and in a radio broadcast of August 5 stated:

> The ordeal has shown us the type of friends we used to hail and call supporters of helpless peoples and who, as now has been confirmed, want to enter the Sudan and Africa with another face of colonialism. We shall not accept the Soviet Union or any other state as our colonizer.[38]

The following day Nimeri again attacked the Soviet leaders as colonizers:

> The Soviets used to think Sudan is a nation which follows them but we will teach them a lesson and show them Sudanese originality. We will not accept colonization from the Soviet Union or any other country.[39]

Despite the polemical attacks between the USSR and the Sudan, diplomatic relations between the two states were not broken, although Nimeri recalled his ambassador from Moscow and expelled the counselor to the Soviet Embassy along with the Bulgarian ambassador. For their part the Russians appear to have held up economic and military aid to the Sudan while also arranging demonstrations of Arab students outside the Sudanese embassy. Interestingly enough, however, the demonstrating students not only carried anti-Nimeri placards but they also criticized Egyptian President Anwar Sadat.[40] The Egyptian leader, who had been instrumental in assisting Nimeri to regain power, not only did not condemn Nimeri's execution of the Communists, but in a major speech on July 30 after the executions, he publicly praised Nimeri and denounced the Sudanese Communists.[41] For Sadat to so defy the Russians on a matter of such importance to them (they had mounted a huge propaganda campaign to save the lives of Mahgoub and El-Sheikh) was a clear indication that treaty or no treaty, Soviet influence with the Sadat regime was quite limited.

To make matters worse, Heikal published a long article in his weekly column in *Al-Ahram* on July 30 in which he severely criticized the Sudanese Communists and, by implication, the USSR. In the article, broadcast the same day on Radio Cairo, Heikal asserted that the Communists should limit themselves to small groups of intellectuals so that the Communist ideology might become "one of the elements of fertility in the national experiment," but that they must understand that they could not be "the seed or the tree itself."[42] In addition, in a clear statement showing the limits of the Arab "Revolutionary Democrats' " willingness to cooperate with local Communists and the USSR, Heikal stated:

> The national-liberation movement by its progressive nature, isolates the reactionary right, but this does not automatically make the Marxist left the alternative.[43]

All in all, Soviet disappointment with Sadat must have been great indeed, for the most that the Egyptian leader would do for them, once Nimeri had completed his repression of the Sudanese Communists, was to issue a joint communique with Soviet leader Boris Ponamarev, who was visiting Egypt on the nineteenth anniversary of the Egyptian Revolution, which stated that hostility to Communist causes only "harmed the people's aspirations, served the interests of the imperialists, and caused dissension within the Arab revolutionary struggle."[44]

That this was only lip service, however, became evident on August 21, 1971, when Sadat flew to Khartoum and delivered a speech on Sudanese radio in which he strongly praised Nimeri and hailed the "victory of the people's will" that had brought Nimeri back to power.[45] In addition to dissatisfaction over Sadat's foreign policy, the Russians could not have been very pleased with a number of the Egyptian leader's domestic actions at the time, which included the jailing of a number of Communist sympathizers, a major speech on August 8 to Egyptian trade union leaders emphasizing national unity over class struggle,[46] and his increasing encouragement of foreign and domestic capital.

Meanwhile, as the events in the Sudan unfolded, the Soviet leaders received another major shock when Henry Kissinger arrived in Peking and announced the visit of U. S. President Richard Nixon to Communist China in early 1972. These developments meant that the long-feared Sino-American rapprochement had become a reality, and it became imperative for the Soviet leaders to adjust their policies accordingly.[47]

All in all, the spring and early summer of 1971 had not proven to be very successful seasons for Soviet policy in the Middle East, and it was not long before a reevaluation of a number of Soviet policies was under way.

REAPPRAISAL OF SOVIET POLICY

The events of May-July 1971 seem to have led to an "agonizing reappraisal" of Soviet policy toward the Middle East. The ousting of a number of pro-Russian figures in Egypt; the abortive Communist-supported coup d'etat in the Sudan, which resulted in the destruction of the strongest Communist party in the Middle East and a sharp deterioration in Soviet-Sudanese relations; Egyptian President Sadat's decision to back Nimeri's policies in the Sudan instead of those of the Soviet Union; the surprisingly rapid rapprochement between the United States and Communist China, which must have seriously complicated Soviet security planning—all seem to have prompted a major reevaluation of Soviet policy throughout the Middle East.

The first indication of a new Soviet position came in a revised evaluation of the Arab Federation, which was to take effect on September 1, 1971, following ratification votes in Egypt, Libya, and Syria. Instead of the effusive comments about the growth of "anti-imperialist" unity in the Arab world so prominent in early descriptions of the federation, the new Soviet evaluation was considerably cooler in tone—and for good reason. It must have been galling for the Russians to listen to the tribute given to the federation on August 2, 1971, by Nimeri after he had been restored to power with the help of the leaders of two of the federation's member nations:

> The attitude of the Tripoli Charter states. . . . The attitude of the sis-
> terly UAR, of beloved Libya, kind Syria and the attitude of the

other Arab sisters which cabled congratulations on the people's restoration of their revolution shows that our people's destiny and fate
is one, *and has primarily proven the efficiency of the Tripoli Charter.*[48] [emphasis added]

The federation appeared to be moving in an anti-Communist and anti-Soviet direction as a result of the summer's events, a direction that could only be reinforced if the now militantly anti-Communist Sudanese regime of Nimeri should
join. Consequently, the Russians began to argue that for the federation to be
successful there had to be room in it for Communists and other "progressive
forces." In a detailed analysis of the obstacles in the path of Arab unity—an analysis that continued to reflect Soviet fears of increased American influence in
the Arab world—the Soviet commentator R. Petrov stated in an article in *New
Times:*

> Another view [of Arab unity], often voiced in some nations *even at
> top levels* is that the movement for unity is the "supreme national
> cause" of all Arabs, irrespective of their social affiliation and politi-
> cal views, regardless of the socio-political systems of the various
> states. The proponents of this approach maintain that to resolve this
> national task it is essential to make use of any kind of support from
> without, whether it comes from the socialist countries or the capital-
> ist. *It has been said for instance, that it is enough merely to neutral-
> ize or limit the role of the United States which, since it backs Israel,
> allegedly holds the "key" to the settlement of the Middle East con-
> flict.*
>
> Lately, reactionary and right wing nationalist forces in Arab coun-
> tries, egged on by the imperialists, have sought to raise the sinister
> flag of anti-communism. *They are trying to persuade the ordinary
> people that it is possible to draw on the support of the socialist
> countries in combating imperialism and the Israeli aggression and at
> the same time wipe out the local Arab communists and ban the com-
> munist parties.*
>
> The fallacy of this position is obvious. Experience, the Arabs' in-
> cluded, has shown that imperialism can be successfully combated
> only if all the national progressive forces stand united. *Any attempt
> to exclude the communists and their parties from the common strug-
> gle can only weaken the united front* and play into the hands of the
> imperialist forces and their agents.
>
> All true friends of the Arab people . . . are confident that in spite
> of the efforts of imperialism, international Zionism and the Arab re-
> actionaries to tie up the Arab unity movement *in the straitjacket of
> nationalism and traditional conservative views,* the Arab peoples will

overcome the obstacles raised by ill-wishers to bar their way to free-dom.[49] [emphasis added]

In making this appeal not only for Arab Communists but also for the Arab Communists *parties*, the Russians seemed to have decided that their original scheme—the dissolution of the Arab Communist parties and the participation of Communists in national fronts *as individuals*—had not proved efficacious, and that Soviet interests would be better served if the Communist parties retained their independent existence. This was to be a theme increasingly emphasized during subsequent months, as the Russians urged Syria and Iraq to establish national fronts where the Communists could participate as parties, albeit subordinate ones.

The events in the Sudan and Sadat's "anti-revolutionary" acts in Egypt provided an opportunity for the Arab Communists, long unhappy with the Soviet Union's preference for the one-party regimes of the revolutionary democracies, to air openly their criticisms. Writing in the *World Marxist Review* in September 1971, Nicholas Shaoui, Secretary General of the Lebanese Communist Party, stated, after commenting on the events in the Sudan and the Arab liberation movement:

The *Working Class*, the most revolutionary and united class and the one most interested in extending and deepening the liberation movement, *must be the center around which all the progressive and patriotic forces are brought together.*[50] [emphasis added]

The Soviet Union's reply to this demand came from Rotislav Ulianovsky, Ponamarev's deputy on the International Committee of the CPSU Central Committee, who cautioned the Arab Communists against any premature thrust for power (the Sudanese case was implied although not specifically mentioned). While Petrov had appealed to the Revolutionary Democrats to allow the Arab Communists to participate in national fronts, Ulianovsky was telling the Arab Communists that their participation would be a subordinate one for a long time to come:

Petty-bourgeois ideology, which usually has a nationalist and anti-imperialist spearhead and religious overtones, dominates the masses in one form or another *and will evidently do so for a long time to come....* The working class movement in most Afro-Asian countries is too weak, too poorly organized and too closely connected with its petty-bourgeois environment, while the positions of scientific socialism are not strong enough to warrant counting on them alone.[51] [emphasis added]

Ulianovsky went on to maintain that the Soviet policy of supporting the national democratic parties was to be continued:

> A realistic revolutionary approach to the matter reveals that socialism must very often be built not out of the ideal matter that an advanced working class alone can be, but of poor material that objective reality puts at the revolutionary's disposal. . . .
>
> The masses . . . can be gradually led to an understanding of scientific socialism. Marxists bring out and foster the tender shoots of genuine socialism in petty-bourgeois concepts that will probably persist in Afro-Asian countries for years. We believe that this is the right line to follow. It proceeds from the idea that the national democratic parties, above all their left-wing groups, can, after starting from non-Marxist national socialism advance toward scientific socialism and, in the course of struggle and contradictions, finally adopt it. . . .
>
> In terms of present and future interests, the important thing is not so much the fact that national democracy is still a non-Marxist trend as its actual fight against imperialism, against capitalism as a social system and the revolutionary democrats' constructive efforts to build a new society. This is what determines the Marxist attitude to revolutionary democratic programs and parties.[52]

While in effect telling the Arab Communists that they had to be satisfied with the "anti-imperialist" policies of the Revolutionary Democrats (which, of course, were in line with the foreign policy interests of the USSR, if not the domestic interests of the local Communist parties), Ulianovsky then told the Communists that they had to endure stoically the persecution they received from the nationalist leaders:

> Anti-communist measures carried out in a number of countries unquestionably make it difficult to achieve mutual understanding between Marxist-Leninists and national democrats, between progressive forces generally. Even when they are temporary, these measures affect both the substance of national democracy and the course of the national liberation movement. *However, proletarian parties do not yield to emotion, but proceed from objective class analysis.*[53] [emphasis added]

Ulianovsky went on to tell the Arab Communists that they were not yet ready to take leadership of the national liberation movement, although they should play an active role in it:

> In a number of countries, national democratic parties are ruling parties playing the leading role in the national-liberation movement and

in noncapitalist development. *The problem of leadership is not solved—and this applies to communist and national democratic parties alike—by declarations about who plays or should play the leading role, but by the actual position of the parties concerned.*[54] [emphasis added]

Ulianovsky concluded by telling the Communists that their alliance with the national democrats was to be a long-range one, and he justified the task he had assigned to the Communists in Marxist terms:

This alliance is not a passing development, but a long-range and lasting perspective. It came into being at the general democratic stage of the national liberation revolution. To continue and consolidate it at the socialist stage *would fully meet the objective requirements of social progress. This is, to our mind, one of the most important theoretical and practical aspects of the problem of the Marxist-Leninist approach to the Revolutionary democrats' non-Marxist socialism today.*[55] [emphasis added]

In addition to a new evaluation of the Arab Federation and a new role for the Arab Communist parties, a third major Soviet policy change took place in regard to the Soviet Union's relations with Israel—the federation's main enemy and a nation occupying territory belonging to two of the three member nations of the federation. A delegation of Israeli figures—all opposed in one way or another to Israeli Premier Golda Meir's policy in the Arab-Israeli conflict—were invited to Moscow at the beginning of September 1971 for a one-week visit. The Soviet press played up the "progressive" nature of the group, although only one was a Communist, and intimated that there were forces in Israel interested in changing its orientation in the world. *Pravda* stated on September 8, 1971:

The members of the group declared that they opposed the anti-Soviet statements of Israel's ruling circles. "The Israeli people are tired of war and the country's one-sided orientation toward the Imperialist Americans," M. Eidelberg [a member of the Soviet Israeli friendship movements] stated.[56]

In addition to the visit of the "progressive" Israeli delegation to Moscow, there were a number of other indications of a Soviet attempt to improve relations with Israel, including the granting of visas to Israelis attending international conferences in the Soviet Union (in previous years Israelis were often barred from international conferences in the USSR) as well as particularly warm and cordial treatment for such visitors once they arrived.[57]

All of this pales, however, before the most important decision of all taken by the Soviet leadership in regard to Israel—the decision to sharply increase Jewish emigration from the USSR to Israel from an average of 300 per month to 3,000 per month. It had long been one of the most cherished dreams of Israeli leaders to obtain Soviet consent for Russian Jews to emigrate to Israel, and this had been one of the factors complicating Soviet-Isreali relations almost since the founding of the Jewish state in 1948.[58] While there may have been a number of domestic political considerations that motivated the decision of the Soviet leaders to allow increased emigration, the foreign policy implications of the decision were of great importance. In the first place, large numbers of the departing Jews were of military age, and a relatively significant proportion were professionals (doctors, engineers, scientists) who could make an important contribution to the Israeli war effort. Thus, while the Russians were supplying Egypt with advisers and modern weapons with which to fight Israel, they also were supplying Israel with both military manpower and individuals with skills vital to both the military and civilian sectors of the Israeli economy.[59]

There have been a number of hypotheses offered to explain the Soviet decision on allowing large-scale Jewish emigration. A number of scholars argue that the Jews are "infecting" other Soviet minorities with their nationalism, and for this reason the Russian authorities wish to get rid of them. Others argue that the release of the Jews is a sop to Western opinion, since the plight of Soviet Jews is now a cause celebre in the Western world; that by giving way on this relatively unimportant issue (to the Soviet leadership), the USSR could improve its relations with the West (which deteriorated sharply after the invasion of Czechoslovakia), an improvement made necessary by need for foreign trade and the Sino-American rapprochement. Indeed, the Russians had long overestimated Jewish and Zionist influence in Washington, and by allowing increased numbers of Jews to emigrate to Israel, the Soviet leadership may have hoped to gain the support of the "Zionist lobby" for Soviet objectives. A third school of thought contends that the exodus of Soviet Jews to Israel is an overt sign of Soviet displeasure with the Sadat regime and is a means of bringing pressure upon it in the pattern of Victor Louis' trip in June.[60]

There is also a fourth hypothesis that bears some examination. Given the events of the summer, the Russians had clearly decided not to back Egypt in any new war against Israel; yet, without a war, it appeared impossible to secure the opening of the Suez Canal, a major goal of Soviet policy. Following the Sino-American rapprochement, it must have seemed urgent for the Russians to build up their southern flank against China, and the USSR's signing of a long-term treaty with India in August 1971 was one way of implementing this policy. An open canal, in addition to enabling the Soviet Union to supply India more rapidly in case of a war with Pakistan, an eventuality that appeared more and more inevitable as the summer wore on, would also enable the USSR to supply its northeastern flank against China more effectively than the highly vulnerable Trans-Siberian Railroad. Finally, with British withdrawal from the Persian Gulf scheduled for the end of 1971, an open canal would enable the Russians to move their Mediterranean fleet there speedily if the need developed. Yet the canal could not be opened without the agreement of Israel, and in the absence of Soviet willingness to exert military force against the Jewish state, it may well be that the Soviet decision to increase Russian Jewish emigration, when coupled with other moves to improve Soviet-Israeli relations, might have been, in part at least, a signal to the Israeli government that they might expect further benefits should they be willing to open the canal on the proper terms.[61]

A fourth significant Soviet policy change that followed the reversals in the Sudan and Egypt was a major effort to broaden the base of Soviet ties in the Middle East. Having concentrated their attention over the past few years in the core area of the Arab world (Egypt, Syria, Iraq), the Russians now moved to improve their position in a number of other states as well. There was a flurry of diplomatic activity between the Soviet Union and the Middle East beginning with a visit by the premier of the People's Democratic Republic of Yemen (South Yemen) to Moscow on September 30. Next came Kosygin's state visits to Algeria and Morocco in the first ten days of October, Egyptian President Sadat's trip to Moscow on October 12, and a visit by Yasir Arafat of the PLO (again at the invitation of the Soviet Afro-Asian Solidarity Organization) on October 20. Indeed, the virtual squeezing of Sadat's visit between Kosygin's trip to North Africa and Arafat's visit to Moscow may well have been an indication to the Egyptian leader that the Soviet Union was not dependent on its position in Egypt for influence in the Arab world, but that it was ready and able to court a number of other Arab leaders as well—including some of Sadat's chief Arab opponents.

The Soviet Union did not restrict itself to established Arab states in its efforts to rebuild its position in the Arab world, but turned to the two main Arab guerrilla organizations as well. At the beginning of September 1971, the Soviet Afro-Asian Solidarity Organization invited a delegation from the Popular Front for the Liberation of Oman and the Arab Gulf (PFLOAG) to Moscow for the first time, following a major Soviet press buildup of their successes against the pro-Western ruler of Oman. This was followed a month later with an invitation to Arafat by the same organization. Of particular interest in the Arafat visit was *Pravda's* description of the talks:

> The Palestinian and Soviet sides noted the importance of the unity of all progressive forces of the Arab world and the necessity for the further strengthening of their alliance with the true friends of the Arab people—the countries of the Socialist commonwealth. In this connection, emphasis was laid on the *danger of attempts to undermine Arab-Soviet friendship, to split the ranks of the Arab anti-imperialist movement, and to tear it from the common anti-imperialist front.* These attempts inflict damage on the Arab People's liberation aspirations and national interests and serve only the interests of international imperialist and Zionist circles.[62] [emphasis added]

While the Russians were now trying to enlist Arafat and his organization in their renewed drive for influence in the Arab world, the Palestinian guerrillas also stood to gain from the visit. Following his return from Moscow, Arafat stated that the talks with the Soviet leaders had been "very successful" and that he had found the Moscow climate "warmer" than on his previous visit in February 1970.[63] The situation had changed markedly for both sides since that time. Badly mauled by the Jordanian army in September 1970 and July 1971, Arafat's forces were greatly weakened and the Palestinian guerrillas were no longer the independent force in Arab politics they once were. Since the guerrillas were in far greater need of Soviet support than at the time of Arafat's February 1970 visit, the Russians may have assumed that the PLO would be more open to Soviet influence. Consequently, although the Chinese Communists continued to back the PLO (a delegation from Fatah, the largest guerrilla group in the PLO, went to Peking two weeks before Arafat's visit to Moscow and got a pledge of continued Chinese assistance from Chou En-lai[64]), the Russians, by reportedly pledging training, medical care, and equipment to the Palestinians, seemed for the first time to be attempting to bring them under the Soviet wing. Interestingly enough, the Soviet invitation to the PFLOAG guerrillas had also come at a time when the guerrilla organization had been weakened because of the efforts of the new Sultan of Oman, who had been trained at Sandhurst, and his British officers.

While the Russians were moving to improve relations with the PFLOAG and the PLO, they did not neglect their relations with the governments with which the two guerrilla organizations were at odds. The Russian government signed a number of agreements with Hussein's regime in Jordan, including one that provided Soviet experts to assist the Jordanians in exploration for minerals; it concluded an $8 million arms deal with Lebanon in early November;[65] and it invited the head of the Yemeni Arab Republic (North Yemen), an opponent both of the regime in South Yemen and the PFLOAG, for a state visit to Moscow on December 7, 1971. The Soviet Union even welcomed good relations with the conservative governments of the new Persian Gulf States, Bahrein, Qatar, and the Union of Arab Emirates—regimes that the PFLOAG had sworn to overthrow.[66]

The explanation for these apparently contradictory Soviet moves seems to lie in the Russian leaders' attempt to broaden as much as possible the Soviet base of operations in the Middle East. Given the rapid changes, coups d'etat, and counter coups d'etat so endemic to Arab politics, the Russians seem to have decided to strive for as much influence as possible with all the actors within the Arab world so as to be on reasonably good terms with whoever might emerge victorious in the numerous power struggles, while at the same time trying to be in a position to reinforce anti-Western trends in the region wherever possible.

One consequence of the broadening of the Soviet thrust into the Arab world was a corresponding limitation of the Soviet relationship with Egypt. As discussed above, the Soviet leaders were quite disenchanted with Sadat following his ouster of Ali Sabry and Shaari Gomaa and his support of Nimeri. Additional areas in which the Russians were clearly unhappy with Sadat were the greater freedom he gave to private capital and his reconciliation with a number of Egypt's leading landowners and capitalists whose property had been expropriated under Nasser. Sadat's ending of the arbitrary seizures of private property that had occurred under Nasser encouraged Egyptians again to make investments in shops and land. In addition, Sadat made a bold move to attract foreign capital by establishing a hard-currency bank for international trade and development. [67]

The Russians made public their criticisms of Sadat's regime in mid-August, following the execution of the Sudanese Communists. In an article in *New Times* sharply critical of the new leadership of Egypt's Arab Socialist Union (Sabry had been one of its leaders before he was purged, and the head of the ASU delegation to the 24th CPSU Congress had met the same fate[68]), the Soviet commentator V. Lykov, after pointedly reminding the Egyptians no less than three times of the importance of Soviet aid, commented:

> There is no discounting the difficulties the Egyptians are confronted with in accomplishing what they have set out to do. The role that belongs in this to the ASU [Arab Socialist Union] would be hard to overrate. *But the ASU is still very young and its new functionaries are younger still in organizational, political experience.* Survival of a specious, purely formal approach is still very strong. There also persists, as a legacy of the past, fear of participation by the broad working masses in conscious working activity. And *local reactionaries do their best to cultivate the idea that people of the Marxist way of thinking must not be allowed to share in active political life, even under ASU slogans.*
>
> The success of the ASU program will be solidly assured if the masses, including the progressive intellectuals, see it as their own vital concern, the tangible future of their country. And so, the key to its successful fulfillment to movement in the long term, toward socialist reconstruction lies above all in the active enlistment of the masses. That applies to the armed forces too. The greater their political understanding, the firmer will be the forces' stand in any and every situation, the more confidently will they defend their country, knowing what social gains they are fighting for. And then there will be true unity of rear and front, and a guarantee against any attempts to use the army against the country's reconstruction along socialist lines, such as there have been in some other countries.[69] [emphasis added]

Relations between the USSR and Egypt continued cool in September. In that month came the visit of British Foreign Secretary Sir Alec Douglas-Home to

Cairo, the first visit of a British Foreign Secretary to Egypt since the Suez war of 1956. It proved to be a successful visit, in that it resulted in an agreement on compensation for British subjects whose property had been nationalized, and it paved the way for a British share in the financing of the Sumed pipeline from Suez to Alexandria. Douglas-Home's successful visit to Cairo, which followed by only four months the visit of U.S. Secretary of State William Rogers, seemed to indicate another move to the West by Sadat's regime—a development not greeted with favor in Moscow, considering the enormous Soviet investment in Egypt.[70]

Thus, as the date of Sadat's trip to Moscow approached, Soviet-Egyptian relations seemed to have hit a new low. Writing on the first anniversary of Nasser's death (and only two weeks before Sadat's scheduled visit), *Pravda* columnist Pavel Demchenko stated:

> The imperialist states and in particular the United States are doing their best to undermine [Soviet-Egyptian] relations and isolate Egypt from the Socialist states. It is no secret that the reactionary elements in Egyptian society would like to forget the course aimed at unifying the progressive anti-imperialist elements which had been pursued by the late President.
>
> The attempts of the imperialists and their allies within Egypt to destroy Nasser's policy were thwarted by the signing of the Soviet-Egyptian treaty of friendship and cooperation in May of this year. However, the attempts to cloud Soviet-Egyptian relations, as an Egyptian journalist put it, have not ceased.[71]

It was one of the goals of Sadat's trip to Moscow to remove the "dark cloud" over Soviet-Egyptian relations, as the Egyptian leader told a group of Egyptian university professors before his departure.[72] Nevertheless, the primary issue in Soviet-Egyptian relations, at least as seen from the Egyptian side, was not easy to resolve. Sadat had already committed himself to the thesis that 1971 was to be the "year of decision" in Egypt's conflict with Israel, and it appeared to be his main goal to obtain Soviet support for military operations against the Israelis. On August 19, 1971, the editor of *Al-Ahram*, Mohammed Heikal, had pointedly stated:

> Any Arab defeat which the USSR does not help prevent will bring the Arab world and the Soviet position in it to the pre-1952 condition when Imperialism was the absolute master and in full control of the Arab area.[73]

In an even more open example of an Egyptian attempt to exploit the Soviet Union, the Egyptian government spokesman, Tahsin Beshir, interviewed by the foreign editor of the London *Times* in an article appearing on October 7,

1971, commented that Sadat was preparing "to bring about a superpower confrontation between the U.S. and the USSR" if Israeli troops did not withdraw from the Sinai Peninsula. With what might be termed brash effrontery, Beshir went on to say that Sadat would be able to manipulate the Soviet leaders to do what he wanted because "the Middle East is the only area outside Europe where the Soviet Union could exercise power and therefore it could not afford to offend Egypt."[74]

The Russians, however, who had given Egypt huge sums in economic and military aid, and who almost had been drawn into a military confrontation with the United States in June 1967, were not then willing to let themselves be so exploited. In the official Soviet description of the Moscow talks between Sadat and the Russian leaders, there were frequent references to "a spirit of frankness" and "exchanges of opinions"—indications that there were a number of disagreements. In his speech of October 12, Sadat continued his theme that war was the only way to secure Israeli withdrawal and that he expected the Soviet Union to support Egypt in its time of need:

> We have proceeded from the conviction that force and force alone is the way to exert pressure on Israel and eliminate aggression against our lands. Force and force alone is the path of opposition to any aggression that may be undertaken against our territory by Israel—this hotbed of aggression that imperialism has created in Arab soil. . . .
> The peoples of the Soviet Union have always stood by us. They have been our friends in happy and difficult times. *Our people believe that the Soviet Union will stand by us at a time when we shall have to decide our destiny and the destiny of freedom on our soil and throughout the Arab world.* Such is our faith in your position, in the position of all socialist states, in the position of all freedom-loving and peace-loving peoples.[75] [emphasis added]

By contrast, Soviet President Podgorny's speech emphasized the need for a peaceful solution to the Arab-Israeli conflict, and the joint communique issued at the end of the talks was a clear reflection of Soviet, not Egyptian, priorities. The UN resolution of November 22, 1967, was repeatedly stressed, and anti-Communism and anti-Sovietism "resolutely condemned." The most the Egyptians were able to extract from the discussions was a somewhat vague statement that the two sides "agreed on measures aimed at the further strengthening of Egypt's military might."[76]

Most galling of all for the Egyptians, however, must have been the Soviet insertion into the communique of the following statement, which seemed to commit the Egyptians to a peaceful settlement:

> The Soviet side noted with satisfaction that Egypt's constructive position with respect to the achievement of a *peaceful* settlement of

the Near East crisis and its clearly expressed desire to reach—through
the mediation of Gunnar Jarring, the special representative of the
U.N. Secretary General—a just settlement on the basis of the fulfillment of all provisions of the November 22, 1967 Security Council
Resolution and the pullback by Israel to the lines of June 4, 1967,
enjoy the support of all *peace-loving* states and peoples.[77] [empha-
sis added]

In an effort to maintain some positive ties to the Sadat regime following
the unsuccessful visit, the Russians gave final approval on November 1 for the
construction of a $110 million aluminum plant at Nag Hammadi, which when
completed would have an output of 100,000 tons of aluminum per year.[78]

In the period following the Soviet-Egyptian talks, the Soviet government
in its public statements on the Middle East continued to emphasize the need for
a peaceful settlement of the Middle Eastern conflict. Despite Sadat's increasingly
bellicose speeches, the Russians clearly indicated that they would not support an
Egyptian attack on Israeli-held territory—"year of decision" or not. The Russians were not willing to risk a confrontation with the United States, whose
president had just been invited to visit the Soviet Union in May 1972, and who
was in the process of planning his trip to China, for the sake of a rather fickle
Arab ally. In addition, the Russians had other concerns at the time, the most important of which was the growing conflict between India and Pakistan.

Limitations of space preclude an extensive analysis of the Soviet role in
the Indo-Pakistani war of 1971. It is nonetheless necessary to discuss briefly the
effects of the conflict on the Soviet position in the Middle East. The USSR's aid
to Hindu India against Moslem Pakistan was unpopular among the Egyptian
masses (Egypt served as a transit point for Soviet equipment going to India), although Sadat made no official comment condemning the USSR.[79] However,
Kaddafi, the Islamic fundamentalist leader of Libya, openly denounced the Soviet role as "confirming the Soviet Union's imperialist designs in the area."[80] In
addition to putting the Russians' Arab supporters in an embarrassing position,
the war also enabled Iran to conquer more easily the three strategically placed islands at the head of the Persian Gulf, which the Shah of Iran had long coveted.
Iraq, Iran's main opponent in the competition for control over the Persian Gulf
following the British withdrawal, appealed in vain for assistance against the
Iranian move. Egypt, which was Iraq's main opponent in the Arab world, was
neither in the position nor in the mood to render support, and the semiofficial
Egyptian newspaper *Al-Jumhuriyah* had said in response to an earlier Iraqi plea
by Iraqi President Al-Bakr that the "bigger Arab powers cannot, under present
circumstances, take part in defending the Arab character of the three islands because they are preoccupied with the Israeli aggression."[81] The Soviet Union,
which was involved in a deterring action against the United States during the war
and had no desire to worsen relations with both Iran and Pakistan, remained si-

lent.[82] Iraq, more isolated than ever, was thus limited to breaking diplomatic relations with England, which was accused of "collusion," and expelling 60,000 Iranian citizens from her territory in reprisal for the Iranian seizure of the islands.[83] Iraq's growing isolation, however, and her military inferiority with respect to Iran were to lead the Arab nation into a treaty with the Soviet Union several months later. A second consequence of the Iranian action that the Soviet leaders found quite positive was Libya's decision to nationalize British Petroleum's interests in Libya because of Britain's "complicity" in the Iranian action. This was the first purely political nationalization of a Western-owned oil company in the Arab world, and the Soviet leaders evidently hoped it was the forerunner of many to come.

By the start of the new year, therefore, the Russian position in the Middle East was a mixed one. On the one hand, the Soviet leaders had considerably strengthened their strategic position in relation to China by backing India in a successful war against Pakistan. With Pakistan no longer a major threat, India could concentrate its forces against China, thus complicating China's security problems considerably—given the Russian buildup along China's northern border. On the other hand, Soviet popularity in the Arab world had dipped even further because of its aid to Hindu India against Moslem Pakistan and because of the Soviet decision to increase sharply Jewish emigration to Israel. The Jewish immigration was a particularly sore point for Arab leaders even before the decision to increase it, as the Kuwaiti newspaper *Al-Rai Al-Am* had stated on March 21, 1971:

> We know very well that every Jew arriving in Israel becomes a soldier in its army. . . . Mindful that Moscow has always been careful to give us only defensive weapons, we can now see the difference between these weapons and the manpower it is sending to Israel to use the offensive weapons already there. The Russians, like the Americans, want us to remain at the mercy of the enemy so we will always need Moscow and remain under its control.[84]

In addition, Soviet-Sudanese relations remained poor. Since Sadat's "year of decision" had passed without a war, the Egyptian leader began openly blaming the Soviet Union for lack of support in Egypt's confrontation with Israel.[85] Consequently, as the new year began, the main Soviet tactical goal seemed to be to arrest the growing wave of anti-Sovietism in the Arab world.

THE SOVIET-IRAQI TREATY AND THE SOVIET EXODUS FROM EGYPT

The Soviet leadership's efforts to arrest the rising tide of anti-Sovietism and anti-Communism in the Arab world initially centered around an effort to utilize the Communist parties of the Middle East to counter these negative trends. The congress of the newly legalized Lebanese Communist Party in Beirut in early January 1972 provided a good opportunity for this, since the party congress attracted government-party delegations from Egypt, Syria, and Iraq, as well as Communist parties from the Middle East, the Soviet Union, and Eastern Europe. One of the main functions of the congress was the denunciation of Communist China, which, having been recognized by Turkey and Iran during the summer and Lebanon in November, was becoming increasingly active in Middle East affairs. The congress resolutions also condemned rightist trends in the Arab world, and the Soviet Union received support for the convening of a congress of all the "progressive and patriotic organizations of the Arab countries" whose goal was to be the mapping out of a "general line of struggle against imperialism, Zionism, and reaction."[86] The goal of the Soviet leaders in arranging such a conference was spelled out by Lebanese Communist Party member Nadim Abd Al-Samad in an interview with *Pravda* on January 26, 1972:

> The Central Committee of the Lebanese Communist Party feels that there is an urgent need to convene a pan-Arab conference of progressive forces now. This is all the more necessary under conditions of increasing pressure on the Arab liberation movement. One of the forms this pressure takes is the attempt by certain circles to arouse anti-communist and anti-Soviet sentiments.[87]

A second facet of the Soviet leadership's use of the Arab Communist parties to curb anti-Sovietism in the Arab world was their call to the leaders of Iraq and Syria to accept the Communists as junior partners in a national front. This theme was clearly spelled out in an article by Ulianovsky in *New Times* titled "The Arab East: Problems of a United Progressive Front," in which the author claimed that both the Syrian and Iraqi Communists had made numerous concessions to the ruling Ba'ath Party in order to enter the national fronts of their countries, and that the Communists clearly recognized the Ba'ath as the "leading force" in each front.[88] In calling for the participation of Communist parties as junior partners in a national front, the Soviet leaders had thus clearly given up their earlier plan of having the Communist parties dissolve. Their experiences with the effects of a dissolved Egyptian Communist Party may have convinced them of the futility of that approach. By clearly emphasizing the junior partner character of Communist participation in the national fronts, the CPSU evidently hoped to allay the fears of the Ba'athist leaders that the Communist parties would utilize their positions to seize power. The apparent Soviet hope was that by working within the framework of a national front, the Communist parties could more effectively influence the foreign and domestic policies of the Ba'athist regimes than they could either as individuals within the regime or as illegal opposition parties outside them.[89]

While perhaps welcoming the Soviet abandonment of the policy of calling for the dissolution of the Arab Communist parties, Syrian and Iraqi Communists were not as enthusiastic about entering coalitions where they would be subordinate to the Ba'ath, whatever the benefits to Soviet foreign policy. The Syrian Communist Party actually split over this issue (among others), and the CPSU was very hard put to mend the breach, which pitted the majority of the Syrian Communist Party's Central Committee against the pro-Russian general secretary, Khalid Bakdash.[90]   Given Assad's March 1972 description of the proposed national front, which stated that the Ba'ath party would have the "majoritarian presence in all institutions of the Front" and that the Ba'ath were given the *exclusive* right to carry on "political recruitment, organization, and propaganda in the ranks of the armed forces and among the student masses," it is not surprising that many Syrian Communists felt that joining the national front under these conditions might well mean the effective end of the Syrian Communist Party.[91] In any case, Assad cleverly selected Communists from each of the two factions to serve in his government, thus playing them off and weakening the Syrian Communist Party still further.

While the Russians were upgrading the importance given to the Communist parties of the Middle East, their relations with Egypt remained cool. Sadat made yet another trip to the Soviet Union in February 1972, but he was in a much weaker position than on his previous visit. His bluff on war with Israel had been called, and student riots had broken out in Cairo two weeks before he left for Moscow. The Russians, with Nixon's visit to the USSR only three months away, were in no mood to pledge support for an Egyptian military venture against Israel. Indeed, according to Heikal, Sadat complained: "In October you promised me equipment that hasn't arrived; more was promised by Podgorny in May and hasn't arrived; more was promised by Ponamarev in July and it hasn't arrived. Why the delay?"[92]   Nonetheless, despite Sadat's complaint, the joint communique following the visit stressed the UN resolution of November 22, 1967, and the need for a peaceful settlement of the Arab-Israeli conflict. As a sop to the Egyptians, the Russians made another vague allusion to giving the Egyptians military aid by stating that "the two sides again considered giving Egypt assistance in the field of further strengthening its defense capability and outlined a number of concrete steps in this direction."[93]   The absence from the talks of Egyptian Defense Minister Mohammed Sadek, however, suggested that these "concrete steps" might be a long time in coming. It is interesting to note that following his return from Moscow, Sadat declared that the Egyptians would have to "prepare themselves for an extended political and military struggle" in order to recover the Israeli-occupied territories.[94]

While the Soviet Union's relations with Egypt remained cool, they rapidly warmed with Iraq. Just as in the 1958-59 period, when Soviet displeasure with the Egyptian regime of Nasser led it into a close relationship with Nasser's Arab rival, Premier Kassem of Iraq, so too in 1971-72, when the Soviet leaders grew disenchanted with Sadat, they moved to improve relations with the regime of Sadat's arch rival in the Arab world, Iraqi President Hassan Al-Bakr.

Mention has already been made of the large loan given to the Iraqi government on April 8, 1971, despite Soviet opposition to a number of Iraq's policies. Following the ouster of Ali Sabry and Shaari Gomaa, the two individuals in the Egyptian regime closest to the Soviet Union, the Russian attitude toward Iraq's Ba'athist regime became much more favorable. Thus, in an article on July 14, 1971, entitled "Iraq on the Path of Changes," *Pravda* columnist R. Petrov praised the Ba'athist regime for having properly reconsidered the policies of its previous period in power in 1963, when it had actively suppressed and slaughtered Iraqi Communists. Petrov was particularly pleased with the Iraqi regime's announced desire to create a national front that would unite "all progressive anti-imperialist organizations, including the communist party of Iraq." While warning that the Iraqis still faced many difficulties—not the least of which was the "remnants of anti-communism and mistrust of Iraqi communists in the Ba'ath party and in the military," Petrov concluded his analysis on a positive note:

> However, in leading Iraqi circles as a whole, every year brings increased understanding of the importance of establishing an atmosphere of genuine trust and cooperation among all the progressive forces of the people.[95]

Soviet-Iraqi relations grew still warmer following the abortive coup in the Sudan several days later. Faced by a hostile Saudi Arabia and Iran to her south and east, and with her western neighbor Syria having joined the Arab Federation led by Egypt, Iraq was isolated both in the Arab world and in the Middle East as a whole. The Iraqis had probably hoped that by supporting the military coup d'etat against Nimeri, the Sudan might be weaned away from its ties with Egypt and into a close relationship with Iraq. When the coup failed and Nimeri returned to power, the Soviet Union was the only country that exceeded Iraq in its condemnation of Nimeri's activities—albeit for different reasons.[96]

Iraq's isolation grew stronger as its Persian Gulf rival Iran seized control of the three strategically placed islands in the Persian Gulf during the Indo-Pakistani war, and all Iraqi appeals for assistance to her fellow Arab states were in vain. At the same time the truce between the Iraqi government and the Kurds had broken down, with Kurdish leader Mullah Mustafa Barzani accusing the Iraqi government of trying to assassinate him and of not fulfilling the agreement of March 11, 1970.[97] The Iraqi government then began arresting large numbers of Kurds, while other Kurds returned to Barzani's mountain fortresses to prepare for war. To make matters worse for the narrowly based Ba'athist government, Iranian Foreign Minister Abbas Khalatbari stated in early December 1971 that Iran would aid the Iraqi Kurds should civil war between the Kurds and the Iraqi government break out again.[98] Meanwhile, the Iraqi government continued to have difficulties in its negotiations with the Western oil companies. Frustrated and isolated, Iraq turned to the Soviet Union. One week after Sadat had departed from Moscow, the number-two man and heir apparent of the Iraqi regime, Saddam Hussein, came to the Soviet Union for a one-week visit. In his welcoming speech, Kosygin continued the usual Soviet line of praise for the evolution of the Ba'athist regime:

> We see that important changes are taking place in the life of the Republic of Iraq. . . . The efforts of the Ba'ath party and other progressive parties and organizations of Iraq aimed at the creation of a National Front of all the country's progressive forces will undoubtedly facilitate the movement of the Iraqi people along the path of progressive social and economic transformation.[99]

Saddam Hussein's speech, however, was considerably more explicit and included an outright request for an alliance with the USSR:

> The conviction is growing among our people that it is necessary to unite the progressive forces in every Arab country and to strengthen the ties between our countries—Iraq and the Soviet Union. . . . While highly appreciating the fraternal assistance that your great country is giving us and other Arab states, we are at the same time looking forward to the day when there will be *qualitative progress* in the nature of relations between us.
>
> We think that the firm strategic alliance between our peoples, parties and governments is the foundation on which economic, technical, cultural and other relations are being built and will continue to be built.[100] [emphasis added]

For reasons of its own, the Soviet Union was also interested in a treaty arrangement. In the first place it would give the Russians another strong point in the Arab world and make it less dependent on its position in Egypt. Perhaps even more important, a treaty with Iraq would strengthen the Soviet Union's position in the Persian Gulf at a time when politics in the oil rich region were in a great state of flux.[101] Nonetheless, there must have been some fears in the Kremlin that the Iraqis might use an alliance with the Soviet Union as a strategic cover for an attack on Iran—much as India had utilized the alliance it signed with the USSR in August 1971 as a diplomatic base from which to launch its attack on Pakistan. It was perhaps for this reason that the joint communique released on February 18, 1972 merely stated:

> The two sides have agreed, taking the present exchange of opinions into account, to study additional measures that could be undertaken

in the near future adequately to strengthen the relations that have developed between the two states and to raise these relations to a new and higher level, formulating them into a treaty.[102]

The Russians also obtained Iraqi approval to include in the joint communique the by-now ritual condemnation of "imperialist attempts to disseminate anti-communism and anti-sovietism in the Arab world."

In mid-March the Iraqis made one last attempt to end their isolation in the Arab world by proposing an alliance between Egypt, Syria, and Iraq—allegedly as a means of dealing with King Hussein's plan to establish a federation of the eastern and western banks of the Jordan River. Having once again been rebuffed by their fellow Arabs, and spurred by the announcement of President Nixon's forthcoming visit to Iran, the Iraqis turned once more to the Soviet Union. This time their wish was granted. On April 9, 1972, during Kosygin's visit to Iraq to inaugurate the northern Rumelia oil fields, which the Russians were helping to develop, a treaty was signed between the two countries.

The treaty bore a number of similarities to the Soviet-Egyptian treaty signed 11 months earlier. Lasting for 15 years, the treaty provided that Iraq and the USSR would contact each other "in the event of the development of situations spelling a danger to the peace of either party or creating a danger to peace." In addition, the two sides agreed not to enter into any alliance aimed against the other. The Soviet commitment on military aid, however, was even more vague than in the case of the Egyptian treaty, stating merely that the two sides "will continue to develop cooperation in the strengthening of their defense capacity."[103]

Thus, in less than one year, the USSR had signed treaties with three of the major nations along its southern periphery: Egypt, India, and Iraq. This was a diplomatic undertaking in many ways reminiscent of the brief period in 1921 when the Soviet Union signed treaties with Turkey, Afghanistan, and Iran. The Soviet-Iraqi treaty, however, contained some possible dangers for Soviet policy makers. In the first place, it was more than likely that Iraq, emboldened by the treaty, would be more aggressive in its relations with Iran. Second, by signing the treaty, the Soviet leadership seemed to have written off the Kurds, whose leader, Barzani, complained to a *Le Figaro* correspondent on April 10 (the day after the treaty was signed) that the weapons that Iraq would receive under the treaty would be used against the Kurds.[104]

Despite the treaty it is apparent that serious disagreements remained between the two countries. Thus, the final communique reported that the negotiations took place in an atmosphere of "frankness" and that "exchanges of opinions" had occurred between the two sides.[105] The Russians may well have been concerned that the Iraqis would use the newly signed treaty with the USSR as support in its conflict with Iran and hence advised the Iraqis to be cautious. Any such Soviet concern was evidently justified, because on April 10, 1972—the day after the signing of the treaty—Iran reported that Iraq had precipitated five border clashes. As if to emphasize the real Iraqi purpose in signing the treaty, the semiofficial Baghdad newspaper *Al-Jumhouria* commented that "the treaty has filled the hearts of the Iranian leaders with fright."[106] Another result of the treaty with which the Russians could not have been too happy was a further deterioration in Iraqi-Libyan relations as Kaddafi branded the treaty "imperialist." (This is of particular interest, since a Libyan delegation had visited the Soviet Union from February 23 to March 4, 1972, and had signed an agreement on economic and technical cooperation with the USSR at that time.)

A more positive effect of the Soviet-Iraqi treaty for the Russian leaders was the announcement on June 1, 1972—less than two months after Kosygin's visit to Iraq—that the Iraqi government had nationalized the Iraq Petroleum Company (IPC) oil field at Kirkuk (one of the three main oil fields owned by the Western consortium). As mentioned above, the Iraqis had been involved in a long wrangle with the IPC, which had cut production in the Kirkuk field by 44 percent in March because of a drop in Mediterranean oil prices. There is little doubt that the Russians actively encouraged the Iraqi nationalization decision. Soviet spokesmen had long urged the Arab states to nationalize their oil holdings and thus strike a blow at "Western imperialism"; and by February 1972 Soviet spokesmen had begun to point out that unlike the situation at the time of the Arab oil boycott after the June 1967 war, both Western Europe and the United States were now vulnerable to Arab oil pressure.[107] On March 14, 1972, Radio Moscow reminded the Arabs that the former chairman of the U.S. Joint Chiefs of Staff, Arthur Radford, had said that the loss of Middle East oil to the West would be a catastrophe, and the broadcast went on to emphasize what it called the "growing sentiment" among the Arabs to use oil as a weapon to exert pressure on the United States because of its "anti-Arab policies."[108] In April 1972 the Soviet journal devoted to the United States, *SSha,* published an article emphasizing Western dependence on Middle East oil and noting the statement of President Nixon's adviser Peter Flanigan that if the United States loses the petroleum of the Near East, its "influence on Western Europe and Japan will be greatly weakened."[109]

Meanwhile, the Western oil companies were steadily retreating in the face of price demands from the Organization of Petroleum Exporting Countries (OPEC), and the oil-producing nations were now also demanding an increasing percentage of the companies' oil for their own use. Consequently, the Soviet leaders may have seen the IPC nationalization as another major blow to the whole structure of Western oil holdings in the Middle East and a reinforcement of the trend leading eventually to the full nationalization of Arab oil and the consequent weakening of the Western alliance system headed by the United States. In the meantime, the increasing Soviet involvement in the development of Iraq's oil industry, highlighted by the northern Rumelia agreement, would be a demonstration to the Arabs that if cut off by the West, they could turn to the

USSR as an alternative source of oil development capital. Indeed, a week *before* Iraq's nationalization, *Pravda* commentator Irina Pogodina stated:

> The recent commissioning of oil fields in North Rumelia, which were opened up with USSR assistance, has created new opportunities for the Iraqi people in their struggle against domination by foreign monopolies. . . . Iraq's fruitful cooperation with the socialist states, which is developing successfully, has created auspicious conditions for the country's achievement of *full* economic independence.[110] [emphasis added]

The Soviet government was quick to hail the Iraqi announcement of the Kirkuk nationalization and the subsequent decision by Syrian Premier Hafiz Assad to nationalize the IPC pipeline complex radiating across Syria. Writing in *New Times,* Pavel Demchenko stated:

> The decision of the Iraqi and Syrian governments to nationalize the property of the Iraq Petroleum Company (IPC) struck a telling blow at the mighty oil empire foreign capital has built up in the Middle East and North Africa in the past half-century. . . .
> The implications of this go far beyond the purely economic aspect and throw light on the potential contained in united action by Arab countries to gain control over their own natural resources which in the independence and strengthening of their anti-imperialist positions . . . [111]

Nonetheless, despite their enthusiastic acceptance and encouragement of the nationalization decision, the Iraqi government's action was not without cost to the Soviet leaders. The day after the nationalization, Iraqi Foreign Minister M. S. A. Baki flew to Moscow in quest of economic and technical assistance to help compensate for the expected losses and difficulties resulting from nationalization. Lacking a tanker fleet of its own, and possessing only a limited refining capacity, Iraq was hard put to market its oil. To make matters worse, the regime had also lost about $780 million in hard-currency revenue as a result of the nationalization. While the Russians may have welcomed the increased dependency of the Iraqi regime, a situation that could lead to closer cooperation in exploiting the unstable situation in the Persian Gulf (assuming such cooperation could be achieved without unduly alarming Iran), the Russians would have to pay for this dependency. Thus, five days after Baki's arrival, an agreement was signed stipulating that the Soviet Union would help Iraq transport its oil, build a refinery in Mosul (near the Kirkuk field) with an annual capacity of 1.5 million tons, and help prospect for oil in southern Iraq. The Russians also agreed to give further assistance to the Baghdad-Basra oil pipeline. This agreement, like previous Soviet-

Iraqi ones, stipulated that the USSR would be paid for its assistance by importing Iraqi oil.[112]

The Soviet assistance, however, was far from meeting all of Iraq's needs.
The Iraqi regime faced a severe shortage of hard currency—something the Russians with their own hard-currency problems (aggravated by the need to buy
large amounts of wheat abroad) could not supply. The Iraqi government sought
to diversify its export outlets by gaining markets in hard-currency areas, and
agreements were signed with both France and Italy covering part of the output
of the Kirkuk fields. Despite these moves, however, the Iraqi government was
still forced to institute an austerity program to compensate for its decreasing
supply of vitally needed hard currency.[113]

While Soviet-Iraqi relations on a state-to-state level continued to improve,
the Russians were not without criticism of the Iraqi government's domestic policies. *Izvestia's* political commentator, V. Kudryavstev, writing one week after
the IPC nationalization, complained that the Iraqi popular front (containing
Communists and other "progressives"), which the Ba'athist government of Iraq
had promised as far back as 1970, had not yet come into existence:

> *The tasks confronting Iraq under its program of social and economic*
> *transformation are so great that the Baath party alone cannot cope*
> *with them. It would be an illusion to believe that this program can*
> *be fulfilled without the cooperation between the Baath on the one*
> *hand and the Iraqi Communist Party and the Democratic Party of*
> *Kurdistan on the other. . . .* In March 1970, I had occasion to talk to
> Saddam Hussein, Deputy General Secretary of the Baath regional
> leadership and Vice-Chairman of the Revolutionary Council; at that
> time he was already talking about the necessity of creating a national
> front of all the country's progressive forces, especially since the
> March 11, 1970 agreement on the peaceful solution of the Kurdish
> problem had facilitated the implementation of this task. But now
> two years have gone by, and still there are only talks about the crea-
> tion of this vitally necessary front.[114] [emphasis added]

By June 1972, it might have occurred to the Russians that the Iraqi call
for a popular front, together with the inclusion of two Iraqi Communists in
nominal positions in the Iraqi cabinet that occurred in May 1972, could well
have been a ploy to gain Soviet support—much as the Syrian Ba'athist regime's
decision in 1966 to allow the return of Syrian Communist Khalid Bakhdash
from exile was a ploy to get Soviet assistance for the Syrian regime. Whether or
not the Russians would be able to exploit Iraq's new dependency to force the
creation of a genuine "popular front" remained very much in doubt, and Iraqi
actions, such as the decision to permit the United States to open an "Interest
Section" in the Belgian embassy in Baghdad in August 1972 seemed to indicate

that the Iraqis were interested in limiting their dependence on the USSR. Nonetheless, despite conflict over the Ba'ath regime's internal policies, in the realm of foreign policy it appeared as if the two governments were working closely together and the immediate prospects were of even greater cooperation in the future.

While Soviet-Iraqi cooperation was increasing, the Soviet relationship with the Sadat regime in Egypt was running into further difficulties. Egyptian President Sadat, who had not been able to get the desired support from the Soviet Union in his conflict with Israel, faced serious criticism at home. The prolonged "no war-no peace" situation was causing increasing frustration, as Israel, which was receiving a continual flow of American military and economic assistance, seemed ever more firmly entrenched in the occupied Sinai Peninsula.

Two months after his unproductive visit to Moscow in February, Sadat made yet another visit to the Soviet capital—this time just before the Nixon-Brezhnev summit talks, which both Sadat and Israeli Prime Minister Golda Meir feared might lead to an imposed Soviet-American Middle East settlement injurious to their interests. As he later remarked in a speech to Egypt's Arab Socialist Union, Sadat told Brezhnev during his Moscow visit that Egypt would never agree either to a limitation of arms shipments to the Middle East or to a continuation of the "no war-no peace" situation, or to the surrender of "one inch of Arab lands" in an imposed peace by the superpowers. Perhaps even more important, however, Sadat once again expressed his desire for advanced weapons (fighter-bombers similar to the Phantom, which could reach the Israeli heartland, and ground-to-ground missiles) along with Soviet support for renewed hostilities against Israel.[115] The Russians, however, with more important global issues at stake (such as the U.S. reaction to a major North Vietnamese offensive into South Vietnam and continued difficulties in completing the SALT agreement), proved unwilling to sacrifice their relations with the United States on behalf of a small ally—and a relatively fickle one at that. Although the joint communique at the end of Sadat's visit contained the statement that Egypt had a right to use "other means" (*drugie sredstva*) to regain territories occupied by Israel should a peaceful solution prove impossible, the Russians committed themselves to nothing more than "considering measures aimed at further increasing the military potential of the Egyptian Arab Republic."[116] Far more to the point was the communique released after the Soviet-American summit conference, which reaffirmed the two superpowers' "support for a peaceful settlement in the Middle East in accordance with Security Council Resolution No. 242," and declared their willingness to play a role in bringing about a settlement in the Middle East "which would permit, in particular, consideration of further steps to bring about a military relaxation in the area."[117] In addition, each power pledged to warn the other in the event that a dangerous local conflict threatened to arise and "to do everything in their power so that conflicts or situations do not arise which would seem to increase international tensions," and also not to seek "unilateral advantage at the expense of the other."[118]   *New Times* correspondent Y. Potomov strongly emphasized the Soviet Union's interest in Soviet-American cooperation and in a peaceful solution to the Arab-Israeli conflict in a commentary on the significance of the Soviet-American talks on the Middle East:

> It is in place to emphasize in this connection the great significance of the support expressed in the joint Soviet-American communique on the talks between the Soviet leaders and the U.S. President for a *peaceful* settlement in the Middle East in accordance with the Security Council resolution of November 22, 1967. . . . All who really seek *peace* in the Middle East and the world should bar the way to the reckless adventurist forces that are prepared to sacrifice the interest of *peace* and security of the peoples for the sake of their own selfish interests.[119] [emphasis added]

Having thus been rebuffed once again by the Soviet leadership in his quest for effective support against Israel, and beset by an increasing sense of frustration as well as a rising level of discontent in Egypt, Sadat began to plan a major shift in Egyptian foreign policy. It should be noted that frustration with the perceived lack of Soviet support was by no means confined to Sadat. In March, a seminar sponsored by *Al-Ahram* on Soviet policy toward the Middle East and attended by Soviet and Egyptian delegates revealed a great deal of mutual hostility; the Egyptians complained that the Russians were promoting Communist ideology in the Arab world, while the Soviet delegates complained about the prominence of the petty bourgeois and the hostility displayed toward Egyptian Communists. Particularly sharp in his criticism was Ismail Fahmy, a senior counselor at the Egyptian Foreign Ministry (and later to become Egypt's Foreign Minister), who complained that the "no war-no peace" situation in the Middle East was being used by the Soviet leaders to further their own interests.[120]   Then, in early April, a number of prominent Egyptians on the right of the Egyptian political spectrum, including Abd Al-Latif Baghdadi and Kamal Ad-Din Hussein, who like Sadat were among the original group of officers who overthrew King Farouk in 1952, complained in a memorandum to the Egyptian president:

> It is now time to reconsider the policy of extravagant dependence on the Soviet Union. That policy, five years after the defeat, has not deterred the aggression nor has it restored the rights. . . . The relationship with the Russians must return to the natural and secure framework of relationships between a newly independent country which is anxious to protect that independence and a big state whose strategy —by virtue of ideology and interests—embodies the desire to expand its influence. . . . It is time now for Egypt to return to a secure area between the two superpowers. . . . There is no doubt that going be-

yond the limits of that area was one of the causes of the catastrophe. The policy of alliance with the devil is not objectionable only until it becomes favorable to the devil.[121]

Sadat made this note public in an interview with the Beirut daily *Al-Hayat* on May 18, probably as a trial balloon to gauge public opinion toward an anti-Russian shift in Egyptian foreign policy. The *Al-Hayat* interview was followed the next day by the publication of the discussions of the *Al-Ahram* seminar, and in June and early July by a series of editorials by the editor of the Egyptian daily *Al-Ahram*, Mohammed Heikal, who not only continued the theme that Egypt should seek a more neutral position in world affairs, but went one step further by asserting, as had Ismail Fahmy, that the Soviet Union, just like Israel and the United States, was actually profiting from the continuation of the "no war-no peace" situation.[122]

In addition to Egyptian dissatisfaction with the lack of Soviet support, there were a number of other serious irritants in Soviet-Egyptian relations. Friction was increasing between the Soviet military advisers and Egyptian officers, and Egyptian Defense Minister Mohammed Sadek frequently complained to Sadat about alleged slurs made by the Russian advisers as to the capability of the officers and troops under his command. In addition, the Soviet bases in Egypt had been declared off limits to Egyptians, even, on occasion, to Sadat himself, and this revived unpleasant memories of the situation that had occurred when the British controlled Egypt only 20 years before.[123]

The Russians, however, also had some grievances. Sadat's increasingly close alignment with Libya's Kaddafi, then the most vocal anti-Soviet leader in the Arab world, was not well received in the Kremlin, and the Soviet efforts to bring Iraq into a closer tie with Egypt may be considered an attempt to counter this trend. Perhaps even more serious was the growing Soviet displeasure at what appeared to be a partial restoration of capitalism in Egypt. Georgi Mirsky, one of the Soviet Union's top experts on Egypt, made the following rather caustic comments about domestic developments in Egypt on the eve of the twentieth anniversary of the Egyptian Revolution:

> In many villages, richer peasants, who profited from the agrarian reforms and who hold the village elders and other local chiefs in the hollow of their hands, call the tune. In urban areas, even though the state controls 85 percent of the industrial production, there is a strong private sector which incorporates not only shopkeepers and artisans, but also growing numbers of middlemen, profiteers, building contractors and other such bourgeois elements. The higher paid bureaucrats display a tendency to link up with the private sector. All these elements, as progressive Egyptian and foreign newsmen note, today represent the main danger at home to Egypt's socialist

orientation; for the Revolution, as they emphasize, has a long way to go before every goal is accomplished.[124]

If there remained any Egyptian hope for possible Soviet support in a war against Israel, it was dispelled in late June with the publication of the report of a team of Soviet Communists who were sent to Syria in an attempt to make peace between the two contending factions of the Syrian Communist Party, one of which was pro-Moscow and the other independent. This report, which was leaked to the Beirut daily *Al-Rayah* by the independent faction of the Syrian Communist Party, contained a number of specific criticisms of Arab and Arab Communist policy. In the first place, the Russians voiced a great deal of skepticism about the possibility of genuine Arab unity because of the lack of a "joint economy." Second, the Russians rejected the slogan of "Arab nationalism" for Arab Communists, stating that "to run after popularity through nationalism will only have a bad result." Most important of all, the Russians came out for a political rather than a military solution to the Arab-Israeli conflict: "The reason is not only that we do not want war, but because war will result in disasters for the progressive Arab regimes"—a clear indication that the Russians showed little confidence in the fighting ability of the "progressive Arab regimes," including Egypt.[125]

Another factor that must have caused considerable concern to Sadat during the prolonged period of "no war-no peace" was that Egypt's position of leadership in the Arab world, which had once been paramount under Nasser, seemed to be slipping away. Thus, despite Sadat's bitter denunciations of the United States in May and June 1972 because of its support for Israel, the regime in North Yemen, once closely aligned with Egypt, announced the restoration of diplomatic relations with the United States on July 2, 1972. At the same time, Sudanese Premier Jaafar Nimeri, whom Sadat had helped to restore to power following the coup d'etat against him less than a year before, spoke very warmly of U.S. aid to the war-ravaged southern section of his country and stated that the Sudan was "seriously considering" the reestablishment of diplomatic relations with the United States, an action that took place less than three weeks later.[126]

Thus, Sadat, beset by internal frustration and rising domestic discontent, and whose leadership was under increasing challenge in the Arab world, decided on a dramatic action before the twentieth anniversary celebration of the Egyptian Revolution to electrify his country and end the malaise that had been deepening in Egypt because of the apparently interminable continuation of the "no war-no peace" situation. Following the failure of a final arms-seeking trip by Egyptian Premier Aziz Sidky to Moscow on July 14, and complaining that "while our enemy has a friend in the world (the United States) which acts rashly and escalates, we have a friend (the USSR) which calculates and is cautious," Sadat announced on July 18, 1972 the "termination of the mission of the Soviet military advisers and experts, the placing of all military bases in Egypt under

Egyptian control, and the call for a Soviet-Egyptian meeting to work out a new relationship" between the two countries.[127]

There is little doubt that these moves were popular both among the Egyptian masses and among the officer corps that is the backbone of the Sadat regime. To foreign observers the whole country appeared invigorated during the celebration of the twentieth anniversary of the revolution just two days later.[128] Yet a greater degree of domestic popularity was clearly not the only motive for Sadat's action. The Egyptian leader was seeking to regain a freedom of action in foreign affairs and break out of the cul-de-sac that the Egyptian relationship with the USSR had gotten Egypt into. Apparently acting on the recommendation of the note addressed to him on April 4, 1972, Sadat was endeavoring to place Egypt "on the more secure ground between the two superpowers." His reasoning seemed to be that since the Soviet Union had been unable to get Israel to withdraw from the occupied territories by diplomatic means, and was unwilling to expel her by force, Egypt would turn to the United States and Western Europe for assistance.

Despite the close American tie to Israel, the Egyptians had not forgotten that it was primarily American pressure that had forced the Israelis to withdraw from the Sinai in 1957. Indeed, Heikal had editorialized on August 21 in *Al-Ahram* that "no one can convince Egypt that the United States is incapable of bringing pressure on Israel."[129] High-ranking American officials such as Henry Kissinger and President Nixon had made no secret of their desire to get the Russians out of Egypt and thereby weaken the entire Soviet position in the eastern Mediterranean. Deprived of their air bases in Egypt and lacking aircraft carriers to provide air cover for their fleet, the Russians were clearly put at a tactical disadvantage with respect to the American fleet in the Mediterranean, and Sadat must have assumed that the United States would be grateful for his expulsion of the Russians. The weakening of the Soviet presence in the Mediterranean was also of benefit to Western Europe, and Sadat may have hoped that the Europeans might reciprocate by bringing pressure on Israel by withholding Common Market tariff concessions then under negotiation as well as by selling Egypt advanced weaponry.

Egypt's move toward a more nonaligned position was officially expressed by Egyptian Minister of Information, Mohammed El-Zayyat (the man who was to become foreign minister one month later), in a news conference for foreign journalists on July 22:

> We joined Nehru and Tito in non-alignment and we urged other emerging nations to do the same. We have *never deviated from this road.* This is the foundation of our behavior and it is important for the understanding of everything.[130] [emphasis added]

On the same day, the government-controlled Cairo newspapers prominently displayed a declaration by Ismail Sabri Abdullah, minister of State for Planning, advocating an "open-door" policy for foreign investments. The statement cited the existence of a new law, made public in September 1971, giving guarantees for foreign investments. This open appeal for Western investment in Egypt was a marked policy change from the days when Nasser was nationalizing Western factories.[131]

In addition to courting support in the West, a second facet of Sadat's new policy was a move toward further union with oil-rich Libya. Indeed, on July 23, only six days after the exodus of the Russians, Libyan leader Kaddafi saw fit to publicize his offer to Sadat of a union of Egypt and Libya—something that had been under consideration since Sadat's unsuccessful trip to Moscow in February 1972. Considering the major benefits that would flow to Egypt as a result of such a union, particularly access to Libya's immense oil revenues, and the strongly anti-Communist and anti-Soviet position held by Kaddafi at that time, it is conceivable that the expulsion of the Russians might have been the condition demanded by Kaddafi before the Egyptians could gain access to Libya's hard-currency reserves, then estimated by some Western sources at $3 billion.[132] In addition, Sadat's ouster of the Soviets would certainly win favor in the eyes of the rabidly anti-Communist King Faisal of Saudi Arabia.[133]

On July 31 Kaddafi and Sadat met at Tobruk, and two days later an agreement was reached to establish a "unified political leadership" to work out plans for the unification of the two countries in finance, education, and political and constitutional organization by September 1973.[134] There were numerous advantages that would accrue to Egypt as a result of such a union. In the first place, as mentioned above, Egypt would gain access to Libya's approximately $3 billion in hard-currency reserves as well as an estimated $2.5 billion in yearly oil revenues. With some of this money, Sadat could not only pursue an independent path of economic development at home should the Russians renege on their promised capital loans to Egypt—but Egypt now could also buy advanced weapons on Western markets. It was rumored that the Egyptians had already begun to shop in England for Rapier antiaircraft missiles and Chieftain tanks. Second, the defense potential of Egypt would clearly be improved by Sadat's ability to position Egyptian aircraft and tanks in Libya, out of the range of Israeli aircraft, until he was ready to use them, and by the fact that Libya was receiving tanks and armored personnel carriers from Italy and Mirage jet fighters from France. Interestingly enough, the French government, which had placed an embargo on exports of weapons to "combatants," stated that the Mirages would continue to flow to Libya until the Libyan-Egyptian union took "more concrete shape" (that is, until September 1973). This assured Libya of at least 18 more Mirages, and many observers doubted that the French government, which had sought to increase its influence in the Arab world under both de Gaulle and Pompidou, would cease to supply the first-class jet fighter-bombers even after that date.[135] Finally, the fact that the United States had major oil holdings in Libya would give Sadat a means of pressure against the United States to weaken its support of Israel.

The Soviet Union, of course, lost heavily by Sadat's decision to expel the Soviet military advisers from Egypt and eliminate Soviet control over Egyptian air and naval bases, although, perhaps to demonstrate Egypt's dependency on the USSR, the Soviet leadership decided to make a more extensive withdrawal than Sadat seems to have wanted.[136] Thus, in addition to the Soviet military advisers, Moscow withdrew its instructors in Egyptian military schools, the SAM-6 missiles (as well as their personnel), and the aircraft operated by Soviet airmen as part of Egypt's integrated air defense system.[137] While, as a result of the exodus, the USSR was far less likely to be dragged into a war with the United States in the Middle East—and this must have sweetened their departure somewhat[138]— nonetheless, the end result of the exodus was that the USSR's strategic position in the eastern Mediterranean was clearly weakened. Without control over the airfields in northern Egypt, it was unable to give air cover to the Soviet Mediterranean fleet, and without the airfield in southern Egypt near Aswan it lost control over a major strategic foothold in northeast Africa. While the Soviet navy did retain the right to visit Egyptian ports, even this was contingent upon a modicum of Egyptian goodwill (indeed, as Soviet-Egyptian relations hit a new low in April 1976, Sadat deprived them of this right as well),[139] and in July 1972 Sadat may have seen this as a bargaining chip to assure the continued flow of Soviet economic aid and/or, at the minimum, the completion of aid projects already under way.

What made matters worse for the Russians was that while their position in the Middle East worsened the positions of their two main rivals for influence in the area, the United States and China, were strengthened. Mention has already been made of the resumption of diplomatic relations between North Yemen and the United States on July 2, 1972, and between the Sudan and the United States on July 19, 1972. U.S. relations also improved with Algeria as the American Federal Power Commission approved plans for the El Paso Gas Company to import $1 billion in natural gas from Algeria (although neither the company nor Algeria was very happy about the price), and the Algerian government promptly returned both the aircraft and the million dollars in ransom that a group of Black Panthers had hijacked to Algeria. Even the militant Iraqi government perceived the need to allow an American government presence in Baghdad and, as mentioned above, an agreement was reached in late August for two American foreign service officers to open an American Interest Section in the Belgian embassy in the Iraqi capital.

The increased American presence in the area was also highlighted by the trip of Secretary of State William Rogers to Kuwait, North Yemen, and Bahrein (where the United States had a small base) in July, and the opening of a "home port" for the United States Sixth Fleet in Piraeus, Greece, in early September. The home-port arrangement enabled the Sixth Fleet to increase its service in the Mediterranean by sharply reducing the separation period between the sailors and their families, many of whom took the opportunity to move to Greece.[140]

The Chinese Communists, jubilant over the Egyptian decision to expel the Russians, were also moving to improve their position. Taking advantage of Soviet mistakes in the Sudan the previous summer, the Chinese supplied the Nimeri government with $80 million in loans following the abortive coup, along with military equipment. Ethiopia, the Sudan's strategically placed southern neighbor, was the recipient of an $87.5 million loan in October 1971, and the Chinese further improved their position in northeast Africa by signing two civil air agreements with the Ethiopian government in May and July 1972.[141] During the summer of 1972, the Chinese also hosted representatives of the North Yemeni and South Yemeni governments in Peking, and in September the wife of the Shah of Iran was an honored guest in the Chinese capital as the Chinese Communists sought to capitalize on the strain in Soviet-Iranian relations following the Soviet-Iraqi treaty.

After a long period of coolness, Sino-Egyptian relations also began to improve, a process hastened by the Soviet departure from Egypt, which received considerable attention in the Chinese press. Following his unsuccessful visit to Moscow in February 1972—an event that increasingly appeared as a turning point in Soviet-Egyptian relations—Sadat approved a sharp increase in Egyptian trade with Communist China from $12.5 million to $85 million per year. Sadat may have also hoped that his expulsion of the Russians would induce the Chinese to allow Egypt to make use of the unused portion of the $90-million loan that the Chinese had promised in 1965, and the Egyptian leader dispatched an economic delegation to China, possibly for this purpose, in early August.[142]

A rapprochemnt between the two countries (after a period of strained relations in which the Chinese Communists had been accused of stirring up the student riots in Cairo in February 1968), when coupled with China's moves in the Sudan, Ethiopia, and North and South Yemen, and the recent improvement in Sino-Iranian relations, all presaged an increase in influence for China in the Middle East, a prospect that probably made the Russians little happier than did the resurgence of American influence in a region that the Russians had endeavored to make their private sphere of influence.

With its expulsion from Egypt, the Soviet Union had thus suffered another major blow to its influence in the Middle East, while the Middle Eastern positions of its two main rivals, China and the United States, had sharply improved in the "zero-sum game" competition for influence in the region. The Middle East, however, remained a highly volatile region. Fortunately for the Soviet leadership, events within the region were soon to give the USSR an opportunity to recoup some of its lost prestige.

NOTES

1. *Pravda*, October 4, 1970.
2. Translated in *Current Digest of the Soviet Press* (hereafter CDSP) 22, no. 42: 15.

3. Victor Kudryavtsev, "The Political Consolidation in the UAR," *New Times,* no. 43 (1970): 7.

4. New York *Times,* October 16, 1970. See also Michael Field, "Iraq—Growing Realism among the Revolutionaries," *New Middle East,* no. 29 (February 1971): 27; and R. D. McLaurin, Mohammed Mughisuddin, and Abraham R. Wagner, *Foreign Policy Making in the Middle East* (New York: Praeger, 1977), pp. 124-25.

5. For an analysis of the events in Syria, see J. Gaspard, "Damascus after the Coup," *New Middle East,* no. 28 (January 1971): 9-11.

6. *CDSP* 22, no. 48: 25.

7. Ibid., p. 26.

8. Mohammed Heikal, *The Road to Ramadan* (New York: Quadrangle, 1975), pp. 117-18.

9. For a translation of the speeches and the final communique, see *CDSP* 23, no. 5: 1-6.

10. For an analysis of the origins and development of the federation, see Peter K. Bechtold, "New Attempts at Arab Cooperation: The Federation of Arab Republics 1971-?" *Middle East Journal* 27, no. 2 (Spring 1973): 152-72.

11. *CDSP* 22, no. 45: 17-18.

12. Ibid., p. 18.

13. *Pravda,* February 2, 1971. Translated in *CDSP* 23, no. 5:3.

14. In opposition both to the Jarring talks and to the proposed federation, the Iraqi regime tried to organize a "Progressive Arab Front" in cooperation with the Popular Democratic Front for the Liberation of Palestine (PDFLP). See *Middle East Monitor* (hereafter *MEM*) 1, no. 6 (April 15, 1971): 1.

15. Cited in "Review of the Soviet Press," *New Middle East,* no. 31 (April 1971): 9.

16. *Documents of the 24th Congress of the Communist Party of the Soviet Union* (Moscow: Novosti Press Agency Publishing House, 1971), pp. 23-24, 28.

17. Boris Ponamarev, "Under the Banner of Marxism-Leninism and Proletarian Internationalism: The 24th Congress of the CPSU'" *World Marxist Review* (hereafter *WMR*) 14, no. 6 (June 1971): 13.

18. Aziz Mohammed's speech was printed in *Pravda,* April 9, 1971.

19. For the text of the federation, see *MEM* 1, no. 7 (May 1, 1971): 3-5. The joint declaration at the time the federation was announced stated: "The three presidents affirm that the Democratic Republic of the Sudan and its struggling Arab people, who have contributed—under the leadership of Chairman Ja'afar Muhammed an-Nimeri and his brother members of the Revolutionary Command Council—earnestly and effectively to the progress of action within the framework of the Tripoli charter, will remain active in the unionist struggle and in close contact with the Federation of Arab Republics until it is able to join."

20. Cited in "Review of the Soviet Press," *New Middle East,* no. 33 (June 1971): 45-46.

21. Ibid., p. 46.

22. Perhaps the best analysis of these events is P. J. Vatikiotis, "Egypt's Politics of Conspiracy," *Survey* 18, no. 2 (Spring 1972): 83-99. See also Peter Mansfield, "After the Purge," *New Middle East,* no. 33 (June 1971): 12-15.

23. For an analysis of the Sadat peace initiative and Rogers' continuing efforts to bring about an Arab-Israeli settlement, see William Quandt, *Decade of Decisions: American Policy toward the Arab-Israeli Conflict 1967-1976* (Berkeley: University of California Press, 1977), pp. 136-43.

24. *New Times,* no. 19 (1971): 16.

25. See Raymond Anderson, "Egypt Is Seeking to Win U.S. Favor," New York *Times,* March 12, 1971.

26. Another of the men purged by Sadat was Abdel-Mahsen Abdel Nur, secretary general of the Arab Socialist Union, who had headed the ASU delegation to the 24th CPSU Congress the previous month. For a discussion of the men purged, see Jaan Pennar, *The USSR and the Arabs: The Ideological Dimension* (New York: Crane Russak, 1973), pp. 84-88.

27. *New Times*, no 21 (1971): 16.

28. The text of the treaty is found in *New Times*, no. 23 (1971): 8-9. For a reasoned analysis of the treaty, see Nadav Safran, "The Soviet-Egyptian Treaty," *New Middle East*, no. 34 (July 1971): 10-13.

29. *Pravda*, May 29, 1971. Translated in *CDSP* 23, no. 22: 5.

30. Ibid.

31. *Pravda*, June 2, 1971.

32. Ibid., June 5, 1971.

33. Shimon Shamir, "The Marxists in Egypt: The 'Licensed Infiltration' Doctrine in Practice," in *The USSR and the Middle East*, ed. Michael Confino and Shimon Shamir (Jerusalem: Israel Universities Press, 1973), p. 313.

34. For a discussion of these events, see Anthony Sylvester, "Mohammed vs. Lenin in Revolutionary Sudan," *New Middle East*, no. 34 (July 1971): 26-28.

35. Dmitry Volsky, "Changes in the Sudan," *New Times*, no. 30 (1971): 11. This issue of *New Times* appeared in the brief interval between the time Nimeri was overthrown and the time he returned to power.

36. *CDSP* 23, no. 29: 3-4.

37. Ibid., p. 5.

38. Radio Sudan (Obdurman), August 5, 1971.

39. *Agence France* Presse, August 6, 1971. Cited in R. Waring Herrick, "Sudan in Sino-Soviet Relations since the July Countercoup," *Radio Liberty Report* (February 7, 1972).

40. Cited in report by Bernard Gwertzman, New York *Times*, July 30, 1971.

41. *OFNS* report from Cario by Colin Legum, cited in Jerusalem *Post*, August 9, 1971.

42. Pennar, op. cit., p. 50.

43. Ibid.

44. For the text of this communique, see Nicholas Shaoui, "The Middle East Crisis and the Arab Liberation Movement," *WMR* 14, no. 9 (September 1971): 31.

45. Radio Sudan (Obdurman), August 21, 1971.

46. *International Herald Tribune*, August 9, 1971.

47. For an analysis of the effect of the Sino-American rapprochement on Soviet policy, see George Ginsburgs, "Moscow's Reaction to Nixon's Jaunt to Peking," in *Sino-American Detente and Its Policy Implications*, ed. Gene T. Hsiao (New York: Praeger, 1974), pp. 137-59.

48. Radio Sudan (Obdurman), August 2, 1971.

49. R. Petrov, "Steps toward Arab Unity," *New Times*, no. 35 (1971): 22.

50. Shaoui, op. cit., p. 34.

51. Rostislav Ulianovsky, "Marxist and Non-Marxist Socialism," *WMR* 14, no. 9 (September 1971): 121-22.

52. Ibid., pp. 122, 125.

53. Ibid., pp. 125-26.

54. Ibid., p. 126.

55. Ibid., p. 127.

56. Translation in *CDSP* 23, no. 36: 21.

57. Jewish Telegraph Agency (JTA) report in *Jewish Exponent* (Philadelphia), September 10, 1971. The warm treatment of Israelis by the Soviet government during this pe-

riod was to stand out in sharp contrast to the official hostility during Israeli participation in the World University Games in the summer of 1973. See Chapter 4, p. 130.

58. On this point, see the study of Soviet-Israeli relations from 1948 to 1970 by Avigdor Dagan, *Moscow and Jerusalem* (New York: Abelard-Schuman, 1970).

59. For a recent Soviet attempt to play down the significance of Jewish emigration to Israel, see "Zionist Fabrications and the Reality," *New Times,* no. 16 (1972): 12-13. Interestingly enough, the author of the article, Soviet Deputy Minister of Internal Affairs, Boris Shumilin, pointedly remarked that "from the Arab countries alone some 800,000 Jews have gone to Israel."

60. A similar Soviet motive may be seen in Romania's permission to 100,000 Romanian Jews to emigrate to Israel in the 1959-60 period when Soviet-Egyptian relations were at a low point. In 1959 Romania was still a docile satellite of the USSR (it was not to take an independent position until 1962), and it is unlikely that the Romanian government could have taken such a step without Soviet permission, if not actual prodding. There is some evidence, however, that the Romanian government gained financially from its decision to let its Jews go, and the money it received from the Jewish exodus helped finance its ambitious industrialization plans. (Interview with David Ben-Gurion, the late prime minister of Israel, Sde-Boker, Israel, August 1, 1971).

61. *Der Spiegel* reported that Victor Louis had offered a yearly emigration quota for Soviet Jews and a pledge not to transfer Soviet troops east of the Suez Canal if Israeli troops withdrew from it. Cited in *New Middle East,* no. 36 (September 1971): 43. For an analysis of the changing Soviet position on the issue of Soviet Jewish emigration, see Robert O. Freedman, "The Lingering Impact of the Soviet System on the Soviet Jewish Immigrant to the United States," in *The Soviet Jewish Emigre,* ed. Jerome M. Gilison (Baltimore: Baltimore Hebrew College, 1977), pp. 32-58.

62. *Pravda,* October 30, 1971. Translated in *CDSP* 23, no. 44: 18.

63. New York *Times,* January 1, 1972.

64. Ibid.

65. *Al-Nahar* (Beirut), November 4, 1971. Cited in *MEM* 1, no. 19 (November 15, 1971): 3. For a background to the arms deal, which was as much related to domestic political pressures as to defense needs, see E. Romane, "Soviet Arms to Lebanon?" *Radio Liberty Report* (July 28, 1971).

66. See *New Times,* no. 8 (1972): 6. The Popular Front for the Liberation of Oman and the Arab Gulf was later to change its name—and apparently its goal—to the Popular Front for the Liberation of Oman (PFLO).

67. For a discussion of these policies, see the New York *Times,* January 31, 1972, "Economic Review of Africa," pp. 60, 67.

68. See note 26.

69. *New Times,* no. 34 (1971): 8.

70. For a suspicious Soviet account of the British official's visit, see *New Times,* no. 39 (1971): 17.

71. *Pravda,* September 28, 1971, translated in *New Middle East,* no. 38 (November 1971): 12.

72. New York *Times,* October 12, 1971.

73. Cited in *New Middle East,* no. 37 (October 1971): 39.

74. Cited in ibid., no. 38 (November 1971): 4.

75. *Pravda,* October 1971. Translated in *CDSP* 23, no. 41: 6-7.

76. Ibid., pp. 7-8.

77. Ibid., p. 7.

78. See the report by William Dullforce in the Los Angeles *Times,* November 3, 1971. Announcement of the agreement may have been an economic sop to Egypt to compensate

for the failure of the USSR to provide the needed military support. On the other hand, it may also be viewed as an attempt to keep up the underlying pattern of economic cooperation, despite political differences. Thus, it would be similar to the Soviet decision in late 1958 to build the Aswan Dam despite increasingly sharp differences with then President Nasser over political issues.

79. For a review of Arab opinion on the war, see *MEM* 2, no. 1 (January 1, 1972): 3-4.

80. Cited in the Jerusalem *Post*, December 17, 1971.

81. *Al-Jumhuriyah*, July 1, 1971. Cited in *MEM* 1, no. 12 (July 15, 1971): 5.

82. For an analysis of the triangular relations of the USSR, the United States, and China in the politics of the Indian subcontinent, see William J. Barnds, "China and America: Limited Partners in the Indian Subcontinent," in Hsiao, op. cit., pp. 226-48.

83. Deportation of Iranian citizens who lived in Iraq near the Shii holy cities of Karbala, Najaf, and Kaziman had been used as a political tactic by the Iraqi government on earlier occasions when it had wished to demonstrate its displeasure with Iranian policies. The fact that the ruling elite of Iraq are Sunni Moslems, while the vast majority of the Iranian population, including the Shah, are Shii Moslems, has exacerbated the conflict between Iran and Iraq.

84. Cited in *MEM* 1, no. 6 (April 15, 1971): 2.

85. For Sadat's speech explaining his decision not to go to war in 1971, see *New Middle East*, no. 41 (February 1972): 42.

86. For a description of the congress, see *New Times*, no. 5 (1972): 15.

87. *CDSP* 24, no. 4: 19.

88. *New Times*, no. 41 (1972): 18-20. A more theoretical treatment of this problem is found in Ulianovsky's article, "O edinom anti-imperialisticheskom fronte progressivnikh sil v osvobodivshikhsia stranakh" [On the unity of the anti-imperialist front of progressive forces in the newly independent states], *Mirovaia ekonomika i mezhdunarodnye otnosheniia*, no. 9 (September 1972): 76-86.

89. The full theoretical implications of the new Soviet policy on national fronts remained to be worked out, however, and throughout 1972 and 1973, the pages of *Mirovaia ekonomika i mezhdunarodnye otnosheniia; Kommunist; Narodii Azii i Afriki; International Affairs;* and *World Marxist Review* were filled with articles analyzing the different ramifications of the new policy.

90. For an excellent treatment of the rift in the Syrian Communist Party, see the *Radio Free Europe Research Reports* by Kevin Devlin (April 13, 1972, June 7, 1972, and August 23, 1972).

91. Kevin Devlin, *Radio Free Europe Research Report* (April 13, 1972), p. 5. Thanks to the split in the Syrian Communist Party, the outside world got a close view of Soviet attitudes both toward the Arab Communists and toward Arab nationalism. The report of the Soviet commission seeking to heal the rift was "leaked" by the dissident Communist faction and broadcast in Arabic from Beirut and then monitored and translated by the Foreign Broadcast Information Service. For a brief examination of the report, see the analysis by Paul Wohl in the *Christian Science Monitor*, August 21, 1972. The report of the Soviet commission did not differ very greatly in its analyses of Arab society from both Soviet and Arab Communist analyses appearing in the *World Marxist Review*.

92. Heikal, op. cit., p. 158.

93. *Pravda*, February 5, 1972. Translated in *CDSP* 24, no. 5: 10.

94. Cited in *New Middle East*, nos. 42-43 (March-April 1972): 66.

95. *CDSP* 23, no. 28: 17.

96. In his July 30, 1971 critique of the USSR and Arab Communism following the coup in the Sudan, Heikal had commented: "The Sudanese Communist Party then turned to

strange alliances, including elements in contact with the Iraqi Ba'ath Party which is a suspect party all around." Haim Shaked, Esther Souery, and Gabriel Warburg, "The Communist Party in the Sudan 1946-1971," in Confino and Shamir, op. cit., p. 362.

97. *L'Orient le jour,* November 18, 1971. Cited in *MEM* 1, no. 20 (December 1, 1971): 4.

98. Cited in *MEM* 2, no. 1 (January 1, 1972): 2-3.

99. *Pravda,* February 12, 1972. Translated in *CDSP* 24, no. 7: 7.

100. Ibid., p. 8.

101. There was an unsuccessful coup d'etat in the gulf sheikhdom of Sharja on January 25, 1972, while there was a successful one on February 22, 1972, in another sheikhdom, Qatar.

102. Translated in *CDSP* 24, no. 7: 8.

103. The text of the treaty is found in *New Times,* no. 16 (1972): 4-5.

104. Cited in *MEM* 2, no. 9 (May 1, 1972): 4.

105. *Pravda,* April 10, 1972.

106. UPI report from Beirut, cited in Jerusalem *Post,* April 21, 1972; Radio Tehran, April 15 and 16, 1972.

107. See I. Bronin, "Arabskaia neft—SSha—zapadnaia Evropa"[Arab oil—the USA—Western Europe], *Mirovaia ekonomika i mezhdunarodnye otnosheniia,* no. 2 (February 1972): 31-42.

108. Cited in Foy D. Kohler, Leon Goure, and Mose L. Harvey, *The Soviet Union and the October 1973 Middle East War* (Miami: Center for Advanced International Studies, University of Miami, 1974), p. 80.

109. A. K. Kislov, "The United States in the Mediterranean: New Realities," *USA,* no. 4 (1972): 23. Cited in Kohler et al., op. cit., p. 27. For an analysis of Soviet policy toward the Arab oil weapon, see Robert O. Freedman, "The Soviet Union and the Politics of Middle Eastern Oil," in *Arab Oil: Impact on the Arab Countries and Global Implications,* ed. Naiem Sherbiny and Mark Tessler (New York: Praeger, 1976), pp. 305-27.

110. *Pravda,* May 24, 1972. Translated in *CDSP* 24, no. 21: 14.

111. Pavel Demchenko, "Arab Oil for the Arabs," *New Times,* no. 25 (1972): 10.

112. *Izvestia,* July 22, 1972. Translated in *CDSP* 24, no. 29: 18-19.

113. For a discussion of Iraq's efforts to overcome these difficulties, see the report by John Cooley in the *Christian Science Monitor,* June 21, 1972.

114. *Izvestia,* June 8, 1972. Translated in *CDSP* 24, no. 24: 13-14.

115. The full text of Sadat's speech, which gave the Egyptian leader's view of the development of Soviet-Egyptian relations, was in the Radio Cairo Domestic Service broadcast, July 24, 1972.

116. Text of the communique in *Pravda,* April 30, 1972.

117. The text of the joint Soviet-American communique, which gave very little space to the Middle East situation, can be found in *New Times,* no. 23 (1972): 36-38.

118. Ibid.

119. Y. Potomov, "A Just Peace for the Middle East," *New Times,* no. 24 (1972): 16.

120. Cited in *MEM* 2, no. 12 (June 15, 1972): 4.

121. Translated in "Egypt and the USSR: Implication of Economic Integration," *Radio Liberty Dispatch,* July 13, 1972, p. 6.

122. For a survey of the Egyptian press at the time of Soviet exodus, see the report by Ihsan A. Hijazi in the New York *Times,* July 19, 1972.

123. For a perceptive view of the domestic situation in Egypt at the time of the Soviet exodus, see P. J. Vatikiotis, "Two Years after Nasser: The Chance of a New Beginning," *New Middle East,* no. 48 (September 1972): 7-9.

124. Georgi Mirsky, "The Path of the Egyptian Revolution," *New Times,* no. 30 (1972): 23.

125. For the text of this most interesting report, see *Al-Rayah*, June 26, 1972, pp. 12-21. Translated in special supplement to the *Foreign Broadcast Information Service Daily Report*.

126. For a discussion of the domestic and foreign background to the Yemeni and Sudanese decisions, see the report by John Cooley in the *Christian Science Monitor*, July 5, 1972; and the report by Henry Tanner in the New York *Times*, July 18, 1972.

127. Text of the statement in the New York *Times*, July 19, 1972. Sadat has explained his quarrel with Moscow and his decision to terminate the services of the Soviet advisers and regain control of Egypt's bases in a number of speeches. See, for example, his interview with *Al-Nahar* on March 29, 1974; his speech of April 3, 1974 (Cairo Radio); his interview with *Akhbar Al-Yom* on August 3, 1974; and his Mena interview of September 22, 1974.

128. See the report by Henry Tanner in the New York *Times*, July 24, 1972.

129. Cited in the report by John Cooley in the *Christian Science Monitor*, July 24, 1972.

130. Cited in the report by Henry Tanner in the New York *Times*, July 23, 1972.

131. Ibid.

132. For a discussion of the potential benefits to Egypt of the union, see Malcolm Kerr, "The Convenient Marriage of Egypt and Libya," *New Middle East*, no. 48 (September 1972): 4-7.

133. For a discussion of Faisal's anti-Communist attitudes, see Edward Sheehan, *The Arabs, Israelis and Kissinger* (New York: Reader's Digest Press, 1976), pp. 64-65.

134. For the text of the agreement, see the New York *Times*, August 3, 1972.

135. Reuters (Paris), cited in Jerusalem *Post*, August 4, 1972. The observers were later proven correct, since despite clear evidence that the Libyan government had sent its Mirages to Egypt for use in the October 1973 war against Israel, the Pompidou government continued to sell Mirages to Libya.

136. On this point, see Galia Golan, *Yom Kippur and After: The Soviet Union and the Middle East Crisis* (New York: Cambridge University Press, 1977), pp. 24-25.

137. Ibid., p. 25.

138. According to Alvin Z. Rubinstein in his study of Soviet-Egyptian relations—*Red Star on the Nile* (Princeton: Princeton University Press, 1977), p. 201—the primary reason for Moscow's decision to pull out of Egypt so extensively and so quietly was to encourage detente.

139. See p. 88.

140. This agreement was not particularly popular, however, among either sections of the Greek people who perceived it as an endorsement of the Greek military dictatorship, or among a number of U.S. Senators.

141. New York *Times*, September 4, 1972.

142. For a thorough examination of Chinese policy toward Egypt and the rest of the Arab world at this time, see W. A. C. Adie, "Peking's Revised Line," *Problems of Communism* 21, no. 5 (September-October 1972): 54-68.

4

From the 1972 Exodus
to the October 1973
Arab-Israeli War

SOVIET POLICY UP TO THE MUNICH MASSACRE

Despite the major loss to the Russians' Middle Eastern position, the initial Soviet reaction to Sadat's expulsion decision was relatively mild, although as time went on and as Soviet-Egyptian relations began to deteriorate sharply, the Russian commentators became more explicit in their criticism of Egyptian policy. The communique on the Soviet exodus, printed in *Pravda* on July 20, 1972, was terse:

> The Soviet military personnel in the Arab Republic of Egypt have now fulfilled their mission. In consideration of this fact and *after a suitable exchange of opinions* between the two sides, it has been deemed expedient to bring back to the Soviet Union those military personnel who were assigned to Egypt for a limited period of time. These personnel will return in the near future.
>
> As was noted by ARE President A. Sadat in his address to the July 18, 1972 session of the Arab Socialist Union Central Committee, the measures now being taken "in no way affect the basic principles of Egyptian-Soviet friendship."[1] [emphasis added]

More to the point was an article in the pro-Moscow Lebanese Communist daily *Al-Nida* on July 19, 1972, which accused Sadat of surrendering to "the U.S. imperialist and reactionary influence" and charged the Egyptian leader with giving the impression that the USSR was to blame for Arab suffering resulting from the continued Israeli occupation of Arab land.[2] The following day *Al-Nida* presented what it said was the background to the expulsion decision:

It was obvious that Egypt was experiencing an acute struggle and
that the Egyptian right was launching a rabid campaign aimed at
striking at the friendship and cooperation with the Soviet Union and
at paving the way for acceptance of the US capitulationist solution.
. . .

The decision taken by Sadat was to end the struggle that had been
going on in Egypt for some time. . . . The struggle reached a climax
when Lt. General Sadek, who is known for his hostility to the Soviet
Union, called on Sadat at the head of a military delegation. Sadat
was asked to take a decision for removal of the Soviet advisers from
Egypt and to reconsider the foundations of Soviet-Egyptian relations. The request was accompanied by a threat of interference by
the Army command openly to impose the decision and to interfere
in the political affairs [of Egypt].[3]

Pravda itself warned on July 23, 1972 (the day after Egyptian Information
Minister Mohammed El-Zayyat's press conference, in which Egypt's nonalignment was stressed), that in a number of countries, including Egypt, "right-wing
reactionary forces" were trying to undermine Soviet-Arab friendship.[4]

Soviet-Egyptian relations worsened further following the Egyptian rejection of a note from Brezhnev to Sadat requesting a high-level meeting. On August 13, 1972, El-Zayyat stated that "there were many things to be settled before a Soviet-Egyptian summit meeting could settle future relations."[5] On August 19, 1972, Sadat told the Egyptian People's Council that he had rejected the
"language, contents and type" of the message he had received from Brezhnev.
The Egyptian leader further stated that the Soviet Union's refusal to supply the
requested arms "aimed to drive us to desperation and the brink of surrender,"
but that Egypt would, God willing, obtain the needed arms elsewhere.[6] Two
days later it became evident where Sadat was looking for arms. In an interview in
Le Figaro Sadat blamed the Russians for not understanding Egyptian psychology
and stated that the Western Europeans now owed Egypt a response to the "initiative" he had taken to help them.[7]

The deterioration in Soviet-Egyptian relations intensified as a war of words
broke out between Soviet and Egyptian newspapers in mid-August. The editor of
the Cairo daily *Akhbar-Al-Yom*, Abdul Koddous, rumored to be a close personal
friend of Sadat, charged the Russians with expansionist designs in Egypt, failure
to supply the needed weaponry, and dividing the Middle East into spheres of influence with the United States in a "new Yalta agreement."[8]

On August 29, *Izvestia* strongly attacked Koddous and indirectly warned
Egypt of the danger of losing Soviet diplomatic support:

The editor-in-chief of *Akhbar-Al-Yom* dares to slander the USSR, al-
leging that it is not fulfilling the article of the treaty referring to cooperation between the USSR and the ARE in the military field. . . .

This "absurd allegation" may gladden the imperialists and the Israeli rulers, but is capable only of harming the Egyptian people and
their just struggle to eliminate the consequences of the Israeli expansion.[9]

New Times columnist Y. Potomov joined in the attack on Koddous and
clearly warned the Egyptians that their weakened position had put them at Israel's mercy:

> Koddous and some of his colleagues have at times lost their bearings,
> forgetting on which side of the barricades are the enemies of the
> Egyptian and other Arab peoples. One of the cardinal features of the
> present propaganda campaign conducted against the Arab peoples is
> its patently anti-Soviet slant. . . . One of the favorite devices used by
> the enemies of the Arab peoples is the myth of "Soviet presence" in
> countries which draw on the generous aid of the Soviet Union in up-
> holding their freedom and independence.
>   Particular emphasis is placed on discrediting Soviet military aid to
> the Arab countries. Not only imperialist propaganda but also the
> right-wing forces in Arab countries acting in unison with it spare no
> effort to smear this aid. They circulate fabrications to the effect that
> the USSR does not supply the Arab countries enough weapons to
> combat the aggressor because it allegedly seeks to perpetuate a "no
> war-no peace" situation in order to preserve its "military presence" in
> the area.
>   Evidently, some people in the West and also in Tel Aviv *assume
> that Egypt has now seriously weakened itself* and that hence the
> time has come to bring out the old projects for "direct" negotiations
> and interim agreements without any definite clear-cut commitment
> by Israel to withdraw its troops from the occupied countries.[10] [em-
> phasis added]

The Egyptian press, however, refused to be cowed by Soviet attacks, with
Koddous even proposing on September 2, 1972 that the Soviet press, like Brezhnev, take a holiday on the Crimea. The next day Moussa Sabry, a columnist for
the Egyptian daily *Al-Akhbar,* went even further than Koddous in his attacks on
the USSR by asserting that the Russians had been involved in the anti-Sadat plot
led by Ali Sabry in May 1971.[11]

There is no telling how much further the deterioration in Soviet-Egyptian
relations might have gone[12] when a group of Palestinian terrorists killed 11 Israeli athletes at the Olympic Games in Munich and set off a chain of events that
greatly upset the pattern of Egyptian diplomacy. But before the consequences of
this event are considered, it is necessary to examine Soviet policy toward other
sections of the Arab world following the USSR's expulsion from Egypt.

As their relations with Egypt deteriorated rapidly, the Russians sought to shore up their positions elsewhere in the Arab world. In Syria, Premier Assad did not follow Sadat's example by expelling his Soviet military advisers, although there is some indication that he extracted a large price in Soviet aid for his "restraint." Soviet-Iraqi relations grew still warmer, and the Russians made a deliberate point of contrasting their improved relations with the Iraqi Ba'athist regime with the chill in Soviet-Egyptian relations. The Soviet leaders also moved to increase their influence within the Palestinian guerrilla movement through both endorsements in the Soviet press and shipments of weapons. Finally, by imposing a prohibitive exit tax on educated Russian Jews seeking to emigrate to Israel, the Russians moved to counter Arab criticism that, while professing aid to the Arab cause, the Russians were in fact contributing to Israel's war potential.

Syrian leader Hafiz Assad, despite frequent protestations of Syrian-Soviet friendship, had been careful to keep the Russians at arm's length. As mentioned above, his faction in Syria's Ba'ath party had ousted the more pro-Soviet Jedid faction in November 1970. Unlike either Egypt or Iraq, the other two areas of primary Soviet influence in the area, Syria had resisted Soviet requests to sign a 15-year treaty of friendship and cooperation. Nonetheless, Assad was more than willing to accept large amounts of Soviet economic aid, and the Russians were involved in a large number of construction projects in Syria, the most important of which was the Euphrates Dam.[13]

The Soviet Union was also the major supplier of weapons to Syria, and Russian advisers helped train the Syrian army and air force, although their numbers were far more limited than in Egypt. Like Egypt, Syria had a serious security problem with respect to Israel, and periodic clashes had erupted on the Syrian-Israeli border since the June 1967 war. Following the Lod massacre of May 29, 1972, in which a group of Japanese terrorists working for one of the Palestine guerrilla organizations killed 26 people at Lod Airport near Tel Aviv, the Israeli army made a number of strikes deep into Lebanon in an effort to destroy the guerrilla bases. In one strike, in an area only 25 miles from Damascus, the Israelis captured four high-ranking Syrian officers together with their Lebanese liaison officer.[14] These Israeli actions may have prompted Assad's visit to Moscow in early July, which resulted, according to the joint communique, in an agreement "on measures for the strengthening of the Syrian Arab Republic's military potential" and in an agreement on economic and technical cooperation.[15]

It was perhaps because of his heightened sense of vulnerability to Israel, or because the Russian "presence" in Syria was far less significant than in Egypt, or perhaps even to extract still more Soviet aid, that Assad did not follow Sadat's example by expelling the Soviet advisers from Syria. In an interview published in the Beirut newspaper *Al-Anwar* on August 10, 1972, and partially reprinted in *Pravda* the next day, Assad was quoted as saying:

> The interests of the Syrian people require the continuation of the
> Soviet military specialists' mission in our country. The Soviet special-

ists have been working in Syria for a long time, and I believe that the necessity for continuing their mission is not subject to discussion.[16]

Assad went on to say, however (in a section of the interview *Pravda* did not publish), that "we here in Syria and Egypt wish the Soviet Union would meet our request [for arms] in a better and more effective manner."[17]

While Soviet-Syrian relations remained good, if a bit distant, the USSR's relations with Iraq continued to improve rapidly, with frequent exchanges of delegations between the two countries. The Russians demonstratively publicized their improved position in Iraq as a counter to their worsened relations with Egypt. Thus, on July 21, 1972, only four days after the Soviet exodus from Egypt began, *Izvestia* made public the details of the Soviet-Iraqi aid agreement of June 7, 1972. In addition, the Russians made frequent use of statements by Iraqi leaders to justify Soviet policies in the Middle East, as the Iraqis took the leading role in combating "anti-Sovietism" in the Arab world. A *New Times* article in late August by I. Gavrilov claimed that the Iraqi people were "unanimous in their opposition to [anti-Soviet] ideological subversion by imperialism and Arab reaction," and cited the following report from the Baghdad *Observer* as "characteristic to their attitude":

> The imperialists and reactionaries are currently acting in unison to undermine Arab-Soviet friendship. This is part of a sweeping design whose object is to deprive the Arab people of powerful Soviet support, disunite the progressive Arab countries in general, and isolate the regime in Iraq in particular.[18]

Another source utilized by the Russians for combating the rising tide of anti-Sovietism in the Arab world was the Palestinian guerrillas. A delegation of the Palestine Liberation Organization headed by Yasir Arafat made a prolonged visit to Moscow on July 17-27—just at the time when Sadat was expelling the Russians from Egypt. *Pravda*, on July 28, cited the PLO's statement of their appreciation of Soviet support for the Palestinian cause and their declaration that

> all attempts by the imperialist and reactionary circles to disrupt the friendship between the national liberation forces in the Arab world and the Soviet Union and other socialist states are incompatible with the interests of the Arab peoples.[19]

In return for their ringing endorsement of Soviet policy toward the Arab world, Arafat's group for the first time reportedly got direct shipments of Soviet arms (hitherto they had gone to the Arab governments on whose soil PLO units were stationed),[20] as well as much greater Soviet press coverage in their struggle against Israel and the antiguerrilla elements in Lebanon. Writing an extensive feature article in *Pravda* on August 29, Pavel Demchenko described the history of the growth of the guerrilla movement and bitterly attacked Israel for its mistreatment of the Palestinians. Perhaps hoping to maintain the Soviet tie to the Hussein regime in Jordan, however, Demchenko made no direct mention of Hussein's bloody destruction of the guerrilla movement in his country in September 1970 and July 1971, which had led a number of the guerrillas to cross the Jordan River to surrender to the Israelis rather than to Hussein's troops. The Soviet journalist was, however, critical of "acts of desperation," such as hijackings of passenger planes and the blowing up of nonmilitary targets, which did "serious damage to the entire Palestinian Resistance Movement and made its support by progressive and democratic forces more difficult."[21]

Demchenko was also critical of the right-wing and anarchistic groups in the Palestinian movement, which he considered tools of the Israelis and Arab reactionaries who were "using them to set a barrier on the path to organizational and political unity." Demchenko's solution to the dilemma of the Palestinians and their relative ineffectiveness, which he candidly admitted, was the unification of the Palestinian resistance in the framework of a national front—similar to the national front policy the Soviet leaders were promoting in Syria and Iraq:

> The facts indicate that the forces of imperialism and reaction have clearly stepped up their activity in the Arab East recently, setting themselves the goal of weakening the national liberation struggle of the Arab peoples and liquidating the Palestinian Resistance Movement. Naturally, this creates new difficulties for the movement and insistently confronts it with a number of cardinal problems, problems that are now being widely discussed by the progressive Arab public.
>
> Among these problems is the determination, on the basis of the actual correlation of forces, of the place and role of the Palestinian movement in the common front of the Arab peoples. What is involved here, among other things, is cooperation with the progressive Arab governments in the struggle for the elimination of the consequences of the Israeli aggression, the settlement of the Near East crisis, and the liberation of the occupied territories. This calls for advancing slogans and setting tasks corresponding to each stage of the struggle, i.e., for the delineation of strategic and tactical tasks. Faik Warrad, a member of the Palestine National Council, has written as follows on this score:
>
> "The experience of the Arab people of Palestine and of other peoples indicates that the policy of 'all or nothing' does not serve the people's interests. Every true revolutionary must take into account the alignment of forces and their correlation at every separate stage and, consequently, must distinguish what is possible and realistic from what is impracticable."

This task can be fulfilled only after the unification of the ranks of the Palestinian movement *within the framework, for instance, of a national front with a political program that will take into account the diversity of the situation and of the forms of struggle* and will help to begin work among the Palestinians in occupied territory and among the refugees, especially in Jordan, since without a mass base the movement cannot develop.

The first shifts in this direction have already become evident. At a session held in Cairo several months ago, the Palestinian National Council came out for the unification of the resistance movement. Since that time, the movement's press has been unified, and a single information agency has been set up. In July the Soviet Union was visited by a PLO delegation headed by Yasir Arafat, the chairman of its executive committee. During the talks that took place, the PLO representatives reported that at present the consolidation of the ranks of the Palestinian resistance is continuing and its *unity growing stronger on a progressive anti-imperialist* basis. . . . Recent facts make it possible to draw the conclusion that attempts to isolate the Palestinian movement, to assign it a special mission in the Arab East, are receding into the past. What is gaining the upper hand is the realization that a just solution to the Palestine problem can be achieved only within the framework of a common liberation struggle of the Arab peoples and that the natural allies of the Palestinian resistance movement are the Arab and international progressive forces, the Soviet Union and other socialist countries.[22] [emphasis added]

In addition to their drive for support in Syria, Iraq, and among the Palestinian guerrillas, the Russians also sought to gain support throughout the Arab world by their decision on August 3, 1972, to charge what amounted to a prohibitive "head tax" on educated Jews seeking to emigrate to Israel. While this decision may also have been made to secure a large amount of desperately needed hard currency from Jewish communities around the world wanting to ransom their brethren in the USSR—hard currency that would pay for wheat imports from the United States—the head tax also had the effect of drastically curtailing the number of educated Jews able to emigrate to Israel.[23] This, in turn, would reduce the increasingly bitter Arab complaints that the Russian supply of skilled manpower to Israel was enhancing Israel's military capabilities.

Despite these Soviet moves to improve their position in the Arab world following the exodus from Egypt, on balance their position in the Middle East was considerably weakened. Indeed, there is no telling how much further this process would have gone when a group of Palestinian terrorists killed 11 Israeli athletes at the Olympic Games in Munich, and set off a chain of events that greatly upset the pattern of Egyptian diplomacy and gave the Russians an excellent opportunity to strengthen their position in the Middle East.

LIMITED RECONCILIATION WITH EGYPT

The immediate effect of the terrorist acts in Munich was to strike a major blow at Sadat's hopes to persuade the Western European and American leaders to bring pressure on Israel to withdraw its troops from occupied Egyptian territory. Hardest hit were Egypt's relations with West Germany, where the terrorist acts took place. Willy Brandt, whose government had painstakingly negotiated the resumption of diplomatic relations with Egypt less than three months earlier (after a seven-year break following West Germany's establishment of diplomatic relations with Israel in 1965), criticized the lack of Egyptian assistance in his efforts to negotiate a settlement with the terrorists. In response, the Egyptian leadership asserted that West Germany was trying to evade responsibility by making false charges against Egypt and other Arab nations. The German government then began to take strong action, including deportation, against Arabs residing in West Germany who were accused of conspiring with terrorist organizations, and this brought a warning from the new Egyptian Information Minister, Abdel Hatem, that "arbitrary measures against Egyptians were continuing and escalating in Germany, and these extraordinary measures may call for similar Egyptian action."[24] The deterioration of Egypt's relations with West Germany, her second leading trade partner (after the USSR) and a potential source of both economic and technical assistance, reached the point in mid-September that Egypt's new Foreign Minister, Mohammed El-Zayyat, canceled a scheduled visit to West Germany, which was part of a planned tour of Western European capitals in search of support against Israel.

Zayyat did complete a trip to England, but here again terrorist activities hampered Egyptian diplomacy. Just as Zayyat arrived in London the Israeli agricultural attache, Ami Shachori, was killed by a letter bomb mailed to the Israeli embassy—an action that inflamed English public opinion against the Arabs.

The United States, whose close alignment with Israel Sadat had hoped to sever by his expulsion of the Russians, stood even more strongly behind the Israeli government following the Munich massacre. Indeed, the American Ambassador to the United Nations, George Bush, vetoed a Security Council resolution condemning Israel for its reprisal raids against Palestinian guerrilla bases in Syria and Lebanon, following the Munich killings, that did not also condemn the terrorist acts that provoked the reprisal raids.

The events at Munich, with their repercussions on Egypt's relations with Western nations, probably hastened the pace of the Egyptian-Libyan union as Sadat became ever more dependent on Libyan support. On September 18 Sadat and Kaddafi reached an agreement that proclaimed Cairo as the capital of the union and provided for a single government, a single political party, and a single president elected by popular vote.[26] The process of union may also have been speeded by increased Egyptian fears of an Israeli attack following the Munich massacre, fears that the Russians did everything possible to encourage.

The Israeli government was under great domestic pressure to avenge the athletes murdered at Munich and did not hesitate long. Having suffered a similar terroristic attack at Lod Airport only three months before, the Israelis apparently decided to attempt to strike a telling blow against the guerrillas by launching a series of air strikes deep into Lebanon and Syria against suspected terrorist bases. The air assault was followed a week later by an armored strike into Lebanon aimed at destroying as many guerrillas and guerrilla bases as possible. Lebanese and Syrian resistance was relatively ineffectual as the Israeli forces roamed at will in the two countries. Three Syrian bombers, counterattacking Israeli positions in the Golan Heights, were shot down.[27] The Israeli assaults, coming on the heels of similar although far more restricted ground strikes into Lebanon following the Lod massacre in June, served once again to underline Syria's vulnerability in relation to Israel, as did numerous statements by Israeli leaders, such as Deputy Premier Yigal Allon, that Israel would henceforth take "active measures" to "deny the Arab terror organizations the necessary bases, facilities and other assistance in their inhuman war."[28]

The Soviet Union seized upon the opportunity presented by the Israeli attacks to launch a special airlift of weapons to Damascus to reinforce the Syrian defenses. This airlift, which generated front-page headlines in both the Arab and Western press, underscored the Soviet argument that the Arabs could only turn to the USSR in their time of need.

Soviet propaganda has been emphasizing this theme ever since Sadat's expulsion order. A week before the Munich massacre, Dmitry Volsky, in a *New Times* article titled "A Frank Talk with Some Arab Colleagues," wrote:

> Isn't it a fact that the US and NATO Mediterranean bases and the US Sixth Fleet which has now obtained a convenient new harbor in Greece, have repeatedly been used for pressure on Arab countries? From which it is clear what damage would be done in the interests of these countries by undivided US and NATO naval control in the Mediterranean? . . . If Iraq and Syria have today successfully challenged a mighty oil concern like Iraq Petroleum, which has leading powers behind it, could they have done it without enjoying the firm support of the Soviet Union and the Socialist community?[29]

Following the Israeli attacks on Lebanon and Syria, the Russians warned the Arabs that they could expect further Israeli attacks and that they could not hope for support from the West. An editorial in *New Times* pointedly stated:

> By bombing Palestinian refugee camps in Lebanon and Syria and villages in these countries and Jordan, killing and maiming hundreds of civilians, Tel Aviv has again shown the world the brigand nature of its policy. And its spokesmen let it be known that they do not mean

to rest content with this. They openly threaten further aggressive action against Arab countries. None other than Israel's Chief of General Staff, General Elazar, has declared that air strikes "are not the
only means" his army has used and continues to use. Another member of the Israeli command, asked by a newsman whether Egypt
might come under attack, replied "I will answer with an Arab prov-
erb—everyone in his turn."

Public opinion in the Arab countries is drawing the inference from
Israel's provocative actions which the imperialists are encouraging.
What if not encouragement is the US veto in the Security Council on
a resolution condemning Tel Aviv's barbarous acts? *All of it is helping the Arabs to realize how illusory are hopes that the imperialists
are prepared to help curb the Israeli expansionists and eliminate the
consequences of their aggression.* And the danger of such illusion is
greater than ever now. For Tel Aviv is using them not only to hold
on to the occupied territories but to make new aggressive moves
against the Arab states.[30] [emphasis added]

In an effort to increase Arab fear of Israeli attacks still further—and thus
make the Arabs feel constrained to turn to the USSR for assistance—the Russians subsequently even began to propagate the old myth about Israel's alleged
desire to expand her borders "from the Nile to the Euphrates." Writing in *New
Times* at the end of September, V. Rumyanstev claimed that the Israelis

are seeking not only to induce the Arabs to accept the annexation of
the territories seized in 1967, but to accustom them to the Zionist
idea of creating a "Greater Israel from the Nile to the Euphrates."[31]

The Russians also utilized the Israeli attacks on the Palestinian guerrilla
camps to dramatize their position as supporters of the Palestinians and thus to
win more influence in the Palestinian resistance movement. While the Western
press unanimously condemned the Munich murders, the Russian press was far
more moderate in tone, referring to them only as a "tragic incident."[32] The Russians, however, denounced the Israeli attacks on Palestinian refugee camps
(which often housed guerrilla bases) while most of the Western press accepted
the Israeli raids as legitimate reprisals for the Munich massacres. The Russians
underlined their concern for the Palestinian cause at this crucial time by airlifting medical supplies to Lebanon to help treat the victims of the Israeli attacks,
and the guerrillas claimed that the USSR was now shipping them arms directly.[33]
Although receiving an increasingly sympathetic treatment in the Soviet press,
the Palestinian movement also once again came in for some Soviet advice. V.
Kornilov, writing a feature article in *New Times*, continued the Soviet criticism
of such extremist groups as Black September, and once again emphasized the

need for unity among the Palestinians, although his discussion of the possibilities of unity were a bit less optimistic than pre-Munich Soviet commentaries on the Palestinian movement:

> What the extremist groups have done and are still doing has not brought about any change for the better in the tragic lot of the Palestinians. Nor could it. On the contrary, what they have done, paradoxical as it might seem, has been grist to the mill of the Zionist ringleaders. Tel Aviv exploits the acts of terror perpetrated by the Palestinian extremists to pass off its pre-planned acts of aggression against Lebanon and Syria as "retaliation," and to step up its propaganda campaign against the Palestinians and Arabs generally, a campaign the Western bourgeois press has joined. All this damages the prestige of the Palestinian movement, and seriously. . . .
>
> In short, despite Israeli terror, despite the machinations of imperialism and Arab reaction, a trend is emerging, *albeit with difficulty*, towards the gradual consolidation of the Palestinian resistance movement. There is an increasing awareness within the PLO that for the Palestinian movement to achieve any measure of success it needs a clear cut political program which, proceeding from reality, would set explicit, feasible tasks. Most leaders of the various Palestinian organizations are coming to see more and more distinctly that both the extremism of certain groups like the Black September organization and the attempts of reactionaries in the Arab world to harness the Palestinian movement to their own interests are equally prejudicial to the cause for which many Palestinian Arabs are ready to give their lives—the liberation of Israeli-occupied territory.[34] [emphasis added]

The events at Munich and the Israeli response to them occasioned a trip to Moscow by Iraqi President Hassan Al-Bakr, and his visit of September 14-19, 1972, underlined the close cooperation now existing between the USSR and Iraq.[35] At a banquet honoring Al-Bakr, Soviet President Podgorny took the opportunity to once again attack the "slanderous assertions" aimed at undermining Arab-Soviet friendship.[36] Podgorny also emphasized a theme that was becoming increasingly prominent in Soviet policy statements about the Arab world—the close relationship between Arab unity on an "anti-imperialist basis" and the unity of the "progressive forces" within each Arab state.[37] This theme was more fully developed in a *New Times* article by R. Ulianovsky, deputy head of the CPSU Central Committee's International Department, entitled "The Arab East: Problems of a United Progressive Front," in which the author appealed to the Ba'ath leadership in both Syria and Iraq to follow through on their promises to implement their national fronts. He stated that once the fronts were established, genuine Arab unity could be achieved.[38]

One of the goals of the new Soviet position on Arab unity may have been to counter the union movement between Egypt and Libya that was developing on an anti-Communist basis. It may also have been aimed at settling the smoldering dispute between the rival wings of the Ba'ath parties ruling in Damascus and Baghdad, each of which had good relations with the Soviet Union but poor relations with the other. If such a development were to occur, it would wean Syria away from its confederation with Egypt and Libya and end Iraq's isolation in the Arab world. This would also provide a bloc of relatively pro-Soviet Arab states in the eastern segment of the Arab world.

Yet there still seemed to be little possibility of unity on the Soviet terms. In both Iraq and Syria, the Communists and other "progressives" remained relatively powerless, and the inherent conflict among the various elements in the national fronts of the two nations was not overlooked by Ulianovsky:

> It is not accidental that the internal and foreign enemies of the national democratic regimes are trying to set the participants of the progressive coalitions against each other. Resorting to underhand machinations, they either seek to bar the communists from the united front or insist on the dissolution of the communist and other left parties.[39]

In an effort to overcome such difficulties, throughout 1972 and early 1973, numerous Soviet conferences and articles in Soviet scholarly journals were devoted to working out the theoretical and practical aspects of Communist participation in national fronts. One conference, held under the auspices of the *World Marxist Review* at the time of Al-Bakr's visit, brought together Soviet and nonruling Communist party delegates along with representatives from Egypt's Arab Socialist Union and the Iraqi and Syrian Ba'ath parties to discuss "problems of anti-imperialist unity." The editor-in-chief of the *World Marxist Review*, K. Zarodov, began the discussion of the national front problem by stating:

> The question requiring further theoretical investigation concerns the united front of progressive forces in national movements with maturing social contradictions. In some countries they grow into class antagonisms; that being so, is there a political perspective for a United Front?[40]

Zarodov went on to answer his own question, and he then gave the current Soviet interpretation of the meaning of "class struggle" in the developing countries:

> Many Afro-Asian communist parties give an affirmative answer. Broad political unity of the nation's healthy progressive anti-imperialist forces is made possible by the fact that the national liberation revolution has not fully discharged its democratic mission. Hence,

though contradictions between individual classes and social groups persist, there is still a considerable area of common interest in resolving crucial national issues. . . .

Political development guided by a united front does not eliminate or preclude class struggle. *In fact, unity of the nation's progressive forces is a principal form of class struggle in present-day Afro-Asian conditions.*[41] [emphasis added]

Zarodov concluded by telling the Communists in the Afro-Asian countries, much as Ulianovsky had done the year before, that they had to endure anti-Communist actions by the nationalist leaders for the sake of maintaining the anti-imperialist coalition:

> In countries ruled by Revolutionary democrats, the Communists see their patriotic and class duty in facilitating progressive change. At times they point to shortcomings in the work of revolutionary democratic regimes. But this is the constructive advice of sincere friends and allies. But some Revolutionary Democratic leaders at times seem unable or reluctant to distinguish between friends and foe, ally and enemy. Unfortunately, the leaders of a number of countries, who, on the whole, take an anti-imperialist stand, regard cooperation with the communists as little short of retreat from national revolution or betrayal of national tradition. . . . We have a situation in which communists are faced by the dual task of supporting Revolutionary-democratic leaders and at the same time working for the consistent application of democratic policy principles. The struggle, therefore, is not against the Revolutionary democrats, but for alliance with them; the struggle is for the comprehensive and vigorous pursuit of socialism.[42]

A second issue raised at the conference was the need for the national democratic transition stage for Third World states. Soviet spokesmen supported the principle, but it was challenged by Lebanese Communist Party member G. Batal, who questioned the "categorical need" for a transition stage at which the general democratic tasks were given priority over the "building of socialism." Batal went on to imply that the social backwardness should not be a barrier to Communists seizing power:

> Given revolutionary government capable of directing the process, a country's backwardness, the relative weakness of its working class, and inadequate social differentiation are not obstacles to socialist construction. The Democratic Republic of Vietnam is proof of that.[43]

A further challenge to the Soviet position came from Jordanian Communist Party member K. Ahmad, who complained that there was still "no general, thought-out and developed theory to disclose the essence of what we term non-capitalist development." And, in a challenge to Soviet theorists who had worked for almost a decade to work out just such a formulation, Ahmad asserted:

> That theory must neither be a utopia based on a random collection of elements relating to another era, nor the result of hasty innovative generalizations or bold extrapolations that are practically useless, even as a hypothesis.[44]

While Soviet theorists and Arab Communists debated various aspects of the national front policy, Iraqi President Hassan Al-Bakr made it quite evident that he had not come to Moscow only for lectures on the desirability of national fronts. Instead, he was seeking Soviet support in Iraq's sharpening conflict with Iran over the Persian Gulf, and it appears that he succeeded in moving the Soviet leaders even closer to the Iraqi side. Thus, in a major speech, Al-Bakr condemned

> actions against the historical rights of the Arab nations in the Persian Gulf, and attempts to impose colonialism on the countries of this area.[45]

The final communique echoed the same theme, although in somewhat milder terms:

> The two sides declared their full support for the struggle that the Arab peoples of the Persian Gulf are waging to rebuff the imperialists' aggressive plans which are jeopardizing their freedom and independence. They affirmed that the peoples of the Persian Gulf must be guaranteed the right to decide their own destiny without outside interference.[46]

Of even greater importance to Iran-Iraqi relations, however, was the Soviet-Iraqi agreement

> on *concrete* measures for the further strengthening of the defense capability of the Republic of Iraq with a view to increasing the *combat readiness* of its armed forces.[47] [emphasis added]

Perhaps to counter the impression of the Soviet Union's "leaning to one side" in the Iran-Iraq conflict, the Russian leaders invited the Shah of Iran and his wife (who had just returned from Peking) to visit Moscow on October 10, less than a month after Al-Bakr's departure. Reports circulated both in Moscow and Beirut that Al-Bakr had requested that the Russians mediate the Iran-Iraq conflict since, given Iraq's difficulties following the nationalization of Iraqi Petroleum Company's Kirkuk fields and continued problems with the Kurds, the Iraqis were in no position to see an escalation of their conflict with Iran.[48] If this was indeed the Soviet goal (and in a dinner speech Podgorny referred to "the need for an improvement in the relations between Asian states"),[49] no mention of such an agreement was made in the final communique. Nonetheless, the Soviet Union and Iran did agree to a 15-year economic treaty, which, while increasing the Soviet share of Iran's trade, still left it far behind the shares of the United States and West Germany—Iran's most important economic partners.

The two nations also reached an agreement on Soviet assistance in enlarging the Isfahan metallurgical works to bring its capacity up to four million tons of steel per year, along with other projects. Nevertheless, differences of opinion clearly remained, and the final communique referred to the talks as having taken place in a "frank" atmosphere and stated that the two sides had "exchanged opinions concerning the situation in Asia."[50]

The purpose behind the Shah's trip to Moscow, which so closely followed Al-Bakr's visit to the Russian capital, bore close resemblance to the reason for the visit of Soviet President Podgorny to Turkey immediately after the signing of the Soviet-Iraqi treaty in April. It appears in both cases that the Russians had hoped that the improvement in the USSR's relations with Iraq, then a nation on poor terms with both Turkey and Iran, would not lead to a deterioration in either Soviet-Turkish or Soviet-Iranian relations. While in the case of Iran the economic agreements may have helped assuage some of Iran's anger, the final Soviet-Iranian communique contained many indications of strained relations, and Podgorny's visit to Turkey resulted in an even more limited communique, the "Declaration on the Principles of Good-Neighbor Relations with the Turkish Government." The Turks, clearly unhappy at the strong Soviet support for Archbishop Makarios on Cyprus and the appearance of Soviet weapons in the hands of antigovernment Turkish terrorists, were in no mood to enter into a closer relationship with the USSR. Indeed, one of the principles listed in the declaration stated that "the present Declaration in no way affects commitments earlier assumed by each of the states in regard to third countries . . . and international organizations," thus tacitly emphasizing Turkey's continued close relationship to the United States and its participation in NATO.[51]

While the Soviet Union was shoring up its positions elsewhere in the Arab world and trying to maintain a balance in its relations between Iran and Iraq, Soviet relations with the Sadat regime in Egypt remained very tense. Although, despite Soviet predictions, Egypt was not hit by an Israeli retaliatory strike (possibly to avert the possibility that Egypt might be forced to call the Russians back), Sadat was clearly discomfited by the events in Munich. With his attempts to win over Western Europe and the United States for the time being, at least, having come to naught, and condemned both at home and throughout the Arab world for failing to protect Syria and Lebanon from Israeli attacks, Sadat decided to try to stabilize Egypt's relations with the USSR before they deteriorated any further.

Consequently, on September 28, 1972, the second anniversary of Nasser's death, Sadat delivered a major policy address in which he sought to regain some of the momentum in Middle Eastern events. In the first place he issued a call for the establishment of a Palestinian government in exile, which he pledged to support, stating—and here he was in close agreement with the Russians—that the divisions within the Palestinian movement hurt it more than Israel or King Hussein. Second, he officially rejected the proposal offered by U.S. Secretary of State William Rogers earlier in the month at the UN for an interim agreement and proximity talks. Using bitter language, perhaps reflecting his frustration at the failure of the United States to reward Egypt for expelling the Russians, Sadat stated: "Mr. Rogers is a man who is not living in this age. . . . There will be no partial settlement and no direct negotiations." Finally, and perhaps most important of all, Sadat changed his tone toward the Russians. The Egyptian leader declared that he had sent a letter to Brezhnev that was "friendly and cordial in spirit."[52]

Conceivably the reply Sadat was expecting was delivered by Hafiz Assad, Premier of Syria, who made a hurried trip to Cairo after returning from a secret visit to Moscow. In any case it was revealed only two days after Sadat's speech that Egyptian Premier Aziz Sidky would undertake a trip to the Soviet Union on October 16.[53] Nonetheless, the tone in the government-controlled Egyptian press remained quite cool to the USSR until the very eve of Sidky's departure. Thus, Sadat himself, in an interview published in the Lebanese weekly *Al-Hawadess* on October 5 and reprinted in Cairo newspapers two days later, stated that a peaceful settlement as desired by the Russians meant "surrender to American and Israeli terms," and complained openly that

> the Russians had become a burden to us. They would not fight and
> would give our enemy an excuse for seeking American support and
> assistance.[54]

Two days later, Sadat's confidant, *Al-Akhbar* editor Abdul Koddous (by now a bête noire of the Russians), warned that the Egyptian people must expect "tough negotiations" in Moscow and that all Assad's visit to Moscow accomplished was the invitation of Sidky.[55] In this article, of which the Chinese reprinted selected excerpts in the Peking *Review*, the Egyptian editor also belittled the value of Soviet assistance and argued that the Russians had utilized their position in Egypt to exploit the Egyptians:

> The Soviet Union benefited from military centers in Egypt so that it
> became an existing power in the Mediterranean. In addition, Egyp-

tian airfields did away with the need of building aircraft carriers which would have cost the Soviet people millions of dollars. The Soviet Union employed these airfields for its international purposes and transported arms to India via these airfields during the war with Pakistan. Again, the Soviet Union benefited since Egypt was an important factor in its rapprochement with the United States, which is based on freezing the situation in the Middle East. On the other hand, Egypt did not benefit from this peaceful coexistence between the two superpowers. In fact, Egypt did not benefit from this friendship which did not prevent the immigration of Soviet Jews to Israel.[56]

This, however, was the last negative comment in the Egyptian press before Sidky's departure. Perhaps prompted by an incident in Cairo's Hussein Mosque on October 12, where an Egyptian captain tried to stir a mass protest by calling for immediate war with Israel,[57] or counseled by his advisers to set a more favorable climate for Sidky's visit, Sadat had changed his tone considerably by October 15, when, in a speech to Egypt's People's Assembly, he stated that Egypt would never have a "two-faced" foreign policy but would always value fully the friendship of the Soviet Union. In addition, the Egyptian leader called the Soviet-Egyptian friendship "strategic" and not "tactical," while warning the United States that it would have to "pay a price" for its support of Israel. Sadat also declared that he was eager to see Sidky's mission succeed.[58]

However eager Sadat may really have been, there appear to have been real limits on the accomplishments of Sidky's trip to Moscow. In the first place, unlike his earlier trip in July, the Egyptian premier did not get to see Brezhnev, but had to be satisfied with meeting Kosygin and Podgorny. Second, there was no mention of continued Soviet aid, either military or economic, in the final communique, which described the talks as having taken place "in an atmosphere of frankness and mutual understanding." About the only thing that Egyptians could point to from the talks (assuming there were no secret protocols) was a rather pro forma Russian pledge, frequently found in joint communiques, that the Russian leaders had accepted an invitation to come to Egypt, although no date was set for their visit.[59]

Upon Sidky's return to Egypt, a general debate was begun in the top ranks of the Egyptian leadership about the proper relationship with the USSR. The editor of *Al-Ahram*, Mohammed Heikal, a man often at odds with the USSR, counseled renewed friendship with the Russians in his weekly column in the October 20, 1972 issue, stating that "a sound, healthy relationship with the USSR is vital." Heikal went on to urge that Egypt continue to seek its weapons from the Russians because other suppliers were politically unreliable:

We are able to get some weapons from sources other than the USSR under certain conditions and in certain quantities; just the same, I am worried about unknown factors in the international arms market.[60]

On October 25, 1972, Sidky delivered his report to a mixed Arab Socialist Union-government meeting, stating that the Russians had promised to resume aid to Egypt, although he did not mention precise quantities. Sadat followed with a speech in which he told the assembled delegates that "it was up to them" whether Egypt should continue to rely primarily on Soviet support or should end her cooperation with Moscow. He somewhat restricted their parameters of choice, however, by stating that there was little hope in the foreseeable future of replacing the USSR as Egypt's principal supplier of arms. Sadat went on to say that if Egypt should choose continued cooperation with the Soviet Union, its scope would never return to the pre-July 18 situation.[61]

The Egyptian leadership apparently decided on continued cooperation with the Russians, because on the very next day Defense Minister Sadek, one of the most anti-Russian of the Egyptian leaders, was either fired or else resigned from his position. This may well have been one of the prices exacted by the Russians for renewed aid; in any case, his ouster was followed by that of the navy commander, Rear Admiral Fahmy Abdel Rahman, another of the outspoken anti-Soviet Egyptian leaders. Sadek was replaced by Ahmed Ismail, Egypt's military Intelligence director, who, unlike Sadek, neither had alienated the Russians nor possessed sufficient popular appeal to pose a challenge to Sadat himself.[62]

Sadek's fall from the second most powerful position in Egypt gave rise to a great deal of speculation both in Egypt and abroad. While most commentators saw Sadek's ouster as the price demanded by the Russians for a resumption of military aid (and the arrival in Egypt of Sam-6 antiaircraft missiles together with Russian technicians soon after Sadek's "resignation" reinforced this belief[63]), Abdul Koddous, writing a front page article in *Akhbar-Al-Yom*, sought to put an end to such speculation. According to Koddous, Sadek had been dismissed because of insubordination and failure to carry out Sadat's orders when the Egyptian president discovered that "some directives to General Sadek had not reached the various commands, while others had not been implemented."[64]

A related factor that could have contributed to Sadek's dismissal was the rising tide of unrest in the Egyptian army—the base on which Sadat's power rested. There had been a mutiny among Egyptian soldiers stationed at the canal in late September. This had been followed by the incident at the Hussein Mosque on October 12 and what the BBC reported as an abortive military coup on October 21.[65] Sadat may well have been displeased with Sadek's inability to control dissension in the army; this, together with the Egyptian general's continuing refusal to accept the necessity for a limited rapprochement with the Soviet Union, may have led to Sadek's ouster.

Whatever the actual reason for Sadek's resignation, the Russians were clearly happy to witness the departure of the most outspokenly anti-Soviet leader in the Egyptian hierarchy. While *Pravda* reported his ouster in a brief two-column story on October 28, 1972, under the title "Resignation Accepted," the Soviet party newspaper gave much more space to a speech by his successor, Ahmed Ismail, four days later. The new Egyptian defense minister spoke warmly of Soviet economic and military aid to Egypt, and stated that the USSR had fulfilled all the obligations it had pledged to Egypt. In addition, Ismail strongly attacked the United States for its aid to Israel and asserted that "nothing good" could be expected from the United States. Ismail also echoed the Soviet line on the goals of American policy in the Middle East:

> The goal of American policy is to isolate the Arabs from the USSR and keep the Soviet Union as far as possible from the Middle East. The United States is also seeking to prevent unity in the ranks of the Arabs.[66]

Despite the warmth of his speech toward the Soviet Union, however, Egypt's new defense minister also reportedly told Western diplomats soon after taking office that "the Egyptian Army Command will never again allow Russian advisers to get key command and advisory posts in the Egyptian armed forces"— a policy goal that Ismail evidently shared with Sadat.[67]

Nonetheless, thanks to the Munich massacre and the sharp upsurge in fighting between Israel and the Arabs that followed it, the Soviet position in the Middle East had markedly improved from its low point in early September, as the Arabs felt more dependent on Soviet military supplies for their sharpening conflict with Israel. The Soviet leadership may have concluded from this that a limited degree of warfare in the region was a net bonus for the Soviet Union, as long as it did not escalate into a war between the two superpowers, since during the period of relative Middle Eastern calm (September 1970 to September 1972) the Russian position had deteriorated steadily. Indeed, the Soviet position had improved so much as a result of the post-Munich developments that on October 26, 1972, Sudanese President Jaafar Nimeri, who had clashed so bitterly with the Russians the year before over the abortive Communist-supported coup d'etat against his regime, announced that the Sudan would restore full diplomatic relations with the Soviet Union by the end of the year.[68] In addition, the Soviet leadership must have welcomed the deterioration in relations between the Arabs and the West, particularly the United States and West Germany, which occurred after the Munich terrorism. Interestingly enough, one of the comments made by the terrorists about the goals of their operation coincided with a similar objective of Soviet policy:

> The operation was aimed at exposing the close relations between the treacherous German authorities and United States imperialism on the one hand and the Zionist enemy's authorities on the other.[69]

Thus, thanks to another twist in the volatile politics of the Middle East, developments in the region began to take a turn favorable to the USSR, and the Soviet leadership now sought to reinforce this trend, although a number of serious problems still hampered their overall policy toward the region.

TO THE NIXON-BREZHNEV SUMMIT

While the Russians had clearly improved their position in the Middle East by the end of October, they still faced a number of problems in their attempts to expand their influence in the region. In the first place, North Yemen (the Yemeni Arab Republic) and South Yemen (the People's Democratic Republic of Yemen—PDRY) were on the verge of full-scale war, and the Russians must have been very concerned when the South Yemeni premier, Ali Nasser, stated in an interview with the Beirut newspaper *L'Orient le jour* on October 6 that "the Soviet Union will not stand with folded arms in the event of an invasion of South Yemen."[70] Relations were scarcely better between Iran and Iraq, and serious clashes between the Kurds and Iraqi government forces made the situation at the top of the Persian Gulf even more difficult for Soviet policy makers. Another problem facing the Russians was their limited position in Egypt, which was still the most important Middle Eastern state despite Sadat's problems. Finally, the Russians continued to worry about American influence in the region and the possibility that a disheartened Egypt might yet agree to a Middle Eastern settlement on American terms.

In an effort to settle the Yemeni conflict, the USSR had long advocated union between the two Yemens, since this would enable the Russians to avoid being dragged into a war between them while still enabling Moscow to maintain influence in the geographically strategic area at the Bab-El-Mandeb Strait, which controlled the entrance to the Red Sea, whose importance would sharply increase if the canal were to be reopened. Talks designed to halt the fighting between the Yemens were postponed in mid-November so that South Yemeni President Salem Ali Rubayi could visit Moscow at the end of the month.[71] In evaluating the progress of the PDRY at the time of Rubayi's visit, *New Times* correspondent Yuri Gvozdev called the conflict between the two Yemens "imperialist instigated."[72] The joint communique published at the conclusion of the visit on November 26 stated that the Soviet side "greeted with satisfaction" South Yemeni measures to end military operations on the border with North Yemen, and "supported PDRY efforts for the normalization of relations between the two Yemens."[73] The Soviet leadership was, consequently, more than satisfied when, only two days later, the two Yemens signed an agreement to unite. Nonetheless, the accord was a fragile one, and the statement by North Yemen's ambassador to France in mid-December that King Faisal of Saudi Arabia supported Yemeni unity on an "Islamic basis" might well have convinced the Russians that the

Saudi monarch was continuing his efforts to overthrow the socialist regime in South Yemen.[74]

If the Soviet leaders proved able to score a moderate success in calming tensions between North and South Yemen, they faced a far more difficult task in the Iran-Iraq conflict. Soviet-Iranian tensions had sharply increased since the signing of the Soviet-Iraqi treaty in April 1972, and the Soviet decision to give Iraq more weaponry during Al-Bakr's visit to Moscow in September further angered the Iranians. Complicating Soviet-Iranian relations at this time was yet another factor—their support for opposite sides in the guerrilla war raging in the Dhofar region of Oman. While the USSR (and Iraq and the PDRY) supported the Popular Front for the Liberation of Oman and the Arab Gulf (PFLOAG) with military supplies, Iran supplied both troops and equipment to the Sultan of Oman's forces. Interestingly enough, however, perhaps in an effort to minimize this area of disagreement, the Soviet Union's official descriptions of the Sultan's forces in 1972 referred only to "British mercenaries," and not to Iranian troops.

Events in February and March 1973 were to force the Russians to quicken their diplomatic efforts to keep the Iran-Iraq conflict under control. On February 10 both Iraq and the USSR were publicly embarrassed by the disclosure that 300 Soviet-made machine guns and 60,000 rounds of ammunition had been found in the Iraqi Embassy in Islamabad, Pakistan.[75] The weapons were evidently destined for the Baluchistani Liberation Front, which demanded that an independent Baluchistan be made up of Baluchistani-populated territories now controlled by both Iran and Pakistan. The Soviet leadership, whose relations with the new Bhutto regime in Pakistan were slowly improving following the Indo-Pakistani war of 1971, referred to this incident as a "regrettable circumstance,"[76] although they could not have been overjoyed by this public disclosure of their linkage, however slight, to an attempt to partition the territory of two states with which they were trying to maintain good relations.

Less than two weeks later came the announcement that Iran had concluded the largest single military sales agreement ever arranged by the U.S. Defense Department—a $2-billion order for U.S. weaponry consisting of helicopter gunships, supersonic interceptors, Phantom jet bombers, and C-130 cargo planes, along with other military equipment.[77] The arms race in the Persian Gulf was now on with a vengeance. It was perhaps in an effort to slow down this arms race—and avoid new arms requests from Iraq—that Soviet Premier Aleksei Kosygin, in a visit to Iran to celebrate the opening of the Soviet-built Isfahan steel works on March 15, pointedly stated:

> We are pleased that good relations have developed between our countries and we intend to do everything in our power to make Soviet-Iranian relations even firmer in the future . . . and we feel that [this] corresponds to the interests of the people of the other Asian countries as well, *particularly those bordering the Soviet Union and*

Iran, insofar as their security and peaceful future to a certain extent is bound up with the foreign policy course of their neighbors, including the Soviet Union and Iran. But if we want the security of the states to be based not on an arms race—no genuine security can be built on such a foundation—but on the continuing relaxation of tensions and the strengthening of mutual trust among countries, then the efforts of each party concerned are required. Conversely, the militant policy of any one country will inevitably inflame the situation in an entire region, and often throughout the world, forcing its neighbors to take some kind of measures to defend their national interest.[78] [emphasis added]

As soon as Kosygin returned to Moscow, however, Iraq took its turn to inflame the Persian Gulf conflict. On March 20 Iraqi troops crossed into Kuwaiti territory and seized two Kuwaiti border posts. The very next day Iraqi Vice-President Saddam Hussein made a hurried visit to Moscow to confer with the Russians about the situation. The lack of Soviet enthusiasm for the Iraqi move can be seen by the *New Times* comment on this episode. Citing "Arab capitals" (a usual Soviet technique to express displeasure indirectly) the *New Times* article stated:

The dispute has caused anxiety in Arab capitals, inasmuch as Zionist and imperialist quarters have seized upon it to sow dissension in the Arab world and to weaken the Arab Front of struggle to eliminate the consequences of the Israeli aggression. The leaders of a number of Arab countries have urged the Iraqi President and the Emir of Kuwait to make every effort to resolve the conflict without delay.[79]

Thus, by invading Kuwait, the small Gulf state between Iran and Iraq, the Iraqis had not only inflamed their conflict with Iran still further but they had also apparently made even more difficult the "anti-imperialist Arab unity" the Russians were striving to create.

While the Iraqi troops eventually pulled out of Kuwait, although no final agreement was reached, the Shah made it quite clear that Iran would go to Kuwait's aid if she requested assistance. In addition, in an interview with a correspondent of the *Christian Science Monitor,* the Shah called for a NATO-like pact for the Gulf's riparian states and announced that Pakistani and Iranian army chiefs of staff had begun consultations in Tehran.[80]

While the conflicts between North and South Yemen and between Iran and Iraq were serious problems for Soviet policy makers dealing with the Middle East, the central Soviet problem was American influence in the Middle East and the lingering possibility that the United States and Egypt might yet work out a Middle Eastern arrangement contrary to Soviet interests. To avoid such a possibility, the Soviet leaders stepped up their efforts in encouraging the Arabs to unite their efforts against Israel. The Soviet tactic seems to have been that were the Arabs to work together, the moderately pro-Russian regimes of Syria and Iraq (together with the Palestinian Liberation Organization, whose leader, Yasir Arafat, was echoing the Soviet line in return for Soviet economic and military support) would prevent any anti-Russian policy from being adopted. Fortunately for the Russians, two developments in the Middle East helped facilitate their policy. On the one hand, the Arab-Israeli conflict reached new heights of intensity following Israel's shooting down a Libyan airliner in February and the Israeli raid on the PLO headquarters in Beirut in April. Second, Egypt was also following a policy of trying to unite the Arabs for a confrontation with Israel, although Sadat's willingness to work closely first with Libyan leader Mu'ammar Kaddafi and subsequently with Saudi Arabia's King Faisal was not particularly to the liking of the Russians, because Arab unity on an Egyptian-Libyan or Egyptian-Saudi Arabian axis would fall far short of the Arab unity on the "progressive, anti-imperialist" basis that the Soviet leaders had long espoused.

In one of the first major Soviet policy statements following their expulsion from Egypt, the Russians had been concerned about just such a development:

> The reactionary elements and certain nationalist elements seek to compromise the very ideas of Arab-Soviet friendship and to counterpose appeals for "reliance on Arab forces alone" to the slogan of strengthening the united Arab front and militant solidarity with all the forces of progress on an anti-imperialist basis. . . .
>
> A fact well worth noting is that Arab reaction's anti-Soviet sallies have been accompanied by the weaving of plots against progressive Arab regimes—plotting that is supported by Saudi Arabia, which is performing the role of promoter of imperialist policies in the Arab East. . . .
>
> The Arab peoples realize the necessity of strengthening national and pan-Arab unity; however, as the Lebanese newspaper *Al Shaab* points out, in present day conditions such a consolidation can be effected only on an anti-imperialist and progressive social basis and not at the expense of Arab-Soviet friendship.[81]

In an effort to promote the "anti-imperialist" Arab unity they were seeking, the Soviet leadership helped sponsor two pan-Arab congresses of "progressive forces" in November. On November 11, an international seminar with the theme "Oil as a Weapon in the Struggle against Imperialism and Israeli Aggression" was convened in Baghdad. According to the Soviet description of the seminar, which was attended by a Soviet delegation as well as delegations from Arab countries, the object of the conference was to "expose the plunder of the Arab countries by the imperialist monopolies, and the link between these monopolies and Israel."[82] At the end of November, an all-Arab Popular Congress of the Palestine Revolution was held in Beirut under the sponsorship of the Arab Communist parties. The congress set up the Arab Front for Participation in the Palestinian Resistance, and a declaration approved by the meeting pledged to "liquidate the imperialist presence and its strategic and economic interests in the Arab homeland."[83] Attending the conference were the Communist parties of the Arab world, along with delegations from the Iraqi, Syrian, South Yemeni, Algerian, and Egyptian governments and representatives of the USSR and Soviet bloc states in Eastern Europe. An editorial in the February 1973 issue of the *World Marxist Review* hailed the formation of the Arab Front as evidence of the increasing cohesion of the anti-imperialist forces in the Arab world:

> The formation, at a conference in Beirut last November, of the Arab Front in support of the Palestinian Revolution, in which communists, revolutionary-democrats, and other patriotic parties and organizations of 14 Arab countries are represented, is evidence of the increasing cohesion of the anti-imperialist forces.[84]

While the Soviet leadership was working for Arab unity "on an anti-imperialist basis," Egyptian leader Anwar Sadat was convening a number of pan-Arab conferences in November and December in an effort to build a united Arab front against Israel. Having sought first Soviet and then American support against Israel, and having failed in both quests, Sadat, under great domestic and foreign pressure to go to war, decided that the only solution for Egypt was to mobilize the capabilities of the Arab world—including its oil power—against Israel and its supporters.[85] In a major policy speech on December 28, Sadat stated that Egypt "realized the limits of Soviet aid" and that Egypt would take "new initiatives to make the battle a pan-Arab one." Replying to Syrian demands that Egypt go to war immediately to relieve the pressure on Syria, which was engaged in almost daily battles with Israel at the time, Sadat remarked, "Egypt could not allow international circumstances to determine the course of events in the Middle East" but "had to impose its will on circumstances."[86]

The Soviet press commented favorably on Sadat's pan-Arab battle plan, and the Russians utilized the opportunity to remind the Arabs that the United States, Israel's main supporter, was becoming very vulnerable to the oil pressure Sadat had recommended. Thus in a *New Times* article in late January, Victor Kudryavtsev, one of the main Soviet commentators on the Middle East, stated:

> Egyptian newspapers report that the Cairo government submitted to the [Arab] joint defense council a plan providing for proportional contribution by the Arab countries to the common struggle with the means available to them—military, economic or financial. It is noted that stress is laid in this plan on the need to work out a joint oil policy.

A coordinated Arab policy in this sphere could be especially effective inasmuch as Israel's main backer, the United States, is displaying an increasing interest in the oil deposits of the Persian Gulf and in Libya. Reference is made in Cairo to a survey made by a U.S. Senate committee showing that in the coming years between 20 and 30 per cent of U.S. fuel requirements will be met with Middle East oil. The Egyptian plan, newspapers say, also envisages an increase in the financial contribution by the oil-rich Arab countries to the common struggle against the aggressor.[87]

Kudryavtsev also warned the Arabs, however, that "experience has convinced the Arab peoples that they can achieve real unity only on a clearly expressed anti-imperialist basis and by promoting friendship and cooperation with the Soviet Union."[88]

In the very next issue of *New Times,* Dmitry Volsky, another key Soviet commentator on Middle East affairs, warned against Saudi Arabia's increasingly important role in the Arab world:

What lies behind the activization of Saudi foreign policy? And what is this thing called the "phenomenon of Saudi Arabia" which the Western press is so zealously touting? . . .

The Saudi monarchy . . . is bent on becoming the bulwark of reaction throughout the Arab world generally. Year after year it spends dozens even hundreds of millions of dollars on what it calls "Arab Policy," the aim of which is to thwart social and economic reforms in other Arab states and subvert their cooperation with the socialist countries. Saudi "dollar diplomacy" is out to rally the Arab nations not for struggle against imperialism and Israeli aggression, for stronger national independence and social and economic advancement, but on purely religious foundations. Riyadh endlessly thumps the drum of the "jihad" or "holy war" that King Faisal has declared against "Communism-Zionism," that fantastic invention of present day obscurantists.

And, as if to discredit Faisal even further, Volsky added:

There is no doubt that Saudi oil could effectively influence Israel's American patrons. But here is what King Faisal said in an interview with the Cairo weekly *Al-Mussawar:* "It is useless to talk about the use of oil as a tool against the United States. It is dangerous even to think of it." Sheikh Ahmed Yamani, the Royal Minister for Oil and Mineral Wealth, explaining the King's viewpoint, says: "It is our opinion that the best way for the Arabs to use their oil is as a basis for closer cooperation with the West, especially the United States."[89]

The Russians had good grounds for attacking Saudi Arabia on this point, because in late September Sheikh Yamani had come to the United States and, in a speech to the Middle East Institute in Washington, stated that Saudi Arabia would raise production from 6 to 20 million barrels of oil per day by 1980 to satisfy the increasing U.S. oil needs, in return for assured entry into the U.S. market.[90] Nonetheless, less than six months later Saudi Arabia was threatening to cut oil supplies to the United States, and within a year Saudi Arabia had joined in an oil embargo against the United States. The cause for this policy transformation may be found in the two Middle Eastern developments during this period mentioned earlier: the escalation of the Arab-Israeli conflict and the realignment of alliance relationships throughout the Arab world, which saw a weakening in the Egyptian-Libyan union movement, and the creation of an Egyptian-Saudi Arabian axis, which by October was to emerge as the dominant factor in Middle Eastern politics.

As Egypt was seeking to mobilize the other Arab states for a confrontation with Israel, on February 21, 1973, an incident occurred that was to inflame passions throughout the Arab world against Israel to a fever pitch. On edge because of Palestinian guerrilla threats to hijack an airliner and crash it into an Israeli city, Israeli air force pilots shot down a Libyan Jet Liner en route from Tripoli to Cairo, which had strayed deep into the Israeli-occupied Sinai Desert and whose pilot had refused Israeli orders to land.[91] The Soviet Union seized upon this incident to link the United States to the Israeli action, in an attempt to discredit the U.S. efforts to mediate the Middle Eastern conflict then in progress and weaken the American position in the Middle East. As New Times columnist V. Katin stated:

> The world press directly links this brigand attack in the air with the intrusion of Israeli troops into Lebanon on the same day. These two sallies testify to the dangerous escalation of Israel's aggression in the Middle East. Tel Aviv is in fact extending the geography of its aggressive actions to Arab countries which were not attacked in 1967. There is also this point. These new provocations were staged on the eve of Golda Meir's visit to the United States. By whipping up military tension, the Israeli government seeks to create a situation in which it will be easier to wrest aid from the backers of Zionism in other countries, particularly the United States.
>
> It is now perfectly obvious that the Israeli rulers' patrons share the responsibility for their crimes.[92]

The Middle Eastern situation heated up further at the beginning of March when two American diplomats were murdered by Palestinian Arab terrorists in the Saudi Arabian Embassy in Khartoum, the Sudan. A week after this event, and perhaps partially in response to it, the United States announced the sale of

24 more Phantom and 24 Skyhawk bombers to Israel. Following this announcement, from which the Soviet Union again made propaganda capital, Egyptian President Sadat reorganized his cabinet by firing Premier Aziz Sidky and assuming the premiership himself along with the post of military governor. Sadat stated at the time that he "reluctantly decided" to assume the leadership himself when he got word of the U.S. commitment to deliver additional Skyhawk and Phantom jets to Israel—a development that followed closely upon the failure of the visit of Sadat's security adviser, Hafiz Izmail, to Washington. In his speech the Egyptian president also mentioned that war could not be delayed and that Egypt's relations with the USSR had resumed a "correct friendly pattern."[93]

While the Soviet leadership welcomed the further deterioration in Egyptian-American relations, there is some question as to how friendly they felt toward the Sadat regime. In an effort to stabilize his domestic position before the battle with Israel, Sadat had embarked on a wholesale purge of the Arab Socialist Union, expelling a large number of leftist intellectuals, including Lutfi Al-Kholi, the only Marxist on the Arab Socialist Union's Central Committee and the man who had earlier praised Sadat's national front.[94] This was clearly a reversal of the national front system the Russians had been urging on Syria, Iraq, and Egypt. In addition, Soviet comments on domestic developments in Egypt began to assume an increasingly negative tone, as it appeared, through his encouragement of foreign investment and domestic capitalism, that Sadat was embarking on a program to restore Western-style capitalism to Egypt.[95] Nonetheless, the Russians evidently decided not to let these negative factors stand in the way of improved Soviet-Egyptian relations, and, following February visits by a Soviet military delegation to Cairo, and by Hafiz Izmail and Ahmed Ismail to Moscow,[96] large quantities of Soviet arms were flowing again to Egypt by March. Thus, on March 24, Abdul Koddous, the newspaper èditor close to Sadat who had been in the forefront of the Egyptian media attack on the lack of sufficient Soviet support the previous summer, could report in an *Akhbar-Al-Yom* column that Egypt had now secured "a steady flow of arms from the USSR."[97] Interestingly enough, however, the USSR was apparently not yet sending Egypt the kinds of weapons (fighter-bombers and ground-to-ground missiles) that Sadat had called for the previous summer, as Koddous stated:

> The type of arms does not matter so long as we can use them to strike and repel enemy strikes. In other words, I do not believe that Egypt, as it imports arms from the USSR these days is facing a problem of the type of arms now that it has solved the problem of securing a steady flow of arms.[98]

Indeed, according to Heikal, between December 1972 and June 1973, Egypt received more arms from the USSR than in the whole of the two preceding years, and Sadat said, "They are drowning me in new arms."[99] Nonetheless, Sadat probably realized that in the absence of the strategic arms he wanted, and because of Israel's military power, his war against Israel would have to be a limited one, fought as much for diplomatic and political goals as for military ones.[100] Consequently, with Egypt now receiving a steady flow of Soviet arms, Sadat turned his attention to developing his relationship with Saudi Arabian King Faisal, whose oil leverage over the United States was a critical factor in the Egyptian strategy against Israel. Faisal's willingness to use the oil weapon may have been partially due to the pressures on him generated by the escalating Arab-Israeli violence in the Middle East, which reached yet another peak on April 9. On that day, Israeli commandos raided Beirut and killed the three Palestinian guerrilla leaders thought by the Israelis to be the masterminds behind the terrorist campaign against Israeli citizens in Europe and responsible for the murder of the Israeli athletes in Munich. As might be expected, the Soviet Union seized upon this incident to discredit the United States further by linking it to the Israeli action, and to again urge the Arabs on to "anti-imperialist Arab unity." Writing in *New Times*, Dmitry Volsky asserted:

> An examination of the Beirut provocation leads many observers to the conclusion that it was carried out with direct assistance from Western Secret Services. In its statement the Palestine Liberation Organization, for example, accused the CIA of complicity in the murders. . . .
>
> The need to unite on an anti-imperialist basis is one of the main conclusions of the Beirut events made by all progressive Arab opinion. The importance of unity is being stressed by papers in Cairo, Damascus and Baghdad. Unity is the motto of numerous protest manifestations now sweeping the Arab world. Concerted actions by the Arab peoples, with the support of their friends, can create an insurmountable barrier in the path of Tel Aviv's encroachments.[101]

Still another factor that might have encouraged Faisal to consider using the oil weapon was the rapid deterioration of the position of the Western oil companies in the Middle East and the increasingly acute energy crisis in the United States, which was making front-page headlines in the Arab press. On January 23, 1973, the Shah of Iran dictated to the Western-owned oil companies operating in Iran a choice that amounted to little more than a threat that if they did not agree to Iranian terms they would lose access to the Iranian oil once their current contracts expired. The oil companies capitulated to the Shah by March 1.[102] The previous day the Western-owned oil companies that formed the Iraqi Petroleum Company signed an agreement with the Iraqi government in which they meekly consented to the nationalization of their Kirkuk fields (which had occurred the previous June) in return for 15 million tons of oil.[103]

Meanwhile, Libyan leader Mu'ammar Kaddafi had been cleverly playing off the Western oil companies in his country against each other, thereby securing increasing control over them while at the same time raising the price for Libyan oil, and neither the oil companies nor governments seemed able to do anything about it.[104]

Whatever the cause, by the middle of April, Faisal was threatening the United States that Saudi Arabia would not increase its oil production to meet American needs unless the United States modified its stand on Israel.[105] Following this warning, the United States, Britain, and France all scurried to sell Faisal modern weaponry, a development further underlining Saudi Arabia's growing importance in the Middle East and the West's growing vulnerability to the oil weapon.

In his May Day speech, Sadat hailed the Saudi warning to the United States as further proof of growing Arab unity. Sadat claimed in the speech that he now had Syrian, Kuwaiti, Algerian, Saudi, Moroccan, and even Iraqi support for the forthcoming battle with Israel, which he termed necessary to prevent "domestic explosions" in Egypt and elsewhere in the Arab world because of frustration over the "no war-no peace" situation. At the same time he pointedly reminded the Russians:

> Regarding a peaceful solution, our friends in the Soviet Union must know the true feeling of our people. From the first moment we believed that what was taken by force can only be regained by force. Our friends in the USSR must know that the peaceful solution which the US has been talking about is fictitious.[106]

At this point, however, although urging the Arabs to use their oil weapon against the United States, and sending a steady supply of weapons to Egypt and Syria, the Russians appeared not yet willing to back Egypt in a war against Israel, although Sadat, having coordinated his military plans with Assad (who was also receiving large shipments of Soviet arms), apparently wanted to go to war in the latter part of May.[107] Instead, with the Brezhnev visit to Washington approaching, the Soviet leadership limited itself to supplying weaponry (for which they were reportedly now receiving hard currency)[108] and trying to discredit further Israel and its U.S. supporters. The latter was done in the United Nations and other public forums, including those specifically convened for the purpose,[109] as the USSR continued its efforts to stimulate and reinforce anti-Western trends in the Middle East. The outbreak of very serious fighting in Lebanon in early May, which pitted the Palestinian guerrillas and their Lebanese supporters against the Lebanese government, may have been another factor in the Soviet Union's urging of caution on the Arabs.

As Brezhnev prepared to go to Washington, however, criticism of the lack of sufficient Soviet support for the Arab cause again began to rise. The Soviet-

American detente had reached the point that on June 11 a Soviet newsman was invited to the U.S. Sixth Fleet change-of-command ceremony aboard the aircraft carrier John F. Kennedy in the Mediterranean.[110] Three days later, the Egyptian newspaper *Al-Gomhouria*, which had been friendly to the USSR in the past, warned that Egypt might still resort to force in the Middle East—even at the expense of Soviet-American detente.[111]   On June 22 Mohammed Heikal bitterly criticized the USSR in a column in *Al-Ahram* for cutting aid to Egypt while the United States was doubling aid to Israel (another U.S. arms deal to Egypt had just been announced, probably in compensation for the proposed U.S. arms shipment to Saudi Arabia). Heikal also asserted: "The United States knows what it wants in the Middle East while the USSR does not. What Moscow does not want is another Arab defeat that would destroy Soviet residual presitge in the Middle East."[112]

Thus, by the time of the Nixon-Brezhnev summit, the Soviet position was a mixed one. On the one hand, the U.S. position had deteriorated sharply, primarily because of its increasing dependence on Arab oil and the apparent willingness of Saudi Arabia to use the oil weapon. In addition, the increasingly bitter Arab-Israeli conflict had radicalized feeling in the Middle East to the point that Libya shut down its oil fields for a day, and Iraq and even pro-Western Kuwait shut down their oil fields for an hour in mid-May in protest against Western support for Israel. On the other hand, Egyptian-Soviet relations, while improved, remained tense; and Libyan leader Mu'ammar Kaddafi, whose nation was set to enter into union with Egypt, continued to complain as bitterly about Soviet imperialism and aid to Israel (through the emigration of Soviet Jews) as he did about the United States. Finally, the escalation of the conflict between Iran and Iraq in the Persian Gulf region, a conflict exacerbated by Iraq's invasion of Kuwait, continued to pose difficult problems of choice for the Soviet leadership.

FROM THE SUMMIT TO THE OCTOBER WAR

As in the 1972 summit, the leaders of the two superpowers appeared to pay little attention to the Middle East in their June 1973 meeting. Indeed, only 89 words out of a total of 3,200 in the final communique issued on June 24 dealt with the Middle Eastern situation, and it appeared as if Nixon and Brezhnev wanted to downplay the conflict deliberately, lest it interfere with their pursuit of detente. Thus, the joint communique failed to mention UN Resolution no. 242—hitherto the basis of the Soviet policy for a settlement of the Arab-Israeli conflict. The text of the communique stated:

> The parties expressed their deep concern with the situation in the Middle East and exchanged opinions regarding ways of reaching a Middle East settlement. Each of the parties set forth its position on this problem.

Both parties agreed to continue to exert their efforts to promote the quickest possible settlement in the Middle East. This settlement should be in accordance with the interests of all states in the area, be consistent with their independence and sovereignty, and should take into due account the legitimate interests of the Palestinian people.[113]

As might be expected, the Egyptian reaction to the summit communique was swift and bitter. On June 25 *Al-Ahram's* managing editor, Ali Hamadi El-Gammal, asserted in a column:

Although we did not expect the talks between the two leaders to produce a specific position with regard to the crisis, we never thought that the problem would meet this strongly negative attitude on their part.[114]

The Arab reaction to the summit's treatment of the Arab-Israeli conflict was, in fact, so negative that the Russians felt constrained to publish a special statement on Soviet policy toward the Middle East. Issued by TASS on June 27, it reiterated the main tenets of Soviet policy frequently stated in the past, including the need for total withdrawal of Israeli troops to the 1967 borders, a "peaceful solution" based on UN Resolution no. 242, recognition of the "legitimate interests and rights of the Palestinians," and Soviet support for the Arab states affected by "Israeli aggression" in 1967.[115]

But bitter Arab reaction to a perceived lack of Soviet support at the summit was not the only Middle East problem the Soviet leaders faced following the Brezhnev-Nixon meeting. The Iran-Iraq conflict heated up even more as the dispute between the Kurds and the Iraqi government moved closer to a full-scale war. To complicate matters even more for the Russians, the United States and China moved even closer to the Iranian side. In the middle of June, China openly came out for Iran. Visiting Foreign Minister Chi Peng-fei stated that Iran was fully justified in its arms buildup because "as the Shah has said, the situation on the eastern and western sides of Iran is a very serious threat to Iran."[116] Then, in late June, the Iranian Foreign Ministry, in its annual report, charged Iraq with numerous frontier violations in Kurdistan and elsewhere. At the same time, Kurdish leader Mullah Mustafa Barzani, in an interview with a Washington *Post* reporter, openly appealed for American aid and held out the prospect of Iraqi oil in return:

We are ready to do what goes with American policy in this area, if America will protect us from the wolves. If support were strong enough, we could control the Kirkuk oil field and give it to a U.S. company to operate. It is in our area, and the recent nationalization of the Western-owned field was an act against the Kurds.[117]

The most serious problem of all for the Russians, however, was the attempted overthrow of the Al-Bakr regime on June 30, in which the number-three man in the Iraqi regime, Abd Al-Khaliq Al-Samarrai, and the chief of security, Nazim Kazar, were heavily implicated, with Kazar apparently being the mastermind behind the plot.[118] In reporting this development, *New Times* urged the Al-Bakr regime to learn from this experience by finally implementing the "progressive national front" of the Iraqi Ba'ath Party, the Iraqi Communist Party, and the Kurdish national party it had long promised.[119] Perhaps because it was severely shaken by the coup d'etat attempt against it, the Al-Bakr regime agreed on July 17 to sign the pact for the national front. While the Iraqi Communists agreed to sign as well, the Kurds refused, and hostility between Kurds and the government degenerated into a situation close to full-scale war.[120]

On the same day as the signing of the national front agreement in Iraq came another event the Russians welcomed—the overthrow of the monarchy in Afghanistan by General Muhammad Daud, who proclaimed Afghanistan to be a republic. Daud, as premier between 1953 and 1963, had established good relations with the USSR, and he was also known for encouraging a "Pashtunistan" separatist movement in Pakistan's Northwest Frontier Province. Were Daud to reactivate this policy, and his speech of July 17 indicated he would do just that,[121] Pakistan's security problems, already complicated by the Baluchistani problem, would become more acute, thereby complicating Iran's security problems as well.

Iran's Premier Abbas Hoveida visited the Soviet Union in early August to discuss the Middle Eastern situation, and *New Times* made it clear, perhaps to reassure the Iraqis, that the broadening of Soviet-Iranian cooperation was "by no means at any third party's expense."[122] Nonetheless, the Iraqi regime, beset by its sharpening internal conflict with the Kurds, who continued to refuse to join the national front, apparently needed more reassuring. By late September the USSR had sent a number of TU-22 Blinder bombers to Iraq.[123] The fact that the number-two man in the Iraqi regime, Saddam Hussein, had openly spoken about improved relations with the United States and Britain to a group of Western correspondents and had declared that Iraq followed a policy of "nonalignment" may have also played a role in the Soviet decision to send the bombers.[124]

As the Iran-Iraq conflict, now exacerbated by strife between the Iraqi government and the Kurds (who were supported by Iran) continued to simmer, the Soviet leadership also had to face the increasingly strident calls by Sadat for war and the Egyptian leader's efforts to unite the Arab states in pursuit of this goal. On July 11, Sadat's national security adviser, Hafiz Izmail, journeyed to Moscow for what were termed "frank and friendly" talks. Upon his return Izmail stated that Egypt and the USSR were in "total accord" on their future relationship and assessment of the Middle Eastern situation.[125] Nevertheless, in a speech following Izmail's return, Sadat stated that he was not fully satisfied with the results of the visit and that the Russians had told Izmail that detente could be expected to last from 20 to 30 years.[126] Sadat then warned the Soviet leaders in a speech on Radio Cairo on July 22 that detente would lead to the isolation of the USSR from the "national liberation movement," a warning certain to anger the USSR, because little more than a month away was the fourth nonaligned nations conference, in Algiers, where the Russians and Chinese would be certain to compete again for the allegiance of the developing nations of the Third World.[127]

While Soviet-Egyptian relations remained strained, despite the steady flow of Soviet armaments, the Soviet leadership could perhaps gain some satisfaction that the Libyan-Egyptian merger project was foundering badly. After visiting Egypt for two weeks in late June and early July, Kaddafi had made little headway in convincing the Egyptians whom he met that the advantages of their union with Libya outweighed the disadvantages. According to Moussa Sabry, writing in *Al-Akhbar* on July 8, "legal, economic and religious differences stood in the way of the union," as did Egyptian misgivings about the Libyan "cultural revolution," Libyan policy regarding Israel, and Kaddafi's disapproval of Egypt's relationship to the Soviet Union, limited as it was.[128]

Stung by the failure of his visit to Egypt, Kaddafi then organized a "peoples march" of 20,000 Libyans to Cairo to force the merger— only to have this tactic fail as well.[129] Finally, an embittered Kaddafi, in a speech broadcast on Radio Tripoli on July 23, stated that "only a cultural revolution similar to Libya's could make the Egyptians a fighting people." In an evident response to the increasingly close relations between Faisal and Sadat, Kaddafi added, "There could be no truce with Arab reactionaries in league with the United States."[130]

The Soviet leaders were clearly pleased by the failure of the Egyptian-Libyan union and Libya's increasing isolation in the Arab world, since Kaddafi, with his militant anti-Sovietism, had constantly opposed Soviet policies in the Middle East. While applauding Kaddafi for his policy of nationalizing foreign oil companies, the Russians continually attacked him for his "third international force" theory, which rejected both capitalism and communism and claimed to offer a new socialist ideal based on the Koran. What particularly irked the Soviet leaders was that in many ways Kaddafi's theory, which stressed the need for Third World countries to oppose both NATO and the Warsaw Pact, bore a close relationship to the doctrines of China's Mao Tse-tung.[131]

Although the Russians were pleased with the failure of the Egyptian-Libyan union project, they could not have been too happy with Sadat's subsequent choice of Saudi Arabia to be his principal Middle Eastern ally. Sadat, who recognized the fact that he had to unite as many of the Arab states as possible in a coalition to confront Israel, knew that Kaddafi had alienated too many other Arab leaders, including King Hussein and King Faisal, to make this coalition a viable one.[132] Thus, as Egypt's relations with Libya cooled, they became much closer with Saudi Arabia, culminating in a visit by Sadat to Saudi Arabia on August 23 in which Sadat probably informed Faisal of the coming war with Israel (although it is doubtful that the exact date was set), and he urged Faisal to use the oil weapon against the United States. Arab-Israeli tension had reached yet another peak at the time of Sadat's visit, following Israel's diversion of a Lebanese airliner from a flight between Beirut and Baghdad to an Israeli airbase. The goal of the Israeli action, which the Arabs branded as "air piracy," was to capture Palestinian terrorist leader George Habash. In addition, U.S. vulnerability to Arab oil pressure was becoming increasingly apparent following a series of "energy talks" by President Nixon and statements by presidential assistants on the "energy crisis," many of which were given prominent attention in the Soviet media.[133] Indeed, official American recognition of the U.S. oil vulnerability had reached the point by early August that, in an interview on Israeli television on August 7, Joseph Sisco, then Assistant Secretary of State for Near Eastern Affairs, told the Israelis that while U.S. and Israeli interests were parallel in many instances, they were not always parallel, and he cited oil as one of the nonparallel cases.[134] In any case, by the end of August, King Faisal had become convinced that the time had come to unfurl the "oil weapon," and in a speech on NBC-TV the Saudi monarch warned the American people that, while he did not want to put restrictions on oil exports to the United States, "America's complete support of Zionism makes it extremely difficult to continue to supply oil to the United States or even to maintain friendly relations with it."[135] Despite Faisal's threats to use the oil weapon, by early September the increasingly close relationship of Egypt and Saudi Arabia became a matter of concern for the Soviet leadership, which had long viewed Saudi Arabia in a very negative way. An article in *New Times* discussing the new trends in inter-Arab politics stated:

> The Press in both Arab and Western countries has of late been focusing on the policy of Saudi Arabia. The reactionary Saudi monarchy, which receives large revenues from the oil monopolies, holds a conspicuous place in the plans of international imperialism. The imperialists, capitalizing on the difficulties experienced by the Arab countries because the settlement of the Middle East problem is dragging out owing to sabotage by Israel, are using the Saudi monarchy as a tool in their efforts to isolate those countries from the Soviet Union and the rest of the Socialist community, with an eye to abolishing the progressive Arab regimes. . . . At the same time, the Saudi reaction, stinting no money, is out to attain its own hegemonistic goals in the Middle East, to undermine the positions of the national democratic forces, and to block progressive reform in this area.
>
> Tripoli Radio, the Libyan station, routinely terms the Saudi King an "imperialist agent" and "traitor" to the Arab cause. The Libyan station has bitterly criticized the Egyptian regime for seeking close contacts with him. King Faisal, Arab diplomats here say, is strongly interested in preventing a merger between Egypt and Libya. It was noted in the foreign press that Kaddafi's unexpected arrival in Cairo

late in August came precisely at a time when President Sadat was on a confidential visit to Saudi Arabia and other Arab countries.[136]

As Egypt moved toward Saudi Arabia and what appeared as a right-wing orientation in domestic and international politics (both the Arab Communists and the Soviet press continued their criticism of Sadat's domestic policies during the summer), the Soviet leadership sought to counter this negative trend by up-grading its relations with the Palestine Liberation Organization, which had become one of the centers of anti-Western influence in the Arab world. In August, PLO President Yasir Arafat was invited as an honored guest to the World University Games in Moscow, and the PLO was permitted to open an office in East Berlin.[137] At the same time the Soviet government vehemently denied rumors that it was planning to sell a large quantity of cement to Israel (to be used for immigrant housing), and the Israeli team at the University Games met severe harassment from Soviet authorities—a marked contrast to the warm reception given to Arafat.[138]

Despite the added Soviet attention given to Arafat and the PLO, Egypt was still the prime mover in Arab politics. In August the Soviets became engaged in a dialogue with Egypt over Sadat's plans to go to war, arguing that war was not necessary to regain the lost Arab lands, since time was on the side of the Arabs. The Russians argued that through the judicious use of the oil weapon, the Israelis could be forced to withdraw because of pressure from the United States, and that this process could be achieved without war—thanks to the existence of the Soviet-American detente. This rather intricate reasoning was most fully expressed by Dmitry Volsky, an associate editor of *New Times,* in a major article in early August:

> The Arabs know the cost of bloodshed as well as anyone else. And the conditions in the world are increasingly favorable *to paying no such price* for the elimination of the consequences of Israel's aggression. . . .
>
> The new climate developing in world affairs is highly unfavorable to the Israeli militarists, it operates against their annexationist designs. The world press has noted repeatedly, for example, that with tensions in Europe lessening Israel's stock in Europe has been falling. . . .
>
> Many observers believe, for instance, that the energy crisis in the West, notably the United States, whose interest in Arab oil is, in the general view, increasing, will affect American Middle East policy, but more important, to our mind, than such adventitious factors is the inherent trend of the continuing struggle between the forces of progress and reaction, in which the balance is shifting more and more in favor of the progressive forces. The Middle East is no exception in this respect.

The Progressive Fronts in Iraq, Syria and South Yemen have strengthened. The progressive Arab countries are building up their friendship and cooperation with the Socialist states. . . . The attempts of Right nationalistic quarters parading pseudo-patriotic extremist slogans to impose their own conceptions on leading Arab countries and *steer them into adventurist courses* are meeting with no success.[139] [emphasis added]

The Egyptians, however, were evidently not convinced by these arguments or by the Soviet decision to allow North Koreans and North Vietnamese to help train the Egyptians and Syrians,[140] and Abdul Kouddous' newspaper, *Akhbar-Al-Yom*, came out with a series of articles attacking detente because it subordinated Arab interests to the interests of the superpowers. The Russians appeared to take this attack quite seriously, as *Pravda* warned on August 28:

It looks as if the political line of this Cairo newspaper is acquiring a rather specific coloration. What purpose do the articles serve? The impression is being created that we are dealing with an attempt to sow distrust toward the Soviet Union among the Egyptian public and to distort the meaning of its support for the just cause of the Arab peoples who are struggling to liquidate the consequences of Israeli aggression.

Such misinformation, of course, cannot harm the time-tested Soviet-Egyptian friendship. It is to be hoped that such attempts to sow seeds of distrust among our people will be properly rebuffed in Egypt itself.[141]

On the eve of the fourth conference of the heads of state of nonaligned countries in Algiers on September 5, Volsky published yet another article in *New Times* describing the benefits to the Third World of Soviet-American detente:

An unbiased examination of the international situation shows that the development of Soviet-U.S. contacts has already had a salutary effect on the third world. Transition from confrontation to stable peaceful coexistence makes it harder for the aggressive neo-colonial quarters to impose their diktat on the newly-emerged national states. In this respect the significance of the Agreement on the Prevention of Nuclear War signed on 22 June this year cannot be overestimated. Recall, for instance, this stipulation of the agreement: Each Party will refrain from the threat or use of force against the other party, against the allies of the other party, and against other countries under circumstances which may endanger international peace and security. The parties agree that they will be guided by these considerations in the formulation of their foreign policies and in their actions in the field of international relations. . . .

Given a different world balance of strength, different international conditions, might the imperialists not have resorted to the most dangerous moves against, say, Iraq when it nationalized Iraq Petroleum, *or against the Popular Unity Government in Chile? . . .*

Such, then, are the facts. They show that with the introduction of peaceful co-existence into Soviet-U.S. relations Soviet support for the national liberation movements will increase rather than diminish, and opportunities for cooperation between the socialist nations and the developing countries will be greater. More, in a climate of detente, when the newly independent states can feel more secure and the system of neo-colonialist blocs is breaking down, these countries gain new opportunities to pursue independent home and foreign policies.[142] [emphasis added]

Volsky must have soon regretted these words because less than a week later, the "Popular Unity" government of Salvador Allende in Chile was overthrown, and Allende, who together with Brezhnev had been the recipient of the Lenin Peace Prize in May, was killed. While it is not in the purview of this study to go into the background and development of the events of Chile, it is very clear that the Soviet leadership was bitterly disappointed over the fall of the Allende government. As shown above, the Allende government was an excellent example proving that the Soviet policy of detente was working, and its overthrow appeared to indicate the opposite, particularly to a number of already suspicious leaders in the Middle East. Indeed, in a *New Times* editorial following the coup in Chile, the Russians acknowledged this effect of the coup on detente:

A concentrated offensive is being waged against detente and its practical achievements. The object is at all costs to impede the progress of this process of such vital importance to the peoples.

Unfortunately, it must be said that the psychological pressure applied by the enemies of international detente is not without effect. One Arab newspaper, for instance, affirmed the other day that the reactionary military coup in Chile was nothing short of a consequence of detente.[143]

Two days after the coup, to which the Soviet media directly linked the United States,[144] came a major air battle in the Middle East between Israel and Syria, which resulted in the Israelis shooting down 13 Syrian planes while losing only one of their own. These events may have at least partially undercut the supporters of detente within the Soviet Politburo—perhaps to the point where they agreed to respond by increasing shipments of Soviet weaponry such as tanks and antiaircraft missiles to Syria and Egypt, and agreed to Sadat's decision to go to war, although the USSR still refrained from supplying the Arabs either with fighter-bombers or with ground-to-ground missiles in sufficient quantity to pose a strategic threat against Israel. There is some evidence, however, that up to 30 SCUD ground-to-ground missiles may have arrived in Egypt at least a month before the war,[145] and if this is true, they did serve as a strategic deterrent to an Israeli attack against Egypt's heartland. These shipments of weapons were to prove sufficient for the Egyptians—who were to use the antiaircraft missiles as a cover for the crossing of the canal and the tanks to spearhead the breakthrough—to make a final decision for war.[146] The Russians must have learned about Sadat's decision in late September, because they began to withdraw nonessential technicians and other civilians from both Syria and Egypt well before the outbreak of the fighting on October 6, and launched Cosmos satellites on September 21 and October 3,[147] most probably to gain information on Egyptian and Israeli troop concentrations.

In thus giving their tacit support for the Egyptian decision to go to war—in the viewpoint of this writer it was clearly an Egyptian and not a Soviet decision[148]—the Soviet leaders may have been motivated by a number of considerations. In the first place, it was conceivable that Sadat was again bluffing, as he had appeared to be many times in the past, and that he needed the additional weapons primarily for domestic considerations. Second, should Sadat go to war and be defeated—and this was the virtually unanimous feeling of the Western intelligence community and probably of a number of Russians as well—the Sadat regime would very likely fall, perhaps to be replaced by a more pro-Soviet Egyptian regime led by Ali Sabry. At the very minimum an outbreak of war would further inflame Arab feelings against the United States, much as the 1967 war had done, thus weakening the U.S. position in the Arab world still further. The Soviet leadership may well have seen the possibility that the war would bring a further nationalization of Western oil companies—the trend was already well under way—and possibly even an oil embargo against the United States and Western Europe, which, unlike the situation in 1967, would be a major blow to the economies of the Western world. Such developments would mean a sharp increase in influence for the USSR in its "zero-sum game" influence competition in the Middle East with the United States, and possibly even tip what the Soviet leaders called the "world balance of forces" toward the USSR.[149] Perhaps in an effort to secure such gains, the USSR failed to inform the United States of the coming war, despite an explicit agreement to do so reached at the 1972 Brezhnev-Nixon summit, where the two powers pledged to warn each other in the event that a dangerous local conflict threatened to arise, and a similar pledge that they would not seek "unilateral advantage" at the expense of the other.[150] On September 28, a week before the war, Soviet Foreign Minister Andrei Gromyko had visited Nixon and Kissinger (who was now officially Secretary of State) at the White House and told the American leaders nothing about the war, despite his almost certain knowledge about it by that late date.

In giving its support for Sadat's decision to go to war, however, the Soviet leadership took its biggest Middle Eastern gamble since February 1970, when it had agreed to Nasser's request for a Soviet-manned air-defense system. In taking that move in 1970, the Soviet leaders had gambled successfully that the Nixon administration, then still bogged down in Vietnam, would make no equivalent countermove. In 1973 the Soviet leaders may have reasoned that the Nixon administration, although out of Vietnam, was now so burdened with Watergate, an ailing economy, and the "energy crisis" that regardless of Soviet action during the war, Nixon could not afford to jettison his detente policy with the USSR, which had proven to be one of his administration's few successes. However, following revelations over the cost to the American consumer of U.S. wheat sales to the Soviet Union, and attacks on detente by Soviet dissidents Andrei Sakharov and Aleksandr Solzhenitsyn, who warned against detente without democratization in the USSR, increasing numbers of Americans, even before the outbreak of the war, were beginning to question both the meaning and value of detente with the Soviet Union.[151] Consequently, the Soviet decision to support the Arabs could only provide ammunition for the enemies of Soviet-American detente; but the Soviet leaders, perhaps still smarting from the defeat in Chile, evidently decided that the benefits of aiding the Arabs outweighed the costs of angering the United States. Nonetheless, Soviet caution in the initial stages of the war indicated that the Soviet leaders were hedging their bets on their support of the Arabs until the Arab forces had secured some military successes.

Ironically, while giving their support to Sadat's decision to go to war, the Soviet leadership remained critical of a number of his policies. An article appearing in *Pravda* on the third anniversary of Nasser's death (only eight days before the outbreak of the war) attacked those who "posed as the defenders of Nasserism and tried to impose upon the masses false interpretations of the views of the late President"—particularly as to relations between Egypt and the socialist states.[152] The Arab Communist parties of Lebanon, Syria, Iraq, Jordan, Algeria, and the Sudan, meeting on the eve of the war, were far more explicit in their criticism of the Egyptian leader, attacking him for his policy of close cooperation with King Faisal, "who plays a leading role in Imperialist plans"; for his policy of "weakening the bonds of alliance and friendship" between Egypt and the USSR; and for his encouragement of Egypt's private sector and foreign capital at the expense of the public sector.[153]

Despite these differences with Sadat over both domestic and foreign policies, the Soviet leadership gave him their support during the October war. It is conceivable that the Soviet leaders felt that wartime cooperation would serve to overcome the serious differences between the two countries. In addition, the fact that Sadat had managed by mid-September to effect a reconciliation between Syria and Jordan clearly established him as the leader of an Arab alignment, which now included not only the radical states of Syria and Libya but also the conservative, pro-Western states of Jordan and Saudi Arabia. This made

Egypt once again the fulcrum of Middle Eastern politics, and the Soviet leaders may well have thought that Soviet aid to Egypt during a war that would pit Israel, and most likely the United States (at least in a support capacity), against the Arab world would help create the "Arab unity on the anti-imperialist basis" they had so long desired. If this was indeed the Soviet hope, it was not destined to be fulfilled. For despite extensive cooperation between the USSR and Egypt during the war, once the fighting was over, Sadat was to return to his earlier patterns of domestic and foreign policy—much to the consternation of Soviet officials, who were to see both the collapse of their long-hoped-for anti-imperialist Arab unity and a major turn by the Egyptian president toward the United States.

NOTES

1. Translated in *Current Digest of the Soviet Press* (hereafter *CDSP*) 24, no. 24: 18.

2. New York *Times,* July 20, 1972.

3. Cited in *Middle East Monitor* 2, no. 15 (August 1, 1974): 6.

4. *Pravda*, July 23, 1972. The statement quoted was in Pavel Demchenko's article on the twentieth anniversary of the Egyptian Revolution.

5. Cited in the report by John Cooley in the *Christian Science Monitor*, August 16, 1972.

6. Cited in the report by John Cooley in the *Christian Science Monitor*, August 21, 1972.

7. Cited in the report by Flora Lewis in the New York *Times*, August 22, 1972.

8. See note 5.

9. Translated in *CDSP* 24, no. 35: 5.

10. Y. Potomov, "Middle East Alliance against Progress," *New Times*, no. 34 (1972): 5.

11. Cited in the New York *Times*, September 4, 1972.

12. The Egyptians even began to charge that there were Israeli spies among the Soviet advisers in Egypt! See the report by John Cooley in the *Christian Science Monitor*, September 15, 1972.

13. For a list of the most important Soviet construction projects in the Arab world, see V. Smirnov and I. Matyukhin, "USSR and the Arab East: Economic Contacts," *International Affairs* (Moscow), no. 9 (September 1972): 83-87.

14. See the report in the New York *Times*, June 21, 1972.

15. *Pravda*, July 9, 1972.

16. Ibid., August 11, 1972. Translated in *CDSP* 24, no. 32: 20.

17. Cited in the report by John Cooley in the *Christian Science Monitor*, August 12, 1972.

18. I. Gavrilov, "Arab Press on the Middle East Situation," *New Times*, no. 36 (1972): 8.

19. Translated in *CDSP* 24, no. 30: 17.

20. See the reports by Eric Pace in the New York *Times*, September 18 and 21, 1972.

21. Pavel Demchenko, "The Palestinian Resistance and Reactionaries' Intrigues," *Pravda*, August 29, 1972. Translated in *CDSP* 24, no. 35: 2.

22. Ibid., pp. 3-4. For an Arab Communist view of the Palestinian resistance movement and its problems, see Naim Ashhab, "To Overcome the Crisis of the Palestine Resistance Movement," *World Marxist Review* 15, no. 5 (May 1972): 71-78.

23. Until August 3, Soviet Jews seeking to emigrate had to pay an exit fee of approximately $1,000. The new exit fee structure was determined by the amount of education each individual had, and ranged from $5,500 for technical school graduates to $40,000 for a scholar with a doctoral degree. For a discussion of the context of the Soviet action, see Robert O. Freedman, "The Lingering Impact of the Soviet System on the Soviet Jewish Immigrant to the United States," in *The Soviet Jewish Emigre*, ed. Jerome M. Gilison (Baltimore: Baltimore Hebrew College, 1977), p. 47.

24. Reuters report from Hamburg, cited in the Jerusalem *Post*, September 22, 1972. West Germany, in addition to reestablishing diplomatic relations with Egypt after the seven-year break, had also been engaged in negotiations with other Arab states with whom diplomatic relations had been broken off since 1965.

25. See the report of John Allen May in the *Christian Science Monitor*, September 21, 1972. According to an AP report from London cited in the Jerusalem *Post*, September 15, 1972, Egypt was seeking $220 million in arms from England.

26. *Middle East Monitor* 2, no. 19 (October 1, 1972): 3.

27. See the report by Terrence Smith in the *Christian Science Monitor*, September 10, 1972.

28. Cited in the report by Francis Offner in the *Christian Science Monitor*, September 23, 1972.

29. Dmitry Volsky, " A Frank Talk with Some Arab Colleagues," *New Times*, no. 37 (1972): 4.

30. *New Times*, no. 38 (1972): 1.

31. V. Rumyanstev, "Syria on the Alert," *New Times*, no. 40 (1972): 8. For an examination of the "Nile to Euphrates" myth, see Mervyn Harris, "From Nile to Euphrates: The Evolution of a Myth," *New Middle East*, nos. 42-43 (March-April 1972): 46-48.

32. *Pravda*, September 7, 1972.

33. See the report by Eric Pace in the New York *Times*, September 22. 1972.

34. Y. Kornilov, "Meetings with the Fedayeen," *New Times*, no. 42 (1972): 24-25.

35. At the very beginning of an article entitled "The Middle East Situation," written at the time of Al-Bakr's visit, Dmitry Volsky wrote: "In the present complex alignment of forces in the Middle East, a positive role is increasingly being played by Soviet-Iraqi relations." *New Times*, no. 39 (1972): 6.

36. Podgorny's speech, which appeared in *Pravda* on September 15, is translated in *CDSP* 24, no. 38: 22.

37. Ibid.

38. *New Times*, no. 41 (1972): 18-20. A more theoretical treatment of this problem is found in R. Ulianovsky, "O edinom anti-imperialisticheskom fronte progressivnikh sil v osvobodivshikhsia stranakh" [On the unity of the anti-imperialist front of progressive forces in the newly independent states], *Mirovaia ekonomika i mezhdunarodnye otnosheniia*, no. 9 (September 1972): 76-86. See also his book *Sotsialism i osvobodivshikhsia strany* (Moscow: Nauka, 1972).

39. *New Times*, no. 41 (1972): 18-20.

40. "New Stage in the National Liberation Movement: Problems of Anti-Imperialist Unity" (an international conference held under the auspices of the *World Marxist Review*), *World Marxist Review* 15, no. 11 (November 1972): 61.

41. Ibid.

42. Ibid.

43. Ibid., p. 64.

44. Ibid., p. 67.

45. *Pravda*, September 15, 1972. Translated in *CDSP* 24, no. 38: 23.

46. *Pravda*, September 20, 1972. Translated in *CDSP* 24, no. 38: 23.

47. Ibid.

48. See the report by John Cooley in the *Christian Science Monitor*, October 13, 1972.

49. Ibid.

50. *Pravda*, October 22, 1972.

51. The text of the declaration is found in *New Times*, no. 17 (1972): 5.

52. Cited in report by Henry Tanner in the New York *Times*, September 29, 1972.

53. See the report by Henry Tanner in the New York *Times*, October 1, 1972.

54. See the report by Juan de Onis in the New York *Times*, October 6, 1972, and the report in the Jerusalem *Post*, October 6.

55. See the report by Henry Tanner in the New York *Times*, October 8, 1972.

56. *Peking Review* 15, no. 42 (October 20, 1972): 21.

57. For a description of this incident, see the report by John Cooley in the *Christian Science Monitor*, November 7, 1972.

58. Cited in the report by Henry Tanner in the New York *Times*, October 16, 1972.

59. The text of the communique is found in *Pravda*, October 19, 1972.

60. Cited in report by John Cooley in the *Christian Science Monitor*, October 24, 1972.

61. Cited in the report by Henry Tanner in the Jerusalem *Post*, October 27, 1972.

62. For a description of the possible effects of these leadership changes, see the report by John Cooley in the *Christian Science Monitor*, November 10, 1972.

63. See the report by William Beecher in the New York *Times*, November 12, 1972.

64. Cited in the report by William Dullforce in the Washington *Post*, October 30, 1972. *Pravda*, November 1, 1972, in reporting a speech by Egypt's new defense minister, Ahmed Ismail, gave the same version. The directives apparently were for the Egyptian army to prepare for war with Israel. On this point, see Galia Golan, *Yom Kippur and after: The Soviet Union and the Middle East Crisis* (New York: Cambridge University Press, 1977), p. 37.

65. See the report by John Cooley in the *Christian Science Monitor*, October 25, 1972.

66. *Pravda*, November 1, 1972.

67. See the report by John Cooley in the *Christian Science Monitor*, November 13, 1972.

68. New York *Times*, October 27, 1972.

69. For the "declaration" on the Munich massacre by the Black September terrorist movement, see *Middle East Monitor* 2, no. 18 (September 15, 1972): 4-6.

70. Cited in the New York *Times*, October 7, 1972.

71. AFP report cited in the New York *Times*, November 12, 1972.

72. Yuri Gvozdev, "Democratic Yemen: Problems and Aims," *New Times*, no. 48 (1972): 15.

73. *Pravda*, November 26, 1972. The communique is translated in *CDSP* 24, no. 47: 14.

74. Cited in *Middle East Monitor* 3, no. 1 (January 1, 1973): 3.

75. This incident is described in *Middle East Monitor* 3, no. 5 (March 1, 1973): 1.

76. *New Times*, no. 18 (1973): 11.

77. New York *Times*, February 22, 1973.

78. *Pravda*, March 16, 1973. Speech translated in *CDSP* 25, no. 11: 25.

79. *New Times*, no. 14 (1973): 7.

80. See *Middle East Monitor* 3, no. 11 (June 1, 1973): 2-3; and the report by John Cooley in the *Christian Science Monitor*, May 29, 1973.

81. L. Medvenko, "Subversive Activity of Imperialism and Reaction against the Arab States' National Interests," *Pravda,* August 19, 1972. Translated in *CDSP* 24, no. 33: 17.

82. *New Times,* no. 47 (1972): 13.

83. See the report by Anan Safadi in the Jerusalem *Post,* December 1, 1972.

84. "Marching Together: The Role of the Communists in Building a Broad Alliance of Democratic Forces," *World Marxist Review* 16, no. 2 (February 1973): 112.

85. There had been serious unrest in the Egyptian armed forces, and it had spread to the normally docile Egyptian Parliament as well as to the universities and to the media.

86. Cited in Reuter's report in the New York *Times,* December 29, 1972. For a discussion of Sadat's preparations for war, see Golan, op. cit., pp. 36-39.

87. Viktor Kudryavtsev, "On the Arab Diplomatic Front," *New Times,* no. 4 (1973): 12. The Russians had long been urging the Arabs to use their oil weapon. For an early theoretical treatment of the possible effects of oil pressure, see I. Bronin, "Arabskaia neft—Ssha —zapadnaia Evrope" [Arab oil—the USA—Western Europe], *Mirovaia ekonomika i mezhdunarodnye otnosheniia,* no. 2 (February 1972): 31-42.

88. Kudryavtsev, op. cit., p. 13.

89. Dmitry Volsky, "King Faisal's Holy War," *New Times,* no. 5 (1973): 26-27.

90. Cited in *Middle East Monitor* 2, no. 20 (November 1, 1972): 4-5.

91. The best treatment of this tragedy is found in *Aviation Week and Space Technology,* March 5, 1973, pp. 26-28.

92. V. Katin, "Tel-Aviv's Atrocious Crime," *New Times,* no. 9 (1973): 20-21.

93. Washington *Post,* March 27, 1973. For an analysis of the failure of Hafez Izmail's visit to Washington, see Mohammed Heikal, *The Road to Ramadan* (New York: Quadrangle, 1975), pp. 200-3; and William B. Quandt, *Decade of Decisions: American Policy toward the Arab-Israeli Conflict 1967-1976* (Berkeley: University of California Press, 1977), pp. 154-55. Quandt argues (p. 123) that U.S. arms shipments to Israel were part of the Nixon Doctrine, in which U.S. allies became regional peacekeepers.

94. Cited in the report by William Dullforce in the Washington *Post,* February 5, 1973.

95. For a contemporary Soviet view of the USSR's relations with Egypt, see N. A. Ushakova, *Arabskaia respublika Egipet* (Moscow: Nauka, 1974). Chapter 3 of this book indicates Soviet displeasure with Egypt's economic turn to the West after 1970.

96. For a description of these visits, see Golan, op. cit., pp. 39-40.

97. Cited in *Brief: Middle East Highlights* (Tel Aviv), no. 54:3 (hereafter *Brief*).

98. Ibid.

99. Heikal, op. cit., p. 181.

100. Ibid.

101. Dmitry Volsky, "The Beirut Crime," *New Times,* no. 16 (1973): 12-13.

102. For a description of these oil developments, see *Middle East Monitor* 3, no. 6 (March 15, 1973): 1-2.

103. Ibid., p. 1.

104. Interestingly enough, following these events, *Pravda* on March 14, 1973, urged the United States to solve its energy problems by investing in Soviet oil and natural gas. For an excellent account of the difficulties facing any such U.S. investment, see John P. Hardt, "West Siberia: The Quest for Energy," *Problems of Communism* 22, no. 3 (May-June 1973): 25-36. See also Arthur Jay Klinghoffer, *The Soviet Union and International Oil Politics* (New York: Columbia University Press, 1977), chap. 12.

105. See report in the Washington *Post,* April 18, 1973, and in the Jerusalem *Post* (AP report), April 20, 1973. See also Klinghoffer, op. cit., p. 178.

106. Cairo Radio, May 1, 1973, reprinted in *Middle East Monitor* 3, no. 10: 3-4. Nonetheless, in April the USSR had made a move to aid the Arab war effort by bringing a group

of Moroccan troops to Syria (Golan, op. cit., p. 57). Sadat also discussed Soviet-Egyptian relations in a *Newsweek* interview on April 9, 1973.

107. On this point see Golan, op. cit., p. 37.

108. *Le Monde,* September 2-3, 1973, cited in Golan, op. cit., p. 40.

109. Compare the International Conference for Peace and Justice in the Middle East, Bologna, Italy, May 13, 1973. For a description of the results of the conference, see *New Times,* no. 21 (1973): 16-17.

110. New York *Times,* June 14, 1973.

111. Cited in the report by John Cooley in the *Christian Science Monitor,* June 20, 1973.

112. Ibid.

113. Text of communique is found in *New Times,* no. 26 (1973): 23.

114. Cited in the New York *Times,* June 26, 1973.

115. Reprinted in *Middle East Monitor* 3, no. 14 (July 15, 1973): 1.

116. Radio Tehran, cited in the *Middle East Monitor* 3, no. 13 (July 1, 1973): 6.

117. Cited in report by Jim Hoagland, Washington *Post* services, in the Milwaukee *Journal,* June 24, 1973.

118. For a Baghdad Radio description of the plot, see *Middle East Monitor* 3, no. 14 (July 15, 1973): 5-6. For a discussion of the attempted coup, see R. D. McLaurin, Mohammed Mughisuddin, and Abraham R. Wagner, *Foreign Policy Making in the Middle East* (New York: Praeger, 1977), pp. 126-27.

119. *New Times,* no. 28 (1973): 17.

120. For a description of the composition of the national front and of the Kurdish opposition to it, see *Middle East Monitor* 3, no. 18 (October 1, 1973): 1.

121. See the text of his speech in *Middle East Monitor* 3, no. 15 (August 1, 1973): 4-6.

122. *New Times,* no. 33 (1973): 6. The article also cited another Kosygin speech opposing arms races.

123. See the reports in the New York *Times* and *Christian Science Monitor,* October 2, 1973.

124. Cited in the report by Juan de Onis in the New York *Times,* July 15, 1973.

125. *Brief,* no. 62: 1.

126. Ibid.

127. Cairo Radio, July 22, 1973.

128. Cited in *Brief,* no. 61: 2.

129. For a Soviet comment on the march, see *New Times,* no. 30 (1973): 16-17.

130. New York *Times,* July 24, 1973.

131. For a detailed Soviet critique of Kaddafi's theories, see *Liturnaia gazeta,* no. 23, 1973. Translated in *CDSP* 25, no. 28: 13-14.

132. Kaddafi also posed a domestic challenge to Sadat, as he had the potential of becoming a rallying point for the Moslem fundamentalists in Egypt, who were still a powerful political force.

133. Compare articles in *New Times,* nos. 25 and 27, 1973. See also the article on the Organization of Petroleum Exporting Countries in the September 1973 issue of *Mirovaia ekonomika i mezhdunarodnye otnosheniia,* pp. 129-33.

134. New York *Times,* August 7, 1973.

135. Cited in *Middle East Monitor* 3, no. 18 (October 1, 1973): 4.

136. Y. Potomov, "The Egypt-Libya Merger Project," *New Times,* no. 36 (1973): 11.

137. See the report of Arafat's visit in *New Times,* no. 35 (1973): 2. On the PLO office, see the New York *Times,* August 19, 1973.

138. On the cement, see the report in the *Christian Science Monitor,* July 25, 1973; on harassment, see the report in the Jerusalem *Post,* August 31, 1973.

139. Dmitry Volsky, "New Opportunities and Old Obstacles," *New Times*, no. 32 (1973): 15.

140. Cited in the New York *Times*, August 16, 1973.

141. Translated in *CDSP* 25, no. 35: 18.

142. Dmitry Volsky, "Soviet-American Relations and the Third World," *New Times*, no. 36 (1973): 4-6.

143. *New Times*, no. 39 (1973): 1.

144. See, for example, Radio Moscow Domestic Service September 13 and 14, 1973.

145. By the end of the war, SCUD missiles had reached Egypt, but it is unclear as to whether they arrived in August, September, or October. In his study *Arms for the Arabs: The Soviet Union and War in the Middle East* (Baltimore: Johns Hopkins Press, 1975), p. 101, Jon D. Glassman refers to reports of the missiles being dispatched to Egypt in August and September. Golan, op. cit., p. 66, indicates that the SCUDs had probably arrived by late August 1973.

146. For a discussion of the quantities and types of weaponry with which Egypt and Syria went to war in October 1973, see Glassman, op. cit., pp. 105-6, 113-15.

147. Golan, op. cit., p. 279. The Egyptians were concerned that the withdrawal of Soviet civilians might signal Israel and the United States about the coming attack. (Heikal, op. cit., pp. 34-35, 243-44, gives a description of how the Russians were informed of the war and their reactions.)

148. For a different view of the Soviet position on the eve of the war, see Uri Ra'anan, "Soviet Policy in the Middle East 1969-1973," *Midstream* 30, no. 10 (December 1973): 23-45; and Jon Kimhe, "The Soviet-Arab Scenario," ibid., pp. 9-22.

149. On this point, see Foy D. Kohler, Leon Goure, and Mose L. Harvey, *The Soviet Union and the October 1973 Middle East War* (Miami: Center for Advanced International Studies, University of Miami, 1974).

150. See Chapter 3, pp. 82-83.

151. See the Sakharov interview with *Der Spiegel*, September 17, 1973. For a Soviet attack on Sakharov because of the interview, see Moscow Radio, September 20, 1973.

152. *Pravda*, September 28, 1973.

153. Cited in the report in the New York *Times*, October 6, 1973.

5

The Soviet Union and the October War

SOVIET POLICY DURING THE WAR

As a well-coordinated Syrian-Egyptian attack struck at Israeli positions in the Sinai Desert and the Golan Heights, the initial Soviet reaction to the war was a very hesitant one. This may have been because the Soviet leadership had some doubts as to the capabilities of the Syrian and Egyptian armies to carry out their offensive successfully—even against an overconfident and poorly prepared Israel.[1] Alternatively, the Soviet leaders may have had some second thoughts about the desirability of sacrificing detente for the sake of a rather fickle Arab ally. In any case, if we are to believe Sadat's account of the first day of the war, the Russians tried to get him to accept a cease-fire after only six hours of fighting, by claiming that Syria had requested a cease-fire.[2] Even when Sadat rejected the Soviet ploy, the Soviet media downplayed the war, with *Pravda* giving far more space to the events in Chile than to the Middle Eastern conflict.[3] It was only after three days of fighting, when it appeared that the Arab side was in fact winning, that the Russians, perhaps sensing the possibility of finally being able to rally the Arabs into the long advocated "anti-imperialist" alignment and strike a blow at U.S. interests in the Middle East, moved to increase their involvement in the war, yet at the same time keeping their involvement within limited bounds.[4] On October 8 Brezhnev sent the following note to Algerian President Houari Boumedienne and similar notes to other Arab leaders:

> Comrade President, I believe that you agree that the struggle waged at present against the Israel aggressor for the liberation of Arab territories occupied since 1967 and the safeguarding of the legitimate rights of the people of Palestine affect the vital interests of all Arab countries. In our view, there must be fraternal Arab solidarity, today

more than ever. Syria and Egypt must not remain alone in their struggle against a treacherous enemy.[5]

Meanwhile, Soviet propaganda denouncing Israel began to rise in intensity and the USSR began a massive airlift and sealift of weapons to Syria and Egypt, the first time in an Arab-Israeli conflict that the USSR had aided the Arabs during the actual fighting. Nonetheless, both Brezhnev's note to Boumedienne and the airlift served to demonstrate that the USSR expected the Arabs, not the USSR, to do the fighting, although the Soviet Union would provide with the necessary supplies.

By October 10, however, the war had already begun to turn on the Syrian front as the Israelis, choosing to deal with one enemy at a time, were repelling the Syrians from the territory they had captured on the Golan Heights in the first few days of the fighting. While the USSR was pouring weaponry into Syria (in the first few days of the airlift Syria received the bulk of the supplies), and placing three Soviet divisions on alert, the Russian leaders also were concerned about the deterioration of the Syrian position and apparently urged Sadat to settle for a cease-fire in place.[6] Sadat, however, rejected the Soviet call, as well as a similar British request for an in-place cease-fire on October 13, deciding instead to exploit his battlefield successes (Egyptian troops had seized the Bar-Lev line, which lay along the Suez Canal, and had penetrated ten kilometers into the Sinai Desert) to capture the strategic Gitla and Middi passes—something Moscow urged,[7] once it was clear that Sadat would not accept a cease-fire, probably because the end result of the Egyptian move (the drawing of Israeli pressure away from Syria) would have been the same.

Meanwhile, as Soviet weapons poured into Syria and Egypt, the U.S. government was coming under increasing pressure to mount an airlift of its own to aid Israel. Perhaps hoping that the Soviet-American efforts for a cease-fire then under way would be successful, Kissinger, at a news conference on October 12, seemed to downplay the Soviet airlift:

We do not consider the [Soviet] airlift of military equipment helpful. We also do not consider that Soviet actions as of now constitute the irresponsibility that on Monday evening I pointed out would threaten detente.[8]

In their analysis of this Kissinger statement, the Soviet leaders may have felt that the American administration was now so wedded to detente that the USSR was free to take even further action to influence the outcome of the war. If the Soviet airlift, sealift, and vocal exhortations to the Arabs were not deemed "irresponsible," then perhaps other acts would not be either. In any case, knowing that Sadat had rejected the cease-fire in place, the USSR stepped up its airlift and sealift operations, and there were reports that Soviet technicians had driven tanks from Syrian ports to the battlefields. On the diplomatic front, the USSR now fully backed Sadat's opposition to a cease-fire unless it meant a withdrawal of Israeli forces back to the borders Israel held before the June 1967 war.[9]

Interestingly enough, while supplying the Syrians and Egyptians (and later the Iraqis) with increasing amounts of weaponry, the Soviets made a number of moves to appeal to the United States in an effort to keep the spirit of detente alive. Thus, instead of reducing or cutting off the flow of Soviet Jews to Israel during the war, they actually increased emigration.[10] In addition, Soviet radio broadcasts to the United States during the war emphasized that the Soviet Union was not against Israel as a state—"only against its conquests."[11] Nonetheless, these Soviet gestures had little weight in American government circles when compared with the huge Soviet arms airlift to Egypt and Syria, and the United States began an airlift to Israel on October 14, announcing on October 15 that the "massive airlift of Soviet weaponry to the Arabs threatened to upset the military balance against Israel."[12]

Meanwhile, as in the 1967 war, Algerian President Boumedienne had flown to Moscow, asking for more support for the Arab cause, and once again he had not received all the aid he asked. Although following his visit TASS published a Soviet pledge to "help in every way" the Arab recapture of territory seized by Israel in the 1967 war, the communique reporting Boumedienne's talks with the Soviet leaders stated that they had taken place in a "frank atmosphere"—the usual Soviet code word for serious disagreement.[13]

Nonetheless, the aid provided by the Soviet Union to the Arabs was sufficient to evoke increasing American ire, and in a speech during the visit of Danish Premier Jorgensen, Kosygin acknowledged this development by stating:

> The opponents of detente are trying to use every pretext to revive the atmosphere of the cold war. . . . They are trying in every way to exploit for these purposes the resumption of hostilities in the Middle East.[14]

One of the leading American opponents of detente was Melvin Laird, once secretary of defense and now an adviser to President Nixon. On October 16 he attacked the Russians for disrupting U.S. efforts to achieve a cease-fire and pointedly complained, "We are not getting action to support the concept of detente."[15]

While the Russians were not ready for a cease-fire in place on October 16, the Israeli crossing of the Suez Canal that day and the subsequent enlargement of their salient on the west bank of the canal quickly changed the Soviet leaders' minds. On October 16 Kosygin flew to Cairo and met for three days with Sadat, in an apparent effort to get the Egyptian leader to agree to a cease-fire in place before Egypt's military position deteriorated too badly (and the USSR might be forced to intervene directly).[16] On the same day, 11 Arab countries meeting in Kuwait announced that Arab oil exports to countries "unfriendly to the Arab cause" would be reduced each month by 5 percent until the Israelis withdrew to the 1967 prewar boundaries.[17] Thus the oil weapon, whose use had been urged by the Soviet leaders both before and during the war, had now been employed. If this action, or the visit of Saudi Arabian Foreign Minister Umar Al-Saqqam and other Arab diplomats to the White House to see President Nixon the same day, was meant to deter the United States from granting further assistance to Israel, the attempt was a failure. On October 19 Nixon asked Congress for $2.2 billion in aid for Israel. Highlighting American support of Israel, Moscow Radio again appealed to the Arabs to cut off the flow of oil to the West:

> Favorable conditions now exist for Arab use of oil as an economic
> and political weapon against capitalist states which are supporting Is-
> rael aggression.[18]

Libya announced it was cutting off all oil exports to the United States that day. Saudi Arabia, once the United States' closest ally in the Arab world, followed suit the next day, with Kuwait, Qatar, Bahrein, and Dubai acting similarly on October 21.

The use of the oil weapon, however, could not stop the rapid deterioration in the position of the Egyptian army—a development that led to Kissinger's flying to the Soviet Union on October 20 at the Soviet leaders' "urgent request."[19] The result of Kissinger's visit was a "cease-fire in place" agreement—a major retreat for the Russians from their previous position calling for a return to the 1967 boundaries as a price for the cease-fire. The Soviet-American cease-fire agreement, which was approved by the Security Council in the early hours of the morning on October 23, did not terminate the fighting; both sides, despite agreeing to the cease-fire, continued fighting to improve their positions. The Israelis got much the better of the fighting, however, and by October 24, with Israeli troops only an hour from Cairo, Sadat was forced to appeal to both the United States and the USSR to send troops to police the cease-fire.[20]

At this point the Soviet Union's Arab client was about to suffer a major defeat, which would have meant a major defeat for Soviet prestige as well, now that the USSR had openly backed the Arabs. Therefore, the Soviet leaders decided to pressure Israel and the United States by dispatching Soviet transport planes to the bases of its alerted airborne troops. At the same time Brezhnev sent a stiff note to Nixon that reportedly stated: "I say it straight that if the United States does not find it possible to act together with us in this matter, we should be faced wtih the necessity urgently to consider the question of taking appropriate steps unilaterally."[21] While the Soviet leader may have been bluffing, Nixon decided not to take any chances, and he called a nuclear alert. It now appeared not only that detente had died but also that the two superpowers were on the verge of a nuclear confrontation.[22] Perhaps because this was the last thing the

Soviet leaders wished to see develop out of the Middle Eastern war, Brezhnev quickly backed off from his threat to intervene unilaterally. The United States, equally unwilling to see the conflict develop any further, brought pressure on Israel and stopped the Israeli army before it had destroyed the surrounded Egyptian Third Army and marched onto Cairo, although, as will be shown below, Kissinger had additional motives in doing so. The superpowers then decided to bring the issue back to the United Nations, and a UN emergency force was established to police the cease-fire, although the two superpowers were later to wrangle about the composition of the UN force.

As the war came to a close, Soviet policy makers who had been hesitant about the war at the start were able to total up a number of significant gains for the Soviet Union's position in the Middle East, although a number of these gains were to turn out to be transient ones. Perhaps the main Soviet gain was the creation of the "anti-imperialist" Arab unity they had advocated for so long and the concomitant apparent isolation of the United States from its erstwhile allies in the region. Not only had Syria, Iraq, Egypt, Jordan, Algeria, Kuwait, and Morocco actually employed their forces against Israel but even such staunch one-time allies of the United States as the conservative regimes of Kuwait and Saudi Arabia, in addition to sending troops to the front, had declared an oil embargo against the United States, while the tiny Gulf sheikhdom of Bahrein had ordered the United States to get out of the naval installation it maintained there.[23] Thus, as early as the second week in the war, Dmitry Volsky could exultingly declare in *New Times*:

> It is no secret that Tel-Aviv has always banked—and of late quite openly—on differences between the Arabs. And not without reason, for the relations between some Arab states, including states with progressive orientations, did indeed leave much to be desired. Today, however, in the hour of trial, soldiers of different Arab countries are fighting shoulder to shoulder against Israeli expansionism. . . . This solidarity of the Arab countries which have laid aside their differences, is a new and very important factor in the Middle East situation, the significance of which will evidently grow as time goes on.[24]

Evaluating the lessons of the war six weeks later, Georgi Mirsky, perhaps the dean of Soviet commentators on the Middle East, further emphasized this theme:

> The third myth dispelled [by the war] related to the alleged fragility and illusoriness of Arab solidarity. Today this solidarity, founded on the sense of Arab brotherhood and an awareness of facing a common enemy, is an incontestable fact, one that was confirmed in the course of the October fighting. Iraqi, Moroccan, Jordanian and Saudi troops fought side by side with the Syrian army; the Palestinians,

and the Kuwaits also saw action, and Algerian aircraft took part in the air war.

But perhaps even more important is the solidarity of the oil-producing Arab states. Although the Arab press has spoken a great deal in recent months about the oil weapon, not everybody took it seriously and many were astounded when after the outbreak of hostilities in October even such countries as Saudi Arabia and Kuwait announced an oil boycott of countries supporting Israel (including a total embargo on oil exports to the United States).[25]

In addition to the establishment of Arab unity on an anti-American basis, and the consequent sharp deterioration of the U.S. position in the Middle East, the Soviet leaders could draw great satisfaction from the fact that their extensive aid to the Arabs, and the conspicuous lack of anything except verbal support from the Chinese, had greatly reinforced the Soviet position as champion of the Arab cause and the cause of the "national liberation" movement throughout the world, while undercutting that of the Chinese. The Russians claimed that by delaying enactment of the cease-fire by the United Nations, the Chinese had actually hurt the Arab cause by enabling the Israeli army to gain more territory. As an article in *New Times* put it:

> The latest aggravation of the Middle East crisis once again showed the Arabs who their real friends are. No amount of demagogy will conceal the fact that at this critical hour for the Arab peoples Peking played into the hands of Israel. "The policy of the P.R.C.," the Beirut *Al-Shaab* wrote on October 31 "does not accord with the interests of the Arab nation or the revolutionary concept of the national liberation struggle against world imperialism and Zionism." The efforts made by the Chinese leaders to undermine Arab-Soviet friendship, to weaken international solidarity with the struggle of the Arabs to liquidate the consequences of the Israeli aggression, are condemned by public opinion in the Arab countries. "Our people," the Syrian *Al-Thawrah* wrote "are well aware of the purpose of these efforts. They know that the object is to shake the Arabs' faith in their own strength and in our friends in order to impel us towards compromise and capitulation." The Lebanese press has stressed that Maoist slander cannot discredit the Soviet Union in the eyes of the Arab peoples who have seen for themselves that "Phantoms were shot down with weapons supplied in Egypt and Syria by the U.S.S.R. and not with Chinese verbiage."[26]

Yet another important benefit for the Soviet Union from the war was the reconciliation between Iran and Iraq. On October 8 Iraq announced its desire to restore diplomatic relations with Iran, and the Iraqi government asked Iran to accept this gesture so that Iraqi troops could be moved from the border with Iran to Syria to join the fighting against Israel. The Iranian government accepted the offer, perhaps in the expectation that it could later trade on its solidarity with the Arabs to get them to agree to a rise in the price for oil.[27] The Russians also must have been satisfied with the reconciliation between the Ba'athist regimes of Syria and Iraq, who had quarreled bitterly before the war over Iraq's decision to build an oil pipeline through Turkey to enable Iraqi oil to flow to the Mediterranean without the constant threat of the Syrians cutting it off.[28]

On the strategic level, the Soviet world position was greatly enhanced by the war. NATO faced its biggest crisis since the Suez war of 1956 because of West European opposition to the supplying of Israel from U.S. bases in Europe. Differences over policy toward the oil embargo exacerbated the strains within the alliance still further. Meanwhile, the Common Market was split by the failure of Britain, France, Italy, and West Germany to come to the aid of fellow EEC member Holland, which was also hit by a total oil embargo. While the Russians welcomed the conflicts within NATO and EEC, they nonetheless expressed some concern that Western Europe might yet adopt a "go it alone" strategy and establish its own defensive alliance.[29]

Thus, the Soviet Union had scored a number of gains as a result of the war, although Soviet-American detente had suffered a major blow, with large numbers of Americans both inside and outside the government now openly opposing Nixon's detente policy toward the Soviet Union and the trade and strategic arms policies that went with it. In addition, the fact that the United States and the Soviet Union experienced a nuclear confrontation during the war could not have been too welcome to the Soviet leaders. On balance, however, the Soviet Union's position in the world, and particularly in the Middle East, had been greatly improved by the war, as the position of their main competitor, the United States, had worsened considerably. It appeared as if the Soviet Union had won a major, if not decisive, victory in the "zero-sum game" competition with the United States for influence in the Middle East. Nonetheless, just as the USSR's position, which had been gravely weakened by its expulsion from Egypt in July 1972, had improved sharply only a few months later as a result of the Munich massacre, so too the United States, at a low point in Middle Eastern prestige at the close of the war, was to improve its position radically, several months later, thanks to the astute diplomacy of Henry Kissinger and a reordering of priorities by Anwar Sadat.

THE ISRAELI-EGYPTIAN DISENGAGEMENT AGREEMENT

After the end of the war, the Soviet leadership faced the choice of either trying to capitalize on the serious rifts in NATO and the EEC and further undermining the U.S. position in the Middle East or trying to improve relations with the United States, thereby demonstrating their primary interest in the long-term benefits of arms limitation and trade. While, on the one hand, continuing to stress the value of detente, and even claiming that the detente relationship had prevented a nuclear war between the superpowers during the Middle Eastern conflict, the Soviet leaders nonetheless chose to urge the Arabs to maintain their oil embargo against the United States—an act clearly not consistent with the U.S. concept of detente, since the embargo was both weakening the American economy and challenging American leadership of the NATO alliance. If the Soviet leaders felt that their verbal endorsements of detente would appease the American people or their government, they were gravely mistaken. Thus, in early November, President Nixon, long an advocate of increased trade with the Soviet Union, decided to have the congressional leadership postpone consideration of an administration bill giving most-favored-nation trading status to the Soviet Union.[30]   A New York *Times* editorial several months later summed up many Americans' feelings on the Soviet endeavor to maintain both detente with the United States and the oil embargo against the United States:

> The propaganda campaign by Radio Moscow in Arabic urging the Arabs to continue their oil embargo against the United States . . . has been a useful reminder of the Kremlin's double standard on detente.
>
> The Arab oil embargo was both discriminatory and illegal, a violation of treaty obligations and international trade rules. Yet while Moscow was supporting it, Soviet officials fanning across the United States to promote trade, were vociferously protesting discriminatory —though legal—American tariffs on Soviet exports. . . . Events in the Middle East make it increasingly clear that, in Moscow's view, detente has very narrow limits.[31]

While Soviet-American relations had clearly suffered as a result of the war, the Arab unity created by the war, which the Soviet leaders had welcomed so warmly, began to disintegrate almost as soon as the war ended. Thus, the Ba'athist regime in Iraq, despite the presence of the Iraqi Communists in a national front, and despite close ties to the USSR, rejected the Soviet-supported cease-fire agreement as being "against the will of the Arab masses," much as it had rejected the Soviet-supported UN Resolution no. 242.[32] The Al-Bakr regime was, in fact, so opposed to the cease-fire that it refused to attend the Algiers summit conference of Arab leaders, which took place in late November to coordinate Arab strategy. Similarly opposed to the cease-fire was Libyan leader Mu'ammar Kaddafi, who characterized it as "a time bomb offered by the United States and Soviet Union."[33]   To make matters worse for the Russians, bloody fighting erupted between the Kurds and the Iraqi Communists from November 7 to 20.[34] It was followed the next month by renewed frontier clashes between Iraq and

Iran, which soon escalated into such severe battles that the Russians had to publicly admonish the Iraqis in a *New Times* report of the clashes.[35] Iraq, whose isolation both in the Arab world and in the region as a whole had impelled the Al-Bakr regime to request an alliance with the Russians in the first place, was thus for all intents and purposes again isolated, except for its somewhat improved—although still tenuous—relationship with Syria, to whom it had sent extensive military aid during the war.

A far more serious problem for the Soviet leaders after the war lay in Egypt, where Soviet influence, partially restored by massive shipments of military equipment, including, at the end of the war, SCUD ground-to-ground missiles,[36] had again begun to erode. By the end of the war the primary alignment in the Arab world was the Egyptian-Saudi Arabian alliance, with the Egyptians supplying the military power and the Saudi Arabians the oil leverage. Kissinger clearly recognized this when he helped negotiate the cease-fire, thereby saving Sadat from probable political ruin, as his armies seemed to be on the verge of being overrun by the Israelis. Kissinger also probably remembered Sadat's past efforts to improve relations with the West and his evident dislike for the Russians, whom he had openly opposed on a number of occasions since becoming Egypt's president in October 1970. Thus, Kissinger may have decided that he had a unique opportunity to win over Egypt—and perhaps the rest of the Arab world as well (or at least the oil-rich states)—by forcing the Israelis to accept a cease-fire and then working out an exchange of prisoners (November 7) and finally a complete disengagement agreement (January 18), which resulted in Israel's withdrawal not only from its salient near Cairo but also from the east bank of the Suez Canal, enabling the Egyptians to control both banks of the canal for the first time since 1967.[37] In the process Kissinger managed to secure the reestablishment of diplomatic relations between the United States and Egypt. In fact, relations between Egypt and the United States warmed up so rapidly that there soon began a steady stream of American businessmen to Egypt, which under Sadat's economic policies provided a warm haven for foreign investments. This process culminated in the visit to Cairo of David Rockefeller, chairman of the Chase Manhattan Bank, which then announced it was planning to open a string of "full-service banks" in Egypt.[38] Not only had Kissinger managed to do this all by himself—leaving out the Russians, who had provided the weaponry to enable the Arabs to go to war in the first place but he also managed to secure Sadat's help in lifting the Arab oil embargo, thus splitting the "anti-imperialist Arab unity" the Russians had worked so diligently to maintain.

As might be expected, the Soviet leadership was far from happy with these developments. *Pravda* articles on November 10 and 16 implicitly criticized Sadat for accepting the Kissinger-mediated agreement without following the Soviet lead in demanding an Israeli withdrawal to the cease-fire lines of October 22. As American influence in Egypt began to rise despite the Soviet warnings, the Russian leaders sought to counter this by deepening their relationship with the Palestine Liberation Organization—one of the most anti-American forces in the Middle East—by floating a "trial balloon" for the establishment of a Palestinian state. Thus, a joint communique issued with visiting Yugoslav leader Josef Tito that was published on the front page of *Pravda* on November 16, stated: "The lawful *national* rights of the Palestinian Refugees must be implemented as part of a peace settlement."[39] Five days later Canadian Foreign Minister Mitchell Sharp commented in a press conference after conferring with Soviet leaders that the USSR would give the Palestinians strong support.[40] Arafat himself was in Moscow from November 19 to 26 for discussions about the future of the Palestinians.[41] This burst of Soviet activity on behalf of the Palestinians came just before the Arab summit conference in Algiers called by Sadat to coordinate Arab strategy, and helped enhance the stature of the PLO at the conference, which recognized the PLO as the "sole legitimate representative" of the Palestinian people. In thus giving stronger backing to the Palestinians than ever before, it appeared as if the Soviet goal—in addition to countering the Egyptian-American rapprochement—was to establish a Palestinian state on the West Bank of the Jordan River and in the Gaza Strip. These areas were occupied by Israel since the June 1967 war; earlier they had been administered by Jordan (the West Bank) and Egypt (the Gaza Strip) after the two Arab states had occupied the territories during the 1948-49 Arab-Israeli war (instead of allowing them to be the basis of a Palestinian Arab state, as the UN resolution of November 1947 had decreed). It would appear that the Russians worked for the establishment of a Palestinian state (they had to convince many Palestinians as well as the Western powers) not only to defuse the Arab-Israeli conflict (if this was their aim at all) but also to secure another area in the Middle East where they could exercise influence, along with South Yemen, Iraq, Syria, and, to a lesser degree, Egypt, where their influence was declining. It may have also been Soviet reasoning that the emplacement of a pro-Soviet regime in the midst of such pro-Western states as Israel, Jordan, and Lebanon would serve to weaken further the position of the United States in the region, while strengthening that of the USSR.

In addition to consolidating their relations with the Palestinians, the Soviet leaders sought to offset the growing Egyptian-American rapprochement by emphasizing the direct U.S. military threat against the Arabs and continued American support of Israel, while at the same time urging the Arabs to maintain their "anti-imperialist" unity. Thus, in greeting the Arab summit conference that took place in late November, the Soviet leadership stated:

> At the present time the matter of regulating the Near East conflict is entering a practical and very crucial stage. Now, as never before, the fate of peace in the Near East is largely dependent on the coordinated policy of the Arab states and on the further strengthening of their solidarity and unity of action with other peace-loving forces.[42]

Similarly, *Pravda* on December 4 displayed satisfaction with the results of the Arab summit, although the fact that neither Libya nor Iraq attended the meeting detracted from the unity the Soviet leaders were seeking:

> The conference in Algiers reflected the increased degree of unity which was tempered and passed a rigorous test during the October 1973 war. This unity is founded on anti-imperialism and serves the just cause for which the Arab countries' peoples are fighting. . . .
>
> The Soviet Union's position received a high evaluation at the conference in Algiers. The participants in the conference expressed profound satisfaction with the political and military assistance that the Soviet Union and the other socialist states have rendered the Arab countries and expressed the desire to develop Arab-Soviet cooperation.[43]

While the Russians were being praised for their support at the Algiers conference, the Egyptians were going ahead with their plan announced on December 9 to give the American Bechtel Company the contract to build the Suez to Mediterranean oil pipeline that had long been under discussion. The investment was to be jointly financed by Kuwait and Saudi Arabia—the very nations that had placed the embargo on oil to the United States.[44] Three days later *Pravda* warned the Arabs that American naval maneuvers in the Indian Ocean were aimed against them:

> The appearance of ships of the US Seventh Fleet off the southern coast of the Arabian Peninsula arouses grave anxiety in a number of Asian countries located in immediate proximity to the Indian Ocean. According to reports from the France-Presse wire services, Israeli troops "based on some islands in the Red Sea" i.e. approximately in the same locality—are also on the move. . . .
>
> At a time when a tense situation persists in the Near East, the appearance of the Seventh Fleet off the coasts of the Arab states looks like a maneuver having nothing to do with the creation of conditions conducive to a peaceful settlement in the Near East. . . . The Seventh Fleet . . . as is known, took a most active part in the aggressive war against the Vietnamese people.[45]

The Soviet Union continued to urge Arab unity as the first Arab-Israeli peace conference in 24 years opened in Geneva on December 22. The conference, however, was boycotted by the Syrians, who claimed that Israel's interests would be served by the conference and that the United States and Israel were engaged in "maneuvers that would lead us into an endless wilderness."[46] The fact that the USSR had strongly supported the conference—to insure Soviet participation in any peace settlement—made the Syrian remarks take on an anti-Soviet as well as an anti-American character. The USSR may also not have been made too happy by Syria's decision at this time to allow the opening of an American-manned Interest Section in Damascus—a step on the road to restoring full diplomatic relations. Nonetheless, despite the lack of Arab unity evidenced by the Syrian boycott, the Soviet Union championed the cause of the Arab states and the Palestinian Arabs at the conference and demanded the total withdrawal of Israeli troops to the 1967 prewar boundaries. Representing the Soviet Union was Foreign Minister Andrei Gromyko, whose speech set forth a number of points that the Soviet leadership claimed were basic to an Arab-Israeli peace settlement. Gromyko's primary emphasis was on the need for a complete and total Israeli withdrawal from all Arab territory it occupied in the June 1967 war.[47] He also called for the inviolability of the borders of the states in the region and spoke of the necessity to ensure respect for and recognition of the sovereignty, territorial integrity, and political independence of all states in the Middle East. Interestingly enough, he called Israel's borders, as of June 4, 1967, the legitimate borders of that nation, thus apparently confirming once and for all the Soviet leadership's recognition of these borders rather than the November 1947 borders set down by the UN partition decision, which were still published in official Soviet maps of the Middle East. In another apparent gesture to Israel (and perhaps to its supporters in the United States), the Soviet foreign minister stated that "the Soviet Union has no hostility toward the state of Israel as such"—only to its policy of annexing conquered Arab territory. Gromyko also held out hope for an improvement of Soviet-Israeli relations when Israel "confirmed by its deeds its readiness for an honest and mutually acceptable settlement." (Gromyko was to raise this issue again in a private meeting with Israeli Foreign Minister Abba Eban after the start of the Geneva conference, in which the Soviet foreign minister reportedly stated that the USSR "does not regret" its role as a catalyst in the creation of Israel and promised Soviet aid against anyone acting against "the existence and sovereignty of the State of Israel."[48]

In still another apparent gesture to Israel, Gromyko spoke of the need for the parties to the conflict themselves to work out a peace settlement (direct negotiations had long been an Israeli demand). He also raised the possibility of establishing demilitarized zones on the basis of reciprocity, and the temporary stationing of international personnel in certain areas—if such an arrangement were to be decided "on a basis mutually acceptable to the parties concerned."

Gromyko did not stress the Palestinian issue in his presentation; this was to be one of the main differences between his December 1973 peace proposal and subsequent Soviet peace pronouncements, particularly those of 1976 and 1977. He did emphasize, however, the need for ensuring "justice" with respect to the Arab people of Palestine and for safeguarding their "legitimate rights" (although he did not stipulate what those rights were). He also stated the necessity for the participation of representatives of the Arab people of Palestine in solving the Palestinian problem.

All in all, Gromyko's presentation at the Geneva peace conference may be considered as fitting into a peace plan that called essentially for a return to the status quo ante of June 4, 1967, with mutual pledges not to resort to war. As far as Israel's claims to anything more than this from the Arabs, Gromyko stated:

> Israel's Arab neighbors have declared their readiness to reach agreement on a settlement on the basis of the well-known Security Council Resolutions which clearly express the principle that all states involved in the conflict have the right to exist.

This was hardly the reassurance that Israeli leaders were looking for (they wanted a peace settlement with open borders, and trade and diplomatic relations), although it appeared to be all the USSR was willing to propose at the time.

The Soviet Union, as cosponsor of the Geneva conference, was able to use its position to temporarily move into the center of Middle Eastern diplomacy— but this was to be its last chance to do so for almost a year and a half, since the Geneva conference soon adjourned and was not to be reconvened. After the conference ended, there were meetings of the Arab oil-producing countries and the Persian Gulf oil-producing countries, which took measures that the Russians greeted with satisfaction. The Persian Gulf oil-producing states more than doubled the "posted price" per barrel of crude oil—in effect, therefore, quadrupling the price they charged for it. This move was certain to aggravate the balance-of-payments problems of the West European states, thus further hampering both Common Market and NATO unity, as it appeared that the Western nations might have to engage in a trade war to pay for their oil imports.[49] Indeed, France broke Common Market unity on January 19, 1974 by its unilateral decision to float the franc, to help meet the crisis caused by the rise in oil prices.[50] The Russians also profited from the fact that, as a net exporter of oil, their hard-currency income would rise with the market price of oil they sold to the West European nations and Japan. The decision of the Arab oil producers to maintain their oil embargo against the United States was also warmly welcomed, although the *Izvestia* article discussing these developments urged the Arabs to go one step farther and nationalize the holdings of the Western oil companies, much as Iraq had done.[51]

The Soviet media continued their twin themes of the American threat to the Arab states and continued American support for Israel throughout the first part of January 1974. Israeli Defense Minister Moshe Dayan's visit to the United States in early January was described as a quest for more American arms.[52] The Soviet media also played up U.S. Defense Secretary James Schlesinger's warning to the Arabs on January 7 that they risked the use of force against them if they carried their oil embargo too far.[53] Nonetheless, *Pravda* complained on January 6 of "attempts to sow discord between the Arab states and their true friends" while also taking the opportunity to blast Libya for "leaking oil" to the United States.

The Soviet leaders, however, were apparently caught by surprise by the Kissinger-arranged Israeli-Egyptian disengagement agreement on January 18, and the new Egyptian foreign minister, Ismail Fahmy, who had clashed with the Russians in the past, had to make a hurried visit to Moscow immediately thereafter to explain the Egyptian position. The Russians put into *Pravda*'s description of the talks the assertion:

> It was stressed that an important factor in the struggle for a just settlement in the Near East is the close coordination of the actions of the Soviet Union and Egypt at all stages of this struggle including the work of the Near East Peace Conference and all the working groups which come of it.[54]

The Russians probably put this assertion in the description because Soviet-Egyptian coordination was anything but close. Meanwhile, the Russians were also warning the Arabs about U.S., West European, and Japanese plans to increase their investments in Arab countries, and about the "oil for technology" deals a number of West European states and Japan were in the process of signing with Arab states in an effort to assure themselves of a secure oil supply. As *Pravda* stated on January 20:

> As the *Wall Street Journal* frankly writes, "a theory has even cropped up among entrepreneurs which reasons that economic and political changes will come with the industrialization of Arab countries." In other words, economic considerations are interwoven with the hope that the influence of the dollar will lead to an "erosion" of Arab unity and a consolidation of the position of the Western powers clientele in the Near East.[55]

The fact that following the disengagement agreement Sadat began to urge the lifting of the embargo was a further blow to the Russians. *Pravda*, in a feature article by "Commentator" on January 30, warned against the disengagement agreement leading to only a partial settlement of the Near East conflict:

> It should be emphasized that the agreement on troop disengagement can be a positive step only if it is followed by other fundamental measures aimed at ensuring the withdrawal of Israeli troops from all occupied Arab territories and guaranteeing the legitimate rights of the Arab people of Palestine. Without the solution of these problems, which are cardinal to a Near East settlement, a lasting peace cannot be achieved, and the possibility of new military outbreaks, fraught with serious international convulsions, cannot be ruled out. *It can be said that the positive significance of the concluded agreement de-*

pends to a decisive extent on its linkage with other fundamental questions of a settlement. . . .

The question of the return of Syrian territory is just as acute as the question of the return of all other Arab territories occupied by Israel. The problem of troop disengagement as a first step in resolving the question of the return of these territories directly affects Syria as well. This is especially important in view of the fact that the ruling circles of *Israel and imperialist reaction persistently follow a line aimed at weakening the unity of the Arab countries.*[56] [emphasis added]

Yet this appeared to be the direction in which Middle Eastern events were moving. Even the decision by the United States to host a conference of energy-consuming nations did not serve to arrest the slow splintering of the facade of Arab unity. While the Russians hailed the decision of the mid-February Arab mini-summit meeting not to lift the embargo, an article in *New Times* about the Arab meeting clearly recognized the dilemma:

In this intricate situation, the Arab press believes joint Arab action and co-ordinated Arab policies are of the utmost importance. All the more so since the Israeli militarists, who still count on being able to avoid withdrawing from occupied Arab territories, are trying to set the Arab countries at loggerheads with one other. . . . Further, the fomenting of Arab differences has a definite place in the designs of the Western oil monopolies, who are out to use the present energy crisis to preserve and even multiply the profits derived from Middle East oil.[57]

By this time, however, it appeared to be only a matter of time until the embargo was lifted, since now Sheikh Yamani as well as Sadat spoke openly about lifting it. In this atmosphere Kissinger made yet another journey to the Middle East at the end of February, this time shuttling back and forth between Damascus and Jerusalem and procuring from the Syrian leaders the list of Israeli prisoners of war the Israelis had demanded as a precondition for talks with Syria. At this point it appeared that once again Kissinger would be able to pull off another diplomatic coup. This, apparently, was too much for the Russians. Having seen the United States replace the USSR as the leading foreign influence in Egypt—however temporarily—the Russian leaders had no desire to see the process repeat itself in Syria. Consequently, Gromyko, who had just paid a surprise visit to Cairo (and the joint communique that followed his visit revealed just how far the Soviet position in Egypt had deteriorated[58]), followed Kissinger to Damascus. The Soviet-Syrian communique issued upon Gromyko's departure was far more bellicose than the Soviet-Egyptian communique and demanded a fixed timetable for Israeli withdrawal from all occupied territory, threatening a "new eruption" of war that would bring about "a threat to peace and security in the Middle East and throughout the world" if Arab demands were not met.[59] Strengthened by new shipments of Soviet arms, and encouraged by Soviet support, the Syrian regime of Hafiz Assad, less willing (or able) to make peace with Israel than Egypt, upon Gromyko's departure began a war of attrition against Israeli positions in the Golan Heights.

Apparently, the Soviet and Syrian leaders hoped that by heating up the conflict in the Golan Heights (the war of attrition included artillery, tank, and air battles), they would be able to prevent the oil-rich states from lifting the oil embargo against the United States. While Syria stepped up its level of fighting, the Soviet Union urged the Arab states in very strong terms to maintain their oil embargo. Thus, on March 12 Radio Moscow broadcast:

> If today some Arab leaders are ready to surrender in the face of American pressure and lift the ban on oil before the demands [for a total Israeli withdrawal] are fulfilled, they are challenging the whole Arab world and the progressive forces of the entire world which insist on the continued use of the oil weapon.[60]

While urging continuation of the oil weapon, the Soviet media also belittled Kissinger's mediation efforts, with *Pravda* on March 17 calling them "a mountain that gave birth to a mouse." Nonetheless, despite Syria's war of attrition and the Soviet campaign to maintain the oil embargo, Kissinger's diplomatic efforts were successful. On March 19 the oil embargo against the United States was lifted by the major oil-producing Arab states, although as a sop to the Syrians, Algeria stated that it would reexamine its embargo policy on June 1. In any case, Arab unity on the oil embargo was clearly broken as Libya and Syria refused to go along with the majority decision to lift the embargo.

The termination of the oil embargo can be considered a significant defeat for Soviet diplomacy in the Middle East. The Soviet leadership had come out strongly for the maintenance of the oil embargo as a means of keeping the Arab world unified against the United States, and the USSR had greatly profited from the disarray in both NATO and the EEC caused by the embargo.[61] Egypt's decision to support an end to the embargo—despite all the aid the USSR had given her before and during the October war—was yet another indication of the sharp diminution of Soviet influence in Egypt and the corresponding rise in American influence. Consequently, following the termination of the oil embargo, the Soviet leadership once again reconsidered its Middle Eastern policies in an effort to halt the pro-American trend that was emerging in the region.

THE ISRAELI-SYRIAN DISENGAGEMENT AGREEMENT

The Soviet response to the termination of the oil embargo was threefold. In the first place, the Soviet leadership launched a public attack on Sadat in an effort to isolate him both inside Egypt and from other Arab leaders. Second, the USSR stepped up support to both Syria and Iraq, lest the two clients of the Soviet Union be attracted to the Egyptian-Saudi Arabian alignment, which, backed by the United States, held out the promise of both economic and technological assistance. Finally, the USSR moved to improve relations with Libya, its erstwhile Middle Eastern enemy, which moved closer to the Soviet Union in response to the Egyptian-American rapprochement. In pursuing these policies, however, the Soviet leadership was careful to maintain contact with the United States while Kissinger was working for a Syrian-Israeli troop disengagement. In pursuing this policy, the Russians sought both to maintain the semblance of detente and also to avoid the repetition of their earlier experience when Kissinger had worked out an Egyptian-Israeli disengagement without the participation of the Soviet Union.

Soviet-Egyptian relations began to deteriorate very rapidly following the end of the oil embargo. Just as in 1971, when Sadat had refused to support Soviet policy in the Sudan, here again he had strongly opposed a major Soviet Middle Eastern policy, despite all the economic and military aid that the Soviet Union had given Egypt. The USSR retaliated against Sadat for his opposition on the embargo issue by branding him a traitor to Nasser's heritage—an obvious attempt to undermine Sadat's position among the Egyptian public and among Egyptian elites who still revered Nasser's memory.[62] At the same time the Soviet leaders voiced a great deal of concern as to the erosion of their position in Egypt. The editor-in-chief of *New Times*, Pavel Naumov, in describing his visit to Egypt in late March, stated: "What is in question is the country's [Egypt's] future."[63]

Sadat, however, was not cowed by the Soviet attacks and replied in kind by charging the Soviet ambassador, Vladimir Vinogradov, with lying to him on the first day of the war about Syria's desire for an immediate cease-fire.[64] He followed up this charge in a major speech on April 3 in which he stated that he had expelled the Russians in July 1972 because they had defaulted on promised arms deliveries to Egypt.[65] Then, on April 18, Soviet-Egyptian relations hit a new low when Sadat announced his decision to cease relying exclusively on the Soviet Union for arms.[66] The Egyptian leader, in a New York *Times* interview three days later, which was widely reprinted in the Egyptian press, asked the United States to supply Egypt with arms because the USSR had used the supply of weapons and ammunition as an "instrument of policy leverage to influence Egyptian actions."[67] While the United States was not yet willing to commit itself to arms sales to Egypt, U.S. officials had discussed loans of up to $250 million as a means of improving Egyptian-American relations.[68] In pursuing this policy of improving relations with the United States, Sadat was attempting to "drive a wedge" between the United States and Israel, while at the same time aiding the Egyptian economy. For his part, Kissinger, in offering Egypt economic aid, was trying to raise the threshold of any Egyptian decision to support Syria in its war of attrition against Israel.[69] While each side was approaching the improvement in relations from a different perspective and with different goals in mind, to many outside observers (including the Russians) it appeared by the end of April that the Egyptian-American rapprochement was turning into an alignment. Perhaps in an effort to prevent this new alignment from solidifying, Brezhnev sent Sadat what the Egyptian leader termed a "conciliatory note" on April 24, an action that Sadat reciprocated two days later.[70]

Meanwhile, despite two Palestinian terrorist attacks against Israeli settlements at Kiryat Shemona (April 12) and Maalot (May 15), it appeared by the latter part of May that the Israeli-Syrian disengagement negotiations, mediated by Kissinger, might well meet with success. Consequently, the Soviet leadership took a more positive posture toward Egypt, whose prestige in the Arab world was sure to rise if the Syrians followed the Egyptian lead in working out a disengagement settlement. On May 19, with the third anniversary of the Soviet-Egyptian treaty approaching, Brezhnev sent a new ambassador to Egypt bearing a friendly message for Sadat.[71] Two days later Arab diplomats announced that the Soviet Union had resumed arms shipments to Egypt.[72] Soviet press comment on the treaty's anniversary was far more limited than on the past two anniversaries, however, and a *New Times* article commemorating the occasion implicitly acknowledged Soviet concern over the deepening American involvement in Egypt:

> The Soviet-Egyptian Treaty of Friendship and Cooperation is subjected to unceasing attacks by forces that would undermine Soviet-Egyptian friendship and thereby deprive the Arabs of support in their just struggle.[73]

While welcoming the limited rapprochement that had occurred with the USSR by the end of May, Sadat was busy seeking other sources of military and economic assistance. In addition to improving relations with the United States, Egypt hosted a meeting of Arab defense and foreign ministers on May 20 in which a decision was taken to establish a cooperative Arab arms industry, with Egypt the site of the initial projects. Significantly, Iraq, the USSR's closest ally in the Arab world, boycotted the conference; Libya, whose premier had just visited the Soviet Union, sent only a low-level delegation.[74] In addition to planning this alternate source of weaponry, in case the USSR should again cut off or limit arms deliveries, or if the desired weapons could not be purchased in the United States or Western Europe, Sadat also acquired an additional source of developmental capital in May when Iran signed a $750 million loan agreement with Egypt.[75] While the arms industry would take years to develop, and the Iranian loan, while highly welcome, could meet only a fraction of Egypt's staggering economic needs, these two actions nonetheless gave Sadat bargaining room in his relations with both the Soviet Union and the United States. By the end of May, the Soviet leaders found Sadat less dependent than before the October war on Soviet military and economic aid.

While Sadat's decision to help end the Arab oil embargo against the United States led to a sharp deterioration in Soviet-Egyptian relations, Libyan leader Mu'ammar Kaddafi, who like the Russians opposed an end to the oil embargo, drew closer to the USSR. In many ways Libya's turn to the Soviet Union resembled that of Iraq in 1972. Isolated regionally, Kaddafi was on poor terms not only with Sadat, who had declined Libya's merger offer and allied with King Faisal, one of Kaddafi's chief Arab enemies but also with Sudanese Premier Jaafar Nimeri, who accused Kaddafi of a number of subversive plots against his regime.[76] To make matters worse for Kaddafi, even his relations with the leaders of fellow Arab radical Algeria were severely strained. Isolated in North Africa as well as throughout most of the Arab world, and angry at Egypt's move toward the United States, Libya turned to the Soviet Union for support, despite the fact that Kaddafi had earlier attacked the USSR in the strongest terms as an "imperialist power." The rapprochement began on April 7 with a two-hour meeting in Paris between Libya's new premier, Abdul Jalloud (Kaddafi had given up the premiership while retaining overall direction of Libya's foreign and domestic policies), and Soviet President Nikolai Podgorny when the two men were in the French capital to attend French President Georges Pompidou's funeral.[77] *New Times* correspondent Aleksei Zlatorunsky helped set the tone for an improvement in Soviet-Libyan relations in early May with a generally sympathetic article describing Libya's development since her 1969 revolution. The article praised Libya's "clear-cut anti-imperialist stand" and her "vigorous support for the African forces of National Liberation," although Zlatorunsky also took the Libyan leadership to task for "rash actions" in behalf of Arab unity.[78] Libya's past hostility toward the Soviet Union was not totally overlooked either, as Zlatorunsky pointedly stated:

> The fact also remains that Libya's anti-imperialist, and on the whole progressive position has been weakened by occasional anti-communist sallies on the part of certain Libyan leaders and press organs.[79]

In sum, however, the article gave a positive view of Libyan development, and the Soviet correspondent concluded his article by offering Libya Soviet support:

> We wish the Libyan people success on the hard road of struggle to strengthen national independence and progress. In this struggle they can rely on the support of the socialist states, the natural allies of all national-democratic forces.[80]

It appears as if the Libyan leaders were eager to take up the Soviet offer of support, because soon after the *New Times* article appeared, Libyan Premier Jalloud arrived in Moscow seeking Soviet aid. In welcoming the Libyan leader at a dinner given in his honor, Soviet Premier Kosygin emphasized the Soviet Union's willingness to forget the past differences between the two countries in the interest of working together in the future:

> If we were to compare that which unites Libya and the Soviet Union to those things on which our views do not coincide, there would be no doubt that the preponderance would fall on the side of that which unites us. This means, above all, the identity or closeness of our position in the struggle against imperialism and colonialism, for the reconstruction of international relations on a just, democratic basis and for the affirmation of and respect for the right of peoples to independent development, including sovereignty over their own natural resources and the implementation of progressive social and economic transformation. . . . As far as differences in views are concerned, evidently they are largely in the field of ideology. But we have never wanted to impose our ideology on others.[81]

Kosygin went on to emphasize Soviet support of the Arab cause and opposition to U.S. diplomatic efforts in the Middle East:

> The Soviet Union condemns the policy of aggression that Israel is pursuing, with the support of outside imperialist forces, and it believes that there can be no lasting and just peace in the Near East without the withdrawal of Israeli troops from all Arab territory occupied in 1967 and later and without guaranteeing the legitimate national rights of the Arab people of Palestine. Any agreements on troop disengagement must be regarded as preliminary steps on the road to an overall settlement and must be followed by other measures to implement the well-known UN Security Council resolutions.
>
> We emphasize this aspect of the matter because the plans of the aggressor and its protectors to substitute some sort of half measures that create only a semblance of detente in the Near East for an all-encompassing Near East settlement have come to light recently.[82]

In concluding his discussion of Soviet policy in the Middle East, Kosygin stated that he hoped the development of Soviet-Libyan relations would serve the interest of Arab solidarity in their struggle against Israel "on an anti-Imperialist basis."[83]

In his speech in reply, Abdul Jalloud, in a manner reminiscent of Iraqi Vice-President Saddam Hussein's speech of February 1972, emphasized Libya's isolation and need for Soviet support:

> We would like to emphasize, in all sincerity, that we are now under pressure from imperialist and reactionary forces. We would like all

forces of progress and truly revolutionary forces to come out against this situation, under cover of which the rights and positions that the progressive forces in our region have won as a result of long struggle are being infringed and nullified.[84]

While the Libyan delegation had come to Moscow primarily for political and military support, the Soviet leaders saw in the visit not only a useful opportunity to counter Sadat's move toward the United States but also a means of strengthening the Soviet economy. In his speech Kosygin also called for an agreement to arrange Soviet-Libyan trade on a long-term basis, and the final communique issued at the conclusion of Jalloud's visit announced the establishment of a Soviet-Libyan intergovernmental commission for this purpose.[85] In addition, the two sides pledged to develop "the highest possible mutually advantageous trade turnover."[86] In calling for a sharp increase in trade, the Soviet leaders may have hoped to gain access to Libya's large hard-currency reserves—a development that would enable the Soviet Union to step up its purchases on Western markets.[87] In addition, the Russians may have hoped to exchange Soviet technology and equipment for Libyan oil, which could be resold on Western markets or used to fulfill the USSR's own increasing domestic oil needs.[88]

Despite the general cordiality of Jalloud's visit, differences remained, and the final communique reported the talks as having taken place "in a spirit of frankness and mutual understanding."[89] Indeed, Soviet-Libyan relations had markedly improved over the prewar period, when mutual hostility was their primary characteristic. Soviet-Libyan cooperation on Middle Eastern affairs had reached the point by May that Libyan-financed newspapers in Beirut printed Soviet attacks on Sadat's policies.[90]

While Soviet-Libyan cooperation had now become a factor in Middle Eastern politics, the Soviet leadership did not neglect its ties with Iraq, which had been its leading Middle Eastern partner since 1972. Although weakened by war with the Kurds and continual confrontation with Iran, Iraq provided a useful center for anti-Western and anti-Egyptian propaganda.[91] The most pressing issue for the Iraqi leaders at this time was their confrontation with the Kurds. The Soviet leadership, faced by the defection of Egypt, now apparently pledged Soviet military support for a massive Iraqi drive against the Kurds—despite the fact that such a policy might trigger a war between Iraq and Iran—in return for continued Iraqi support of Soviet positions on the larger Middle Eastern issues. A trip to Moscow by Iraqi Vice-President Saddam Hussein at the end of February was used by the Soviet leadership to demonstrate Arab cooperation with the USSR, and the communique issued at the end of his visit (and published on *Pravda*'s front page) stated:

The two sides believe that the Arab states' solidarity on an anti-imperialist basis and the consolidation of their cooperation with the Soviet Union and other countries of the socialist commonwealth is a major condition for the success of the Arab peoples' struggle against Israeli aggression and for the strengthening of their national independence and economic and social progress.[92]

On March 14, the date on which the Iraqi government's "autonomy" plan for the Kurds was due to come into effect, *Pravda* came out in full support of the Iraqi government. In describing the autonomy agreement and Kurdish leader Mustafa Barzani's opposition to it, *Pravda* columnist Pavel Demchenko stated:

The obstacles to a resolution of the Kurdish question still have not been overcome. Foreign agents are still interfering in Kurdish affairs. The activity of the rightist elements which have penetrated the Kurdish Democratic Party as a result of its class heterogeneity and which are trying to arouse separatist sentiments, is becoming more evident.[93]

As the Kurdish opposition mounted, the Iraqi leaders decided to mount a major offensive against the Kurds to try to end the Kurdish separatist threat (and the danger to the Kirkuk oil fields claimed by the Kurds) once and for all. Possibly to inspect Iraqi preparations for this offensive, Soviet Defense Minister Grechko paid a visit to Iraq between March 23 and 25 for what *Pravda* reported as "a detailed discussion of questions relating to the present state and future development of Soviet-Iraqi cooperation in the military and other spheres."[94]

As the Iraqi government began to mount its offensive against the Kurds in April, *Pravda* took a harder line than ever before against them, while linking the Kurdish opposition to "imperialist forces":

According to foreign press reports, military operations have begun between the Kurds and government troops in the northern regions of Iraq. The Kurdish leaders have refused to acknowledge the law of autonomy of the Kurds, issued by the Iraqi government in March of this year, although it guarantees the 2,000,000 Kurds in Iraq democratic national and social rights within the framework of the Iraqi Republic.

Reports indicate that in making this decision, the Kurdish leaders were not free from interference by imperialist and other reactionary forces who are trying to sow discord between the Arab and Kurdish populations of Iraq and weaken the progressive regime in that country. For these purposes they are supplying the Kurdish extremists with weapons and ammunition and considerable financial support. The foreign "benefactors" are inciting those elements among the Kurdish leadership that oppose progressive changes in Iraq.[95]

Echoing a similar theme, a *New Times* article on Iraq in the middle of May took the opportunity to tie the Kurdish rebellion to the growing American activity in the Middle East:

> While exerting pressure on Egypt, Syria and South Yemen, certain quarters in Washington and the Arab reactionaries are at the same time searching for allies inside the progressive Middle East countries. In Iraq they have pinned their hopes on the right-wing elements among the Kurds.[96]

Thus, the Iraqi government had embarked on a full-scale offensive against the Kurds, supported by the USSR, although the offensive raised the possibility of war between Iraq and Iran—an eventuality clearly not desired by the Soviet leadership.[97]

While the Soviet leaders worked to improve relations with Libya and solidify their ties with Iraq, the central Soviet concern during the postembargo period was their relations with Syria. The Soviet leaders were clearly concerned that Syria might follow Egypt's example and move toward the West in return for economic and technical aid. The Syrian government's decision on March 13 to lift restrictions on the movement of private capital in and out of Syria and to permit the Syrian private sector to sign loan agreements with foreign investors must have added to the Soviet concern.[98] By supporting Syria in its war of attrition against Israel, the Soviet leaders hoped to avert a Syrian turn to the West while at the same time isolating Sadat as the only Arab leader to have reached an agreement with Israel. In addition, the Soviet leadership may have entertained the hope that should fighting intensify sufficiently, the Arab oil-producing states might be forced by Arab public opinion to reimpose the oil embargo, and Sadat himself might be forced to return to war.[99] Yet in pursuing their policy of encouraging Syrian belligerence, the Soviet leaders had to toe a very narrow diplomatic line. A new summit meeting with the United States was on the horizon, and important strategic arms limitation issues between the two superpowers were under active consideration. In addition, the Soviet Union's relations with China had taken another turn for the worse as the Chinese government refused to return the crew of a Soviet helicopter that had crashed on Chinese territory.[100] Consequently, the Soviet leaders adopted a policy of support for Syrian belligerency while at the same time maintaining close contact with Kissinger's mediation efforts. This dual policy would underscore Soviet support for the Arab cause while also enabling the Soviet leadership to claim a share of the credit should Kissinger succeed in persuading the Syrians and Israelis to accept a disengagement agreement. In addition, a series of meetings between Kissinger and top Soviet leaders would help create a positive atmosphere for the convening of a summit conference between Nixon and Brezhnev.

The first high-level Soviet-American meeting after the lifting of the oil embargo came on March 29, when Kissinger journeyed to Moscow for talks with the Soviet leadership. While strategic arms issues were the main topic of consideration—and Kissinger later reported that no "conceptual breakthroughs" had been reached—the two superpowers also discussed the Middle Eastern situation. The final communique, however, stated only that the "two sides would make efforts to promote the solution of the key questions of Near East settlement." [101] Interestingly enough, while Western press reports of Kissinger's talks in Moscow portrayed them as being relatively unsuccessful, the Soviet media challenged this interpretation. Thus, on March 30, *Izvestia* commented:

> The mood and content of the talks did not at all correspond to the pessimistic accompaniment that certain Western media provided for H. Kissinger's mission. [102]

While making this gesture toward Soviet-American relations, the Soviet leaders went out of their way to emphasize their support for Syrian President Hafiz Assad during his visit to Moscow in mid-April. Assad was met at the Moscow airport by all three of the primary Soviet leaders (Brezhnev, Kosygin, and Podgorny), and the Syrian president's visit received major front-page coverage in both *Pravda* and *Izvestia*. In his dinner speech welcoming Assad, Brezhnev pointedly attacked Kissinger's diplomatic efforts in the Middle East:

> Against the background of reduced tensions, the aggressors and their protectors may once again attempt to evade a fundamental all-inclusive solution to the [Middle East] problem. It is by no means happenstance that recently "ersatz plans" as I would call them for a Near East settlement have been launched. [103]

The Soviet leader did, however, call for reliable guarantees for the security of all countries in the Middle East—something that the Syrians, who were not yet ready to recognize Israel's legitimacy, may not have appreciated. In any case, following five days of talks, which the final communique described as taking place in an atmosphere "of frankness and mutual understanding," the Soviet leadership agreed to "further strengthen" Syria's defense capacity and stated once again that Syria had a "lawful inalienable right" to use "all effective means to free its occupied lands." And, to underline the Soviet desire to play a role in the peace talks, the joint communique stated:

> The Syrian side reemphasized the importance of the Soviet Union's participation in all stages and in all areas of a settlement aimed at establishing a just and lasting peace in the Near East. [104]

Soviet attention switched back to the United States at the end of April, when Gromyko met with Kissinger in Geneva as the American secretary of state was en route to the Middle East for further negotiations with Syria and Israel. While the main topic of the talks was Nixon's forthcoming visit to Moscow, for which no date had been set, *Pravda* also reported that the two leaders

> exchanged opinions concerning the current situation in the talks on the Near East settlement and concerning the next stage of these talks. The two sides agreed to exert their influence in favor of a positive outcome of the talks and to maintain close contact with each other while striving to coordinate their actions in the interests of a peaceful settlement in the region.[105]

Kissinger, however, gave a far less optimistic view of the talks, stating only that in regard to his forthcoming mediation efforts, "I expect we'll have Soviet understanding, and I hope cooperation."[106]

Meanwhile, however, opposition to the proposed Nixon trip to Moscow was growing in the United States. Arguing that the United States had been cheated in its wheat deal with the Soviet Union, that the United States had been placed at a disadvantage by the SALT 1 agreement, and that the Soviet Union had proven an unworthy partner because of her aid to the Arabs during the October war and her support of the oil embargo, a growing number of prominent Americans opposed a new summit. *Pravda*'s political commentator Yuri Zhukov, in acknowledging this opposition, claimed it was organized by a "dirty coalition of reactionary forces made up of imperialist circles, the American military-industrial complex, West German revanchists, NATO generals, and Zionists and adventurers of every stripe."[107] At the same time, Zhukov hailed the forces in the world working for detente, lavishing particular praise on West German Chancellor Willy Brandt, and stating that Kissinger's meetings with Brezhnev and Gromyko "inspired confidence that the forthcoming Soviet-American summit talks will be a new step forward in making the process of detente irreversible."[108]

Gromyko met Kissinger yet another time on May 7, as the Soviet leadership continued to demonstrate its desire to remain closely involved with the disengagement talks while also fostering detente. For his part, Kissinger humored the Soviet desire, evidently hoping that the frequent meetings would serve to limit Soviet obstructionism of a peaceful settlement. Only two days later, however, Soviet concern about detente must have been sharply reinforced when West German Chancellor Brandt was forced to resign over a spy scandal involving East Germany. At this point, with both Pompidou and Brandt having departed from the European political scene, and with a Watergate-weakened Nixon under increasing attack by the opponents of detente in the United States, Brezhnev may have seen the whole structure of his detente policy toward the West in danger of collapse. The Soviet leader may have decided that overt obstructionism to a Syrian-Israeli disengagement agreement on American terms was becoming too great a threat to Soviet-American relations. This feeling may have been rein-

forced by the fact that despite two bloody Palestinian terrorist attacks on Israeli settlements, the latter killing 24 Israeli schoolchildren at Maalot on May 15,
Kissinger had nonetheless managed to work out the outlines of an agreement by
the latter part of May. Consequently, as the Syrians and Israelis were in the process of ironing out the last details of their agreement on May 29, Gromyko made
yet another visit to Damascus, hoping to salvage some prestige for the USSR
from the American-mediated agreement. Gromyko received from the Syrian government an acknowledgment of the USSR's right to participate in all stages of a
peace settlement, much as Assad had given the Russians during his April visit to
Moscow.[109] In addition, perhaps as an additional sop to the Soviet leadership—
which in reality had played little role in the negotiations and which could well
have been afraid that Syria, tempted by promises of American aid, might follow
Egypt into the American camp—the joint communique issued upon the conclusion of Gromyko's visit stated:

> The Soviet Union and the Syrian Arab Republic affirm the durabil-
> ity of the relations that have been established between them and the
> durability of the friendship between the peoples of the two coun-
> tries, and they declare that *they will let no one disturb these rela-
> tions and this friendship.*[110] [emphasis added]

Nonetheless, it is clear that the Soviet leaders were worried about just such
an eventuality. *New Times* correspondent Alexander Ignatov, in describing the
situation in Syria following the disengagement agreement, used much the same
terms Pavel Naumov had used two months before in describing Egypt. The Soviet journalist commented that despite the 1966 Ba'ath revolution, the "internal
struggle in Syria" between those advocating the private sector and a Western
orientation and those advocating promotion of the state sector and stronger ties
with the Soviet Union "is still going on."[111]

In general, Soviet comment on the Syrian-Israeli disengagement agreement,
which returned to Syria all the land it had lost in the 1973 war as well as the city
of Kuneitra lost in 1967, and set up a UN force—renewable semiannually—on the
Golan Heights between the Syrian and Israeli armies, stressed two main points:
that the USSR had played a major role in bringing about the agreement, and that
it was only the first step toward a much more comprehensive settlement. *New
Times* associate editor Dmitry Volsky, in a review of the agreement, also took
the opportunity to warn the Arabs that it was not in their interest to have the
USSR excluded from the peace negotiations:

> Certain quarters continue their efforts to discredit the Soviet Un-
> ion's Middle East policy. There are obviously some who would like
> nothing better than to "squeeze out" the Soviet Union and leave the
> Arab countries to face alone the combined forces of Zionism and
> Imperialism.[112]

The Syrian-Israeli disengagement agreement ended the period of direct military confrontation between Israel and the Arab states dating back to the October war, although Palestinian terrorist attacks continued to plague the Israelis. The threat of renewed warfare, for the time being at least, had receded as both sides began to concentrate on diplomatic preparations for a renewal of the Geneva peace conference. In this atmosphere the United States set the date for Nixon's visit to the USSR—indeed, a Syrian-Israeli disengagement agreement may well have been the price exacted by Kissinger for the visit—and the Soviet leadership could perhaps hope that the momentum toward "irreversible detente," interrupted by the October war, had now been restored. Nevertheless, as a result of the disengagement agreement, American prestige rose sharply in the Arab world, and it appeared to many observers that the United States was in the process of replacing the Soviet Union as the dominant foreign influence among the Arabs, a view that was to be reinforced by Nixon's triumphant tour of the Middle East in mid-June. [113]

SOVIET POLICY UP TO THE VLADIVOSTOK SUMMIT

Before his scheduled visit to the Soviet Union on June 27, U.S. President Richard Nixon set out on a multination tour of the Middle East to reap the political benefits of the disengagement agreement so painfully negotiated by his secretary of state. Kissinger, before the Nixon trip, in an apparent effort to limit Soviet concern over the rising American prestige in the area, had stated in a press conference: "We have no intention of trying to eliminate Soviet influence in the Middle East. We are not even in a position to do so."[114] However, it is doubtful that the Soviet leaders were persuaded by this statement. In their "zero-sum" view of Middle Eastern influence they were quite concerned that the sharp rise in American prestige in the region meant a concomitant drop in Soviet influence. In addition, they might even have considered Kissinger's statement a bit naive—if they really believed it—since they had long been trying to eliminate Western influence from the Middle East. In any case, Nixon received a hero's welcome in Egypt as the man who had forced the Israelis to withdraw from the Suez Canal. And he received a warm welcome in Syria, where American aid in getting Israel to withdraw not only from its gains in the 1973 war but also from the city of Kuneitra, which had been captured in 1967, was highly praised. During Nixon's visit to Damascus, diplomatic relations between Syria and the United States were restored. The Soviet leadership could not have been too happy with Syrian Deputy Premier Muhammad Hazdar's statement on June 20 that Syria was ready for "an open-minded dialogue with any foreign capital that wants to participate in Syria's development."[115]

During his trip Nixon signed a large number of economic and technical agreements with Arab leaders, the most important of which was a pledge of

American assistance in the development of atomic energy in Egypt.[116] Following Nixon's visit American prestige rose to a new high in the Arab world and the Soviet leaders were clearly concerned about this unwelcome trend. Soviet reporting of Nixon's Middle Eastern trip, as might be expected, downplayed its significance. Thus, before Nixon's departure, Dmitry Volsky, after taking the New York *Times* to task for "wishful thinking" in its description of the disengagement agreement as leading to "dramatic shifts in the American position in the Arab world," may have engaged in a bit of wishful thinking himself in stating that the Arab states "are sufficiently mature politically to take sober stock of the lessons of the recent past and the modifications the USA is obliged to introduce into its Middle East policy."[117] Volsky also reminded the Arabs that the United States remained Israel's main supporter as well as a direct military threat to the Arabs itself because of its plans to construct a military base on Diego Garcia, which was termed a "spearhead against the southern fringe of the Arab world."[118] *Pravda*, in describing Nixon's trip on June 16, echoed many of the same concerns:

> Reactionary bourgeois propaganda is now trying in every way possible to minimize the role of the Soviet Union in the Near East settlement. The right wing press maintains that the Soviet Union, so they say, does not have anything to do with this settlement, that U.S. policy allegedly will lead to the "elimination of Soviet influence in the Near East." . . .
>
> At the present time U.S. President Richard Nixon is traveling through the Near East. The United States has supported Israel for a long time, and this has undermined its relations with the Arabs. The Arabs have justifiably seen the United States as an accomplice of the Israeli aggressors. The new international climate makes it possible to change the nature of American-Arab relations, however, some "cold-war" advocates would like to place their own interpretation on the U.S. President's trip and use it in a campaign to undermine Arab-Soviet friendship. Such attempts are being suitably rebuffed by the Arabs themselves.[119]

Despite the deprecatory treatment accorded Nixon's visit to the Middle East, the Soviet media hailed the American president's visit to the Soviet Union at the end of June as proof that detente was working. While the primary Soviet interest in the summit was to achieve progress in the areas of strategic arms limitation and Soviet-American trade, Sino-Soviet and Sino-American relations also could not have been too far from the minds of the Soviet leaders. Just as Nixon was arriving in Moscow, U.S. Senator Henry Jackson, long a foe of the USSR and one of the leading Democratic candidates for president in 1976, was on his way to Peking at the invitation of the Chinese, who had timed his visit to coincide with the Nixon-Brezhnev talks.[120] The Moscow summit's emphasis was on trade and strategic arms, and the presence of Henry Jackson in Peking underlined the triangular relationship among the United States, the Soviet Union, and Communist China. However, the Middle Eastern situation was not overlooked. In their final communique Brezhnev and Nixon stated, in regard to the Middle East:

> Both sides believe that the removal of the danger of war and tension in the Middle East is a task of paramount importance and urgency, and therefore, the only alternative is the achievement, on the basis Security Council Resolution 338 [which ended the October war] of a just and lasting peace settlement, in which should be taken into account the *legitimate interests of all peoples in the Middle East, including the Palestinian people,* and the right to existence of all states in the area.
>
> As co-chairmen of the Geneva Peace Conference on the Middle East, the USSR and USA consider it important that the conference resume its work as soon as possible, *with the question of other participants from the Middle East Area* to be discussed at the conference. Both sides see the main purpose of the Geneva Peace Conference, the achievement of which they will promote in every way, as the establishment of a just and stable peace in the Middle East.
>
> They agreed that the USSR and the USA will continue to remain in close touch with a view to coordinating the efforts of both countries toward a peaceful settlement in the Middle East.[121] [emphasis added]

Soviet propaganda highlighted the final communique's emphasis on the role of the Palestinians in a peace settlement in an effort to reinforce the USSR's relations with the Palestine Liberation Organization, as a counter to Sadat's Westward move and the possibility of a similar move by Syria. Gromyko had met PLO leader Yasir Arafat on a regular basis during the negotiations for the Syrian-Israeli disengagement agreement, and these meetings had been given prominent attention in the Soviet press. Despite their military weakness, the Palestinian guerrilla organizations still enjoyed a great deal of popularity among the more radical Arab states and among large sectors of the Arab public as well. The Soviet leaders, just as after the October war, hoped that by increasing their ties to the Palestinians they would strengthen a major anti-Western force in the Middle East and reap the benefits of guerrilla popularity in the Arab world. For their part, the Palestinian Arabs were now in greater need of Soviet aid than ever before because the Israeli disengagement with Syria—which Palestinian terrorist groups had tried to prevent with attacks on the Israeli settlements of Kiryat Shemona and Maalot—had left the Palestinian Arabs alone, at least for the time being, in their confrontation with Israel, despite pledges of support by Arab leaders.

Following the Syrian-Israeli disengagement agreement, the Palestinian National Council convened in Cairo to determine the direction of the Palestinian movement. The council was a quasi-parliamentary organization composed of representatives from almost all the varied Palestinian organizations. After a great deal of debate, the Palestinian National Council worked out a ten-point program, not all of which was to the liking of the Soviet leadership.[122] In its first point, the program rejected participation in the Geneva conference under Resolution no. 242 so long as it dealt with the Palestinian Arabs only as a "refugee problem."[123] The second point stated that the PLO would struggle "by all means, foremost of which is armed struggle, to liberate Palestinian Land," while opposing any agreement with Israel.[124] Although disagreeing with the Palestinians' refusal to come to Geneva or deal with Israel, the Soviet leadership warmly welcomed the ninth point of the program, which stated that the PLO "will struggle to strengthen its solidarity with the socialist countries and the world forces of liberation and progress to foil all Zionist, reactionary and imperialist schemes."[125]

In commenting on the meeting of the Palestinian National Council, *New Times* correspondnent Viktor Bukharov, citing Arab newspapers, indirectly rebuked the Palestinian guerrillas for rejecting participation in the Geneva conference and for other "extremist" positions.[126] In addition, Bukharov returned to an earlier Soviet theme, arguing that unity was a vital necessity for the Palestinian guerrilla organizations. While describing the Palestinian movement in generally favorable terms, Bukharov reserved his warmest praise for the decision of the PLO executive to admit representatives of the Palestinian National Front.[127] This was a guerrilla organization made up primarily of West Bank Arab Communists, who, once dormant, were now carrying out acts of sabotage against the Israelis. The admission of the Palestinian National Front into the PLO drew such warm Soviet praise because it served both as an excellent example of the success of the national front strategy the Soviet leaders had been urging on the Arab world and as a way they could influence the PLO from the inside.[128]

While the USSR was exhorting the Palestinian guerrilla organizations to unify, and warning them against "extremist positions," it was simultaneously exploiting the Israeli reprisal raids induced by guerrilla attacks to underline the "aggressive nature" of Israel and its ties to the United States. The Soviet goal in this maneuver was to prove to the Arabs that the Soviet Union was their only true friend. *Pravda*, on June 23, denounced Israeli attacks on the "peaceful inhabitants of Lebanon," comparing it to Nazi attacks during World War II, while branding as "absurd" Israel's justification for the attacks as responses to actions by the Palestinian guerrillas operating from Lebanon. Then, following an attack by Palestinian terrorists operating from the Lebanese port of Tyre against the Israeli coastal town of Nahariyah in late June (the attack was timed to coincide with Nixon's arrival in Moscow), the Israelis retaliated with attacks against three

Lebanese ports in an effort to deter the Lebanese government from granting naval staging areas to the terrorists. The Soviet leadership seized upon these Israeli attacks to offer aid to Lebanon against Israel and to pose again as the champion of the Arabs.[129]

As Arab-Israeli tensions heightened once again following the Palestinian terrorist raids against Israel and Israeli reprisals and preemptive attacks against the Palestinian guerrilla bases in Lebanon, the Soviet leadership may have hoped for the repetition of the situation of September 1972. At that time an anti-Soviet and pro-American trend was reversed by the massacre of Israeli athletes at Munich and the subsequent Israeli attacks on Lebanon and Syria, which made Soviet military aid a vital necessity for the Arab states. In any case, in early July 1974 an Arab League Defense Council meeting was called to deal with Israeli attacks on Lebanon, and Soviet comment on the conference hailed Arab "solidarity" in support of Lebanon while once again stressing Soviet support of the Arab cause.[130]

The Soviet leaders were not content, however, with merely encouraging Arab support of the Palestinians and Lebanese in the face of Israeli reprisal attacks. With the reconvening of the Geneva peace conference under active discussion, the Soviet leaders continued their efforts to persuade the Palestinians to participate in the Geneva conference, with the ultimate goal of creating a Palestinian Arab state on the West Bank and in Gaza. *Izvestia* correspondent Igor Belyayev, in a key article on the Middle East on July 9, stated:

> Back in November 1947, the 1947 UN General Assembly adopted a resolution on the division of Palestine into two independent states—Jewish and Arab. Israel was created in 1948. The Arab Palestinian state never became a reality. . . .
>
> The Palestinian Arabs must now have the opportunity to decide their own fate. The Geneva Peace Conference on the Near East can and must be the most suitable place for a discussion of their legitimate rights.[131]

While the Soviet leadership thus came out more strongly than ever before in favor of a Palestinian state and tried to win the Palestinian Arabs over to their point of view, the Soviet Union's relations with Egypt again deteriorated and the Soviet leaders utilized the Palestinian issue in an effort to isolate and embarrass Egyptian President Sadat. The effusive Egyptian welcome given to Nixon, far greater than the Egyptian welcomes given to Khrushchev in 1964 or to Podgorny in 1971, together with the numerous Egyptian-American agreements signed during Nixon's visit, clearly angered the Soviet leaders, who saw Egypt moving farther and farther into the American camp, despite all the military and economic aid the USSR had given Egypt and the risks the Russians had taken on Egypt's behalf. Soon after the end of the Soviet-American summit, the Soviet leadership demonstrated its displeasure with Sadat's policies by abruptly postponing the scheduled Moscow visit of Egyptian Foreign Minister Ismail Fahmy, which was supposed to lay the groundwork for a Sadat-Brezhnev "summit."[132] This snub, however, did not deter Sadat, who had just received a $200 million loan from Germany, from improving relations with the United States still further in mid-July. On July 17 and 18, he signed agreements safeguarding American investments in the Egyptian economy and allowing four major American banks (Chase Manhattan, First National City, American Express, and Bank of America) to begin operations in Egypt.[133] As mentioned above, Sadat's strategy at this time was both to strengthen the Egyptian economy and to use his new economic ties with the United States to "drive a wedge" between the United States and Israel, while playing off the United States against the USSR. The Soviet leaders, however, perceived the United States as the primary "wedge driver" in the relationship, viewing the American goal as splitting Egypt off from the USSR—a process that seemed well on the way to success by mid-July.

Egypt's relations with the Soviet Union deteriorated further on July 18 when Sadat, in an interview with the Lebanese weekly *Al-Hawadess,* accused the Russians of trying to restrict Egypt's freedom in determining its foreign policy. The Egyptian leader also criticized the Russians for delaying Ismail Fahmy's visit to Moscow until October.[134] The Soviet leadership responded to Sadat's attacks and to his turn to the United States in a major *Izvestia* article on the Middle East by its editor, L. Tolkunov, who made a detailed attack on "anti-Sovietism in Egypt." Tolkunov began the article by indicating Soviet concern over both American diplomatic efforts in the Middle East and the Arab leaders who supported them:

> Bilateral contacts through someone else's mediation constrict the possible framework of the Arab states' political activeness. Some of these countries are trying to do a balancing act, to draw dividends from both poles as it were; from the US and Western European countries on the one hand, and from the Soviet Union and the National Liberation movement on the other.[135]

Tolkunov went on to remind the Arabs that "in itself" the establishment of diplomatic relations between the United States and a number of Arab states has in no way affected the "provocative aggressive nature of Israel's course." The Soviet editor then attacked "anti-Sovietism in Egypt" as he commented on the growing economic ties between the United States and Egypt:

> Some people in Egypt want to prepare the ground for the broad penetration of Western capital into the country and the simultaneous "liberation" of Egypt from Soviet "economic dependence." Under the same flag, steps are being taken to strengthen economic ties with

Western countries, a subject that Egyptian journalists are writing a great deal about. But the most sober-minded people in Cairo are asking: What will too close ties between the Egyptian economy and Western circles really give the Egyptian people? Can they, these circles, provide effective and disinterested assistance to Egypt? Many people in Cairo are talking about the illusory nature of the idea that the Western countries will show much favor toward Egypt if it retreats further from cooperation with the Soviet Union.[136]

While Tolkunov attacked Sadat's economic policy, *New Times* correspondent Y. Potomov was attacking Sadat for his agreement with Jordan's King Hussein that the Jordanian monarch, and not the PLO, represented the Palestinians living in his kingdom—including the West Bank.[137]   While Sadat was later to change his position on this, Potomov seized the opportunity to use the PLO and Libyan leader Mu'ammar Kaddafi to demonstrate that Sadat was isolated from the mainstream of Arab thinking on the Palestinian question:

> The leaders of the PLO and several other Arab countries disagree with the proviso contained in the communique on the recent talks between President Anwar Sadat of Egypt and King Hussein of Jordan that "the Palestinian Liberation Organization is the legitimate representative of the Palestinians with the exception of those dwelling in the Hashemite Kingdom of Jordan." The communique has been trenchantly criticized by the press in a number of Arab countries.
>
> On July 23 PLO Executive Chairman Yasir Arafat met Libyan leader Muammar Kaddafi. According to Libyan newspapers, they were of one mind in noting that the Jordanian communique cut across the decisions of last year's Arab summit conference in Algiers which recognized the PLO as the sole legitimate representative of the entire Palestinian people.[138]

In the same article, however, Potomov indicated Soviet concern over current Middle East trends:

> Forces trying to spot a weak link in Arab ranks are . . . stepping up their activities. Cashing in on the difficulties the Arab countries are experiencing due to the protracted Israeli aggression, *these forces are endeavoring with the assistance of local reactionaries, to pluck one state after another out of the united Arab front resisting imperialist aggression.*[139] [emphasis added]

The Soviet embrace of the Palestinian cause, which was part of the overall Soviet strategy of encouraging anti-Western trends in the Middle East, reached a new high at the end of July when the Soviet leadership invited Yasir Arafat to come to Moscow. At the time of Arafat's visit the Soviet press gave unprecedented coverage to the Palestinian question, including a six-page report in *New Times* and a 3,700-word article in *Izvestia*.[140] During the talks with Arafat and his delegation the Soviet leadership again emphasized its recognition of the PLO as the "sole legitimate representative of the people of Palestine,"[141] thus indirectly attacking Sadat. According to the description of the talks in *Pravda*, the USSR also expressed its support for the participation of the PLO at the Geneva conference "on an equal basis with the other participants," and agreed to the opening of a PLO mission in Moscow.[142] In return, the PLO delegation, which included a Jordanian Communist (probably as a sop to the Russians), gave its usual lip-service praise of the Soviet Union for its "unvarying support and assistance," and for its "principled policy."[143]

Soon after Arafat's departure, however, the Soviet Union was confronted by a problem far more important to the Soviet leadership than the Palestinians: the sudden resignation of U.S. President Richard Nixon, who had been the architect of the detente policy with the USSR. Gerald Ford, his successor, in his speech to a joint session of Congress after assuming the presidency, pledged continuity in American relations with the Soviet Union—a pledge given wide play by the Soviet press[144]—and also pledged to retain Henry Kissinger as secretary of state. Nonetheless, the accession to power of a man neither burdened by Watergate nor wedded to the detente policy must have been of great concern to the Soviet leaders. They may well have recalled the changes made by Anwar Sadat in Egypt's relations with the Soviet Union when he acceded to the presidency in October 1970.

Gerald Ford came to power in the United States at a time when politics in the Middle East were in a great state of flux. Alignments among the states in the region and between regional states and extraregional powers were constantly changing. While Egypt had moved toward the United States, Libya had moved toward the USSR; but these alignments were neither stable nor permanent, and the Arab oil-producing states were accumulating huge sums of money, so much that the Western economies were groaning under the strain of paying quadrupled prices for Arab oil—a development that held a number of dangers for the future development of Arab relations with the West. At the same time the Cyprus conflict had broken out anew and the Arab-Israeli conflict, while temporarily defused, remained fundamentally unresolved and the danger of a new outbreak of war loomed on the horizon.

Indeed, despite the Israeli-Egyptian and Israeli-Syrian disengagement agreements worked out so painfully by Kissinger, by the time of Ford's accession to the presidency there were indications that in the absence of further steps toward an Arab-Israeli peace agreement, another war could erupt in the very near future —possibly upon the November 30 termination of the mandate of the UN force stationed between Israel and Syria. The Israeli government was complaining about Syrian violations of the disengagement agreement, and about the huge influx of Soviet arms to Syria. For its part, Syria was protesting what it termed Israeli preparations for a new war, including a one-day mobilization of Israeli reservists.[145]

In an attempt to keep the momentum for peace under way, Kissinger and Ford entertained a parade of Middle Eastern leaders in August and September, as the U.S. leaders sought to work out the optimum approach for the next stage of the peace talks. Visiting Washington during this period were Egyptian Foreign Minister Ismail Fahmy, Syrian Foreign Minister Abdel Halim Khaddam, Jordan's King Hussein, Saudi Arabian Foreign Minister Omar Saqqaf, and finally, in mid-September, Israel's new Premier, Yitzhak Rabin. The Israeli Premier, under intense domestic pressure not to yield any more land without concrete Arab moves toward peace, had a number of discussions with Ford and Kissinger.[146] Following these meetings, he presented a formula for Arab "non-belligerency" that he said would be an acceptable price for another Israeli withdrawal. In return for a further withdrawal in Sinai, Rabin stated, Egypt could demonstrate its good intentions by ending its economic boycott of Israel. Rabin chose Egypt as the target of Israel's diplomacy not only because withdrawal in the Sinai was far more acceptable domestically in Israel than pullbacks on the Golan Heights or on the West Bank but also because he felt that Egypt held the key to a permanent Arab-Israeli peace. In discussing Egypt on the U.S. television program "Meet the Press," Rabin stated:

> If you looked back through the history of the Arab-Israeli conflict, you would realize that the Arab world didn't do anything without Egypt leading them into it, either to war or out of war. . . .
> I think there are hopes—at least I hope there are signs that in Egypt . . . there is some sort of readiness for peace.[147]

While one of the goals of Rabin's trip to Washington was to coordinate strategy in the peace negotiations, a second goal was to acquire sufficient weaponry should the peace negotiations fail. It would appear that Rabin was successful in his quest for arms, because in a news conference at Blair House on September 13 Rabin stated, "We reached an understanding on our on-going military relationship in a concrete way with concrete results."[148]

As might be expected, the Soviet leadership, unhappy that Washington continued to be the center of Middle Eastern diplomacy, seized upon the Rabin visit to underline U.S. support for Israel. An editorial in *New Times* commented:

> Israeli Premier Yitzhak Rabin has completed his four-day visit to the United States. Before his departure from Tel-Aviv he declared "Israel needs much more aid from the United States—far more than it was receiving before the Yom Kippur War. . . . "

As former Ambassador to the United States, he knows his way about in Washington. And, as former Chief of General Staff, he is quite at home getting new arms shipments.

According to press reports, the United States has agreed to complete the delivery of 50 Phantom fighter-bombers by next summer. Tel-Aviv will also get from 200-250 M-60 tanks and laser-guided missiles. All this will be part of the United States' "current aid" to Israel for which Congress has appropriated $2,200 million. American officials say Rabin has also "achieved progress" concerning the long-range programme of American arms shipments to Israel. It is quite possible that it is the promise of these deliveries that has prompted the Premier to take, as he himself has said, a "tough stand" on the Middle East settlement.[149]

While the Arab leaders could not have been too happy with the support secured by Rabin in Washington, less than a week after the Israeli premier's visit another event occurred to irritate Arab-American relations. President Ford, deciding to try to come to grips with the inflation problem that threatened to undermine the economies of the NATO allies and Japan—a problem exacerbated (although not caused) by the quadrupling of oil prices—issued both an appeal for cooperation between the world's food and energy producers and a veiled threat as to what might happen should cooperation not be forthcoming. Speaking at the United Nations on September 18 Ford stated:

> The United States recognizes the special responsibility we bear as the world's largest producer of food. That is why Secretary of State Kissinger proposed from this very podium last year a World Food Conference to define a global food policy. And that is one reason why we have removed domestic restrictions of food production in the United States. *It has not been our policy to use food as a political weapon, despite the oil embargo and recent oil price and production decisions. . . .*
>
> Now is the time for oil producers to define their conception of a global policy on energy to meet the growing need—and to do this without imposing unacceptable burdens on the international monetary and trade system. *A world of economic confrontation cannot be a world of political cooperation.*[150] [emphasis added]

Ford followed up his UN speech on food and energy with an even stronger warning at the Ninth World Energy Conference in Detroit five days later:

> Sovereign nations cannot allow their policies to be dictated or their fate decided by artificial rigging or distortion of world commodity

markets. . . . Exorbitant prices can only distort the world economy, run the risk of a worldwide depression and threaten the breakdown of world order and world safety. It is difficult to discuss the energy problem without lapsing unfortunately into doomsday language. The danger is clear. It is very severe.[151]

Kissinger echoed a similar warning in his address to the United Nations on September 23 when he said, "The world cannot sustain even the present level of prices, much less continuing increases."[152]

Reaction from the oil-exporting states—most of them Arab—to the U.S. demand for a lowering of oil prices was strong and often bitter. The Beirut newspaper *Al-Nahar* went so far as to claim in a headline, "America declares war against oil-rich Arabs."[153] Indeed, fear over possible U.S. military intervention to seize Middle Eastern oil fields had reached the point by September 25 that U.S. Defense Secretary James Schlesinger stated at a news conference that the United States was not contemplating military action against the oil-producing countries in the Middle East, but rather was trying to find a solution to rising oil prices through "amicable discussions."[154]

As in the case of Rabin's visit to Washington, the Soviet leadership seized upon Ford and Kissinger's warnings at the United Nations in an effort to undermine the U.S. position in the Middle East. In discussing the UN speeches, *Pravda* correspondent Yuly Yakhontov stated:

> The oil-producing countries are being accused of having artificially created the economic difficulties of the oil-consuming countries. The U.S.A. even threatened to halt economic aid and shipments of food to states who raise oil prices or reduce oil production. . . .
>
> The U.S. statement produced a . . . violent reaction in the Near and Middle East. The Iranian newspaper *Kayhan* termed Washington's action as nothing less than "interference in the internal affairs of sovereign states." "The peoples of Arab countries will not bow to threats of force or tolerate intervention in their internal affairs and economic policies" declared the Beirut newspaper *Ash Sharq.*[155]

It was with this background of Arab irritation over U.S. policies that Kissinger embarked on yet another trip to the Middle East in early October. The main target of the U.S. secretary of state's diplomacy was Egypt, as both the United States and Israel felt that another Israeli-Egyptian agreement would be the logical "next step" in the process of securing a final Arab-Israeli peace settlement, although Kissinger also held out the hope for an Israeli-Jordanian accord. Unfortunately for Kissinger, however, Sadat was not to prove as accommodating to the United States as on previous occasions. The Egyptian leader, unhappy at the very slow pace of promised U.S. economic and nuclear assistance, and desiring to maintain himself as the leader of the Arab world in the face of challenges from Libya and Iraq, was unwilling to agree to the cessation of the Arab economic boycott against Israel desired by Rabin, or make any other political concession to Israel in return for another Israeli withdrawal. Sadat, however, was too clever a diplomat to reject Kissinger's approaches directly. Instead, he took a step toward the PLO and stated that any further Israeli-Egyptian agreements were contingent upon Israeli withdrawals from the Golan Heights and the West Bank, in the latter case ceding the territory to the PLO rather than to King Hussein. In adopting these policies, Sadat abrogated his earlier agreement with Hussein, and made Kissinger's mediation efforts considerably more difficult, given the PLO's continuing terrorist activities against Israel and its professed policy of dismantling the Jewish state. In choosing to support the claim of the PLO to represent all Palestinians, Sadat also adopted a policy favored by the Soviet Union, and the two nations drew closer together as Kissinger's peacemaking activities waned.

Sadat's policy shift was first made evident on September 22, one week after Rabin's trip to Washington. At a "coordination conference" in Cairo attended by Egypt, Syria, and the PLO, and boycotted by King Hussein, the Arab leaders took two steps of major importance to the Arab-Israeli peace negotiations. First, they agreed "to reject any attempt to carry out partial political settlements, considering the Arab cause as one cause." Second, the participants agreed that the PLO was the "sole legitimate representative of the people of Palestine."[156]   In agreeing to these two points, Sadat effectively told the United States that a Jordanian-Israeli agreement could not be sanctioned, since only the PLO could speak for the West Bank, and that Egypt could not follow a "go it alone" policy apart from its allies. Three days after this conference, in a taped appearance on the U.S. television program "The Today Show," Sadat stated his refusal to personally meet Rabin, and intimated that he was willing to shift Egypt's position back to the Soviet Union by stating that Egypt's foreign minister, Ismail Fahmy, scheduled to visit Moscow in mid-October, would be discussing Soviet arms supplies to Egypt during his visit.[157]

Given Sadat's unwillingness to come to an agreement with Israel, and Egypt's other policy changes, it is not surprising that Kissinger's diplomatic efforts made little progress during his visit to Cairo in early October. Kissinger did, however, obtain Sadat's agreement to a six-month extension of the UN force stationed between the Israeli and Egyptian armies in the Sinai Desert—possibly because, without a resumption of the constant flow of Soviet arms and spare parts he had before the October war, Sadat was unable to demonstrate that he could exercise the option of returning to war, should he so decide. Indeed, Fahmy left for Moscow in an apparent effort to obtain Soviet arms several days after Kissinger's visit to Cairo.

While the paramount Egyptian interest expressed during Fahmy's visit to Moscow was a need for more Soviet arms, the Soviet leaders had other goals in mind. The Russians were clearly still unhappy at the Westward turn in Egypt's economy, and a *Pravda* article, published on the eve of Fahmy's visit, continued the Soviet leadership's criticism of the Egyptian government's policies weakening the state sector of the Egyptian economy and fostering foreign investment.[158] In addition, in a major policy speech in Kishinev on October 11, just before Fahmy arrived in Moscow, Soviet party leader Brezhnev made clear his opposition to the type of personal diplomacy carried on by Kissinger with the Egyptians. The Soviet leader also called for a speedy resumption of the Geneva conference, where the USSR would be an equal partner with the United States in overseeing Middle Eastern peace negotiations, and, in the strongest official show of support to the Palestinian cause to date, openly called for a "national home" for the Palestinians.[159] Possibly reflecting the still cool nature of Soviet-Egyptian relations, no mention of renewed Soviet arms deliveries to Egypt was made in the joint communique issued at the conclusion of Fahmy's visit. This was in marked contrast to Brezhnev's promises of continued Soviet military aid to Syrian President Hafiz Assad, who had stopped off in Moscow September 27 on his way to a state visit to North Korea.[160] Nonetheless, the Soviet leadership did agree to a visit by Brezhnev to Cairo in January 1975, and the Brezhnev visit would clearly facilitate Sadat's policy of playing the two superpowers off against each other. In return, however, the Egyptians agreed that "a complete and final settlement to the Middle East Crisis can be achieved only within the framework of the Geneva Conference."[161] The two sides also agreed that a final peace settlement could be achieved "only if the legitimate rights of the Arab people of Palestine, including their right to a homeland, are guaranteed," and that the PLO should take part in the Geneva conference on an equal footing with the other participants.[162]

The Soviet press played up the results of the Egyptian foreign minister's visit as the Soviet leadership, despite its disappointment with Sadat in the past, saw an opportunity to demonstrate its ties to the most powerful of the Arab states. An editorial in *New Times* stated:

> It is no secret . . . that those who do not want to see close friendship between the Soviet Union and the Arabs have been working hard to drive a wedge between our country and Egypt. The results of the talks the Egyptian delegation led by Ismail Fahmy had in Moscow show that hopes on this score entertained by the reactionaries are groundless. . . .
>
> Leonid Brezhnev's visit to Cairo next January and his meeting with President Anwar Sadat, agreed upon during the Moscow talks, will undoubtedly be a landmark in the development of Soviet-Egyptian relations. The decision concerning the Brezhnev-Sadat meeting, the Cairo *Al-Akhbar* stresses, "is convincing proof of the depth and enduring quality of Soviet-Egyptian relations. These are not tran-

sient relations nor are they engendered by some extraordinary circumstances."[163]

Having secured Brezhnev's promise to visit Egypt, thus once again demonstrating his ability to play off the Soviet Union against the United States, Sadat turned his attention to the summit conference of Arab leaders at Rabat, Morocco, where the conflict between Jordan and the PLO threatened once again to split apart the coalition of Arab states headed by Egypt. Sadat's support of the PLO at the Rabat summit was in line with his agreement with Syria and the PLO in late September, and with the Soviet-Egyptian communique of mid-October, although many Western observers seemed shocked by the Egyptian position, which they had erroneously felt would be more "moderate." After several days of intense debate, the other Arab states won King Hussein's agreement to a declaration that the PLO was the "sole and legitimate representative of the Palestinian people and had the right to establish the independent Palestinian authority on any liberated Palestinian territory." Perhaps in return for his agreement to renounce Jordan's claims to the West Bank, Hussein was promised a $300 million grant by the oil-rich Arab states. Other Arab states securing funds at the Rabat summit were Egypt and Syria, which obtained $1 billion annually over a period of four years, and the PLO, which was awarded $50 million.[164]

The Soviet press hailed the Rabat decision recognizing the PLO, and it may have appeared to the Soviet leadership that the radical, anti-Western position of the PLO had won over a number of moderate and pro-Western Arab leaders. Indeed, Dmitry Volsky, writing in *New Times,* claimed that the Rabat conference's decision was proof of the Arab states' growing unity on an anti-imperialist basis—the type of unity the Soviets had so long desired:

> The intentions of Tel-Aviv and its backers are sufficiently transparent. Their aim is to substitute for the Geneva conference "separate talks" with this or that Arab country with a view to preventing a solution of the cardinal issues involved in a Middle East settlement and reducing matters to "partial measures." Associated with all this are attempts to place the Palestinian movement in isolation within the Arab world itself in order subsequently to deal with it separately.
>
> The Rabat summit clearly demonstrated that the designs the Israeli aggressors have been harboring failed of their object. The Conference showed the Arab countries fully able to embody their resolve for unity in concrete decisions and political practice. . . .
>
> There is of course a long way to go before the decisions taken are translated into reality. *Nevertheless, the important thing is that the process of Arab consolidation is gaining headway. It is gaining headway, moreover, on an anti-imperialist platform* and with the support of all progressive forces, primarily the USSR which, as the Soviet

leaders emphasized in their message to the Rabat summit, will continue to "do everything to secure a genuinely just Middle East settlement."[165] [emphasis added]

Arab unity at the Rabat conference was not as strong as the Soviet press made it appear, however. Libyan leader Mu'ammar Kaddafi boycotted the conference, and Iraqi leader Saddam Hussein stated at the end of the conference, in a clear disagreement with Sadat: "Should the PLO go to Geneva or become a party to the contacts being held with the United States, Iraq's commitment to this draft resolution would be null and void."[166] Hussein's statement also clearly demonstrated that despite extensive Soviet military aid, and assistance in the war against the Kurds, on this important Middle Eastern policy the two states were diametrically opposed, since the Soviet Union had long advocated a PLO role at Geneva.

While the Arab world may not have been totally unified in its policies toward the PLO, and while the terrorist organization had itself split, with George Habash of the PFLP openly denouncing Arafat and the Rabat decisions, nonetheless the Middle East appeared much closer to war as a result of the Rabat conference. Given Arafat's continuing call for the replacement of Israel by a "democratic secular state," the Israelis began to gird for war as even a leader of Israel's dovish Mapam party, Dov Zakin, stated, "If you take the Rabat decisions literally, there is no alternative to war."[167]

In an effort to prevent the outbreak of war, Kissinger made yet another visit to the Middle East in early November. At this point Sadat was able to play the role of a "moderate," telling Kissinger, "We shall always be, in Egypt, ready to regain whatever land we can ... I can't see at all that the Rabat conference has put any block in the step-by-step approach."[168] The Egyptian leader made it be known, however, that while he would agree to another Israeli withdrawal, he could not make any political agreements with Israel to obtain it.[169] In taking this position, Sadat indicated to Kissinger that if he wished to keep the momentum of his personal diplomacy toward peace, Egypt would be happy to cooperate so long as Kissinger could secure another Israeli withdrawal at no political cost to Egypt.[170]

If Sadat had hoped that through this diplomatic maneuvering Kissinger would now be forced to bring pressure on Israel for an unconditional withdrawal in order to recoup his personal prestige and secure a continuation of the American-sponsored peace effort, the American secretary of state's task was made infinitely more difficult by Arafat's speech at the United Nations on November 13. In his UN address, Arafat repeated the PLO call for the dismantlement of Israel and warned that if his demands were not achieved, the PLO would continue its terrorist attacks.[171] The United States strongly opposed both the PLO's program to dismantle Israel and its terrorist attacks, one of which occurred during the UN debate. The U.S. ambassador to the United Nations, John Scali, gave a very strong speech in favor of Israel's right to existence as a sovereign state.[172] For its part, the USSR, while hailing Arafat's visit to the United Nations, was careful to continue to emphasize, as it had done in the past, that while the PLO had a right to a state, Israel also had a right to exist.[173] Indeed, given the strong American support for Israel, and a summit conference between Ford and Brezhnev coming up on November 23, the Soviet leadership clearly had no desire to alienate important segments of American opinion by supporting the PLO's demands to dismantle Israel, particularly with new agreements of strategic arms limitations to be discussed at the summit and the USSR's need for American technological inputs and long-term grants for the next Soviet Five-Year Plan, then in an advanced stage of preparation.

Despite both Soviet and American statements that Israel had a right to exist, it appeared that after Arafat's visit to the United Nations, war loomed ever closer. Indeed, in mid-November, the Syrian government, long a champion of the PLO, refused to comment on whether it would permit a six-month extension of the mandate of the UN force between Syrian and Israeli lines on the Golan Heights, which was due to expire at the end of the month. The Israelis, not wishing to be caught by surprise, as they were in October 1973, began to prepare for war. Following a report that 20 Soviet ships were unloading arms at Syrian ports, the Israelis began to mobilize reservists and move them to the Golan Heights. For a while it looked as if war was imminent until the personal intervention of Henry Kissinger succeeded in cooling the situation.[174] Nonetheless, the war scare did serve to remind both Brezhnev and Ford that they would have to deal with the Middle East, as well as with arms control, at their summit in Vladivostok. Although the details of the summit negotiations on the Middle East are not yet known, it is probable that Ford specifically asked Brezhnev to restrain the Syrians and convince them to accept an extension of the UN force. Given Syria's need for a continued supply of Soviet weaponry to fight a new war, the Soviet Union was not without leverage in this situation. In any case, at the end of the month the Syrians did agree to extend the UN force, although to what degree the Syrian decision was due to Soviet pressure, internal politics, or Egypt's unwillingness to support Syria in a new war is not yet known.

The Middle East occupied a relatively small, although not insignificant, section of the communique issued by the two leaders at the conclusion of their meeting at Vladivostok, which was devoted primarily to working out a new nuclear arms limitation agreement. The section of the communique dealing with the Middle East stated:

> In the course of the exchange of views on the Middle East both sides expressed their concern with regard to the dangerous situation in that region. They reaffirmed their intention to make every effort to promote a solution of the key issues of a just and lasting peace in accordance with United Nations Resolution 338, with due account

taken of the legitimate interests of all peoples of the area, including the Palestinian people and respect for the *right of all states of the area to independent existence.*

The sides believe that the Geneva Conference should play an important part in the establishment of a just and lasting peace in the Middle East and *should resume its work as soon as possible.*[175] [emphasis added]

While rather vague as to details, the communique appears to have been a compromise between the two sides. On the one hand, the statement supporting all the Middle Eastern states' right to an "independent existence" explicitly repudiated the PLO program of dismantling Israel. Indeed, the Soviet Union's support of the PLO, at least as reflected in the joint communique, was weaker than in the Nixon-Brezhnev communique issued four months earlier.[176] On the other hand, however, by agreeing to a resumption of the Geneva conference, the United States seemed to be acceding to the Soviet desire to play a more active role in the peace negotiations. Nonetheless, since no date was set for the resumption of the Geneva talks, and since similar language had been used in the July communique, the United States kept alive the possibility of more activity by the peripatetic Kissinger.

Indeed, soon after the conclusion of the Vladivostok talks, Kissinger was once again to start work on another disengagement agreement, although it was to be more than ten months until his efforts met with success.

NOTES

1. For an example of the Israeli leaders' lack of mental preparedness for the war, see Defense Minister Moshe Dayan's lecture to the Israeli Command and Staff College on August 9, 1973. Reprinted in *Brief: Middle East Highlights* (Tel Aviv), no. 63, 1973 (hereafter *Brief*).

2. Sadat interview in *Al-Anwar* (Beirut), March 29, 1974, cited in the report by Henry Tanner in the New York *Times*, March 30, 1974. For an Egyptian view of the war, which deals in some detail with Soviet policy, see Mohammed Heikal, *The Road to Ramadan* (New York: Quadrangle, 1975). For an Israeli view of the war, see Chaim Herzog, *The War of Atonement* (Boston: Little, Brown, 1975). For specialized studies of Soviet involvement in the war, see Galia Golan, *Yom Kippur and After: The Soviet Union and the Middle East Crisis* (New York: Cambridge University Press, 1977); Jon D. Glassman, *Arms for the Arabs: The Soviet Union and War in the Middle East* (Baltimore: Johns Hopkins, 1975); and William B. Quandt, *Soviet Policy in the October 1973 War*, R-1864-ISA (Santa Monica, Calif.: Rand Corporation, 1976). See also Alvin Z. Rubinstein, *Red Star on the Nile* (Princeton: Princeton University Press, 1977), chap. 8. For a Soviet view of Soviet wartime policy (which contends that Syria wanted an early cease-fire), see the so-called Vinogradov Document (the reported talk of the Soviet ambassador to Egypt, Vladimir Vinogradov), published in *Al-Safir* (Beirut) on April 16, 1974, and translated in *Journal of Palestine Studies*, no. 12 (Summer 1974): 161-63. For a balanced account of U.S. policy during the war, see

William B. Quandt, *Decade of Decisions: American Policy toward the Arab-Israeli Conflict 1967-1976* (Berkeley: University of California Press, 1977), chap. 6.

3. See *Pravda*, October 7-9, 1973, and Radio Moscow reports of October 6-9, 1973.

4. The Soviet Union had placed a number of "spy" satellites into the air over the Middle East before the war, and they were brought down at intervals during the war so that the Soviet leadership could be kept abreast of the military situation. The author was told during interviews with Soviet officials in Moscow in May 1974 that the reason for the Soviet delay of three days in taking a strong stand was because the Soviet leadership wished to see how the fighting was going.

5. For the text of the message, see Radio Paris (Domestic Service), October 9, 1973.

6. For a detailed examination of the Soviet airlift and sealift, see Quandt, *Soviet Policy in the October 1973 War*, pp. 18-27. For a description of the Soviet alerts, see Golan, op. cit., p. 122; and Glassman, op. cit., p. 161. On Soviet recommendation of a cease-fire, see the "Vinogradov Document," p. 162; Heikal, op. cit., pp. 212, 216-17.

7. See Heikal, op. cit., p. 220; Vinogradov Document, loc. cit.

8. The text of the news conference was published as a State Department Bureau of Public Affairs news release, October 12, 1973.

9. For an assessment of Soviet maneuvering on the cease-fire issue, see Golan, op. cit., p. 127.

10. Cited in UPI report from Moscow in the New York *Times*, November 2, 1973. See also the New York *Times*, October 19, 1973.

11. Compare Radio Moscow in English to North America, October 15, 1973.

12. Cited in the report by Bernard Gwertzman in the New York *Times*, October 16, 1973. For a reasoned explanation of the delay in the American decision to send arms to Israel, see Walter Laqueur and Edward Luttwak, "Kissinger and the Yom Kippur War," *Commentary* 58, no. 3 (September 1974): 33-40. See also Quandt, *Decade of Decisions*, pp. 179-84.

13. *Pravda*, October 16, 1973.

14. Ibid., October 15, 1973.

15. Cited in the report by Bernard Gwertzman in the New York *Times*, October 17, 1973.

16. Heikal, op. cit., p. 232.

17. Cited in *Middle East Monitor* 3, no. 20 (November 1, 1973): 3.

18. Radio Moscow, October 18, 1974.

19. Cited in the report by Bernard Gwertzman in the New York *Times*, October 21, 1973.

20. Cited in *Middle East Monitor* 3, no. 20 (November 1, 1973): 5. According to Heikal, op. cit., p. 251, all Egypt wanted was observers. Given the desperate situation Egypt faced, however, it appears probable that, had Kissinger not stopped the Israelis, who were only an hour from Cairo, Egypt would have welcomed a Soviet troop commitment.

21. This was the text of the note published in the Washington *Post*, November 28, 1973.

22. The American alert and the exact nature of Soviet moves are not yet fully clear. For Kissinger's statement about the alert at a press conference and a description of the alert, see the New York *Times*, October 26, 1973.

23. For a detailed description of the actions of the Arab states during the war, see *Middle East Monitor* 3, nos. 19 and 20 (October 15, 1973 and November 1, 1973).

24. Dmitry Volsky and A. Usvatov, "Israeli Expansionists Miscalculate," *New Times*, no. 42 (1973): 10.

25. Georgi Mirsky, "The Middle East: New Factors," *New Times*, no. 48 (1973): 18-19. The other "myths" that Mirsky claimed were dispelled by the war were (a) Israel would

always enjoy military superiority; (b) Arab weaponry was inferior to that of Israel; and (c) detente had no value (Mirsky said that, thanks to detente, a worse "flare-up" was avoided).

26. G. Apalin, "Peking Provocations," *New Times*, nos. 45-46 (1973): 29-30. Apalin also claimed, as did much of the Soviet media, that the Chinese attempted to use the Middle Eastern war "to provoke a confrontation" between the United States and the USSR.

27. A close study of Radio Tehran's announcement of its agreement with Iraq, however, would probably have convinced the Russians that the Iranians remained deeply suspicious of Iraq and that the agreement would probably not last too long. See Radio Tehran Domestic Service, "Commentary," October 8, 1973. The Shah was quoted in *Al-Hayat* (Beirut) on November 22, 1973, as saying he had put some Iranian aircraft at the disposal of Saudi Arabia during the war. See *Middle East Monitor* 3, no. 22 (December 1, 1973): 1.

28. A description of this dispute is in *Middle East Monitor* 3, no. 19 (October 15, 1973): 3.

29. See *Pravda*, November 21 and December 9, 1973.

30. New York *Times*, November 5, 1973.

31. Ibid., March 16, 1974. Ironically, at a time when the USSR was encouraging the oil embargo against the United States (October 23-31, 1973), 189 U.S. firms were displaying oil field equipment at a Moscow exhibition (cited in Arthur Jay Klinghoffer, *The Soviet Union and International Oil Politics* [New York: Columbia University Press, 1977], p. 266 n.). Interestingly enough, however, while the USSR was encouraging the Arab oil embargo, it was itself selling oil to the United States. On this point, see Klinghoffer, op. cit., pp. 175-76; and Marshall Goldman, *Detente and Dollars* (New York: Basic Books, 1975), p. 98.

32. Cited in *Brief*, no. 68: 2.

33. Ibid.

34. *Middle East Monitor* 3, no. 22 (December 1, 1973): 1. Interestingly enough, in a report on these clashes, *New Times* took a far more moderate position on the Kurds than it was to take only two months later. See Vladimir Shmarov, "The Baghdad Dialogue," *New Times*, no. 5 (1974): 10; compare it to *Pravda*, April 26, and Alexander Ignatov, "Iraq Today," *New Times*, no. 21 (1974): 22-25. For the reason for the Soviet change, see pp. 161-63.

35. *New Times*, no. 8 (1974): 13.

36. See AP report, cited in *Brief*, no. 69: 3. For a discussion of the delivery of the SCUDs, see Chapter 4, pp. 132-33.

37. For analyses of Kissinger's diplomacy, see Edward R. F. Sheehan, *The Arabs, Israelis and Kissinger: A Secret History of American Diplomacy in the Middle East* (New York: Reader's Digest, 1976); Matti Golan, *The Secret Conversations of Henry Kissinger* (New York: Quadrangle, 1976); Quandt, *Decade of Decisions*; and Heikal, op. cit. Sheehan is very critical of the Israelis, almost to the point of bias. Golan, an Israeli, is very critical of Kissinger, although he also has a number of critical comments about the Israeli government and especially about Yitzhak Rabin, who became prime minister in June 1974. Heikal is critical of Sadat's policy in the postwar period. The most balanced of the studies is Quandt's.

For a Soviet analysis of Kissinger's diplomacy that draws heavily on Sheehan's and Golan's studies, see Yevgeny Primakov, "Sbalansirovanii kurs' na Blizhnem Vostoke ili staraia politika inimi sredstvami" [A balanced course in the Middle East or the old policy pursued by other means], *Mirovaia ekonomika i mezhdunarodnye otnosheniia*, no. 12 (1976): 33-51, and no. 1 (1977): 51-60.

38. Cited in the report by Theodore Shabad in the New York *Times*, February 5, 1974. Egypt's bureaucracy, however, remained an impediment to foreign investors.

39. *Pravda*, November 16, 1973. The communique also demanded Israeli withdrawal to the October 22 cease-fire lines.

40. Washington *Post*, November 21, 1973.

41. Galia Golan, op. cit., p. 140. Reportedly the USSR had sent a memo to Arafat, Hawatmeh, and Habash at the end of October 1973, seeking their views as to a possible West Bank-Gaza state.

42. *Pravda*, November 27, 1973. Translated in *Current Digest of the Soviet Press* (hereafter *CDSP*) 25, no. 48.

43. Translated in ibid., no. 49: 18.

44. Cited in the report by John Cooley in the *Christian Science Monitor*. See also *Middle East Monitor* 4, no. 1 (January 1, 1974): 1-2.

45. *Pravda*, December 12, 1973. Translated in *CDSP* 25, no. 50: 21.

46. See the report by Bernard Gwertzman in the New York *Times*, December 19, 1973.

47. Gromyko's speech (*Pravda*, December 22), translated in *CDSP* 25, no. 51: 1-4.

48. For a detailed report on the Eban-Gromyko talks, see Matti Golan, op. cit., pp. 138-41.

49. For an excellent analysis of the dangers to the world economy caused by the precipitous rise in oil prices, see Walter J. Levy, "World Oil Cooperation or International Chaos," *Foreign Affairs* 52, no. 4 (July 1974): 690-713.

50. See *Izvestia*, January 23, 1974, for a Soviet view of the French action.

51. Ibid., December 30, 1973.

52. Ibid., January 9, 1974.

53. *New Times*, no. 3 (1974): 13.

54. *Pravda*, January 25, 1974. Translated in *CDSP* 26, no. 4: 25.

55. Translated in ibid., no. 3: 14.

56. Translated in ibid., no. 5:11-12.

57. *New Times*, no. 8 (1974): 16.

58. The communique was published in *Pravda*, March 6, 1974, and referred to the talks as having taken place in a "businesslike atmosphere"—the usual Soviet terminology for low-level cooperation.

59. The communique was published in *Pravda*, March 8, 1974.

60. Radio Moscow, March 12, 1974 (cited in the New York *Times*, March 13, 1974). See also Moscow Radio Peace and Progress, March 13, 1974.

61. For Soviet analyses of the effect of the oil embargo on the United States and Western Europe and its relation to the energy crisis, see Y. Primakov, "Energeticheskii krizis v kapitalisticheskikh stranakh" [The energy crisis in capitalist states], *Mirovaia ekonomika i mezhdunarodnye otnosheniia* (hereafter *MEIMO*), no. 2 (February 1974): 65-72; V. Spichkin, "Energeticheskii krizis v Ssha" [Energy crisis in the USA], *MEIMO*, no. 3 (March 1974): 85-98; and V. Cherniavina, "Energeticheskie problemy stran EEC" [Energy problems in EEC countries], *MEIMO*, no. 4 (April 1974): 56-65. See also B. V. Rachkov, "Energeticheskie problemy Soedinenykh Shtatov" [Energy problems in the United States], *Ssha*, no. 3 (March 1974): 29-43.

62. *Pravda*, March 25, 1974. *Pravda* was quoting a group of "prominent" Lebanese "public figures" who appealed to Sadat to stop the attacks on Nasser and his policies. For a description of other anti-Sadat actions taken by the Soviet leaders at the time, see the New York *Times*, March 26, 1974.

63. Pavel Naumov, "In Egypt Today," *New Times*, no. 12 (1974): 24.

64. Cited in the New York *Times*, March 29, 1974.

65. Radio Cairo, April 4, 1974.

66. Cited in the New York *Times*, April 19, 1974.

67. New York *Times* interview, April 22, 1974.

68. In his foreign assistance message to Congress on April 24, Nixon officially requested $250 million in aid for Egypt along with $350 million for Israel and $207.5 million for Jordan. Interestingly enough, the president also requested $100 million in a "Special Re-

quirements" fund, which many observers saw as earmarked for Syria to help in its postwar reconstruction efforts—if the Syrians agreed to a disengagement agreement. For the text of Nixon's message, see news release, Bureau of Public Affairs, Department of State, April 24, 1974. For speculation on U.S. aid to Syria, see the New York *Times*, April 25, 1974.

69. For a further development of this point, see Robert O. Freedman's testimony before the Foreign Affairs Committee, U.S. House of Representatives, May 14, 1974, *The Middle East, 1974: New Hopes, New Challenges* (Washington, D.C.: U.S. Government Printing Office, 1974). U.S.-Egyptian cooperation at the time was highlighted by U.S. assistance in the clearing of the Suez Canal, a project in which U.S. helicopters and a U.S. aircraft carrier participated.

70. See the reports in the New York *Times*, April 25 and 28, 1974.

71. Jean Riollot, "Moscow Cries 'Wolf' in the Middle East," *Radio Liberty Report*, May 21, 1974.

72. New York *Times*, May 25, 1974.

73. "The Foundation of Soviet-Egyptian Relations," *New Times*, no. 22 (1974): 17.

74. *Middle East Monitor* 4, no. 11 (June 1, 1974): 1.

75. See the report in *Middle East Monitor* 4, no. 12 (June 15, 1974): 2-3.

76. On April 24, 1974, Egypt officially charged that Kaddafi had been involved in the attempt to overthrow Sadat's government on April 18. On May 11, 1974, Nimeri accused Kaddafi of trying to overthrow his government. See the report in the New York *Times*, May 12, 1974.

77. New York *Times*, April 8, 1974.

78. Aleksei Zlatorunsky, "Libya and Its Problems," *New Times*, nos. 18-19 (1974): 35.

79. Ibid., p. 36.

80. Ibid.

81. *Pravda*, May 15, 1974. Translated in *CDSP* 26, no. 20: 17.

82. Ibid.

83. Ibid., pp. 17-18.

84. Ibid., p. 18.

85. *Pravda*, May 22, 1974. Translated in *CDSP* 26, no. 20: 18.

86. Ibid.

87. Several months later an article appeared in the Soviet foreign trade journal, *Vneshniaia torgovlia*, that indicated a frank Soviet interest in Arab states with "spare capital." See R. Klekovsky, "Fruitful Co-operation between the CMEA States and the Arab Countries," *Foreign Trade* (Vneshniaia torgovlia), no. 8 (August 1974): 16-19.

88. For a discussion of the sharp increase in Soviet imports of oil, natural gas, and other raw materials from developing countries from 1970 to 1973, see A. Ivanov, "Soviet Imports from Developing Countries," *Foreign Trade*, no. 9 (September 1974):38-43.

89. *Pravda*, May 22, 1974.

90. See the report by Juan de Onis in the New York *Times*, May 5, 1974.

91. Compare the Afro-Asian Peoples' Solidarity Organization session in Baghdad in late March 1974, which denounced "Imperialism and Maoism." For a report on the AAPSO meeting, see Dmitry Volsky, "Whose Minefields?" *New Times*, no. 14 (1974): 8-9.

92. *Pravda*, February 28, 1974. Translated in *CDSP* 26, no. 9: 19. Nonetheless, Soviet-Iraqi disagreement on a number of issues remained, and the report of the 8th Congress of the Ba'ath party, published on March 8 by the Iraqi News Agency, supported the slogan of alliance with the USSR "despite disagreement or lack of identity of view between us and them on a number of problems" (Galia Golan, op. cit., p. 197).

93. Pavel Demchenko, "Autonomy for Iraq's Kurds," *Pravda*, March 14, 1974. Translated in *CDSP* 26, no. 11: 21.

94. *Pravda*, March 27, 1974. Translated in *CDSP* 26, no. 13: 18.

95. *Pravda*, April 26, 1974. Translated in *CDSP* 26, no. 17: 17.

96. Alexander Ignatov, "Iraq Today," *New Times*, no. 21 (1974): 24.

97. Chances of Soviet involvement in such a war would rise if, as the Washington *Post* reported in early October, Soviet pilots were flying missions against the Kurds. See the report by Michael Getler in the Washington *Post*, October 5, 1974.

98. See the report in *Middle East Monitor* 4, no. 7 (April 1, 1974): 1.

99. Moscow Radio Peace and Progress echoed this theme on May 16, 1974.

100. *Pravda*, March 29, 1974, printed a very stiff Soviet note to the Chinese about this incident.

101. The communique was printed in *Pravda*, March 29, 1974.

102. *Izvestia*, March 30, 1974. Translated in *CDSP* 26, no. 13: 11. According to Quandt, however, Kissinger's meeting with Brezhnev was the "toughest and most unpleasant" he ever had with the Soviet leaders, who accused him of violating pledges that Middle Eastern peace negotiations would take place at Geneva (Quandt, *Decade of Decisions*, pp. 236-37).

103. *Pravda*, April 12, 1974. Translated in *CDSP* 26, no. 16: 2.

104. *Pravda*, April 17, 1974. Translated in *CDSP* 26, no. 16: 5-6.

105. *Pravda*, April 30, 1974. Translated in *CDSP* 26, no. 17: 14.

106. New York *Times*, April 30, 1974.

107. *Pravda*, May 3, 1974. Translated in *CDSP* 26, no. 18: 9.

108. Ibid.

109. *Pravda*, May 30, 1974.

110. Ibid. Translated in *CDSP* 26, no. 22: 5. In addition, both the USSR and Syria published a letter from Brezhnev to Assad on May 31, 1974, that expressed Brezhnev's "satisfaction" over the agreement, and over the fact that Syria and the USSR had acted "in unison" during the talks, but also warned that the agreement was only "a step along the road to a final Near East settlement" (Galia Golan, op. cit., p. 232).

111. Alexander Ignatov, "This Spring in Damascus," *New Times*, no. 24 (1974): 26-27.

112. Dmitry Volsky, "Step toward Settlement," *New Times*, no. 23 (1974): 9.

113. For an essay developing this viewpoint, see Bernard Gwertzman's "News Analysis" in the New York *Times*, June 1, 1974.

114. Cited in the report of Kissinger's news conference by Leslie Gelb in the New York *Times*, June 7, 1974.

115. Cited in *Middle East Monitor* 4, no. 13 (June 30, 1974): 1. According to Quandt (*Decade of Decisions*, pp. 246-48), Nixon reportedly also told Assad he was in favor of Israel's withdrawal all the way to the old borders.

116. The text of the joint Sadat-Nixon statement, titled "Principles of Relations and Cooperation between Egypt and the United States," outlining nuclear energy cooperation and other areas, was published in the New York *Times*, June 15, 1974.

117. Dmitry Volsky, "Arab East: Miracles and Realities," *New Times*, no. 24 (1974): 12.

118. Ibid., p. 13.

119. *Pravda*, June 16, 1974. Translated in *CDSP* 26, no. 24: 21.

120. *Izvestia*, July 7, 1974, carried a negative description of the Jackson visit.

121. This document, along with the other agreements and documents of the summit, may be found in the document section of *New Times*, no. 28 (1974): 21-32. The document pertaining to the Middle East is found on p. 23.

122. A description of the meeting, together with the ten-point program, is found in *Middle East Monitor* 4, no. 13 (June 30, 1974): 3-4.

123. Ibid., p. 4.

124. Ibid.

125. Ibid.

126. Victor Bukharov, "Palestinian National Council Session," *New Times*, no. 25 (1974): 12.

127. Ibid., p. 13.

128. For a detailed description of the activities of the Palestinian National Front on the Israeli-occupied West Bank, see the report by Terence Smith in the New York *Times*, August 23, 1974. This was one of the few successes of Soviet policy toward the Arab Communists, however, as Arab Communists had bitterly attacked the Soviet policy of encouraging Arab solidarity with "Arab reactionaries" such as King Faisal. See, for example, Kerim Mroue, "Use the Opportunities of the New Situation in the Middle East," *World Marxist Review* 17, no. 3 (March 1974): 92.

129. See the report by Juan de Onis in the New York *Times*, July 12, 1974.

130. Georgi Shmelyov, "Solidarity the Keynote," *New Times*, no. 28 (1974): 10.

131. *Izvestia*, July 9, 1974. Translated in *CDSP* 26, no. 27: 21.

132. Cited in the report by Henry Tanner in the New York *Times*, July 11, 1974.

133. *Pravda* printed a description of the agreements in its issue of July 18, 1974. The agreements were signed during U.S. Treasury Secretary William Simon's visit to Cairo.

134. New York *Times*, July 19, 1974.

135. *Izvestia*, July 25, 1974. Translated in *CDSP* 26, no. 31: 2.

136. Ibid., p. 4.

137. Sadat was not explicit as to whether Hussein could be considered the representative of the West Bank Palestinians. It appears as if he signed the agreement with Hussein to encourage prospects of a military disengagement agreement between Israel and Jordan that would give Hussein part of the West Bank. Earlier in the month Israeli Information Minister Aharon Yariv had floated a trial balloon (that was quickly shot down) that Israel might negotiate with the Palestinian guerrilla organizations if they would acknowledge the existence of Israel as a Jewish state and agree to cease hostile actions against it. See the reports in the New York *Times*, July 12 and 22, 1974; and Matti Golan, op. cit., pp. 220-22.

138. Y. Potomov, "Middle East Settlement: Urgent Task," *New Times*, no. 31 (1974): 22.

139. Ibid.

140. *New Times*, no. 32 (1974): 26-31. The same issue of the journal carried a front-page editorial supporting the PLO and a two-page interview with Yasir Arafat (pp. 10-11), who hailed the Palestinian National Front and warmly praised the Soviet Union for its aid. See also *Izvestia*, July 30, 1974, for the extensive article on the Palestinians.

141. *Pravda*, August 4, 1974. Translated in *CDSP* 26, no. 30: 5.

142. Ibid.

143. The fact that Arafat met with both Ponamarev and Ulianovsky probably indicated that there were discussions about the links between the PLO leadership and the Arab Communists.

144. Compare Iona Andronov, "The Change-over in the White House," *New Times*, no. 33 (1974): 6; and *Pravda*, August 11, 1974.

145. For a discussion of the renewed threat of war, see the article by Terence Smith in the August 18, 1974, issue of the New York *Times*.

146. In mid-September, Rabin's government had a majority of only one seat in the Israeli Parliament. Rabin had replaced Golda Meir as premier in early June, following conclusion of the Syrian-Israeli disengagement agreement, when Meir had retired. For a description of Rabin's diplomatic difficulties, see Matti Golan, op. cit., chap. 7.

147. Cited in the report by Bernard Gwertzman in the September 16, 1974, issue of the New York *Times*.

148. Cited in the report by Bernard Gwertzman in the September 14, 1974, issue of the New York *Times.*

149. *New Times*, no. 38 (1974): 17.

150. News release, Bureau of Public Affairs, Department of State, September 18, 1974.

151. Ibid., September 23, 1974.

152. Ibid.

153. Cited in the report by John Cooley in the September 25, 1974, issue of the *Christian Science Monitor.*

154. Cited in the report by John Finney in the September 26, 1974, issue of the New York *Times.*

155. *Pravda*, September 29, 1974. Translated in *CDSP* 26, no. 39: 21.

156. For the text of the agreement, see *Middle East Monitor* 4, no. 18 (October 1, 1974): 4.

157. Cited in the report by Wolf Blitzer in the September 27, 1974, issue of the *Jerusalem Post.* Sadat was also negotiating with France and Britain for weapons at this time. France began supplying Mirage jet fighter-bombers to Egypt in late November, thereby strengthening Sadat's bargaining position with the Soviet Union.

158. *Pravda*, October 10, 1974.

159. Ibid., October 12, 1974.

160. Ibid., September 28, 1974.

161. "Fruitful Talks," *New Times*, no. 43 (1974): 17.

162. Ibid.

163. Ibid. See also *Pravda*, October 17, 1974.

164. For a description of the results of the Rabat conference, see *Middle East Monitor* 4, no. 21 (November 15, 1974): 2-4.

165. Dmitry Volsky, "After the Rabat Meeting," *New Times*, no. 45 (1974): 10-11.

166. Cited in *Middle East Monitor* 4, no. 21 (November 15, 1974): 4.

167. Cited in the New York *Times*, October 30, 1974.

168. Cited in the report by Bernard Gwertzman in the November 7, 1974, issue of the New York *Times.*

169. Compare report by Henry Tanner in the November 9, 1974, issue of the New York *Times.*

170. While apparently getting no promises of U.S. pressure on Israel, Sadat did obtain a promise from Kissinger to sell Egypt 200,000 tons of wheat and sorghum at long-term, low-interest, reduced price rates. Given the rapid rise in Egypt's population, and its inability to feed its population without outside assistance, the role of food assistance is likely to grow in importance in the Egyptian-American relationship. Interestingly enough, the promise of 200,000 tons of grain was in addition to a 100,000-ton promise made to Ismail Fahmy when he visited Washington in August.

171. For the text of Arafat's speech and the reply by Israel's representative, Yosef Takoah, see the November 14, 1974, issue of the New York *Times.*

172. The text of Scali's speech is in the November 22, 1974, issue of the New York *Times.* A terrorist raid on the Israeli town of Bet Shan on November 19, during the UN debate on Palestine, killed four Israelis and wounded 19. The raid was carried out by the Popular Democratic Front for the Liberation of Palestine, an organization supporting Arafat within the PLO.

173. Compare Gromyko's speech to the United Nations on September 24, 1974. See also *Pravda*, November 14 and 15, 1974.

174. For an analysis of the war scare, see the report by John Cooley in the November 18, 1974, issue of the *Christian Science Monitor.*

175. The text of the communique is found in the November 25, 1974, issue of the New York *Times.*

176. See pp. 168-69.

6

The Road to Sinai II

SOVIET POLICY FROM VLADIVOSTOK TO THE COLLAPSE OF THE KISSINGER MISSION

In the period following the Vladivostok conference, the Soviet leadership returned to its major Middle Eastern themes by calling for a speedy resumption of the Geneva peace conference (with PLO participation on an equal basis), emphasizing Soviet opposition to any "partial settlements" of the Arab-Israeli conflict, and urging the maintenance of Arab unity on an "anti-imperialist" basis. The Soviet relationship with Egypt, once its primary Arab ally, which had improved somewhat because of Fahmy's visit to Moscow in October, again deteriorated as Brezhnev abruptly canceled his scheduled January visit to Cairo and an angry Anwar Sadat responded with some strong words criticizing Soviet arms supply policy. While the USSR's ties with Egypt remained strained, the Soviet leadership continued to strengthen its relationship with the PLO and with Syria, which the USSR, through massive military aid and diplomatic support, now sought to establish as the leader of its long-desired anti-imperialist Arab coalition. Finally, the Russians continued to follow their old policy of trying to capitalize on situations not of their making to enhance the Soviet position in the Middle East. Thus, the Soviet media gave great emphasis to such developments as Kissinger's threat of military action against the Arabs in case of "oil strangulation," CENTO maneuvers near the Persian Gulf, and continued American military aid to Israel, in an effort to undermine the American position in the Arab world.

The central Soviet concern during the November 1974-March 1975 period was that another American-orchestrated disengagement accord would be realized. Such a development would enhance U.S. prestige in the region while undermining that of the USSR, in what both superpowers perceived as a "zero-sum game" competition for influence in the Middle East. To thwart such an eventual-

ity, the Soviet leadership sought to rebuild the Arab unity "on an anti-imperialist basis" that had reached its high point during the October 1973 Arab-Israeli
war, when virtually the entire Arab world was arrayed against Israel and the
United States. One of the critical elements of the Arab coalition that the Soviet
Union was seeking to forge was the Palestine Liberation Organization (PLO),
whose leader, Yasir Arafat, was now a frequent visitor in Moscow. With PLO
prestige in the Arab world on the upswing after the Rabat conference and Arafat's appearance at the United Nations, the Russians hoped to capitalize on their
relations with the PLO to enhance the Soviet position in the Arab world. Thus,
when Arafat visited Moscow in late November 1974, the Soviet media gave a
great deal of emphasis to a *Pravda* interview in which Arafat hailed the USSR as
"a true and sincere friend of the Arab peoples."[1] Indeed, the Soviet leadership
cited this interview to refute Chinese Communist claims, during Brezhnev's
meeting with Ford at Vladivostok, that the USSR had given insufficient support
to the Arab and Palestinian causes.[2]

A second part of the Arafat interview, however, was later to prove to be an
embarrassment to his Soviet hosts. In praising Brezhnev's scheduled January visit
to Egypt, Syria, and Iraq, the Palestinian leader stated:

> These visits undoubtedly will become a major political event and ob-
> viously will demonstrate to the whole world how firm are the bonds
> of friendship linking the Arab peoples and the peoples of the great
> land of the Soviets. These visits will help chart the new strategic di-
> rection of all anti-imperialist and anti-Zionist forces. Like the peo-
> ples of Egypt, Syria and Iraq, and like all those who cherish the
> cause of establishing a just and lasting peace in the Middle East, we
> Palestinians say to L. Brezhnev from the bottom of our hearts, Wel-
> come![3]

Unfortunately for the Russians, the welcome they were to receive in Egypt
was considerably colder than the one promised by Arafat. Despite a relatively favorable Soviet press treatment of Egyptian developments in November and December, as well as a large propaganda buildup for the Brezhnev visit, Sadat
proved unwilling to reach an agreement on key issues with the Russians, and the
Soviet leader abruptly canceled his trip at the end of December. According to
Sadat, the cause of the cancellation lay in the USSR's unwillingness to grant
Egypt the kind of weapons she wanted, as well as the Soviet leadership's refusal
to accede to an Egyptian request for a deferral of debt payments to the USSR.[4]
What apparently especially rankled Sadat was the fact that Syria had been able
to get not only the arms she desired but also a deferral of her very large debt to
the Soviet Union. While the Soviet leadership, in clearly favoring Syria over
Egypt, sought to demonstrate the rewards available to those Arab states that cooperated with the USSR, Sadat publicly aired his complaints about the USSR to

the Arab world, in an apparent effort to embarrass the Russians into granting the Egyptian requests. Sadat's anger at the Russians may also have stemmed in part from what appear to have been leftist-inspired riots in Egypt on New Year's Day, when students and workers protested poor living conditions. Indeed, when asked if the riots had had any effect on Soviet-Egyptian relations, Sadat replied, "Our relations are between one state and another. There is no room for meddling in our internal affairs."[5]

While the Soviet position in the Arab world suffered as a result of the cancellation of Brezhnev's visit and the new acrimony in Soviet-Egyptian relations, the course of events soon gave the Soviet leaders a chance to improve their position vis-a-vis that of the United States. Inflation had turned to recession in the industrialized West, and unemployment soon rose to near-record proportions. In this atmosphere Kissinger had an interview with the U.S. magazine *Business Week* in which he threatened to use force if the oil producers "strangled" the industrialized world. In replying to the question "Have you considered military action on oil?" Kissinger stated:

> [It would be] a very dangerous course. We should have learned from Vietnam that it is easier to get into a war than to get out of it. I am not saying that there's no circumstance where we would not use force. *But it's one thing to use it in the case of a dispute over price, it's another where there is some actual strangulation of the industrialized world.*[6] [emphasis added]

Taken in context, Kissinger's remarks appear little more than the common-sense expression of a statesman stating that his country would fight rather than be strangled to death. Nonetheless, the reaction in the Arab world to Kissinger's *Business Week* interview was bitter, with even Anwar Sadat terming the American leader's statement "very regrettable."[7] As might be expected, the Soviet leadership, which had just lost some ground in the Middle East by canceling Brezhnev's visit to the region, seized on Kissinger's comments to demonstrate that the United States was a major threat to the Arab world—a theme that Soviet propaganda had been echoing since the 1973 war. *Pravda*, on January 7, 1975, printed two stories about the "oil war" and charged that the West was resorting to military blackmail against the Arab oil-producing countries; and the Soviet leaders may have entertained the hope that the Arab oil-producing states, concerned with Kissinger's "threat," might draw closer to the USSR for protection. Indeed, as Dmitry Volsky, an associate editor and Middle Eastern specialist of *New Times*, stated:

> The Arabs are proud and freedom-loving peoples. They cannot be brought to their knees by threats of armed force, especially now when they have friendship with the Soviet Union to draw on. And this

friendship will continue to grow despite all the efforts to the contrary exerted by its opponents.[8]

The imbroglio over U.S. oil intervention came at an inopportune time for
American diplomacy, as Kissinger was in the midst of preparations for another
trip to the Middle East, once again trying to bring about a second Egyptian-Israeli disengagement agreement. Israeli Foreign Minister Yigal Allon had visited
Washington in early December for talks aimed at working out a plan for the disengagement process, and he returned to Washington in mid-January for further
discussions with Kissinger. Pavel Demchenko, writing in *Pravda* on January 19,
indicated Soviet concern that a second-stage settlement might soon be completed:

> Israel is trying to push through plans for separate deals with individ-
> ual Arab countries. Foreign newspapers report that Israeli Foreign
> Minister, Y. Allon, has now been sent to Washington with precisely
> this in mind. While there he supposedly has stated Israel's consent to
> withdraw an additional several kilometers from the Sinai Peninsula,
> and from the Jordan River, in exchange for political concessions on
> the part of Cairo and Amman and for new generous credits and arms
> shipments from the U.S.A.
>
> It is not hard to see that if there actually is such a plan, it com-
> pletely ignores the interests of Syria and the Palestinians and counts
> on a split in the Arab countries' front and on their virtual rejection
> of an overall political settlement in the Near East in favor of partial
> deals. It is no wonder that these reports have aroused lively commen-
> tary in the Arab press. For example, Egypt is accused of intending to
> sign a separate agreement with Israel, Cairo's *Al-Ahram* writes.[9]

As Kissinger was preparing to depart for the Middle East in February, the
USSR stepped up its efforts to prevent a partial settlement. Soveit Foreign Minister Andrei Gromyko visited Syria and Egypt in early February, prior to Kissinger's trip to the two Arab states. In Damascus, Gromyko received Syrian agreement for the immediate resumption of the Geneva conference and even got Syrian consent to have the date of the meeting set for "no later than February or
early March 1975"—an action aimed at enabling the Russians to prevent any major accomplishments by Kissinger before the conference resumed its work. Syria
also again agreed to Soviet participation "in all areas and at all stages" of Middle
Eastern peace efforts, thereby assuring, at least on paper, that the USSR would
not again be isolated from any peace settlement that Kissinger might be able to
work out. In return, the Soviet foreign minister emphasized the USSR's willingness to continue "to strengthen the defense capability of Syria," and even went
so far as to indicate the USSR's preference for Syria as the leader of the Arab
anti-imperialist coalition:

The Soviet Union gave a high approval of the efforts made by the Syrian Arab Republic to strengthen inter-Arab solidarity and to consolidate the Arab states' unity of action to counteract the plans of imperialism and international Zionism.[10]

Thus, the USSR began openly to back Syria as the center of an Arab grouping of states that would, the Soviet leaders hoped, support Soviet policy regardless of any action taken by Egypt. For his part, Assad was in need of Soviet aid, given the unlikelihood of another Israeli withdrawal on the Golan Heights prior to a final peace settlement and Israel's stated unwillingness to attend any peace conference to work out a final settlement so long as the PLO, which was backed by Syria, was allowed to attend. Indeed, the impasse between Israel and Syria became very severe at this point because Syria refused to attend any peace conference unless the PLO attended as an equal partner.

Perhaps because the USSR now clearly favored Syria over Egypt, Gromyko's reception in Cairo was considerably cooler than the one he received in Damascus. The joint communique issued at the conclusion of his talks with Sadat stated that they had taken place in a "friendly and businesslike atmosphere"— a clear indication that serious conflict had arisen. Nonetheless, Egypt was to agree to an "immediate resumption of the Geneva talks"—although, in contrast with Syria, no fixed date was set—and the Egyptians also agreed that the USSR should participate in "all areas and all stages"of a Middle Eastern peace settlement. The joint communique ended with a pledge that both sides were determined to expand and deepen Soviet-Egyptian cooperation.[11]

Perhaps in return for Egypt's limited willingness to support the Soviet position, and also perhaps in hopes of avoiding any further Egyptian movement into the American camp during Kissinger's forthcoming trip to Cairo, the Soviet leadership decided to resume arms shipments to Egypt following Gromyko's visit.[12] Evidently they hoped that Gromyko's mission had succeeded in averting any new "separate deal" inimical to Soviet interest, and a *New Times* article describing Gromyko's trip to the two Arab capitals stated:

What is especially important is that these visits have demonstrated anew that the Soviet Union and the Arab countries agree in principle on the approach to a Middle Eastern settlement. For it is no secret that there has been considerable speculation on this score in the Western (and not only the Western) press.[13]

Meanwhile, on the eve of Kissinger's February trip to the Middle East, the Soviet leadership also sought to emphasize its role as defender of the Arabs against the U.S. military threat. *Izvestia*, on February 6, issued a veiled warning against the use of U.S. troops to "prevent the strangulation of the capitalist economy" in the event of a new oil embargo:

It is not difficult to realize that an attempt at the armed recoloniza-
tion of the Arab East would lead to consequences in comparison with
which the present economic chaos and political disaster (in the capitalist world) would seem like the embodiment of order and stability.[14]

The Soviet warning, however, did not still American voices calling for the seizure
of the Arab oil, for an article in the March 1975 issue of *Harper's* detailed the
hypothetical American seizure of the Saudi Arabian oil fields. The Soviet press
seized upon this and similar articles to reinforce their contention that the Arabs
needed the USSR for protection against the United States. Indeed, the Soviet
media now coupled this message with continued detailed descriptions of CENTO
maneuvers near the Persian Gulf oil fields and of American military aid to Israel.
It was even asserted that Israel was now willing "to assume the role of a strike
force for the oil monopolies."[15]

American posturing on the issue of seizing the Arab oil fields, while perhaps aimed at deterring another oil embargo, did not enhance the American diplomatic position in the Arab world as Kissinger, following a brief Middle Eastern
visit in February, set out once more in early March on what was labeled as the
decisive shuttle to bring about a second-stage disengagement between Egypt and
Israel.[16] The U.S. position in the region had been harmed in other ways as well.
The Cyprus conflict continued to poison relations between Greece and Turkey,
both NATO allies of the United States. As a result of a perceived lack of U.S.
support, Greece withdrew, in part, from NATO and Turkey not only refused to
participate in NATO exercises but also threatened to close U.S. bases if promised
arms assistance, eliminated by the U.S. Congress, was not restored.

While the Greek-Turkish conflict clearly weakened the U.S. position in the
eastern Mediterranean, the Iran-Iraq conflict, which had posed similar problems
for the Soviet position in the Persian Gulf, came to an end. On March 6 the Iranian and Iraqi governments signed an agreement delineating their long-disputed
border and agreeing to cease assistance to dissident groups within each other's
territory.[17] This meant a termination of Iranian aid to the Kurds, who were then
in the midst of a life-and-death struggle with the advancing Iraqi army. With the
end of the Iran-Iraq conflict, and an inevitable end in view for the Kurdish struggle for autonomy, the Soviet position in the Persian Gulf seemed to be greatly
enhanced. The long-feared possibility that the USSR would be drawn into a war
between Iran and Iraq was now eliminated, and the USSR could move to improve its relations with Iran as well as Iraq while also assuring itself of a continued flow of oil from Iraq and an uninterrupted flow of natural gas from Iran.[18]

Kissinger's mediation efforts in the Middle East were also affected by
Southeast Asian developments during his shuttle between Cairo and Jerusalem.
The Cambodian government of Lon Nol, allied to the United States, was on the
verge of being toppled by Cambodian Communist forces besieging the capital

city of Phnom Penh. The situation in South Vietnam was scarcely better, and it appeared that the U.S. Congress' unwillingness to send any more military assistance to the American allies in Southeast Asia spurred the Communist offensives in the two countries. It may well have been the feeling in both Cairo and Damascus that just as the U.S. Congress had tired of pouring aid into Cambodia and South Vietnam, so it would eventually tire of aiding Israel. In addition, strengthened by new shipments of Soviet arms, Sadat (as well as Assad, whom Kissinger also visited during the shuttle) could adopt a strong bargaining position vis-a-vis both the United States and Israel.

Nonetheless, despite continued professions about Arab unity during the shuttle, it is clear that Syria, as well as the Soviet Union, was very concerned that Sadat might yet agree to a second-stage disengagement agreement with Israel. To combat the possibility of being isolated against Israel should this occur, the Syrian government, in early March, offered to join the PLO in a joint command[19] and also signed a far-reaching economic and political agreement with its erstwhile enemy, the regime of King Hussein of Jordan.[20] At the same time, by taking the first steps toward a PLO-Syrian-Jordanian alignment, Assad was also moving toward a position of leadership in the Arab world. The USSR strongly endorsed the effort by Assad to establish the PLO-Syrian-Jordanian alignment because it had the potential of leading pro-Western Jordan into the Soviet camp, thereby helping to establish the "anti-imperialist" Arab unity the USSR desired.[21]

The Israelis, meanwhile, seriously concerned by what they perceived as an Iranian sellout of the Kurds—and cognizant of the fact that they were almost totally dependent on Iranian oil should they give back the Abu Rodeis oil fields that Sadat demanded—took a hard bargaining stance with Kissinger. Indeed, for the first time since the October war, Israel seemed to unite with public opinion backing Premier Rabin's opposition to Kissinger's terms and to a blunt warning from President Ford;[22] and such hardliners of the right as General Arik Sharon joined such "doves" of the left as Aryeh Eliav and Abba Eban to demand meaningful concessions from Egypt before any settlement could be agreed upon. The end result was the failure of Kissinger's mission and the temporary end of the U.S. diplomatic initiative in the Middle East.

FROM DISENGAGEMENT FAILURE TO DISENGAGEMENT SUCCESS: THE SOVIET UNION AND MIDDLE EASTERN DIPLOMACY, APRIL-SEPTEMBER 1975

The failure of Kissinger's Middle Eastern disengagement efforts led President Ford to call for a total reassessment of U.S. policy toward the Middle East, and the United States temporarily stepped back from her central position in Middle Eastern diplomacy. With the United States abandoning center stage, the

Soviet Union took the initiative in trying to secure a Middle Eastern settlement through diplomatic efforts. Nevertheless, despite a parade of visitors from Arab countries to Moscow in April, Kosygin's trips to Libya and Tunisia in May, and a number of Soviet gestures toward improving relations with Israel, the USSR proved no more successful in securing a Middle Eastern peace settlement than the United States had been. The lack of Arab unity, now exacerbated by a sharply increased conflict between the USSR's closest Arab allies, Syria and Iraq, hampered any common Arab stand, as did increasing inter-Arab conflict in Lebanon.

Meanwhile, following the fall of Cambodia and Vietnam to Communist forces and a major turn to the left in Portugal, detente came under very severe attack in the United States, and the Soviet leaders sought to use such events as the Apollo-Soyuz joint space flight and the Helsinki conference on European security to demonstrate the continued viability of detente between the two nations. Although the U.S. position in the world now appeared weakened, the Soviet Union continued to express concern that a second-stage disengagement agreement in the Middle East might yet be worked out. As Kissinger began to revive his efforts during the summer, after a successful meeting between Ford and Sadat in Austria in early June, Soviet concern grew apace. Soviet-Egyptian relations hit a new low during this period as the USSR stepped up its criticism of Sadat's policies, but the USSR proved unable to prevent Kissinger from working out a three-year disengagement agreement between Egypt and Israel in late August.

The failure of Kissinger's disengagement efforts in March led to an agonizing reappraisal of the totality of U.S. policy toward the Middle East.[23] While this major reappraisal was under way, it was clear that no new American peace initiatives would be forthcoming. In such a situation, the Soviet Union stepped forward and, for the first time since the 1973 war, the Soviet leadership took the diplomatic initiative, once again calling for the resumption of the Geneva peace conference to work out a settlement that would secure a total withdrawal of Israeli forces from all Arab territory occupied in the 1967 Six-Day War; establish a Palestinian state; and guarantee the right to existence of all states in the Middle East—including Israel. Yet even while the Soviet leaders were successively entertaining leaders of Egypt, Iraq, Syria, and the PLO in Moscow, they continued to be concerned about a new U.S.-sponsored disengagement agreement. Indeed, the *New Times* article discussing the failure of Kissinger's mission indicated the nature of Soviet concern:

> Ever since the October 1973 war, Israel and its imperialist backers have exerted a great deal of effort to break up the United Front of the Arab states and to persuade them to enter into separate deals that would outwardly appear to be a step forward while actually impeding the Arabs' struggle for a comprehensive settlement. . . .

Had their strategy succeeded, a wedge would have been driven between Egypt and Syria and the solution of the Palestine question, which lies at the root of the Middle East problem, would again have been postponed.[24]

It was to prevent such a wedge from being driven and to forge a united Arab stand on a peace settlement that representatives of Egypt, Iraq, Syria, and the PLO were invited to Moscow in April. The first to arrive was the Iraqi regime's second in command, Saddam Hussein. At the time of Hussein's visit to Moscow, Iraq and Syria were strongly at odds over a number of issues, including the amount of water Syria was willing to allow to flow into Iraq from the Euphrates Dam, thus gravely diminishing the possibility that the Syrian-PLO-Jordan entente, which had come into being in March, might also attract the Iraqis. It was perhaps for this reason that Kosygin, in his welcoming speech, urged the Arabs to take a more unified stand lest they be at a disadvantage in dealing with Israel and the United States at the Geneva conference.[25] The joint communique issued at the end of Hussein's visit stated that there had been an "exchange of opinions" on the Middle Eastern situation, indicating that there had been disagreement on a number of issues, although Iraq did join with the USSR in reaffirming the need for the "cohesion of the Arab states on an anti-imperialist basis" and the need to strengthen Arab cooperation with the socialist countries. Both sides also affirmed the "legitimate rights" of the Arab people of Palestine, including their right to self-determination.[26]

Following Hussein to Moscow was Egyptian Foreign Minister Ismail Fahmy. Egypt's relations with Syria had improved somewhat at the time of Fahmy's visit, in part because of the failure of Kissinger's mission and the meeting of Sadat and Assad at the funeral of Saudi Arabian King Faisal at the end of March. However, her relations with another of the Soviet Union's allies, Libya, had deteriorated still further, with Sadat going so far as to say that Kadaffi was "100% sick" and that his actions were "directed by the devil."[27] This, in turn, led Libya to threaten to break diplomatic relations with Egypt. Like the Libyans, the Soviet leaders were not too positively inclined toward Egypt; and in his welcoming speech, Gromyko said that the USSR was prepared to deepen and enrich its policy of cooperation with Egypt, but "only if Egypt and the Egyptian leadership pursue the same policy with respect to the USSR."[28] Once again disagreements were evident in the discussions between the two sides, as *Pravda*'s description of the talks referred to them as having taken place in a "businesslike atmosphere." Nonetheless, the *Pravda* description also stated that Egypt did agree that "any partial measures and decisions on them must be a component, inalienable part of a general settlement, and must be adopted in the framework of the [Geneva] conference on the Near East"[29]—a stipulation that Egypt was to show no hesitation in disregarding several months later.

The third in the parade of Middle Eastern visitors to Moscow in April was Syrian Foreign Minister Abdel Khaddam. Khaddam's visit coincided with the arrival in Syria of Soviet Chief of Staff Victor Kulikov, thus underlining the close military relations between the two countries.[30] Indeed, the joint communique issued at the conclusion of the meeting stressed the importance of "strengthening the defense capability of the Syrian Arab Republic" and denounced "separate agreements." In addition the USSR again hailed Syria for her "efforts to consolidate Arab solidarity" and strengthen the Arab countries' "unity of action." Nonetheless, the reference to an "exchange of opinions" in *Pravda*'s description of the talks indicated that disagreement was present.[31] In this case it was probably not only over Soviet unhappiness at the escalating Syrian-Iraqi quarrel over the Soviet-built Euphrates Dam waters but also over Gromyko's blunt statement to his Syrian colleague that no peace was possible without the guarantee of Israel's right to exist, and that the USSR was prepared to guarantee Israel's existence.[32] While the timing and content of Gromyko's speech were clearly intended as a signal to Israel, given Syria's unwillingness to recognize Israel's existence, the Syrian foreign minister's failure to reply in public to Gromyko's initiative was perhaps an indication that Syria was not yet ready to embrace this Soviet position on the prerequisites for a Middle Eastern peace settlement.

If the Syrian government proved unwilling to recognize Israel's existence during Khaddam's talks in Moscow, the next Arab visitor to the Soviet capital, Yassir Arafat, was even less prepared to do so. The most both sides were able to agree on was the need for the PLO and the Arab states to coordinate their efforts "against any bilateral separate deal outside the context of a comprehensive settlement of the Arab-Israeli conflict."[33] Arafat, whose forces in Lebanon were now engaged in occasional battles with Lebanese Phalangists, also supported the Soviet position that the policy of partial settlement was "aimed at dividing the Arab countries" and "isolating them from their valuable allies, the Socialist countries, and drawing them into the sphere of imperialist domination."[34]

One week after Arafat's departure from Moscow, Soviet Premier Alexei Kosygin left the Soviet capital for a journey to Libya, which, over the last year, had become one of the Soviet Union's primary allies in the Middle East. Just as in the previous year when Jalloud had visited Moscow, the Libyan prime minister openly called for Soviet aid. After warmly praising the USSR for its economic and military assistance, Jalloud went on to say: "I would like to say that there are possibilities for further development of this assistance so that, relying on it, we would be able to defeat Zionism and imperialism, in the same way that the defeats in Vietnam and Cambodia took place."[35]

Kosygin's reply was equally frank. Despite the Libyan government's stated opposition to the existence of the state of Israel, Kosygin publicly reiterated what had now become the standard Soviet peace plan: complete withdrawal of Israeli troops from Arab territories occupied in 1967, the implementation of the legitimate rights of the Palestinian people (including the right to the creation of their own state), and the guaranteeing of the "independent existence and development of all states in the region."[36] In addition Kosygin, mindful of the strained relations between Libya and Egypt, sought to play down the seriousness of the differences dividing the Arab world while at the same time urging them on to greater unity to solve their problems:

> Allow me to say candidly that the achievement of peace in the Near East depends directly on the Arab countries' unity in the struggle against imperialism and aggression. *We believe that the differences among the Arab countries in approaching a Near East settlement are transient in nature.* We also are convinced that they will be able to overcome these differences, subordinate their actions to the task of strengthening unity in the anti-imperialist struggle, and unite on the path to progress and peace . . . if we are to bring the future closer, unity, the unification of all the progressive forces of the Arab peoples and deepened cooperation among the Arab states are necessary. [emphasis added]

Kosygin also noted that the "overall balance of forces in the world had changed in favor of Socialism," thus enabling the Communists to triumph in Vietnam and Cambodia.

Soon after Kosygin's visit, large amounts of Soviet military aid began to arrive in Libya, and the Egyptian press went so far as to accuse Kadaffi of granting the USSR base rights in Libya in return for this aid, a charge vehemently denied by the USSR.[37]

From Libya, Kosygin went on to Tunisia, one of the pro-Western Arab states, where his welcome, while not as warm as that in Libya, was nonetheless cordial. In summing up the Kosygin visits to the two North African countries, *Izvestia* stated that they had demonstrated the importance of Soviet-Arab cooperation. The article also stated that Kosygin was convinced that despite "differences among the Arab countries in their approaches to the settlement of the Near East conflict," the Arab countries would "be able to overcome these disagreements, put the fundamental interests of the Arab world first and foremost, and subordinate their actions to the strengthening of unity in the anti-imperialist struggle."[38]

While the Soviet leadership was seeking to produce a coordinated and unified Arab approach to the peace talks, it did not overlook the necessity of gaining Israeli agreement for the Soviet peace plan. Mention has already been made of Gromyko's offer to guarantee Israel's existence in his welcoming speech to Syrian Foreign Minister Khaddam and Kosygin's public support of Israel's right to exist in Libya. In addition, the Soviet leadership sent two high-ranking diplomats on a secret mission to Israel, reportedly to convey the same message personally and to sound out the Israelis on possible terms for reconvening the Geneva conference.[39] A number of articles also appeared in the Soviet press openly offering Israel improved relations with the Soviet Union if it were to agree to Soviet conditions for peace. Thus, in a *New Times* article with the title "Growth of Peace Sentiment in Israel," columnist J. Schreiber stated:

> Judging from their public statements, realistically-minded represen-
> tatives of Israeli public-opinion are increasingly coming to see that
> if Israel renounced its present policy and unequivocally declared for
> a just settlement of the conflict, the way would be opened to a nor-
> malization of relations with the Soviet Union and other countries of
> the socialist community.[40]

Similarly, an associate editor of *New Times*, Vladimir Shelepin, in a column answering a Moroccan reader's question as to why the USSR supported the
partition of Palestine at the United Nations in 1947, and the subsequent establishment of the state of Israel, replied that the Jewish community in Palestine
had become an "objective fact" by 1947 that could not be ignored. Shelepin
then pointedly stated, "The road to peace in the Middle East does not lie
through the cancellation of the 1947 U.N. Resolution"[40] —a position advocated
by a number of the more radical Arab states, such as Libya and Iraq.

Despite all of these diplomatic efforts, however, the Soviet leaders were ultimately to prove no more successful than the United States had been in working
out the mechanics of a peace settlement. While the overall Soviet position in the
world had improved with Communist victories in Vietnam and Cambodia (although the new Cambodian regime quickly allied itself to Communist China), a
sharp movement to the left in Portugal that brought Communists near to the
point of taking full power, and a general crisis of confidence in the United States
(which was plagued not only by a severe recession but also by serious doubts as
to its policies in a post-Vietnam world), little could be shown for the extensive
Soviet diplomatic efforts in the Middle East. Meanwhile, opposition to detente
in the United States, which had begun to rise after the 1973 Arab-Israeli war,
was now reaching a new height, with a number of influential Americans charging
that detente had become a smoke screen for the expansion of Soviet power
throughout the world. The Soviet leaders, suffering from a poor harvest and hoping to conclude another strategic arms agreement with the United States, could
not help but be concerned about these developments. Nonetheless, President
Ford's deliberate failure to meet with Soviet dissident Aleksandr Solzhenitsyn
"lest it disturb detente,"[42] and Ford's repeated efforts to convince Congress to
pass a law giving the USSR trade benefits without any conditions as to its emigration policy[43] (the Soviet Union had abrogated its trade agreement with the
United States in January 1975 because Congress had imposed such conditions),
may well have convinced the Soviet leaders that the American government now
needed good relations with the Soviet Union more than the USSR needed a good
relationship with the United States. In any case, the Soviet leadership seized
upon such events as the joint Soviet-American space flight (Apollo-Soyuz), visits

of U.S. Congressmen, and the Conference on European Security at Helsinki to dramatize the positive achievements of detente.

While Soviet-American cooperation may have been visible in outer space and in Helsinki, the two superpowers continued to compete sharply for influence in the Middle East. The main area of competition remained Egypt, whose president, Anwar Sadat, had agreed at the end of March both to a three-month extension of the UN force in the Sinai and to reopen the Suez Canal despite the failure of Kissinger's disengagement mission. Sadat also arranged to meet Ford in Salzburg, Austria, in early June. These events, when coupled with the announcement of Israeli Premier Yitzhak Rabin's planned visit to Washington several weeks later, seemed to indicate that the United States was resuming its efforts to obtain a second-stage Egyptian-Israeli peace agreement. Indeed, on the eve of Sadat's meeting with Ford in Salzburg, *Izvestia* launched yet another attack on "partial agreements," this time openly castigating Egypt for its continued willingness to deal with Kissinger and contrasting Egypt's position with the "principled position" of Syria:

> People in some Arab capitals continue to maintain that the "key to peace" in the Near East is in the hands of the U.S.A. which supposedly is able to exert some kind of decisive pressure on Israel. . . . Experience has shown that certain circles in the U.S.A. have no intention of exerting pressure on Israel, and particularly not in the Arabs' favor. For these circles, especially after the loss of Vietnam, the Arab-Israeli conflict is only a means of consolidating their positions in the Near East, which have been seriously undermined as a result of the social and national-liberation revolutions in the Arab countries. . . .
>
> What was Egypt's attitude to the Kissinger plan? *The very fact that talks were held with the American Secretary of State was evidence that Cairo is not rejecting the search for an accord on the question of a partial withdrawal.*
>
> Syria's position is very clear. It would regard an Egyptian-Israeli agreement as a separate agreement, one at variance with the spirit of Arab unity. . . . [This is] in keeping with Syria's principled position which organically links a Near East settlement with the creation of an independent Palestinian Arab state.[44] [emphasis added]

While the Soviet Union praised Syria's "principled position," she might have been somewhat concerned about the development of Syria's economic relations with the West, and with the United States in particular.[45] In addition, the fact that Sadat had journeyed to Salzburg via Damascus at least implicitly indicated Syria's support for the trip. Syrian Foreign Minister Khaddam's visit to Washington, soon after Rabin's, may also have provided evidence to the Russians that Syria continued to keep her diplomatic options open. A more serious concern for the Soviet leadership was the exacerbation of relations between Syria and Iraq, the USSR's two primary allies in the Middle East. An editorial in *New Times* was indicative of Soviet concern:

> Certain quarters in the West and the Zionists would like to capitalize on the complications between Iraq and Syria to undermine the unity of the progressive national patriotic forces in the Arab East. Developments show that hostile forces always seek to take advantage of the difficulties arising in independent Arab countries, particularly those following an anti-imperialist policy. That explains the alarm caused in the Arab capitals by the Iraqi-Syrian differences. The situation there was described as a "dangerous test for all Arabs."[46]

Although the Syrian-Iraqi dispute over the Euphrates Dam was to recede somewhat, the hostility between the rival wings of the Ba'ath party ruling in Damascus and Baghdad remained acute, and Syria's reported willingness to defend Kuwait in the event of an Iraqi invasion did little to improve Syrian-Iraqi relations.[47] Interestingly enough, however, although Syria and Iraq differed on a number of critical issues, they both agreed that it was in their national interests to improve economic relations with the West. Indeed, Iraq followed Syria's example in this regard and, blessed with a large amount of oil revenue and no longer having to spend large amounts of money on a war against the now-defeated Kurds, turned toward the West in expenditures for national development, thereby reducing her economic dependence on the Soviet bloc.[48] Perhaps to avert the impression that Iraq was sliding into the economic camp of the West, as Egypt already seemed to have done, the Soviet media gave major coverage to the cooperation agreement reached between Iraq and the Council for Mutual Economic Assistance (the Soviet bloc's counterpart of the Common Market), which was designed to plan multilateral economic projects.[49]

While the USSR displayed considerable concern about developments in Syrian-Iraqi relations, she was very well disposed toward the steady improvement in Syrian-Jordanian relations, which reached a high point when Assad visited Amman in mid-June and the Syrian and Jordanian governments announced the formation of a permanent joint high commission to coordinate military, political, economic, and cultural policies.[50] While to the Soviet leadership, which had sent representatives to Jordan on several occasions during the spring, this development may have appeared to be yet another step toward the creation of a Syrian-Jordanian-PLO entente that would isolate Egypt and become a center of "anti-imperialist Arab unity" in the Arab world, both Syria and Jordan had other reasons for improving relations. Mention has already been made of Assad's desire to cover his flank in case another Egyptian-Israeli disengagement agreement were to be consummated. In addition, an agreement with Jordan would serve as a counter to Iraq, which, in the early spring, had made several moves to improve relations with Egypt and Saudi Arabia as well as Iran.[51]

The Jordanian-Syrian rapprochement also met a number of King Hussein's needs. In the first place, an improved relationship with Syria would strengthen Hussein's position against the PLO, which had not forsaken its pledge to overthrow him[52] but was now dependent on Syria for most of its support—particularly since hostilities had begun to break out in Lebanon. Consequently, in return for Jordan's agreeing to close cooperation with Syria, Hussein may well have extracted a pledge from Assad to keep the PLO under control and prevent any subversive or overt actions against the Jordanian government. Second, the rapprochement would keep open the Syrian border for the transit of Jordanian goods—the border had frequently been closed in the past by Assad because of Hussein's attacks on the Palestinians—and this would facilitate Jordan's economic development. Third, a major arms deal was under negotiation between Jordan and the United States, and the Jordanian movement toward Soviet-backed Syria may have been expected to be seen in Washington as a first step toward an arms purchase from the USSR. This, coupled with the Soviet diplomatic visits to Jordan in the spring, could well have been a ploy to obtain the maximum in arms from the United States. If this was one of Hussein's goals in moving closer to Syria, however, he failed to consider the growing power of the U.S. Congress, which vetoed the large arms agreement the Ford administration was eventually to promise Jordan. The final arms supply arrangement was considerably less than the Jordanian monarch had hoped for.[53] A final Jordanian goal in the rapprochement with Syria was similar to the Syrian goal in moving toward Jordan—a desire to avoid being isolated against Israel in case an Egyptian-Israeli disengagement agreement was worked out.

As Jordan and Syria moved closer together, Sadat made an attempt to speed up his negotiations with Israel by threatening, on July 15, not to renew the mandate of the UN Sinai force set to expire on July 23. Sadat backed down from this decision, however, and agreed to renew the mandate when he saw the image he had so carefully nurtured of himself as an Arab "moderate" begin to fade in American eyes.[54] Following the renewal of the UN mandate, bargaining between Israel and Egypt resumed in earnest, and on August 6 the Egyptian newspaper *Al-Ahram* published an article stating that it was Sadat's policy to live in peace with Israel, if the latter withdrew to her 1967 borders.[55] The United States was even more interested in a second-stage Egyptian-Israeli agreement than before, because her position in the eastern Mediterranean had suffered a major blow on July 25 when Turkey decided to halt operations of American troops at their Turkish bases because the U.S. Congress had halted arms aid. As might be expected, the Soviet Union hailed the Turkish decision and urged the nation to go one step further and pull out of NATO entirely.[56]

With the rise of anti-American spirit in Turkey, and also in Greece, where the United States lost home port privileges for the Sixth Fleet, it became imperative for the United States to work out a peace agreement between Egypt and Israel, not only to shore up the faltering American position in the eastern Mediter-

ranean but also to restore confidence in American leadership, which had suffered severe reverses in Vietnam, Cambodia, and Portugal. As the U.S. leadership
stepped up its efforts to achieve the disengagement agreement, the Soviet leadership increased its public attacks on Egyptian policy and again began to try to isolate Egypt from its Arab neighbors, perhaps hoping that the power of Arab public opinion might prevent Sadat from making the agreement.

In following this strategy, the Soviet leaders may have hoped that if Sadat's policies could be portrayed in a sufficiently negative light, the oil-rich Arab
states might be swayed by the power of Arab opinion to withhold the economic
aid on which Egypt depended. In retaliating against this Soviet policy, Sadat began to publicly denounce the Soviet Union for her failure to support Egypt, only
to be accused of anti-Sovietism and selling out to the West by the Soviet press.
On July 15, *Pravda* openly attacked the government-controlled Egyptian newspaper *Al-Akhbar* for deliberately trying "to mislead millions of Egyptians and
citizens of other Arab countries to pervert the USSR's policy in the Near East,
and, in the final analysis, to sow anti-Soviet sentiments among the Arabs." The
article went on to state:

> It is not difficult to figure out what foreign and domestic forces' in-
> terests it is that the authors of the anti-Soviet articles appearing in
> the Cairo press are playing up to, and who is interested in sowing dis-
> cord between the peoples of Egypt, Libya and other Arab countries,
> on the one hand, and the Soviet Union, their natural ally, on the
> other.[57]

A second step in the USSR's anti-Sadat policy was the decision of the Soviet leadership to revive the Egyptian Communist Party, which had been dissolved 11 years before in a Soviet attempt to influence Egypt's single political
party, the Arab Socialist Union, from within.[58] The program of the newly recon-
stituted Egyptian Communist Party was published in the pro-Libyan Lebanese
newspaper *As-Safir* on August 4, and it consisted of a scathing attack on Sadat's
domestic and foreign policies. While officially eschewing a call for the overthrow
of Sadat's regime, the party gave notice that it would seek to exploit "patriotic
trends within the Egyptian armed forces" and would "struggle to strike at agent
forces in the regime which seek to implement the imperialist designs and remove
these forces from the ruling alliances."[59]

Nonetheless, neither Soviet press attacks nor the revival of the Egyptian
Communist Party served to deter Sadat from working out a three-year disengagement agreement with Israel (which was to be compensated for its withdrawal by
large amounts of American military aid and a U.S. pledge not to deal with the
PLO until it accepted UN Resolution no. 242 and recognized Israel's right to
exist), under Kissinger's mediation, in the latter part of August.[60] Throughout
these negotiations, *Pravda* kept up its efforts to isolate Sadat by citing Western

reports of Israeli withdrawal concessions as "militarily meaningless."[61] It also stated that the negotiations ignored such important questions as a withdrawal from the Golan Heights and from the banks of the Jordan, as well as a recognition of the legitimate rights of the Palestinian Arabs.[62] The Soviet press also cited Arab newspapers denouncing the agreement as a threat to Arab unity.[63] Its strongest criticism, however, appeared on August 29, when the agreement was just about to be concluded. In a feature article titled "The Main Problems Are Not Settled," *Pravda* cited Syrian Foreign Minister Abdul Khaddam's denunciation of the agreement as "not a step toward peace, but a step toward war."[64]

As the disengagement talks reached their successful conclusion, perhaps the only positive development the Soviet leadership could detect was a move toward still closer cooperation between Syria and Jordan. On August 22, Hussein journeyed to Damascus to sign an agreement with Syria for the establishment of a Syrian-Jordanian supreme leadership council to coordinate the foreign policy and military activities of the two countries.[65] In addition, the two states issued a joint communique on August 25 stating that peace in the Middle East could come about only through the complete withdrawal of Israeli forces from all occupied Arab territories and the assurance of the legal rights of the Palestinian Arabs. Soviet approval of the intensification of Syrian-Jordanian cooperation can be noted from the fact that the joint communique received front-page coverage in *Pravda*.[66]

Thus, the USSR proved unable to prevent the second Israeli-Egyptian disengagement agreement, despite its attempts to isolate the Sadat regime both within Egypt and throughout the Arab world. Given these Soviet efforts, one must question Kissinger's and Ford's evaluations that the USSR deliberately kept quiet during the Middle Eastern negotiations lest she upset detente and prevent Ford's journey to Helsinki for the European Security Conference.[67] It would appear, rather, that despite the Soviet leadership's strong opposition to the second Egyptian-Israeli disengagement agreement, they had proved powerless to prevent it, much as they proved unable to influence the earlier Egyptian and Syrian disengagement agreements.

SOVIET POLICY TOWARD THE MIDDLE EAST AFTER THE SECOND EGYPTIAN-ISRAELI DISENGAGEMENT AGREEMENT

The Soviet leadership was clearly discouraged by the second Egyptian-Israeli disengagement agreement, which seemed to herald both a resurgence of American influence in the Middle East and a further erosion of the Soviet position. Following the agreement, the USSR redoubled her efforts to isolate Sadat and to denigrate his domestic and foreign policies. At the same time, the USSR drew closer to Syria, which considered herself abandoned by Egypt in the Arab confrontation with Israel. The Syrians also found themselves confronted by a civil war in Lebanon between Christians and Moslems, with Libya and Iraq—nations with whom Syria had been at odds—funneling money to some of the leftist Moslem groups. With a possible conflict facing them on two fronts, therefore, the Syrians drew closer to the USSR, and seemed to play the role of leaders of the anti-imperialist bloc of Arab states ascribed to them by the Russians. The USSR also maintained close contact with the PLO, and the Soviet leaders indicated that the USSR would not be unhappy if the Palestinian forces, together with Lebanese Moslems, overturned the Christian power structure and swung Lebanon away from its traditional pro-Western position.

Meanwhile, the USSR was having difficulties in other parts of the Middle East. Although Soviet-Kuwaiti relations seemed to improve following the visit of Kuwait's foreign minister to Moscow, Soviet hopes for an increased role in the Persian Gulf following the end of the Iran-Iraq conflict appeared to be thwarted as the leading local power, Iran, took a more assertive position. Indeed, the USSR began openly to criticize Iran both for her continued cooperation with CENTO and for her intervention in Oman to help the Sultan defeat the Popular Front guerrillas, who were aided by Soviet-backed South Yemen. On the other side of the Arab world, the old feud between Algeria and Morocco was rekindled as the two countries, which had gone to war in 1963, maneuvered for control of the phosphate-rich Spanish Sahara. The USSR, which had endeavored to maintain good relations with both nations, was therefore caught in a dilemma not unlike the one that had plagued her in the Iran-Iraq confrontation.

Finally, Soviet relations with the United States, both in the Middle East and in other areas, such as Portugal and Angola, became increasingly strained. In addition, while the USSR continued to call for a resumption of the Geneva conference, the United States (and Israel) refused to attend if the PLO were present, and no conference materialized. Nonetheless, both Syria and the USSR were able to maneuver a resolution through the UN Security Council making the continued stationing of UN forces on the Golan Heights conditional upon the participation of the PLO in the January 1976 Security Council debate on the Middle East.

The Soviet Union launched a strong attack on the second-stage settlement as soon as it was completed. The USSR opposed it not only because it "sowed discord in the Arab world" but also because the agreement called for the stationing of American civilian technicians (rather than UN troops) to monitor the six electronic surveillance posts that Israel agreed to evacuate (along with the Abu Rodeis oil fields). In complaining about this development, *Pravda* stated:

> Commentators are reasonably asking why it is necessary to violate this [UN] system and replace an already existing international mechanism with unilateral national control by only one of the powers, whose pro-Israeli position is no secret to anyone.[68]

To show their displeasure over the agreement, the Russians boycotted the signing ceremony in Geneva. Interestingly enough, the United States also did not attend the session, despite all the hard work Kissinger had put in to secure the agreement—reportedly to avoid embarrassing the USSR.[69] Whether the USSR would have boycotted such a ceremony in deference to the United States if Soviet representatives had worked out an agreement in the face of U.S. opposition is a very open question. Indeed, Soviet leadership may well have interpreted the American action as yet another case of American weakness, similar to Ford's failure to meet Solzhenitsyn the previous month.

If the United States was taking a rather soft stand toward Soviet opposition to the disengagement agreement, Sadat was not. The Egyptian president, whose long-postponed trip to the United States had been announced the day after the agreement was concluded, launched a blistering attack on the Soviet Union for "flagrant incitement and an attempt at splitting the ranks of the Arab nation."[70] The Soviet response to Egypt's signing of the pact was twofold. In the first place, Soviet media attacks on the Sadat regime's foreign policy increased in intensity, reaching a new crescendo on the eve of Sadat's trip to the United States at the end of October.[71] Second, the Russians played up American promises of large-scale, long-term military aid to the Israelis (including nuclear-capable Lance missiles and, initially, long-range Pershing missiles), implying that as a result of the agreement, Israel was in a far better military position than before (and Sadat had therefore sold out the Arab cause).[72] Finally, in meetings with Arab heads of state and Arab political organizations,[73] the Russians sought to denigrate Sadat's policies, and thereby so isolate the Egyptian leader that no other Arab head of state would be tempted to follow his path in working out separate deals mediated by the United States.

A feature article in *Pravda*, appearing on the eve of Sadat's visit to the United States, typified Soviet criticism of Sadat:

> Recently, the Egyptian press has been carrying more and more comments that are meant to cast aspersions on the Soviet Union and on its policy in the Near East question, especially with respect to Egypt. Some go almost to the point of claiming that the Soviet Union is to blame for the fact that the Egyptian leadership is now being criticized by other Arab countries in connection with the recent separate Egyptian-Israeli agreement. . . .
>
> The fact that the Soviet position most fully meets the fundamental interests of the Arab peoples has been graphically confirmed yet again by the critical attitude of other Arab states toward the recent Egyptian-Israeli agreement on the partial withdrawal of Israeli troops from the Sinai. It is being criticized because, under the terms of the agreement, Egypt, to which the aggressor has returned an *infinitesimally small* part of its territory, has at the same time taken away the

urgency of the question of the liberation of the part of its own territory—almost 90% of the Sinai that remains under Israeli occupation
—and of the other Arab states' territories seized by Israel. Also a
blow has been dealt to efforts aimed at guaranteeing the legitimate
and unalienable rights of the Arab people of Palestine. . . .

The signing of an agreement of this sort could not fail to strike a
blow at the unity of the Arab peoples. It is not for the best of motives that some people are now trying, as the saying goes, to lay the
blame at someone else's door, flinging reproaches at the Soviet
Union for "undermining Arab unity."

These reproaches are obviously being sent to the wrong address.
*There has been no meeting between Soviet and Arab leaders, there
has been no Soviet-Arab document, in which the Soviet side has not
emphasized the importance of the solidarity of the Arab states and
of strengthening the unity of their actions* in the struggle against Israel's continuing aggression. In its practical activity, *the Soviet
Union is doing everything it can to facilitate the solidarity of the
Arab states and peoples on an anti-imperialist basis.*[74] [emphasis
added]

Indeed, the USSR was making an intense effort to rally the Arabs behind
the anti-imperialist banner, although with only mixed success. Just as in the period following the failure of Kissinger's mission in March, a parade of high-ranking Arab visitors came to Moscow. This time, however, the visitors came not
only from the "progressive" Arab states and organizations (Iraq, Syria, Libya,
and the PLO) but also from such conservative states as Jordan and Kuwait. The
key to Soviet policy in the Arab world, however, remained Syria, which denounced the Egyptian agreement with Israel as "shameful and disgraceful"[75] because it did not contain a commitment by Israel to negotiate the return of the
Golan Heights to Syria. Assad came to Moscow on October 9, and the joint announcement describing the meeting stated that "no one would be allowed to disrupt or damage" the friendship between the two states.[76] The trip was evidently
a profitable one for the Syrians since, one week later, Assad refused to enter into
negotiations with the United States on a disengagement agreement similar to
that worked out by Egypt and Israel.[77] This may have occurred because the Is-
realis had spoken only of "cosmetic arrangements" on the Golan Heights until a
full peace treaty was signed, and even then it appeared doubtful whether Israel
would give up all of the Golan Heights because of her security problems in the
northern Galilee.[78] In addition, in an interview with the Kuwaiti newspaper *Al-
Rai Al-Am*, Assad, whose support of the Palestinians had helped secure his domestic legitimacy, stated: "Syria will never accept American offers to mediate a
similar disengagement accord on the Golan Heights because such an accord will
be mainly designed to separate Syria from the Palestine question."[79]

In return for taking this stand, which scuttled American moves to keep the shuttle momentum alive, Assad was promised new shipments of Soviet weapons, including advanced Mig-23s, which more than made up for Egypt's pulling out its warplanes from Syria as relations between the two Arab nations sharply deteriorated. The Mig-23s arrived in Syria in the middle of November, thereby strengthening Syria's position as yet another deadline for the extension of the mandate for the UN force in the Golan Heights approached.[80] Syria used the approaching deadline to strengthen its demands for changes in UN Security Council Resolution nos. 242 and 338 favorable to the Palestinians, as its price for renewing the mandate. When the United States opposed the Syrian position, Assad reduced his requirements to a demand that the PLO be permitted to participate in the Security Council debate on the Middle East in January 1976. The United States did not oppose this Syrian ploy, probably in order to keep the momentum toward a peace settlement (or at least the appearance of such a momentum) alive. This Syrian maneuver, backed by the USSR, which used the opportunity to embarrass the United States, won the PLO increased diplomatic stature by enabling its representatives to address the Security Council for the first time, and won Syria new prestige in the Arab world, confirming its position as champion of the Palestinians.

While the PLO was winning more prestige in the United Nations, it was facing greater difficulty in the Middle East and becoming ever more dependent on Syria. Civil war had broken out in Lebanon, and the various PLO groupings allied to Moslem factions found themselves in almost daily battle with Christian Lebanese forces. Indeed, they may have feared a repetition of the events of 1970, when Hussein had bloodily suppressed the Palestinian guerrillas in Jordan. At the same time, the PLO's relations with Egypt had deteriorated very sharply. Zuheir Mohsen, head of the military department of the PLO, had called Sadat "a traitor and conspirator" for signing the agreement with Israel, and promised an all-out Palestinian offensive against the Sadat government.[81] In addition, a Palestinian group seized the Egyptian Embassy in Madrid and another tried to hijack an Egyptian plane in Beirut. In retaliation for PLO opposition, Sadat closed down the PLO radio station in Egypt, much as Nasser had done five years earlier when the Palestinians had opposed the Egyptian-Israeli cease-fire negotiated by U.S. Secretary of State William Rogers.[82]

While the PLO forces suffered from a severely strained relationship with Egypt and were encountering difficulties in Lebanon, the Soviet leadership appeared to be reevaluating its own strategy toward them. As early as April 12, Viktor Kudryavtsev, Vice-Chairman of the Soviet Committee for Solidarity with Asia and Africa, wrote an extensive article in *Izvestia*, in which he described the Palestinian resistance movement both as an aid to Soviet policy opposing separate agreements and as an instrument for social change in the Arab world. Kudryavtsev envisioned the Palestinian "resistance movement" as a "kind of motor making it possible for the national liberation movement in the Arab East not to get stuck at intermediate stages, seduced by the promises of imperialist sirens, but to develop further along the path of progress."[83]

Three days later, Kudryavtsev published another article on the Palestinian resistance movement, noting with satisfaction (and perhaps a bit of wishful thinking) that the Palestinian movement had become committed to social change, although he also expressed concern that the PLO might be subverted by reactionary forces in the Arab world:

> It was gratifying to hear from the leaders of the Palestine Resistance Movement that if the struggle against Zionist aggression and imperialist intrigues in the Near East is to be successful it is necessary to launch a struggle against internal Arab reaction, which is an ally and bulwark of forces alien to the national interests of the Arab peoples. It is no secret that the P.R.M. is a movement of socially very heterogeneous strata of the Arab people of Palestine, and that a struggle is taking place in this movement over the working out of correct guidelines for activity, guidelines that are in the interest of the Palestinians themselves, over goals and over methods of achieving them. But, under the impact of events as they develop in the Near East, the P.R.M. today no longer regards itself as a "supraclass, nonsocial" organization involved only in the accomplishment of a concrete national task. According to the Palestinians, a confrontation between the P.R.M. on the one hand and the Arab reactionaries and conservative circles on the other is becoming inevitable under the impact of the ongoing development of the revolutionary process in the Near East and the polarization of forces in the Arab national-liberation movement.
>
> In this connection, our conversational partners' concern not only for the creation of their own statehood but—and this is the main thing—over what this statehood will be like, their concern that it not lose the progressive nature that characterizes the movement itself, is understandable. The point is that under the impact of the imperialists' setbacks in the Near East, it must be expected that their tactics will become still more insidious and refined. *Certain circles interested in keeping the Near East within the framework of their own interests would like to turn the future state of the Palestinian Arabs into a kind of trap for the P.R.M. To confine this movement within certain boundaries, taking advantage of economic difficulties, to subordinate it to the interests of the monopolies and their local agents, to emasculate the progressive content of the Palestine Resistance Movement, to eliminate or at least to restrict the influence of the democratic elements in it, to shift it from the front lines far into the rear—these are the reactionaries' hopes. For this reason, the P.R.M.*

*leaders are even now doing a great deal of work to ensure that the
future state will be progressive, taking into account the inevitability
and necessity of social changes that should consolidate in the Arab
countries the fruits of their anti-imperialist and anti-Zionist struggle.*

*During our stay in Syria and Lebanon when the results of U.S.
Secretary of State H. Kissinger's mission were still unknown, Syrian
President H. Assad proposed that a united military and political
leadership for Syria and the Palestine Liberation Organization be
created, something that other Arab countries could join too. All the
people with whom we talked drew attention to the great political
significance of this proposal. The initiators of this undertaking had,
as it were, warned the imperialists that, despite everything, a core of
anti-imperialist Arab unity exists and will continue to exist. Furthermore, in spite of whatever difficulties may arise in the Near East, for
one reason or another, the movement of the Arab people of Palestine will never be deprived of a territorial base for its struggle.* One
cannot fail to see in this step a manifestation of the irreversibility of
the positive processes that are taking place in the Near East in our
time.[84] [emphasis added]

It is interesting to note the Soviet emphasis on the PLO as an agency for
social change in the Middle East, particularly given Yasir Arafat's opposition to
Marxism—and the Marxist groups within the PLO—and his willingness to accept
aid from any and all Arab states, including the conservative Arab states of Kuwait and Saudi Arabia. It was perhaps for this reason that Kudryavtsev's article
went on to praise the Marxist Palestinian leader Naef Hawatmeh (leader of the
Marxist Popular Democratic Front for the Liberation of Palestine) as "a politically experienced and erudite person" with whom Kudryavtsev had a "very useful and profound conversation."[85] The subsequent Soviet decision to invite Hawatmeh to Moscow in December for a week of negotiations[86] indicated that the
USSR might be considering trying to groom him as an alternative to Arafat in a
newly established Palestinian state, or at least to use him as a means of leverage
on Arafat to prevent him from agreeing to a settlement not to the liking of the
USSR.

Meanwhile, it appeared that Arafat was moving a bit closer toward the Soviet view of a peace settlement. In a visit to Moscow in late November 1975, in
addition to denouncing the policy of partial agreements and praising Soviet support, Arafat agreed with his Soviet hosts that a peace agreement could be
achieved by the withdrawal of Israeli troops from all Arab territories "occupied
by aggression" and by the satisfaction of the legitimate national rights of the
Arab people of Palestine, including their right to create their own national state
on Palestinian territory in accordance with UN resolutions.[87] While the terminology was vague, Arafat seemed to be giving up his vision of a "democratic-secular"

state that he had discussed at the United Nations the year before and to be moving toward the Soviet concept of an independent Palestinian state. However, the vagueness of the terminology left him a great deal of room to maneuver, and the fact that *Pravda* mentioned "an exchange of opinions" indicated that disagreement was still present.

While the Soviet leaders were seeking to move the PLO toward the Soviet view of a peace settlement, and using the organization to aid Soviet policy in the Arab world, Moscow was encountering resistance to the spread of Soviet influence in the Persian Gulf. Perhaps expecting that upon the conclusion of the Iran-Iraq conflict, the major barrier to Soviet influence in the region had been eliminated, the USSR found herself confronted not only by the Iraqi-Syrian conflict but also by a more assertive Iran, which, while occasionally quarreling with the United States over the cost of oil, nonetheless closely cooperated with the latter in CENTO affairs. In addition, by improving relations with the now conservative regime of Egypt and with Saudi Arabia, the Shah seemed to be in the process of establishing a conservative, anti-Soviet grouping of states in the Middle East that would undermine Soviet efforts to establish "anti-imperialist" Arab unity. Indeed, part of the program of the newly revivified Egyptian Communist Party attacked the Sadat regime for "strengthening its relations with the regimes which are agents of the U.S. imperialism, such as Iran," as well as for "increasing its cooperation with the reactionary Arab regimes and establishing a Cairo-Riyadh axis."[88]

Soviet disappointment about the trend of developments in the Persian Gulf was directly expressed in an article by Kudryavtsev in the October 4 issue of *Izvestia*:

> Now that detente has begun to influence the course of events in Asia, some circles in the Middle East, not without the knowledge of CENTO's prime movers, of course, have started a campaign for the creation of new military-political blocs in the zone of the Persian Gulf and the Indian Ocean.
>
> Touching upon the subject of the security of the Persian Gulf countries, the Teheran newspaper Kayhan, for example, stressed that the organization of such security could become the lever with which to "get the great powers out of this region". *Apparently reflecting the mood at the top, the newspaper made no distinction between the policy of the USSR and that of the U.S.A. in the Indian Ocean.* But the U.S.A. is making no secret of the fact that the expansion of its base on Diego Garcia and the strengthening of its military presence in the Indian Ocean will enhance its ability to pressure the countries of South Asia and the petroleum-producing countries of the Middle East. The advocates of the expansion of CENTO are evidently seeking to meet the American plans in this area halfway, espe-

cially as this conforms to the policy of neo-colonialism, which in this instance is aimed at making the Asian countries themselves the agents of imperialist policy.[89] [emphasis added]

The USSR stepped up its criticism of Iran two weeks later as an article in *Pravda* criticized Iran for its large defense budget and its close ties with the West.

Many observers feel that the large arms burden that Iran has assumed is hindering its economic development. "In terms of percentage of gross national product, Iran's defense budget is larger than that of any NATO power", writes the *London Times*. Reports have filtered into the press recently to the effect that certain Iranian circles are even planning to activate CENTO or create another bloc in the Persian Gulf to "defend its oil riches". It is clear that the realization of such a dangerous idea, which runs counter to the spirit of the times, could not only lead to political complications but could also increase the country's military expenditures. . . .

As it becomes more economically developed, Iran is forming increasingly closer ties with the international capitalist market and is more frequently subject to the effects of inflation, currency and financial disorders and market fluctuations. Entire branches of Iranian industry are tied to giant multinational companies. For instance, there are plans to build a synthetic fibers complex near Isfahan in cooperation with Dupont, which will receive 40% of the stock. Foreign capital is being introduced into new or nascent industries, such as chemicals, metallurgy, machine building, electronics, aircraft and helicopter assembly, atomic energy and copper and uranium processing. Even if international companies do not receive a controlling share of the stock, they exercise an influence through patents, skilled personnel and market connections.[90]

The Soviet Union was also clearly unhappy with Iranian policy in Oman, where Iranian troops were aiding the Sultan in suppressing the guerrillas of the Popular Front for the Liberation of Oman, who were aided by Soviet-backed South Yemen, which now appeared close to war with Oman.[91] Indeed, a feature article in early January 1976 on the situation in southern Arabia and the Persian Gulf by *New Times* associate editor Dmitry Volsky not only continued the Soviet attack on Iran's policy of cooperation with CENTO but also pointedly stated:

Disquieting . . . is the news from southern Arabia. The People's Democratic Republic of Yemen has officially announced that since mid-October Democratic Yemen has been subjected to attacks by

Iranian troops and mercenaries in the service of the Sultan of neighbouring Oman. According to the London "New Statesman" no less than 2,000 British nationals, among them combat officers and flyers, are serving in the Sultan's army, besides which the Sultan has invited several thousand Iranian troops. But even with the help of the British mercenaries and the Iranians, it has proved impossible to crush the popular uprising in Dhofar, the western province of the Sultanate. The rebels have been placed in an extremely difficult position, but they are continuing military action. In these circumstances the opponents of the liberation movement are tempted to resort to a device that was widely but unsuccessfully used during the Vietnam war —to carry hostilities over to the territory of the neighbouring state, especially since the strengthening of the progressive regime in Democratic Yemen is exercising a growing influence on public sentiment and the psychological climate throughout the area. Some quarters probably would not be averse to turning the Arabian South, like Lebanon, into a new seat of tension to divert the attention of the Arab peoples away from the struggle for a just settlement of the Middle East conflict. All this clearly shows with what dangers to stability the "stabilizing force" concept is fraught. More, along with the U.S. arms, so-called "technical assistance field teams" consisting of U.S. servicemen have appeared in Iran and Saudi Arabia. By 1980 there will be as many as 150,000 Americans there, the Pentagon estimates on the basis of the contracts concluded to date. In effect the prospect is one of "invisible occupation", which, needless to say, cannot be taken as an indication of striving to strengthen national independence. Besides, the threats of direct intervention in the oil-producing countries have not yet been withdrawn.

According to the "Washington Post", official U.S. spokesmen regard the Persian Gulf as a backdoor to the Arab world.[92]

It was perhaps to counter what it perceived as a developing Saudi Arabian-Iranian-American alliance grouping in the Persian Gulf region that the Soviet leadership invited the Kuwaiti foreign minister, Sheikh Sabah Al-Ahmad Al-Jaber Al-Sabah, to Moscow at the beginning of December. For the Kuwaitis, the visit also held important possibilities, since Kuwait continued to fear an invasion by Soviet-supported Iraq, which, while moving to improve relations with other Persian Gulf states, had not renounced her claims to Kuwaiti territory. In addition, the Kuwaitis were interested in diversifying their arms purchases, hitherto supplied by the West, at least in part because of Western oil threats. The USSR, which had long used the supply of arms as a means of political influence, proved willing to meet the Kuwaiti requests. The USSR may have perceived the Kuwaiti foreign minister's visit and the supply of arms as the first steps toward detaching

Kuwait from its pro-Western stance in the Middle East, much as it hoped to do with King Hussein's regime in Jordan.[93] While the joint communique published after the visit referred to a number of "exchanges of opinions"—thus indicating disagreement—both sides did agree to the following declaration concerning the Persian Gulf:

> Peace and security in this [Persian Gulf] area could be strengthened by prohibiting *foreign interference in the affairs of this region*, by in-suring freedom of navigation in the Persian Gulf, and by establishing trust and good-neighborly cooperation among *all the states* in the gulf zone on the basis of *noninterference in each other's internal af-fairs and respect for the right of each* to free and independent devel-opment.[94] [emphasis added]

Thus, both sides seemed to get what they wished. Kuwait obtained, at least on paper, Soviet support for her independence against Iraq, while the USSR obtained Kuwait's support of her position opposing "foreign [U.S.] interference in the region."

Indeed, in his *New Times* article the following month, Volsky referred to this Soviet-Kuwaiti declaration as an indication of the type of "detente policy" the Russians wished to see in the Persian Gulf:

> There is only one way to normalize the situation in the Persian Gulf, and that is to extend to it the general principles of detente. A con-crete programme for the application of these principles here has al-ready been outlined. It found reflection in the joint Soviet-Kuwaiti communique published in early December.[95]

While the USSR was endeavoring to promote its version of detente in the Persian Gulf, events in North Africa were moving toward war. As Spain with-drew from the phosphate-rich Spanish Sahara, both Morocco, itself a major phosphate exporter, which wished to annex the territory, and Algeria, which wished it to be independent (and under Algerian influence) began their maneu-vering, with Mauritania supporting Morocco in return for the southern third of the disputed territory. The end result was that Morocco and Mauritania annexed the area. Algeria then provided support to the Polisario Liberation Front, which began to wage guerrilla war against Morocco and Mauritania in an effort to win independence for the former Spanish Sahara.

The situation posed an old dilemma for the Soviet leadership: which side to support in a conflict when the optimum Soviet policy is to maintain good re-lations with both countries. If, given the closer tie between the USSR and Alge-ria—a tie reinforced by Algeria's willingness to transship Soviet war materiel to the Soviet-backed faction in Angola[96]—the USSR were to support Algeria, Morocco would be alienated. In such a situation, any hopes the Soviet leadership may have entertained of winning Morocco to its side, much as it was trying to do with other conservative Arab states like Kuwait and Jordan, would be dashed. This, indeed, appeared to be the outcome, as the Soviet press supported independence for the Spanish Sahara.[97] The Moroccan navy captured, off the coast of the former Spanish Sahara, a Soviet cargo ship that contained arms and three Algerian officers—an indication that the weapons were bound for anti-Moroccan forces in the former Spanish colony.[98]

While the conflict in North Africa posed a dilemma for Soviet diplomacy, it also appeared to hold some benefit for the USSR. Libya, a Soviet client state long isolated in the Arab world, signed a pact with Algeria at the end of December calling for the two nations to coordinate their policies in support of the Polisario Liberation Front, and for each nation to consider an attack on the other as an attack on herself.[99] The Libyan-Algerian pact was one of a number of moves made at the time by the Libyans in an effort to escape their isolation in the Arab world. Libyan Prime Minister Jalloud had gone to Iraq at the beginning of January, reportedly to coordinate policies opposing any settlement with Israel.[100] Also, several weeks earlier a Libyan-Kuwaiti agreement had been signed to establish joint military industries to produce aircraft and other weapons.[101] Whether either of these latter moves by Libya would be of benefit to the Soviet Union, however, was an open question. Both Libya and Iraq have continued to oppose the Soviet Union's three-point plan for peace in the Middle East because it stipulates Israel's right to exist, and closer coordination of what has been called their "rejectionist front" policies is not likely to make the Soviet diplomatic position any easier. Second, the establishment of the Libyan-Kuwaiti joint arms industry, if ever realized, could make Libya more independent of Soviet weapons supplies. Nonetheless, the establishment of an arms industry is a long-term undertaking, and even if it were not done under Soviet technical supervision, the USSR may have seen the move as another step toward detaching Kuwait from the pro-Western camp of states in the Arab world.

The Soviet Union may also have viewed the steady improvement of Libyan-Turkish relations in the same light, particularly since it coincided with a Soviet effort to reduce Turkey's ties to NATO. Indeed, Premier Kosygin visited Turkey at the end of December and the two countries agreed to draw up "a political document on friendly relations and cooperation."[102] Nonetheless, this rather vague statement could be interpreted more as an expression of Turkish unhappiness with American policy than as a real move toward the USSR, because the Soviet leadership continued to strongly condemn the Turkish occupation of northern Cyprus.

While Soviet diplomacy was active throughout the entire Middle East, from Morocco to Kuwait, in the period following the second Egyptian-Israeli disengagement agreement, Soviet-American relations continued to be a major concern for the Soviet leaders. Strategic arms negotiations remained stalled, Sino-

Soviet relations continued to be strained (despite China's return of the Soviet helicopter crew captured in 1974), and the worst Soviet harvest in a decade made the USSR once again dependent on large imports of American grain. At the same time, the Soviet Union had suffered a defeat in Portugal as the Portuguese Communists were driven from their positions of power in the government —a development viewed with great relief by Washington because of Portugal's membership in NATO and the U.S. bases in the Azores. The Soviet leadership moved quickly to counter this defeat, however, by stepping up aid to Soviet-backed forces fighting in the Angolan civil war. This Soviet aid, which consisted of heavy weapons and the airlift of thousands of Cuban troops, turned the tide of battle and enabled the Soviet-backed side to score a string of victories against Western-backed forces. This development, however, angered Ford and Kissinger, who were already on the domestic political defensive against such critics of detente as presidential candidates Ronald Reagan, Henry Jackson, and George Wallace.

Nonetheless, the Soviet leadership must have been satisfied with such events as Ford's firing of Defense Secretary Schlesinger, a strong critic of detente,[103] and the resignation of Daniel Moynihan as U.S. Ambassador to the United Nations. Indeed, while Ford had gone out of his way to avoid embarrassing the Soviet Union and "endangering detente" by refusing to meet Solzhenitsyn, Moynihan, whose resignation may have been prompted by a lack of White House support, showed no hesitation in quoting Andrei Sakharov, another leading Soviet dissident, during a UN debate on amnesty for political prisoners—despite a request by the chief Soviet UN delegate, Yaakov Malik (who had seen the advance text of the speech), that the passage be deleted because Sakharov was "an enemy of the Soviet people."[104] The Soviet leaders may also have been encouraged by Ford's rather cool reception during his trip to China and by the American president's public refusal to use the threat of withholding U.S. grain shipments to the USSR as a lever for gaining Soviet concessions on Angola.[105] Indeed, Soviet press coverage of Ford continued to be positive, portraying him as one of the leading U.S. advocates of detente.[106]

Detente was not very visible in the Middle East, however, as the two superpowers sought to weaken each other's positions. The Soviet Union continued to seek to attract such Western allies as Kuwait, Jordan, Greece, and Turkey to her side while reinforcing ties to Syria, Libya, Iraq, and the PLO. The United States, for her part, sought to reinforce ties with once pro-Russian Egypt, Saudi Arabia, and Israel while increasing trade with such ostensibly pro-Soviet states as Syria and Iraq and even hinting, through the so-called "Saunders Document," at a change in policy toward the PLO.[107] The Soviet Union also continued to demand the reconvening of the Geneva peace conference, with the full participation of the PLO (a note sent to the United States on November 9 made this demand), and on December 18 rejected an American plan to hold a preparatory conference without the PLO as "an intention to avoid convening the Geneva Conference."[108] Indeed, the Soviet leaders sought to use the January 1976 Security Council debate on the Middle East, at which the PLO would be represented, as a partial substitute for the Geneva conference and as a vehicle for propagandizing their own position on the Middle East. Thus, on the eve of the meeting, the Soviet government issued what turned out to be the first of the series of official peace plans that it would present in 1976.[109]

While hitherto the general outlines of the Soviet peace plans were contained in speeches by Brezhnev, Kosygin, or Gromyko, now an official document was issued setting forth the Soviet government plan in greater detail. The strategy in issuing the peace proposal just before the convening of the Security Council debate seems clear. Given the continued success of the United States in securing partial disengagement agreements, with the concomitant postponement of the Geneva peace conference (of which the Soviet Union was a cosponsor), the Soviet leadership seems to have hoped to transform the Security Council session, where the PLO would be present (Israel boycotted the session because of the presence of the PLO), into a vehicle for speedily reconvening the Geneva conference. Indeed, the Soviet statement was rather explicit on this point:

> The main result of the discussion of the Middle East situation in the Security Council should be the creation of the necessary conditions for the resumption and effective work of the Geneva Conference.

At the same time, the statement exhibited continued concern at U.S. efforts to prevent the reconvening of the Geneva conference through partial agreements:

> Certain states that have long been encouraging Israel's aggressive policy continue putting spokes in the wheel of the process of an overall political settlement in the Middle East. They continue striving to bypass the Geneva Conference, and are seeking separate deals that overlook key problems of the settlement. They clearly hope to find weak links among Arab countries, and gain an influence and control over them.

While the tactics of the Soviet leadership in presenting its peace plan just prior to the Security Council session may have been novel, the substance of the peace plan was not. The only difference was an even stronger emphasis than before on the rights of the Palestinians; the statement called for ensuring the legitimate rights of the Palestinians, "including their inalienable right to the creation of their own state," while also emphasizing the opinion of the "overwhelming majority" of states that all directly interested parties, including the Palestine Liberation Organization, should take part in the Geneva conference's work from the beginning and with equal rights.

The Security Council debate, however, proved ineffectual in setting the framework for Geneva: Israel boycotted the session. The USSR won a small propaganda victory, however, when the United States vetoed an anti-Israeli resolution. In commenting on the Security Council meeting, an *Izvestia* editorial on January 28 bemoaned the fact that the USSR had not been able to "create the necessary preconditions for the resumption and effective work of the Geneva Conference," but also emphasized the rising stature of the PLO, which it credited as being the legal representative of the Arab people of Palestine.

While the Security Council debate may have been a temporary victory for the PLO and the USSR, the PLO was soon to find itself in severe difficulty in Lebanon as its erstwhile ally, Syria, came into direct conflict with it. As a result, the Soviet leaders were to find themselves in the uncomfortable position of having to choose between the Syrians and the Palestinians as the civil war in Lebanon escalated.

NOTES

1. *Pravda*, November 28, 1974.

2. Ibid., December 5, 1974.

3. Ibid., November 28, 1974. Translated in *Current Digest of the Soviet Press* (hereafter *CDSP*) 26, no. 48: 18.

4. Excerpts from Sadat's speech were printed in the New York *Times*, January 9, 1975.

5. Cited in report by Jim Hoagland in the January 9, 1975, issue of the Washington *Post*.

6. The entire *Business Week* interview (issue of January 13, 1975) was reprinted by the Bureau of Public Affairs, U.S. Department of State.

7. Cited in report by Juan de Onis in the January 10, 1975, issue of the New York *Times*.

8. Dmitry Volsky, "Blackmailing the Arabs," *New Times*, no. 2 (1975): 11.

9. *Pravda*, January 19, 1975. Translated in *CDSP* 27, no. 3: 20.

10. *Pravda*, February 4, 1975. The joint communique is translated in *CDSP* 27, no. 5: 15.

11. *Pravda*, February 6, 1975. The joint communique is translated in *CDSP* 27, no. 5: 16.

12. Cited in report by Drew Middleton in the February 19, 1975, issue of the New York *Times*. The weapons were said to include Mig-23 aircraft.

13. D. Antonov, "Urgent Task," *New Times*, no. 7 (1975): 6.

14. *Izvestia*, February 6, 1975. Translated in *CDSP* 27, no. 6: 11.

15. Compare *Izvestia*, February 11, 1975; *New Times*, no. 9 (1975); *New Times*, no. 12 (1975).

16. Compare report by Joseph Harsch in the March 7, 1975, issue of the *Christian Science Monitor*. For descriptions of Kissinger's diplomacy during the shuttle, see Edward R. F. Sheehan, *The Arabs, Israelis and Kissinger* (New York: Readers Digest Press, 1976), chap. 11; Matti Golan, *The Secret Conversations of Henry Kissinger* (New York: Quadrangle, 1976), chap. 7; and William B. Quandt, *Decade of Decisions: American Policy toward the Arab-Israeli Conflict 1967-1976* (Berkeley: University of California Press, 1977), chap. 7.

Sheehan's report has a clear anti-Israeli slant, almost to the point of bias. Golan's book reflects the Israeli viewpoint and is bitterly critical of Kissinger and severely critical of Rabin as well. Quandt's analysis is the best of the three.

For a Soviet analysis of Kissinger's diplomacy that draws heavily on the Golan and Sheehan studies, see Yevgeny Primakov, "Sbalansirovanii kurs' na Blizhnem Vostoke ili staraia politika inimi sredstvami" [A balanced course in the Middle East or the old policy pursued by different means], *Mirovaia ekonomika i mezhdunarodnye otnosheniia*, no. 12 (1976): 33-51, and no. 1 (1977): 51-60.

17. For the text of the Iran-Iraq accord, see *Middle East Monitor* (hereafter *MEM*) 5, no. 6 (March 15, 1975): 4-5.

18. For an analysis of Soviet interest in Iraqi oil and Iranian natural gas, see Arthur J. Klinghoffer, *The Soviet Union and International Oil Politics* (New York: Columbia University Press, 1977), pp. 122-39.

19. The offer to the PLO is cited in Associated Press report from Damascus, New York *Times*, March 9, 1975.

20. See *MEM* 5, no. 5 (March 15, 1975): 2, for a description of the agreement with Jordan.

21. *Izvestia*, April 15, 1975.

22. Compare Golan, op. cit.

23. See Sheehan, op. cit., and Quandt, op. cit., for a description of the reassessment.

24. O. Alov, "Wanted: A Genuine Mid-East Settlement," *New Times*, no. 14 (1975): 8.

25. *Pravda*, April 15, 1975.

26. Ibid., April 17, 1975.

27. Cited in report by Henry Tanner in the April 18, 1975, issue of the New York *Times*.

28. *Pravda*, April 20, 1975.

29. Ibid., April 23, 1975.

30. Cited in the *Christian Science Monitor*, April 24, 1975.

31. *Pravda*, April 27, 1975.

32. Ibid., April 24, 1975.

33. Ibid., May 5, 1975.

34. A. Usvatov, "Palestinian Delegation in Moscow," *New Times*, no. 19 (1975): 24.

35. *Pravda*, May 14, 1975. Translated in *CDSP* 27, no. 20: 10.

36. *Pravda*, May 14, 1975. Translated in *CDSP* 27, no. 20: 10-11.

37. *Pravda*, May 27, 1975. Soviet terminology about "bases" can be deceptive, however, since the Soviet leaders have a definition of a "base" that differs from the Western one. Thus, the USSR denied it had a base in Somalia despite on-the-spot evidence collected by an American Congressman.

38. *Izvestia*, May 21, 1975. Translated in *CDSP* 27, no. 20: 14.

39. Compare reports by Dev Muraka in the April 25, 1975, issue of the *Christian Science Monitor* and by Wolf Blitzer in the April 25, 1975, issue of the Jerusalem *Post*.

40. J. Schreiber, "Growth of Peace Sentiment in Israel," *New Times*, no. 26 (1975): 10.

41. *New Times*, no. 28 (1975): 31.

42. For a description of the Solzhenitsyn affair, see the report by James Naughton in the July 18, 1975, issue of the New York *Times*.

43. On the trade situation, compare report by Yuri Kornilov in *Selskaya zhizn*, July 6, 1975), translated in *CDSP* 27, no. 27: 18. See also *New Times*, no. 28 (1975): 5.

44. *Izvestia*, May 29, 1975. Translated in *CDSP* 27, no. 22: 10.

45. See the reports by John Cooley in the June 26, 1975, and July 23, 1975, issues of the *Christian Science Monitor*.

46. *New Times*, no. 25 (1975): 17.

47. *Al-Hawadeth* (Beirut), cited in Associated Press report in the Jerusalem *Post*, August 29, 1975.

48. See the report by Juan de Onis in the March 19, 1975, issue of the New York *Times*, which cited Jawad Hashem, director of the economic staff of Saddam Hussein, as stating: "What we want is the best technology and the fastest possible fulfillment of orders and contracts." See also the report by Mohammed Azhar Khan in the July 8, 1975, issue of the *Christian Science Monitor*. For an Arab analysis of the development possibilities in Iraq, see "Iraq Looks Forward to Long-Term Growth," *The Middle East*, no. 7 (April 1975): 57-58.

49. *Pravda*, July 10, 1975; *Izvestia*, July 13, 1975; *New Times*, no. 31 (1975): 17.

50. See the report by Henry Tanner in the June 13, 1975, issue of the New York *Times*.

51. For an analysis of Iraq's improvement in relations with Egypt, its long-time Arab enemy, see "Egypt and Iraq Rivalry Gives Way to Cooperation," *The Middle East*, no. 9 (June 1975): 51-52. See also *MEM* 5, no. 6 (March 15, 1975): 1-2.

52. Point Five of the Palestine National Council program of June 1974 called for the establishment of a "national-democratic" government in Jordan.

53. For an analysis of the evolution of the arms negotiations, see *The Near East Report* 19, no. 38 (September 17, 1975): 159; and no. 39 (September 24, 1975): 167.

54. Compare editorial in New York *Times*, July 23, 1975.

55. For a translation of excerpts of this key article, see *MEM*, 5, no. 16 (September 1, 1975): 3-4.

56. V. Shmarov, "Turkey: Control over Bases," *New Times*, no. 32 (1975): 12-13.

57. *Pravda*, July 15, 1975. Translated in *CDSP* 27, no. 28: 7, 24.

58. For the background to this event, see Robert O. Freedman, "The Soviet Union and the Communist Parties of the Arab World: An Uncertain Relationship," in *Soviet Economic and Political Relations with the Developing World*, ed. Roger E. Kanet and Donna Bahry (New York: Praeger, 1975), pp. 100-34.

59. *As-Safir*, August 4, 1975. Translated in the *Foreign Broadcast Information Service: Daily Report* 5 (August 13, 1975): D2-D13.

60. For analyses of the last stages of the shuttle, see Sheehan, op. cit., Golan, op. cit.; and Quandt, op. cit.

61. *Pravda*, August 12, 1975.

62. Ibid., August 18, 1975.

63. Ibid., August 26, 1975.

64. Ibid., August 29, 1975. Sadat also claimed that the USSR lied to Arafat about the contents of the Sinai II agreement, in an effort to prevent Egypt from signing it. See report by Flora Lewis in the December 7, 1977, issue of the New York *Times*.

65. For a description of the agreement, see *MEM* 5, no. 17 (September 15, 1975): 2-3.

66. *Pravda*, August 26, 1975.

67. Compare report by Godfrey Sperling in the August 21, 1975, issue of the *Christian Science Monitor*.

68. *Pravda*, August 30, 1975. Translated in *CDSP* 27, no. 35: 13. For the text of the agreement, see *MEM* 5, no. 17 (September 15, 1975): 3-6.

69. Reuters report from Geneva in the September 5, 1975, issue of the New York *Times*.

70. Excerpts from Sadat's speech were printed in the September 5, 1975, issue of the New York *Times*. Sadat also blasted the USSR on September 28 for failing to deliver promised weaponry.

71. The Soviet attacks also concentrated on Sadat's opening of the Egyptian economy to foreign capital, with *Pravda* on November 23, 1975, going so far as to imply that Egypt was losing its "economic independence."

72. Compare *Pravda*, September 17 and 21, 1975.

73. These organizations included not only the PLO but also such bodies as the Arab Front in Support of the Palestine Revolution. For the background of this group see p. 119 in text.

74. *Pravda*, October 25, 1975. Translated in *CDSP* 27, no. 43: 1-2.

75. Cited in Associated Press report from Damascus in the September 6, 1975, issue of the New York *Times*.

76. *Pravda*, October 11, 1975.

77. *Al-Rai Al-Am* (Kuwait), cited in Associated Press report from Kuwait in the October 19, 1975, issue of the New York *Times*.

78. Indeed, soon after the disengagement agreement with Egypt, Israeli Premier Rabin stated that there was "virtually no chance" for an interim agreement with Syria. See the report by Henry Kamm in the September 6, 1975, issue of the New York *Times*.

79. *Al-Rai Al-Am*, October 19, 1975.

80. Compare report by Bernard Gwertzman in the November 18, 1975, issue of the New York *Times*. Gwertzman called the planes Mig-25s, but the available evidence indicates that they were advanced Mig-23s. For an analysis of the capability of this aircraft, see Jon D. Glassman, *Arms for the Arabs* (Baltimore: Johns Hopkins Press, 1975).

81. Cited in United Press International report from Beirut in the September 6, 1975, issue of the New York *Times*.

82. Cited in the *Christian Science Monitor*, September 12, 1975.

83. *Izvestia*, April 12, 1975. Translated in *CDSP* 27, no. 15: 2.

84. *Izvestia*, April 15, 1975. Translated in *CDSP* 27, no. 15: 2-3.

85. *Izvestia*, April 15, 1975. Translated in *CDSP* 27, no. 15: 3.

86. *Pravda*, December 20, 1975.

87. Ibid., November 29, 1975. For an analysis of the changing position of the USSR toward the PLO, see Galia Golan, *The Soviet Union and the PLO* (Jerusalem: Soviet and East European Research Center, Hebrew University, 1976).

88. *As-Safir*, August 4, 1975. Translated in *Foreign Broadcast Information Service: Daily Report* 5 (August 13, 1975): D2-D3.

89. *Izvestia*, October 4, 1975. Translated in *CDSP* 27, no. 40: 20.

90. *Pravda*, October 20, 1975. Translated in *CDSP* 27, no. 42: 20.

91. The Washington *Post* on December 24, 1975, and the New York *Times* on December 25, 1975, carried reports that Oman threatened war against South Yemen.

92. Dmitry Volsky, "Security or Confrontation," *New Times*, no. 2 (1976): 9.

93. For a description of the arms deal, see the report by John Cooley in the January 12, 1976, issue of the *Christian Science Monitor*. In an earlier effort to improve Soviet-Kuwaiti relations, a delegation from the Supreme Soviet visited Kuwait in February 1974.

94. *Pravda*, December 9, 1975. Translated in *CDSP* 27, no. 49: 23.

95. Volsky, "Security or Confrontation," loc. cit.

96. Cited in report by Jim Hoagland in the January 19, 1976, issue of the Washington *Post*.

97. Compare analysis by V. Sidenko in *New Times*, no. 44 (1975): 17. In mid-November, Morocco broke off diplomatic relations with East Germany over this issue, possibly as a signal to the USSR.

98. Cited in Associated Press report from Morocco in the January 6, 1976, issue of the New York *Times*.

99. See reports in the Washington *Post*, December 30, 1975, and January 1, 1976.

100. Cited in the *Christian Science Monitor*, January 2, 1976.

101. Compare Reuters report in the December 19, 1975, issue of the Jerusalem *Post*.

102. *Pravda*, December 30, 1975.

103. *Izvestia* on November 6, 1975, indicated that Schlesinger had been fired because of his opposition to detente.

104. Cited in the New York *Times*, December 19, 1975.

105. Cited in report by Philip Shabecoff in the January 6, 1976, issue of the New York *Times*.

106. Compare *Izvestia*, November 6, 1975; *New Times*, no. 50 (1975): 11.

107. For excerpts of a U.S. State Department paper by Deputy Assistant Secretary of State Harold Saunders indicating a possible shift in the U.S. position on the PLO, see *MEM* 5, no. 23: 3-4. For an analysis that argues that Kissinger had carefully gone over the document, see Quandt, op. cit., p. 278.

108. *Pravda*, December 20, 1975.

109. Ibid., January 10, 1976. Translated in *CDSP* 28, no. 2: 6.

7

The Soviet Union and the Civil War in Lebanon

SOVIET DIPLOMACY FROM SYRIA'S INTERVENTION IN LEBANON TO KOSYGIN'S TRIP TO DAMASCUS: JANUARY-JUNE 1976

The civil war in Lebanon was one of a number of events in the Middle East that illustrate the essentially reactive nature of Soviet diplomacy in the region, for the Soviet leadership sought to react to a situation that it not only had not caused, but that it had a great deal of difficulty trying to shape to fit its goals in the region. While it is not in the scope of this book to deal in detail with the various factions and religious and ethnic groups constituting the mosaic of Lebanese society, or with the causes of the Lebanese civil war of 1975-76, a brief outline of the situation is necessary as a background for the analysis of Soviet policy during the war.[1] Essentially, the Lebanese National Pact, a system for sharing power between Christian and Moslem Lebanese that had been established in 1943, was no longer effective.[2] At the time it was established, the Christian Arabs, who already controlled the economy of Lebanon, were given the greater share of political power through the offices of the president and army commander, as well as a 6:5 ratio of seats in the Lebanese Parliament. The system, which survived the Lebanese civil war of 1958, began to break down in the late 1960s as Lebanese society began to polarize and the spirit of compromise present in the first two decades of the National Pact began to fade.

In part, the problem lay in a lack of good leadership; neither Charles Helois, who was president from 1964 to 1970, nor Suliman Franjieh, in power from 1970 to 1976, was able to stem the tide toward greater sectarianism—indeed, some of their actions helped promote it.[3] A more important cause, however, lay in the desire of the Moslems for a greater share of the political and economic power in Lebanon, which they felt was their due as their numbers increased more rapidly than those of the Christians and Moslem Arab prestige rose

as a result of the 1973 Arab-Israeli war. In addition, the sharp increase in inflation, which most hurt the Lebanese poor (who are predominantly Moslem), reinforced the call for political and economic change. Complicating the internal
Lebanese situation further was the presence of approximately 400,000 Palestinian Arab refugees who, organized by the PLO in the aftermath of the 1967 Arab-
Israeli war, became an autonomous, albeit internally divided, element in Lebanese society following the Cairo agreement of 1969, which gave the PLO control
over the Palestinian refugee camps throughout Lebanon and a base of operations
in the southern part of the country.

The Palestinian presence affected Lebanese politics in two ways. In the
first place, by launching attacks on Israel from Lebanese soil, the Palestinians
brought Israeli reprisals against Lebanon that the weak Lebanese army was unable to repel. As a result, many Lebanese Moslems (most of them Shii) were
forced to flee northward, adding to the social unrest in the country. This led the
Lebanese Christians, particularly the Maronites, to call for the expulsion or control of the Palestinians in order to avert the danger of Israeli attacks. On the
other hand, the Sunni Moslems sought to use the heavily armed Palestinians as a
political instrument to increase their share of power in Lebanon at the expense
of the Maronites. Complicating this situation further was the assistance given by
radical Palestinian groups to left-wing Moslems such as Kamal Jumblatt, who
wanted to go much further than the traditional Moslem leaders, such as Rashid
Karami and Saab Salam, in restructuring Lebanese society. The fact that Palestinian groups, particularly after the 1973 war, obtained large amounts of aid
from Iraq, Libya, and especially Syria, and then passed on part of it to their Lebanese Moslem allies, further complicated the situation. In addition, the Christian
Lebanese, themselves divided among a number of groups, of which the Maronites
of Pierre Gemayal were the strongest, also were arming.

Thus, by the spring of 1975 Lebanon was increasingly polarized. The Lebanese Christians, feeling threatened by both the Moslem Arabs and the Palestinians, sought to oust the Palestinians from Lebanon as a means of protecting their
own position in the country. The Moslem Lebanese, and particularly the left-
wing Moslems under the leadership of Jumblatt, wanted a much greater share of
power in the state. And the various factions of the PLO wanted to be free to use
Lebanon as a base for attacking Israel.

As the Lebanese civil war began to worsen in the summer of 1975, the
USSR clearly showed her preference for the leftist Moslem-PLO alignment
(known as the National Front), apparently hoping that its success would move
Lebanon from the pro-Western Arab camp to the pro-Soviet group then consisting of Iraq, Libya, South Yemen, the PLO, Algeria, and Syria. Given the facts
that the PLO, and particularly Arafat's Fatah faction, could be considered one
of the USSR's primary allies in the Middle East, and that Jumblatt, head of the
left-wing Moslems, was both a Lenin Prize winner and the man who, as minister
of the interior, had legalized the Lebanese Communist Party in 1970, the Soviet
hopes could be seen to have a solid basis.

Nonetheless, as the Lebanese civil war grew in intensity in the late summer and early fall, the USSR expressed concern that the Palestinians might be overcome by Lebanese "reactionaries." When the civil war became even more severe in mid-December, *New Times* correspondent Anatoly Agaryshev offered an analysis of the Lebanese situation in which he expressed Soviet hopes for the future direction of the country:

Will Lebanon resume the unique role it played until recently in the capitalist world's trade and finances? This is the question all Lebanese are asking today.

The reactionary forces responsible for unleashing the fratricidal conflicts want to preserve the system of free enterprise which has multiplied their capital.

Not all the Lebanese businessmen belong in this category of course. *There are some who are sensible enough to see that Lebanon's past and future are linked not only with the capitalist West but with the Arab world as well. Consequently, they reason, Lebanon cannot be a bystander in the Middle East conflict. Her place is with the Arab states resisting Israeli aggression.* They realize that the one to gain most from the bloodshed in Lebanon is Israel. It is noteworthy that this is the opinion not only of Moslem businessmen but of some Catholic Maronites too. There are many Christians in the progressive front—workers as well as petty and middle bourgeoisie.[4] [emphasis added]

Agaryshev went on to describe what he saw as one of the central problems in Lebanon:

What complicates the situation is that the number of paramilitary organizations involved in the conflict is growing. Some of them are extreme-Rightist. Besides the Kataeb Party, there is the Cedar Defence Front, a reactionary clandestine organization that is called the Lebanese Ku Klux Klan. What it is like may be gauged by the slogans its members paint on house walls in Beirut: "No to the Palestine movement! No to Arabs! No to Communism!"

Big landowners, tribal chieftains and prominent politicians maintain their own private armies.

The presence of such paramilitary formations cannot but aggravate the situation in the country. The very fact that they exist proves that by provoking bloody clashes the Lebanese reactionaries are doing a service to external imperialist forces that seek to weaken the Arabs and dismember Lebanon. These forces are whipping up the Lebanese conflict with the object of striking a blow at the political role of the Palestine movement and getting the Middle East conflict settled after the imperialist recipe.[5]

As the civil war escalated still further in January 1976, the Soviet leaders, seeing both Syria and the PLO (despite its loosely federated nature) as useful allies in the struggle against American influence in the Arab world, and having witnessed the close Syrian-PLO cooperation in the Security Council debates, evidently hoped that Syrian-PLO cooperation would continue in Lebanon as well, a country in which Syria had a major security and economic interest.[6] Nonetheless, Syrian-Palestinian relations were not without their problems. While Syria was now clearly projecting herself as the champion of the Palestinians in the Security Council, the Palestinians themselves may have had some doubts.[7] Under tight control in Syria, they were not permitted to launch attacks against Israel from Syrian soil, and one of the major forces within the loosely federated PLO was Saiqa—a Syrian-dominated Palestinian guerrilla organization.[8] In addition, several of the Palestine Liberation Army (PLA) brigades were located on Syrian soil and were under the command of a pro-Syrian Palestinian officer, Masbah Al-Budeiry, whose wife was the sister-in-law of Syrian Defense Minister Mustapha Tlass. Consequently, when Assad sent several battalions of the PLA into Lebanon on January 20, in an effort to stop the fighting, the left-wing Moslem-Palestinian alignment may have seen the move as directed as much at securing Syrian control over Lebanon as in aiding the Palestinians and bringing order to the country.

Whatever its motivation, this Syrian move helped lay the groundwork for an agreement for a more equal sharing of power in Lebanon, whereby Parliament would be evenly divided between Christians and Moslems, and the Sunni Moslem prime minister would be elected by the Parliament instead of being appointed by the Christian president, as had been the case under the old system. These moves brought a temporary calm to Lebanon, and the Christian right, which was ceding some of its power in these reforms, received assurances from the Syrians that the Palestinians would honor their agreements with Lebanon and limit their activities in Lebanon according to the Cairo agreement of 1969—long a goal of the Christian Maronites.[9]

The initial Syrian move into Lebanon was hailed by the Russians, who the previous week had claimed, in an *Izvestia* editorial, that Israel and the "forces of imperialism" were encouraging the civil war in Lebanon in order both to "strike a new blow against the Palestinian Resistance Movement" and to break up Lebanon by creating a separate Christian state "which would give the forces of imperialism and Zionism another weapon, along with the State of Israel, with which to combat the movement of the peoples of the Arab East for freedom, true independence and social progress."[10]

While Syria shared the Soviet goal of preventing the partition of Lebanon—an event that might precipitate an Israeli take-over of the southern part of the country up to the Litani River—the Syrians were not averse to promoting their own interests in Lebanon as well. Thus, a week after the intervention, elements of the Syrian-dominated Saiqa guerrillas attacked two pro-Iraqi newspapers, killing seven journalists in the process.[11] This event, however, did not diminish Soviet enthusiasm for the Syrian move, for on February 10 *Pravda* stated, in a commentary on the "positive changes" in Lebanon:

> These positive changes are the result of the implementation of an accord reached between the opposing sides through the mediation of Syria. . . . Many observers feel that the current agreement has succeeded where others failed because it was concluded on a more thoroughgoing basis and with the participation of Syria as a guarantor of its implementation. The Palestine Liberation Organization has also played a constructive role in the development of the normalization process.[12]

The Soviet Union's close relations with Syria were underlined during Brezhnev's keynote address to the 25th Party Congress on February 24. In his speech Brezhnev placed the Arab friends of the USSR in rank order, with Syria clearly leading the list.

> Now I shall say something about our relations with the Arab countries. During the past five-year period we established a good mutual understanding with Syria. *We act in concert on many international problems, above all those of the Middle East.* The conclusion of the Treaty of Friendship and cooperation with Iraq, on the basis of which our relations are developing, was an important event. Cooperation with Algeria and South Yemen is expanding and deepening. Significant steps have been taken to develop Soviet-Libyan ties. Friendly ties with the Palestine Liberation Organization have grown stronger.[13] [emphasis added]

The Soviet party leader also discussed the deterioration of the USSR's relations with Egypt, although he took a positive attitude toward the long-term prospects of those relations.

> Recently, certain forces have been making persistent attempts to undermine Soviet-Egyptian relations. As far as the USSR is concerned, we remain faithful to our principled line of strengthening these relations. This was reflected in the Treaty of Friendship and Cooperation between the USSR and Egypt which we regard as a long-term basis for relations in the interest of not only our countries, but also the entire Arab world.[14]

In the course of his speech, Brezhnev again offered the Soviet peace plan for the Middle East, which included three major points: Israeli withdrawal from all territory captured in the 1967 war; the recognition of the "legitimate rights" of the Palestinians, including their right to a national state; and the guarantee of the security of all states in the region and their right to independent existence and development. In addition, Brezhnev stated the USSR's willingness to participate in international guarantees for the security and borders of all the states in the Middle East. In an apparent nod to Israel, the Soviet leader stated the USSR's willingness to develop relations with all countries in the Middle East: "We have no prejudice against any of them." Finally, Brezhnev said that the USSR was prepared to work to end the arms race in the Middle East (long an American goal), but only after an overall settlement had been reached.[15]

The relatively optimistic presentation by Brezhnev of the USSR's position in the Arab world at the 25th Party Congress, however, was soon overtaken by events. The first blow to Brezhnev's analysis of Soviet-Arab relations came less than three weeks after the Party Congress, when Egyptian President Anwar Sadat abrogated the 15-year Treaty of Friendship and Cooperation signed with the USSR in 1971 (which the Soviet party leader had deemed the "long-term basis" for Soviet-Egyptian relations). In justifying the treaty's cancellation, Sadat complained that the USSR not only had withheld needed equipment from Egypt but also had refused to allow India to supply jet-engine spare parts to Egypt. He also stated that the USSR was following a policy of "imperialism and neo-colonialism" in the developing countries.[16]

The timing of the treaty cancellation was opportune for the Egyptian leader, since the Ford administration had already moved to ask the U.S. Congress to lift the embargo on arms to Egypt by selling the Egyptians C-130 military transport planes. Needing congressional approval for the sale, the Ford administration exploited Sadat's treaty abrogation, with Kissinger going so far as to say that not to approve the C-130 sales "would be a slap in the face to Sadat following so closely his decision with regard to the Soviet Union."[17] The arms deal ultimately went through, although not without opposition, and Sadat may well have seen this as the first installment on much larger future shipments of American weaponry. Interestingly enough, however, Sadat may also have envisioned the treaty abrogation as a ploy to get a resumption of arms from the USSR, since, despite initial press reports, he did not immediately cancel the Soviet navy's right to use Egyptian ports.[18]

If the Egyptian leader was seeking a change in the Soviet position, however, it was not forthcoming. TASS called the treaty abrogation a "new manifestation of the unfriendly policy Sadat had been pursuing for a long time."[19] In addition, the Russians stepped up their attacks on the Westward turn of Egypt's economy, stating that the only ones to profit from it were Egypt's "fat cats" while the masses suffered.[20] They also attacked Sadat for violating Nasser's legacy:

Egypt's departure from the principles of the July 1952 Revolution signified the gradual liquidation of the economic and social gains achieved under Nasser.[21]

Then, in a major broadside on April 1, *Pravda* publicized a statement given to the Egyptian government following the termination of the treaty. In the strongest attack on Sadat to date, the Russians claimed that Egypt "distorted everything connected with cooperation with the USSR, especially in the military field, in a bid to justify its policy of deals with the aggressor and his backer." Furthermore, the Soviets claimed:

> The policy of Egypt's present leadership runs counter to the genuine interests of the Egyptian people and the peoples of other Arab countries ... [and] benefits only the enemies of the Egyptians and other Arab peoples, the forces of imperialism, Zionism and reaction.[22]

Needless to say, this was not the response Sadat was looking for, and on April 2 the Egyptian Foreign Ministry rejected the Soviet note, with Egyptian Vice-President Husni Mubarak calling it an "interference in Egypt's internal affairs."[23] Several days later, Sadat formally moved to cancel the Soviet navy's rights to use the ports of Alexandria, Port Said, and Matruh.[24]

The United States was not the only Soviet opponent to express satisfaction at the further deterioration of Egyptian-Soviet relations. Soon after the treaty of friendship was abrogated, Communist China came out strongly in support of the Egyptian action and offered Egypt 30 engines and spare parts for its Migs, reportedly free of charge.[25] In addition, Egyptian Vice-President Mubarak was invited to China in mid-April, and the *Renmin Ribao* editorial that greeted his arrival seized the opportunity to attack the USSR:

> Egypt's bold decision to abrogate the Egyptian-Soviet friendship and cooperation treaty, and its victory in countering Soviet social-imperialist threats, intimidation, disruption and sabotage, are a new development in the Egyptian people's struggle to safeguard their national independence and state sovereignty. ... The Egyptian people ... have courageously denounced and laid bare the crimes perpetrated by Soviet revisionism in Egypt. ... This has set an example for the people of all countries, especially of the Third World, in their struggle against hegemonism.[26]

While the Chinese received a great deal of propaganda benefit from the treaty cancellation and the Mubarak visit, and attempted to exploit these developments to weaken the Soviet position in the Third World, Egypt was also to benefit. In addition to strong political support, the Egyptians secured assistance from China through an agreement that reportedly assured Egypt of a steady flow of spare parts for Soviet-built weaponry.[27] Given the fact that Chinese planes are several generations behind Soviet models, however, it appeared that the military significance of the protocol for Egypt was, at least initially, considerably less than the political. Indeed, this was the main Soviet reaction to Egypt's turn to China, as *Sovetskaia Rossiia* deprecated the results of the visit:

> The results of Mubarak's visit to Peking show that in playing its "Peking Card" the Egyptian side was again gambling on anti-Sovietism, while Peking used the visit to encourage in every way possible the anti-Soviet direction of President A. Sadat's policy. . . .
>
> As for the essence of the agreements reached during the talks, it should be noted that, although the Cairo Press is rhapsodizing over "Peking's readiness to assist Egypt" the foreign press reports that Peking evinced no particular generosity during the talks. On the military side, the press agencies report that China agreed to supply Egypt with spare airplane parts. As UPI notes, "the protocol on military aid signed by China and Egypt has more symbolic than real significance. . . . "
>
> Mubarak's visit to Peking has shown once again that imperialism and Maoism are pursuing one and the same goal: to split and weaken Arab unity and to undermine friendship and cooperation between the Arab peoples, including the Egyptians, and their natural and dependable ally—the Soviet Union.[28]

Despite this deprecation of the Mubarak mission in Peking, the Soviet leadership could not have been pleased with the further deterioration of their relations with Egypt. By abrogating the friendship treaty with the USSR, by excluding the Soviet fleet from Egyptian port facilities, and by demonstrably moving to improve relations with China, the Sadat regime had further distanced itself from the USSR, thereby making a rapprochement between the two states far more difficult. Interestingly enough, however, Sadat did not go all the way in his break with the USSR. In his May Day speech one week after Mubarak's return from China, Sadat held out the hope of improved relations with the Russians—a ploy he had used in the past after a serious conflict with the USSR. This time, at least, the USSR did not rise to the bait. Moscow Radio, while noting Sadat's May Day speech, continued the Soviet attack on the Egyptian leader for distorting Soviet policy.[29] Nonetheless, despite the mutual propaganda attacks, trade continued at a high level between the two countries and a new trade agreement was signed on April 28.[30]

While the USSR's relations worsened with Egypt, the situation in Lebanon also deteriorated. Far from bringing peace to the country, the initial Syrian intervention in Lebanon, which was essentially political in nature, was soon followed by an intensification of fighting that the Syrians had great difficulty controlling. Complaining that the Syrian-mediated agreement had not gone far enough in giving them their just share of power in Lebanon, the left-wing Moslems became restive, while the Palestinians became concerned about increasing Syrian control over their operations. The rising Moslem opposition helped precipitate the defection of a number of Moslem soldiers from the Lebanese army and their formation into a separate Moslem "Lebanese Arab Army" under Lt. Ahmed Khatib, a Moslem with close ties to the Palestinians and leftist Moslems.[31] Troops proclaiming allegiance to the new "Lebanese Arab Army" quickly moved to control army posts in a number of sections of Lebanon, including several near the Israeli border.

As the Lebanese army, already weakened by the civil war, began to disintegrate,[32] the commander of the Beirut military garrison, Brig. Gen. Abdel Aziz Al-Ahdad, staged a pseudo coup d'etat, proclaimed himself military governor, and demanded the resignation of Lebanese President Suliman Franjieh and Prime Minister Rashid Karami. The general also offered a pardon to Khatib's rebel soldiers, stating that they had genuine grievances.[33] While neither Franjieh nor Khatib accepted Ahdad's demands, his call for Franjieh's resignation was a popular one, and two-thirds of Lebanon's Parliament signed a petition calling for his resignation.[34] This was followed by a drive by Khatib's forces on the presidential mansion at Baabda to physically oust Franjieh.

Interestingly enough, however, Syria stepped in at this point and, using Saiqa troops, the Syrians were able to stop the army columns before they could reach the palace.[35] The left-wing Moslems under Jumblatt, now cooperating with the rebel Arab army, resented the Syrian move, however, and resumed military operations in Beirut and in the Lebanese mountains near Beirut. Artillery bombardments from these attacks forced Franjieh to flee to Zuk Mekail, near the Christian-controlled city of Junieh, which had become the de facto Christian capital of the country. Backed by the momentum of their military offensive, Jumblatt and other Moslem leaders, including Khatib, stated that there would be no cease-fire until major changes were made in the constitutional system of Lebanon and until Franjieh resigned. Meanwhile, the leftist Moslem alliance continued its drive in Lebanon's mountain areas, seeking to link up with left-wing Christian villages and seize control over the Beirut-Damascus highway.[36]

The Syrians were faced with a major dilemma posed by the left-wing Moslem victories. Partition of Lebanon now appeared to be a real possibility, with a Christian mini-state in the north (except for Tripoli, which was under Karami's control) and a leftist-dominated state in the south. It was also conceivable that the left-wing Moslems, together with their Palestinian allies, might soon dominate the entire country. What made the situation so menacing for the Assad regime was that a left-wing, Moslem-controlled state was likely to have close ties with Iraq—Syria's main enemy in the Arab world—and Libya, with whom Syria's relations were strained.[37] In addition, such a state, with close ties to the Palestinians, might well precipitate an Israeli attack upon it by permitting Palestinian attacks on Israel, thus leading to a possible Syrian-Israeli conflict at a time when the Syrians were not ready for war.

It was to prevent such a development that the Syrians began to cut off military supplies to the Palestinians (the PLO had been supplying the leftists with arms) at the end of March and brought pressure on them to stop the leftist Moslem military push. In addition, Syria blockaded Lebanese ports to prevent military supplies from reaching the leftists. A week later, despite Iraqi threats—and perhaps no longer trusting the loyalty of the Syrian-led PLA or of Saiqa forces—Syria moved her troops across the border into a frontier region of Lebanon to reinforce the shaky truce that had finally been agreed upon.[38] In response, Jumblatt and his leftist allies issued a formal statement "calling the attention of our Syrian brothers to the gravity of military involvement through the entry of the Syrian army in an illegitimate manner."[39]

The developments in Lebanon posed a major problem for the Soviet Union. In the first place, the Russians were confronted with the possibility of a split between two of their major Arab allies, the PLO and Syria, over events in Lebanon while relations between Syria, the USSR's number-one Arab ally, and Jumblatt, long a friend of the USSR, reached the breaking point. There was also the possibility of a split between Jumblatt and his Palestinian allies, who were caught in the middle of the Assad-Jumblatt squabble. What made matters worse for the Soviet leaders at this point was that the United States, which had long been inactive in the Lebanese crisis, suddenly dispatched a special envoy, L. Dean Brown, to Lebanon to try to mediate the conflict while elements of the U.S. Sixth Fleet moved to a position near Lebanon in case an evacuation of U.S. citizens was ordered.

Brown's mission, which followed unsuccessful mediation attempts by France and the Vatican, was dispatched after talks in Washington between King Hussein, now one of Assad's closest Arab allies, and the Ford administration, but it met with strong Palestinian disapproval; both Fatah leader Yasir Arafat and PDFLP leader Naef Hawatmeh condemned the mission. Hawatmeh, who was close to the Soviet leadership, went so far as to contend that Brown was "trying to manipulate differences between warring Lebanese Christians and Moslems and between Syria and the Palestinian guerrillas."[40] Clearly, the Soviet leaders must have feared that since both the United States and Syria had the common goal of restricting the leftist Moslems and Palestinians in Lebanon, the two nations might well coordinate their actions. The effect of such a development, should it prove successful, would be a warming of Syrian-American relations and the further splintering of the "anti-imperialist" Arab unity the Russians had sought to create.

In discussing the events in Lebanon, an article in *Pravda* on April 8, under the authoritative "Commentator" by-line, stated:

At present, a new cease-fire agreement has been achieved in Lebanon with the help of Syria's mediatory efforts, and consultations are taking place among the interested Lebanese parties. This is a new and positive element in the development of the situation in Lebanon and it can only be welcomed. Nevertheless, the situation in the country remains tense, the contradictions are still acute, and much combustible material has accumulated. . . .

What is needed now is a maximum effort to consolidate the cease-fire that was achieved with such difficulty and to use it effectively to normalize the situation and to restore a stable peace and tranquility in Lebanon. This has real prospects for the preservation of a united, integral and independent Lebanese state. . . .

The normalization of the situation in Lebanon is an important factor making for cohesion in the front of Arab forces struggling to eliminate the consequences of Israeli aggression and to establish a just and lasting peace in the Middle East.[41]

One week later, after the Syrian intervention, *New Times* correspondent V. Nikolayev indicated Soviet concern over developments in Lebanon:

The imperialist and reactionary elements have tried to take advantage of the situation to provoke quarrels among the various national patriotic contingents, the Palestine Resistance Movement, and neighboring Syria, which is mediating in an effort to put an end to the fratricidal bloodshed and find a mutually acceptable settlement.[42]

Nikolayev also supported the Syrian position opposing intervention by other Arab armies in the civil war, using the opportunity to criticize Egypt (which had proposed a pan-Arab force) while also condemning the U.S. position on Lebanon:

Egypt's idea of Arabizing the conflict, that is of introducing army units of different Arab countries into Lebanon has met with no support from Lebanese political groups. Other proposals to "internationalize" the conflict have also been rejected. . . .

The Beirut Press has qualified as a threat of direct interference in Lebanese affairs the news of the appearance of seven ships of the U.S. Sixth Fleet off the coast of Lebanon, allegedly for a "possible evacuation" of U.S. nationals from that country.[43]

The same issue of *New Times* carried another article strongly endorsing Syria's role in Lebanon (one that completely overlooked Syria's clash with Jumblatt) and emphasizing the close relations between the USSR and Syria. Discussing "Ancient Syria Today," Alexander Klimov wrote:

> The Syrian government is justifiably uneasy about the bloody clashes in neighboring Lebanon. The efforts undertaken by the reactionary forces to unleash a civil war in that Arab country are qualified in Syria as an attempt to divert the Arabs' attention from the crucial issue, that of establishing a just and lasting peace in the Middle East. One proof of Syria's growing prestige in the Arab world is that the parties involved in the Lebanese conflict have all agreed to Syria's mediation in finding a solution to the internal crisis in Lebanon and ending the bloody confrontation.
>
> In her efforts to achieve a just settlement in the Middle East, Syria cooperates with the Palestine Resistance Movement, the Soviet Union, other Socialist countries, and anti-imperialist forces in the Arab world and elsewhere. The firm mutual understanding between the Soviet Union and Syria was noted by CPSU General Secretary Leonid Brezhnev when he said at the Party's 25th Congress that "we act in concert on many international problems, *first and foremost that of the Middle East.*"[44] [emphasis added]

Both Klimov and Brezhnev would soon have reason to question the accuracy of the party secretary's statement.

Despite these pro-Syrian articles in the Soviet press, the Soviet leadership could only have been concerned by the change in American policy toward the civil war in Lebanon. Until Brown's mission the United States had condemned outside intervention in Lebanon, but on April 14 Kissinger called the Syrian intervention in Lebanon "constructive."[45] News Secretary Ron Nessen emphasized this point several days later, stating, "If you look at the nature and the intent of what Syria is doing in Lebanon, overall they've played a constructive role."[46] In addition to verbal support, U.S. policy makers, by mediating with the Israelis, had helped to prevent any Israeli military response to the Syrian moves in Lebanon. Finally, L. Dean Brown had been at least partially successful in his mission; the Lebanese Parliament approved an amendment—under Syrian urging—to allow the selection of Franjieh's successor before his term of office expired.

Neither American nor Syrian actions, however, succeeded in ending the fighting that increasingly marred the truce, although an agreement between the PLO and Syria on April 16 seemed to improve Syrian-PLO relations. The Russians expressed satisfaction with the accord, particularly Article 5, which stipulated that the two sides would reject American solutions and plans for Lebanon.[47] The PLO's Moslem allies in Lebanon, however, stepped up their pressure as fighting increased sharply, despite Franjieh's belated statement of his willingness to resign. Meanwhile, despite the fighting, an election "campaign" took place and it soon became clear that the Syrians were backing one candidate for the presidency, Elias Sarkis, while Jumblatt's forces were backing his rival, Raymond Edde. It was against this confused background of communal conflict, widespread fighting, growing hostility among key members of their "anti-imperialist" Arab coalition, and the possibility of increased Syrian-American cooperation that the Soviet leadership suddenly unveiled their Middle Eastern peace plan on April 29.

Using the civil war in Lebanon as the reason for the call for a "radical" solution of the Middle Eastern conflict, the Soviet statement again stressed the three central components that the Soviet leaders considered necessary for a peace settlement (withdrawal of Israeli troops from all Arab territories conquered in 1967; satisfaction of the "legitimate" national demands of the Arab people of Palestine, including their right to establish their own state; and international guarantees for the security and inviolability of all Middle Eastern states and their right to independent existence and development). The Russians, in a change from earlier peace statements, also acknowledged the possibility of a two-stage Geneva conference—something advocated by the United States—in which the initial stage would "solve all the organizational questions that might arise." Nonetheless, by stipulating that the Palestine Liberation Organization had to take part in *both* stages of the conference, the Soviet leaders seem to have negated the possibility of that meeting because the United States, to say nothing of Israel, refused to deal with the PLO until it recognized Israel.

In addition to the substantive peace suggestions in their statement, the Soviet leaders used the document to stress some of their own evaluations of events in the Arab world and to warn the Arabs against cooperating with the United States. In the first place, the document stressed Israel's development of nuclear weapons—and the fact that the United States was sending Israel weapons capable of carrying them. Second, the Arabs were told of the "real aims" of the United States and its allies in the Middle East:

> The real aims of those who would like to put off the solution of the problem of the Middle East settlement endlessly and indefinitely should be clear to any objectively minded person. The preservation of the present situation in the Middle East fully accords with their long-term plans of establishing their control over the Middle East area, over its tremendous oil resources and important strategic positions.
>
> It is precisely for their sake that those who pursue aims that have nothing in common with the genuine interests of the peoples of the Middle East would like to weaken the Arab states to the maximum, push them off the road of progressive social development, range them against one another and compel them to act in disunity. . . .
>
> Obvious attempts are being made to strike a blow at the forces of the Palestine Resistance Movement and draw Arabs into a fratricidal war against Arabs. This is the real meaning of the events in Lebanon. This is even more emphasized by such provocative actions as the concentration of Israeli troops on Lebanon's southern borders and

the sending of U.S. naval ships to Lebanese shores, although they have no business there.[48]

All in all, the Soviet peace plan of April 29 can be seen as basically a propagandistic device to thrust the USSR back into the center of Middle Eastern politics at a time when, from the point of view of the USSR, the situation was deteriorating dangerously in Lebanon.[49]

The Soviet peace proposal, however, led neither to a general peace in the Middle East nor to peace in Lebanon. Instead, fighting again increased, so much so that the scheduled elections for a new Lebanese president had to be postponed for a week. When they finally were held, the leftist Moslem forces under Jumblatt boycotted the elections and called for a general strike, demanding that elections be postponed until the Syrian troops were removed from Lebanon.[50] Without the aid of the Palestinians, however, Jumblatt was unable to prevent the elections, as Arafat's forces reportedly protected a convoy of representatives who went to Parliament through a neighborhood controlled by Arafat's Fatah forces.[51]

While the Russians could not have been pleased with the now open split between Jumblatt and Assad, which seemed irrevocable after the election of Elias Sarkis, who was perceived as a Syrian tool by Jumblatt, they could at least draw consolation from the fact that Arafat and Assad, who continued to meet regularly, remained allied, albeit very loosely. Nonetheless, Arafat moved to a rapprochement with Egypt's Anwar Sadat in early May as a means of countering pressure from the Syrians.[52] At the same time, as if to balance his turn to Egypt, Arafat moved to reinforce his ties with the USSR, and in an interview granted to a *Pravda* correspondent on May 5 he was fulsome in his praise of the USSR. After hailing Brezhnev's speech to the 25th CPSU Congress and the USSR's April 29 statement, Arafat appealed for Soviet support:

> Here in the Near East, where imperialist intrigues are growing more intense, we are now experiencing one of the most complex and cruel stages of the National Liberation struggle. Therefore, *the support of the USSR, which consistently advocates the liquidation of the consequences of the Israeli aggression, is of truly tremendous significance for us.*
>
> We express our great appreciation to the friendly Soviet Union for its assistance and support. *This solidarity will undoubtedly contribute to further successes for the just cause of the Palestine revolution and of the Arab National Liberation movement.*[53] [emphasis added]

Arafat's move toward Egypt and his effort to reinforce ties to the USSR were not the only Arab diplomatic developments in May. As the fighting continued to rage in Lebanon, Saudi Arabia, together with Kuwait, sought to mediate the conflict between Syria and Egypt. The Soviet leaders were not happy with this development, since they perceived Saudi Arabia as being solidly in the American camp—indeed, Saudi Arabia, with its new oil wealth, had become the bete noire of Soviet policy in the area.[54] The Russians were clearly concerned that following the American diplomatic intervention in Lebanon, in which there was considerable evidence of tacit Syrian-American cooperation (L. Dean Brown left Lebanon after Sarkis' election), a successful mediation effort by Saudi Arabia, which was a significant contributor of assistance to the Syrian economy, might pull Syria into the American-supported Egyptian-Saudi axis. Thus, as might be expected, Radio Moscow, in an Arabic broadcast to the Middle East on May 12, took a dim view of such mediation:

> It is obvious that the aggravation of Egyptian-Syrian relations harms the just Arab cause. It is therefore self-evident that there is an intention to settle them. It has been reported that a meeting is being planned in this connection in Riyadh between Egyptian and Syrian top officials. The Saudi Arabian Kingdom was among those who initiated this meeting. This plan is drawing attention, not just in the Arab countries, and this is not surprising because the issue to be discussed is the settlement of relations between the two Arab countries which are the main target of the imperialist Israeli aggression.
>
> Many political commentators and observers are now wondering: On what basis and by what means, and more important, for what purpose are the efforts for reconciliation between Egypt and Syria being made? What adds to the urgency of this question is *the fact that Riyadh is known for its effective sharing of U.S. policy in the Middle East and that the aims of this anti-Arab policy is also known full well.*[55] [emphasis added]

On the following day, Radio Moscow was even more clear in its criticism of the proposed conference:

> It is extremely clear that ruling circles in the West are pinning specific hopes on the [Riyadh] meeting, expecting that Egypt and Saudi Arabia, which are coordinating their policies with those of the U.S., will be able to exert pressure on Syria to refrain from criticizing the American step-by-step policy, and particularly the Egyptian-Israeli Sinai agreement; the adjustments being introduced to the foreign and domestic Egyptian policies, etc.
>
> The Financial Times of London wrote frankly that convincing Syria to end its altercation with Egypt, and weakening Syria's condemnation of the Sinai agreement, are indeed among the objectives of the meeting due to be held in Riyadh.[56]

While Saudi Arabia was seeking to move Syria toward a rapprochement with Egypt, there was increasing evidence of a near break between the PLO and Damascus—a development the Russians had wished to avoid at all costs. Thus, on May 14 a number of Palestinian leaders, following clashes between Syrian-controlled forces and pro-Iraqi leftist Moslems in Tripoli, issued a statement condemning the Syrian action and demanding a withdrawal of Syrian forces.[57] In addition, Arafat directly challenged Syrian control over the Palestine Liberation Army by ordering the PLA to withdraw from Tripoli.[58] This move was to lead to a sharp deterioration in Syrian-PLO relations, although Assad did invite Arafat to Damascus to discuss the situation. He was followed to Damascus by Libyan Prime Minister Abdul Jalloud, who apparently sought both to lessen Syrian-PLO tensions and to mediate between Syria and Iraq. Jalloud then went to Beirut and issued a statement in which he both backed the left-wing Moslem-PLO alignment in Lebanon and urged the "reunification" of Syria and the left-wing Moslem forces.[59] After his departure, it was announced that Libya, Iraq, and Algeria had formed an alliance with the leftist-Moslem-Palestinian side in the civil war.[60] At the same time, the Riyadh meeting between Egypt and Syria fell through despite the last-minute diplomatic efforts of Saudi Arabia to salvage it. This event must have been greeted with satisfaction by the Russians, although Moscow Radio was to deny that the USSR had opposed the meeting, as charged by the Kuwaiti newspaper *Al-Rai Al-Am.*[61] Following the flurry of diplomatic action, fighting in Lebanon sharply escalated, with Syrian forces again tangling with left-wing Moslem troops and France offering to send troops to Lebanon.[62]

At this point, despite Syria's clashes with Jumblatt's forces and the Palestinians, Assad was in an enviable diplomatic position—although one not without its domestic difficulties.[63] On the one hand, he was being courted by the rejectionist alliance, headed by Libya, who was urging him to consolidate his ties with the Moslem leftists and Palestinians in Lebanon, reconcile himself to Iraq, and join in opposition to U.S. peace initiatives in the Middle East. On the other hand, Assad was being courted by Saudi Arabia, who was urging him to be reconciled to Egypt. At this point the Soviet leaders decided to send Premier Aleksei Kosygin to visit Iraq and Syria, in a probable effort both to effect a reconciliation between the two countries and to personally urge Syria to join the rejectionist front and stay out of the pro-Western grouping of Arab states led by Saudi Arabia. The need for such a personal intervention on the part of the Soviet leader was made even more clear on May 26, when L. Dean Brown, in discussing his Lebanese mission with David Binder of the New York *Times*, said that the Ford administration probably "made a mistake" in discouraging the Syrians from sending troops into Beirut in April[64]—a statement that might well have been interpreted as a signal that the United States would not oppose such a move in the future.

In any case, now courted by all sides, and consequently in an excellent diplomatic position, Assad made his move. First, to cover his flank with Israel, he agreed to the renewal of the mandate for the UN troops in the Golan Heights

—this time, without any conditions. Next, he authorized the Syrian-controlled newspaper *Ash-Sharq* in Lebanon to indicate that Syria would join Libya, Iraq, and Algeria in the rejectionist front.[65] Utilizing this report as a smoke screen— much as he seemed to use Syrian newspaper attacks on the United States and L. Dean Brown to cover his tacit cooperation with the United States in Leba- non—Assad gave the order for his troops to embark on a major invasion of Leba- non. Unfortunately for the Russians, the invasion order was given, and the troops were already moving, when Kosygin was in the air between Baghdad and Damascus. The Soviet leader was thus presented with a fait accompli when he ar- rived in the Syrian capital.

FROM THE KOSYGIN VISIT TO THE RIYADH CONFERENCE

The Soviet leadership's decision to send someone with the stature of Kosy- gin to Iraq and Syria was an indication of its grave concern over the course of events in the volatile Arab world. Kosygin's apparent goal was to help reconcile Iraq and Syria while also keeping Syria out of the Saudi Arabian camp, but this was not an easy task. Syria and Iraq had long been feuding over the allocation of water from the Soviet-built Euphrates Dam, the transit of Iraqi oil through Syr- ia, Syrian aid to the Kurdish rebels, Iraqi opposition to Syrian moves in Leba- non, and periodic attempts by one government or the other to overthrow its Ba'athist rival. The immediate issue at hand during Kosygin's visits was Lebanon, and the Soviet leader, while appearing to agree with the position of each of his hosts, succeeded only in contradicting himself. When he left the Middle East, the Arab world was in far greater disarray than when he arrived. Indeed, any hopes he and the other Soviet leaders might have had for creating an anti-imperi- alist Arab bloc in which Syria and Iraq would cooperate seemed, at that point, almost totally dashed.

Given the apparent goals of Kosygin's mission, it is not surprising that the communique issued at the end of the Soviet-Iraqi talks referred to them as hav- ing taken place in a "friendly atmosphere of frankness and mutual understand- ing"—diplomatic code words for disagreement.[66] Nonetheless, Kosygin seemed to go out of his way to placate his Iraqi hosts on the Lebanese issue. Thus, in a special television broadcast, Kosygin stated:

> Lebanon must be protected from any imperialist interference in its domestic affairs, because the right to decide upon them belongs only to the people of that country. *It is a legitimate right that must be re- spected by everybody.*[67] [emphasis added]

In an even more explicitly pro-Iraqi (and anti-Syrian) statement on Lebanon, the final Soviet-Iraqi communique said: "The two sides affirm that a positive solu-

tion to the Lebanese crisis can be achieved by the Lebanese people themselves."
Finally, the communique (which was broadcast by Radio Moscow in Arabic) en-
dorsed the long-sought policy goal of the USSR of creating an anti-imperialist
Arab bloc:

> The Soviet Union and Iraq believe that the main condition for the
> success of the struggle against imperialist and Zionist aggression lies
> in the cohesion of the Arab countries based on anti-imperialism and
> also on consolidation and cooperation among themselves and their
> friends, above all with the Soviet Union and other Socialist coun-
> tries.[68]

Having thus taken a relatively pro-Iraqi position on the Lebanese situation,
Kosygin boarded his plane for Damascus. With the Soviet premier in the air, Assad gave the order for his troops, camped in the eastern border regions of Lebanon, to fan out to the north, west, and south, relieving besieged Christian Arab
villages and securing Syrian control over most of the country. While the Syrian
troops, during Kosygin's visit, did not directly clash with the Palestinians who
commanded the road to Beirut, the Syrian move clearly put Kosygin in a very
awkward position. The Syrians, for their part, seem to have sought to put Kosygin at ease—at least on the subject of Syrian-American cooperation. Thus, at a
dinner given in honor of Kosygin on June 2, Syrian Prime Minister Mahmoud Al-
Ayubi took a very pro-Soviet and anti-American stand while apparently supporting the Soviet goal of an anti-imperialist Arab unity:

> The Arab nation and the Syrian Arab people look upon the Soviet
> Union as a true friend and powerful ally. . . .
> One of the most prominent results of the October War was the
> solidarity demonstrated by the Arab countries in compliance with
> the entire Arab peoples' will. This solidarity could have led to a radi-
> cal change in the balance of forces in the Middle East conflict, if the
> U.S. had not been quick to bend every effort and use all of its pres-
> tige to undermine this solidarity and fan up disunity among the Arab
> countries, particularly among the countries engaged in a confronta-
> tion with their Israeli enemy.[69]

Al-Ayubi went on, however, to state that Syria had a rightful claim on Soviet weaponry because Syria was on the "front line" of the international struggle
against imperialism.

> In the military sphere, the weapons which you supplied to us be-
> came a means for repulsing the expansionist, imperialist, and Zionist
> aspirations in the region. The stronger Syria is in military terms, the

greater the degree to which this will be a factor for the security of the forces of freedom and progress in our region. We are on the front line of the international struggle for the consolidation of the ideals of freedom, democracy, socialism and of the right of the peoples to self-determination. Syria bears for itself and for others a considerable share of the burden in the practical confrontation with world imperialism.[70]

The Syrian premier also stated, perhaps to the unhappiness of his Soviet guest, that Syria would continue to pursue its policy course in Lebanon.[71]

In his own dinner speech, Kosygin was far more circumspect in regard to Lebanon than he had been in Iraq, stating only that the "Soviet Union regards as impermissible imperialist interference in Lebanon's affairs in any form whatever." He also came out in support of the need for Lebanese unity—perhaps the only factor in the Lebanese situation that the USSR, Syria, and Iraq could agree upon.[72]

The joint communique issued at the end of the Soviet-Syrian talks characterized them as having taken place in an "atmosphere of friendship and mutual understanding" during which a "detailed exchange of opinions" took place—diplomatic expressions for disagreement. On the Lebanese issue, relatively little was said other than that Syria and the USSR "affirmed their resolve to continue work to end the bloodshed, to restore security and peace in Lebanon, and to ensure its integrity, independence, and sovereignty"—a statement tacitly supporting the Syrian position. Perhaps most important of all, however, the Russians indicated that they would not take a retaliatory military action against Syria for its move into Lebanon. The final communique, after listing a series of areas of Soviet assistance to Syria (including the strengthening of Syria's "defense capability"), stated: "The two sides unanimously affirmed their desire to continue expanding and improving these relations on a solid, long-term basis."[73]

On balance, it would appear that Kosygin's visits to Iraq and Syria did little more than reinforce the USSR's bilateral relations with each country, thereby perhaps forestalling the possibility of a Syrian or Iraqi move toward the United States.[74] Nonetheless, the Syrian invasion of Lebanon, which the USSR had been able neither to forestall nor to reverse, threatened, for the first time, to pit Syrian forces directly against the Palestinians, a development that would gravely weaken what the Soviet leadership had termed the "anti-imperialist core" of the Arab world.[75] It would also pose a very painful problem of choice for the Soviet leadership. Nonetheless, a *New Times* editorial in early June, calling for the rapid resumption of the Geneva conference, sought to put the best possible face on the Kosygin trip, stating:

The visits Aleksei Kosygin has just paid to Iraq and Syria, the announcement that King Hussein of Jordan is to visit Moscow, and many other things are evidence that, despite the intrigues of anti-Sovieteers of every hue, Soviet-Arab cooperation remains one of the most important positive factors in the Middle East.[76]

The initial Soviet response to the Syrian invasion was mixed—perhaps reflecting confusion in the top leadership. On the one hand, the Soviets permitted a protest demonstration of about 300 Lebanese and Palestinian students outside the Syrian Embassy.[77] Several days later, however, on June 6, Radio Moscow, in a broadcast to the Arab world of a *Pravda* commentary, gave a qualified endorsement of the initial Syrian move into Lebanon:

> In Lebanon, all attempts by the national forces to seek ways leading to the establishment of a political settlement of the crisis have failed. As reported by Syrian papers, units of the Syrian army are now in Lebanon, and their presence has helped ease the situation in a number of regions in the country. But the situation in general is still tense and complicated. The imperialist quarters are fully to blame for the tense situation.[78]

The very next day, the Syrians stepped up their military pressure—possibly in response to Palestinian and leftist Moslem attacks on pro-Syrian Saiqa forces—and began a drive on Beirut and Sidon, this time clashing directly with Palestinian as well as leftist Moslem forces.

This new Syrian move apparently caught the Russians by surprise again, and as the fighting heated up, the Soviet leadership changed its position once again. On June 10, *Pravda* published an official TASS statement giving the strongest anti-Syrian criticism to date. The statement also appealed for an immediate cease-fire and warned the Western powers not to intervene—perhaps as a counter to continued discussions about the use of French troops in a peace-keeping force:

> The Syrian Arab Republic has repeatedly stated that the troops it has sent into Lebanon are there to help stop the bloodshed. It is obvious, however, that the bloodshed in Lebanon is not only continuing, but is actually increasing. . . .
>
> It is necessary for all sides that are in one way or another involved in the Lebanese events to stop fighting immediately. As for those countries that, alluding to their stake in the Lebanese situation, have threatened direct military intervention in Lebanese affairs, the Soviet Union is compelled to state: the Middle East is much closer to the USSR than to those who are making such threats.[79]

While the USSR was calling for a cease-fire between its Middle Eastern allies, the Syrian invasion was causing an uproar in inter-Arab politics. Egypt had virtually severed diplomatic relations with Syria after a Syrian student rampage in the Egyptian Embassy in Damascus, which followed a student occupation of the Syrian Embassy in Cairo. The Egyptians also seized on the Syrian invasion to once again champion the Palestinians, and the PLO radio stations in Egypt, which had been closed following Palestinian criticism of the Sinai II agreement, were now reopened.[80] Iraq, Syria's other major Arab opponent, sought to counter the invasion by moving several divisions of troops to the Syrian border, necessitating a similar Syrian deployment. At the same time, all the Palestinian forces except Saiqa[81] united in what was perhaps the only positive development the Russians could cite out of the Lebanese imbroglio, since the USSR had long been urging the unification of the diverse Palestinian groups. Indeed, although the Palestinians were almost certainly driven to this measure by military necessity, the Russians must have taken comfort from the fact that George Habash and other rejectionist front "radicals" were now cooperating with the Fatah "moderates." Nonetheless, without Saiqa and its Syrian backers, both the Palestinian unity and the broader Arab unity the Russians desired were still a long way off.

In addition to unifying among themselves, the Palestinian groups joined with Kamal Jumblatt's forces and Ahmed Khatib's Lebanese Arab Army in a central command to provide a united front against the Syrian invasion. Meanwhile, a number of Arab states, led by Egypt and the PLO, were calling for an Arab League meeting to deal with the Syrian invasion, and a meeting was held as the Syrian-Palestinian fighting intensified. The Syrians, while inflicting heavy casualties on the Palestinians, were themselves suffering losses, particularly in their tank forces, which were engaged in battles near Sidon (Saida) and Bhamdoun.[82] Perhaps sensing the need to regroup his forces after encountering unexpectedly strong Palestinian resistance, and also seeking to diffuse the heavy Arab pressure now directed against him, Assad agreed to the establishment of a peace-keeping truce force composed of Libyan, Algerian, Saudi, Sudanese, Palestinian, and Syrian troops. It soon became clear, however, that the other Arab forces were to be small compared with the Syrian contingent, and the Syrians quickly moved to consolidate their hold in central, eastern, and southern Lebanon. Meanwhile, the PLO demanded another Arab League meeting, claiming that the truce agreement, which had been negotiated by Libyan Prime Minister Abdul Salam Jalloud, called for the full withdrawal of Syrian forces from Lebanon.[83] The most the Syrians would eventually agree to, however, were minor withdrawals from Beirut airport (turning it over to the pan-Arab peace-keeping force) and the region near Sidon.

Jalloud's mediation effort had only limited success, and an effort by Saudi Arabia in the latter part of June to forge a reconciliation between Egypt and Syria met a similar fate. Unlike the abortive meeting in May, however, this time the meeting did take place, albeit only at the prime minister level. The most that was agreed on was the formation of a joint committee to prepare for a meeting of Sadat and Assad and the creation of a military-political committee, headed by each country's foreign minister, to study ways to carry out the recommendations of the 1974 Rabat conference.[84]

While these Arab diplomatic interactions were taking place, the Soviet Union found itself unable to influence the course of events. The most the Soviets could do in support of the Palestinians, who were now confronted by both the Syrian army and the right-wing Christian forces, was to promise shipments of food and medicine[85] and allow the opening of the PLO mission in Moscow. At the same time, however, their criticism of Syria remained limited, although it became a bit more severe as June wore on. Perhaps most interesting of all, however, a note of frustration and bewilderment began to appear in Soviet reporting of Arab affairs, reminiscent of the period in the late summer of 1971 when the USSR suffered a series of reverses in its Middle Eastern policy following the government shake-up in Egypt and the abortive Communist-supported coup d'etat in the Sudan.[86]

An example of this bewilderment over "natural allies" fighting each other can be seen in a *New Times* article in the middle of June by Yuri Potomov, a Soviet journalist who has written extensively on Middle Eastern affairs. He began his article, "The Lebanon Crisis: Who Stands to Gain," by observing:

> The situation in Lebanon and around that country has latterly become so complex that some observers are inclined to consider the logic of developments completely beyond comprehension.[87]

Several weeks later, Dmitry Volsky, another veteran Middle Eastern reporter for *New Times*, commented:

> All against all and each against each, and anarchy is now nearly reality—such is the leitmotif of Western capitalist press comment on Lebanon and the Arab East in general at the present time. There is a lot of talk about "coalitions that unexpectedly spring up and disintegrate", about unsuccessful attempts at mediation in an atmosphere of general suspicion and bellicosity, about the *"political paradoxes" in which, it must be admitted, the Middle East now abounds more than ever before.*
>
> Indeed, could one conceive only a short while ago that the Rightist leaders of the Lebanese Maronites would be receiving arms from Israel and welcoming the presence of Syrian troops in Lebanon or that soldiers of two contingents of the inter-Arab peace-keeping force would start shooting at each other in Beirut airport because relations had become strained to the utmost.[88] [emphasis added]

While the Soviet press was expressing some bewilderment about the Middle East, it was also slowly increasing its criticism of the Syrian intervention. Thus, on June 16 *Pravda* stated:

The situation in Lebanon remains extremely tense despite the fact that the intensity of armed clashes has somewhat abated in recent days. Lebanese national-patriotic forces and the Palestinian resistance movement are adhering firmly to the terms of the cease-fire reached through the mediation of Libyan Prime Minister A. Jalloud.

In recent days, however, according to Lebanese radio, Syrian troops have continued moving west in the Bekaa Valley and the Arkub region. Syrian troops stationed in the Beirut suburb of Uzai yesterday launched artillery and mortar attacks against the position of the national-patriotic forces.[89]

Three days later *Pravda*, after reporting clashes between Syrian troops and the Palestinian-leftist Moslem joint command, quoted a report of the leftist forces:

Instead of withdrawing from Beirut, Saida, and Tripoli, as required by the agreement reached through the mediation of A. Jalloud . . . the Syrian troops have not lifted their blockade of these cities and are continuing to strengthen their positions.[90]

While their criticism of Syria was stepped up, although still kept in a minor key (as if they hoped a PLO-Syrian reconciliation was possible), the Soviets made a gesture to the hard-pressed PLO—but little more than that. On June 22 Mohammed Ibrahim Al-Shaer, head of the permanent mission of the PLO in the USSR, formally opened the long-delayed PLO mission in Moscow. Nonetheless, the handling of that opening—together with subsequent major Soviet criticisms of Syrian policy toward the Palestinians—was relegated to the level of the Soviet Afro-Asian Solidarity Committee, a low-level Soviet foreign policy organ with only semiofficial status. The Russians, however, used the ceremony for maximum propaganda effect, with *Pravda* citing Shaer's statement to emphasize the PLO's appreciation of Soviet support:

In his statement, M. Shaer noted that, at a time when the Palestinian resistance movement is waging a stubborn struggle against imperialist and reactionary intrigues in the Middle East and for the National rights of the Arab people of Palestine, the establishment of a PLO mission in the USSR and the inauguration of its work is seen by the Arab people of Palestine and all progressive Arabs as a convincing demonstration of the firm principled support given by the CPSU and the Soviet state to the national-liberation struggle of the Palestinian people.[91]

One of the reasons why the Soviet leaders seemed to continue soft-pedaling their criticism of Syria may have been their concern that if they pushed Syria too hard, the Syrians might go over to the American-backed Saudi-Egyptian camp. It was for this reason, perhaps, that the Radio Moscow commentary discussing the Riyadh conference of late June took a very pro-Syrian line, emphasizing that the meeting had not taken place in May because Syria wanted to discuss the "negative effects of the Sinai II agreement." Radio commentator Aleksandr Rimoshkin stated, "Syria quite rightly believed that by agreeing to sign a separate agreement with Israel through active U.S. mediation, Egypt had been taken out of the effective participation in the battle against aggression."[92]

As might be expected, the Soviet leaders were heartened by the relative lack of success of the Riyadh conference, and Radio Moscow had the following comment:

> On the official level these [Saudi Arabian ruling] quarters were portraying their organization of the conference in Riyadh as being first and foremost in the interests of Egypt and Syria on the basis of the struggle against Israeli aggression. But it is no secret any longer that in the past Saudi Arabia tried to pressure Egypt with a view to steering it on the road of separate deals with Tel Aviv, and later entering the U.S. sphere of influence. Moreover, it was also trying to exercise similar pressure on Syria by cutting off the financial assistance stipulated by the Rabat summit conference.
>
> Progressive Arab papers pointed out that the Saudi ruling quarters pinned on the Arab Quadripartite Conference their hopes of securing approval for their policy with regard to a Middle East settlement. Egyptian delegates also pinned their hopes on the conference.
>
> However, the outcome of the conference has failed the hopes of the organizers. It appears that the capitulationist line in matters connected with a settlement in the Middle East reflected in the Sinai agreement has been exposed so much that it cannot possibly be imposed on anyone except those who have fallen victim to it.[93]

While the Soviet leaders were seeking to keep Syria out of the Egyptian-Saudi Arabian camp, they were finding it increasingly difficult to downplay their criticism of Syrian policy in Lebanon as the predicament of the Palestinian forces became more and more serious. Because of the Syrian invasion, the Palestinian and Moslem forces had to concentrate their troops on the fronts opposing the Syrian army, and this, in turn, enabled the Christian rightist forces to take the offensive against their Lebanese and Palestinian enemies. The first Christian targets were the Palestinian refugee camps of Jisr Al-Pasha (which, interestingly enough, contained primarily Christian Palestinian refugees) and Tel Zaatar, which lay in the Christian suburbs of Beirut and served to block the lines of communication between the Christian section of Beirut and the Christian villages in the Lebanese mountains.

By the latter part of June, both camps were under siege and Arab League mediator Abdel Salam Jalloud, whose sympathies all along had appeared to be on the side of the leftist Moslem-Palestinian bloc, gave up his efforts on June 29. He returned to Libya, warning that he would "escalate" Libyan support for the Palestinians and their allies.[94] The next day the Jisr Al-Pasha refugee camp fell to the advancing Christian forces, and their pressure intensified against Tel Zaatar. At the same time the joint Palestinian-leftist Moslem command accused the Syrians of aiding the Christian attacks, and at a meeting of the Arab League in Cairo on July 1, Arafat made the same accusation.[95] In an attempt to relieve the pressure on Tel Zaatar, leftist forces launched an attack from Tripoli on July 5 against the northern heartland of Christian Lebanon, temporarily capturing the town of Chekka. They were subsequently driven out, however, not only from Chekka but also from the formerly leftist-held town of Enfe.[96] The Palestinians accused the Syrians of aiding the Christian counteroffensive and of shelling the refinery of Sidon to prevent the leftist alliance from getting gasoline. The situation had thus become quite desperate for the Palestinians, with Arafat reportedly going so far as to appeal to his erstwhile enemy, Anwar Sadat, on July 9 "to take swift revolutionary measures to stop the gravely deteriorating situation before it is too late."[97]

Under these circumstances, it would appear that the Russians felt constrained to take some kind of action if they wished to maintain credibility with the Palestinians. Thus, Syrian Foreign Minister Khaddam was invited to Moscow for talks between July 5 and 7. The Soviet leaders evidently did not succeed in getting the Syrians to ease their pressure on the Palestinians (no communique was issued at the end of the visit), because three days after Khaddam's departure the Soviet Afro-Asian Solidarity Organization issued a statement containing the strongest Soviet criticism of Syria up to that point. The criticism remained relatively mild, however, as the bulk of the blame for the Lebanese situation remained assigned to the "imperialists":

> The progressive Arab public has correctly assessed the Lebanese crisis as an insidious new plot of imperialism and Israel's ruling circles aimed against a just settlement of the Middle East conflict and at disuniting the Arab peoples in their struggle for the liberation of the Arab territories occupied by Israel. *The involvement of Syrian military units in the Lebanon conflict has further complicated the situation....*
>
> On behalf of broad circles of the Soviet public, the Soviet Committee for solidarity with Afro-Asian countries appeals to all the hostile parties in Lebanon for an immediate cease-fire and an end to the bloodshed. Soviet people are convinced that the Lebanese crisis can and must be settled by the Lebanese themselves without any outside interference, with the participation of all interested parties and on the basis of guarantees of the independence, sovereignty, and territorial integrity of Lebanon.[98] [emphasis added]

This form of rhetorical support, while undoubtedly welcome, was not all that the Palestinians either needed or expected. Indeed, in a cable to a specially convened Arab foreign ministers meeting in Cairo, Arafat reportedly stated, "Our non-Arab friends abroad will come to our rescue if Arab countries fail to help us."[99] In addition, the leftist-controlled Beirut Radio reported that the USSR was preparing for "urgent action" to prevent the defeat of the leftist Moslem-Palestinian forces in the civil war.[100] The USSR never confirmed such reports although on July 19 *Le Monde* published a letter reportedly sent from Brezhnev to Assad on July 11 in which the Soviet leader called for the withdrawal of Syrian forces, blamed the Syrians for the cease-fire not taking hold, and warned the Syrians that the prospects for "further strengthening" Moscow's relations with Syria would be damaged if they did not comply with Soviet wishes. The authenticity of this letter cannot be verified, although there were reports of a slowdown in Soviet military shipments to Syria.[101]

What the Russians clearly did do was to increase their public criticism of Syria in *Pravda* and other publications, although, it should be noted, the criticism still remained rather limited. Thus, on July 15, *Pravda* published the press conference of PLO mission head Mohammed Al-Shaer, in which he stated rather pointedly:

> Domestic reactionary forces, with all-round support from foreign imperialist circles, have launched a broad offensive against detachments of the Palestinian resistance movement and Lebanese National Patriotic forces. *The fact that regular Syrian formations are taking part in these operations is cause for deep regret and bewilderment.*[102] [emphasis added]

The next day *Pravda* published an extensive analysis of the Lebanese situation by Pavel Demchenko in which Demchenko, in addition to the normal Soviet criticism of "imperialism" and Israeli interference in Lebanese affairs, criticized Franjieh for not stepping down and making way for Elias Sarkis, indicating that such a move might help "normalize" the situation. As for Syria's role in the Lebanese events, Demchenko had the following comments:

> The discord that arose between Syria and the PLO leadership has turned out to be real "manna from heaven" for all those interested in prolonging the Lebanese crisis. Events took a truly dramatic turn when in early June Syria brought its troops into Lebanon.
> The PLO leadership assessed the appearance of Syrian troops in Lebanon as an act directed against the Palestinian Resistance movement. Fighting broke out with new force. PLO units found themselves under fire from the rear and the front—from the Syrians and from Rightist Lebanese formations.

... Inter-Arab differences have to all intents and purposes helped untie the hands of the Bloc of Lebanese Rightist forces ... [which] has launched wide-scale military operations with the aim of gaining control of part of Lebanon north of Beirut, driving the Palestinians out of that area, and thereby achieving the de facto partition of the country.

... The situation remains complex.... News agencies are also reporting about initial preparations for a meeting between representatives of the Syrian government and the PLO for the purpose of normalizing relations between the two.

A way out of the present crisis, which in fact is not limited to one country, can be found primarily along lines of the restoration of mutual understanding and unity of action among the Arab liberation and progressive forces, including the Palestinian movement.[103] [emphasis added]

While the Soviet leaders continued to hope for an improvement in PLO-Syrian relations, they had to be concerned about the further deterioration of their overall position in the Middle East during this period, a development caused by an abortive coup in the Sudan on July 2 that was apparently aided by one of the USSR's Arab allies, Libya.[104] This event not only led to a sharp deterioration in Sudanese-Libyan relations but also to a major strain in Soviet-Sudanese relations, which had never fully recovered from the damage caused by the abortive Communist-supported coup of July 1971.[105] As Sudanese President Jaafar Nimeri said in a New York *Times* interview in early August 1976, "Behind Colonel Kaddafi we think there is another power, one of the powers of the world, a power who is seeking some influence in the Nile Valley."[106]

An important consequence of the Libyan-backed coup attempt was the decision by Egypt and the Sudan to conclude a mutual defense treaty on July 15. Significantly, the announcement of the pact came after three days of talks among Nimeri, Sadat, and King Khalid of Saudi Arabia in the Saudi port city of Jidda. It was also announced that all three countries would establish "joint organizations and institutions for close political, military and economic cooperation."[107] While somewhat vague, this tripartite agreement, together with the Egyptian-Sudanese defense agreement, served to bring the Sudan, once a relatively close ally of the USSR, more firmly into the Western-supported Egyptian-Saudi grouping of Arab states. It also reinforced Libya's isolation in northeast Africa, for now the Sudan, as well as Egypt, stood in opposition to it. As might be expected, the Soviet Union was not happy about this development, with a *New Times* report giving the following evaluation:

The results of the Egyptian-Sudanese-Saudi contacts met with a mixed response in the region. The Teheran press, for instance, said the Egyptian-Sudanese Treaty "has no direct relation to the Arab-Israeli crisis", and is spearheaded against Libya. Many draw attention to the fact that Saudi Arabia's reactionary monarchist regime has been drawn into the realm of Egyptian-Sudanese relations.[108]

Soviet unhappiness with Saudi Arabian activities, however, was not limited to the closer ties with Egypt and the Sudan. The Saudis have moved to improve relations with yet another old Soviet ally, South Yemen (the People's Democratic Republic of Yemen), and the Soviet leadership displayed some concern that the poor, albeit Marxist, Arab state might also be drawn into the Saudi orbit. Relations between Saudi Arabia and South Yemen were restored on March 10, 1976, following the winding down of the South Yemeni-supported insurgency in the Dhofar region of neighboring Oman, and the Saudis have reportedly given a total of $100 million in grants to their southern neighbor.[109] Soviet concern over the development of Saudi-South Yemeni relations may be seen in a report on South Yemen by *New Times* correspondent V. Alexandrov. In an otherwise positive report on the transformations of South Yemeni society under its Marxist rulers, Alexandrov noted:

> The radical reforms have undermined the material and political base of the Right-Wing opposition. The well-to-do sections of the population in town and country, whose interests have been infringed by the revolution, and the political emigres who have found refuge and support in certain Arab countries still entertain hopes of restoring the old order, if only partially. These elements pin their hopes, to some extent, on normalization of relations with neighboring Saudi Arabia in the belief that the establishment of political and business contacts between Aden and Riyadh might lead to the de-ideologization of the progressive South Yemeni regime, the erosion of the revolution.[110]

Saudi policies were to prove a problem for Soviet policy makers in yet another area of the Middle East. Following the breakdown of the Jordanian-American negotiations for the purchase of an antiaircraft missile system in April 1976, Jordan began negotiations with the Soviet Union to purchase such a system, and in May the commander of the Soviet air force, Deputy Defense Minister Marshal Pavel S. Kutakhov, journeyed to Jordan for discussions. Kutakhov was the highest-ranking Soviet official ever to visit the traditionally pro-Western Arab state. The Soviet Union apparently entertained high hopes for the mission, and Radio Moscow, in praising the Jordanians for awarding Kutakhov the Jordanian Independence Medal, stated that "wide quarters of the Jordanian public, in stressing the principled stand of the Soviet Union on the Middle East problem, have been persistently demanding that Soviet-Jordanian cooperation be expanded."[111]

No missile agreement was signed during the Kutakhov visit, however, and King Hussein himself set out for Moscow the following month. While Hussein may well have been using his negotiations with Moscow as a ploy, much as he had done in the past, to arrange better financial terms for an American arms deal (it was unlikely that Saudi Arabia would be willing to finance a Soviet air defense system), the Soviet Union nonetheless gave extensive propaganda coverage to his visit. In advance of Hussein's arrival, *New Times*, as it often does when foreign dignitaries visit the USSR, published an article on Jordan. The author, Anatoly Repin, after describing the expansion of Soviet-Jordanian relations in the recent past, concluded by stating:

> In short, our ties are becoming ever more diversified. Nevertheless, *not all the possibilities have yet been used.* It is hoped that King Hussein's visit to our country will contribute weightily to the expansion of Soviet-Jordanian cooperation.[112] [emphasis added]

Unfortunately for the Russians, however, Hussein's visit did not lead to military cooperation, although, in a possible attempt to increase his bargaining power with the United States, Hussein had stated on the eve of his visit to Moscow, "It is no secret that we have begun to investigate the possibilities of providing our armed forces with an air defense system of Soviet manufacture. We are now in the preliminary stage of this investigation."[113] The joint communique issued at the end of Hussein's trip to the USSR described the talks as having taken place in a businesslike atmosphere—the usual Soviet description of low-level cooperation—and referred to an "exchange of opinions" on international problems. It made no mention of any arms agreement, although the USSR did agree to give Jordan assistance in oil exploration, in building a power transmission line, and in establishing vocational and technical training centers.[114]

Following the failure of his arms-seeking mission to Moscow, and reportedly under heavy pressure from his main financial supporter, Saudi Arabia, Hussein once again turned to the United States for arms. On July 31 the Ford administration announced that a general agreement had been worked out at a reduced cost of $540 million (to be financed by Saudi Arabia) to sell the air defense system to Jordan.[115] The deal for the 14-battery Hawk missile system was finally consummated in early September.[116]

Thus, as their overall position in the Arab world deteriorated, the Russians could ill afford to alienate Syria. Yet the continued deterioration of the position of their Palestinian allies, whom they also valued (albeit not as highly), put them under increasing pressure to take some kind of action. As mentioned above, the Soviet leadership was hoping for a PLO-Syrian reconciliation and greeted with enthusiasm the report that a PLO-Syrian meeting had been arranged. That meeting, however, did not fulfill Soviet expectations, despite the mediating role played by Libyan Prime Minister Jalloud, who continued to try to effect a reconciliation between the two sides. While the agreement, signed by Syrian Foreign Minister Khaddam and PLO leader Farouk Kaddoumi, established a cease-fire and stipulated that all sides would abide by both the Syrian-sponsored agreement of February 1976 regulating Christian-Moslem relations in Lebanon and the 1969 Cairo agreement regulating the activities of the Palestinians in Lebanon, the joint communique contained a clause that attacked the Sinai II agreement.[117] This created an uproar as Arafat, in an effort to mollify Egypt, repudiated the clause. The agreement itself came under attack within the PLO, since it made no mention of any Syrian withdrawal from Lebanon.[118]

As a result of this development, Syrian-Egyptian relations, temporarily calmed by the Riyadh conference of late June, were again inflamed. The Soviet leadership, ever seeking to foster a reconciliation between the PLO and Syria, took a positive, albeit guarded, view of the agreement, with *Pravda* commentator Pavel Demchenko on August 4 calling it a "step toward the normalization of Syrian-Palestinian relations." The *Pravda* article also cited the Syrian newspaper *Al-Thawrah*'s comment that the agreement signified that "the natural state of affairs is being restored and that recognition of the lasting importance of relations between Syria and the Palestinian movement has proven stronger than all the artificial, extraneous matters and complications that have arisen during the events in Lebanon." Still expressing Soviet displeasure over the Syrian involvement in Lebanon, however, Demchenko added:

> At the same time, the press in a number of Arab countries has called attention to the fact that the agreement circumvents the question of the withdrawal of Syrian troops from Lebanon.

The Soviet commentary concluded with the report that, despite the agreement, fighting continued in Lebanon with rightist assaults on Tel Zaatar, and that therefore the agreement could be considered only "a first encouraging step leading to the reduction of tension."[119]

Tension, however, was not reduced; both Syrian and Christian forces moved to improve their positions as fighting continued to rage. The Syrians consolidated their positions near Jezzine (east of Sidon), clashing with Palestinian-leftist forces in the process, while the Christian Lebanese forces stepped up their assault on Tel Zaatar, which finally fell on August 12. The fall of Tel Zaatar enabled the Christian forces to begin to press against the leftist-Palestinian positions in northern Lebanon and in the mountains east of Beirut. The Palestinians, finding themselves caught in a pincer between the Syrians and the Christians, and with their supplies virtually cut off by Israeli and Syrian blockades of the ports under their control, began a major recruitment drive to strengthen their forces and appealed to the Arab states and the USSR for aid. In the most explicit Palestinian call for Soviet aid to date, Salah Khalaf (Abu Iyads), second in command to Arafat, complained:

> What have you given us? We do not want you to tell us to reach an understanding with the Syrians. You have lost many of your positions in

the Arab world because you did not understand the conspiracy. We are not asking the impossible; we want a ship carrying flour and hoisting the Russian flag to come to Saida and defy Israel.[120]

While the Soviets were not prepared to militarily challenge either Syria or Israel, the Soviet press did step up its criticism of Syrian policy in Lebanon. Thus, *Pravda* on August 18, in a report of a meeting between Lebanese Communist Party leader N. Shawi and Andrei Kirilenko of the CPSU, cited the Lebanese Communist Party's opinion favoring the withdrawal of Syrian troops from Lebanon. The Russians also seized on the visit of two American diplomats to the Christian Lebanese capital of Jounieh, together with a television interview by L. Dean Brown, to claim that the United States was supporting the partition of Lebanon.[121] The same *Pravda* article cited a left-wing Beirut newspaper report that the success of the Christian drive in northern Lebanon was aided by the Syrian blockade of Tripoli.[122]

The strongest criticism of Syrian policy, however, came on August 27, when another statement by the Soviet Afro-Asian Solidarity Committee explicitly asked the Syrian troops to leave Lebanon and again appealed for the restoration of anti-imperialist Arab unity:

> People in the Soviet Union are firmly convinced that the Lebanese conflict can and must be settled peacefully and democratically by the Lebanese themselves in the interests of ensuring the territorial integrity, independence, and sovereignty of Lebanon. Soviet people actively support the position of the PLO and the Lebanese National Patriotic forces, *a position in favor of a settlement of the Lebanese crisis without outside interference, and share the world public's opinion that the withdrawal of Syrian troops from Lebanon would be of great importance in resolving the Lebanese crisis.* Needless to say, the normalization of the situation in Lebanon would be significantly facilitated by Syria's cooperation with its natural allies in the anti-imperialist struggle—the Palestinian resistance movement and Lebanon's National Patriotic forces. This would undoubtedly promote the restoration and consolidation of the front of Arab forces waging a struggle against Israeli aggression and the expansionist plans and aspirations of imperialism and reaction and for ensuring a just peace in the Middle East.[123] [emphasis added]

Pravda's "International Week" column two days later emphasized this point:

> The withdrawal of Syrian troops from Lebanon would be of great importance in resolving the Lebanese crisis as would Syria's cooperation with its natural allies in the anti-imperialist struggle—the Palestinian

resistance movement and Lebanon's National Patriotic forces. This would facilitate the restoration and consolidation of the front of Arab forces.[124]

Pravda continued its attack on Syrian policy in a very strong article under the "Commentator" by-line on September 8, arguing that "essentially, the Lebanese rightist groupings, the imperialist circles, Israel, and the Arab reactionaries are now in a single formation against Lebanon's National Patriotic forces and the Palestinian resistance movement." It pointedly added:

> Whatever considerations may have guided Damascus when it sent its troops into Lebanon, this decision turned against the Palestinian movement and allowed the rightists to inflict telling blows on detachments of Palestinians and Lebanese National Patriotic forces. It is understandable why the Lebanese progressive organizations, the PLO, and many countries of the Arab—and not only the Arab—world are demanding that Syrian units be withdrawn from the country.[125]

The Soviet article went on, however, to express some hope for a compromise peace agreement when Sarkis took office on September 23, but warned that "There must not be a settlement that means infringing the Palestinians' rights or does not take account of the National Patriotic forces' legitimate demands." Interestingly enough, it warned not only rightist leaders against sabotaging any compromise agreement but also "ultra-leftist elements within the Palestinian movement and the front of patriotic forces" against "rejecting out of hand" all peace proposals—a statement that caused considerable consternation among Lebanon's left-wing Moslems and Palestinians, who wondered if the USSR was changing its policy.[126]

Perhaps to determine the exact line of Soviet policy, Farouk Kaddoumi, head of the PLO Executive Committee's Political Department, journeyed to Moscow for talks with Gromyko the following week. *Pravda*'s report of the discussions described them as having taken place in a "friendly atmosphere," and emphasized that both sides desired to normalize the situation in Lebanon. *Pravda*'s description of the talks made no mention of the need for a Syrian withdrawal, however.[127] The Soviet leadership may have simply given up on it, particularly after Assad had reportedly rejected, on September 11, a Soviet note from Brezhnev personally requesting the withdrawal of Syrian forces.[128] Indeed, the Soviet leaders, with Sarkis' assumption of the presidency approaching on September 23, may have seen this as a good opportunity to work out a compromise agreement—something that was also stressed in *Pravda*'s September 8 statement. The fact that both leftist Moslem leader Jumblatt and Fatah leader Salah Khalaf, in interviews in Beirut in September,[129] praised Sarkis and said they could work with him may also have prompted the Soviets to moderate their stand toward Syria. Reports of cooperation in mid-September between Syria and Israel to effect family reunions on the Golan Heights,[130] which the Russians may have seen as further evidence of the tacit Syrian-Israeli cooperation already evident in Lebanon, may have been another factor in the changed Soviet policy. Whatever the cause, in a clear gesture to Assad on September 27, *Pravda* published a Syrian report of Assad's speech to his troops on the Golan Heights that justified Syria's intervention in Lebanon.

Unfortunately for the Russians, however, they were once again overtaken by events. While PLO chief Arafat announced a cease-fire in honor of Sarkis' inauguration, Arab terrorists, whom the Syrians branded as Fatah members, seized the Semiramis Hotel in Damascus on September 26.[131] Assad responded by hanging the terrorists and launching a new offensive in Lebanon against the mountain salient above Beirut held by the Palestinians and leftist forces. The operation was coordinated with rightist attacks from the west and, before a truce was arranged, the two forces captured a large section of the narrow salient that projected into the Christian-controlled region of Lebanon. The renewal of the Syrian rightist offensive caused a rapid reversal in Soviet policy; another Soviet Afro-Asian Solidarity Committee statement was issued on September 30, this one the strongest yet in its criticism of the Syrian actions. The statement also clearly expressed Soviet frustration at developments in Lebanon:

> A major step aimed at restoring peace was the announcement by Yasir Arafat, Chairman of the Palestine Liberation Organization Executive Committee, of a unilateral cease-fire by Palestinian detachments in all combat sectors in Lebanon so as to create favorable conditions for the materialization of President Sarkis's peace initiative. ... Lebanon's National Patriotic forces expressed willingness to cooperate with the Patriotic forces expressed willingness to cooperate with the new President in the interests of halting the bloodshed and peacefully resolving the country's internal problems ... important political contacts were established and intensive consultations began between various political forces of the country. The fighting began to die down in a number of areas.
>
> Now, however, everything is threatened again. Lebanon's right-wing forces, encouraged from without by imperialist circles and relying on the direct support of Israel, responded to the constructive cease-fire steps taken by the Palestine Liberation Organization and the National Patriotic forces with a new military attack. ...
>
> Now no one can doubt any longer the existence of an extensive conspiracy by imperialism and the Arab reaction against the Palestine Resistance Movement, which has shown itself an active and steadfast fighter against imperialist intrigues and Israeli aggression. This conspiracy is also aimed at the National Patriotic forces of Lebanon.

Particularly alarming to the world community and also to the Soviet people is the fact that Syrian troops, stationed on Lebanese soil since June of this year, are now participating in military operations against the Palestine Liberation Movement and Lebanon's National Patriotic forces.[132] [emphasis added]

A second Soviet reaction to the new Lebanese developments was to launch yet another peace initiative, much as the Soviet leaders had done at the end of April when Lebanese events began to take a course that threatened Soviet policy. Unlike the April initiative, however, this was given to the concerned states (United States, Egypt, Syria, Jordan, and Israel), as well as the PLO, before it was made public by *Pravda* on October 2. The Russians again cited events in Lebanon as the reason for the need for an overall peace settlement, and called for the resumption of the Geneva conference in October-November 1976--almost immediately. In addition to the three by-now traditional points in the Soviet peace plan (the need to ensure Israel's independent existence and security was specifically spelled out this time), the new Soviet proposal called for the cessation of the state of war between the Arab states and Israel.[133] While clearly a gesture toward Israeli demands, the Soviet Union's continued adherence to the principle of PLO participation in both stages of the Geneva conference on an equal footing eliminated the chances of a quick resumption of the conference, since both Israel and the United States remained opposed to PLO participation before it agreed to recognize Israel.

The Soviet peace plan did not bring peace to Lebanon, however, although there was a temporary lull in the fighting as Syria, having once again proven its military superiority over the Palestinians, halted before its forces crushed them. Instead, the Syrians agreed to meet with the Palestinians at Chtaura, a town in eastern Lebanon under Syrian control, under the mediation of Hassan Sabry El-Kholy, an Egyptian diplomat. While a tentative agreement was reached at Chtaura,[134] a series of Palestinian terrorist attacks against Syrian embassies in Italy and Pakistan precipitated a Syrian attack, and Syrian forces drove toward Beirut and Sidon. As might be expected, the Soviet leadership reacted angrily to the new Syrian move—particularly since they apparently held high hopes for the achievement of a mediated peace agreement between Syria and the PLO at Chtaura. *Pravda* made the following comments on October 18, emphasizing its support of the PLO:

The situation in Lebanon has again sharply deteriorated. Following the September 28 attack by rightist Christian and Syrian troops against positions of the Palestinians and progressive forces in the Lebanese mountains, a broad offensive has been launched in recent days throughout practically the entire country. Syrian military units are currently waging an offensive against the Palestinians at the approaches to Beirut and near the big Lebanese port of Saida. The Lebanese reactionaries, relying on Israeli military support, have launched military actions in Southern Lebanon.

It is noteworthy that the escalation of military action in Lebanon occurred under circumstances in which there had been a seeming breakthrough in the political negotiation aimed at bringing about a cease-fire and a peaceful settlement of the Lebanese crisis. It has been reported just recently that a real possibility of agreement had appeared in talks in the town of Chtaura among representatives of Syria, Lebanon and the Palestine Liberation Organization; and al-Kholy, an Arab League representative, even stated that an agreement in principle had already been achieved and would soon be made public.

However, the hopes that had begun to arise of a change for the better in the Lebanese situation was dashed by this new military offensive. It seems that although on the one hand Syrian representatives agreed to cease-fire talks, on the other hand, Syrian troops are thwarting efforts toward a peaceful settlement, and the bloodshed is resuming. To whose advantage is this?

It is a secret to no one that the blows now being struck are directed against those whom international imperialism and local reaction have long tried to destory—*the Palestinian Resistance Movement which stands at the forefront of the anti-imperialistic struggle in the Middle East.* Is it not clear, then, that if the Palestinian Resistance Movement falls out of the anti-imperialist front in this region it will be a grave blow to the entire Arab cause.[135] [emphasis added]

The *Pravda* article concluded with yet another appeal for a cease-fire.

A cease-fire was soon achieved—and a relatively lasting one this time—but not under Soviet mediation. Instead, Saudi Arabia, the USSR's bete noire in the Middle East, was the country instrumental in achieving the cease-fire, along with a reconciliation between Egypt and Syria. This diplomatic feat was accomplished in the Saudi Arabian capital of Riyadh.

THE RIYADH CONFERENCE AND ITS AFTERMATH

After 56 unsuccessful truces, peace came to Lebanon (despite intermittent shelling, terrorism, and fighting along the Lebanese-Israeli border) on the fifty-seventh. In Riyadh, Saudi Arabia, the heads of state of Egypt, Syria, Saudi Arabia, and Kuwait (the primary Arab military powers and their chief financial supporters), together with a much weakened, though not yet subdued, PLO (in the person of Yasir Arafat) and the newly inaugurated Lebanese president, Elias Sar-

kis, worked out an agreement that, in effect, transformed Lebanon into a protectorate of Syria. (Neither the Lebanese leftists under Jumblatt nor the Christian
rightists were direct parties to the agreement.) The agreement stipulated that a
30,000-man peace-keeping force—the vast majority of which would be Syrian
troops—would maintain order under the command of Lebanese President Elias
Sarkis, who had come into office with the backing of Syria.[136] In addition, the
PLO agreed to observe the Cairo accord of 1969, which, if observed, would mean
that the Palestinians would no longer participate in Lebanese politics on the side
of the left-wing forces of Jumblatt—yet another victory for Syria and a point
greeted warmly by the Lebanese Christians. The PLO, however, was to remain
intact and would move to bases in southern Lebanon, where it could be in position to attack Israel.[137]

This development may also be seen as a partial victory for Syria, which
had long sought to use the PLO as both a political and a military weapon in its
arsenal against Israel. If it were now to be based in southern Lebanon, where it
would be dependent on Syrian logistic support, the PLO could be made to serve
just such a Syrian purpose. It was only a partial victory for Syria, however, since
Assad was unable to secure the leadership changes in the PLO he appeared to
want,[138] and an Arafat-led PLO could be seen to maintain at least partial autonomy from Syria. Finally, Syria also gained by receiving both financial aid and
pan-Arab approval for its venture in Lebanon, thereby emerging from its position of relative isolation in the Arab world caused by the invasion of Lebanon.

Another major diplomatic development to come from the Riyadh conference was the reconciliation between Syria and Egypt, which was to blossom into
yet another movement for a Syrian-Egyptian union by the end of the year (but
it was to prove abortive once again).[139] With the American elections due in the
very near future and a general expectation that the United States would move
for a Middle Eastern peace agreement soon thereafter, it appeared that both
Syria and Egypt realized that their bargaining position vis-a-vis Israel would be
much stronger once their quarrel was patched up. In addition, their main financial supporter, Saudi Arabia, had a significant amount of economic leverage to
indicate to the states that it was in their interest to cease their conflict. As a result, Syria ended its propaganda attacks on Egypt for the Sinai II agreement, and
Egypt ended its attacks on Syria for its intervention in Lebanon. The fact that
Saudi Arabia had successfully mediated the end not only to the Lebanese war
but also to the Syrian-Egyptian rift, served to underline its growing importance
in Arab affairs.

The decision of the six leaders at Riyadh was brought to the larger Arab
League meeting in Cairo for ratification. Of the 21 members of the Arab League
(the PLO had been admitted as a full member in early September at the urging
of Egypt, which at the time was seeking to embarrass Syria) 19 voted in favor of
the agreement, with only Iraq and Libya—the Soviet Union's most important remaining Arab allies—opposing it.[140] Iraq tried to get the Cairo meeting to discuss

the continued presence of Syrian troops in Lebanon, but failed. As a result, Syrian-Iraqi relations hit a new low and the Iraqis temporarily closed their border with Syria and recalled their chief of mission in Damascus, claiming that "the masses will settle accounts with the reactionary regimes of Saudi Arabia and Kuwait whose riches underpin the treachery."[141]

The events in Riyadh were greeted with both hesitation and suspicion in Moscow. While the Soviet leaders could only have been relieved that the PLO, one of their main Middle Eastern allies, was preserved, the facts that the cease-fire had been arranged under Saudi auspices, and that the Saudis had brought about the reconciliation between Syria and Egypt, must have been of serious concern, for it may well have appeared that Syria was being attracted to the Saudi-Egyptian camp. The first major authoritative comment on Riyadh—albeit a rather hesitant one—came from Brezhnev in a general speech to a CPSU Central Committee meeting on October 25, during which he reviewed the events in Lebanon and stated Soviet policy goals for that country:

In Lebanon, the forces of internal reaction, armed and encouraged by the Western powers and supported by *Israel and Saudi Arabia*, have gone on the offensive against the local national-patriotic forces. However, the main force of their blows is aimed against detachments of the Palestinian Resistance Movement, i.e. against one of the anti-imperialist detachments of the Arab world. Unfortunately, Syria has also been drawn into the orbit of military operations.

... We are of the opinion that it is very important to settle, in a spirit of mutual goodwill, relations between the Palestinian and Lebanese patriots on the one hand and neighboring Syria on the other. This is necessary to restore the unity of the anti-imperialist forces in the Arab East.

As is known, a conference of the heads of state of Saudi Arabia, Egypt, Syria, Kuwait and Lebanon and Chairman Arafat of the Palestine Liberation Organization's Executive Committee was held recently. An agreement was reached on a cease-fire, the creation of an inter-Arab security force and the normalization of the situation in Lebanon.

From all indications, this agreement, at least as far as the cease-fire is concerned, is generally being observed. We shall see what happens in the future.

Needless to say, we take a positive attitude toward the very fact of an accord ending the war in Lebanon. *We should like to hope that the process of the normalization of the situation there will take place on a healthy basis, without detriment to the Lebanese patriotic forces or the Palestinian Resistance Movement.*[142] [emphasis added]

Echoing Brezhnev's concern that the Riyadh agreement might lead to the weakening of the position of the Palestinian-leftist Moslem alignment in Lebanon, *New Times* columnist Alexei Prignetov warned:

> If, however, further attempts are made to resolve the Lebanese conflict at the expense of the Palestine Resistance and the National Patriotic forces, the Riyadh agreement will share the fate of the preceding agreements. It will not survive.[143]

While the Soviet leadership was displaying concern as to the future of two of its allies in Lebanon, it was also clearly worried about the activities of Saudi Arabia—the main force behind the Riyadh agreement. In an article extremely frank in its criticism of Saudi Arabia, *New Times* correspondent Y. Tsaplin wrote:

> To put it in a nutshell, the reactionary feudal and monarchic regime in Saudi Arabia has become the main bulwark of international imperialism in the Arab East. Its brisk diplomatic activity and rapid arms build-up with American assistance are aimed at tying the hands of the progressive anti-imperialist forces in that region.
> ... Riyadh acts as a sort of charge d'affaires of the U.S. administration in the Middle East. It helps to promote military cooperation of the Arab countries with the United States, often paying for American deliveries out of its own treasury.
> ... The Arab reactionaries, led by the Riyadh regime, are out to split the progressive national forces in the Arab world and thus weaken their influence on the elaboration of a single Arab policy.[144]

Following the Riyadh conference, peace came, albeit fitfully, to Lebanon as the Syrian-dominated peace force established its control over the country—to the point of censoring the free-wheeling Beirut press. While the war had essentially come to an end—although both the Christian and Palestinian-Moslem sides stockpiled weapons to be ready for a new outbreak of fighting—the Soviet leaders were soon to encounter another major challenge to their Middle Eastern position when the newly elected American president, Jimmy Carter, undertook a major peace initiative.

NOTES

1. For a study of Lebanon dealing with the causes and early stages of the civil war, see Enver M. Koury, *The Crisis in the Lebanese System* (Washington, D.C.: American Enterprise Institute, 1976). For a survey of Soviet literature on Lebanon, see Jacob M. Landau, "Lebanon in Some Soviet Publications," *Middle Eastern Studies* 12, no. 2 (May 1976): 209-12.

2. For a discussion of the National Pact, see Abdo I. Baaklini, *Legislative and Political Development: Lebanon, 1842-1972* (Durham, N.C.: Duke University Press, 1976), pp. 109-12.

3. Compare "Lebanon's Tug of War," *The Middle East* (London), no. 19 (May (1976): 23-26. See also Koury, op. cit., chap. 4.

4. A. Agaryshev, "Beirut: Days of Trial," *New Times*, no. 51 (1975): 25.

5. Ibid.

6. See Chapter 6, p. 211. Following the 1973 war, Syrian leaders expressed fear of an Israeli attack upon Syria via Lebanon's Bekaa Valley. In addition, approximately 500,000 Syrians worked in Lebanon and many Syrians considered Lebanon to be a protectorate of Syria. It should also be noted that a number of Syrians, having never reconciled themselves to the French action after World War I that took Syrian territory and gave it to Lebanon, continue to hope for the eventual incorporation of Lebanon (and Jordan) into a "Greater Syria."

7. For a good survey of Syrian-PLO relations that covers the early stages of the Lebanese civil war, see "Syria at the Crossroads," *The Middle East*, no. 21 (July 1976): 6-11. For an earlier study covering the PLO's relationships with a number of Arab states, see William Quandt et al., *The Politics of Palestinian Nationalism* (Berkeley: University of California Press, 1973), especially sections II and III.

8. Iraq, like Syria, had its own Palestinian group in the PLO, the Arab Liberation Front. Other PLO organizations included Fatah, which was the largest and relatively independent, and three small Marxist Palestinian groups: the Popular Front for the Liberation of Palestine (PFLP) of George Habash; the Popular Democratic Front for the Liberation of Palestine (PDFLP), led by Naef Hawatmeh; and the Popular Front for the Liberation of Palestine-General Command (PFLP-GC), led by Ahmed Jibril, who was sympathetic to Syria and later was ousted from the leadership of the PFLP-GC because of it.

9. For a description of the February 1976 agreement, see the text of Lebanese President Franjieh's speech on February 16, 1976, in *Journal of Palestine Studies*, nos. 19-20 (Spring-Summer 1976): 271-72.

10. *Izvestia*, January 14, 1976. Translated in *Current Digest of the Soviet Press* (hereafter *CDSP*) 28, no. 2: 7.

11. Cited in report by Henry Tanner in the February 2, 1976, issue of the New York *Times*.

12. *Pravda*, February 10, 1976. Translated in *CDSP* 28, no. 6: 19.

13. *Pravda*, February 25, 1975. Translated in *CDSP* 28, no. 8: 7.

14. Ibid.

15. Ibid.

16. Cited in report by Thomas W. Lippman in the March 15, 1976, issue of the Washington *Post*.

17. Cited in *Near East Report* 20, no. 13 (March 31, 1976): 2.

18. Compare Washington *Post*, March 16, 1976.

19. TASS report, March 16, 1976, cited in *Pravda*, March 16, 1976.

20. *Izvestia*, March 24, 1976. See also the attack in *Pravda* on March 10, 1976. For a review of earlier Soviet criticism of changes in the Egyptian economy, see pp. 172-73.

21. *Izvestia*, March 25, 1976. Translated in *CDSP* 28, no. 12: 19.

22. *Pravda*, April 1, 1976.

23. Cited in AP report from Cairo in the Baltimore *Sun*, April 3, 1976.

24. Cited in report by Flora Lewis in the April 5, 1976, issue of the New York *Times*.

25. Middle East News Agency report from Cairo, cited in the March 26, 1976, issue of the Washington *Post*.

26. *Peking Review* 19, no. 17 (April 23, 1976): 5-6.

27. Cited in Reuters report from Peking in the April 22, 1976, issue of the New York *Times*. For the possible military implications of the agreement, see the analysis by Fox Butterfield in the April 23, 1976, issue of the New York *Times*.

28. *Sovetskaia Rossiia*, April 27, 1976. Translated in *CDSP* 28, no. 17: 20.

29. Radio Moscow (in Arabic), May 3, 1976 (commentary by Alexander Timoshkin).

30. The agreement kept the USSR as Egypt's main trading partner, but the fact that Egypt was exporting more to the USSR than it was importing indicated that Egypt was repaying its large debt (New York *Times*, May 9, 1976). Egypt had a similar export surplus in 1974 and 1975. For a summary of Soviet-Egyptian trade in 1974 and 1975, see *Vneshniaia torgoviia SSSR v 1975* (Soviet Foreign Trade in 1975) (Moscow: Statistika, 1976), p. 12.

31. Cited in report by Joe Alex Norris, Jr. (Los Angeles *Times*), in the March 13, 1976, issue of the Washington *Post*.

32. A number of Christian soldiers joined Col. Antoine Barakat, a Maronite, whose artillery was to shell Beirut regularly during the war.

33. Cited in report by James M. Markham, in the March 12, 1976, issue of the New York *Times*.

34. Cited in report by James M. Markham in the March 14, 1976, issue of the New York *Times*.

35. Cited in report by James M. Markham in the March 16, 1976, issue of the New York *Times*.

36. Cited in reports by Henry Tanner in the March 27 and 28, 1976, issues of the New York *Times*.

37. For a survey of Libyan-Syrian relations, see "Federation of Arab Republics Remains Inactive," *The Middle East*, no. 12 (October 1975): 35-36.

38. For a description of the Syrian troop movement, see the report by James M. Markham in the April 10, 1976, issue of the New York *Times* and the report by Jonathan C. Randal in the April 10, 1976, issue of the Washington *Post*.

39. Cited in report by James M. Markham in the April 12, 1976, issue of the New York *Times*.

40. Cited in AP report from Beirut in the April 8, 1976, issue of the Baltimore *Evening Sun*. For a description of the USSR's relations with Hawatmeh, see Chapter 6, p. 213.

41. *Pravda*, April 8, 1976. Translated in *CDSP* 28, no. 14: 4.

42. V. Nikolayev, "Trying Days for Lebanon," *New Times*, no. 16 (1976): 10.

43. Ibid., pp. 10-11.

44. Alexander Klimov, "Ancient Syria Today," *New Times*, no. 16 (1976): 25.

45. Cited in report by Don Oberdorfer in the April 15, 1976, issue of the Washington *Post*.

46. Cited in report by Edward Walsh in the April 20, 1976, issue of the Washington *Post*.

47. For the text of the document, see *Journal of Palestine Studies*, nos. 19-20 (Spring-Summer 1976): 275. For the Soviet reaction to the agreement, see *Pravda*, April 17, 1976.

48. *Pravda*, April 29, 1976. Translation issued by *Moscow News*, no. 19 (May 15-22, 1976).

49. On April 29, 1976, the author happened to be conducting interviews at the U.S. State Department when the Soviet peace plan was received via teletypewriter. He was informed that the USSR had not given the document to the United States before making it public.

50. Cited in report by Douglas Watson in the May 8, 1976, issue of the Washington *Post*.

51. Cited in report by Henry Tanner in the May 9, 1976, issue of the New York *Times*. For a statement on the elections by Jumblatt, see *Journal of Palestine Studies*, nos. 19-20 (Spring-Summer 1976): 277-78.

52. Arafat's move, however, was not uniformly accepted in the PLO. While WAFA (the Palestinian news agency) warmly welcomed Sadat's May 1 speech, which offered Egyptian support to the Palestinians, both Saiqa and the PDFLP publicly stated that the WAFA commentary did not represent PLO thinking. For a report on this incident, see "PLO Mends Fences with Egypt," *The Middle East*, no. 20 (June 1976): 86-87.

53. *Pravda*, May 5, 1976. Translated in *Foreign Broadcast Information Service: Daily Report*, May 7, 1976. (Hereafter *FBIS*.)

54. For the Soviet view of Saudi Arabia before the Lebanese civil war, see Chapter 4, pp. 120-21.

55. Radio Moscow (in Arabic), May 12, 1976 (commentary by Alexander Timoshkin).

56. Ibid., May 13, 1976 (unattributed commentary).

57. For the text of the statement, see *Journal of Palestine Studies*, nos. 19-20 (Spring-Summer 1976): 281-82.

58. Cited in the report by Henry Tanner in the May 15, 1976, issue of the New York *Times*.

59. The text of Jalloud's statement may be found in *Journal of Palestine Studies*, nos. 19-20 (Spring-Summer 1976): 286-87.

60. Cited in AP report from Beirut, in the May 22, 1976, issue of the Baltimore *Sun*.

61. Radio Moscow (in Arabic), May 20, 1976 (unattributed commentary).

62. For an analysis of the Lebanese reactions to the French troop offer, see the report by Henry Tanner in the May 23, 1976, issue of the New York *Times*.

63. There were persistent reports that the majority Sunni Moslems of Syria were unhappy that Assad, an Alawite (Shii) Moslem (as were most of his entourage) had aided the Christian Lebanese. In addition, there were reports of Syrian Ba'athist unhappiness that Assad was intervening to oppose the left-wing forces under Jumblatt as well as the Palestinians. On the other hand, however, the flow of Lebanese refugees into Syria, along with the return to Syria of Syrians who had been working in Lebanon, placed a mounting burden on the Syrian economy. Assad sought to answer his domestic critics, and justify his policy in Lebanon, in a major speech on July 20, 1976. See the report by James M. Markham in the June 7, 1976, issue of the New York *Times*, and the report by Douglas Watson in the June 5, 1976, issue of the Washington *Post*, describing Assad's domestic position. Assad's July 20 speech is found in *FBIS: Daily Report, Middle East and North Africa*, July 21, 1976.

64. Cited in the report by David Binder in the May 27, 1976, issue of the New York *Times*.

65. Cited in the report by Henry Tanner in the May 29, 1976, issue of the New York *Times*.

66. *Pravda*, June 1, 1976. Translated in *CDSP* 28, no. 22: 4.

67. TASS report, May 31, 1976, in *FBIS: Daily Report, Soviet Union*, June 1, 1976.

68. Radio Moscow, May 31, 1976.

69. *Pravda*, June 3, 1976. Translated in *CDSP* 28, no. 22: 4.

70. *Pravda*, June 3, 1976. Translated in *FBIS: Daily Report, Soviet Union*, June 7, 1976.

71. *Pravda*, June 3, 1976.

72. Ibid.

73. Ibid., June 4, 1976.

74. Kosygin did, however, meet with the Communist party of each state that was nominally a member of the country's ruling front, and the Kosygin visit may have been good for their morale. For a study of the attitudes of the Arab Communists toward Soviet policies, see Robert O. Freedman, "The Soviet Union and the Communist Parties of the

Arab World: An Uncertain Relationship," in *Soviet Economic and Political Relations with the Developing World*, ed. Roger E. Kanet and Donna Bahry (New York: Praeger, 1976), pp. 100-34.

75. See Chapter 6, p. 213.

76. "The Middle East Needs a Just Peace," *New Times*, no. 24 (1976): 1.

77. Cited in News Dispatch Report in the June 4, 1976, issue of the Washington *Post*.

78. Radio Moscow (in Arabic), June 6, 1976, citing a *Pravda* commentary of the same day.

79. *Pravda*, June 10, 1976. Translated in *CDSP* 28, no. 23: 18-19.

80. Cited in report by William Blakemore in the June 8, 1976, issue of the *Christian Science Monitor*.

81. Cited in report by Douglas Watson in the June 6, 1976, issue of the Washington *Post*.

82. Cited in report by Douglas Watson in the June 9, 1976, issue of the Washington *Post*.

83. Cited in AP report from Beirut in the June 14, 1976, issue of the Baltimore *Sun*.

84. Cited in report by James F. Clarity in the June 25, 1976, issue of the New York *Times*. For a description of the Rabat agreement, see *Middle East Monitor* 4, no. 21 (November 15, 1974): 2-4.

85. TASS dispatch, cited in report by William Blakemore in the June 22, 1976, issue of the *Christian Science Monitor*.

86. See Chapter 1, p. 7.

87. Yuri Potomov, "The Lebanon Crisis: Who Stands to Gain," *New Times*, no. 26 (1976): 10.

88. Dmitry Volsky, "The Lebanese Drama and the Middle East," *New Times*, no. 29 (1976): 10.

89. *Pravda*, June 16, 1976. Translated in *CDSP* 28, no. 24: 11.

90. *Pravda*, June 19, 1976. Translated in *CDSP* 28, no. 25: 20.

91. *Pravda*, June 23, 1976. Translated in *CDSP* 28, no. 25: 19.

92. Radio Moscow (in Arabic), June 25, 1976 (commentary by Alexander Timoshkin).

93. Radio Moscow, June 28, 1976 (unattributed commentary).

94. Cited in New York *Times* report, June 30, 1976.

95. Cited in report by Ihsan A. Hijazi in the July 1, 1976, issue of the New York *Times*.

96. Cited in AP report from Beirut in the July 10, 1976, issue of the New York *Times*.

97. Cited in AP report from Beirut in the July 10, 1976, issue of the Baltimore *Sun*.

98. *Pravda*, July 11, 1976. Translated in *CDSP* 28, no. 28: 11.

99. Cited in AP report from Beirut in July 13, 1976, issue of the Baltimore *Evening Sun*. This report was later denied by a Palestinian official in Cairo, according to an AP report from Beirut published in the July 14 issue of the Baltimore *Sun*.

100. Cited in AP report from Beirut in the July 14, 1976, issue of the Baltimore *Sun*.

101. For a detailed description of this reported letter, see *Middle East Intelligence Survey* (Tel Aviv) 4, no. 8 (July 16-31, 1976): 61. Interviews by the author with U.S. government officials support the reports of a slowdown in Soviet arms shipments to Syria.

102. *Pravda*, July 15, 1976. Translated in *CDSP* 28, no. 28:24.

103. *Pravda*, July 16, 1976. Translated in *CDSP* 28, no. 28: 10-11.

104. For a description of the coup attempt, see "Sudan: Invasion or Coup?" *The Middle East*, no. 22 (August 1976): 92-94.

105. Ironically, in an interview in the April 1976 issue of *The Middle East* (p. 27), Nimeri had stated that the Sudan's relations with the USSR were being "normalized." For a

description of the 1971 abortive coup and its effects on Soviet-Sudanese relations, see Chapter 3, pp. 57-61.

106. Cited in report by John Darnton in the August 10, 1976, issue of the New York *Times*.

107. Cited in the July 20, 1976, issue of the Washington *Post*.

108. "Egyptian-Sudanese-Saudi Contacts," *New Times*, no. 31 (1976): 11.

109. The restoration of relations is cited in report by Joseph Fitchett in the March 12, 1976, issue of the Washington *Post*; information on the grants is cited in AP report from Cairo in the May 12, 1976, issue of the Baltimore *Sun*.

110. V. Alexandrov, "Dynamic Progress,"*New Times*, no. 42 (1976): 15.

111. Radio Moscow (in Arabic), May 23, 1976 (commentary by Rafael Artunov).

112. Anatoly Repin, "Jordan Today," *New Times*, no. 25 (1976): 13.

113. Cited in AP report from Vienna in the June 16, 1976, issue of the New York *Times*.

114. *Pravda*, June 29, 1976.

115. Cited in report by Don Oberdorfer in the August 1, 1976, issue of the Washington *Post*.

116. Compare AP report in the September 6, 1976, issue of the Washington *Post*.

117. For the text of the agreement and the communique, see *Journal of Palestine Studies*, no. 21 (Autumn 1976): 188-89.

118. Cited in report by Henry Tanner in the July 31, 1976, issue of the New York *Times*.

119. *Pravda*, August 4, 1976.

120. Cited in a report from Beirut in the August 17, 1976, issue of the New York *Times*.

121. *Pravda*, August 24, 1976.

122. Ibid.

123. *Pravda*, August 27, 1976. Translated in *CDSP* 28, no. 33: 6.

124. *Pravda*, August 29, 1976. Translated in *CDSP* 28, no. 33: 6.

125. *Pravda*, September 8, 1976. Translated in *CDSP* 28, no. 36: 8.

126. Ibid.

127. *Pravda*, September 18, 1976.

128. Cited in report by James F. Clarity in the October 2, 1976, issue of the New York *Times*.

129. For the texts of the interviews, see *Journal of Palestine Studies*, no. 22 (Winter 1977): 182-89.

130. Cited in report in the September 16, 1976, issue of the Washington *Post*.

131. Cited in report by William Blakemore in the September 27, 1976, issue of the *Christian Science Monitor*.

132. *Pravda*, October 1, 1976. Translated in *CDSP* 28, no. 39: 15.

133. *Pravda*, October 2, 1976.

134. Cited in a report in the October 9, 1976, issue of the New York *Times*. For a description of the events at Chtaura, see Imad Kaisi, "Lebanon: Once Again 'No Victor and No Vanquished,'" *The Middle East*, no. 26 (December 1976): 16-20.

135. *Pravda*, October 18, 1976. Translated in *CDSP* 28, no. 42: 21.

136. According to a report by Henry Tanner in the October 28, 1976, issue of the New York *Times*, Ahmed Iskender Ahmed, the Syrian Information Minister, stated on Damascus Radio, "The Syrian forces in Lebanon will form the backbone of the Arab peace-keeping force."

137. For a discussion of subsequent events in Lebanon, see Chapter 8, pp. 308-9.

138. For a description of Syrian attitudes to the PLO leadership, see "Impossible Task Facing Palestine Council," *The Middle East*, no. 27 (January 1977): 35.

139. For a discussion of the deterioration of Syrian-Egyptian relations in 1977, see Chapter 8, pp. 313-14.

140. Cited in report by James F. Clarity in the October 20, 1976 issue of the New York *Times*.

141. Cited in *Middle East Intelligence Survey* 4, no. 15 (November 1-15, 1976): 120. For a description of Iraq's position in the Arab world after the Riyadh conference, see "Iraq: Left out in the Cold," *The Middle East*, no. 26 (December 1976): 71-72.

142. *Pravda*, October 26, 1976. Translated in *CDSP* 28, no. 43: 9.

143. Alexei Prignetov, "Lebanon: First Steps toward Settlement," *New Times*, no. 44 (1976): 15.

144. Y. Tsaplin, "Teamed up," *New Times*, no. 48 (1976): 23.

8

The Soviet Union and the Quest for an Arab-Israeli Peace Settlement

SOVIET POLICY FROM THE END OF THE LEBANESE CIVIL WAR TO THE ISRAELI ELECTIONS OF MAY 1977

The termination of the civil war in Lebanon by the Riyadh conference, which legitimized the presence of Syrian troops in Lebanon while at the same time preserving the PLO, albeit in a weakened state, posed a number of problems for the Soviet leadership. In the first place, there was a clear need to improve relations with Syria after the sharp deterioration in Soviet-Syrian relations caused by the war, lest the Syrians gravitate further into the Western-supported Egyptian-Saudi camp. Second, because the USSR had given little more than lip-service support to the PLO during its battles with the Syrian army, Moscow had to move to improve relations with the Palestinians. In addition, with the election of Jimmy Carter, the USSR faced a leadership change in the United States, with whom relations had cooled considerably over the past 12 months, thanks in large part to Soviet activities in Angola. Finally, the end of the civil war in Lebanon, which was followed by the reconciliation of Syria and Egypt, and the apparent taming of the PLO, together with the advent of a new administration in Washington, once again focused efforts on bringing about an Arab-Israeli peace settlement.

While there had been some movement toward peace in the aftermath of the June 1967 Arab-Israeli war,[1] serious discussions about a peace settlement did not take place until after the October 1973 Arab-Israeli war, and by the end of the Lebanese civil war there were two concepts of an Arab-Israeli settlement under serious consideration by the states who were the central parties to the conflict (Egypt, Syria, Jordan, and Israel). The PLO, whose charter called for the destruction of Israel, was exhibiting a great deal of concern that one or the other form of settlement would be imposed upon it.

Essentially, the two concepts of a peace settlement, which will be called Model I and Model II, had the following central characteristics. The Model I peace agreement called for the return by Israel of all or almost all of the land it captured in the 1967 war and the establishment of the status quo ante bellum in relations between Israel and its Arab neighbors. That is, essentially, a continuation of the armistice agreement that existed between 1949 and 1967, with no diplomatic, economic, or cultural relationships between Israel and its Arab neighbors. The only difference between such a peace plan and the 1949-67 situation would be that genuine demilitarized zones[2] would be emplaced in border areas and that the Arab states would formally foreswear their previous plan to destroy Israel, while Israel would promise not to go to war against them. Variations of the Model I peace concept provided for the passage of Israeli shipping through the Straits of Tiran and through the Suez Canal. In addition, a number of the proponents of the Model I plan called for the establishment of a Palestinian state or entity on the West Bank and Gaza Strip after their evacuation by Israel, although there were sharp differences of opinion as to whether such a Palestinian state or entity would be linked to Jordan, and whether it would have to permanently commit itself to live in peace with Israel. The main supporters of the Model I peace plan were the USSR, Egypt, and Syria, with Jordan reluctantly going along with the concept of an independent Palestinian entity. Support for such a plan also came from some quarters in the U.S. State Department (which saw in it much of the defunct Rogers Plan) and some of the West European states.

The Model II peace plan differed from Model I primarily in the situation that was to result from the withdrawal of Israeli forces from the bulk of, if not all of, the territories captured in 1967. The proponents of the Model II plan called for the establishment of diplomatic, trade, and cultural relations between Israel and its Arab neighbors as part of any peace agreement, contending that only in this way could Israel be assured that the Arab states had finally "accepted" her as a legitimate entity in the Middle East. Not surprisingly, the main proponents of this peace plan were found in Israel, although it also had many supporters in the United States, including a number of influential congressmen and senators and the newly elected president, Jimmy Carter.[3] The supporters of the Model II peace plan tended to be divided on the desirability of establishing a Palestinian state on the West Bank and Gaza Strip, with those in Israel primarily favoring a strong link between any such entity and Jordan, if not a return of the West Bank directly to Jordan, while a number of Americans were more sympathetic to an independent Palestinian state, albeit one pledged to live in peace with Israel.

While the Soviet leaders were noting the sharpened interest in an Arab-Israeli peace settlement in the aftermath of the Lebanese civil war,[4] they also had to be concerned about the state of Soviet-American relations, which had clearly worsened in the last year of the Ford administration. Soviet activity in Angola, together with a primary election campaign against Ronald Reagan, a conservative Republican, had put President Ford on the defensive about Soviet-American relations. On March 1, 1976, Ford announced in an interview with a television reporter that the word "detente" was no longer the proper one to describe Soviet-American relations.[5] While the Soviets reacted rather mildly to this event— New Times said rejecting the word was not the same as rejecting the policy of relaxing tensions[6]—some of the concrete developments in Soviet-American relations did concern the Soviet leaders.

In the first place, following an unsuccessful visit to Moscow in January 1976, Kissinger had announced to the Senate Finance Committee that because of Angola, the Ford administration no longer planned to ask Congress to lift the trade restrictions it had voted against the USSR.[7] In addition, he stated that he now opposed the multibillion-dollar U.S. investments in the USSR to develop Soviet oil and natural gas that he had previous advocated.[8] Yet another signal of the chill in Soviet-U.S. relations came in mid-March, when three Soviet-American cabinet-level meetings were called off by the United States.[9] Perhaps most serious of all to the Soviet leaders, however, was the virtual halt to progress in the strategic arms limitation talks. Indeed, in a speech to the Conference of European Communist Parties at the end of June, Brezhnev publicly decried the delay in reaching a strategic arms agreement.[10] Consequently, once the election campaign was over (the USSR attributed a large part of the cooling off of Soviet-American relations to campaign pressures), the Soviet leadership set about sending signals to the incoming Carter administration that it was interested in improved relations and would look forward to Soviet-American cooperation in reaching a new strategic arms agreement and a Middle Eastern settlement.

A major signal to the Carter administration came during the meeting of the American-Soviet Trade and Economic Council at the end of November 1976, when Brezhnev appealed for an end to the "freeze" on the strategic arms discussions and for a new agreement based on the Vladivostok accord. He also used the opportunity to call for an end to U.S. trade discrimination against the USSR, stating that U.S. firms lost between $1.5 and $2 billion because of it.[11] Two weeks later Pravda published a major article by Georgi Arbatov, one of the top Soviet experts on the United States, evaluating the state of U.S.-Soviet relations. After criticizing the "enemies of detente," Arbatov praised President-elect Carter's "positive" statements about improving Soviet-American relations and seeking ways to limit arms. Arbatov then went on to call for the resumption of the Geneva Middle East peace conference as quickly as possible.[12] Next, on December 28 Pravda praised Carter's appointments of Cyrus Vance and Zbigniew Brzezinski to key foreign policy posts, although not without reservations. Several days later Brezhnev gave an interview to a U.S. correspondent in which he said that a strategic arms agreement would be the most important step the United States and USSR could take to strengthen their relations, and he hailed President-elect Carter for statements expressing a similar interest.[13] The most important Soviet signal, however, came the day before Carter's inauguration when

Brezhnev, in a speech in Tula, noted that the SALT I agreement would expire in October 1977 and appealed for the "consolidation" of the Vladivostock accord, and for a resumption of the Geneva Middle East peace conference. He also reiterated the point that Israel had the right to "state independence and a secure existence," but added that "the Arab people of Palestine have the same right."[14]

While reestablishing positive relations with the United States was perhaps the main Soviet priority on the international scene in the November 1976-January 1977 period, rebuilding Soviet-Syrian relations was the highest Soviet priority in the Middle East. The Soviet leaders clearly wished to keep Syria out of the Western-backed Egyptian-Saudi Arabian camp, but the price of this was at least a tacit recognition of Syrian dominance in Lebanon. Writing in late December, *Pravda* commentator Pavel Demchenko tried to take a positive view of developments, and hailed what he saw was the normalization in Lebanon and the rebuilding of Syrian-PLO cooperation. He was not without his criticism of certain Syrian activities, however, including the censorship imposed on the Lebanese Communist newspaper *An-Nida*, along with a number of other Lebanese newspapers:

> Lebanon is gradually returning to normal life . . . already it is clear that the pan-Arab peace-keeping force has accomplished its first objective—to stop the bloodshed in Lebanon. . . .
>
> *At the same time, such actions by divisions of the pan-Arab forces as their seizure of nearly all the progressive and independent newspapers published in Beirut, including the newspaper An Nida, the organ of the Lebanese Communists, have generated public unrest in this country.* It has been remarked here that under their statute these forces have no right to interfere in Lebanese internal matters. . . .
>
> Ranking among the gratifying events is the resumption of relations between Syria and the Palestine Liberation Organization (PLO) which were disrupted during the happenings in Lebanon. The PLO Central Council met in Damascus recently with representatives of almost all the Palestinian organizations (38 of the council's 42 members) participating. The very fact that the Syrian capital was chosen for the meeting says, one would think, a good deal in itself. The statement published following the Central Council session applauds the "resumption of normal relations between the PLO and Syria" and expresses confidence that "these relations will be maintained and improved in the interests of the common struggle".
>
> Attempts are now being made to eliminate the split within the PLO itself, which was occasioned by differing appraisals of the events in Lebanon. It has also become known here that Syria's ruling Arab Socialist Renaissance Party is arranging contacts with represen-

tatives of Lebanon's National Patriotic forces. F. Ansari, a member of the ASRP leadership, told us that Syria's relations with the Palestinian Resistance Movement and Lebanon's National Patriotic forces are of a strategic nature and cannot be disrupted by temporary, transient factors. Among such factors he specifically listed the recent tragic events in Lebanon.[15] [emphasis added]

While the Soviet leaders seemed pleased with the Syrian-PLO rapprochement—such as it was—they could only have been concerned with the "unity" accord reached between Syria and Egypt in late December and the meeting of Syria, Jordan, Egypt, the PLO, Saudi Arabia, Kuwait, Bahrein, Qatar, and the United Arab Emirates in Riyadh in early January. Both of these events served to further underline the growing importance of Saudi Arabia in Arab politics and the apparent attraction of Syria to the Egyptian-Saudi axis in the Arab world.

While Soviet relations with Syria gradually improved following the end of the fighting in Lebanon, the USSR's relations with Egypt, once the linchpin of its Middle Eastern strategy, remained sour. Although immediately following Carter's election, Egyptian Foreign Minister Ismail Fahmy met with Soviet Foreign Minister Andrei Gromyko in Bucharest, there was little noticeable improvement of relations following the two days of talks, and *Pravda*'s description of them (there was no joint communique) referred to an "exchange of opinions" on a number of subjects.[16] When severe riots occurred in Egypt two months later and Sadat blamed them on Egyptian Communists, Soviet-Egyptian relations hit a new low as the USSR exploited the opportunity to blame the riots on the liberalization of the Egyptian economy and its opening to Western capital.[17] Relations between the Soviet leadership and the Sadat regime deteriorated still further the following month when a *Pravda* editorial attacked Sadat's memoirs, then being published, as "lies, slander, and falsification."[18] In an effort to discredit Sadat, the *Pravda* editorial went so far as to accuse him of defaming Nasser—a ploy used earlier by the USSR to try to weaken Sadat's political base.[19] Yet another cause of conflict between the two states was Egypt's aid to Zaire in putting down a rebellion supported by the Angolan regime that the USSR had helped bring to power in 1976 and with which it had established very close ties.

While Soviet-Egyptian relations were deteriorating, the USSR sought to reinforce its relations with its remaining Arab allies, Libya and Iraq, and tried, albeit unsuccessfully, to bring them around to the Soviet view of a Middle Eastern settlement. In early December, Libyan leader Mu'ammar Kaddafi visited the USSR, the first visit of a major leader of the "rejectionist front" Arab states since the end of the Lebanese civil war. In his dinner speech welcoming Kaddafi, Soviet President Podgorny reiterated the Soviet position that "a settlement in the region was dependent on Israeli troop withdrawals from land occupied in 1967," thus again indicating Soviet approval for Israel's borders as of June 4, 1967. Podgorny also called for insuring the right of the Palestinians to have their own state, and for the resumption of the Geneva conference, where a full settlement of the Arab-Israeli conflict could be worked out.[20]

As had been the pattern in previous Soviet-Libyan meetings, the Libyans were very frank in stating their opposing positions. After emphasizing the "strategic" (long-term) nature of Libya's relationship with the USSR, a statement that may have proved comforting to the leaders of the USSR after their recent experiences with Egypt and Syria, Kaddafi went on to present Libya's solution to the Arab-Israeli conflict—"the expulsion of the racists [Israelis] from Palestine." Realizing that his views differed very sharply from those of his Soviet hosts, Kaddafi then made a gesture toward their position by stating, "Of course we respect the viewpoint of others." He went on, however, to deprecate the importance of convening the Geneva conference, which was a Soviet goal.[21]

As might be expected, the communique issued at the end of the four days of meetings between Kaddafi and the Soviet leaders referred to an "atmosphere of frankness," thus reflecting the clear disagreement between the two sides on the nature of an Arab-Israeli settlement. Nonetheless, the Russians praised Libya for "the active role it is playing in the realization of Arab unity," thereby apparently awarding Libya the same role the USSR had previously credited to the Syrians. In addition, both sides emphasized the need to strengthen Arab unity on an "anti-imperialist, progressive basis." No mention was made in the communique of the Geneva conference or Israel's right to exist, possibly because the Russians, with very few allies left in the Arab world, did not wish to alienate Libya by trying to pressure her to adopt such a position. In a further effort to cement ties to the radical Arab state, the Russians promised to deepen relations in economic, cultural, technical, scientific, and "other" fields—the latter term usually indicating military assistance.[22]

The next rejectionist front leader to visit Moscow was Saddam Hussein of Iraq. Just prior to his visit at the end of January, *Pravda* printed an extensive article by Pavel Demchenko citing the readiness in the Middle East for a general settlement of the Arab-Israeli conflict and for the resumption of the Geneva conference. It also indicated that the PLO was ready to accept a West Bank-Gaza state and would even go to a peace conference—if invited under the proper circumstances:

Lately, statements have been appearing more and more frequently in the Arab and Western press saying that attempts to solve the Middle East problem in parts or by stages have failed. . . . Even the creator of "diplomacy by small steps", Henry Kissinger, was forced to state recently that "the moment has come when the all encompassing approach logically becomes the next step".

There is also much talk in foreign newspapers that 1977 is the time for resuming the Geneva peace conference on the Middle East . . . Egypt and Syria recently published a communique proclaiming full support for the Geneva Conference. . . . Jordan is also prepared to participate in the conference. As for the Palestine Liberation Organization, its position was set down in the 13th session of the National Council of Palestine in 1974 and calls for "the establishment of independent national power of the people in any part of the Palestinian land that is liberated". It appears from a number of statements by PLO leaders that such power can be established on the West Bank of the Jordan and in the Gaza Strip. The National Council favors PLO participation in the search for a Middle East settlement, provided the Palestinian question is treated as a political question, i.e. that the aim is to satisfy the people's national rights and is not limited solely to the refugee problem.[23]

While Demchenko emphasized the willingness of the Arab states to go to Geneva, he neglected to mention that by the end of January both Syria and Egypt had spoken of a link between a Palestinian entity and Jordan, in a possible gesture to Israel meant to expedite the beginning of peace negotiations. Such a development could hamper the independence of action of the PLO, something neither its leaders nor the USSR wanted. In addition, the PLO did not appear to be as forthcoming as Demchenko indicated. Indeed, the Palestine National Council meeting, initially scheduled for December 1976, was postponed until March 1977 while its Central Committee, meeting in Damascus on December 12, made no decision about a willingness to set up a West Bank-Gaza state or even form a government in exile to attend a Geneva-type peace conference.

In any case, by the time of Saddam Hussein's arrival it seems clear that the USSR was continuing to push for its threefold peace plan in the Middle East and was trying to win the Arabs—particularly those in the rejectionist front—over to its point of view. Unfortunately for the Soviet leaders, however, they met with little more success with Saddam Hussein than they had with Mu'ammar Kaddafi. In his welcoming speech Kosygin put forth the position that a settlement required the withdrawal by Israel from all territories occupied in 1967, and he openly stated that peace and security could not be established in the Middle East without guaranteeing the right of independent existence to all the states involved in the conflict, and unless the state of war among them was ended. Kosygin also emphasized the necessity of insuring the right of the Palestinians to set up their own state, and he advocated the resumption of the Geneva conference—even if it should experience "difficulties."[24]   Saddam Hussein, like Kaddafi before him, took a hard line on a peace settlement, although he was not quite so explicit, stating that while Iraq favored peace and stability, it rejected those plans that impose "capitulationist decisions on our people to rob them of their historic rights." Unlike Kaddafi, however, he made no mention of the undesirability of a peace conference.[25]

The final communique, which described the talks as taking place in a "businesslike, friendly atmosphere" (indicating a rather low level of agreement between the two sides), emphasized continued Soviet aid to Iraq, particularly in the oil and military fields.[26] As far as a Middle Eastern settlement was concerned, the two sides agreed that it could come about only if "all occupied Arab territory" was liberated and the "legitimate and unalienable national rights of Palestine's Arab peoples be completely satisfied"—terminology open to varied interpretations. Perhaps as a sop to the Soviet leaders, who had continued to express concern that Iraq would be economically wooed away from the USSR by the West, the Iraqis agreed to put in the communique the statement that the USSR and Iraq would "firmly rebuff any attempts to damage Soviet-Arab friendship."[27]

While the Soviet leaders had at least made an effort to win the Arab rejectionists over to their point of view on Israel's right to exist, they did not prove successful. There is, of course, a real question as to how hard they tried. Following the events in Lebanon, Iraq and Libya were the two strongest allies the USSR had left in the Arab world, and the Soviet leadership may not have wished to alienate them by pressing too hard on this point—particularly since if the main confrontation states (Israel, Egypt, Syria, and Jordan) agreed on a peace settlement, there was little either Iraq or Libya could do to prevent one. In addition, the two Arab states were major suppliers of oil to the USSR and, although the USSR was itself a major oil producer and exporter (indeed, oil was her leading hard-currency export), there were a number of reports that she would become a net importer of oil sometime in the 1980s. While specialists differed in evaluating the validity of these reports (of which the CIA report of April 1977 was the most important), the oil question may nonetheless have been a factor (although most probably a secondary one) in the Soviet leadership's decision not to try to press Iraq and Libya on a peace settlement.[28]

As the USSR was endeavoring to secure a resumption of the Geneva conference in order to bring about its conception of an Arab-Israeli peace settlement, the newly inaugurated American president, Jimmy Carter, was trying to promote a settlement as well. After dispatching his secretary of state, Cyrus Vance, to the Middle East in February, Carter invited to Washington a series of Middle Eastern leaders, beginning with Prime Minister Yitzhak Rabin of Israel. Carter sought to set his Israeli visitor at ease at the beginning of their talks by publicly coming out for "defensible borders" for Israel and indicating that these borders might extend beyond the "permanent and recognized borders" reached in a peace settlement.[29] As might be expected, such a pronouncement was strongly opposed by Arab leaders and exploited by the Soviet press.[30] One week later, however, in response to a question at his "town meeting" visit to Clinton, Massachusetts, Carter stunned the Israelis by publicly coming out for a "homeland" for the Palestinians. Although his speech emphasized a Model II plan for peace, in which Israel would be a fully accepted member of the Middle Eastern community, having ties of trade, tourism, and cultural exchange with Jordan, Lebanon, Egypt, and Syria, and the Palestinians would have to give up their "publicly professed commitment to destroy Israel,"[31] this was still the first time an American president had publicly mentioned a Palestinian homeland—something that remained an anathema to most Israeli leaders.

It would appear that Carter was deliberately signaling the Palestinians by his comments, since the Palestine National Council was meeting in Cairo at that time amid a great deal of speculation that it would moderate its position toward Israel. Carter apparently hoped that by using the term "Palestinian homeland," he might reinforce trends for moderation among the Palestinians by indicating that the United States was willing to come out in support of a Palestinian entity of some type. Given the fact that Syria and Egypt had earlier spoken of such an entity linked to Jordan, Carter's comment that "the exact way to solve the Palestine problem is one that first of all addresses itself right now to the Arab countries"[32] may have been seen as support for such a position. Indeed, the Russians may well have been concerned that were a Palestinian state to be linked to Jordan, which had established close ties to Syria, then yet another instrument that they hoped to use to oppose U.S. policy in the Arab world might be lost.[33] In a *New Times* article in early March, Oleg Alov was critical both of Sadat's plan for a confederation of Jordan and a Palestinian state, and of Israel's demands, as enunciated in a speech by Rabin, for a Model II peace settlement.[34]

Carter's hopes for moderation at the Palestine National Council session, however, were not realized. Militancy won out and there was no change in the council attitude toward Israel, with Article 9 of the 15-point program specifically calling for the "liberation of all the occupied Arab lands" and for the "return of the national established rights of the Palestinians without peace, reconciliation, or recognition."[35] While neither the USSR nor the United States could have been pleased at the militancy against Israel evidenced at the Palestine National Council meeting, the Russians may have at least drawn comfort from Article 4 of the program, which rejected "all kinds of American capitulationist settlements and all liquidationist projects." In addition, Article 8, which called for "strengthening the Arab front participating in the Palestinian revolution and deepening cohesion with all forces participating in it in all Arab countries in order to cope with the imperialist and Zionist designs," was similar to the Soviet goal of establishing an anti-imperialist Arab unity, albeit for a different ultimate purpose.[36]

In commenting on the Palestine National Council session one week later, *Pravda* columnist Yuri Glukhov chose to emphasize what he saw as the positive outcome of the conference—the growing solidarity among the Palestinians, and their rejection of "capitulationist plans."[37] He also hailed the Palestinian readiness to deal with progressive, democratic forces in Israel (Article 14 of the program), although he conspicuously failed to mention the council's statement that these forces had to be anti-Zionist—thus eliminating a number of Zionist Jews who advocated the establishment of a Palestinian state alongside Israel. Finally, Glukhov endorsed as a "just demand" the council demand (Article 15) that the PLO be represented as an "independent member in all conferences and meetings bearing on the Palestine problem," a position effectively negating a number of proposals for a joint Palestinian-Jordanian entity at the Geneva talks.

While President Carter was apparently trying to signal the Palestinian Arabs at the council meeting with his statement about a Palestinian homeland, Brezhnev was also sending out signals. Relations with the United States, which looked promising at the start of the Carter administration, had deteriorated sharply because of U.S. advocacy of the human rights issue. With Secretary of State Cyrus Vance on his way to Moscow to begin the negotiations on a new strategic arms agreement, Brezhnev used the opportunity of a speech to the Soviet Trade Unions Congress (much as he had done with his earlier speech at Tula) to urge an improvement in Soviet-American relations, and offered another Soviet Middle Eastern peace plan as part of his signal.[38] While his emphasis once again was on the necessity of reaching a strategic arms agreement (he also took the opportunity to denounce "interference in the USSR's internal affairs on any pretext"), Brezhnev also mentioned the need for "concerted action" by both the United States and the USSR "to achieve a just and lasting peace in the Middle East," and went on to speak in detail about a Middle Eastern peace settlement.

Interestingly enough, Brezhnev began his discussion by stating that while it looked as if the Geneva conference was "gradually becoming more of a reality," he went on to say that the conference was "not an end in itself" and that "the main thing is that its work should yield fruitful and just results." Perhaps indirectly indicating to the Palestinians and other Arabs that they would have to deal directly with Israel, Brezhnev then said, "It goes without saying that the drawing up of peace terms in all details is primarily a matter for the conflicting sides." Following this caveat, he discussed the four-point peace plan first mentioned during the height of the Lebanese civil war in October, which stipulated the total withdrawal of Israeli troops from lands occupied in 1967; the securing of the inalienable rights of the Arab people of Palestine, including their right to self-determination and statehood; the right of all states in the Middle East to "independent existence and security"; and the termination of the state of war between Israel and its Arab neighbors.

Brezhnev then went on to make a number of additional points that seemed directed at gaining Israeli and U.S. approval. First, he spoke of a staged Israeli withdrawal, perhaps to give Israel a greater sense of security about withdrawing, although his timetable of "several months" indicates that this was more of a gesture than a genuine attempt to allay Israel's security concerns. Second, Brezhnev spoke of clearly defined borders between Israel and its Arab neighbors after an Israeli withdrawal, borders that would be "final and inviolable." This was a clear indication, similar to Gromyko's speech at the Geneva conference in 1973, that Israel's prewar 1967 borders would be the ones recognized by the USSR. In another apparent attempt to make Israel feel more secure, given the nature of the prewar 1967 boundaries, Brezhnev also favored the establishment of demilitarized zones on both sides of the respective borders (but only if the respective states agreed) and the stationing of a UN emergency force or UN observers in these zones for "some clearly stipulated period of time." This was a move to allay Israel's fears, since such an arrangement would prevent unilateral expulsion of the UN troops, which had been one of the causes of the 1967 war. Brezhnev also spoke of guarantees for any peace settlement, indicating, as the USSR had done in the past, that the Soviet Union was prepared to be a guarantor; and he suggested that the guarantor states could have observers in UN contingents "in the respective [demilitarized] zones." Finally, after stating that these were the USSR's "preliminary ideas" about a peace settlement that it was "not imposing on anyone," Brezhnev said that the Soviet Union was receptive to other peace plans and again offered to reach an agreement to help end the arms race in the Middle East once a peace settlement was reached.

Despite the detailed Middle Eastern peace plan, which went further to meet Israeli demands than any other Soviet offer since the 1973 war (although it remained essentially a Model I plan that Israel rejected), the Soviet leadership's talks with Vance did not go well. The disagreements were not so much on the Middle East, however, as on strategic arms. Nonetheless, *Pravda*'s description of the talks cited the two nations' agreement that coordinated actions by the United States and USSR "are essential for the achievement of a just and durable peace in the Middle East," and noted that an agreement had been reached to hold a Vance-Gromyko meeting in Geneva in May to "broaden the exchange of opinions on the Middle East, including the question of the resumption of the Geneva Conference."[39]

The interim period between the Soviet-American discussions of the Middle East was to prove an active one indeed in Middle Eastern diplomacy. President Carter continued his round of talks with Arab leaders, seeing Anwar Sadat and King Hussein in Washington and arranging to meet Hafiz Assad in Europe. The Soviets themselves were not idle, as first Tunisian Prime Minister Hedi Nouria, then Arafat, and then Assad journeyed to Moscow.

Arafat's visit, coming right after the conclusion of the Palestine National Council session, where he was able to reassert his authority over the movement following its losses in Lebanon, may well have been a difficult one for the Palestinian leader. In his Trade Unions Congress speech, Brezhnev had negated one of the fundamental principles adopted by the Palestinians—the destruction of Israel —and in doing so had been very explicit in supporting Israel's right to exist. Nonetheless, each side needed the other. To the Russians, the PLO served as a radical force in inter-Arab politics that the USSR sought to manipulate against American strategy in the Arab world. To the PLO, the Russians served as a source of military and diplomatic support, and a check, albeit only a limited one (as the civil war in Lebanon indicated), on Syrian efforts to control the PLO.

Arafat was preceded to Moscow by Tunisian Prime Minister Hedi Nouria, and the Palestinian leader could not have welcomed Kosygin's speech to Nouria, which called for a guarantee of the rights of all states involved in the Middle Eastern conflict to independent existence.[40] When Arafat arrived in the USSR, he met first with Andrei Gromyko and then with Brezhnev. Moscow Radio reported "a thorough exchange of views" on the Middle Eastern situation between Gromyko and Arafat, and noted the "urgent need to resume as soon as possible the work of the Geneva Conference"—a major change from the degree of necessity noted by Brezhnev in his Trade Unions Congress speech only two weeks before.[41]

Further emphasizing Israel's right to exist, in April, Moscow Radio Peace and Progress broadcast to the Arab world, in Arabic, the following statement attributed to Brezhnev:

> Leonid Brezhnev has stated that naturally Israel has the right to have an independent state and a secure entity, but the Palestinian Arab people also have such a right.

Brezhnev met Arafat the same day, and *Pravda* printed a report of the meeting, together with a picture, on its front page.[42] Brezhnev hailed the Palestinian resistance movement as one of the leading forces of the Arab national liberation movement and once again stated that the USSR considered the creation of an independent Palestinian state "an inseparable part of an all-encompassing Middle East settlement." Arafat thanked the USSR for her support of the Palestinian Arabs' struggle for "their legitimate national rights" and reaffirmed that the Palestinians would continue to fight against the "intrigues of imperialism and reaction." Given the obvious disagreements between the two sides, no joint communique was issued. For the Soviet leadership, however, the visit had the positive effect of reaffirming Soviet-Palestinian relations and their joint opposition to U.S. peace initiatives, after a number of Palestinians had criticized the Russians for a lack of support during the Lebanese civil war.

One week later Hafiz Assad journeyed to Moscow. He was welcomed at the airport by Brezhnev, a clear signal from the Soviet leadership of its desire to improve relations with Syria in order to overcome the tensions caused by Syrian intervention in the civil war in Lebanon. Brezhnev's speech at a dinner honoring Assad echoed this theme as he offered to broaden Soviet-Syrian relations "in all fields" and urged coordination of action on the Middle East.[43] In addition, however, Brezhnev reiterated to Assad the Soviet position that Israel had the right to "state independence and a secure existence." Interestingly enough, while also coming out for a Palestinian state, he stressed the point that "not a single decision affecting the Arab people of Palestine should be taken without the Palestinians or against their will." While Brezhnev made this assertion in the context of a statement advocating the convocation of the Geneva conference "without delay" (thus apparently backtracking from the position he took on the urgency of reconvening Geneva in his Trade Unions Congress speech one month before), the implications of his comments appeared contradictory. Indeed, they seemed to indicate that if the Palestinians refused to recognize or to live in peace with Israel, even under the Soviet peace formula, the USSR would necessarily have to acquiesce in their decision. While Brezhnev probably intended this statement to oppose "reactionary" Arab (or Syrian) attempts to impose a peace settlement on the Palestinians "against their will," such phraseology was open to different interpretations, and the PLO leadership could also invoke it to oppose the Soviet peace plan.

Assad's speech in reply to Brezhnev was similarly warm in tone, and he characterized Soviet-Syrian relations as being "strategic" in nature.[44] He further stated that Soviet-Syrian relations had successfully come out of what had "obviously" been a "difficult time," and that different points of view could not undermine the relations between the two nations if "the principles of mutual respect and sincere cooperation were observed." Nonetheless, he then gave a long and rather impassioned defense of the Syrian invasion of Lebanon, in part justifying it to his Soviet listeners as stemming from "an ardent desire to preserve the Palestinian revolution." As far as a settlement was concerned, Assad was silent, although he did mention the complete withdrawal of Israel from the lands it occupied in 1967 and its recognition of the Palestinian Arabs' right to self-determination. He also supported the Soviet Union's call for the rapid reconvening of the Geneva conference.

The reconciliation between Syria and the USSR, noticeable in the tone and content of Brezhnev's and Assad's speeches, was consolidated in the joint communique issued at the conclusion of the visit, although it was evident that a number of areas of disagreement remained.[45] The communique referred to "a constructive exchange of opinions on a number of issues, including the ways of achieving a just and lasting peace in the Middle East." Nonetheless, in an effort to rebuild relations with Syria, the USSR promised measures "for a further rise in the level of the Syrian Arab Republic's defense capabilities,"[46] and joined with Syria in advocating only two of the Soviet peace plan's principles: the total withdrawal of Israeli troops from all Arab territory occupied in 1967 and the satisfaction of the national rights of the Arab people of Palestine, including their right to creation of their own independent state. The other Soviet principle, stating the right of existence of all states in the Middle East, was conspicuous by its absence from the communique, and there was also no mention of the termination of the state of war between the Arabs and Israel. For its part, Syria supported the Soviet goal of the "earliest possible convocation of the Geneva Conference" while emphasizing the "importance of the role of the USSR as cochairman." In return, the Soviet leaders publicly acknowledged the Syrian quasi protectorate over Lebanon by joining Syria in "expressing satisfaction with the progress taking place in the normalization of the situation in Lebanon."

Thus ended Assad's visit, one that had been profitable for both sides, although suspicions apparently still lingered. Assad had received promises of increased military aid and Soviet approval for the Syrian role in Lebanon. With an improved relationship with the USSR, he could set forth to negotiate with Jimmy Carter from a stronger bargaining position. The Russians also gained, although probably not as much. They could point to a rebuilding of their ties to Syria after the civil war in Lebanon and to Syrian support for a quick reconvening of the Geneva conference. Nonetheless, Syria continued to maintain its close relations with both Egypt and Saudi Arabia, and the USSR could no longer count on her, as at least some Soviet leaders had once hoped, to be the linchpin for the anti-imperialist Arab unity the USSR had advocated for so long.

Indeed, by the time of Assad's visit to Moscow, Syria's ties to Egypt and Saudi Arabia had become a serious concern to the Soviet leadership. The Soviet concern was particularly acute over developments in the Red Sea area. Prompted by Libyan intrigues against their regimes, Egypt and the Sudan had signed a mutual defense treaty in July 1976, following talks in Riyadh, where the two Arab states and Saudi Arabia announced plans to foster closer political, military, and economic cooperation.[47] While the immediate target of this alignment appeared to be Libya, developments in Ethiopia and along the Ethiopian-Sudanese border soon raised the possibility of a direct clash between the Sudan and Ethiopia, a development that could commit Egypt and Saudi Arabia as well. Earlier, the prospect of such a clash would have been viewed differently by the USSR, given the fact that Ethiopia had been a major U.S. ally in northeast Africa while the Sudan had received Soviet support. Much had changed in recent years, however, as Soviet-Sudanese relations, once very warm, had sharply deteriorated after the Communist-supported coup d'etat against the Nimeri regime in July 1971, while Ethiopia, under the military government that had overthrown Emperor Haile Selassie in September 1974, moved the country out of the American orbit and toward the USSR.

While limitations of space preclude an extensive discussion of Soviet policy toward the new Marxist regime in Ethiopia,[48] it appears clear that it was the Ethiopians who were the more aggressive in seeking a close relationship. The Soviet leaders, although welcoming the "progressive transformations" being undertaken by the Marxist regime in Ethiopia, at least initially, seemed cautious about offering arms aid to the Ethiopians.[49] There were a number of reasons for the Soviet caution. In the first place, the Marxist regime was highly unstable, with numerous executions and assassinations continually taking place in the upper ranks of its leadership. Second, it was beset by a major insurrection in its northeast province of Eritrea, where two "liberation" armies, the Eritrean Liberation Front and the Eritrean Peoples Liberation Front, were fighting against the Ethiopians.[50] While in conflict between themselves, the two forces were nonetheless receiving military assistance from a number of Arab states, including Iraq, one of the USSR's few close allies in the Arab world. Third, Ethiopia's relations with the Sudan were strained, in part due to Sudanese support for the Eritreans.

Fourth, and perhaps from the Soviet point of view most serious of all, the Ethiopian regime was beset by a guerrilla war in its southeastern region of Ogaden, where antiregime guerrillas were supported by Somalia—hitherto a major arms client of the USSR and a state whose self-proclaimed Marxist government had given the USSR important military bases. Somalia had long-standing claims to Ogaden, which it considered part of "Greater Somalia,"[51] and complicating

Somali-Ethiopian relations further was the approaching independence of the French colony of Djibouti, an area located along the Red Sea between Ethiopia and Somalia that, because of the Eritrean fighting, was now Ethiopia's only secure outlet to the Red Sea. This outlet would be lost if Somalia, which claimed Djibouti, were to absorb the colony, the majority of whose population was Somali. Consequently, the Soviet leadership faced the risk that any overt support of Ethiopia might jeopardize its close ties to Somalia. In addition, by lining up with non-Arab Ethiopia against both the Sudan and Somalia, the USSR would be alienating almost all of the Arabs (initially Libya alone among the Arabs supported Ethiopia; South Yemen was later to offer Ethiopia aid as well) at a time when it was still seeking to forge them into a united "anti-imperialist" front against the West.

Despite these considerations, however, the Soviet Union was ultimately to embrace Ethiopia ideologically and send it military assistance, although throughout the process it sought to maintain its ties with Somalia, in an effort to prevent the Somali regime from defecting to the U.S.-supported Egyptian-Saudi axis. One of the factors precipitating the Soviet decision to support Ethiopia may have been the February 1977 upheaval in the Ethiopian military regime, in which, after a great deal of internecine strife, Col. Mengistu Haile Mariam, the Ethiopian strongman, was finally able to consolidate his position. Second, at the end of February, Nimeri, Assad, and Sadat met in Khartoum to discuss, among other things, the future of the Red Sea, and they reportedly called for its transformation into a "lake of peace."[52] While on the surface the statement appeared innocuous, several days later the Syrian newspaper Al-Ba'ath called for the restoration of the Red Sea's Arab character, and claimed the waterway had always been an "Arab lake."[53] Such a statement could be seen as directed not only at Israel, which borders the Red Sea at Eilat, but also at Ethiopia, which has an extensive Red Sea coastline and, to a lesser degree, even at the USSR, a major user of the waterway for transporting goods between the eastern and western sections of the USSR and for its trade with Asia.

In an effort to avoid a Somali-Ethiopian confrontation, and keep Somalia from joining the Saudi-Egyptian-Sudanese alignment, the Soviet leadership made use of both Fidel Castro, then touring Africa, and Soviet President Podgorny, also on an African journey, to suggest a federation of Somalia and Ethiopia (along with South Yemen and the territory of Djibouti).[54] Unfortunately for the Russians, Somali leader Siad Barre rejected their proposal,[55] then met with the leaders of the Sudan, North Yemen, and South Yemen is what appeared to many observers as yet another anti-Ethiopian meeting of Arab Red Sea states. What may have been particularly alarming to the USSR in this process was the participation of South Yemen, as well as Somalia, in such a meeting, since the Saudi Arabians had been making major efforts to wean the South Yemenis away from their alignment with the USSR. Indeed, the Western-supported Arab bloc of states seemed to be capitalizing on Soviet support for Ethiopia in its confrontations with the Moslem Eritreans, Sudan, and Somalia, in an effort to try to win over both the Somalis and the South Yemenis.

It was perhaps to prevent such a development and to personally argue for an Ethiopian-Somali federation that Soviet President Podgorny made a surprise visit to Somalia at the beginning of April, but apparently to little avail, as Barre continued to refuse to cooperate with the Ethiopians.[56] By the middle of April, therefore, the situation in the Red Sea and at the Horn of Africa had become a matter of serious concern for the Russians. A major article in *Izvestia*, by Viktor Kudryavtsev, summarized the main areas of Soviet worry:

> The progressive Arab and African press has recently reported with great alarm about stepped up activity by imperialist forces and their agents in the Red Sea region. . . . *In certain circles in the Arab countries, the Red Sea has come to be referred to as an "Arab lake", a term that reeks of nationalism*, especially because not all of the coastal countries are Arab, to say nothing of the national affiliation of the ships passing through the Red Sea, only a very small percentage of which are Arab. . . . For some people, emphasizing that the Red Sea is an Arab lake is something they must do in order to speculate on nationalism and to pit the Arab countries against Ethiopia, which has 625 miles of Red Sea coastline, its only outlet to the sea.
>
> The reactionary press is combining the nationalistic campaign that is stirred being up over the Red Sea's "security" with a no less virulent campaign against Ethiopia, which is going through difficult days in which a new, independent and progressive rule is being formed in a stubborn struggle against a feudalism that is unwilling to leave the political stage. . . . The recent Ethiopian-Cuban communique in connection with Fidel Castro's visit to Addis Ababa says, quite correctly, "the two sides condemned counterrevolutionary activity of imperialism and its puppets in the Red Sea area" and noted the need for progressive forces of that region to coordinate their struggle against the intrigues of the common enemy—imperialism.
>
> Saudi Arabia is playing an active role in all Red Sea affairs. The French bourgeois newspaper *L'Aurore* has written that Saudi Arabia is attempting to put together a bloc of Arab countries in the Red Sea region by "offering these countries considerable financial aid". In another article, *L'Aurore* notes that Riyadh, directly or through other countries "is attempting to draw such countries as Somalia and South Yemen into the conservative camp it heads, since it is unable to tolerate their revolutionary socialism any longer". The heightened interest Riyadh is showing in unification trends in the two Yemens, as well as its attempts to play a role as an intermediary between certain Middle Eastern states, should be viewed in this light. . . . *The*

furor over the alleged threat to the security of the Red Sea region, which is said to take the form of rivalry between the two superpowers, has not only anti-Soviet motives but also the objective of splitting the anti-imperialist unity of the Arab states and diverting their attention from the basic task—eliminating the consequences of Israeli aggression.[57] [emphasis added]

In addition to diplomatic support for Ethiopia, the USSR also began to send shipments of weapons to the Ethiopian regime, which by April was confronted with fighting in its Eritrean and Ogaden regions, as well as with a guerrilla threat from the Ethiopian Peoples Revolutionary Party in Addis Ababa, its capital.[58] At the same time, Ethiopian-American relations fell to a new low as the major U.S. communications station in Ethiopia was closed, the U.S. military assistance team was ousted, and the U.S. cultural center was shut down. These events formed the background for Mengistu's visit in early May to the Soviet Union, where he signed a "declaration of basic principles" with the USSR[59] and a joint communique stipulating that as a result of "progressive transformations" in Ethiopia, "new possibilities have emerged" to give Soviet-Ethiopian relations a "qualitatively new character." The communique went on to say that "the USSR and Socialist Ethiopia will make efforts to further expand and deepen bilateral ties in the political, economic, cultural and other fields"—the latter term usually indicating military assistance. The communique also cited the two countries' opposition to "attempts by certain countries to establish their control over the Red Sea in violation of the legitimate rights of other states and peoples of the area and to the detriment of the interests of international navigation."[60]

The warm welcome afforded Mengistu in Moscow, together with the increasing flow of Soviet weaponry to assist his embattled regime, moved Somali leader Siad Barre to convene a press conference (his first in two years) on May 15, in which he warned that the delivery of Soviet arms to Ethiopia posed a danger to which Somalia could not remain indifferent and that could affect Soviet-Somali relations.[61] Sudanese leader Jaafar Nimeri took a much stronger anti-Soviet action three days later, expelling the remaining Soviet military advisers from his country.[62]

While Soviet-Arab relations were increasingly disturbed by Soviet aid to Ethiopia, the Soviets were soon to capitalize on the results of the Israeli election, which took place on May 17, to try to reverse the situation and restore the "anti-imperialist" unity of the Arab states.

THE BEGIN ELECTION VICTORY AND ITS AFTERMATH

The results of the Israeli election came as a major surprise to most observers, for the Israeli Labor Party, which had dominated the nation's governments since the creation of the state of Israel in 1948, lost its plurality and the right-wing Likud party emerged with the most votes. With Likud leader Menahem Begin the likely new prime minister, the Soviet media lost little time in trying to exploit the election, and Begin's postelection statements and actions, to rally the Arabs away from the United States and revive the anti-imperialist Arab bloc the USSR desired. Thus, in a broadcast on May 23, Moscow Radio commentator Sergey Bulantsev stated:

> The very first statements by Begin, the leader of the "Likud" bloc, have confirmed the worst apprehensions of the world press, which said that with power in Israel going to the rightwing, prospects for a peaceful settlement of the situation in the Middle East have worsened considerably. Observers note that in the very first days after the election Begin fully justified his reputation as a "hawk" and fanatical nationalist.
>
> Speaking via American television on Sunday, Begin categorically rejected proposals that Israel return to the borders that existed before its 1967 aggressions against the Arab countries. He also excluded the possibility of participation by the Palestine Liberation Organization in the Geneva peace conference and opposed creation of a Palestinian state on the West Bank of the Jordan. This is not the first statement by Begin that illustrates his extreme militarist position. Speaking last week at the militarized settlement of Qaddum on the West Bank of the Jordan he spoke of his intention to preserve captured Arab territories because they allegedly are part of traditional Jewish lands. He also said that a number of new military Jewish settlements would be created in the near future on the West Bank.[63]

Two days later, a Moscow Radio broadcast to the Arab world raised what was to become a recurrent theme in the postelection period. It sought to deprecate Western reports of a clash between a Begin-led Israel and the United States on Middle Eastern policy, while underlining the continued close ties between the United States and Israel.

> The emergence of new political forces in Israel and the rise of Menahem Begin have not taken place in spite of Washington; they are results of its long and well-known policy toward Israel. Washington's policy of using any means to procrastinate over a Middle East settlement and to consolidate Tel Aviv's control of occupied Arab lands greatly helped create the political climate in Israel that enabled extremists in ruling Israeli circles to win the election. . . .
>
> Growing sectors of Arab public opinion have begun to comprehend this harsh and bitter truth: reliance on a change in Washington's

pro-Israeli policy is only a mirage. The Jordanian *Ar-Ra'y* says: "Arabs must wake up and understand that the U.S. attitude will not change and that it is in line only with expansionist Israeli designs." A growing number of Arab statesmen, newspapers and magazines support the need for a critical analysis of the policy pursued by the Arabs and the drawing up of a realistic course. The Syrian *Al-Ba'ath*, for instance, says: "The victory of Menahem Begin in the elections must make Arabs reject the spirit of apathy that dominates the Arab world at present and reject the illusions about a neat and easy peace. Under present circumstances Arabs must review their calculations and strategy and build without delay strong and good Arab relations based on solidarity in the struggle." Along with the call for the consolidation of Arab unity on anti-imperialist foundations there is growing support for the consolidation of Arab cooperation with socialist countries. In this context the Moroccan *Al-Bayan* wrote: "Life has proved that Arabs should dispense with illusions of changing the U.S. attitude to a settlement in the Middle East and must rely on themselves and on the support of their tested and loyal allies."[64]

The first major opportunity for the Soviet leaders to capitalize on the Begin election in an attempt to re-create an "anti-imperialist" coalition came in early June, when Egyptian Foreign Minister Ismail Fahmy paid a visit to Moscow. Although the visit was arranged before the Israeli elections, it nonetheless provided the Russians with the opportunity to repair Egyptian-Soviet relations, which had reached their lowest point since the 1973 Arab-Israeli war. Despite the Begin election victory, Sadat clearly remained cool to the Russians, and in a news conference on May 29 even questioned whether the Fahmy visit would take place.[65] Perhaps as a signal to the Egyptians of their desire for improved relations, the Russians again reportedly began sending some arms to Egypt, and this may have set the stage for Sadat's decision finally to send Fahmy on June 8.[66]

In any case, Fahmy met with both Brezhnev and Gromyko, and according to the *Pravda* description of the talks, he "exchanged opinions" with the Soviet leaders on both the prospects for Soviet-Egyptian relations and the Middle Eastern situation.[67] Gromyko, in a speech at a luncheon honoring Fahmy, stated that the USSR wanted friendly relations with Egypt in "political, economic and other areas" (the latter term usually meaning military) and appealed for an improvement in Soviet-Egyptian relations, asserting that the USSR would do its part in this regard. He also used the opportunity to strongly emphasize that the USSR stood for the complete withdrawal of Israeli forces from all Arab lands occupied in 1967 and for an autumn reconvening of the Geneva conference with the full and equal participation of the PLO. In addition, Gromyko came out for the right of the Palestinians to create their own state and for "ensuring to all states in the area the right to an independent existence and security." For his part, Fahmy used the opportunity to note Egypt's desire to "retain bridges of contact and cooperation with the USSR," and he urged the USSR to continue to help the Arabs liberate their occupied territories.[68]

The final communique noted that the discussions had taken place in a "businesslike and constructive atmosphere" (a Soviet term for low-level cooperation) and that the two countries had considered "concrete measures" for overcoming the difficulties in Soviet-Egyptian relations. In addition, both agreed on the resumption of the Geneva conference "not later than Autumn 1977," with the participation of the PLO—"the legitimate representative of the Arab people of Palestine—on an equal footing with all other participants." Finally, the two sides agreed to continue meeting alternately in Moscow and Cairo, and Gromyko was invited to visit Cairo, although no date was set for his trip.[69]

The temporary improvement in Soviet-Egyptian relations was not to last, however. On June 26, Sadat attacked members of Egypt's legal leftist party for being "agents of the Soviet Union."[70] Three weeks later, in a speech before Egypt's Arab Socialist Union broadcast by Cairo Radio, Sadat announced that Fahmy's visit to Moscow had failed.[71] Sadat attributed the failure to the USSR, which, after demanding that Egypt sign a new political agreement, had demanded hard currency for military equipment, refused to send replacements for equipment lost in the 1973 war, and generally "behaved rudely and adopted a very hard line." In addition, the Soviet leaders reportedly warned Egypt not to exclude the USSR from the peace-making process in the Arab-Israeli conflict and stated strongly that the USSR stood by Ethiopia in the event of a Sudanese-Ethiopian war—warnings that Egypt rejected. Interestingly enough, in the latter part of his extensive speech, Sadat made an apparent gesture both to the United States and to Israel, offering to "politically and legally recognize Israel in its June 4, 1967 borders" so that "for the first time in its history Israel's legal existence within its borders would be recognized." While rather vague, this nonetheless was the closest statement yet to the Israeli demand for a Model II peace agreement, and a precursor of his visit to Jerusalem four months later.

While Sadat's speech held out the prospects for an improvement in Egyptian-Israeli relations, Soviet-Egyptian relations continued to deteriorate. Not only was Sadat continuing to attack the USSR for its policy in Africa[72] (its alleged aid to the rebels in Zaire, whom Egyptian forces had helped to defeat, and its overt aid to Ethiopia), but three days after his ASU speech Sadat entered into a border war with Libya, one of the few remaining Arab allies of the Soviet Union. While the fighting lasted less than a week, Sadat's action served to prove that there were limits to his patience with Kaddafi, and also perhaps to indicate that neither Egypt nor his regime was as weak as a number of observers—including the USSR—may have felt. Nonetheless, perhaps in an effort to retain some ties to Egypt, still the most militarily powerful of the Arab states, the Soviet leaders kept their public response to the war relatively restrained.

While the fighting was going on, Soviet reaction was limited to an Afro-Asian Solidarity Committee statement (published in *Pravda* on July 26) that appealed to Egypt to stop its attacks, "which serve the interests of imperialism, Zionism, and their ally, Arab reaction," and which hurt the "solidarity of the Arab peoples in their struggle for their just cause, the liberation of the Arab lands occupied by Israel in 1967."[73] Sadat, however, did not reciprocate the Soviet moderation, accusing the USSR of encouraging anti-Egyptian acts by Kaddafi and charging that Soviet helicopters flying from a Soviet aircraft carrier had interfered with Egyptian communications during the fighting.[74] Then, strengthened by shipments of Chinese weapons and promises of American weaponry, Sadat announced the abrogation of export agreements for the sale of cotton and cotton products to the USSR, thus signaling yet a further deterioration in Soviet-Egyptian relations.[75]

While the Libyan-Egyptian border war underlined the difficulties the USSR was encountering in rebuilding Arab unity on an "anti-imperialist" basis, despite the Begin election, the Soviet Union's policy in North Africa was also in serious trouble. Fighting escalated between Ethiopia and Somalia, and it appeared that the USSR and Libya would be isolated against the majority of Arab states who supported Somalia. Despite a visit to the USSR by Somali Vice-President Mohammed Ali Samantar on June 1, the USSR remained unable to convince the Somalis (or the Eritreans) to federate with Ethiopia,[76] and as Soviet aid to Ethiopia increased, Soviet-Somali relations began to deteriorate. Initially, the USSR sought to blame the Sudan for foreign intervention in Ethiopia,[77] but on June 6, as the Ethiopian military position weakened, a formal TASS statement was issued generalizing the Soviet warning against intervention in Ethiopia.

Those who are presently plotting a military adventure against Ethiopia would like nothing better than to set African states against one another, undermine their efforts to strengthen their national independence and obstruct the national liberation struggle against the racist regimes. They are also pursuing the goal of distracting Arab people's attention from their most urgent task—settlement of the Mideast conflict.

The Soviet Union, which builds its relations with Ethiopia in accordance with the Soviet-Ethiopian declaration on the principles of friendly relations and cooperation, is carefully following the development of the situation around Ethiopia.

Tass is empowered to state that the Soviet Union resolutely condemns the actions of those circles that are preparing to mount an aggression against Ethiopia and also those who are urging them on to this dangerous course. They are playing with fire, and those who do so will bear heavy responsibility before the peoples of Africa and the entire world.[78]

This warning, however, did not deter the Somalis from stepping up their military movements into Ethiopia, and there were reports of a cutback in the large Soviet adviser force in Somalia.[79] While the Soviet foreign affairs weekly *New Times* denounced "the ill-intentioned propaganda campaign mounted by the imperialists to vilify Somali-Soviet cooperation" as "utterly groundless,"[80] the Soviet leadership could only have been concerned by the escalation in the fighting and by the American decision, in late July, to offer in principle to sell arms to Somalia.[81] By mid-August, when Somali troops entered Ethiopia in force, TASS published a statement blaming "the imperialists and other reactionary circles for making frenzied efforts to deepen the division between the two countries [Ethiopia and Somalia] . . . to tear Ethiopia and Somalia away from their natural allies and friends . . . and to strike at the progressive revolutionary regimes, first of Ethiopia and then of Somalia."[82] In evaluating the fighting then raging in North Africa, *New Times* commentator Dmitry Volsky observed in early August:

> Who stands behind the attempt to undermine the progressive regimes in North Africa and set the newly independent states at loggerheads, is now seen more and more clearly. *Newsweek* frankly notes in a recent issue "the aim of U.S. policy now is to build up the Saudi-Egyptian-Sudanese alliance as a counterforce to the . . . regimes of Ethiopia and Libya".
>
> Such are the circumstances attending the recent Libyan-Egyptian border clashes and the appearance of the hotbed of tension in the Horn of Africa. In Ogaden, in Ethiopia, Somali regulars have engaged Ethiopian troops.[83]

Meanwhile, as the anti-imperialist coalition of Arab states continued to disintegrate, the Soviet leadership also had to be concerned about the possibility of a Westward turn by some of its remaining allies in the Arab world. Iraq, which was rapidly increasing its trade with the West, was reportedly considering the purchase of a French fighter-bomber,[84] and American Undersecretary of State Philip Habib made a visit to Baghdad in mid-May—the highest-level meeting between the two countries since Iraq broke diplomatic relations with the United States at the time of the June 1967 war. While Iraqi-American relations had not yet reached the point of restoration of formal diplomatic ties, the Soviet leadership could only have been concerned by Jimmy Carter's statement, made public June 11, that the United States was out to challenge the USSR for influence in Iraq.[85]

A similar problem confronted the Soviet Union in South Yemen, once very tightly tied to the USSR. The rapprochement between Saudi Arabia and South Yemen was continuing, and on July 31, for the first time, the South Yemeni president, Ali Salem Rubayi, made an official visit to Riyadh. The South

Yemenis, however, were careful to balance their improving ties with Saudi Arabia with their ties to the USSR, as the South Yemeni prime minister, Ali Nasser Mohammed, visited Moscow on July 29—just before Rubayi's visit to Riyadh—and the interior minister visited Ethiopia one week later, a prelude to South Yemeni aid to Ethiopia.[86] Indeed, given the situation in the Red Sea and South Yemen's dependence on Moscow for arms, it appeared that while South Yemen had made a few steps toward improved relations with Saudi Arabia, it continued to seek good relations with the USSR as well.

While the Soviet Union was suffering a series of Middle Eastern reverses despite the Begin election, the Soviet leaders could perhaps take solace from the fact that the American position also suffered a blow when the United States finally left its naval installations in Bahrein on July 1. The USSR also welcomed the warming of relations between Syria and the PLO, whose conflict in 1976 had brought Soviet-Syrian relations to the breaking point, and the cooling of Syrian-Egyptian relations. The Syrian-PLO rapprochement might have been due to a weakening of Assad's regime[87] and his consequent desire to regain support from the Syrian Ba'athists by again embracing the PLO. A second cause may have been Begin's election and his postelection actions, which provided the Syrians with the opportunity to champion the PLO and thereby strengthen their barring position with Israel. Nonetheless, despite the improvement in Syrian-PLO relations, a development the Soviet press was happy to note, Syria maintained a firm grip over the PLO in Lebanon.

As their overall position in the Middle East continued to deteriorate and the long hoped-for pro-Soviet bloc of "anti-imperialist" Arab states continued to disintegrate, the Soviet leaders stepped up their efforts to exploit the emergence of the Begin government as a means of rallying the Arabs against Israel and the United States. The United States continued to occupy center stage in Middle Eastern peacemaking efforts, with a Washington visit by Saudi Arabian Crown Prince Fahd in May, a visit by Begin to Washington set for July, and yet another Vance trip to the Middle East on the horizon. The Soviet leaders continued to emphasize that the United States stood behind Begin's hard-line positions, and that reports of differences between Israel and the United States (such as the Israeli-American clash over the State Department policy statement of June 27 calling for Israeli withdrawal from Sinai, Golan, and the West Bank) were without a real foundation.[88] Thus, in a *Pravda* article assessing the new Begin government on June 30, Yuri Glukhov stated:

> The makeup of the government shows that the most reactionary and chauvinistic elements have come to power. The world press calls the new Israeli Cabinet a government of "superhawks".
>
> The outspoken claims of the Israeli "hawks" have shocked even official Washington. Certain statements made there in recent days are regarded by a portion of the Western press as an external attempt

to stand aloof from Begin's policy. Many political observers express skepticism in this connection, however. The French newspaper *Aurore* writes that Washington's statements with respect to Israeli plans in the Mideast "contain nothing new, their primary purpose is to calm the Arab states, which are unhappy over the new deliveries of arms to their opponent".

And indeed, the intention to supply Israel with $115 million dollars worth of armored tank and missile equipment has just been announced in the overseas capital. A law forbidding American companies to participate in the boycott of Israel has just taken effect in the U.S., demonstrating once again the "special character" of American-Israeli relations.[89]

Similarly, in an *Izvestia* article three days later, Victor Kudryavtsev deprecated the State Department position paper of June 27, while emphasizing U.S. Vice-President Walter Mondale's declaration that "Israel must not withdraw from occupied Arab lands until it has secured a genuine peace from the Arabs." Interestingly enough, however, Kudryavtsev did not define the expression "genuine peace" in terms of a Model II peace arrangement as Mondale had, but, rather, as "until the Arab countries accept Israeli-U.S. terms for a settlement." Kudryavtsev also somewhat downgraded UN Security Council Resolution no. 242 as a vehicle for reaching a peace agreement while emphasizing General Assembly Resolution no. 3236 (of November 10, 1975), which called for the right of the Palestinian people to national independence and sovereignty in Palestine.[90] The Soviet commentator's emphasis on General Assembly Resolution no. 3236 may have been a response to the continuing discussion among a number of Arab states of a link between Jordan and a Palestinian state as a possible means of getting the Israelis to agree to the establishment of a Palestinian entity of some type. Thus, on July 1, Sadat again came out for a Gaza-West Bank state linked to Jordan.[91] Nine days later, in a joint statement with King Hussein, he called for an "explicit link" between Jordan and the Palestinians.[92]

The Soviet leaders, who continued to strongly support the concept of an independent Palestinian state, used a *Pravda* article to cite Beirut PLO Information Chief Yasir Rabb's statement that no one of the Arab states had the right to speak in the name of the Palestinian people on the problem of creating an independent Palestinian state, and that "if anyone took upon himself the right to speak, a priori, in terms of a linking of this [Palestinian] state with any other state, in this instance Jordan, as was the case during the recent Egyptian-Jordanian summit talks, he challenges not only the Palestinians but the Arab world and world public opinion."[93] Nonetheless, despite Soviet and PLO protestations, plans continued for a Jordan-PLO link, with President Carter endorsing the plan at a press conference on July 12.[94]

All this helped to set the stage for the new Israeli prime minister, Menahem Begin, to visit Washington on July 19. Begin, upon his arrival in Washington, unveiled what could be termed a "procedural" peace plan calling for the opening of the Geneva conference on October 10 to establish a Model II peace, with Israel meeting with its Arab neighbors in "mixed commissions" to settle mutual problems.[95] Begin made it quite clear, however, that the participation of the PLO or any known member of the PLO in the peace talks was ruled out, although he held open the possibility of a non-PLO Palestinian participation in the Jordanian delegation. In addition, he did not rule out, a priori, the possibility of negotiations concerning the West Bank, thus gaining the support of President Carter, who stated that as a result of the Begin visit, the "groundwork" had been laid for the resumption of the Geneva conference—barring unforeseen difficulties.[96]

The Arabs, however, uniformly rejected the Begin plan and, as might be expected, the Soviet leaders sought to take a propaganda advantage of the Begin visit and the $250 million arms agreement reached during the Israeli prime minister's stay—an agreement that included 18 Cobra attack helicopters and U.S. aid in helping Israel develop its own tank[97]—to demonstrate the United States' continuing close ties to Israel. In addition, Begin's decision, immediately upon his return to Israel, to announce the legalization of three hitherto illegal Israeli settlements in the heart of the West Bank provided further grist for the Soviet propaganda mill, since the Begin move appeared to have the tacit endorsement of the American president, despite Carter's later condemnation of the action. Thus, for example, Vladimir Bolshakov, writing the "International Week" column in *Pravda* on July 31, commented:

> It is not surprising that immediately after his talks in the United States, Israeli Prime Minister Begin announced that his government was rescinding the previous cabinet's decision and recognizing previously illegal Israeli settlements on the West Bank of the Jordan as "permanent and legal". In addition a plan for the construction of another twelve settlements was announced.
>
> Despite the fact that the U.S. State Department has officially disassociated itself from Begin's decision, the foreign press writes that this annexationist "legalization" was in fact made possible only by Washington's support for Israel's actions.[98]

Bolshakov then went on to tie the United States and Israel to the fighting going on in North Africa:

> Acting on the principle of "divide and conquer", Washington and its Tel-Aviv henchmen are doing everything in their power to exacerbate the disagreements that exist in the Arab world and North Africa and are trying to provoke conflict among the countries in this region in order to weaken the anti-imperialist front and thwart efforts to undo the consequences of the Israeli aggression of 1967.

The Soviet commentator also claimed that the Begin visit had made the Arab leaders "suspicious" of the U.S. role in Middle Eastern peace negotiations, and in particular the forthcoming Vance visit:

> After Begin's visit to the U.S. it became clear that Israel is destined to play an increasingly active role in the "holy alliance" that imperialism is creating for its "crusade" against progressive forces in Africa and the Arab world. This fact has made Arab leaders suspicious on the eve of the upcoming Middle East trip by U.S. Secretary of State C. Vance.

Despite the negative Soviet description of his forthcoming trip, Secretary of State Vance, just as he had done in February before his first trip to the Middle East, promised to keep in close contact with the Soviet leaders.[99] Indeed, Vance even stated that the Soviet leaders had indicated a willingness to "use their influence" with some of the parties to encourage flexibility.[100] It is difficult to know, of course, whether Vance took the Soviet leaders seriously as to their willingness to encourage flexibility, because, at least from Soviet media statements during the Vance trip, it appeared that the Russians were openly trying to disparage Vance's diplomatic efforts. In any case, even without Soviet obstruction, Vance had a most difficult task to accomplish. The crucial question was how the Palestinians could be represented at the Geneva talks, with Israel opposing PLO representation while the Arabs supported it. At the start of the Vance visit, Egypt, the Arab state that appeared most eager for talks, proposed that Arab-Israeli working groups meet in the United States prior to a Geneva conference, to make arrangements for it.[101] Israel quickly endorsed the proposal,[102] which appeared to be a way to avoid dealing with the Palestinian issue at the early stage of negotiations. The Syrians rejected it, with Assad commenting, "There is a possibility that the working groups would be looked upon as competition for Geneva, and none of us would like that."[103] Interestingly enough, however, Assad was later to propose a unified Arab delegation at Geneva—something the PLO rejected almost as rapidly as they had the Begin proposal.[104] In any case, it was clear by August 6 that Vance's Middle Eastern mission had not met with much success. In a press conference in Amman on that date, Vance reported that while he had made some progress in narrowing the gap between the Arabs and Israelis on the nature of peace he had made no progress on the Palestinian issue.[105]

As Vance's mission began to falter, Carter began to move in an effort to break the impasse. In a *Time* magazine interview released at the beginning of August to coincide with the start of the Vance trip, Carter had stated that if the Palestinian leaders (meaning the PLO) accepted Israel's existence or espoused UN Resolutions 242 and 338 as a basis for negotiations at Geneva, "we would immediately commence plans to begin talks with the Palestine leaders."[106] This was rejected by the Palestinians,[107] but Carter was to try again on August 8, following Vance's report of a lack of progress on the Palestinian issue at his Amman news conference. In a clear gesture to the PLO, Carter stated, after hearing rumors of PLO acceptance of Resolution 242 from Saudi Arabian sources, that "if the Palestinians recognized the applicability of U.N. Resolution 242, then it would open up a new opportunity for us to start discussions with them."[108]

Both the *Time* interview and the Carter press conference statement were significant retreats from the earlier American insistence, made in a pledge to Israel at the time of the 1975 Sinai agreement, that the PLO had to change its charter, which called for the destruction of Israel, before the United States would have any dealings with it;[109] the Israelis, as might be expected, strongly opposed the Carter initiative. While clearly an appeal to the Palestinians to moderate their position so as to enable the United States to deal with them, much as Carter's homeland statement had been a signal to the Palestinians at their National Council meeting in March, the Carter appeal of August 8 was not accepted. Instead, the PLO Central Council, meeting in Damascus on August 26, announced that it would not accept UN Resolution 242 and would not change its charter. In addition, it denounced "all the American and Zionist maneuvers" aimed at hampering the establishment of an independent state under PLO leadership.[110] Following the Central Council meeting, Arafat journeyed to Moscow for consultations, much as he had done after the National Council meeting in March.

The Soviet response to the Vance trip and the American appeal to the PLO was predictable. At the start of the Vance visit, in a broadcast to the Arab world on August 1, Moscow Radio reiterated the three-pronged Soviet plan for a Middle Eastern peace, including the guarantee of an independent existence to all the states of the region, and went on to underline the "special" U.S. commitment to Israel and the "negative attitude" of the United States toward the rights of the Palestinians.[111] The Russians were also quick to attack the Vance-Sadat working group proposal as being a means of avoiding PLO participation in the Geneva talks, and used Begin's endorsement of the idea to discredit Sadat:

> Facts remain facts. Despite the statements that shroud this agreement about adhering to the ideals of Arab solidarity and about the pressing need for the future participation of the representatives of the Palestinian Arab people in the Geneva conference, despite all the existing agreements among the Arab countries, and despite the Rabat agreement, Cairo has agreed to exclude the Palestinians from the game, according to the terminology of statesmen. Is this not in itself a reason to make Begin happy, since one of his major concerns is to liquidate the Palestinian resistance movement? Without doubt the decision on the so-called working party to prepare for the Geneva peace conference, to be headed by Vance—who defends Israel's view-

point—also pleased the Israeli prime minister. This makes it easy for Begin to impose the U.S.-Israeli peace plan on the Arabs, a plan which provides for the annexation of part of the occupied Arab territories and for the elimination of the Palestinian question from the agenda. [112]

The Soviets also hailed Syrian rejection of the working group idea, perhaps seeing in it a further move by Syria away from its alignment with Egypt, and warned that the United States was returning to step-by-step diplomacy to divide the Arabs. [113] *Izvestia* then sought to discredit Carter's appeal to the Palestinians:

> Since the failure with the "working group", the United States has started to flirt with the Palestinians, hinting to them that if they agree to the Geneva conference being convened on the basis of Security Council resolution 242 of 22 November 1967 (the PLO disagrees with the paragraph of the resolution with regards [to] the Palestinians as refugees), Israel would agree to Palestinian representatives participating in Geneva. However, Israel immediately rejected this idea, declaring that it has no intention of releasing the West Bank of the Jordan and the Gaza Strip, which it has occupied, and will not under any circumstances agree to talks with the Palestinians and still less to the creation of a sovereign Palestinian Arab state next to Israel.
>
> Why did C. Vance need to submit a proposal which was obviously going to be unacceptable to Israel, and just after the American-Israeli talks in Washington? To mask his pro-Israeli position behind the imaginary role of an "honest broker" and thereby dull the Arab countries' vigilance. And the main thing is that this American proposal conceals an endeavor to make the Palestinians recognize the existence of Israel in one form or another before the latter will embark on any talks on a general settlement. Therefore, this proposal is also aimed at strengthening Israel's position and encouraging its implacability. [114]

While deprecating the American peace initiatives, the Soviet Union once again thrust itself forward as the champion of the Palestinians, with Moscow Radio on August 10 going so far as to state that a reconvened Geneva conference should base itself not only on Security Council Resolution 242 but also on UN General Assembly Resolution 3236. [115]

In the diplomatic hiatus following the Vance visit to the Middle East, Begin moved to increase Israeli control over the West Bank by setting up three additional settlements and implementing Israeli welfare laws there. As might be expected, the Russians exploited these events to underline the American-Israeli tie while commenting that American protestations against the Israeli actions should not be taken seriously.[116] Indeed, both Moscow Radio and *Pravda* made a point of emphasizing Carter's news conference statement of August 24, in which he said that despite American unhappiness with the Israeli actions, "We don't intend to go farther than our caution to Israel. Obviously, we could exert pressure on Israel in other ways, but I have no intention of doing so."[117] The Russians also used the opportunity to try to discredit Saudi Arabia among its Arab brothers:

> At an OPEC conference Saudi representatives came out in support of the U.S. Middle East policy line. They said: Let us secure the success of this line and thus show the various Arab popular sections why we are pinning hopes on the Americans to such an extent. But despite all the efforts made by Riyadh in support of the U.S. line in the Middle East, it failed to insure its success.
>
> As a matter of fact, such success was simply impossible, because all the U.S. plans for a Middle East settlement met the exclusive interests of Israel and the United States. Consequently, Saudi Arabia now finds itself in the position of an Arab country which shares responsibility for the present deadlock in the Middle East and elsewhere. Events show that the Saudi rulers have always been loyal and faithful protectors of U.S. interests in the Middle East, especially the interests of U.S. oil monopolies with shares in Aramco.[118]

While the USSR was continuing to attack Egypt, Saudi Arabia, the United States, and Israel for their positions on a Middle Eastern settlement, Yasir Arafat journeyed to Moscow for talks with the Soviet leadership at the end of August. Although the PLO had rejected the American initiative, it was clear that a number of Arab states were pressuring the PLO to accept UN Security Council Resolution no. 242 and enter into discussions with the United States. Indeed, Baghdad Radio broadcast an interview with Salah Khalaf (Abu Iyad), a ranking PLO leader, on August 31 in which he cited pressure in this area from Arab sources, although he did not name them.[119] In addition, the PLO could only have been concerned with Assad's suggestion, which was repeated in a New York *Times* interview on August 29, that a unified Arab delegation represent the Palestinians at Geneva. The suggestion, endorsed by Jordan, was rejected by the PLO.[120] Yet another development confronting the PLO was the upcoming UN General Assembly session, which was to be used by the Israeli and the Egyptian, Syrian, and Jordanian foreign ministers for further meetings with Vance and Carter to try to work out a peace settlement. It was in this atmosphere of heightened diplomatic activity that Arafat went to Moscow on August 29, together with Farouk Kaddoumi, Zuheir Mohsen, and other PLO leaders.

During his three-day visit, Arafat met with Soviet Foreign Minister Gromyko (not with Brezhnev, as he had in April) and *Pravda*'s reports of the meetings referred to "an exchange of opinions in an atmosphere of mutual under-standing"[121]—usual Soviet terminology to indicate that significant disagreements remained between the two sides. *Pravda*'s summary of the talks made note of the attempts to exclude both the PLO and the USSR from the Middle Eastern peace efforts and emphasized the two sides' position that the Geneva conference had to be resumed as soon as possible with PLO participation.[122] Gromyko was cited as reiterating the USSR's strong support of the national rights of the Palestin-ians, "including the right to establish their own state and return to their homes in accordance with existing U.N. resolutions." The Soviet leader thereby gave further—if tacit—support to General Assembly Resolution no. 3236. Gromyko also maintained, however, that there could be no lasting peace in the Middle East without the liberation of all the Arab lands occupied by Israel in 1967, thereby again supporting Israel's right to exist in its prewar boundaries. Arafat, however, was apparently not prepared to give any ground on the issue of Israel's right to exist, and *Pravda* stated only that he had "informed the Soviet side on the struggle of the Arab Palestinian people for realization of their national aspi-rations and on the results of the recent session of the PLO Central Council." Arafat also gave his customary thanks to the USSR for its support of the Pales-tinian cause.[123]

As in the past, the Soviet leaders used Arafat's visit to emphasize Soviet-Arab solidarity. Thus, in an Arabic-language program on August 30, Moscow Ra-dio broadcast an interview with Arafat in which the Palestinian leader discussed the talks he had completed in Moscow. After noting that the talks were "frank," Arafat went on to say:

> We . . . briefed our comrades on the imperialist and Israeli attempts
> to impede or hinder the resumption of the Geneva Conference in or-
> der to prevent the friendly Soviet Union from playing a fundamen-
> tal, effective role in the determination of the destiny of the Arab re-
> gion. These moves are clearly aimed at ousting the Soviet Union and
> eradicating the Palestinian presence. Nobody can eradicate the Pales-
> tinian presence. Nor can anyone decide that the Soviet Union should
> play this or that role. It is important to us, as an Arab nation and a
> Palestinian people, that the Soviet Union still plays its full role in the
> events in the Arab region as cochairman of the Geneva conference.[124]

Thus concluded the PLO's talks in Moscow. It appeared that the two sides were still concerned about American peace efforts in the Middle East, despite the lack of success of the Vance mission, and that efforts to avoid exclusion from the peace-making process occupied a good part of their discussion. In addi-tion, apart from Gromyko's comment on the need for Israel to withdraw to its prewar boundaries, there was little overt indication of any Soviet effort to con-vince the PLO of the need to recognize Israel's right to exist. However, Arafat's comment about "frank" discussions and *Pravda*'s report of an "exchange of opinions" may have been indications of disagreement on that point. In any case, soon after Arafat's departure, Moscow Radio Peace and Progress underlined the Soviet Union's commitment to Israel's existence by broadcasting in Hebrew a description of the Arafat visit and the nature of the Soviet commitment to the Palestinians:

> In its conscious opposition to the belligerent policy of the ruling circles in Israel, the Soviet Union does not at all demand the liquidation of the State of Israel. When we demand that the rights of the Palestinian people be guaranteed, we justly assume that there is room in the Middle East both for a sovereign Jewish State and for an independent Arab Palestinian State.[125]

Despite once again making a commitment to Israel's existence, a commitment that was to be publicly repeated by Soviet Foreign Minister Gromyko in his UN speech of September 27,[126] the Soviet leadership made it clear that the peace settlement it had in mind was of the Model I variety by strongly attacking the Israeli demand for open borders—a central part of both the Israeli and the U.S. peace plans. In a front-page editorial titled "The Way to a Genuine Peace," *New Times* stated:

> It is no secret that by "real peace" the Tel Aviv expansionists mean the notorious "open borders" between Israel and its Arab neighbors, the "free movement of people and goods" and even "cooperation in respect of security"—all of which would make Tel Aviv the center of a huge neo-colonialist "empire" in the Middle East.[127]

While castigating the Israeli peace plan, Moscow remained concerned that despite the lack of success of the Vance visit, American diplomatic efforts to reach a Middle Eastern settlement might yet bear fruit. Thus, a TASS broadcast on September 7, citing the Arab press, complained of the lack of unity evident at the Arab League Council meeting of early September, which had as its objective the coordination of Arab policy for the forthcoming UN session. Moscow particularly deplored the strength shown by the "moderate" (pro-U.S.) forces at the meeting.[128] The central Soviet concern remained a fear that Syria, which had swung back and forth since 1973, and possibly even the PLO, might swing over to the Western-supported Egyptian-Saudi axis. While the loosely federated PLO had opposed the U.S. offers in August, there were evidently certain elements within the organization who wanted to take a more positive position toward the United States, if only to drive a wedge between it and Israel. This was particularly evident following the U.S. State Department pronouncement on September 12 that "the Palestinians must be involved in the peace-making process."[129]

While Arafat praised the statement, calling it a "positive step,"[130] his position was contested by both Saiqa leader Zuheir Mohsen and PFLP leader George Habash. Mohsen asserted that "Arabs as well as Palestinians must not be fooled by deceptive American promises."[131] Indeed, he went so far as to say, "The Soviet Union has warned us both, Arafat and myself when we were recently in Moscow, not to have any trust in American promises."[132] If the Saiqa leader was quoted correctly, his statement would seem to put in question Vance's assertion of early August that the Soviet leaders had indicated a willingness to "use their influence to encourage flexibility," at least insofar as the PLO was concerned.[133]

In any case, Moscow soon sought to deprecate the U.S. move, with Radio Moscow calling it a ploy to "avoid strong criticism from the Arabs on the eve of the debate on the Middle East at the U.N.," to "avoid the convening of the Geneva Conference, and to replace the conference with its own mediation."[134] Moscow Radio Peace and Progress carried the criticism one step further, stating that the failure of the U.S. State Department to mention the PLO in the September 12 statement was clearly tied to U.S., Israeli, and Saudi Arabian efforts to bribe West Bank and Gaza Palestinians and thereby achieve a "capitulatory" settlement.[135] In an effort to keep the PLO on its side, Moscow Radio also highlighted Carter's statement several days later, on the eve of Israeli Foreign Minister Moshe Dayan's visit to Washington, that he (Carter) never supported the PLO and was not in favor of an independent Palestinian state.[136] On September 21, *Izvestia* used Carter's comments to downplay U.S. efforts to be an "honest broker" between the Arabs and Israelis during the late September negotiations that the Carter administration was carrying on with Dayan and a number of Arab foreign ministers, claiming that Carter's opposition to the PLO was "diametrically opposed to what many governments of the Arab countries insist on—full recognition of the PLO and the obligatory participation of its representatives in the Geneva Conference."[137]

As might be expected, the Soviet leaders were quick to deprecate the U.S.-Israeli agreement that emerged from Dayan's talks in Washington. In this document the Israelis agreed, for the first time, to negotiate with a united Arab delegation containing Palestinian Arabs—hitherto, Israel had opposed both negotiating with a united Arab delegation and the inclusion of Palestinians among the Arabs, unless they were members of the Jordanian delegation. The Israelis did, however, attach a number of important qualifications to the agreement, including the exclusion of known PLO members, the limiting of the united Arab delegation to the symbolic opening session of the conference, and the limiting of the Palestinian Arabs to the Jordanian delegation after the opening session.[138] While the United States then backed away from some of the Israeli conditions, with U.S. Secretary of State Cyrus Vance calling for a greater degree of Palestinian participation in the Geneva talks,[139] Moscow quickly reinforced Arab opposition to the plan. *Pravda* commented on September 29 that "the leadership and the press of the Arab countries see this step by Israel as an attempt to split the

Arabs' ranks, to force them to make concessions to Tel Aviv, and at the same time to shift the responsibility for failure to reach a settlement onto the Arab states."[140]   Possibly because the idea of a united Arab delegation had initially come from Syria—an idea opposed by both the USSR and the PLO—the *Pravda* article went on to cite a Syrian government spokesman who said the plan was a device "to wreck the Geneva Conference."

With the American diplomatic effort once again in difficulty, President Carter was called upon, at a press conference on September 29, to explain the U.S. position. In response to questions about the role of the PLO at Geneva, Carter stated:

> We're trying to act as an intermediary between Israel and each one of those Arab countries that border their [sic] own country. There are some differences among the Arab nations which we are trying to resolve, concerning a unified Arab delegation or individual Arab delegations and the format which might be used to let the Palestinians be represented.
>
> . . . It is obvious to me that there can be no Middle East peace settlement without adequate Palestinian representation.
>
> . . . If the PLO should go ahead and say "we endorse U.N. Resolution 242, we don't think it adequately addresses the Palestinian issue because it only refers to refugees and we think we have a further interest than that", that would suit us O.K. We would then begin to meet with and to work with the PLO.
>
> Obviously they don't represent a nation. *It is a group that represents a substantial part of the Palestinians.* I certainly don't think they're the exclusive representatives of the Palestinians. Obviously, there are mayors, for instance, and local officials in the West Bank area who represent Palestinians. They may or may not be members of the PLO.[141] [emphasis added]

In addition to this statement, which was the strongest U.S. recognition to date of the political importance of the PLO, and possibly another effort to get it to change its policy, Carter also mentioned the role of the USSR at Geneva:

> At the same time we have a further complicating factor in that we are joint Chairmen of the Geneva Conference, along with the Soviet Union, so in the call for the conference and in negotiations preceding the format of the conference we have to deal with the Soviet Union as well.[142]

Carter's emphasis on the need to deal with the USSR was made very clear only two days later, when a joint Soviet-American statement on the Middle East was issued, a statement that was to cause an uproar in American politics and a major upheaval in U.S.-Israeli relations. The United States appeared to bring the Soviet Union back into the heart of the Middle Eastern peacemaking process, from which, for all intents and purposes, it had sought to exclude the Russians since the 1973 war.

SOVIET POLICY FROM THE JOINT SOVIET-AMERICAN STATEMENT TO THE SADAT VISIT TO JERUSALEM

The joint Soviet-American statement opened a new, albeit brief, period of Soviet-American cooperation in the Middle East. Given the importance of the statement, it is reproduced in full below:

> Having exchanged views regarding the unsafe situation that remains in the Middle East, A. A. Gromyko, member of the Politburo of the CPSU Central Committee and USSR Minister of Foreign Affairs, and U.S. Secretary of State C. Vance have the following statement to make on behalf of their countries, which are cochairmen of the Geneva Peace Conference on the Middle East:
>
> 1. Both sides are convinced that the vital interests of the peoples of this area, as well as the interests of strengthening peace and international security in general, urgently dictate the necessity of achieving as soon as possible a just and lasting settlement of the Arab-Israeli conflict. *This settlement should be comprehensive, incorporating all the parties concerned and all questions.*
>
> The Soviet and American sides believe that, within the framework of a comprehensive settlement of the Middle East problem, all specific questions of the settlement should be resolved, *including such key issues as withdrawal of Israeli armed forces from territories occupied in the 1967 conflict*; the resolution of the Palestinian questions, *including ensuring the legitimate rights of the Palestinian people*; termination of the state of war and establishment of normal peaceful relations on the basis of mutual recognition of the principles of sovereignty, territorial integrity and political independence.
>
> Both sides believe that, in addition to such measures for ensuring the security of the borders between Israel and the neighboring Arab states as the establishment of demilitarized zones and the agreed stationing in them of UN troops or observers, international guarantees of such borders, as well as of the observance of the terms of the settlement, can also be established, should the contracting parties so desire. The Soviet Union and the United States of America are ready to participate in these guarantees, subject to their constitutional processes.

2. The Soviet and American sides believe that the only right and effective way for achieving a fundamental solution to all aspects of the Middle East problem in its entirety is negotiations *within the framework of the Geneva peace conference specially convened for these purposes, with participation in its work of the representatives of all the parties involved in the conflict, including those of the Palestinian people*, and legal and contractual formalization of the decisions reached at the conference.

In their capacity as cochairmen of the Geneva conference, the USSR and the US affirm their intention through joint efforts and in their contacts with the parties concerned to *facilitate in every way the resumption of the work of the conference no later than December 1977*. The cochairmen note that there still exist several questions of a procedural and organizational nature that remain to be agreed upon by the participants in the Geneva Conference.

3. Guided by the goal of achieving a just political settlement in the Middle East and of eliminating the explosive situation in this area of the world, the USSR and the US appeal to all the parties in the conflict to understand the necessity for careful consideration of each other's legitimate rights and interests and to demonstrate mutual readiness to act accordingly.[143] [emphasis added]

An examination of the document indicates concessions by both sides from their previous positions on a Middle Eastern peace settlement, although the Soviet concessions soon proved to be merely paper ones and the United States was also to pull back from commitments it made in the statement. The Soviet concessions were fourfold in nature. In the first place, the document called only for Israeli withdrawal from territories occupied in 1967 (not *all* the territories); second, it made no specific mention of the need to establish a Palestinian state; third, there was no mention of the Palestine Liberation Organization; and fourth, it called for the establishment of normal peaceful relations, a term that implied a Model II peace settlement (and therefore the reversal of the Soviet position emphasized by the *New Times* editorial of early September).

The United States also made four concessions. The first and most important was its agreement to the term "the legitimate rights of the Palestinians" (hitherto she had spoken only of the "legitimate interests of the Palestinians"). Second, the document made no mention of UN Resolution nos. 242 or 338, hitherto the only documents agreed upon by the Geneva participants. Third, the United States came out for a comprehensive settlement, thus publicly ending the step-by-step strategy and appearing to eliminate the possibility of another Egyptian-Israeli separate agreement. Finally, by calling for the resumption of the Geneva conference "no later than December 1977," the United States guaranteed the USSR a major role in the Middle Eastern peacemaking process as an equal, since the United States had never before set a specific date for the reconvening of Geneva.

The U.S. reasoning in bringing the USSR back into the peacemaking process would appear to be based on two assumptions. First, the Carter administration seemed set on an overall peace settlement, and saw Geneva as the only way to bring one about. Therefore, it felt, in the words of President Carter, that it was better not "to have a cochairman who might be publicly and privately opposing any peaceful solution."[144] Perhaps more important, after the lack of success of the Vance mission in August (reportedly, Vance got the idea for a joint statement after his Middle Eastern trip),[145] and realizing that both Syria and the PLO had to be brought into a settlement, the administration apparently believed, as Vance had stated before his August mission, that the USSR could and would use its influence to make both Syria and the PLO agree to a peace settlement.[146]

If these, indeed, were the American assumptions—and the latter, at least, was highly debatable—subsequent Soviet behavior might have raised a few questions about administration reasoning. Within a few days of the Soviet-American statement, the USSR had backtracked from a number of its concessions and returned to its prestatement position on a Middle Eastern peace settlement. In an Arabic-language broadcast on October 3, Radio Moscow interpreted the statement as calling for the *complete* withdrawal of Israeli forces from lands captured in 1967.[147] On the same day, in another Arabic-language broadcast, Radio Moscow presented the statement of the PLO leader in Moscow, Mohammed Shaer, in which he said that the term "legitimate rights" of the Palestinian Arab people meant their legitimate national rights to establish their own national state.[148] Soviet radio broadcasts reversing the joint statement "concessions" continued throughout October, and *New Times* carried a feature article by Oleg Alov in mid-October that also repudiated most of the Soviet concessions made in the joint statement:

> The Soviet Union has always supported and continues to support the just struggle of the Arab peoples, the Palestinians included. That this is its unchanging policy was restated by Andrei Gromyko in his speech at the U.N. General Assembly. The Soviet Union stands for the withdrawal of all Israeli forces from the Arab territories occupied in 1967, the *realization of the legitimate rights of the Arab people of Palestine, including their right to self-determination and independent statehood*, and the ensuring of the rights of all states in this area to independent development and security. The Soviet Union is working indefatigably to have all these questions examined in their totality *at the Geneva Conference with the equal participation of all sides concerned, including the PLO*, the lawful representative of the Arab people of Palestine.[149] [emphasis added]

In the last week of October, Oleg Trayanovsky, the Soviet Union's permanent UN representative, made a statement in the Security Council debate on the Middle East supporting the establishment of a Palestinian state and reaffirming Soviet support for the PLO as the sole lawful representative of the Palestinian people.[150] Several days later, in a major *Pravda* article on October 29, Pavel Demchenko called for the total withdrawal of Israeli troops from all occupied territories and again endorsed the right of the Palestinians to their own state.[151] In early November a feature article in *New Times* again attacked the "open borders" concept, thereby calling into question Moscow's interpretation of the "normalization" of Arab-Israeli relations.[152]

While the USSR was backtracking from its concessions in the joint statement, the Carter administration was coming under very severe pressure for having signed the statement at all. Israel, its friends in Congress, the American Jewish community, AFL-CIO leader George Meany, and a host of other people berated the administration for its concessions to the USSR and for taking steps to impose a Middle Eastern solution with the USSR.[153] Indeed, the pressure on the administration grew so heavy that the president, facing major problems with the Congress over energy and the Panama Canal, and with his position weakened as a result of the resignation of his close friend Bert Lance, quickly moved to placate his critics. In his UN speech on October 4, Carter emphasized the continued importance of UN Resolutions 242 and 338, and stated that the United States was not seeking to impose a peace settlement. In addition, he again came out for a Model II peace settlement and restated his commitment to recognized and secure borders for Israel, although he also mentioned "the legitimate rights of the Palestinians."[154] The president took even a stronger step toward placating his critics two days later when, after a lengthy session with Israeli Foreign Minister Dayan, he told Dayan that Israel would not be required to agree to the wording of the joint Soviet-American statement as a prerequisite for Geneva, and that UN Resolutions 242 and 338 would remain the basis for the resumption of the Geneva talks.[155] In addition, the United States and Israel reached a six-point "working paper" for Geneva that stated:[156]

1. The Arabs will be represented by a unified Arab delegation, which will include Palestinian Arabs. After the opening session, the conference will split into working groups.

2. The working groups will be as follows:
   a. Egypt-Israel
   b. Jordan-Israel
   c. Syria-Israel
   d. Lebanon-Israel

3. The West Bank and Gaza issues will be discussed in a working group to consist of Israel, Egypt, Jordan and the Palestinian Arabs.

4. The solution of the problem of the Arab refugees and of the Jewish refugees will be discussed in accordance with terms to be agreed on.

5. The agreed bases for the negotiations at the Geneva peace conference on the Middle East are U.N. Security Council Resolutions 242 and 338.

6. All the initial terms of reference of the Geneva peace conference remain in force, except as may be agreed upon by the parties.

An analysis of the working paper indicates that while the United States had clearly sought to placate Israel in its most important concerns, Israel also had made concessions. Indeed, the Israelis had gone beyond their September 25 agreement with the United States by agreeing to Palestinians not only in the ceremonial opening session but also in the substantive discussions on the West Bank-Gaza issue. Nonetheless, the Israelis continued to refuse any negotiations with the PLO and, after some contradictory statements from the State Department, they received public U.S. assurance that they did not have to.[157]

As these events unfolded, the Soviet Union, which had warmly welcomed the joint Soviet-American statement, quickly attacked the U.S.-Israeli working paper. Writing in *Izvestia* on October 19, political commentator S. Kondrashov blasted the Israelis for going over the head of the American administration and for appealing to "the instincts of the anti-Soviet lobby to which any signs of cooperation with the Soviet Union are odious" in order to force administration concessions. Kondrashov went on to state:

> This concentrated pressure extracted from President Carter a new and highly dramatic admission of loyalty to the U.S. Near East ally. The President told the leaders of the American Jewish organizations that he would "sooner commit political suicide than harm Israel".
>
> The U.S. administration had to maneuver, without renouncing the joint statement with the Soviet Union, and at the same time humor Israel and its American lobbyists and tactically play down, as it were, the significance of the Soviet-American initiative. An American-Israeli statement was published following Carter's New York meeting with Dayan. As a concession to Tel Aviv it contains the provision that their agreement with the Soviet-American statement "is not an absolute condition of the reconvening and holding of the Geneva Conference". At the same time the White House press secretary said that the Soviet-American statement "remains in force".[158]

Demchenko, in his *Pravda* article of October 29, echoed this theme. After hailing the Soviet-American joint statement as a "renunciation by the United

States of 'stage-by-stage' diplomacy" and as a "realization by Washington's leading circles that the old line has proved ineffective and that, without the participation of the USSR and outside the framework of the Geneva Conference, a solution of the Near East crisis is impossible," Demchenko went on to attack the joint Israeli-U.S. working paper, claiming it was merely a device to enable the Israelis to hold occupied territory and ignore the Palestinian problem.[159]

While Moscow was attacking the working paper, the Arabs were also not showing much enthusiasm about it. Indeed, the PLO rejected it totally.[160] In addition, Syria came out in strong support of the PLO, stating that the PLO must have a role at Geneva.[161] Meanwhile, since the PLO had not renounced its goal of destroying Israel—if anything, the loose federation appeared to take a harder line in October than it had in August[162]—Israel continued to refuse to deal with it. Thus, by the beginning of November, an impasse seemed to have been reached over Palestinian representation at Geneva, with Syria and the USSR actively supporting the PLO and Israel adamantly rejecting it. Sadat sought to break the procedural impasse on November 4 by calling for a working committee to plan the Geneva talks.[163] His initiative was rejected by both Israel and Syria, whose deputy foreign minister, Abdullah Al-Khani, warned in an interview with *Christian Science Monitor* columnist Helena Cobban: "In the end, there is no third alternative between Geneva and war."[164]

Under these circumstances, and with another renewal of the UN force on the Golan Heights less than a month away, the flare-up in fighting in southern Lebanon at the beginning of November took on a particularly ominous tone. Fighting in the region had gone on since the termination of the civil war in the rest of Lebanon by the Riyadh conference of October 1976—the PLO sought to use southern Lebanon as a secure base while Israel, allied to Christian Arabs there, had sought to create a PLO-free buffer area along its northern border. The end result of the conflicting policies had been fighting between the Israeli-backed Christian Lebanese and the PLO that occasionally erupted into major battles. Numerous cease-fire arrangements had been tried, without much success —including an accord reached at Chtaura under Arab mediation in July and one mediated by the United States at the end of September, after Israeli troops had crossed the Lebanese border to help their Lebanese Christian allies. When the Israelis withdrew, they claimed that a reciprocal PLO withdrawal was required.[165] When this did not occur (Arafat publicly refused to withdraw),[166] the tinderbox situation in southern Lebanon required only a spark to set it off.

The spark came on November 6, when Palestinian forces fired rockets from Lebanon at the Israeli city of Nahariyah, killing two Israelis. In addition to ordering return artillery fire, Israeli Defense Minister Ezer Weizman warned that Israeli forces would "act intensively and quickly to restore peace" in the Lebanese border area if Palestinians in Lebanon continued to shell Israel.[167] The Palestinians, however, were not deterred by Weizman's warning and launched a barrage of rockets against Nahariyah on November 8, killing one Israeli and wounding five.[168] The Israelis responded with a major air raid against suspected PLO positions in southern Lebanon. The timing of the Palestinian rocket attacks against Israel did not appear accidental, although the identity of the group actually firing the rockets remains in doubt. An Arab foreign ministers conference was less than a week away (November 12), and the PLO leadership may have reasoned that if they could provoke Israel into a major raid on Lebanon—and following Weizman's public warning, such a provocation could be easily arranged—the Arab states would feel compelled to rally around the PLO at the foreign ministers meeting, and perhaps also at the Arab summit meeting the PLO had proposed in late October.[169] They may also have hoped that such Arab solidarity could compel the United States, if she wished to hold on to her Arab allies, to force the Israelis to accept a PLO presence at Geneva, or at least prevent a settlement inimical to PLO interests.

If this was Palestinian reasoning, it proved faulty. Perhaps realizing that the PLO move might well prevent Egypt from attaining the peace settlement he wanted, Sadat, in what could only be termed a very bold move, offered to end the procedural impasse by going to Jerusalem to talk to the Israeli Parliament if it would help the cause of peace.[170] The boldness and originality of the move, which had a major impact on American public opinion,[171] is underlined by the fact that Sadat's offer came despite—or perhaps in response to—the renewed fighting in Lebanon. It soon became clear that Sadat was setting a new course in Arab-Israeli relations, one with major implications for Soviet policy in the Middle East.

SADAT'S VISIT TO JERUSALEM AND ITS AFTERMATH

At the time of Sadat's decision to visit Jerusalem, Egyptian-Soviet relations had hit a new low, while Egyptian-American relations had continued to improve steadily, with the United States not only supplying Egypt with large amounts of food and economic assistance but also agreeing to rebuild a number of Mig engines in Egyptian planes. In August, Sadat had abrogated cotton shipments (the major Egyptian export) to the Soviet Union, and on September 28 he had accused the USSR of planning to plant bombs in mosques and churches so as to fuel a religious conflict in Egypt.[172] He then threatened to declare a unilateral ten-year suspension of the repayment of Egypt's military debts to the USSR, an action that was carried out on October 26.[173] A more symbolic, but nonetheless important, example of the worsening of Soviet-Egyptian relations was the removal of the Marxist Ismail Sabry Abdullah from his position as head of the Egyptian Institute of Planning and his replacement by an American-educated economist, Ali Abdel Meguid.[174]

As Soviet-Egyptian relations deteriorated, Soviet propaganda attacks against Sadat increased in intensity, with Moscow Radio Peace and Progress, in an Arabic-language broadcast on October 10, accusing Sadat and the Egyptian media of defaming the USSR with their anti-Soviet statements.[175] Despite the Soviet propaganda attacks, however, Moscow realized the continued importance of Egypt both in the Arab world and in the Arab-Israeli conflict, and when Mikhail Sytenko, Deputy Soviet Foreign Minister for Middle Eastern Affairs, visited the Middle East from October 31 to November 7 to press for the reconvening of Geneva, his last stop (after visiting Syria and Jordan) was Egypt, which he visited from November 4 to November 7.[176] Sytenko, however, must have been as surprised as the rest of the world[177] when, only two days after his departure, Sadat announced his willingness to go to Jerusalem—an event that seemed to many observers to be designed at least to postpone, if not to eliminate, the Geneva conference by beginning a two-way Israeli-Egyptian dialogue. Such a move, of course, held the possibility of a separate Egyptian-Israeli settlement, which would freeze the USSR out of the Middle Eastern peacemaking process, into which it had just managed to gain reentry as a result of the Soviet-American joint statement of October 1.

Yet almost before the Soviet leaders had a chance to consider the implications of Sadat's visit for their Middle Eastern strategy, they were to suffer a serious blow to both their Middle Eastern position and their tactical position in the Horn of Africa and the Indian Ocean. On November 13, Somali leader Siad Barre expelled the USSR from its bases in Somalia, and ordered home the Soviet military and civilian advisers working there; he also abrogated the friendship and assistance treaty that Somalia had signed with the USSR in 1974.[178] Until then Moscow had tried to pursue a policy of "riding both camels" in the Ethiopian-Somali conflict, but as full-scale war flared in mid-August and Somali troops drove deep into Ethiopia, the USSR increasingly took the side of Ethiopia. This resulted in a series of warnings from Somali leaders that such Soviet aid jeopardized the Soviet position in Somalia,[179] and Barre himself went to Moscow at the end of August to argue Somalia's case. The Soviet leaders may have felt that they could resist Barre's pleas since, in a change of position, the United States had backed off from its earlier promise of aid to Somalia (as had France), and she therefore had nowhere else to turn.[180] In addition, the fact that at their September meeting, the Arab foreign ministers, perhaps fearing the possible alienation of black Africa, had not given full support to Somalia[181] may have further convinced Moscow it still had leverage over the Somalis.

As Soviet military aid and Cuban advisers moved into Ethiopia, however, Soviet-Somali relations grew tense, and the Somalis claimed that Moscow had cut off military assistance.[182] Meanwhile, the Soviet media emphasized that the USSR was seeking to develop friendly relations with both Somalia and Ethiopia, and blamed the "imperialists" for stirring up the conflict.[183] Nonetheless, on October 19, Moscow appeared clearly to back the Ethiopian side when, in a speech to the Ethiopian press marking the sixtieth anniversary of the Bolshevik Revolution, Soviet Ambassador Anatoly Ratanov stated that Moscow had "officially and formally" stopped arms supplies to Somalia.[184] This led Siad Barre to openly denounce the USSR for supporting Ethiopian "intrigues" and to warn that "the continuation of the present all-out armed support to the Ethiopian regime by the Soviet Union and the influx of Cuban troops put the relations between the two countries and Somalia in great jeopardy."[185] Three weeks later, when the Soviets failed to heed his warning, Barre expelled the Soviet advisers, ousted the Russians from their Somali bases, renounced the Soviet-Somali friendship treaty, broke diplomatic relations with Cuba, and ordered a reduction in the staff of the Soviet Embassy in Somalia.

In reacting to the Somali move, the Soviet leaders, in a TASS statement, commented:

> The Somali government took its action unilaterally and in conditions of the factual war it had unleashed against neighboring Ethiopia. Essentially, behind this action lies dissatisfaction because the Soviet Union did not support Somalia's territorial claims on a neighboring state and refused to facilitate the stirring of fratricidal war in the African Horn. . . . Judging from the present steps, chauvinist, expansionist moods prevailed over common sense inside the Somali government.[186]

The USSR's inability to maintain its position in Somalia had a substantial effect on its overall position in the Horn of Africa and in the Indian Ocean. Its bet on Ethiopia had not yet borne fruit, and not only were Somali forces still inside Ethiopia, and the Eritrean secessionist forces continuing to score victories against the Ethiopian army, but the internecine fighting that had plagued the Ethiopian revolutionary government continued as the number-two man in the government, Lt. Col. Atnafu Abate, was killed.[187] Even if the Ethiopian regime ultimately emerged victorious from all of its battles (and the USSR quickly stepped up aid to Ethiopia following Barre's expulsion order,[188] airlifting not only large amounts of military equipment but also Cuban combat troops and pilots in an ultimate effort to turn the tide of battle), the Soviets had suffered an immediate tactical defeat in the region, with the departure of Soviet advisers from both the Sudan and Somalia in the space of six months, and the loss of the Soviet bases in Somalia.

The weakening of the Soviet position was also evident in the continued move of North Yemen away from the USSR and toward Saudi Arabia and the West,[189] as evidenced by the expulsion of the TASS correspondent from North Yemen in early August, an act that Moscow publicly called "unfriendly."[190] In addition, South Yemen's loyalty could no longer be taken for granted, although Soviet-South Yemeni relations remained close and South Yemen aided Soviet efforts in Ethiopia.[191] At the same time, with its loss of bases in Somalia and the overall weakening of its position in the Horn of Africa, the USSR's position in the Indian Ocean had also deteriorated.[192] Not only did the United States unquestionably have the largest and most formidable base in the region on Diego Garcia, but the overall geopolitical balance in the region[193] had shifted against the Soviets because of the sudden change of government in India. Indira Gandhi, who had been quite sympathetic to the USSR, was ousted by popular vote and replaced by Morarji Desai, who appeared to take a much more neutral position in the Soviet-American struggle for influence in the Third World. Thus, the overall deterioration of their position in the Horn of Africa and in the Indian Ocean (which they were soon to seek to reverse by sending massive amounts of military aid to Ethiopia) must have concerned the Soviet leaders as they sought to deal with an even more serious problem—Sadat's visit to Jerusalem and its implications for Soviet policy in the core area of the Middle East.

Essentially, Sadat's decision to go to Jerusalem presented the Soviet leadership with both a danger and an opportunity. On the one hand, should Sadat and Begin successfully negotiate a moderate peace settlement, there was a very good chance that Jordan, Syria, and moderate Palestinian elements both within and outside the PLO might follow suit. Then the USSR would be isolated in the Middle East, with only radical Libya and Iraq (whom virtually all the other Arab states distrusted) as backers of Soviet policy, along with radical rejectionists within the PLO, and possibly Algeria and South Yemen as well (the latter two Arab states were too far removed from the core of the Arab world to count very much). In addition, Algeria had developed ties to Western powers, while South Yemen had made a few limited moves toward reconciliation with both Saudi Arabia and North Yemen, although the reconciliation was soon to prove short-lived.[194]

On the other hand, however, should the Egyptian-Israeli talks fail to achieve an agreement to which Syria could adhere, there was the possibility that Syria, together with its ally Jordan, its dependency Lebanon, and its PLO force Saiqa, might be drawn to join the rejectionists, thereby isolating Sadat in the Arab world as the sole Arab leader willing to make peace with Israel. Such a development might well hasten Sadat's ouster or, at the minimum, lead to the formation of a large "anti-imperialist" bloc of Arab states that could be expected to be supportive of Soviet policy in its "zero-sum game" competition with the United States for influence in the Arab world. Finally, should the Egyptian-Israeli talks fail, Sadat would be discredited and the United States might feel constrained to push for the immediate reconvening of the Geneva conference, where the USSR would play a major role as cochairman.

Consequently, as Middle Eastern events unfolded, Soviet strategy, which remained highly reactive, could be seen as an attempt to isolate and discredit Sadat in order to, if at all possible, prevent an Egyptian-Israeli agreement from taking place. Or, if an agreement should be consummated despite Soviet efforts (indeed, the USSR had little direct influence over either Egypt or Israel to prevent such an agreement), the Soviet strategy was to try to prevent any other Arab state or group from adhering to it.

While the Soviet leadership was pondering the possible effects of Sadat's move on their Middle Eastern position, Sadat's announcement of his willingness to go to Jerusalem appeared to send a shock wave of uncertainty through the Arab foreign ministers meeting in Tunis, and his additional suggestion that American professors of Palestinian origin be the Palestinian representatives at the Geneva peace conference further complicated discussions. The end result of the meeting was that February 15 was set for the next Arab summit—a maneuver that seemed to give Sadat more time to work out his peace initiative.[195] In addition, Arab unity scored a victory, although it was to prove to be only a temporary one, when both Egypt and the Sudan agreed to resume diplomatic relations with Libya, a development Moscow Radio hailed as "positive."[196] The USSR took a harsher line, however, in its evaluation of Sadat's forthcoming visit to Israel, with *Pravda* on November 15 juxtaposing Sadat's announcement of his willingness to go to Jerusalem with news of Palestinian fears of new Israeli raids into Lebanon. The *Pravda* article also indicated how Israeli Prime Minister Begin had "exploited" Sadat's willingness to go to Jerusalem, "a city illegally declared the capital of Israel in defiance of U.N. decisions."[197] On the same day, in an Arabic-language broadcast, Moscow Radio noted:

> Begin and other Israeli leaders see in the separate dialogue with Sadat an unparalleled opportunity to dent the Arab front and to exclude the Soviet Union from the settlement process.[198]

Following a meeting between Sadat and Assad, in which the Egyptian president proved unable to justify his Jerusalem visit to his Syrian counterpart, Arab criticism of Sadat mounted. The Soviet Union sought to reinforce it with extensive international broadcasts. Thus, the USSR gave prominent attention to the joint statement of the Syrian government, the Syrian Ba'ath Party, and Syria's Progressive Front denouncing the visit. An Arabic-language broadcast on November 17, in discussing the Arab opposition, repeated *Pravda*'s discrediting of Sadat by tying the Egyptian president's visit to Israeli actions in Lebanon:

> What is deplored in many Arab capitals is the fact that Sadat announced his readiness to go to Israel at a time when the Israeli artillery and airforce are engaged in attacks on peaceful villages and Palestinian refugee camps in Lebanon, killing and torturing civilians.[199]

As Sadat's November 20 visit to Jerusalem drew near, Arab opposition increased. The Al-Fatah Central Committee and more radical Palestinian groups denounced it,[200] and Sadat closed Cairo's Voice of Palestine Radio in response to PLO opposition—much as he did when the PLO opposed the Sinai II agreement. Even Saudi Arabia issued a statement mildly critical of Sadat's visit, asserting that the decision to go to Jerusalem "has placed the Arab world in a precarious position," because "any move with regard to a settlement must be within the framework of Arab unity."[201] In addition, Egyptian Foreign Minister Ismail Fahmy, and his designated successor, Muhammad Riad, resigned in protest over the forthcoming visit, as did the Egyptian ambassador to Yugoslavia several days later; the Soviet media played up these events as evidence of Sadat's increasing isolation.[202] Meanwhile, the United States, also caught by surprise by the Sadat move and not wishing to see Sadat isolated, sent messages to Saudi Arabia and Jordan urging support of the Sadat visit to Jerusalem.[203] Carter also reportedly told Soviet Ambassador Anatoly Dobrynin that the United States was unhappy with Moscow's decision to support the Arab radicals opposing Sadat's trip, and expressed the hope that the USSR, as cochairman of Geneva, would use its influence constructively.[204] The American request, however, did not change Moscow's stand, and it was in an atmosphere of rising Arab and Soviet criticism of his visit that Sadat came to Jerusalem.

Sadat apparently had two major goals on his trip. First, by both word and deed, he sought to demonstrate to the Israelis that they were an accepted nation in the Middle East—accepted by the Arab world's most populous and militarily powerful state, Egypt. He reviewed an Israeli honor guard, laid a wreath at the tomb of the unknown Israeli soldier, and spoke to the Israeli Knesset (Parliament) in Jerusalem—thus appearing to legitimize Israel's status as a sovereign state in the Middle East as well as its claim to at least western Jerusalem. In addition, in an attempt to show the Israelis he sympathized with their security fears, he visited Yad Vashem, the Israeli memorial to the victims of the Holocaust. Sadat's words reinforced his deeds, for in his Knesset speech the Egyptian president stated: "In all sincerity, I tell you we welcome you among us with full security and safety. . . . Today I tell you, and I declare it to the whole world, we accept to live with you in a permanent peace based on justice."[205]

But, while he was seeking to reassure the Israelis as to their place in the Middle East, Sadat's second goal was to frankly express Arab demands on Israel, stating that in return for peace and security, Israel was required to make "complete withdrawal" from territories occupied after 1967, including eastern Jerusalem, and permit the "achievement of the fundamental rights of the Palestinians and their right to self-determination, including their right to establish their own state." Sadat also made it very clear—indeed, he repeated the point three times, perhaps as a counter to his Arab (and Soviet) critics—that he had not come to Jerusalem for a separate Egyptian-Israeli deal. In addition, in an apparent effort to show he could champion the Palestinian cause as well as any other Arab leader could, he made Palestinian rights one of the main subjects of his talk. He did not mention the PLO, however, possibly as a gesture to his hosts that would make his comments more palatable, and possibly because he no longer thought the PLO was central to any peace settlement, and he wanted to build up a non-PLO Palestinian following that would favor his peace initiative. Israeli Prime Minister Begin, whose speech followed Sadat's, detailed the trials and tribulations of recent Jewish history, including the Holocaust, as a justification for Israel's need for secure borders; but he also made a major gesture to Sadat by saying, "Everything is open to negotiation."[206]

Sadat's visit to Jerusalem was warmly received, not only in Israel but also in Egypt, where the Egyptian people rallied around their president upon his return. Indeed, an "Egypt-first" spirit seemed to sweep the country, with many Egyptians commenting that it was Egyptians who had done the fighting, and dying, in the Arab cause, while other Arabs had done the talking—and the profiting when oil prices skyrocketed.[207] Arab reaction outside of Egypt to the trip was mixed, with Jordan giving a very cautious approval, Saudi Arabia remaining noncommittal, and only Morocco, Oman, and the Sudan expressing strong approval. Nimeri flew to Cairo to show his support, thereby reciprocating Sadat's assistance to him in the summer of 1971, when Nimeri was greatly in need of support after the abortive coup d'etat that temporarily deposed him.[208] On the other hand, Iraq and Libya, the long-time rejectionists, denounced the trip and— of greater concern for both Egypt and the United States—Syria and the PLO not only denounced the trip but also signed a joint communique that termed the visit part of a "conspiracy by Sadat, Israel and the U.S. to shatter the united Arab policy toward Israel."[209] In addition, the Syrian delegate to the United Nations, in a speech to the General Assembly, denounced Sadat's visit as a "visit of shame" and a "stab in the back of the Arab people"—accusations that prompted Egypt's chief UN delegate, Ahmed Meguid, to walk out of the General Assembly in protest.[210]

Soviet criticism of the Sadat visit was similar in content, if not yet in tone. *Pravda* articles on November 20 and 22 claimed that the United States was behind the Sadat visit, with the article of November 22 deprecating Sadat's support of Palestinian rights in his Knesset speech because he made no mention of the PLO or of PLO participation at Geneva. The article also attacked Sadat for legitimizing Israel's occupation of Arab land by his visit, and for talking peace with the Israelis when Israeli planes and artillery were killing Lebanese civilians.[211] Perhaps the sharpest note of Soviet criticism came in a feature article in *New Times* that compared Sadat's visit to the Holy Roman Emperor's humiliation at Canossa and accused Sadat of trying to bypass the PLO (possibly because Egypt had invited West Bank leaders to Cairo for consultations).[212] It also accused Sadat of seeking to "relegate to oblivion" the joint Soviet-American statement of October 1, in order to make a separate bilateral deal or to postpone Geneva indefinitely.[213] As part of its attack on the Sadat trip, Moscow endorsed the joint Syrian-PLO communique, which Moscow Radio on November 23 termed "strong criticism of the capitulatory step" of Egypt.[214] Another broadcast claimed that Sadat was after a separate settlement at the expense of the Palestinians, and that he wanted to isolate both the PLO and the USSR.[215]

Despite the strong Soviet criticism of the Sadat visit, U.S. Deputy Secretary of State Warren Christopher sought to downplay Soviet negativism, and in a speech to the convention of the Union of American Hebrew Congregations on November 22, he continued to defend the Soviet-American statement of October 1:

> It would be wrong and shortsighted in these weeks of intense diplomacy to pretend that the Soviet Union, as cochairman of the Geneva Conference, does not have an interest in the Middle East or to pretend it does not have a role to play in the outcome of negotiations—a constructive role or a troublesome role. This is why, through our recent joint statement, we sought to engage the Soviets on the most constructive basis at this most critical moment. We do not take lightly the Soviet commitments implied in that statement.[216]

Christopher's comments were in direct contrast with those of former Secretary of State Henry Kissinger, who, in an NBC "Today Show" interview on the same day, suggested that the Carter administration downplay the Soviet role, because the USSR "was responsible for most of the crises in the area" and because it opposed the Sadat trip and discouraged other Arabs from endorsing it. The maximum role the Soviets should play, argued Kissinger, would be to participate in endorsing an agreement that the parties had reached directly.[217]

While Kissinger and the Carter administration were disagreeing about the role of the USSR in the Middle Eastern peacemaking process, Egyptian President Sadat, in a speech to Egypt's Parliament on November 26, made another major diplomatic move by inviting Israel, the Arab confrontation states, the Palestinians, and the two superpowers to a conference in Cairo to prepare for Geneva. In his speech Sadat also took the opportunity to criticize Syria and to appeal for Palestinian support by reminding the Palestinians that it was Syrian, not Egyptian, bullets that had been shot at them (in Lebanon) and that Egypt had not asked for a Palestinian group of its own, as Syria had done. Sadat's strongest criticism, however, was reserved for the Soviet Union, which he blamed for egging on Syria and the Palestinians against Egypt; he accused the USSR of wanting a "no war-no peace" situation in the Middle East to preserve its position in the region.[218]

Sadat's plan to hold a preparatory conference in Cairo had a mixed response. Israel agreed immediately, but the United States, perhaps concerned that such a conference might hinder, rather than help, Geneva—or hoping to convince other states, including the USSR, to attend the Cairo meeting—[219] hesitated several days before giving a positive response. Jordan also hesitated and took a middle-of-the-road position, stating it would not attend either the Cairo conference or the conference of rejectionist Arab forces scheduled for Tripoli in early December.[220] Syria's strongly negative response came immediately, with Foreign Minister Abdel Khaddam stating that not only would Syria not attend the Cairo conference, it would go to the anti-Sadat meeting of Arab rejectionist forces in

Tripoli.[221] Syrian President Assad, however, was keeping his options open; in a news conference on November 28, two days after Khaddam's statement, he sought to downplay Syrian criticism of Sadat, stating that while he considered Sadat to be in error, Syria was not trying to isolate either Egypt or Sadat. Further, in response to a question as to whether the "divorce" of Syria and Egypt was final, Assad said, "The term 'divorce' is not applicable in the relations of brotherly countries. There are divergences over the methods of working for peace, over procedure."[222] Nonetheless, while making this gesture to Sadat, Assad also sent Khaddam to Moscow for consultations with the Soviet leaders.

Khaddam was not the first Arab leader to visit Moscow after the Sadat trip to Jerusalem. PLO Political Department Chief Farouk Kaddoumi had journeyed to Moscow on November 24 for a one-day visit, and the joint communique issued after his talks with Gromyko condemned "imperialist and Zionist plots aimed at dividing Arab countries fighting against Israel."[223] Khaddam's visit, however, was by far the more important, as Moscow sought to win Syria over to the rejectionists and to an anti-American position in the Middle East. The Soviet leaders, therefore, must have been gratified to hear Khaddam's luncheon declaration (which may, however, have been mere lip service) that "Soviet-Syrian relations have withstood all attempts aimed at weakening Soviet-Syrian friendship" and his condemnation of attempts to undermine Soviet-Arab friendship—a possible reference to Sadat's Parliament speech attacking the USSR, although the Egyptian leader was not cited by name.[224]

Gromyko also praised Soviet-Syrian cooperation while condemning Sadat's visit (again the Egyptian leader was not mentioned by name) as an action aimed at wrecking the Geneva conference before it convened. Indeed, he said, the convening of Geneva had been made more difficult by the visit, and the USSR was undertaking consultations with a number of countries in light of the new situation. Gromyko also reiterated that Soviet policy called for the *full* withdrawal of Israeli forces from occupied Arab countries, for the establishment of a Palestinian state, and for the right of all peoples and states in the Middle East to develop in freedom and independence. The USSR sought to get maximum propaganda effect from the Khaddam visit as illustrating close Syrian-Soviet cooperation. A front-page story in *Pravda* on December 1 highlighted Khaddam's talks with Brezhnev and Gromyko, and put a major emphasis on the two nations' desire to "strengthen their friendly relations" and "firmly rebuff any attempts to undermine Soviet-Syrian friendship." The *Pravda* article also emphasized the two states' determination to achieve a comprehensive settlement—without separate deals and with the participation of the PLO.[225]

In order for the anti-Sadat/anti-U.S. coalition that the Russians were hoping to build to achieve maximum success, a reconciliation between Syria and Iraq was needed; but relations between the two Arab states remained very strained. Less than two weeks after Assad had made a gesture toward improving relations with Iraq in mid-October by accepting a new Iraqi ambassador (the first in two years),[226] Syria accused Iraq of attempting to assassinate Abdel Khaddam, the Syrian foreign minister. In mid-November, even after Sadat's visit to Jerusalem had been confirmed, Syria closed its border with Iraq, charging an Iraqi sabotage plot.[227] Nonetheless, on November 28, Assad said he would personally attend the Tripoli rejectionist meeting, where he hoped to patch things up with Iraq because "we are all facing the same dangers."[228] Consequently, the Soviet leadership may have been somewhat optimistic about the possibility of helping create their long-sought Syrian-Iraqi tie, which could serve as the heart of the "anti-imperialist" Arab bloc, when they entertained Iraqi President Hassan Al-Bakr's special envoy, Tariq Aziz, immediately after Khaddam's departure. Indeed, in his luncheon speech Tariq Aziz, after hailing Soviet-Iraqi cooperation and friendship, stated that he had come to Moscow to exchange ideas about what the two countries should do to "strengthen the position of the Arab progressive forces against the imperialist, reactionary and Zionist plots."[229] He also said, however, that Iraq wished to discuss how to deal with the capitulationist policies and stands of certain well-known Arab parties—a term that may well have referred to Syrian leader Hafiz Assad, whom the Iraqis had been attacking since 1973 for accepting UN Resolutions 242 and 338 (resolutions the USSR continued to support), and Sadat.[230]

In any case, Moscow sought to put the best possible light on the two visits, and a number of Moscow Radio broadcasts to the Arab world emphasized the close relations between both Syria and Iraq and the USSR. Indeed, a radio broadcast on December 3 claimed, in referring to the two visits:

> The progressive Arab forces are now fully convinced that their most effective weapon in the continuous, relentless struggle for the triumph of justice and for victory in the anti-imperialist liberation struggle is strong solidarity between them on the one hand and their solid alliance with the socialist world, primarily the Soviet Union, on the other.[231]

Unfortunately for the Soviet leaders, the solidarity they had hoped for between Syria and Iraq was not present at the Tripoli conference. Indeed, the Iraqis walked out of the conference, refusing to sign its final document, the "Tripoli Declaration," because they claimed that the document was to be based on UN Resolutions 242 and 338, which Iraq rejected.[232] Baghdad Radio, citing the Iraqi chief delegate to the conference, Taha Ramadan, also claimed that the cause of the lack of agreement between Iraq and Syria was Syrian insistence on a "capitulatory course."[233] Despite the Iraqi walkout, which could only have been a blow to Moscow's hopes for a strongly unified anti-Sadat Arab bloc, there were two other developments at the conference that the Soviet Union could view favorably, albeit perhaps with reservations. The first was the signing of a Palestinian unity document, which brought George Habash's PFLP back into the PLO fold.

Among the principles of the agreement were rejection of UN Resolutions 242 and 338 and rejection of all international conferences (including Geneva) based on the two resolutions, and a commitment to "no peace or recognition."[234] While the USSR hailed the establishment of Palestinian unity,[235] something it had long advocated, the rejection of UN Resolutions 242 and 338 was a development that the USSR did not favor, and many "old Middle East hands" in Moscow may have wondered how long Palestinian unity would last, given the animosity between Habash and Arafat. A second major result of the Tripoli conference was the signing of the "Tripoli Declaration" by Syria, Algeria, Libya, South Yemen, and the PLO, a document that condemned Sadat's visit to Jerusalem and "froze" political and diplomatic relations with Egypt.[236] (Reportedly, both Assad and Arafat opposed any stronger action against Egypt.)[237] In addition, the declaration called on the Arabs to give political, military, and economic aid to Syria and the PLO. Finally, the declaration announced the formation of a pan-Arab front "to confront the Zionist enemy and combat the imperialist plot." The front would be composed of Syria, the PLO, South Yemen, Algeria, and Libya, but would be open to other Arab countries. The members of the front also agreed to consider aggression against any one member as aggression against all members. Ironically, despite the declaration's condemnation of Sadat, the last point of the declaration, if operative,[238] might be the one with greatest importance for future inter-Arab relations, given Algeria's conflict with Morocco, Libya's fear of an attack by Egypt, the possibility of renewed conflict between South Yemen and North Yemen, and even Syria's continuing confrontation with Iraq.

The Soviet leadership gave a strong endorsement to the decision of the Tripoli conference, even with the nonparticipation of Iraq in the final declaration, evidently hoping that the pan-Arab front created by the conference would be the strong nucleus of the anti-imperialist Arab unity the USSR had sought for so long. They may have been somewhat overoptimistic in their hope, however, given the heterogeneous members of the front who, like Habash's PFLP and Syria, were themselves often in conflict.[239] The USSR also hailed the Tripoli Declaration's statement praising the USSR for its help to the Arab cause and asserting that one of the goals of the Sadat-Israel talks was to harm Arab-Soviet relations.[240] By this time, however, Moscow did not limit itself to statements of approval of the rejectionist conference. In addition to making public her refusal to attend the Cairo conference (she had privately told the United States of her refusal at the end of November),[241] the USSR began to attack Sadat in very harsh terms. A TASS article by Yuri Kornilov on December 5 denounced Sadat for "deliberately lying" by saying he wanted a comprehensive settlement.[242] Kornilov stated in very strong terms that Egypt had "capitulated to imperialism and militant Zionism and had betrayed the Arab people of Palestine." In addition, the Soviet commentator denounced Sadat's efforts to bring non-PLO West Bank Palestinians into the peace discussions, stating that Sadat "dances to the tune of the imperialist circles, striving to bar the PLO from participation in the solution of the Middle East conflict and substitute it by a group of 'Palestine Quislings.'" Other Soviet propaganda organs emphasized the Nazi analogy, claiming that Sadat had been an admirer of Hitler and Nazi Germany.[243]

As Soviet invective against the Sadat visit increased, even U.S. Secretary of State Cyrus Vance felt constrained to protest the Soviet statements, although he did so in mild terms. In a press conference on December 6, Vance stated that the Soviet pronouncements "raised questions about what their ultimate objectives are in the region." Nonetheless, Vance added a positive note: "We still believe that their ultimate objective is to see a comprehensive settlement of the Middle East problem and work as one of the co-chairmen to that end."[244] Vance's statements were not too different in tone from those of President Carter, who, in a press conference on November 30, after the Russians had told the United States of their decision not to go to Cairo, had said, somewhat optimistically:

> In the past I think it is accurate to say that the Soviets have not played a constructive role in many instances because they had espoused almost completely the more adamant Arab position. My own feeling is that in recent months the Soviets have moved toward a much more balanced position as a prelude to the Geneva Conference. . . . I wish that the Soviets had decided to go to Cairo. They decided not to but we'll make as much progress as we can following the leadership of Sadat and Begin . . . with the Soviets not present. And my belief is that the desire of the whole world is so great for peace in the Middle East that the Soviets will follow along and take advantage of any constructive step toward peace. . . . I don't think that they are trying to be an obstacle to peace. Their perspective is just different from ours.[245]

While the United States was still taking an essentially positive view of Soviet policies and intentions, the USSR did not reciprocate the U.S. stand. Indeed, in a commentary on Carter's press conference, TASS accused the United States of striving to impose a separate peace, of bypassing Geneva, and of seeking to pressure other Arab countries to follow Egypt's example.[246]

If the United States was taking a moderate attitude toward Soviet attempts to discredit Sadat and his peace initiative, the Egyptian president was not. Following the Tripoli conference, Sadat not only broke diplomatic relations with the five rejectionist states that had participated (Libya, Algeria, Syria, Iraq, and South Yemen) but also ordered the Soviet Union, Czechoslovakia, Hungary, Poland, and East Germany to close all of their consulates and cultural centers outside Cairo—a step on the road to breaking diplomatic relations, and one the USSR deemed an "unfriendly" action.[247] In addition, Sadat warned the PLO that it jeopardized its role as recognized leader of the Palestinians by participating in the Tripoli conference.[248] He also set the date for the Cairo conference (December 14), vowing he would meet alone with Israel if no other Arab state came.[249]

Meanwhile, the United States decided to send Cyrus Vance on a quick trip to the Middle East to build support for the Sadat mission, also sending Undersecretary of State for Political Affairs Philip Habib to Moscow in what the State Department termed "part of the continuing consultations" between the two countries on the Middle East.[250] While Habib may have been sent in an attempt to mollify the Soviet leaders and get them to tone down their criticism of the Sadat initiative, the Soviet Union sought to use his mission to show the continued important role of the USSR in the Middle East, with an Arabic-language broadcast on December 7 claiming that Habib's visit "indicated once again that peace cannot be achieved in the Middle East without the participation of the Soviet Union."[251] Soviet commentary on Vance's Middle Eastern visit was considerably more caustic, with Moscow Radio on December 9 calling the trip, and the American position in support of the Egyptian-Israeli talks, a "contradiction" of the Soviet-American statement of October 1.[252] In a similar tone, *Pravda* on December 11 said that the Vance trip was nothing more than an attempt to torpedo the Geneva conference by supporting a separate agreement.

Interestingly enough, however, the United States shared the USSR's opposition to a separate peace agreement, albeit for different reasons, and reportedly Vance obtained a pledge from Sadat that he would not seek a separate peace[253] —a rather redundant action, perhaps, given Sadat's very clear statements in Jerusalem. It apparently was designed to reassure Syria and Jordan, whom the United States hoped would join the Israeli-Egyptian talks at a later stage, as well as Saudi Arabia, a key Arab ally of the United States, which Vance had also visited and which was still concerned about Sadat's initiative. Indeed, by the time of Vance's trip to the Middle East (his third since becoming secretary of state), it appeared that the Carter administration, in light of Sadat's Jerusalem visit and subsequent convening of the Cairo conference (and perhaps also because of Soviet obstructionism), had jettisoned its earlier concept of an overall settlement in Geneva.

The new U.S. policy appeared to be a "peace by concentric circles" system in which the final step would be a Geneva conference to ratify earlier agreements —in effect, the strategy suggested by Henry Kissinger in his "Today Show" interview two weeks before. Speaking on the ABC television program "Issues and Answers," Zbigniew Brzezinski, President Carter's national security adviser, articulated the new American strategy of "three concentric circles."[254] The first circle, Brzezinski stated, would include Egypt, Israel, and the United States, "because they want us to be there." The second circle would bring in "the moderate Arabs"—the moderate Palestinians and the Jordanians—to negotiate the issues of Gaza and the West Bank. Finally, Brzezinski said, there is the concentric circle "which involves the Soviet Union and the Syrians, if they choose not to become engaged sooner, and that clearly is Geneva." Interestingly enough, however, Brzezinski denied that the new American strategy in any way changed the U.S. view of the Soviet role in the Middle Eastern peacemaking process.

Moscow, however, took another view, claiming that the U.S. plan, as outlined "quite frankly" by Brzezinski, was aimed at urging Israel and Egypt to conclude a separate agreement, thus "breaking up Arab unity, keeping Israel as the U.S. strike force in the Middle East and bringing the Arab countries into line one by one."[255] *New Times* summed up the Soviet concern thus:

> The aim now is not simply to bring about a "reconciliation" between Cairo and Tel Aviv, but to create what might be called the core of a class alliance among the reactionary forces in the Middle East. Hence the efforts made to camouflage the separate character of the Egyptian-Israeli talks, to draw others into them, and to induce Saudi Arabia, the main backer of the conservative Arab regimes, to consolidate the deal in the making by bringing its financial weight and religious prestige to bear. And then what? The next step . . . would be to muster the hawks and to exert heavy pressure on the Syrians and the PLO, indeed on all the anti-imperialist forces in the area.[256]

In addition to downgrading the Soviet role in the peacemaking process, by relegating it to the last stage of the negotiations, the Carter administration, after having courted the PLO since March, apparently reached the limit of its patience with the Palestinian organization and, at least temporarily, ruled the PLO out of the negotiations. Explaining the changed U.S. policy in a news conference on December 15, President Carter stated:

> The PLO have been completely negative. They have not been cooperative at all in spite of my own indirect invitation to them and the direct invitations by Sadat and Assad, by King Hussein, by King Khalid and Saudi Arabia. The PLO have refused to make any move toward a peaceful attitude. They have completely rejected United Nations Resolutions 242 and 338. They have refused to make a public acknowledgement that Israel has a right to exist—to exist in peace.
>
> So I think they have themselves removed the PLO from any immediate prospect of participation in a peace discussion. But I certainly would not ascribe that sort of intransigence or negative attitude to any of the other parties who have been mentioned as possible participants.
>
> We want to be sure that at least moderate Palestinians are included in the discussions and this is an attitude that's mirrored not only

by myself but also by Prime Minister Begin, President Sadat and others.[257]

The president took a more gentle position on the USSR, stating that the Soviets "have not been very constructive, yet they have not been nearly as much of an obstacle as they apparently were in the past." Carter also expressed the hope that the USSR would again be cooperative "when we go past Cairo toward an ultimate Geneva Conference."[258]

As the president was speaking, the Cairo conference was already under way, despite the Soviet efforts to prevent it. Nonetheless, Moscow must have been heartened by the fact that besides Egypt, no other Arab state had joined the start of negotiations; Vance's efforts to persuade Jordan and Syria to attend had been fruitless. The Soviet leaders, however, were clearly angered at the course of developments in the Middle East, although the ultimate outcome of the negotiations remained in doubt, with the United States hoping the talks would succeed and draw in Jordan, Syria, and the moderate Palestinians, and the USSR hoping that the talks would fail or that Sadat would be so isolated in the Middle East that his regime would fall, and that a large and cohesive "anti-imperialist" bloc of Arab states cooperating with the USSR would be created as a result of his opening to the Israelis.

Brezhnev summed up the USSR's feeling about the Cairo conference in a front-page *Pravda* interview on December 24. The talks, which had adjourned for a special Sadat-Begin conference in Ismailia (following a Begin visit to Washington), were characterized as "the notorious negotiations between the Egyptian and Israeli leaders which are aimed at frustrating a real settlement, and above all, at torpedoing the Geneva Conference even before it begins." Brezhnev also took the opportunity to reiterate the fourfold Soviet peace plan, calling for the withdrawal by Israel from all land occupied in 1967; the right of the Palestinian Arab people to create their own state; the right to independent existence and security for "all states directly involved in the conflict, both the Arab states bordering on Israel and the state of Israel itself"; and the ending of the state of war "between the relevant Arab countries and Israel." Further, he called for the convening of the Geneva conference with the participation of the Palestine Liberation Organization.[259] The Soviet leader was soon to follow up his rhetoric with action.

THE SOVIET RESPONSE TO THE SADAT PEACE INITIATIVE

The first major Soviet action taken after the Sadat visit to Jerusalem was a massive resupply effort for the Ethiopian government which was in deep trouble because of Somali inroads into the Ethiopian heartland and Eritrean successes against Ethiopian troops. On November 26, less than a week after Sadat's visit, the Soviet Union mounted a huge airlift of military equipment and Cuban troops which soon succeeded in turning the tide of battle. The Soviet goals in moving to aid the Ethiopian regime seem clear. In the first place, Moscow feared that Sadat's visit might lead to a Western-supported peace settlement that could effectively isolate the Soviet Union in the region. By aiding Ethiopia, the USSR sought to assure itself of at least a political—and possibly a military—base at the junction of the Middle East and black Africa, one that commanded a large section of Red Sea coastline. In addition, an Ethiopian victory would prevent the Red Sea from being transformed into an "Arab lake" controlled by pro-Western Arab regimes. Third, by demonstrating that it was both willing and able to aid a client regime in need, the USSR hoped to set an example for both its few remaining Middle East allies and for prospective clients as well. The Soviet intervention in Ethiopia was facilitated by the fact that it was primarily Cuban rather than Soviet troops which were used, and the risk of a superpower confrontation therefore somewhat lessened, as well as by what could only be called a confused American reaction to the Soviet move. In the first place, after apparently promising Somalia arms, the administration then reneged on its promise.[260] A second American refusal to aid Somalia was followed by a still greater airlift of Soviet equipment and Cuban troops as the Soviet leadership took advantage of American indecision. Carter's subsequent denunciation of Soviet policy did little to stop the Soviet buildup, and the Russians must have sensed the conflict within the administration between Andrew Young and Cyrus Vance on the one hand and Zbigniew Brzezinski on the other concerning strategy in the Horn of Africa.[261] American warnings may have had some effect in preventing the Ethiopians from invading Somalia after they had driven the Somali troops from the Ogaden by the end of February, but it is more likely that the Ethiopians, perhaps counseled by the Russians, had the more immediate goal of ending the insurrection in Eritrea, a task to which they turned in early March. While the USSR justified its role in aiding Ethiopia, Soviet propaganda accused the United States of setting Arab and African countries against each other to block the formation of "anti-imperialist" unity and of diverting the Arabs from their conflict with Israel to make it easier for Egypt to sign a separate deal with Israel.[262]

All in all, the Soviet efforts to aid Ethiopia in its war with Somalia met with great success, although the subsequent Ethiopian move against the Eritreans held some diplomatic dangers for the USSR since the Eritrean guerrilla forces were backed by Syria and Iraq—nations the Soviet leadership was seeking to forge into an anti-imperialist, anti-Sadat front.

In addition to mounting a major airlift and sealift to Ethiopia, the second major Soviet response to the Sadat peace initiative was to try to isolate Sadat and reinforce the anti-Sadat coalition of Arab states which had come into being as a result of the Egyptian president's visit to Jerusalem. In addition to the visits of Farouk Kaddoumi (November 24) and Syrian Foreign Minister Abdel Khaddam (November 29), Tariq Aziz, the special representative of Iraqi President Hassan Al-Bakr, visited Moscow on December 3; Algerian President Houari Boummdienne on January 12; South Yemeni Prime Minister Ali Nasser

Mohammed on February 1; Libyan Foreign Minister Abdul Jalloud on February 14; Syrian President Hafiz Assad on February 21, and PLO leader Yasir Arafat on March 9. The Soviet leaders seem to have entertained two goals in inviting the Arab leaders to Moscow. In the first place, it was a good opportunity to rein-force Soviet ties with each Arab opponent of Sadat, and Western intelligence reports indicated a sharp increase in Soviet military aid for a number of the rejectionist states, especially Syria, South Yemen, and Libya following the visits.[263] A second goal of the plethora of visits to Moscow may well have been the coordination of the policies of the anti-Sadat forces and their forging into a cohesive "anti-imperialist" front, since all (except Iraq) were members of the Front of Steadfastness and Confrontation. Nonetheless, while the Front of Steadfastness and Confrontation may have been seen by Moscow as the core of this anti-imperialist front, it appeared to lack the cohesion necessary to be an effective organization. Thus at the second meeting of the rejectionist forces in February, Iraq failed to attend at all while Libyan leader Mu'ammar Kaddafi arrived late—reportedly because of a disagreement with Iraq over the activities of the conference.[264] The real test of the Front, however, came in March follow-ing the Israeli invasion of Southern Lebanon, which was precipitated by a PLO terrorist attack against an Israeli bus traveling between Haifa and Tel Aviv. Despite PLO calls for help and Syrian President Assad's announcement that he was opening Syria's borders and airspace to anyone willing to fight Israel, the only help that arrived was a few hundred Iraqis whose purpose appeared to be more to embarrass the Syrians than to fight the Israelis. The USSR itself did little to aid its PLO ally in the face of the Israeli assault other than to refrain from vetoing (at "Lebanese request") a U.S. resolution that set up a U.N. force to police Southern Lebanon and called for an Israeli withdrawal.[265] Moscow did, however, seek to make some propaganda gains out of the invasion, blaming the Israeli-Egyptian talks for being a cover for the Israeli move and the United States for backing it.[266]

In sum, while no other Arab state joined the Egyptians in talking peace with Israel—and for this the Soviet leadership must have been thankful— at this point the anti-Sadat front had not become the major force for anti-imperialist Arab unity that the Soviet Union had desired. Indeed, an Arab summit took place at the end of March with Egypt but without the rejectionist states (a PLO observer did attend), which condemned the "aggressive acts" by foreign forces in the Horn of Africa, a clear reference to the USSR and Cuba.[267] The summit was an indication to the Russians that Sadat was not as isolated as they might have hoped, and subsequent Soviet propaganda warned of Egyptian infiltration of "imperialist and reactionary nationalist influence" into states adopting progressive positions under the guise of references to their national interests being threatened by the "Communist peril."[268]

Moscow's sensitivity on this point was heightened as its relationship with several of the key rejectionist states began to cool in the late spring. In Iraq, the old problem of Iraqi Communist activity resurfaced and the Iraqi regime, perhaps nervous because of a Communist coup in nearby Afghanistan, executed in April 21 Iraqi Communist leaders.[269] The government-controlled press accused the Iraqi Communist Party of subservience to Moscow and seeking to undermine the position of the Iraqi Ba'ath party by forming secret cells in Iraq's armed forces. A second cause for conflict lay in the Iraqi Communist program, issued in April 1978, which criticized the Iraqi government for increasing economic cooperation with the West and for mistreating its Kurdish minority. In addition to conflict between the Iraqi regime and the Iraqi Communist Party, another factor which led to a cooling of Soviet-Iraqi relations was Soviet support for the Ethiopian drive against Eritrea. The issue of local Communist activity also complicated Soviet relations with Syria. While the USSR was sending large amounts of sophisticated military equipment to Syria, the Soviet press was noticeably critical of the Syrian government's domestic policies and called for the strengthening of Syria's Progressive National Front—the only organization in which Syrian Communists were permitted to operate.[270]

In addition to problems in Iraq and Syria, the Soviet leaders faced a threat to their position in South Yemen where a struggle for power was taking place. On one side was South Yemeni President Sulim Rubai Ali, who appears to have been an advocate of improved relations with Saudi Arabia, together with an end to support for the Dhofar rebellion in Oman, and lessened Yemeni involvement in Ethiopia; on the other were Prime Minister Ali Nasser Mohammed and his then close ally Abdel Fattah Ismael, who were strong backers of ties with the USSR and opponents of improved relations with the West. Fortunately for the Russians, their supporters won out in the power struggle in late June and the Soviet position in South Yemen was strengthened.[271] Another event which initially appeared to strengthen the Soviet position in the region was the Communist coup in Afghanistan which took place in April 1978, although the inability of the new regime to consolidate its power was to cause increasing difficulty for Moscow and ultimately lead to a Soviet invasion in December 1979.[272]

While the Soviet leadership was working, albeit without too much success, to solidify the anti-Sadat Arab forces into a cohesive and powerful anti-imperialist front, they were also working to undermine the American position in the Arab world by deprecating U.S. moves to expedite the pace of Egyptian-Israeli negotiations which had become bogged down less than a month and a half after Sadat's visit to Jerusalem.

The steady drumfire of Soviet criticism over the Sadat peace initiative reached a peak in January as *Pravda* on January 8 attacked Carter during his Middle East trip for trying to get the Arabs to agree to "unilateral concessions" to Israel. Following the recall of an Egyptian delegation from Israel in mid-January, the Russians termed the bilateral Egyptian-Israeli talks a failure and called for a return to Geneva, once again emphasizing that the conference could not be used as a screen for separate deals with Israel.[273] Sadat's visit to the United States in early February was also branded as a failure since he was unable to get American pressure on Israel to change its position (although he did get promises of economic assistance).[274] The USSR kept up its criticism of Egypt in the latter part of the month as *Pravda* condemned the Egyptians for their attempted rescue of hostages in Cyprus.[275] Meanwhile, as a result of Soviet activity in the Horn of Africa and attempts by members of the Carter administration to link the Soviet actions to the SALT talks, Soviet-American relations began to deteriorate sharply, and Soviet criticism of the United States mounted. In addition to attacking the United States for its aid to Israel, and minimizing the differences between the Begin and Carter administrations on Middle East policy (there had been a serious clash between Begin and Carter during the Israeli Prime Minister's visit to Washington in March), the Soviet leadership also attacked the United States for its plan to sell advanced aircraft to Saudi Arabia and Egypt as well as Israel. Indeed, *Pravda* commentator Yuri Zhukov went so far as to call this a "profound political change of course":

> At present, the U.S. government has embarked on a profound political change of course, from exclusive support of Israel, its sole ally in the Middle East to the present time, to reliance on a group of states with reactionary regimes . . . on Saudi Arabia . . . and certain other Arab states.[276]

Soviet concern about an American-Israeli-Saudi Arabian-Egyptian alignment grew considerably in May following the insurrection in Zaire and the Franco-American military action to suppress it. Soviet propaganda media gave extensive coverage to the link between a Saudi Arabian "bloc" in the Red Sea and a French-led Afro-Arab intervention force in Africa. The Soviets seemed to fear that such an army, based on the force that suppressed the Zaire revolt, might be used against Angola, one of the USSR's allies in black Africa.[277] In addition, *New Times* went so far as to state that the United States was using the events in Zaire "to demonstrate to the world that U.S. imperialism is still firmly in the saddle, that it is capable of meeting the 'challenge' from the fighting peoples."[278] The journal went on to attack the United States for blackmailing the USSR by "demanding that it give up its support of the liberation struggle of the peoples oppressed by imperialism in exchange for the policy of detente." France, which the USSR had been trying to woo away from the NATO alliance for many years, also came in for sharp Soviet criticism not only for its actions in Zaire, but also for its aid to Morocco and Mauritania against the Algerian-aided Polisario guerrillas in the former Spanish Sahara and for its intervention on behalf of the Chad government against the insurrection in that country which was supported by the Soviet Union's other North African ally, Libya.[279]

All in all, whether or not the USSR (or Cuba) was involved in the Zaire invasion,[280] the Soviet leadership, having scored successes in both Angola and Ethiopia seemed to be taken aback by the strong Western reaction to the Zaire events, and Moscow exhibited concern that the Western move would serve not only to foil future Soviet probes of this sort, but also threaten the existence of such none-too-stable regimes as the Angolan, and possibly even some of the USSR's Middle East allies such as South Yemen.

Meanwhile, although Soviet-American relations deteriorated as a result of the African events, a slowdown in the SALT negotiations, a warming of relations between China and the United States, and the mistreatment of Soviet dissidents and Americans working in the USSR, the two powers continued to talk about the Middle East, although little was accomplished. Vance journeyed to Moscow on April 20 for discussions with Gromyko on SALT and the Middle East, and the Soviet description of the talks referred to an "exchange of views on the Middle East"—the usual Soviet code words for disagreement.[281] Then, in early May, possibly under Soviet prodding or possibly because the Palestinian position in Lebanon was more and more untenable as the PLO came under increasing Syrian control as a result of the Israeli invasion, Arafat gave an interview to the New York *Times* in which he stated that the Soviet-American joint statement of October 1, 1977 "could become a firm foundation for a realistic settlement."[282] The PLO leader also called on both the USSR and the United States to provide guarantees for the existence of Israel and a Palestinian state. The fact that *Pravda*, on May 3, cited the interview appeared to be tacit support for Arafat's statements, which were very close to the Soviet peace plan of May 1977. Nothing came of the Arafat interview, however, nor of the Carter-Gromyko talks later in the month, while the Egyptian-Israeli peace talks remained stalemated through June and July despite a meeting of the Egyptian and Israeli foreign ministers in London and despite American efforts to expedite the peace process. Thus, by September 1978, more than ten months after the Sadat initiative, the Soviet leadership must have viewed their position in the Middle East as a perplexing one. On the one hand, the Egyptian-Israeli talks had not succeeded and Egypt had become somewhat isolated in the Arab world because of Sadat's peace initiative. On the other hand, however, the anti-Sadat front had not proven cohesive, and Sadat remained in power while the Carter administration, for its part, continued to seek a way to bring the Israeli-Egyptian negotiations to a successful conclusion—making a final major effort in early September when Carter invited Begin and Sadat to a summit conference at Camp David, the president's mountain retreat near Washington. The Camp David talks, and the agreements that resulted from them, were to provide Moscow with a major opportunity to improve its Middle East position.

NOTES

1. See Chapter 2, pp. 29-30.
2. Demilitarized zones were also part of Israel's armistice agreement with Syria and Egypt following the 1948-49 Arab-Israeli war, but there were almost immediate disagree-

ments about them. On this point see Howard Sachar, *Europe Leaves the Middle East* (New York: Alfred A. Knopf, 1972), pp. 573-75.

3. For an analysis of Carter's position prior to the inauguration, see Robert O. Freedman, "Brzezinski: The Man behind Carter's Middle East Policies," *The Middle East*, no. 26 (December 1976): 47-49.

4. Compare Oleg Alov, "Middle East: The Diplomatic Front," *New Times*, no. 47 (1976): 12-13.

5. Cited in the report by Murray Marder in the Washington *Post*, March 3, 1976.

6. V. Kuznetzov, "Not 'Only a Word,'" *New Times*, no. 11 (1976): 16.

7. Cited in report by Bernard Gwertzman in the New York *Times*, January 31, 1976.

8. Ibid. For an analysis of these oil and natural gas projects, see Arthur J. Klinghoffer, *The Soviet Union and International Oil Politics* (New York: Columbia University Press, 1977), pp. 265-74.

9. Cited in report by Richard M. Weintraub in the Washington *Post*, March 16, 1976.

10. *Pravda*, June 30, 1976.

11. Ibid., December 1, 1976.

12. Ibid., December 11, 1976.

13. Ibid., December 30, 1976.

14. Ibid., January 19, 1977.

15. Ibid., December 22, 1976. Translated in *Current Digest of the Soviet Press* (hereafter *CDSP*) 28, no. 51: 17-18.

16. *Pravda*, November 5, 1976.

17. Ibid., January 22, 1977.

18. Ibid., February 19, 1977.

19. See Chapter 5, pp. 156-57.

20. *Pravda*, December 7, 1977.

21. Ibid.

22. Ibid., December 10, 1976.

23. Ibid., January 27, 1977. Translated in *CDSP* 29, no. 4: 26.

24. *Pravda*, February 2, 1977.

25. Ibid.

26. For an analysis of Soviet-Iraqi oil relations, see Klinghoffer, op. cit., pp. 134-39.

27. *Pravda*, February 4, 1977.

28. On Soviet oil reserves and future production, see Klinghoffer, op. cit.; *Prospects for Soviet Oil Production*, CIA Report ER77-10270 (April 1977); and Leslie Dienes, "The Soviet Union: An Energy Crunch Ahead?" *Problems of Communism* 26, no. 5 (September-October 1977): 41-60.

29. Cited in *Near East Report* 21, no. 11 (March 16, 1977): 42. Subsequent U.S. statements, however, referred only to "minor modifications" of the 1967 borders.

30. *Pravda*, March 12, 1977.

31. Cited in *Near East Report* 21, no. 12 (March 23, 1977): 47.

32. Ibid.

33. Soviet concern was expressed in a Moscow Radio Peace and Progress broadcast on March 22, 1977. See also *Izvestia*, April 5, 1977.

34. Oleg Alov, "The Settlement Issue," *New Times*, no. 12 (1977): 4-5.

35. The 15-point Palestine National Council Program was translated in the *Foreign Broadcast Information Service* (hereafter *FBIS*), *Daily Report*, March 21, 1977.

36. Moscow Radio, in an Arabic-language broadcast on March 23, emphasized this point.

37. *Pravda*, March 27, 1977.

38. The text of the foreign policy section of Brezhnev's speech was translated in *New Times*, no. 13 (1977): 4-7.

39. *Pravda*, April 1, 1977.

40. Ibid., April 5, 1977. The speech was broadcast in Arabic to the Arab world on Moscow Radio, April 4, 1977.

41. Moscow Radio Domestic Service, April 6, 1977.

42. *Pravda*, April 8, 1977.

43. Ibid., April 19, 1977. The speech received first-page coverage.

44. Ibid.

45. Ibid., April 23, 1977.

46. By this time, the slowdown in Soviet arms shipments to Syria, caused by Syrian action against the PLO in Lebanon, had ended.

47. See Chapter 7, pp. 252-53.

48. For an analysis of the new Ethiopian government and the conflict on the Horn of Africa, see Tom J. Farer, *War Clouds on the Horn of Africa* (Washington, D.C.: Carnegie Endowment for International Peace, 1976).

49. Thus, when an Ethiopian delegation visited Moscow on July 6-12, 1976, the joint communique issued after the visit said, "Questions concerning the expansion of ties in the economic, cultural and other fields were discussed in a spirit of mutual understanding"—a statement that appeared to indicate that no agreement was reached. See *Pravda*, July 14, 1976, for the text of the communique.

50. Compare Farer, op. cit., chap. 2.

51. Ibid., pp. 49-103.

52. This was the terminology used by a Sudanese presidential spokesman, as cited in the report by Geoffrey Godsell in the March 2, 1977, issue of the *Christian Science Monitor*.

53. Cited in a report by Anan Safadi in the March 4, 1977, issue of the Jerusalem *Post*.

54. See the interview with Ethiopian President Mengistu Mariam in the March 15, 1977, issue of the Cuban newspaper *Granma*. Reprinted in the *Granma Weekly Review*, March 27, 1977, p. 3.

55. Cited in *Arab Report and Record*, May 15-30, 1977, p. 408.

56. Ibid.

57. *Izvestia*, April 16, 1977. Translated in *CDSP* 29, no. 15: 5. See also Vladimir Larin, "Ethiopia: Who Gains from the Tension," *New Times*, no. 19 (1977): 10.

58. Cited in the report by David Ottaway in the April 16, 1977, issue of the Washington *Post*. Ottaway reported a secret Soviet-Ethiopian arms deal had been signed in December 1976.

59. *Pravda*, May 9, 1977.

60. Ibid. Other causes for the USSR's decision to aid Ethiopia may have been Moscow's perception of Ethiopia as a gateway to northeast Africa, the utility of Ethiopia's Marxist turn for the CPSU's domestic legitimization, and Ethiopia's large population and natural resources. It may also have been a counter to Soviet losses in Egypt and the Sudan, much as the Soviet embrace of the left-wing Syrian Ba'ath in 1966 was a counter to Soviet losses elsewhere (see Chapter 2, p. 22).

61. Cited in the report by David Ottaway in the May 17, 1977, issue of the Washington *Post*.

62. Cited in AP report from Khartoum, in the May 19, 1977, issue of the Washington *Post*.

63. TASS International Service, May 23, 1977.

64. Radio Moscow in Arabic to the Arab world, May 25, 1977 (unattributed commentary).

65. Cited in a Reuters report from Egypt in the May 30, 1977, issue of the New York *Times*.

66. Cited in a Reuters report from Beirut in the June 4, 1977, issue of the New York *Times*. See also the report by John Cooley in the June 6, 1977, issue of the *Christian Science Monitor*.

67. *Pravda*, June 11, 1977.

68. Ibid.

69. Ibid., June 12, 1977.

70. Cited in the report by John Cooley in the June 29, 1977, issue of the *Christian Science Monitor*.

71. Cairo Radio Domestic Service, July 16, 1977.

72. Both Egyptian and Sudanese attacks on Soviet policy at the OAU conference in early July must have been exceedingly embarrassing to the Russians.

73. Translated in *CDSP* 29, no. 30: 5. For analyses of the war, see *The Middle East*, no. 35 (September 1977): 36-40.

74. Cited in a report in the August 1, 1977, issue of the Washington *Post*.

75. For a description of the Chinese weapons, see the report by Henry Tanner in the June 26, 1977, issue of the New York *Times*. For a description of the proposed American arms sale to Egypt, see the report by Don Oberdorfer in the July 28, 1977, issue of the Washington *Post*. (The American weapons reportedly included pilotless drones and C-130 transport planes; there was later to be a discussion of American technicians going to Egypt to rebuild Soviet Migs.)

76. *Pravda*'s description of the talks in its June 2, 1977, issue referred to "an exchange of opinions." For a description of the Eritrean refusal, see the report by David Ottaway in the June 9, 1977, issue of the Washington *Post*.

77. Compare *New Times*, no. 22 (1977): 14-15; *Pravda*, June 4, 1977.

78. *Pravda*, June 6, 1977. Translated in *CDSP* 29, no. 23: 20.

79. Compare AP report from Nairobi in the July 15, 1977, issue of the Baltimore *Sun* and the report by Ronald Koven in the July 16, 1977, issue of the Washington *Post*. Estimates of the size of the Soviet adviser force were as high as 6,000 men.

80. Y. Tsaplin, "USSR-Somalia—Road of Friendship," *New Times*, no. 28 (1977): 14-15.

81. See the report by Don Oberdorfer in the July 28, 1977, issue of the Washington *Post*. The American offer was later withdrawn because of evidence that Somali regulars were fighting inside Ethiopia.

82. TASS statement, broadcast on Moscow Radio, August 13, 1977.

83. Dmitry Volsky, "Behind the Conflicts," *New Times*, no. 34 (1977): 8-9.

84. Cited in a Washington *Post* report, June 28, 1977.

85. Cited in a report in the Baltimore *Sun*, June 12, 1977. Other nations that Carter mentioned in the "peaceful" influence competition with the USSR were Vietnam, Somalia, Algeria, China, and "even Cuba."

86. *Middle East Intelligence Survey* 5, no. 9 (August 1-15, 1977): 72. Subsequent South Yemeni aid to Ethiopia demonstrated its continued interest in close ties with the USSR.

87. There were widespread reports of corruption that reached to the top of the Syrian power structure (Assad's brother Rifai), and a number of Assad's associates were assassinated.

88. For the text of the State Department policy statement, see the New York *Times*, June 28, 1977.

89. Translated in *CDSP* 29, no. 26: 16.

90. *Izvestia*, July 3, 1977.

91. Cited in AP report from Beirut in the July 2, 1977, issue of the New York *Times*.

92. Cited in UPI report from Cairo in the July 11, 1977, issue of the New York *Times*.

93. *Pravda*, July 15, 1977.

94. The text of the press conference statement is printed in the July 13, 1977, issue of the New York *Times*.

95. For the text of the Begin statement of Israel's peace proposal, see the New York *Times*, July 21, 1977.

96. For the text of Carter's statement, see the New York *Times*, July 21, 1977.

97. For a description of the arms deal, see the report by Bernard Gwertzman in the July 23, 1977, issue of the New York *Times*.

98. Translated in *CDSP* 29, no. 30: 5.

99. See *Near East Report* 21, no. 7 (February 16, 1977): 25; and report by Don Oberdorfer in the July 30, 1977, issue of the Washington *Post*.

100. Cited in the report by Don Oberdorfer in the July 30, 1977, issue of the Washington *Post*.

101. Cited in the report by Don Oberdorfer in the August 3, 1977, issue of the Washington *Post*.

102. Cited in the report by Moshe Brilliant in the August 4, 1977, issue of the New York *Times*.

103. Cited in the report by Don Oberdorfer in the August 5, 1977, issue of the Washington *Post*.

104. Cited in TASS report from Damascus, August 10, 1977, in the *FBIS Daily Report: Soviet Union*, August 11, 1977, p. B-6. Assad was later to make a similar suggestion in an interview in the New York *Times* on August 29, 1977, which the PLO was to quickly reject.

105. Cited in report by Bernard Gwertzman in the August 7, 1977, issue of the New York *Times*.

106. *Time*, August 8, 1977, pp. 24-25.

107. Cited in the report by Daniel Southerland in the August 5, 1977, issue of the *Christian Science Monitor*.

108. Cited in the report by Daniel Southerland in the August 9, 1977, issue of the *Christian Science Monitor*.

109. For the text of the U.S.-Israeli agreement, see Edward R. F. Sheehan, *The Arabs, Israelis and Kissinger* (New York: Readers Digest Press, 1976), p. 257.

110. The text of the rejection was broadcast over Cairo Radio Voice of Palestine on August 26, 1977.

111. Moscow Radio in Arabic to the Arab World, August 1, 1977 (unattributed commentary).

112. Moscow Radio in Arabic to the Arab World, August 4, 1977 (unattributed commentary).

113. Moscow Radio in Arabic to the Arab World, August 5, 1977.

114. *Izvestia*, August 14, 1977. Translated in *FBIS Daily Report: Soviet Union*, August 17, 1977, p. B-4.

115. Moscow Radio in Arabic to the Arab World, August 10, 1977 (Vladimir Bilyakov commentary).

116. Compare Moscow Radio in Arabic to the Arab World, August 19, 1977 (unattributed commentary).

117. Moscow Radio, August 24, 1977; *Pravda*, August 25, 1977. The information was repeated in *Pravda*'s "International Week" column on August 28.

118. Moscow Radio in Arabic to the Arab World, August 21, 1977 (unattributed commentary).

119. Radio Baghdad, August 31, 1977.

120. Cairo Radio, August 30, 1977; Radio Algiers Voice of Palestine, August 30, 1977.

121. *Pravda*, August 31 and September 1, 1977.

122. Ibid., September 1, 1977.

123. Ibid.

124. Moscow Radio in Arabic to the Arab World, August 30, 1977.

125. Moscow Radio Peace and Progress, September 2, 1977 (unattributed commentary).

126. *Pravda*, September 28, 1977.

127. *New Times*, no. 36 (1977): 1.

128. TASS, September 1, 1977. The French newspapers *Le Figaro* and *Le Quotidien de Paris* were also cited to make the same point.

129. Cited in report by Bernard Gwertzman, New York *Times*, September 13, 1977.

130. Cited in Reuters report, New York *Times*, September 14, 1977.

131. Cited in AP report from Beirut, Baltimore *Evening Sun*, September 14, 1977.

132. Ibid.

133. See p. 295.

134. Radio Moscow, in Arabic, September 14, 1977 (station commentary).

135. Radio Moscow Peace and Progress, in Arabic, September 14, 1977.

136. Radio Moscow, in Arabic, September 19, 1977 (unattributed commentary).

137. *Izvestia*, September 21, 1977.

138. Cited in report by William E. Farrell, New York *Times*, September 26, 1977.

139. Cited in report in Washington *Post*, September 27, 1977.

140. *Pravda*, September 29, 1977. Translated in *CDSP* 29, no. 39: 8.

141. The text of the Carter news conference is found in the New York *Times*, September 30, 1977.

142. Ibid.

143. *Pravda*, October 2, 1977. Translated in *CDSP* 29, no. 39: 8-9.

144. Carter interview with newspapermen, cited in *Near East Report* 21, no. 44 (November 2, 1977): 189.

145. Vance mission/idea cited in report by Bernard Gwertzman, New York *Times*, October 8, 1977.

146. Administration views obtained in author's interview with Marshall D. Shulman, special adviser to Secretary of State Cyrus Vance on Soviet affairs, Washington, D.C., December 7, 1977. For other authoritative views of U.S. policy vis-a-vis the Soviet Union in the Middle East at this time, see the testimony of Shulman before the Subcommittee on Europe and the Middle East of the House Committee on International Relations (Department of State: Bureau of Public Affairs, October 16, 1977); and the interview of Secretary of State Vance with the editors of *U.S. News and World Report* (Department of State: Bureau of Public Affairs, October 31, 1977). For an analysis of the joint Soviet-American statement and its background, see the report by Robert G. Kaiser, Washington *Post*, October 7, 1977. National security adviser Zbigniew Brzezinski also took a positive view of Soviet willingness to aid in a peace settlement in an interview with the Canadian Television Network, in which he also stated that the United States had a "legitimate right to exercise its own leverage" to obtain a settlement (cited in report by Dusko Doder, the Washington *Post*, October 3, 1977). The United States was also working at this time to achieve a cooperative arrangement with the USSR in the Indian Ocean, and this may have had an effect on the Carter administration's desire to sign the joint statement with the Soviet Union on the Middle East. Some commentators also have suggested that the joint statement was linked with a U.S. desire to get Soviet agreement in other areas of Soviet-American relations, such as the SALT talks, but this was denied by Vance in his interview with the editors of *U.S. News and World Report*.

147. Radio Moscow, in Arabic, October 3, 1977 (unattributed commentary).

148. Ibid.

149. Oleg Alov, "The Objective: Geneva," *New Times*, no. 43 (1977): 8.

150. TASS, in English, October 28, 1977.

151. *Pravda*, October 29, 1977.

152. Dmitry Volsky, "Middle East: Key to the Puzzle," *New Times*, no. 47 (1977): 21-22.

153. See the report in the New York *Times*, October 3, 1977.

154. For the text of Carter's UN address, see the New York *Times*, October 5, 1977.

155. The text of the brief joint statement released after the talks is found in the report by Bernard Gwertzman, New York *Times*, October 6, 1977.

156. The text of the working paper is found in the report by William E. Farrell, New York *Times*, October 14, 1977.

157. The State Department statement of October 18, by spokesman Hodding Carter III, overrode his own statement of October 14. See the report by UPI in the Washington *Post*, October 15, 1977, and the report by Jim Anderson (UPI), Washington *Post*, October 19, 1977.

158. *Izvestia*, October 19, 1977. Translated in *CDSP* 29, no. 42: 20.

159. *Pravda*, October 29, 1977.

160. Cited in report by Marvin Howe, New York *Times*, October 23, 1977. See also the report by Thomas Lippman, Washington *Post*, October 17, 1977.

161. Cited in report by Thomas W. Lippman, Washington *Post*, October 17, 1977.

162. Compare Judith Perara, "PLO: New Grassroot Unity Emerging?" *The Middle East*, no. 37 (November 1977): 29-32.

163. Cited in report by Murray Marder, Washington *Post*, November 5, 1977.

164. Cited in report by Helena Cobban, *Christian Science Monitor*, November 8, 1977.

165. Cited in report by Dusko Doder and Yuval Elizur, Washington *Post*, September 27, 1977.

166. Cited in report by Marvin Howe, New York *Times*, November 7, 1977.

167. Cited in report in New York *Times*, November 9, 1977.

168. Cited in report by H. D. S. Greenway, Washington *Post*, November 9, 1977.

169. Cited in report in New York *Times*, October 24, 1977.

170. Cited in report by Christopher Wren, New York *Times*, November 10, 1977.

171. An ABC News-Louis Harris poll of 1,200 respondents conducted December 2-4, 1977, revealed that 52 percent said Egypt was making the most important peace initiatives, while 48 percent said Israel was most interested in peace. This was a sharp reversal of Israel's usual 2-1 advantage, said Harris, on the ABC "Today" program (cited in report in New York *Times*, December 9, 1977). Should the Arab-Israeli talks fall through, Sadat would appear to have won a great deal of support in U.S. public opinion that he might be able to use in case a new Arab-Israeli war erupts.

172. Cited in AP report in New York *Times*, September 29, 1977.

173. Cited in report in Washington *Post*, October 27, 1977.

174. Cited in report by Christopher Wren, New York *Times*, October 27, 1977.

175. Radio Moscow Peace and Progress, in Arabic, October 10, 1977.

176. Cited in Reuters report, Baltimore *Sun*, November 6, 1977.

177. Ismail Fahmy, Sadat's foreign minister, stated that he did not hear about the trip until Sadat announced it in Parliament. This may have been one of the reasons for his subsequent resignation (cited in Reuters report, New York *Times*, December 4, 1977). Sadat, however, stated in a *Time* interview that he had told Fahmy in advance (*Time*, January 1, 1978, p. 31).

178. Cited in report by John Darnton, New York *Times*, November 14, 1977.

179. Compare Reuters report, New York *Times*, August 21, 1977, and report by John Darnton, New York *Times*, September 15, 1977.

180. The American explanation was that Somalia was waging an "offensive" war against Ethiopia. See the report by Jim Hoagland in the Washington *Post*, September 1, 1977. The

United States may also have been concerned that its weaponry would be used by Somalia against Kenya, a close ally of the United States in Africa, and a nation against whom Somalia also had territorial claims. For a critical evaluation of U.S. policy, see W. Scott Thompson, "The American-African Nexus in Soviet Strategy," a paper delivered to the Ninth Annual Convention of the American Association for the Advancement of Slavic Studies, Washington, D.C., November 1977.

181. Cited in report in Washington *Post*, September 6, 1977. Most of black Africa had opposed the Somali invasion of Ethiopia for fear of the precedent it might set.

182. Cited in report by Jay Ross, Washington *Post*, September 8, 1977.

183. Compare Radio Moscow, in Arabic, October 6, 1977 (Alexander Timoshkin commentary) and Y. Tyunkov, "The Horn of Africa: Who Gains by It?" *New Times*, no. 38 (1977): 8-9.

184. Cited in report by Milton R. Benjamin, Washington *Post*, October 21, 1977.

185. Cited in report by Roger Mann, Washington *Post*, October 22, 1977.

186. TASS statement, in English, November 15, 1977. The text is found in *FBIS Daily Report: Soviet Union*, p. H-1. Following the Somali action, the USSR began to claim that the United States was shipping Somalia weapons via Iran and Pakistan.

187. Cited in report by Graham Hovey, New York *Times*, November 15, 1977.

188. The level of Soviet aid had reached such proportions by January 1978 that President Carter publicly attacked the USSR for selling "excessive quantities of arms" (New York *Times*, January 13, 1978). Administration spokesmen later linked the SALT talks to Soviet actions in Ethiopia. By March 1978, Somalia had been forced to withdraw its troops from the Ogaden region of Ethiopia as a result of the Soviet- and Cuban-backed Ethiopian offensive.

189. North Yemen, for example, had begun to get U.S. military assistance. For reports on North Yemeni developments, see Fred Halliday, "North Yemen's Hamdi: Walking a Tightrope," *The Middle East*, no. 32 (June 1977): 20; "Yemen without Hamdi: No Changes Expected," *The Middle East*, no. 37 (November 1977): 10-11; and Ray Vicker, "North Yemen Becomes One of the Pivotal Nations in East-West Tilt," *Wall Street Journal*, June 2, 1977. See also Robert Burrowes, "State-Building and Political Institutionalization in the Yemen Arab Republic," a paper delivered to the Middle East Studies Association Annual Convention, New York, November 1977.

190. *Pravda*, August 6, 1977.

191. For a report depicting South Yemen's moves toward a somewhat more independent policy, see Fulvio Grimaldi, "Rubai Ali Steers a New Course for South Yemen," *The Middle East*, no. 36 (October 1977): 19-21.

192. There has been considerable debate about the types of installations that the Soviet Union operated in Somalia. At the minimum, all sides seem to agree that one facility was a missile storage and testing facility—of great importance to what is essentially a "one-shot" Soviet navy. In addition, the Russians appear to have maintained repair facilities (a floating dry dock), and the long runways that the USSR built for Somalia could have enabled Soviet planes with air-to-sea missiles to land. In addition, Somalia served as a good base of operations for Soviet antisubmarine patrols. For a balanced evaluation of the Soviet facility, see Farer, op. cit., p. 111.

193. For a good study of the geopolitics of the Indian Ocean, see A. J. Cottrell and R. M. Burrell, "Soviet-U.S. Naval Competition in the Indian Ocean," *Orbis* 18, no. 4 (Winter 1975): 1109-28.

194. Both Algeria and South Yemen could, however, perhaps be counted on to give lip service to the rejectionist cause for domestic political purposes or to gain more Soviet aid; and Algeria might trade its help to the hard-line rejectionists like Libya and Iraq for support in its confrontation with Morocco over the former Spanish Sahara, which Morocco and Mauritania had annexed. Indeed, the Morocco-Algeria confrontation had heated up considerably

at the time of the Sadat visit, following the capture of French citizens by Algerian-backed Polisario guerrillas and French military moves to try to obtain their release (see the report by Paul Lewis, New York *Times*, November 3, 1977). In addition, King Hassan of Morocco warned on November 6, 1977, that his troops would exercise the right of pursuit of Polisario guerrillas into Algeria—a warning that was rejected by Algeria. Interestingly enough, the United States, while an ally and military supplier of Morocco, was in the process of negotiating major natural gas import deals with Algeria, and by 1976 had become the main trading partner of Algeria (see the report by Jonathan C. Randal, Washington *Post*, November 4, 1977).

195. Compare report by Thomas W. Lippman, Washington *Post*, November 15, 1977.

196. Radio Moscow, in Arabic, November 16, 1977 (unattributed commentary).

197. *Pravda*, November 15, 1977.

198. Radio Moscow, in Arabic, November 15, 1977 (unattributed commentary).

199. Radio Moscow, in Arabic, November 17, 1977 (unattributed commentary).

200. Compare report by Thomas Lippman, Washington *Post*, November 18, 1977.

201. Cited in report by Marvin Howe, New York *Times*, November 19, 1977.

202. Compare TASS report, in English, November 18, 1977.

203. Cited in report by Bernard Gwertzman, New York *Times*, November 18, 1977.

204. Cited in report by Bernard Gwertzman, New York *Times*, November 19, 1977.

205. The texts of Sadat's speech and of Begin's reply are found in the New York *Times*, November 21, 1977.

206. Ibid.

207. Compare report by Michael Parks, Baltimore *Sun*, November 30, 1977.

208. Jordanian approval came in the form of a statement by Jordanian Information Minister Abu Odeh, who said, "This visit has broken the ice and removed the psychological barriers and brought fresh hope" (cited in report by Thomas W. Lippman, Washington *Post*, November 23, 1977). Moroccan approval may be related to Egyptian support of Morocco on the issue of the Spanish Sahara. In addition, the two states had cooperated in aiding the Mobutu regime in Zaire against invaders from Soviet-supported Angola.

209. Cited in AP report, Baltimore *Sun*, November 23, 1977.

210. Cited in report by Kathleen Teltsch, New York *Times*, November 23, 1977.

211. *Pravda*, November 22, 1977.

212. On November 24, Egypt's Arab Socialist Union (the Egyptian political party) invited Palestinian leaders from both Israel and the West Bank for a briefing in Cairo on the Sadat visit to Jerusalem. See the report by Christopher S. Wren in the New York *Times*, November 25, 1977.

213. Yuri Potomov, "President Sadat's Canossa," *New Times*, no. 49 (1977): 8-9.

214. Radio Moscow, in Arabic, November 23, 1977.

215. Ibid. (commentary by Vladimir Bilyakov).

216. Cited in report by Bernard Gwertzman, New York *Times*, November 23, 1977.

217. Ibid.

218. Excerpts from Sadat's address are found in the New York *Times*, November 27, 1977.

219. Reportedly, the United States sought to have Sadat delay the meeting to give her time to get others to attend (compare report by Hedrick Smith, New York *Times*, December 1, 1977).

220. Cited in Reuters report, New York *Times*, November 29, 1977. Technically, Jordan offered to go to both conferences, but only if all the Arab parties attended—a highly unlikely situation, given Syria's rejection of the Cairo conference and Egypt's rejection of the rejectionist conference.

221. Cited in report by Marvin Howe, New York *Times*, November 27, 1977.

222. Cited in report by Marvin Howe, New York *Times*, November 29, 1977.

223. AFP report, *FBIS Daily Report: Soviet Union*, November 28, 1977, p. F-1. Radio Moscow Peace and Progress also broadcast a diatribe by PLO leader Muhammad Ash-Sha'ir on November 23 that severely condemned Sadat.

224. Radio Moscow, in Arabic, November 29, 1977.

225. *Pravda*, December 1, 1977. Reportedly, the USSR sent new shipments of arms to Syria, including tanks and advanced antiaircraft missiles, after the visit (Washington *Post*, January 9, 1978).

226. Cited in report by Michael Parks, Baltimore *Sun*, October 21, 1977.

227. See report by John K. Cooley, *Christian Science Monitor*, October 28, 1977; and UPI report, Washington *Post*, November 16, 1977.

228. Cited in report by H. D. S. Greenway, Washington *Post*, November 29, 1977.

229. Baghdad INA, in Arabic, December 2, 1977.

230. Ibid.

231. Radio Moscow, in Arabic, December 3, 1977 (Alexander Timoshkin commentary).

232. Baghdad INA, in Arabic, December 5, 1977.

233. Ibid.

234. The text of the unity document was broadcast by Radio Tripoli Domestic Service, in Arabic, December 4, 1977.

235. Radio Moscow, in Arabic, December 6, 1977 (unattributed commentary).

236. The text of the Tripoli Declaration was broadcast by Tripoli JANA, in Arabic, December 5, 1977.

237. Doha (Qatar) QNA, in Arabic, December 5, 1977.

238. There is some question, however, as to how seriously Algeria and South Yemen took the Tripoli Declaration. For an Arab view raising some questions about the cohesiveness of the rejectionist alliance, see "The Emerging Realities," *The Middle East*, no. 39 (January 1978): 14.

239. Compare TASS report, in English, December 5, 1977.

240. Ibid. See also A. Usvatov, "The Middle East,"*New Times*, no. 50 (1977): 12-13; and Radio Moscow, "Window on the Arab World," December 5, 1977.

241. *Pravda*, December 4, 1977. (The *Pravda* article called it an "unseemly conference.") Soviet notification of the United States is cited in report by Bernard Gwertzman, New York *Times*, November 30, 1977.

242. TASS report, in English, December 5, 1977 (Yuri Kornilov commentary).

243. Compare TASS reports, in English, December 5 and 6, 1977.

244. Cited in report by Bernard Gwertzman, New York *Times*, December 7, 1977.

245. The text of the Carter news conference is found in the New York *Times*, December 1, 1977.

246. TASS International Service, in Russian, December 1, 1977.

247. Radio Moscow, in Arabic, December 8, 1977.

248. Compare report by Ronald Koven and Thomas W. Lippman, Washington *Post*, December 11, 1977.

249. Cited in report by Flora Lewis, New York *Times*, December 7, 1977.

250. Cited in report by Charles W. Cordry, Baltimore *Sun*, December 5, 1977.

251. Radio Moscow, in Arabic, December 7, 1977 (unattributed commentary).

252. Radio Moscow, in Arabic, December 9, 1977 (station commentary, "What Is Vance's Purpose in the Middle East?").

253. Cited in report by Bernard Gwertzman, New York *Times*, December 11, 1977.

254. Cited in report in New York *Times*, December 12, 1977.

255. Radio Moscow Domestic Service, in Russian, December 18, 1977.

256. Dmitry Volsky, "Middle East Behind the Smoke Screen," *New Times*, no. 52 (1977): 7.

257. The text of the Carter news conference is found in the New York *Times*, December 16, 1977.

258. Ibid. Carter also said, "On SALT, comprehensive test ban, the Indian Ocean, and many other items, we've had a very constructive relationship with the Soviet Union, which I think is constantly improving."

259. *Pravda*, December 24, 1977. Brezhnev's comments limiting the need to end the state of war to Israel "and the relevant Arab countries" (those bordering Israel) may have been made because the USSR had neither the desire nor the ability to convince such states as Iraq and Libya (neither of which bordered Israel) to end the state of war with it.

260. Compare report by Murray Marder in the January 18, 1978 issue of the Washington *Post*. This was in response to a request by Somalia for arms to repel what it feared would be a pending Ethiopian invasion of Somalia. In late July the United States had agreed "in principle" to sell Somalia arms, but suspended the agreement on August 10, 1977. (Compare report by Jim Hoagland in the September 1, 1977 issue of the Washington *Post*.) A major cause of the U.S. change in policy was a concern that its weaponry would be used by Somalia against Kenya, a close ally of the United States in Africa, and a nation against whom Somalia also had territorial claims. For a critical evaluation of U.S. policy, see W. Scott Thompson, "The American-African Nexus in Soviet Strategy," a paper delivered to the Ninth Annual Convention of the American Association for the Advancement of Slavic Studies, Washington, D.C., November 1977. For detailed examinations of the role of the superpowers in the Ethiopian-Somali war, see David Albright, "The Horn of Africa and the Arab-Israeli Conflict," in *World Politics and the Arab-Israeli Conflict* , ed. Robert O. Freedman (New York: Pergamon, 1979), pp. 147-91; and Richard Remnek, "Soviet Policy in the Horn of Africa: The Decision to Intervene," in *The Soviet Union and the Third World: Successes and Failures*, ed. Robert H. Donaldson (Boulder, Colorado: Westview, 1981).

261. See, for example, the Soviet attempt to play off Brzezinski against the State Department in *Pravda*, March 5, 1978. On this point see Robert O. Freedman, "The Soviet Image of the Carter Administration's Policy Toward the USSR: From the Inauguration to the Invasion of Afghanistan," *Korea and World Affairs* Vol. 4 no. 2 (Summer 1980), pp. 229-67.

262. *Izvestia*, January 23, 1978.

263. Compare report by John Cooley in the January 11, 1978 issue of the *Christian Science Monitor*, AP report in New York *Times* on January 12 citing U.S. State Department spokesman Hodding Carter III, and the report by Drew Middleton in the March 27, 1978 issue of the New York *Times*.

264. For a discussion of this incident, see *Middle East Intelligence Survey* Vol. 5 no. 21 (1-15 February, 1978), p. 167.

265. *Pravda*, March 21, 1978.

266. *Pravda*, March 26, 1978.

267. Cited in the report by Christopher Wren in the March 30, 1978 issue of the New York *Times*.

268. *Izvestia*, June 10, 1978.

269. For a description of the background of Soviet-Iraqi conflict over the issue of the Iraqi Communists, see Robert O. Freedman, "Soviet Policy Toward Ba'athist Iraq" in *The Soviet Union in the Third World*, op.cit., pp. 161-91. For a discussion of the 1978 areas of conflict, see the report by Thomas W. Lippman in the June 8, 1978 issue of the Washington *Post* and Tewfik Mishlawi, "Crackdown on Communists in Iraq," *The Middle East* no. 45 (July 1978), pp. 29-30.

270. Compare Andrei Stepanov, "Syria: On Guard," *New Times* no. 16, 1978, pp. 14-15.

271. For a discussion of the events in South Yemen, see the report by John Cooley in the June 28, 1978 issue of the *Christian Science Monitor* and the AP report in the June 28, 1978 issue of the Baltimore *Sun*. A more detailed analysis is provided in Nimrod Novick,

Between Two Yemens: Regional Dynamics and Superpower Conduct in Riyadh's "Back-yard" (Tel Aviv: Center for Strategic Studies, paper No. 11, 1980).

272. See Chapter 10, p. 389.

273. *Pravda*, January 22, 1978.

274. *Izvestia*, February 16, 1978.

275. *Pravda*, February 26, 1978.

276. *Pravda*, March 11, 1978.

277. Compare reports in *Pravda* on May 26, 1978 and June 4, 1978 and Yuri Tsaplin, "Miniblocks in Africa," *New Times* no. 22, 1978, pp. 20-21. See also, Victor Sidenko, "The Lessons of Shaba," *New Times* no. 23, 1978, pp. 8-9.

278. Victor Sidenko, "The Zaire Tunnel," *New Times* no. 24, 1978, pp. 10-11.

279. V. Guryev, "Contrary to the Interests of Detente," *New Times* no. 22, 1978, p. 22.

280. The alleged Soviet/Cuban involvement in the Zaire invasion in some ways resembled the alleged Soviet involvement in the Syrian invasion of Jordan in September 1970. See Robert O. Freedman, "Detente and U.S. Soviet Relations in the Nixon Years," *Dimensions of Detente*, ed. Della W. Sheldon, (New York: Praeger, 1978), pp. 92-96.

281. Y. Katin, "Useful Talks," *New Times* no. 18, 1978, p. 10. See also *Pravda*, April 23, 1978.

282. Cited in New York *Times*, May 2, 1978.

9

The Soviet Reaction
to Camp David and the
Revolution in Iran

The Camp David agreements of September 1978 and the Egyptian-Israeli peace agreement that followed six months later led to a major restructuring of alignments in the Arab world. The fall of the Shah of Iran during the period when the peace treaty was being negotiated, and the subsequent rise of the Ayatollah Khomeini, also affected Middle Eastern relationships and threatened the governments of a number of Arab states in the region as well. These events had as significant an effect on the Middle East as the 1973 Arab-Israeli war, and presented the Soviet Union with a number of opportunities to increase its influence in the region at the expense of the United States.

THE SOVIET REACTION TO CAMP DAVID

Despite the lack of progress in the Egyptian-Israeli discussions in the period between the Sadat visit to Jerusalem and the summit at Camp David, Soviet concerns about a possible Egyptian-Israeli "separate deal" mounted during the 13-day summit which began on September 5, 1978. In addition, the Soviet media emphasized what had now become a familiar theme since the American tripartite arms deal with Israel, Egypt and Saudi Arabia in May—that the United States was seeking to create a new Middle Eastern military organization, with Israel joining the Egyptian-Saudi-Iranian axis. The Soviet leadership seemed particularly concerned that the United States would secure military bases from such a development, with *Pravda* on September 10, going so far as to warn:

Anyone who nurtures plans for a U.S. military presence in the Middle East must take into account that this region is in immediate proximity to the borders of the USSR and other countries of the Socialist commonwealth, who are by no means indifferent to the future development of events there.

   While the outcome of the Camp David discussions did not provide for a U.S. military base in either Israel or Egypt, it was clear that the United States, by virtue of its mediating efforts between Egypt and Israel and its promises to them of economic and military aid, was becoming even more involved in both countries, and the USSR may have sensed that a more formal military relationship might not be far off.[1] There were two agreements signed at Camp David: the rather vague "Framework for Peace in the Middle East," which called for Palestinian autonomy in the West Bank and Gaza (with due regard for Israeli security)—with Egypt, Jordan and Israel helping to arrange the autonomy; and the far more specific "Framework for the Conclusion of a Peace Treaty between Egypt and Israel," which called for the total evacuation by Israel of the Sinai Peninsula in return for Egypt's agreement to station only limited forces there; the establishment of a U.N. force between Israel and Egypt which could be removed only by the unanimous vote of the five permanent members of the United Nations Security Council; and for the establishment of full diplomatic relations between the two countries along with trade and tourism—just the type of peace that Israel had long been advocating. Finally, Egypt and Israel pledged to complete the signing of a formal Egyptian-Israeli treaty within three months.[2]

   Not unexpectedly, the USSR greeted the treaty with hostility. In a major speech at Baku on September 22, Brezhnev denounced what he termed the U.S. attempt to "split the Arab ranks" and force the Arabs to accept Israeli peace terms. In addition, he returned to the old four-part Soviet peace plan, emphasizing that Israel had to withdraw totally from all territory captured in the 1967 war and agree to the establishment of a Palestinian state in the West Bank and Gaza. Brezhnev also repeated the Soviet call for a return to the Geneva Conference, with full participation of the PLO. Interestingly enough, perhaps to balance the American success at Camp David, Brezhnev hailed events in Afghanistan in his Baku speech, emphasizing that the new Communist government which had seized power in that country in April had embarked on the road to socialism.[3]

   If the Soviet reaction to Camp David was hostile, the reaction of most of the Arab states was not much warmer. While President Carter dispatched a series of administration representatives to try to sell the agreement to such key Arab states as Saudi Arabia (a major financial supporter of Egypt), Jordan (which according to the Camp David agreements was to play a major role in working out the West Bank-Gaza autonomy plan), and Syria, they met with little success. Indeed, only three days after the announcement of the Camp David agreements, the Front of Steadfastness and Confrontation met in Damascus. Not only did it condemn Camp David which it termed "illegal," and reaffirm the role of the

PLO as the sole representative of the Palestinian people; it also decided on the need to "develop and strengthen friendly relations with the Socialist community led by the USSR."[4] Reinforcing Soviet satisfaction with this development, PLO Moscow representative Mohammed Shaer stated that the Front for Steadfastness and Confrontation was "the core of a future broad pan-Arab anti-imperialist front."[5]

The Soviet Union, for its part, moved once again to reinforce its ties with key members of the rejectionist front as first Assad, then Henri Boummadienne of Algeria and then Arafat of the PLO visited Moscow in October. The Soviet media hailed the visit of Assad who, it was noted, came as a representative of the Steadfastness Front; and one result of the meeting, besides the joint denunciation of Camp David and of attempts "to undermine Soviet-Arab friendship," was a Soviet decision to "further strengthen Syria's defense potential."[6]

While the visit of Assad to Moscow could be considered a success for the USSR in its efforts to prevent the Camp David agreement from acquiring further Arab support, the Syrian leader's subsequent move toward a reconciliation with Iraq was even more warmly endorsed by Moscow. As discussed above, the Syrian-Iraqi conflict had long bedeviled Soviet attempts to create a unified "anti-imperialist" bloc of Arab states, and, therefore, when Assad announced that he had accepted an invitation to visit Iraq, the Soviet leadership must have seen this as a major step toward creating the long-sought "anti-imperialist" Arab bloc. While many observers saw Assad's visit as a tactical ploy to strengthen Syria's position in the face of the projected Israeli-Egyptian treaty, the USSR was effusive in its praise, with Moscow Radio calling it "an event of truly enormous importance which had considerably strengthened the position of those forces that decisively reject the capitulatory plans for a settlement drawn up at Camp David."[7]

While the Syrian-Iraqi reconciliation can be considered the most positive Arab development from the Soviet point of view to flow from Camp David, the limited rapprochement between the PLO and Jordan that occurred was also deemed a favorable development by the USSR, since it further reduced the chances of Jordanian participation in the Camp David accords and brought Jordan closer to an alignment with the anti-Sadat forces in the Arab world. The USSR itself was moving to tighten its relations with the PLO as Arafat visited the USSR in the latter part of October, and the USSR, for the first time, formally recognized the PLO as the sole legitimate representative of the Palestinian people. The communiqué issued by the two sides after the Moscow talks emphasized the "urgent task to rally and activize all the forces opposing anti-Arab separate deals."[8] Of particular concern for both the PLO and the USSR, perhaps the two actors most likely to suffer if the Camp David formula succeeded in attracting other Arab states, was the Arab summit which was scheduled for November 1 in Baghdad to react to the Camp David agreements. Soviet commentary prior to the conference was divided as to the expected results. Pavel Demchenko recalled that heretofore the lack of Arab unity had "aided the imperialists" and stated that while it was to be hoped that at Baghdad the Arabs, meeting without Egypt, would unify against Camp David, "it should be taken into consideration that the composition of the Baghdad Conference participants is not uniform sociopolitically"[9]—Soviet code words to describe the presence of such pro-Western Arab states as Saudi Arabia, the Sudan, North Yemen, and Oman. Vladimir Kudravtsev, usually a more optimistic Soviet observer, stated that while Egypt's breakaway was a grave loss to the Arab world, the Arabs were "capable of compensating for it by strengthening their unity."[10]

Given the rather hesitant Soviet comments prior to the conference, the Soviet leaders could only have been pleased by its results. Not only were the Camp David agreements condemned, with even Saudi Arabia participating in the condemnation (the Saudis may have been influenced, if not intimidated, by the Syrian-Iraqi rapprochement), but a joint PLO-Jordanian commission was established, an event that appeared to foreshadow further cooperation between these two erstwhile enemies. In addition, another reconciliation took place as the PLO and Iraq, which had been involved in an assassination campaign against each other in the summer, also appeared to end their conflict. Besides these reconciliations, specific anti-Egyptian measures were decided upon at Baghdad. Thus, the Arab League headquarters was to be removed from Cairo, and economic sanctions were planned against Egypt should Sadat go ahead with the signing of the treaty. Finally, the USSR must have been pleased by the Baghdad Conference's formula for a "just peace" in the Middle East: Israeli withdrawal from the territories captured in 1967 and the "right of the Palestinian people to establish an independent state on their national soil."[11] While the latter phrase was open to differing interpretations, the juxtaposition of the two statements seemed to indicate that even such radical states as Iraq and Libya might for the first time be willing grudgingly to accept Israel's existence. Although the Baghdad statement on peace was far from the trade, tourism and normal diplomatic relations wanted by the Israelis, it was very close to the peace formula that had been advocated by the USSR since 1976. In sum, the Soviet leadership was undoubtedly pleased with the results of the Baghdad summit, with one Soviet commentator deeming it "a final blow to imperialist intentions aimed at dissolving Arab unity and pressuring other Arabs to join Camp David."[12] An editorial in *New Times* emphasized Soviet satisfaction with the Arab response to Camp David even more clearly:

> Contrary to the prediction of some skeptics, Baghdad marked a transition from mere verbal avowals of solidarity to practical efforts to overcome differences between the Arab countries and to coordinate their actions. . . . Indicative are the meetings of representatives of Syria and Iraq held to discuss close unity of action between these two countries that used to be at loggerheads with each other. And could it be expected only a few months ago that an official delegation

from the Palestine Liberation Organization would be received in the
Royal Palace in Aman with all honors?[13]

While events in the Arab world seemed to be taking a favorable turn
for the USSR in the aftermath of Camp David, Moscow was also to profit
from the increasingly severe upheavals in Iran. Since the Nixon era, the United
States had depended on Iran to be its "policeman" in the Persian Gulf and
had given extensive amounts of arms to the Shah's armed forces. Indeed, under
the Shah's leadership, Iran had proven to be a major obstacle to Soviet ambitions in the Middle East. Iran's efforts to form a Persian Gulf Security Pact
seemed primarily aimed at keeping out Soviet influence. Iran's military aid
to Oman had helped defeat the PFLO insurgency backed by Moscow's ally,
the Peoples Democratic Republic of Yemen, and Iranian economic aid was
used to try to entice such Middle Eastern states as Afghanistan out of the
Soviet camp.[14] Iran also served as a moderating influence on the Arab-Israeli
conflict,[15] and the increasingly warm relations between Iran and Egypt seemed
to solidify the central American alliance system of the Middle East, composed
of Israel, Egypt, Iran and Saudi Arabia. Consequently, as domestic turmoil
in Iran increased sharply in the fall of 1978, the USSR welcomed the weakening
of the Shah's government and the increasing influence of exiled Muslim religious
leader Ayatollah Khomeini, if at first somewhat cautiously. To be sure, the
USSR now imported natural gas from Iran and the cut-off of natural gas exports
by striking petroleum workers was not welcomed. In addition, as a Muslim
fundamentalist, Khomeini posed a threat somewhat to Soviet control of its
large Muslim population. Nonetheless, most Soviet Muslims are Sunni, not
Shiite like the Ayatollah, and the Islamic threat was, at least for the short
run, essentially a theoretical one. On the other hand, however, if the United
States could be deprived of its major economic and military positions in Iran,
including sophisticated radar stations for checking the telemetry of Soviet
missiles, and if Iran could be detached from the American Middle Eastern
alliance system, the USSR would emerge with a clear gain in its influence
competition with the United States.[16] Thus, perhaps exploiting a November
13, 1978 statement by President Carter that the United States would not intervene in the Iranian situation, Brezhnev issued a warning on November 19 against
U.S. intervention in Iran.[17] At this point Soviet anti-American broadcasts to
Iran were stepped up—despite rather plaintive protests by Hodding Carter
and other State Department officials. Indeed, by claiming the United States
was sending troops and CIA officials to Iran, the USSR seemed to be trying
to inflame Iranian popular passions against the United States, a fairly transparent effort to expedite the elimination of American influence from Iran
as the revolutionary upheaval in Iran increased in intensity. Consequently,
following the departure of the Shah and the installation of the short-lived
Bakhtiar government, senior Soviet Middle East commentator Dmitry Volsky
expressed Soviet satisfaction with the trend of events in Iran:

The plans to knock together a pact in the Persian Gulf area and shore up CENTO have had to be shelved because of the events in Iran. . . . Whatever course the events in Iran may take, one thing is clear: never again will the West be able to rely on that country in its global strategy.[18]

Meanwhile, as it became increasingly evident that Khomeini would come to power, Moscow changed the leadership of the Tudeh Party. In place of the veteran Iraj Eskandrei, Nur Al-din Kianuri took over as first secretary. This may well have been a gesture to Khomeini's Islamic sympathies since Kianuri was the son of the well-known Iranian Islamic leader, Ayatollah Faztollah Nuri.[19]

While events in Iran were taking a marked anti-American turn (and consequently were seen as a net plus by the USSR in its zero-sum game competition for influence with the United States in the Middle East), events in other parts of the world were not moving in such a favorable direction for the Soviet Union. China, in particular, posed increasing problems for the USSR as it moved first to sign a long-term treaty with Japan and then, much to the surprise of most of the world, moved to establish formal diplomatic relations with the United States—the latter development being followed by a trip to the United States by Vice-Premier Teng Hsiao Ping, who used the opportunity to make a number of anti-Soviet pronouncements. On the other hand, however, the rapprochement between China and India slowed considerably following the subsequent Chinese invasion of Vietnam, thus weakening Chinese hopes of overcoming Moscow's policy of using India to contain China, although Peking was to persist in its efforts to improve ties with New Delhi.

While the efforts of Chinese diplomats were unquestionably of concern to Soviet leaders, Soviet attention remained centered on the Middle East peace settlement. Even before the Baghdad Conference, the United States sought to gain Israeli approval for a formal linkage between the two Camp David agreements so as to demonstrate to the other Arab states that Egypt was not deserting the Arab cause. Begin, under severe domestic pressure for having given up too much at Camp David, resisted both the American efforts at linkage and other United States efforts at interpreting the Camp David agreements in ways contrary to what he perceived as Israel's security interests. The end result was a collapse of the negotiations in mid-December 1978 as U.S. Secretary of State Vance delivered to Israel a set of Egyptian-American proposals that the Israelis found objectionable.[20] Commenting on the failure of the Vance mission, Volsky stated:

In the light of stiff Arab resistance to the Camp David deal, a frankly separate treaty, "ourtight capitulation," would mean the complete loss of political face for the Egyptian President.

. . . Evidently, this is what Begin is aiming at. He would like to see the Sadat regime fall into his lap like a ripe apple. However, this does not suit Washington, which has a stake in bringing not only Cairo but also Tel-Aviv closer to the "moderate" Arab states, especially the oil producers—particularly in view of the present crisis in Iran.[21]

While the Soviet leaders continued to deprecate the Carter administration's peace efforts, Moscow also made another of its periodic gestures to Israel. Thus, a group of Israeli parliamentarians representing a number of Israeli parties, including Labour, Mapam, the National Religious Party and the Israeli Communist Party, were invited to Moscow at the invitation of the Soviet Peace Committee.[22] In many ways reminiscent of the dispatch of Soviet representatives to Israel at the time of the United States Middle East policy "reappraisal" in 1975 and Gromyko's private talk with Abba Eban in 1973, it seemed to be a Soviet effort, at a turning point in Middle East affairs, to try to gain Israeli support for the Soviet Middle East peace plan.[23]

In addition to its gestures to Israel, the Soviet leadership also made an effort to improve relations with Saudi Arabia, hitherto its *bête noire* in the Arab world. Seeking to capitalize on the deterioration of American-Saudi relations caused by what the Saudis perceived as an insufficient U.S. response to Soviet activities in Ethiopia and Afghanistan and insufficient U.S. backing for the Shah, and what the United States perceived as the Saudi failure to support Carter's Camp David initiative and Saudi backing both for anti-Egyptian positions taken at the Baghdad Arab summit in November, and the OPEC decision to sharply increase oil prices in December, the Soviet leaders floated a trial balloon, via an article in the Soviet journal *Literaturnaia Gazeta*, that advocated improved Soviet-Saudi relations.[24] While the article evoked no immediate change in Saudi policy, it was clear that the Saudi regime was distancing itself from its close relationship with the United States, a development that was underscored when the Saudis refused an American offer of direct U.S. military aid to deal with the growing threat on their southern border caused by the PDRY's invasion of North Yemen in late February 1979 and the reactivization of the rebellion in Oman following the withdrawal of Iranian troops who had been helping the Sultan put down the Popular Front for the Liberation of Oman guerrillas there.

Indeed, following the collapse of the Shah's regime in Iran and the coming to power of Khomeini, American Middle East policy appeared to be in a shambles. As a result of the Baghdad Conference, Egypt appeared effectively isolated in the Middle East while the Egyptian-Israeli negotiations on achieving a peace treaty remained stalemated. In addition, the confused American response to the events in Iran—the dispatching and then the recalling three days later of a naval task force to the Persian Gulf—seemed to indicate that the Carter administration was unsure of the proper course to follow in the Middle East. Perhaps worst of all, the United States appeared humiliated as its Embassy was seized by leftists in Iran on February 14 (it was held for one day before

being freed by Khomeini's forces)[25] and its ambassador to Afghanistan, now a
Soviet client state, was murdered by terrorists.

Soviet satisfaction with the impact of the events in Iran on the Middle
East situation was summarized by *Izvestia*'s political commentator S. Kondrashov:

> Let us emphasize that the problems of American foreign policy have
> been aggravated since the victory of the national revolution in Iran.
> *The revolution is tantamount to a direct defeat of the United
> States since the structure that Washington erected over many years,
> in which Iran was assigned the role of "policeman of the Persian
> Gulf" has collapsed* . . . .
>
> Another aspect of the situation is that the Iranian revolution,
> which combines the features of a revolution of national liberation
> with those of a religious and Islamic revolution, has stimulated
> opposition by the Islamic Arab states to a separate Israeli-Egyptian
> agreement under Washington's aegis. This is evident, for example,
> in Saudi Arabia's position. The Americans . . . . attempted to intimi-
> date this influential Arab country with the possible consequences of
> Iranian events and to impose on it the traditional American concept
> of "stability" through arms buildup, official or de facto member-
> ship in military blocs, and some form or another of American
> "military presence." The Saudis failed to swallow this bait and
> reacted critically to a concept of "stability" that had just suffered
> its latest failure in Iran . . . in the opinion of political observers,
> Riyadh has taken another step politically away from Washington
> and Cairo. When one looks closely at the position of various Arab
> states, one sees that the spirit of decisive resistance to Camp David,
> which united them at the Baghdad Conference last October, has
> grown even stronger in the atmosphere created by the events in
> Iran . . . .
>
> In Egypt, Sadat has been forced to take a careful look not
> only at Saudi Arabia and the other Arab states that oppose the
> separate deal but also at the events in Iran and the fate of the
> Shah . . . . *Doubts and apprehension have increased among those
> who so closely linked their present and future with Uncle Sam,
> contrary to the interests of their people.*[26] [emphasis added]

The South Yemeni invasion of North Yemen may perhaps be understood
against this background of the apparently weakening American position in the
Middle East. To be sure, the North Yemeni regime was itself weak and had
suffered two major coup attempts as well as the murder of its president in less
than a year.[27] At the same time the PDRY had a long history of conflict with
the North, and relations between the two Yemeni states had alternated between
open warfare and discussions of unification since 1972. Nonetheless, the timing

of the PDRY invasion of American-backed North Yemen does not appear accidental. Coming only a week after the establishment of the Khomeini regime in Iran and the leftist seizure of the U.S. embassy in that country, it appears as if the USSR, in giving its consent to its client's desire to invade North Yemen, was seeking to create a bandwagon effect to further erode American influence in the Middle East. In many ways the situation appeared similar to that of September 1970 when, after a series of American Middle Eastern reverses (the fall of the pro-Western government in Libya, the establishment of a major Soviet military presence in Egypt, and the Soviet-Egyptian violation of the American-mediated cease-fire agreement between Egypt and Israel), Moscow gave its tacit approval for a Syrian move into Jordan to help the Palestinian guerrillas in their war against King Hussein.[28] In both invasions, the USSR could remain in the background, but would profit if the pro-American regime was toppled by the Soviet client state's invasion. Interestingly enough, however, if indeed this was the Soviet goal in both invasions, in neither was it successful. In the case of Jordan, a clear American warning to the USSR, coupled with American-Israeli military maneuvers, managed to limit the Syrian invasion and an Arab League meeting provided the face-saving cover for the Syrian withdrawal (the Syrians, meanwhile, had been badly battered by King Hussein's air force). A similar pattern occurred in the case of North Yemen. The United States coupled open warnings to the USSR about discontinuing logistic support for the South Yemeni invasion with two major military moves of its own. In the first place it dispatched the U.S. aircraft carrier Constellation along with supporting vessels to the Arabian Sea—this time, without recalling them. Secondly, it began a major $390 million military supply effort to North Yemen including F-5 jets, tanks, and armored personnel carriers, together with more than 100 American instructors to aid the North Yemenis in using the new equipment.[29]

In addition to the United States military moves, another factor that may have prompted the South Yemenis and their Soviet advisors to terminate the invasion was the active mediation efforts of an Arab League team led by representatives from Iraq, Syria, and Jordan. The USSR clearly had no desire to alienate any of these three opponents of the Camp David agreements—particularly since in early March President Carter launched a personal effort to achieve the Egyptian-Israeli peace treaty. The end result of the Arab mediation effort was a ceasefire agreement, the withdrawal of the PDRY troops, and an agreement by the presidents of both South and North Yemen to undertake negotiations about the unification of their two countries.

In evaluating the impact of the PDRY invasion of North Yemen on Soviet policy in the Middle East, one can see mixed results for Moscow. On the one hand, were the projected unity talks to be successful, the USSR might be able to expand its influence into North Yemen. This possibility, however, would be countered if Saudi Arabia, which currently exercises considerable influence in North Yemen, were able to extend it southwards, as it has sought to do through offers of economic aid to the PDRY in the past. Secondly, Moscow may not have been too happy that its clients, Syria and especially Iraq, moved to terminate the PDRY invasion before it had a major chance of success. Finally, the invasion of North Yemen, coming on the heels of the fall of the Shah in Iran, seems to have galvanized the United States into taking a more active military role in the Middle East. Indeed, following these two events, serious consideration began to be given in Washington for the establishing of a Fifth fleet and a Rapid Deployment Force for the Indian Ocean/Persian Gulf area.[30]

In sum, therefore, the Soviet gamble on the PDRY invasion of North Yemen—if, indeed, a gamble it was—may turn out to have been a mistake for the USSR, much as Soviet support for the Syrian invasion of Jordan in 1970 turned out to be.

While the USSR was closely following the events in the Yemeni civil war, it had also to be concerned with the renewed American efforts to bring about an Israeli-Egyptian agreement. Thus, Cyrus Vance met with Israeli Foreign Minister Dayan and Egyptian Prime Minister Khalil in Camp David in late February, and the diplomatic momentum was then increased with a Begin-Carter meeting in Washington, and Carter's final (and successful) visit to Egypt and Israel in mid-March. The end result was a peace treaty signed by Begin and Sadat and witnessed by Carter in Washington on March 26, 1979.

The Egyptian-Israeli Peace Treaty was similar to its Camp David prototype in many ways.[31] Thus Israel agreed to give up the entire Sinai Peninsula, in stages, over a three year period and Egypt agreed to limit the forces it would station in the Sinai. As a gesture to Egypt, Israel also agreed to a limited forces zone on its side of the border. In addition, a United Nations force was to be installed along the border between Israel and Egypt, one that could be removed only with the unanimous approval of the permanent members of the United Nations Security Council. A second main principle of Camp David also became part of the treaty: the establishment of diplomatic, economic and cultural relations, along with the passage of Israeli ships through the Suez Canal, and freedom of travel through the Straits of Tiran and the Gulf of Aqaba. Wording about linkage between the Egyptian-Israeli treaty and a more comprehensive peace settlement was included both in the treaty preamble and in a joint letter from Begin and Sadat to President Carter accompanying the treaty in which the two Middle Eastern leaders pledged to begin negotiations within a month of their treaty's ratification to implement the provisions of the Camp David agreement pertaining to the West Bank and Gaza. Sadat and Begin specifically stated that the purpose of their negotiations, in which the United States would "participate fully," and in which Jordan would be invited to participate, "shall be to agree, prior to the elections, on the modalities for establishing the elected self-governing authority and defining its powers and responsibilities." Israel and Egypt set a one year "goal" to complete the negotiations, although no specific deadline was set. Following the talks, which Egypt and Israel pledged to negotiate in "good faith," the inhabitants of the West Bank and Gaza would obtain full "autonomy," the Israeli military government and its civilian administration would be withdrawn, and the Israeli forces would be deployed into specified "security locations." As in Camp David, the issue of the ultimate disposition of the West Bank and Gaza, the nature of "autonomy" and the future role of Israel in the areas were left open.

In addition to agreeing to participate in the negotiations on West Bank autonomy, the United States also pledged increased economic and military aid to both Israel and Egypt and, in a special letter to Sadat and Begin, President Carter pledged that (subject to United States constitutional processes) the United States would intervene in case of an actual or threatened violation of the treaty and would move to establish a substitute multinational force between Israel and Egypt if the United Nations Security Council failed to create one. Israel, still concerned that the Sadat regime or a future Egyptian government might renege on the treaty, received additional American assurances to compensate it for giving up the Sinai in a separate memorandum of agreement with the United States. In it the United States pledged to provide Israel with support in case of a demonstrated violation of the peace treaty, such as a blockade of Israel's use of international waterways, a violation of the treaty provisions concerning Egypt's force limitations in the Sinai Peninsula, or an armed attack against Israel. Additionally, the United States extended to 15 years the pledge first made at the time of the Sinai II agreement of September 1, 1975, to help provide Israel with oil.

As in the case of the Camp David agreements, President Carter quickly dispatched one of his top aides (Zbigniew Brzezinski) to the Middle East to help gain support for the Egyptian-Israeli treaty. Once again, however, the effort did not meet with success as Jordan and Saudi Arabia, which Brzezinski had visited on his trip, voted along with the Arab rejectionists to impose sanctions against Egypt at the second Baghdad Conference, which met after the treaty signing. The sanctions included suspension of Egypt's membership in the Arab League, withdrawal of all Arab ambassadors from Cairo, the severing of all political and diplomatic relations with Egypt, and the cutting off of all economic aid to Egypt.[32] Although these provisions were voted unanimously (the Sudan and Oman did not attend the conference and came out in support of Sadat), it remained to be seen whether the rest of the Arab world could successfully isolate its most populous and militarily powerful member, a possibility Moscow would watch with close attention.

SOVIET PROBLEMS IN THE AFTERMATH OF THE EGYPTIAN-ISRAELI TREATY

As the Egyptian-Israeli treaty negotiations neared completion, the USSR stepped up its criticism of what it disparagingly termed a "separate deal." On the eve of the signing ceremonies, Soviet Foreign Minister Andrei Gromyko was dispatched to Syria where he held talks with Assad, Arafat, and also leaders of the Syrian Communist Party. The purpose of the visit was to coordinate the stands of the USSR and Syria in opposing the Egyptian-Israeli treaty, and the communiqué that was issued following the Assad-Gromyko talks both denounced the "separate deal" and urged Arab unity to oppose it, placing special emphasis on Syrian-Iraqi cooperation and the need to implement the anti-Egyptian Baghdad resolutions.[33] The communiqué's emphasis on the "paramount importance" of developing political ties, however, seemed to sidestep the issue of the continuing Syrian call for more weapons, and in an airport interview Gromyko limited the areas in which the stands of the USSR and Syria coincided to the "Camp David separate deal and the Egyptian-Israeli treaty imposed by the United States."[34]

The Egyptian-Israeli treaty was signed on the same day Gromyko returned to Moscow from Damascus, and, as might have been expected, it provoked a very sharp Soviet reaction. Sadat was attacked for his "capitulation," the United States for its plans to create "a new military-police structure based on the Tel Aviv-Cairo axis," and Israel for trying to "blackmail" moderate Arab states such as Saudi Arabia into backing the "separate deal." China, which had been encouraging Egypt's opposition to the Soviet drive for hegemony in the Middle East, and which had given its tacit support for the Camp David agreements, was also singled out for censure.[35]

By contrast, the second Baghdad Conference, which met soon after the signing of the treaty, received high praise from the USSR as it appeared that most of the Arab world, including such "moderates" as Saudi Arabia, Jordan, and Kuwait, had taken a firm anti-Egyptian position. *Pravda* commentator Arkady Maslennikov, summed up Moscow's satisfaction with Baghdad II:

> The decisions made by the Baghdad Conference of 18 Arab states on the severing of diplomatic and political relations with Cairo and cutting off of its economic support, are putting the Egyptian regime in a position of isolation in the Arab world and, in doing so, are greatly weakening Sadat's position in both foreign and domestic affairs. . . .
>
> The chief source of concern for Washington is undoubtedly the fact that, contrary to expectations, the solidarity of the Arab states and anti-American sentiment in the Middle East have not only failed to diminish as a result of the "Camp David peace" but have considerably increased. . . .[36]

Carrying this theme further, *Pravda* commentator Yuri Glukhov, in his evaluation of Baghdad, noted approvingly:

> Certain participants in the meeting demanded not only the imposition of sanctions on Egypt, but also the application of resolute measures with respect to Washington, including an oil embargo.

And although this proposal was not adopted, the Conference's anti-imperialist mood was itself indicative.[37]

In assessing their position in the Middle East following the completion of the second Baghdad Conference, the Soviet leaders may well have been satisfied at the sharp improvement in their position—and the concommitant weakening of the American position—since the low point of Soviet Middle East fortunes following the end of the civil war in Lebanon in October 1976. Their hopes of a unified, "anti-imperialist" bloc of Arab states (albeit one without Egypt or the Sudan) seemed on the way to being realized as even such one-time allies of the United States, Saudi Arabia, Kuwait, and Jordan criticized the Egyptian-Israeli treaty and the U.S. role in achieving it. In addition, the once hostile Arab Ba'athist states, Syria and Iraq, were now cooperating and this development, together with the ouster of the Shah of Iran and the rise to power of pro-Soviet regimes in Ethiopia and Afghanistan, seemed to tilt the Middle East balance of forces toward the USSR.

Yet the new Middle East situation still posed its problems for Soviet policy makers. In the first place, Iraq, which was the primary leader of the anti-Egyptian forces of the Arab world, and whose diplomatic efforts helped make both Baghdad conferences successful, had distanced itself somewhat from the USSR because of differences over both domestic and foreign policies. Secondly, the situation in Iran remained fluid as anti-Soviet as well as anti-American statements were issued by the new Iranian leaders, and Moscow may have been concerned that Iran might gravitate back toward the West because of its severe internal and external problems. Finally, Moscow was encountering increasing difficulties with its new client regime in Afghanistan as Muslim rebels made increasingly successful inroads against it.

Iraq had been one of the USSR's primary Arab allies since 1972 when Sadat had ousted Soviet military advisors from Egypt, and Iraq and the Soviet Union had signed a Treaty of Friendship and Cooperation. Soviet aid had proven most useful to the Ba'athist leaders of Iraq as they nationalized the Iraq Petroleum Company, developed their military forces to combat the Iranian military buildup, and sought to terminate the rebellion of the Kurds who inhabit the northern section of Iraq. In return for Soviet assistance the Ba'athist regime, in addition to anti-Western pronouncements, made a number of gestures to the USSR which included the appointment of two Iraqi Communists to cabinet positions in 1972 and the establishment of a National Front where the Iraqi Communist Party could legally participate. The latter development, however, occurred after a major coup attempt against the Al-Bakr government in 1973, and may have been more of a ploy to help stabilize the Ba'athist regime than a commitment to allow the Iraqi Communists a genuine role in governing the country. Indeed, by prohibiting the Iraqi Communists from recruiting in the army or Ba'ath Party, the Ba'athists evidently hoped to keep the Communist role to a minimum while at the same time guarding against attempted coup d'états.[38]

The issue of the Iraqi Communist Party and its periodic persecution by the authorities had long been a problem clouding Soviet-Iraqi relations, but it did not emerge as a serious issue until 1978. By this time Iraq, which had greatly profited from the quadrupling of oil prices in 1973, was actively developing its economy and was increasingly turning to the West and Japan, rather than to the USSR and East Europe, for assistance. At the same time Iraq had become disturbed over Soviet aid to the Ethiopian regime which was suppressing the Iraqi-supported Eritreans. Still another issue that had arisen between the two countries was Iraq's decision to maintain good relations with Peking despite the serious Sino-Soviet rift. Indeed, by 1978, Iraq was far less in need of Soviet support than earlier. With its oil fields now operating, its problems with the Kurds essentially solved (although some guerrilla fighting continued), and its long border conflict with Iran terminated by the 1975 Iraqi-Iranian treaty, the Ba'athist regime was moving to take a more independent position in world affairs.

Despite the outward signs of prosperity, however, the Iraqi regime remained very much a police state and the Ba'athist Party, which came to power twice by means of a military coup, was intent on protecting itself against the same tactic. At the same time, the Iraqi Communist Party (ICP) became increasingly unhappy with its virtually powerless position in the Iraqi government and began to openly advocate an increased role for itself in the National Front. In addition, the ICP began to advocate genuine autonomy for the Kurds (the Iraqi government had imposed an autonomy plan that left the central government in control of all key aspects of Kurdish life) and openly opposed the Ba'athist policy of resettling Kurds outside of Kurdistan. Clearly unhappy with the Westward drift of the Iraqi economy, the ICP also condemned the growing power of "private capital" and Iraq's "continuing dependence on the capitalist world market."[39]

In addition to making these open criticisms of Ba'athist policy, the Communists reportedly sought to form secret cells in the Iraqi armed forces and carried on anti-government propaganda among Iraq's Kurds and Shiites—the groups most disaffected with the Sunni Ba'athist rule in Iraq.[40] Given the nature of the Iraqi regime, which has not hesitated to liquidate any outspoken opponents of the regime whether or not they resided in Iraq, it appeared only a matter of time until the crackdowns occurred.[41] While persecution of the ICP became increasingly open in 1977, the Iraqi government decided to execute a number of Communists in the spring of 1978. Possibly reacting to the army-based, pro-Soviet coup in nearby Afghanistan, the Ba'athist regime evidently decided that the crackdown took precedence over its relations with the USSR. Indeed, as Naim Haddad, one of the leaders of Iraq's ruling Revolutionary Command Council bluntly stated, "All Communist parties all over the world are always trying to get power. We chop off any weed that pops up."[42]

The executions cast a pall over Soviet-Iraqi relations, despite the protestations of Iraqi leaders that they wanted good relations with the USSR. Significantly, however, Haddad stated: "the Soviet Union is a friend with whom we can cooperate as long as there is no interference in our internal affairs."[43] Relations improved, however, following the rapprochement between Syria and Iraq and Iraq's diplomatic leadership of the anti-Sadat conference at Baghdad in November 1978. The climate had improved to the point that by December Iraqi strongman Saddam Hussein himself was invited to Moscow.

While the main purpose of Hussein's visit was to coordinate the Soviet and Iraqi positions opposing Camp David, it appears that other issues occupied the discussions as well. These included Soviet-Iraqi trade relations, problems pertaining to Iraq's Communist Party, and the Soviet supply of arms to Iraq following Camp David. In this regard there were a number of reports in the Western press that both Syria and Iraq were asking for sharp increases in Soviet weapons supplies to compensate the Arabs for Egypt's departure from the Arab camp.[44] The USSR, however, reportedly told Syria and Iraq that since they were now cooperating they could pool their weapons.[45] In taking this stand the USSR may have been concerned that if the Syrians and Iraqis were too well armed they might provoke a war against Israel at a time inconvenient for the USSR.[46]

While there appeared to have been progress on the question of economic relations during the talks, the outcome of the military aid question was not as clear with the final communiqué stipulating only that "the sides reiterated their readiness to keep cooperating in strengthening the defense capacity of the Iraqi Republic."[47] Even less was said on the subject of the Iraqi Communist Party, and the only public reference (and a veiled one at that) to this area of conflict in Soviet-Iraqi relations was made in a dinner speech by Kosygin who stated:

> Friendly relations with the Republic of Iraq are highly valued in the Soviet Union and we are doing everything to make them more durable. This is our firm course and it is not affected by circumstantial considerations."[48]

If the Soviet leadership sought to use the Brezhnev-Hussein meeting to secure improved treatment for the Iraqi Communists, it was not successful. Less than a month later, on January 10, 1979, *Pravda* published an editorial from the Iraqi Communist paper *Tariq Ash-Shab* deploring "the widespread persecution of Communists in Iraq and repression against the Communist Party's organization and press," and *Pravda* followed the editorial up three days later by publishing the statement of the December 1978 Conference of Arab Communist parties which similarly condemned Iraq for its treatment of the ICP.[49]

The anti-Iraqi campaign in the Soviet press is of particular interest. In the past, the USSR had grudgingly tolerated attacks on local Communist parties, so long as the regime responsible adopted a proper "anti-imperialist" stance. Indeed, the USSR has even gone so far as to urge the dissolution of Arab Communist parties or their restriction to the role of teachers of "scientific socialism" in Third World countries to avoid such conflicts.[50] It may well be, therefore, that Moscow saw more than just a domestic problem in Iraq's persecution of the ICP, which continued through the first half of 1979. Iraq, in leading the opposition to the Egyptian-Israeli treaty, was seeking to project itself as the leader of the Arab world. In order to accomplish this task successfully, however, Iraq had not only to arrange a rapprochement with Syria; it had to establish a working relationship with Saudi Arabia as well, the Arab world's leading financier, and a growing Persian Gulf military power. The Soviet leadership may have suspected, therefore, that the overt anti-Communist campaign in Iraq was designed to signal to the Saudis that Iraq was no longer a close ally of the USSR, and when Iraqi strongman Saddam Hussein went so far as to state that "We reject the wide expansion by the Soviet Union in the Arab homeland" and that "the Arabs should fight anyone—even friends like the Soviets who try to occupy Saudi land," this may have confirmed Soviet suspicions.[51]

Yet another factor which may have tarnished somewhat Iraq's usefulness to the USSR as leader of the anti-Sadat and anti-American forces in the Arab world was the eruption of a serious quarrel between Iraq and the PDRY, the most Marxist of the Soviet Union's Arab allies. An Iraqi Communist Party member, Taufiq Rushdi, who had been lecturing in South Yemen, was murdered —apparently by a team of Iraqi security men attached to Iraq's Aden embassy. In reprisal, a PDRY force stormed the Iraqi Embassy and seized the gunmen.[52] This incident, which was bitterly protested by Iraq, came on the heels of Iraq's intervention in the PDRY invasion of North Yemen, which cut short any hopes the PDRY had of toppling the North Yemeni regime. Yet another issue exacerbating Iraqi-PDRY relations was the Iraqi move to improve ties with North Yemen by offering SANA a $300-million loan.[53]

While the USSR had to be somewhat concerned about these new directions in Iraqi foreign policy, despite Iraq's continued anti-American rhetoric and leadership in the drive for higher OPEC oil prices (which aided the USSR as a major exporter of oil), another development was calling into question the solidarity of the "anti-Western" bloc in the Middle East which seemed to have come into being following the Iranian Revolution. The problem for the USSR stemmed from developments in Iran which, after the overthrow of the Shah and the Bahktiar regime, had become enbroiled in domestic difficulties that soon spilled over to affect its foreign policy.

One of the central problems which was to cause serious difficulties for the Iranian revolutionary authorities was a diffusion of power.[54] Thus, in addition to the "official" government of Mehdi Bazargan, there was an unofficial, but much more powerful government headed by the Ayatollah Khomeini, himself, and a semi-independent revolutionary court system as well. Opposition to the new regime came from many quarters. In the first place there were two armed guerrilla organizations, the Marxist "Cherika Fedaye Khalk" and the Islamic "Mujaheddin Khalk," which challenged a number of Khomeini's policies. Secondly, there were liberals grouped around Karim Sanjabi, who had briefly served as foreign minister of the new regime, and Hedayat Matine-Daftary, the grandson of former Prime Minister Mossadeq. The liberals openly opposed Khomeini's restrictive policies toward women as well as Iran's Islamic courts and their summary executions. Opposition to Khomeini even came from his fellow religious leaders such as the Ayatollahs Taleghani and Shariat-Madri, who called for a more liberal regime. Underpinning much of the growth of domestic discontent in Iran was the sharp rise in unemployment and the near collapse of the nonoil sector of the Iranian economy. As if these domestic problems and challenges were not sufficient, Iran's revolutionary government also encountered trouble from many of the ethnic minorities who live along Iran's borders. Seizing the opportunity presented by the disintegration of the Shah's regime—and of the Iranian army—a number of Iran's ethnic minorities demanded autonomy. The end result was bloody clashes between the central authorities and Iran's Kurds, Turkomans, Baluchis and Arabs.

Inevitably, some of these domestic conflicts spilled over Iran's borders. Thus as the Kurds agitated for independence, this inevitably affected the Kurds living in Iraq who, after receiving arms from their brethren in Iran, rekindled their war against the Ba'athist regime in Iraq. This, in turn, led to Iraqi bombing of Kurdish border villages in Iran and a sharp deterioration in Iranian-Iraqi relations.[55] Further disturbing relations between the two states were charges by the Iranian governor general of Khuzistan that Iraq had smuggled weapons into the region in which most of Iran's ethnic Arabs live, and an Iraqi crackdown on Shiite religious leaders in Iraq who had maintained close relations with Khomeini.[56] Iran's clash with Iraq also affected its relations with other Arab states when, in response to Iraqi demands that Iran return the three Arab islands in the Straits of Hormuz seized by the Shah in 1971, a religious leader close to Khomeini reasserted Iran's claim to Bahrein, which the Shah had renounced in 1970.[57]

The rise in Iranian-Arab tensions served to further split the camp of the anti-Sadat Arabs, with Kuwait and Bahrein lining up behind Iraq while Libya and the PLO, which had been early supporters of Khomeini, continued to back the Iranians.[58] In the case of the PLO, which had hailed the revolution in Iran as causing a "decisive change in the Middle East balance of power against Israel," support for Iran may have been a defensive move to keep its special relationship with Khomeini since the PLO, which had an office in Ahwaz, a city in Khuzistan, may have been implicated in the Arab drive for autonomy. Indeed, Iran's Deputy Prime Minister Abbas Entezam stated in a press conference on April 12 that "our warm and friendly welcome for the Palestinians could have caused some misunderstanding for them as far as their stand and activities in Iran are concerned."[59]

The growing tension between Iran and Iraq also had its affect on Iranian-Soviet relations, as a front page editorial in a government-supported newspaper, the *Islamic Republic*, claimed that "the ruling clique in Iraq" was plotting against Iran both to "prevent the spread of Iran's Islamic revolution into Iraq" and to "open the road to the warm waters of the Persian Gulf to their big master"—a clear reference to the Soviet Union.[60] The Iraqi-Iranian conflict was not the only problem marring Soviet-Iranian relations, however. As the fundamentalist Islamic regime sought to consolidate its hold, it ran into conflict not only with Iran's ethnic minorities but with the Marxist guerrilla organization, the Cherika Fedaye Khalk, as well. While the Marxist Fedaye group claimed it was independent of Moscow, its aid to ethnic minorities fighting the central government soon associated it in the public mind with the pro-Soviet Iranian Communist party, the Tudeh. Then, when a key leader of the Khomeini regime, Ayatollah Motahari, was assassinated, the crowds demonstrating at his funeral began to shout anti-Communist slogans, a development that cast a further pall on Soviet-Iranian relations.[61]

Another major obstacle to close Soviet-Iranian ties, however, was the guerrilla war in Afghanistan on which the two countries took opposing positions. While Khomeini denied the allegations by the Soviet-supported Afghan regime—allegations that received wide publicity in the Soviet press—[62] that Iran was aiding the Islamic guerrillas fighting the Afghan government, there is no question but that the sympathies of Khomeini and his supporters were clearly behind the Afghani rebels. Indeed, Khomeini ordered broadcast over Iranian state radio a heated exchange between himself and the Soviet Ambassador Valdimir M. Vinogradov in which the Iranian religious leader told the Soviet Ambassador:

> Afghanistan is an Islamic country and their problems should be solved in an Islamic way. Russian interference in Afghanistan also affects Iran. We want Russia to stop interfering in Afghanistan's affairs. . . . The present government in Afghanistan is oppressing people in the name of Communism. We have been informed that 50,000 people have been killed in Afghanistan and that Islamic religious leaders have been arrested there.[63]

As anti-Soviet feelings began to rise in Iran, the Soviet leaders seemed to be unsure as to the proper reaction. Their initial warm support of the new regime's actions such as leaving CENTO, terminating relations with and oil shipments to Israel, and breaking diplomatic relations with Egypt following the Egyptian-Israeli peace treaty began to give way to a number of doubts about the regime. Thus while *Pravda* on March 1 hailed the "process of stabilization of the revolutionary regime," by March 24 the authoritative Soviet newspaper was warning:

> Quite a few difficult problems arising from the multinational structure of Iran's population are on the (Iranian) agenda. Problems artificially created by counterrevolutionary forces and imperialist agents add to the objective difficulties. Enemies of the Iranian people are trying to sow discord and incite clashes among the various

parties, trends and groups that through their joint actions ensured the victory of the revolution.

Reactionary and imperialist agents are using various methods and means of provoking friction between Iran and surrounding states—the USSR in particular. For this purpose, provocational slanderous rumors are being circulated about "Soviet interference in Iranian affairs, the dispatching of 'Soviet agents' and the Soviet Union's interest in 'dismembering' Iran." Obviously, lies about the USSR's "inherent hostility" toward "all Moslem countries" are spread from the same source.

These gentlemen are wasting their energy! They will not succeed in starting a quarrel between Iran and the Soviet Union and alienating the peoples of the two neighboring states.[64]

Despite such disclaimers, however, the USSR soon began to openly criticize the policies of Iran's new government, if at first relatively gently. Thus, on March 29 "local authorities" were accused of allowing "fanatical Afghan elements" to attack the Afghani Embassy in Tehran and the Afghani Consulate in Meshed,[65] and one month later the central Iranian government was criticized for being insensitive to worker demands and for being infiltrated by the Iranian bourgeoisie which "believes that the revolution has already achieved its goals and is completed even though the country's economic foundation and social structure remain unchanged."[66]

The anti-Communist demonstration that accompanied the funeral of the assassinated Iranian leader, Ayatollah Motahari, provoked much sharper Soviet criticism:

Despite the clear-cut position of the democratic forces and despite the facts and circumstances that have already become known, certain groups in Iran see the political murders as a pretext for unleashing a wide-scale campaign against the left-wing of the revolution. Slanderously ascribing the responsibility for the terrorist acts to "Marxists and their allies," these groups would like to exclude the parties and forces that made the greatest sacrifices in the struggle against the Shah's regime and that performed undeniable services in the victory of the revolution from having any further influence over issues of vital importance to the Iranian people.

These groups, whose social and political character may be precisely termed reactionary, have been joined by individual representatives of the Iranian clergy, as evidenced in particular by the address given by the religious figure Rafsanjani at the funeral of the slain Motahari in Qum. His speech contained attacks on Communists and other selfless fighters against the Shah and imperialism, and it also attacked friends of independent Iran, including the Soviet Union.[67]

As the anti-Communist and anti-Soviet forces increased their activity in Iran, the USSR had to be increasingly concerned. On the one hand, even with the rise in anti-Communist feeling in Iran, Moscow was far better off with the neutralist policies of the Khomeini regime than it was with the Shah. Khomeini had pulled Iran out of CENTO, detached Iran from the American Middle East alliance system, advocated sharply increased oil prices, and given support to the PLO, now one of the most pro-Soviet and anti-American forces in the Middle East. In addition, the Khomeini regime continued to clash with the United States over the legacy of the Shah's rule and the rising number of executions of Iranians.

On the other hand, however, Iran's quarrels with Iraq had helped split the anti-Sadat forces in the Middle East, while the insurgency in Afghanistan, which was supported by Iran and opposed by the USSR, along with Iran's internal problems, held the possibility of once again aligning Iran with the West, although most probably not as closely as before. For these reasons, therefore, as the Soviet leaders watched the developments in Iran, their satisfaction over the fall of the Shah had to be increasingly tempered by concern over the future direction of Iran's internal politics and foreign policy.

Indeed, as the summer wore on, Moscow's concern about Iranian developments heightened. While the new government took a number of actions that the Soviet leaders viewed favorably, such as the cancellation of a multi-billion dollar arms deal with the United States (for such weapons as the F-16 fighter, AWACS aircraft, and destroyers),[68] and the nationalization of Iranian banks and a number of industries,[69] Moscow was far less happy with Iran's decision to cease construction of a second natural gas pipeline to the USSR which was to supply natural gas to the Soviet Union as well as West Germany, France, Austria, and Czechoslovakia.[70] Neither was Moscow happy with the demands by the Iranians for higher prices for the natural gas being shipped through the first pipeline.

A far more serious problem for the USSR in its dealings with Khomeini, however, lay in the autonomy drive by a number of Iranian nationalities. While Moscow denied the charges that it was involved in aiding the "secessionists," the Islamic leaders remembered the Soviet role in Azerbaizhan and Kurdistan in World War II and the immediate postwar period. In addition they could not help but notice the statement by Kurdish Democratic Party leader Abder Rahman Ghassemlou, who asserted "We are democrats and we respect all Marxist-Leninist groups. They can work freely in Kurdistan"; or Kurdish religious leader Sheikh Izzedin's assertion, "I believe in socialism and I believe God will be pleased by it too."[71] The fact that the Soviet media viewed Ghassemlou and Sheikh Izzedin positively[72] and that the Tudeh Party openly proclaimed its intention to begin "organizational activity" in Kurdistan[73] may also not have been lost on the Iranian leaders, who viewed the Kurdish separatist drive as treason to Iran. Indeed, the Iranian Deputy Prime Minister Sadek Tabatabai, tied by a family relationship to Khomeini, claimed "what has happened in Kurdistan and Khuzistan and what will happen in Baluchistan is the result of the activities of agitators and agents provocateurs," and he made direct reference to Soviet action in Baluchistan.[74] The USSR reacted sharply to Tabatabai's statement, with *Pravda* on June 22 not only denying Soviet involvement, but also warning "It is impossible to ignore statements of this sort, which are made for the purpose of casting a pall over relations between our two countries."

Yet Moscow was clearly in a dilemma as the Iranians using Muslim fundamentalist and anti-Communist revolutionary guards (Pasdaran) went on the offensive against the Kurds and other Iranian groups seeking autonomy. On the one hand the USSR certainly did not wish to alienate the new Iranian regime and drive it back toward the United States. On the other hand, elements more sympathetic to Moscow than the increasingly fundamentalist regime in Tehran were trying to preserve a modicum of freedom of action in such regions as Kurdistan, and Moscow may well have hoped that, given the still tenuous nature of Khomeini's rule, such forces might yet increase their influence in Iran, and for this reason the USSR did not want to see them destroyed. Consequently, as the summer wore on, Soviet propaganda became increasingly sympathetic to the Kurdish rebels and increasingly hostile toward government attempts to repress them.[75]

Compounding the Soviet problem was the overall crackdown on all liberal and leftist groups by Muslim fundamentalists, a development that reflected the steady erosion of Prime Minister Bazargan's authority. Included among the victims of the Iranian crackdown were not only the Fedayeen and Mujahadeen (one of whose members was imprisoned for spying for the USSR),[76] but also the Tudeh, whose offices were burned, whose newspaper (*Mardom*) was closed, and of whose members two were summarily executed in Kurdistan. The USSR reacted to these developments by publishing, in *Pravda*, the open letters from the Tudeh to the Iranian government protesting these acts,[77] while also publishing, for the first time, an article personally critical of Khomeini in *Izvestia*'s weekend supplement (*Nedelia*), by a senior Soviet correspondent, Alexander Bovin. Bovin's article painted a bleak picture of Iran under the revolutionary regime, noting that "all publications expressing views that differ from official religious-ideological doctrines have been shut down and forbidden," "persons advocating progressive social transformation . . . are being persecuted under the guise of 'hunting communists,'" and "ethnic minorities who want autonomy and equal rights are declared to be traitors." Bovin also blasted the Islamic tribunals headed by Ayatollah Khalkhali (previously he had been praised for rooting out Savak agents tied to the United States) and quoted such statements of Khomeini's as "Islam is a religion of blood." He also warned that the Iranian people would "reap no benefit from the stirring up of religious fanaticism and anti-communist hysteria" and denounced "the endeavor to present the policy and intentions of a friendly country in a false light."[78] Reinforcing the growing Soviet unhappiness with Iran was the Iranian government's decision in early September to ask the United States to resume shipping military spare parts.[79] This move, coupled with the attacks on the Tudeh Party, may have raised the fear in the Kremlin that Iran was shifting back toward the United States. Indeed, in an article discussing Iran's "troubled August" in the Soviet foreign policy weekly *New Times*, Alexander Usvatov stated:

> The attacks on the progressive, democratic forces which took an active part in the anti-Shah movement, and the setting of political, national, and religious groups against one another—in a word, the splitting and undermining of the unity of the front that over-threw the monarchy—play only into the hands of imperialism and reaction.[80]

While the Soviet leaders were watching developments in Iran with increasing concern, they were also preparing for a summit with the United States. After extensive and difficult negotiations both Moscow and Washington had finally agreed upon a SALT agreement. Long a major Soviet foreign policy objective, the USSR greeted the signing of the SALT II agreement at the June 1979 summit in Vienna with a great deal of enthusiasm and, not surprisingly, as in past Soviet-American summits, the Middle East received little official mention. Nonetheless, while the Middle East was very much on the minds of both super-powers, they could find very little to agree on.[81]

In the period before the summit, the USSR had continued to denounce the Egyptian-Israeli peace treaty, as well as the proposed U.S. Middle East strike force which the Soviet media projected as a threat against the Arabs and Iran. Interestingly enough, however, Moscow sent its own naval task force to South Yemen at the end of May,[82] possibly as a subtle means of pressure against North Yemen or as a means of reassurance to the PRDY in the face of the major U.S. military buildup of North Yemen. The United States, for its part, in addition to sending its Middle East peace negotiator, Robert Strauss, to the Middle East earlier than originally scheduled in an effort to expedite the Egyptian-Israeli talks on Palestinian autonomy, announced that it would supply Egypt with 34 F-4 Phantom jets—a clear gesture of support to Sadat in the wake of his continuing isolation in much of the Arab world. China, which like the United States valued Egypt's role as a leading anti-Soviet force in the Arab world, also signed an agreement to give military aircraft to Egypt.[83] The United States also sought to repair the strain in U.S.-Saudi relations, an effort that was at least partially successful, as the Saudis agreed to produce an additional million barrels of oil per day to help meet the serious oil shortage that beset the United States in June.

At the summit itself there was little official mention of the Middle East. According to Radio Moscow, however, Brezhnev openly criticized the Egyptian-Israeli treaty and reiterated the Soviet peace plan.[84] Brezhnev's position on the Middle East was repeated by Gromyko in his news conference following the summit, and the Soviet foreign minister further stated that the USSR opposed the use of the United Nations in policing the treaty, thus calling into question the future mandate of the U.N. force stationed between Egypt and Israel in the Sinai that was due to expire on July 24. Gromyko went out of his way, however, to emphasize once again the Soviet belief that Israel had the right to exist and, while again coming out for an independent Palestinian state, he asserted that it could be a "small" one—yet another means of reassurance to Israel:

> The American side tried to prove that the Soviet Union would be better off supporting the separate treaty between Egypt and Israel, and that it should help to link the U.N., in one way or another, to the treaty and the mechanisms created in order to serve this treaty in the Middle East.
>
> It goes without saying that the Soviet Union could not agree with such a view. Leonid Brezhnev outlined the principled position of the Soviet Union. He clearly stated that the Soviet Union's support for the anti-Arab treaty and any mechanism being created to serve this treaty is out of the question. . . .
>
> Certainly I must say that no one had any doubt that the Soviet Union's principled position on Middle Eastern affairs was and remains the same as it was formulated many years ago. Namely: all the lands captured by Israel from the Arabs must be returned; the Palestine Arab people must be granted the opportunity to create its own, *if only small*, independent state. . . .
>
> All of the countries of that region, *including Israel, and nobody must have any doubt about it*, should have the possibility to exist and develop in the Middle East as independent sovereign states. . . .[85] [emphasis added]

Following the Soviet-American summit, the Middle East situation took a sharp turn for the worse for Moscow. The central focus of the anti-Sadat bloc of Arab states created at the two Baghdad conferences, the Syrian-Iraqi alignment, fell apart, and the two states resumed their quarrel. This was due in part to the fact that Iraq's new President, Saddam Hussein, accused Syria of being involved in a plot to overthrow him, and in part to Syria's unwillingness to subordinate itself to Iraq in the proposed union of the two countries.[86] The July 1979 resumption of the Syrian-Iraqi conflict ruptured the alignment between the Steadfastness Front and the Persian Gulf and freed Saudi Arabia to take a more independent position.

As events in the Arab world moved to the disadvantage of the USSR, the Soviet leadership also had to be concerned with a new attempt by the Carter administration to widen the Camp David process. In the first place, the administration made a series of overtures to the PLO, although the Andrew Young fiasco seemed to abort, at least temporarily, administration efforts to involve that organization. Nonetheless, Moscow was clearly concerned about this as a commentary in *New Times* on the Carter effort noted that "attempts were made to find a weak link in the ranks of the Palestinians and to persuade world opinion that they were divided into 'moderates' and 'radicals' who differed in their approach to the 'new initiatives' of the U.S. administration."[87] A second Carter administration effort to widen Camp David lay in its decision to send arms to Morocco to help the king in his fight with the Polisario rebels in the western Sahara. Given Egypt's willingness to also aid Morocco, it seems clear that the United States was seeking Moroccan endorsement for Camp David. While Morocco was not to respond to the U.S. aid by embracing Camp David, the possibility of such a development could not be ruled out, particularly as Morocco ran into increasing difficulty as it attempted to suppress the Polisario, which was now receiving support from both Algeria and Libya.

In addition to its attempts to gain greater Arab support for Camp David in the postsummit period, the United States also sought to bolster its military position in the Middle East. Thus the United States supported Oman's efforts (which initially proved unsuccessful) to create an anti-Soviet Persian Gulf Security Pact with U.S., English and West German support,[88] while moving to bolster its own military forces in the region as the concept of an American Rapid Deployment Force began to take shape.

In the face of these challenges to its Middle East position, Moscow responded in several ways. In the first place, soon after the Vienna Summit, Moscow again emphatically disassociated itself from the Camp David "deal," and reiterated its refusal to endorse the use of UNEF to police the Egyptian-Israeli treaty. Secondly, it strongly supported the decision of the Nonaligned Conference in Havana which denounced the Camp David agreements. Then, in September, at a time of renewed flux in the regional situation, Soviet Prime Minister Aleksei Kosygin journeyed to Ethiopia and South Yemen to shore up Soviet ties with these two nations which had become Moscow's closest allies in the Middle East over the past few years. Indeed, relations had improved between Moscow and the PDRY to the point by late October 1979 that PDRY Premier Abdel Fattah Ismael visited Moscow and signed a Friendship and Cooperation Treaty with the USSR.[89] Another important element in Moscow's effort to reinforce its Middle East position was the journey of Hafiz Assad to Moscow in mid-October. Assad, who had become a regular fall visitor to the Soviet Union, was now in a far weaker position than ever before. The signing of the Egyptian-Israeli treaty in March left Syria in a weakened position vis-à-vis Israel, while at the same time the breakdown in its relationship with Iraq in July had left it even more exposed. At the same time, besides being bogged down in Lebanon, Assad faced a growing internal threat from the Muslim Brotherhood, which had been assassinating a number of prominent Alawi figures. Adding to Syria's sense of isolation was a cooling of its relationship with Jordan which, undoubtedly to the chagrin of the regime in Damascus, had become increasingly friendly with Iraq, which was granting it large amounts of economic aid. Perhaps in response to these developments which isolated Syria in the Arab world, Assad felt it necessary to demonstrate his willingness to defend the Arab cause by sending up Syrian aircraft to challenge the Israeli planes that were periodically attacking PLO bases in Lebanon. This, of course, may also have been a ploy to demonstrate to Moscow his need for more sophisticated aircraft, since invariably the Syrian jets were shot down by the Israelis. In any case, by the fall of 1979, Syrian dependence on Moscow had increased markedly, and Assad was clearly anxious to improve relations.

For its part Moscow was also interested in improving ties to Syria. With the rebirth of the Syrian-Iraqi quarrel, Moscow's hopes for the creation of an anti-imperialist Arab front had begun to dissipate, while it also had to be concerned about American efforts to expand the Camp David process (as mentioned above the United States had made a number of gestures to the Palestinians during the summer, a process that culminated in the meeting of U.S. United Nations Ambassador Andrew Young with a PLO representative). At the same time, Iraq was further distancing itself from the USSR, and the only close Soviet Arab allies were South Yemen and Libya, countries that all the other Arab states distrusted. For these reasons Moscow was also interested in improving relations with Syria, a pivotal Arab state, one important to the Arab world as a whole and also to the Arab-Israeli conflict. As a result, Assad's October 1979 visit to Moscow was a productive one.

Assad's main quest during his Moscow visit was, of course, weaponry, and he was apparently not to be disappointed in his quest as the final communiqué released after his visit noted that "appropriate decisions were adopted on strengthening Syria's defense potential." For its part, Moscow obtained Syria's support on the need to strengthen Arab solidarity on an anti-imperialist basis and to "rebuff all attempts to undermine Soviet-Arab friendship."[90] On balance, Assad's visit was a successful one and the pattern was set for increasingly warm relations between Damascus and Moscow, a process which was to accelerate rapidly following Syria's support for the Soviet invasion of Afghanistan in January and was to lead to the signing of a Friendship and Cooperation Treaty between the two countries in October 1980.

In sum, Moscow's Middle Eastern position on the eve of the hostage crisis with Iran was a mixed one. On the one hand, the renewal of the Iraqi-Syrian conflict had seriously disrupted the anti-Sadat alignment in the Arab world which Moscow had been encouraging. In addition, Soviet-Iranian relations had taken a turn for the worse. On the other hand, Egypt remained isolated in the Arab and Muslim worlds because of its treaty with Israel, and the United States, so far, had been unable to attract other Arab states or Palestinian Arabs to the Camp David process. The onset of the hostage crisis was to have a major effect not only on Iranian-American relations, but also on the entire American position in the Middle East, and Moscow was to try to exploit this development to improve its own position in the region.

MOSCOW AND THE HOSTAGE CRISIS

By mid-October, the outlook for the Iranian regime of the Ayatollah Khomeini was not very bright. The economy was in a shambles, unemployment was rising, and the Kurds were scoring victories against Khomeini's forces. Meanwhile, Prime Minister Bazargan and his liberal allies were losing out in the power struggle with the Islamic Revolutionary Council as clerical leaders close to Khomeini such as Ayatollah Beheshti and nonclerical Islamic radicals such as Hassan Bani-Sadr expressed growing displeasure with the Bazargan government. As one after another of Bazargan's allies were forced out of office, a rising tide of anti-Americanism seemed to engulf Iran, since the United States was blamed for Iran's increasing problems by Khomeini and his supporters. At the same time, the Tudeh Party was allowed to reopen its newspaper, since Iran's clerical leaders evidently felt they had to mend their fences somewhat with their northern neighbor if they were to mount a major confrontation with the United States. It should be noted in this context that the rise in anti-American propaganda began *before* the Shah came to the United States for medical treatment. His arrival, therefore, came at a time when the anti-American campaign was well underway and the atmosphere already prepared for the action against the embassy. Meanwhile the position of Bazargan, who wanted normalized relations with the United States, was further weakened on November 1, when Iranian television, under the control of his enemies, telecast his meeting with Brzezinski in Algeria.[91] Whether or not Ayatollah Khomeini actually ordered the embassy seizure himself three days later is not yet known; what is clear is that he prepared the atmosphere for the seizure and that he and his entourage were to exploit the hostage seizure to inject a new spirit into Iran's Islamic revolution at a time when Iran was facing serious difficulties.

The initial Soviet reaction to the embassy seizure was somewhat guarded as *Pravda* printed essentially factual accounts of the action of the "students."[92] Several days later, however, as the situation became more clear, the USSR tilted toward a pro-Iranian position, with a Moscow Radio Persian language commentary on November 6 terming the student action "totally understandable and logical."[93] Soviet broadcasts continued in this vein—despite protests by Washington (a situation reminiscent of Soviet behavior the previous fall when the Shah was slipping from power)—until December 5 when *Pravda* itself took a strongly pro-Iranian position, in an article by A. Petrov which, after deploring the U.S. naval buildup near Iran as "flagrant military and political pressure against Iran," stated:

> Instead of setting an example of restraint, responsibility and composure in the present circumstances, redoubling efforts to seek a reasonable way out of this situation and not letting emotions take the upper hand, certain circles in the U.S. are leaning more and more toward the use of force. They claim that this is a response to the

holding as hostages of U.S. Embassy personnel in Tehran, which is contrary to the norms of international law. To be sure, the seizure of the American Embassy in and of itself does not conform to the international convention concerning respect for diplomatic privileges and immunity. However, one cannot pull this act out of the overall context of American-Iranian relations and forget about the actions of the U.S. toward Iran, which are in no way consonant with the norms of law and morality. . . . The indisputability of the principle of immunity of diplomatic representatives cannot serve as justification, and even less as a pretext, for violating the sovereignty of an independent state—another principle that is at the heart of all international law.[94]

Petrov's rather convoluted analysis of international law ended with a warning: "Our country, as Comrade L. Brezhnev has stressed, opposes outside interference in Iran's internal affairs by anyone, in any form and under any pretext. This position of the Soviet Union remains unchanged."

In analyzing the reasoning behind Moscow's pro-Iranian position in the hostage crisis, at a time it was seeking the passage of the SALT II agreement in the U.S. Senate, one can perhaps point to the uncertain handling of the crisis by the Carter administration. The administration's reluctance to impose economic, let alone military, sanctions at a time when the United States was being humiliated on a daily basis by street mobs parading with the sign "America can't do anything" may well have struck the Soviet leadership as a sign of weakness, particularly since President Carter emphasized so strongly that the lives of the hostages were the primary American concern. Indeed, the hostage situation weakened still further the position of the United States in the Middle East as many nations in the region began to wonder openly how likely it was that the United States would come to their aid if it could not even defend its own interests, a perception perhaps reinforced by Washington's passivity after its embassy in Pakistan was stormed and burned later in November. To be sure, when the hostage issue was initially raised in the United Nations, Moscow voted for two Security Council resolutions calling on Iran to free the hostages (after all, its own diplomats could one day find themselves in a similar situation), the latter one on December 4. Yet the *Pravda* article mentioned above which appeared one day after the December 4 vote (and which was broadcast by Tass International Service), seemed to convey the USSR's true feelings. As the hostage crisis went on, it appears that the Soviet leaders saw an excellent opportunity to drive a wedge between the United States and Iran and prevent the rapprochement that they had feared only a few months before. At the same time, Moscow could exploit Carter's decision to send a naval task force toward Iran as a threat not only against that country, thereby reinforcing Iranian-American animosity, but against the Arab oil producers, as well, in an effort to further weaken the American position in the Middle East. Indeed, this was to be the central theme of Soviet propaganda for the next few months. Apparently, Moscow thought that given Carter's strong commitment to the SALT II agreement, and his tendency to overlook Soviet exploitation of Third World crises, the USSR could have its way in Iran and have SALT II also.[95]

The onset of the hostage crisis brought a change in the Iranian government as Prime Minister Bazargan resigned and Khomeini gave full governmental power to the Islamic Revolutionary Council. The change in government was welcomed by Moscow who saw in the liberal Bazargan an individual who was likely to seek good ties with the United States.[96] *Pravda* at first hailed the anti-U.S. statements of Bani Sadr, one of the most influential members of the Islamic Revolutionary Council, in the evident expectation that the anti-U.S. thrust of the hostage seizure would become a basic policy of the new government.[97] Indeed, one of the first acts of the new government was to denounce the 1959 mutual security treaty between the United States and Iran, an action clearly welcomed by Moscow, although the Soviet leadership was far less happy over the government's abrogation of the clauses of the 1921 Soviet-Iranian Treaty that allowed Soviet troops to enter Iran if a foreign military force entered that country.[98]

As might be expected, the Tudeh Party pledged its full support for the new regime and hailed the transfer of power from the "bourgeois liberal" Bazargan government to the revolutionary government,[99] and in an interview in *L'Humanité* which was cited in *Pravda*, Tudeh leader Nur Al-din Kianuri claimed that a "new stage" of the Iranian revolution had begun two aims of which were to "eliminate all manifestations of American domination in Iran and deepen the revolution's class content by enlisting the popular masses in a more active struggle against the upper bourgeoisie." He also called for the establishment of a "broad national front" to rally all available forces, including national minorities, for "the struggle against American domination."[100] Kianouri's concern about the national minorities probably reflected the fact that by November, the Iranian government was fighting not only the Kurds but the Azerbaizhanis as well, and the Tudeh (and Moscow) may have worried that these conflicts would sap the power of the now strongly anti-American regime in Tehran. For its part, Moscow changed its reporting of the struggles of the national minorities to a far more sympathetic evaluation of the central regime and blamed U.S. agents for "organizing separatist actions and provoking unrest in Iran."[101]

In sum, the hostage seizure and the subsequent rift between the United States and Iran was seen by the Soviet Union as a golden opportunity to reinforce its own ties with Iran while weakening the overall position of the United States in the region. Whether or not the Carter administration's lack of firmness in handling the Iranian crisis was a factor in the Soviet decision to proceed with a massive invasion of Afghanistan in late December is only a matter of conjecture.[102] Nonetheless, it must have struck the Kremlin leaders that if the United States was unwilling to intervene in Iran where it had major interests, it was very unlikely to take action in Afghanistan where American interests were almost nonexistent. In any case, the Soviet invasion of Afghanistan was to cause Moscow serious problems throughout the Muslim world, although the USSR was to use its championing of Iranian interests against the United States to try to deflect Muslim criticism.

NOTES

1. In this Moscow was to be correct. See Chapter 11.

2. For the texts of the Camp David agreements and the accompanying letters, see *The Camp David Summit* (Washington: United States Department of State publication no. 8954, September 1978).

3. *Pravda*, September 23, 1978.

4. Leonid Medvenko, "Middle East: Fictions and Realities," *New Times* no. 40, 1978, p. 6.

5. A. Stepanov, "Hour of Trial for the Palestinians," *New Times* no. 41, 1978, p. 7.

6. *Pravda*, October 7, 1978. This issue, however, was to later cause some conflict in Soviet-Syrian relations. See p. 359.

7. Radio Moscow (Domestic Service), October 28, 1978 (International Diary Program).

8. *Pravda*, November 2, 1978.

9. *Pravda*, November 1, 1978.

10. *Izvestia*, November 2, 1978.

11. For a report on the results of the Baghdad Conference, see Baghdad INA, November 5, 1978, in *Foreign Broadcast Information Service Daily Report: Middle East and North Africa*, November 6, 1978, pp. A-13-15.

12. See also Amman Ar-Ra'y, in Arabic, November 6, 1978, in ibid, pp. A-19-20.

13. "Wanted! Not a Bogus Settlement," *New Times* no. 50, 1978, p. 1.

14. Selig Harrison in his article "Dateline Afghanistan: Exit Through Finland" (*Foreign Policy* no. 41, pp. 163-87) argues that Iran's efforts helped to precipitate the Communist coup.

15. Compare R. K. Ramazani, "Iran and the Arab-Israeli Conflict," *World Politics and the Arab-Israeli Conflict*, ed. Robert O. Freedman (New York: Pergamon, 1979), pp. 129-46.

16. For analyses of the Soviet nationalities bordering Iran, see E. Enders Wimbush, "Divided Azerbaizhan: Nation Building, Assimilation and Mobilization between Three States;" and Eden Naby, "The Iranian Frontier Nationalities: The Kurds, the Assyrians, the Baluchis and the Turkomans," in *Soviet Asian Ethnic Frontiers*, ed. William O. McCagg, Jr., and Brian D. Silver (New York: Pergamon, 1979). For an analysis of the preliminary impact of Khomeini on Soviet Moslems, see Alexandre Bennigsen, "Soviet Muslims and the World of Islam," *Problems of Communism*, Vol. 29 no. 2 (March/April 1980), pp. 49-51. For studies of Soviet policy toward Iran, see George Lenczowski, *Russia and the West in Iran, 1918-1948* (Ithaca: Cornell University Press, 1949); Rouhollah R. Ramazani, *Iran's Foreign Policy 1941-1973* (Charlottesville: University Press of Virginia, 1975); and Sepehr Zabih, *The Communist Movement in Iran* (Berkeley: University of California Press, 1966). For a solid study of the causes of the Shah's fall, see Amin Saikal, *The Rise and Fall of the Shah* (Princeton: Princeton University Press, 1980).

17. On the interplay of these statements, see Robert Rand, *Radio Liberty Report* (hereafter *RL*), no. 262/78, November 21, 1978.

18. Dmitry Volsky, "Vicious Circle," *New Times* no. 5, 1979, p. 8.

19. Compare *Middle East Intelligence Service* (Tel Aviv), June 1-15, 1980.

20. For a discussion of these events, see "Epilogue," *World Politics and the Arab-Israeli Conflict*, op.cit.

21. Dmitry Volsky, "Flop or Maneuver," *New Times*, no. 52, 1978, p. 17.

22. For a Soviet description of the visit, see L. Lebedev and Y. Tyunkov, "Useful Exchange of Views," *New Times*, no. 51, 1978, p. 15.

23. For an account of these events, see Robert O. Freedman, *Soviet Policy Toward the Middle East Since 1970*, (New York: Praeger, 1978), pp. 152 and 201-02.

24. For a translation of excerpts of the article, which appeared on January 31, see *Current Digest of the Soviet Press* (hereafter *CDSP*) Vol. 31 no. 5, pp. 5-6. Moscow continued its efforts in February and early March (Compare Radio Moscow in Arabic to the Arab world, March 5, 1979).

25. On February 14, 1979, the embassy was seized for one day; on November 4 it was seized, and the American diplomats held hostage for 444 days (see p. 370).

26. *Izvestia*, March 8, 1979 (translated in *CDSP* Vol. 31 no. 18, p. 23).

27. For a good general background on North Yemen, see Robert W. Stookey, *Yemen: The Politics of the Yemen Arab Republic* (Boulder, Colorado: Westview Press, 1978). For an analysis of the problems facing North Yemen on the eve of the invasion, see Fulvio Grimaldi, "Whose War in the Yemens?" *The Middle East* no. 54 (April 1979), pp. 56-57.

28. For an analysis of the Soviet role in the Syrian invasion of Jordan, see Robert O. Freedman, "Detente and Soviet-American Relations in the Middle East During the Nixon Years," in *Dimensions of Detente*, ed. Della Sheldon (New York: Praeger, 1978), pp. 92-101.

29. For a description of American military aid to Yemen, see the article by Richard Burt, New York *Times*, March 18, 1979. There were, however, later to be serious problems with the American deliveries (see below, p. 418). Most military observers felt that the organization of the three-pronged PDRY invasion of North Yemen could not have been accomplished by the South Yemenis themselves. (Compare report by John Cooley, *Christian Science Monitor*, March 13, 1979.)

30. For a discussion of American thinking on the idea of a "Fifth Fleet," see the article by Charles W. Cordry, Baltimore *Sun*, March 8, 1979.

31. For the text of the Egyptian-Israeli Treaty and the accompanying letters, see *The Egyptian-Israeli Peace Treaty* (Washington: Department of State, Bureau of Public Affairs, Selected Documents no. 11, April 1979).

32. For a list of the actions taken against Egypt and the dynamics of the second Baghdad Conference, see *The Middle East* no. 55 (May 1979), pp. 12, 37-39.

33. *Pravda*, March 27, 1979.

34. Radio Damascus Domestic Service, March 26, 1979.

35. *Pravda*, March 27, 1979.

36. *Pravda*, April 8, 1979 (translated in *CDSP* Vol. 31 no. 14, p. 17).

37. *Pravda*, April 7, 1979.

38. For a detailed treatment of the Iraqi-Soviet relationship, see Robert O. Freedman, "Soviet Policy Toward Ba'athist Iraq," in *The Soviet Union in the Third World*, ed. Robert H. Donaldson (Boulder, Colorado: Westview Press, 1981, pp. 161-91).

39. Compare Baqir Ibrahim, "The Masses, The Party and The National Front," *World Marxist Review* Vol. 19 no. 8 (August 1976), pp. 49-56; and Aziz Mohammed, "Tasks of the Revolutionary Forces of Iraq," *World Marxist Review* Vol. 19 no. 9 (September 1976), pp. 10-18.

40. Tewfiq Mishlawi, "Crackdown on Communists in Iraq," *The Middle East* no. 45 (July 1978), pp. 29-30.

41. For a list of Iraqi actions against "enemies of the regime," see article by J. P. Smith, Washington *Post*, August 6, 1978.

42. Cited in ibid.

43. Cited in Mishlawi, loc.cit., p. 30.

44. Compare Reuters report in The Jerusalem *Post*, November 24, 1978; AP report in the New York *Times*, November 24, 1978; and the article by Ned Temko, *The Christian Science Monitor*, November 30, 1978. See also the broadcast by Radio Kuwait (KUNA) on December 13, 1978 of an *Ar-Ra'y Al-'am* article challenging the USSR to give more military assistance to Iraq and Syria.

45. AP report from Moscow, The Jerusalem *Post*, January 5, 1979.

46. If so, the incident is reminiscent of Moscow's unwillingness to provide Egypt with the weaponry Sadat wanted in 1971 and 1972. There were also reports that following Camp David, the USSR felt it had greater leverage over Iraq and Syria and it could exercise that leverage to obtain improved treatment of the ICP from Iraq and the long-sought friendship and assistance treaty from Syria. (See the Western sources mentioned in n. 44 above.)

47. *Pravda*, December 14, 1978.

48. *Tass*, in English, December 12, 1978 (*Foreign Broadcast Information Service: Daily Report USSR*, December 13, 1978, p. F-3).

49. *Pravda*, January 13, 1979.

50. On this point, see Robert O. Freedman, "The USSR and the Communist Parties of the Arab World," in *Soviet Economic and Political Relations with the Developing World*, ed. Roger Kanet (New York: Praeger, 1975), pp. 100-34.

51. Cited in report by Ned Temko, *The Christian Science Monitor*, April 11, 1979.

52. This incident is discussed in Tewfiq Mishlawi, "Iraq's Foreign Policy Headaches," *The Middle East* no. 57 (July 1979), p. 10.

53. Ibid.

54. For a discussion of the events in Iran, see Robert O. Freedman, "Iran's Revolution and the Mideast Balance of Power," *Jewish Frontier*, Vol. 46 no. 6 (June/July 1979), pp. 4-5, 30.

55. Compare report in Washington *Post*, June 15, 1979.

56. Cited in AP report from Tehran, Baltimore Evening *Sun*, June 6, 1979.

57. Cited in report by William Branigin, Washington *Post*, June 16, 1979.

58. Compare report by Ned Temko, *Christian Science Monitor*, June 18, 1979.

59. For a more detailed discussion of the role of the PLO in revolutionary Iran, see Robert O. Freedman, "Iran's Revolution and the Mideast Balance of Power," loc.cit.

60. Cited in AP report from Tehran, Baltimore Evening *Sun*, June 6, 1979.

61. Cited in the report by John Kifner, New York *Times*, May 4, 1979.

62. Compare *Pravda*, March 19 and April 10, 1979.

63. Cited in report by Jonathan Kandell, New York *Times*, June 13, 1979.

64. *Pravda*, March 24, 1979 (translated in *CDSP* Vol. 31 no. 12, p. 19).

65. *Pravda*, March 29, 1979.

66. *Pravda*, May 2, 1979.

67. *Pravda*, May 5, 1979 (translated in *CDSP* Vol. 31 no. 19, p. 15). See also Mikhail Krutikin, "Iran: Uphill Road of Change," *New Times* no. 19, 1979, pp. 12-13.

68. *New Times*, no. 34, 1979, p. 13.

69. *New Times*, no. 29, 1979, p. 9.

70. Compare New York *Times*, July 19, 1979.

71. These statements were cited in Terry Povey, "Iran's Autonomy Seekers," *The Middle East*, August 1979, pp. 41-43.

72. See Alexander Usvatov, "Iran's Troubled August," *New Times* no. 36, 1979, pp. 10-11.

73. Compare *World Marxist Review Information Bulletin*, nos. 21-22, 1979, p. 68.

74. Cited in *The Middle East*, September 1979, p. 27.

75. Compare *Pravda*, August 26, 1979 and September 4, 1979.

76. Cited in *The Middle East*, September 1979, p. 31.

77. *Pravda*, August 29, 1979 and September 4, 1979.

78. *Nedelia*, September 3-9, 1979 (translated in *CDSP* Vol. 31 no. 35, p. 5).

79. Usvatov, "Iran: Troubled August," loc.cit., pp. 10-11.

80. Ibid.

81. For an analysis of the summit, see Robert O. Freedman, "The Soviet Image of the Carter Administration's Policy Toward the USSR: From the Inauguration to the Invasion of Afghanistan," *Korea and World Affairs* Vol. 4 no. 2 (Summer 1980).

82. UPI report, New York *Times*, May 31, 1979.

83. Cited in report by Christopher Wren, New York *Times*, June 23, 1978.

84. *Tass*, in English, June 17, 1979 (*Foreign Broadcast Information Service*: Daily Report USSR, June 18, 1979, p. AA-11).

85. Radio Moscow Domestic Service, June 25, 1979. For a Soviet view of the general Middle Eastern situation at this time, see the interview of Yevgeny Primakov in the Beirut publication *Monday Morning* (*Foreign Broadcast Information Service*: Daily Report, USSR, July 6, 1979, pp. H-1-11).

86. For an analysis of the resumption of the Iraq-Syria quarrel, see Graham Benten, "After the Coup Attempt," *The Middle East* no. 59 (September 1979) pp. 13-14.

87. O. Volgin, "Palestinians Stand Firm," *New Times* no. 35, 1979, p. 14. The U.S. ambassador to the U.N., Andrew Young, had been forced to resign after an "unauthorized" meeting with the PLO U.N. representative in New York.

88. For an analysis of the Omani plan, see "Gulf Security," *The Middle East* no. 61 (November 1979), pp. 16-18. The Omani effort, however, was to meet with greater success after the outbreak of the Iran-Iraq war when a Gulf Council for Cooperation was formed. See Chapter 10, p. 393.

89. For the text of the treaty, see *Pravda*, October 27, 1979.

90. *Pravda*, October 19, 1979.

91. For an excellent analysis of this period, see Barry Rubin, *Paved with Good Intentions: The American Experience and Iran* (New York: Oxford, 1970), Chapter 9.

92. *Pravda*, November 5, 1979.

93. Commentary by Vera Lebedeva (*Foreign Broadcast Information Service*: Daily Report Soviet Union, November 7, 1979, p. H-4).

94. Translated in *CDSP* Vol. 31 no. 49, pp. 4, 26.

95. For an analysis of the Soviet evaluation of Carter, see Freedman, "The Soviet Image of the Carter Administration's Policy Toward the USSR from the Inauguration to the Invasion of Afghanistan," loc.cit., pp. 229-67.

96. Compare *New Times*, no. 47, 1979, p. 7.

97. *Pravda*, November 11, 1979.

98. For an analysis of the Iranian action, see Robert Rand, *RL Report* No. 337/79, November 7, 1979. For the Soviet view of the treaty, see B. Ponomaryov et al, *History of Soviet Foreign Policy 1917-1945* (Moscow: Progress Publishers, 1969), pp. 42-48.

99. *World Marxist Review Information Bulletin*, nos. 1-2, 1980, pp. 86-87.

100. *Pravda*, November 23, 1979.

101. Compare *New Times* no. 2, 1980, p. 13.

102. For a different view of the connection between the hostage crisis and the invasion of Afghanistan, see Jacques Levesque, "L'Intervention Sovietique en Afghanistan," *L'URSS dans les rélations internationales* (Bordeaux: University of Bordeaux: forthcoming). See also Harrison, "Dateline Afghanistan: Exit Through Finland," loc.cit.

10

The Soviet Invasion
of Afghanistan and
Its Aftermath

THE IMPACT OF THE SOVIET INVASION

The invasion of Afghanistan, which was to create major problems for Moscow in its drive to extend Soviet influence in the Middle East, came after more than a year and a half of rising frustration with the Communist leadership of Afghanistan, which had ruled ineffectually since seizing power in April 1978.[1] The very narrowly based government of Noor Mohammed Taraki was in deep trouble almost from the time it seized power, and the signing of a Treaty of Friendship and Cooperation with the USSR in December 1978 did little to help the Communist regime. Although Soviet military aid and advisers had poured into the country after the coup, and Taraki and his strongman Prime Minister Hafizullah Amin had begun to institute major land reform and social reform programs in the rural areas of Afghanistan, the new government had incurred the wrath of the Islamic religious leaders as well as tribal leaders who resisted Kabul's efforts to extend its control to their areas. While the rebels were divided among themselves, the heavy-handed actions of the central government, which included the physical mistreatment of Muslim Mullahs and the indiscriminate bombing of rebel areas, helped expand the opposition to the Communist regime, and the rebels were also aided by the defection of a number of Afghani soldiers (many of whom belonged to non-Pathan ethnic minorities) and army officers as well. The government's efforts were further hampered by the fierce rivalry between the Khalq faction of the party led by Taraki and Amin and the rival Parcham faction led by Babrak Karmal. By June 1979 fighting was raging in more than three-quarters of Afghanistan's provinces, and an attack had been made in Kabul itself against the government.

The conflict in Afghanistan posed a major threat to Soviet prestige. Having signed a Treaty of Friendship and Cooperation with the Taraki regime, and having hailed the Afghani leader as a fellow revolutionary,[2] Brezhnev felt obligated to aid the new Afghani government—particularly since it shared a long border with the USSR. Consequently, as the Taraki regime began to lose control, the USSR expanded its military aid, sending helicopters and helicopter gun-ships to assist the Afghani government in fighting the rebels in Afghanistan's mountain regions,[3] and there were a number of reports of Soviet involvement in military actions.[4]

In addition to stepping up its military aid to Kabul, Moscow also moved on the diplomatic front to try to curb the Afghani rebels' use of sanctuaries in neighboring countries. Pakistan, the main rebel base, was singled out for Soviet censure, and Moscow exploited the fact that Pakistan was in a difficult position because of its conflict with the United States over the independent Pakistani nuclear development program, which had caused a sharp deterioration in Pakistani American relations. As discussed above, Iran also came in for Soviet censure, and the USSR also accused China, Egypt and the United States of aiding the rebels. Indeed, *Pravda* openly accused the CIA of involvement in the rebellion,[5] a charge that was termed "slanderous and baseless" by the United States.[6]

Neither Soviet charges of outside intervention nor the military aid that the USSR had thus far extended, however, managed to stem the tide which appeared to be flowing against the Taraki regime by June 1, 1979. The Soviet leadership then stepped up its diplomatic efforts to protect Taraki by issuing a formal warning in *Pravda* that stated:

> The USSR cannot remain indifferent to the violations of the sovereignty of the Democratic Republic of Afghanistan, the incursions into its territory from Pakistan, and the attempt to create a crisis situation in that area. . . . What is in question is virtual aggression against a state with which the USSR has a common frontier.[7]

This warning, however, did not serve to end the insurgency which, in any case, was locally based. Consequently, the Soviet leadership increasingly faced the choice of whether or not to commit its own troops (or those of a client state such as Cuba) to help salvage the situation. A major troop commitment held both advantages and disadvantages for Moscow. On the one hand, Soviet military aid to Iraq in 1974 and Ethiopia in 1978, the latter case involving a sizeable Soviet military commitment, had succeeded in helping its allies to crush insurgencies, and Moscow by now had experience in counter-insurgency operations. In addition, the propinquity of Afghanistan's border to the USSR and its treaty with Moscow, to say nothing of Soviet prestige and a desire to prevent the emergence of a solid band of increasingly militant Islamic states along its southern borders (Iran, Pakistan, and if the Muslim-dominated rebels were successful, Afghanistan), all militated for increased Soviet military activity. On the other hand, however, the Taraki regime was in a far weaker position than either the Iraqi Ba'ath in 1974 or even Mengistu's Ethiopian regime in 1978, and an increase in Soviet military activity in Afghanistan might also serve to drive both Iran and Pakistan back toward the United States while at the same time providing ammunition for the anti-SALT elements in the United States at a time when the SALT II treaty, which had to be ratified by the United States Senate, was already under heavy attack there.

The change in government in Afghanistan in September 1979 could only have further disturbed Moscow as Taraki was overthrown (and apparently executed) by Amin, who took full control and soon clashed directly with the Russians, demanding the ouster of the Soviet ambassador. It increasingly must have appeared to the Soviet leaders that Amin, who had studied for three years in the United States (at Columbia University), and who had met frequently with U.S. Ambassador Adolph Dubs (before the latter's assassination), might become an Asian Tito,[8] if he were not overthrown first by the Afghan rebels. Under these circumstances, and benefiting from the hostage crisis in Iran which diverted American attention (and, as mentioned above, noting the very weak American reaction to the hostage seizure), Moscow sent its troops into Afghanistan, deposed (and murdered) Amin, and replaced him with Babrak Karmal.

While the Soviet relationship with Afghanistan dated back to the 19th century, and while Soviet-Afghan relations both in the military and economic spheres had become increasingly close after World War II,[9] the dispatch of more than 80,000 Soviet combat troops to Afghanistan, the first Soviet military move of such magnitude outside the Soviet bloc in Eastern Europe, stirred a great many fears in the Middle East and particularly among the oil producers in the Arab world since Soviet forces, operating from airbases in Afghanistan, were now in fighter-bomber range of the Strait of Hormuz. In addition it created serious problems for Moscow in its relations with the United States (President Carter imposed a partial grain embargo, limited the sale of high technology equipment, withdrew the SALT II treaty from Senate consideration, and cancelled American participation in the Moscow Olympics). The United States also seized upon the invasion to try to rally the Muslim states of the Middle East, many of whom were suspicious of the United States because of its role in Camp David, against the USSR while at the same time stepping up its search for Middle Eastern bases and hastening the deployment of its military forces near the Persian Gulf, which Carter pledged to protect.[10] When the issue of Soviet intervention in Afghanistan came up for a vote in the United Nations in early January, only Ethiopia and South Yemen, among Moscow's Middle Eastern allies, voted against the resolution which condemned the USSR, while Algeria, Syria and North Yemen abstained, with Libya taking a similar position by being absent from the vote.[11] Among the 104 countries voting against Moscow (only 18 states voted with the USSR while 30 abstained or were not present) was Iraq, whose President Saddam Hussein publicly condemned the invasion, thus further demonstrating Iraq's independence of Moscow.[12] Also voting against Moscow were Saudi Arabia, Jordan and Kuwait, all of whom Moscow had hoped to wean away from the West. As far as Iran was concerned, its Foreign Ministry issued a statement condemning the invasion, while its U.N. representative joined with the majority in voting for the anti-Soviet resolution.[13]

In an effort to overcome this Muslim backlash which it feared the United States would be able to exploit, Moscow made several moves. In the first place, its most trusted Arab allies, who formed the Steadfastness and Confrontation Front, organized a meeting in Damascus in mid-January—two weeks before the Islamic Conference of Nations was scheduled to meet to discuss the invasion. The Steadfastness and Confrontation Front used its meeting as a platform to condemn the United States, while pledging its friendship for the Soviet Union and its solidarity with Iran. It also tried to divert the attention of the Arab world away from the Soviet invasion of Afghanistan by emphasizing American support for Camp David and calling for a postponement of the beginning of the Islamic Conference on January 26 because that was the date scheduled for the normalization of relations between Egypt and the "Zionist Entity" (Israel).[14]

Indeed, the Steadfastness Front, or at least key components of it such as Syria, the PLO (primarily the PFLP and PDFLP), and the PDRY became almost adjuncts of Soviet policy during this period. Thus, at the end of January Gromyko visited Syria, and the joint communiqué issued at the end of his visit articulated the themes that Moscow and its Middle East allies were to use over the next few months to try to divert Muslim attention from the invasion of Afghanistan to the activities of "American-supported" Israel in the West Bank and Gaza. Fortunately for Moscow, the expansion of Israeli settlements on the West Bank and the turnabout in the March 1, 1980 U.S. Security Council vote condemning Israeli policies were to prove most fortuitous for Soviet propaganda efforts.

Moscow's invective against Israel reached a new high during Gromyko's visit as the Soviet-Syrian communiqué attacked Israel not only for racial discrimination but also for the "desecration of objects of historical, religious and cultural value to the Arabs." The United States, however, received the brunt of the Soviet and Syrian criticism:

> Under the cover of an artificially fomented uproar over the events in Iran and Afghanistan, imperialist circles and their accomplices are striving to divert the Arab people's attention away from the struggle to liquidate the consequences of Israeli aggression, and are attempting to create a split in the ranks of the Arab and Moslem countries, drive a wedge between them and their friends—the USSR —and subvert the unity and principles of the non-aligned movement. [The USSR and Syria] condemn the continuing campaign by imperialist forces, led by the United States, which are displaying a false concern for Islam while simultaneously supporting Israel's seizure of the Holy places in Jerusalem [and] taking an openly hostile position toward the revolution in Iran.
>
> The facts indicate that imperialism has been and continues to be an enemy of all the Moslem countries as a whole and an enemy of Islam.[15]

The communiqué also mentioned further Soviet provision of military aid to Syria, and indeed, not only Syria but also Iraq, Algeria, South Yemen and Libya reportedly received sharply increased amounts of Soviet weaponry in the postinvasion period as Moscow sought to bolster its position in these countries.[16] An arms deal was also signed with Kuwait in early February as Moscow sought to improve that country's relationship with the USSR.[17]

Nonetheless, while Moscow was seeking—and obtaining—the support of the Steadfastness Front in the post-Afghan invasion period, the Front itself was encountering serious problems. In addition to criticism from other Arab and Muslim states for their position on the Soviet invasion of Afghanistan, many of the Front leaders were encountering internal problems. Mention has already been made of the Muslim brotherhood's attacks against the Syrian government, but, in addition, Libyan leader Kaddafi faced internal unrest, as well as condemnation from other Arab states for supporting an abortive attack against Tunisia. At the same time, Libya and the PLO became embroiled in a conflict because of Kaddafi's displeasure over a lack of PLO aggressiveness against Israel. Meanwhile, the new Algerian President, Chadli Ben Jedid, faced the continuing problem of the Polisario rebellion which was draining Algerian as well as Moroccan resources, and Algeria began to moderate its position toward the United States. Finally, a major power struggle was underway in the PDRY, which culminated five days after the end of the Steadfastness Conference in the ouster of PDRY President Abdel Fattah Ismael, and his replacement by the more pragmatic Prime Minister Ali Nasser Mohammed—the second major government upheaval in South Yemen in less than two years.[18]

Consequently, it was a weakened Steadfastness Front that met in April 1980, and although it managed to work out a rapprochement between the PLO and Libya and denounced the normalization of relations between Israel and Egypt, the meeting was not particularly successful in working out any concrete measures to combat either Sadat or the United States.[19] While diplomatic relations were broken between the Steadfastness Front members and the Sudan, Somalia, and Oman, which still maintained diplomatic relations with Egypt, and while the United States (and its efforts to obtain bases in the Arab world) was severely denounced while Moscow was warmly praised, the Steadfastness meeting was not marked by any solid achievement. Moscow, however, took an optimistic view of the meeting pointing to its decision to establish a joint military command, and other coordinating bodies, and asserted that "the tendency towards the anti-imperialist united action of the Arab people is gaining momentum."[20] The previous failure of the Steadfastness Front members to coordinate their actions, however, must have raised serious questions, even in Moscow, as to the likelihood of success of these organizational moves.

In addition to obtaining the support of the Steadfastness Front, Moscow also appeared to draw somewhat closer to North Yemen with whom it signed a major arms deal. While the North Yemenis may well have turned to Moscow for arms to demonstrate their displeasure with the military supply arrangement made with Washington the previous year, an arrangement that Saudi Arabia, for its own reasons, was delaying, the overall impact of the North Yemeni turn to Moscow seemed to undercut U.S. policy in the Arabian Peninsula and was to raise, once again, questions about the capability of U.S. diplomacy.[21]

A similar development in South Asia was also to weaken the U.S. position while strengthening that of the USSR. An election was held in India that brought Indira Gandhi back to power—the woman who, as prime minister, had been far more friendly to Moscow than her successor, Morarji Desai, had been. While Mrs. Gandhi criticized the Soviet invasion of Afghanistan, she was far more critical of the U.S. aid offers to Pakistan to help counter the Soviet action. Then, when Pakistan's President Zia contemptuously rejected America's $400 million aid offer as "peanuts," American prestige dropped again, while Moscow sought to carefully cultivate India, a process that was to result in Indian recognition of the Vietnamese puppet government in Cambodia, and a major Soviet-Indian arms deal.[22]

In addition to bolstering its ties with India and utilizing the Rejectionist Front to deflect Muslim criticism, Moscow stepped up its support for Iran in its confrontation with the United States in the period after the invasion of Afghanistan. Not only did the USSR veto a U.S.-sponsored U.N. Security Council resolution calling for economic sanctions against Iran; it also strongly reiterated its warning against U.S. military intervention in Iran with Pravda, on January 10, 1980, stating that Moscow would not tolerate any outside interference in Iranian internal affairs. While the USSR sought to project itself as the protector of Iran, it also sought to temper Iranian criticism of the Afghan invasion by having Babrak Karmal, the Soviet-installed leader of Afghanistan, write to Khomeini with an appeal for a common front against U.S. imperialism.[23] To further placate the Ayatollah, his picture was published in two Kabul newspapers.[24] All these efforts, however, came to naught. The two leading candidates for the Iranian presidency, Hassan Bani-Sadr and Foreign Minister Ghotbzadeh both attacked the USSR in campaign speeches in late January 1980, with Bani-Sadr accusing Moscow of wanting to divide Iran and push to the Indian Ocean.[25] At the Islamic Conference, the Iranian representative joined in the general denunciation of Soviet policy and urged the conference to demand the withdrawal of Soviet forces from Afghanistan, although he also demanded that the conference condemn the U.S. economic blocade of Iran and act to eliminate "U.S. imperialist influence in Islamic countries."[26]

The Islamic Conference, which not only condemned the USSR in very strong terms (despite the efforts of the Steadfastness Front) but also suspended the membership of Afghanistan, called on Islamic nations to break diplomatic relations with the country, and urged a boycott of the Moscow Olympics, was a major defeat for Soviet Middle Eastern policy.[27] The Soviet defeat was compounded in early February when Ayatollah Khomeini himself castigated the Soviet invasion for the first time, and pledged unconditional support for the Muslim insurgents fighting the Soviet-backed regime.[28] Iran's newly elected

President Bani-Sadr also denounced the USSR and promised that Iran would send supplies and equipment to the Afghan rebels.[29] By this time, the United States had softened its stance toward Iran, and, as part of its overall effort to rally the Muslim Middle East against the USSR, decided to postpone sanctions against Iran until after Bani-Sadr had a chance to deal with the hostage issue.

As the Iranian leadership issued anti-Soviet statements, Moscow could not help but be concerned that the Iranians might come to agree with the U.S. assertion that the USSR was the greater threat and, with Soviet troops now bordering Iran in two directions, might release the U.S. hostages and turn Iran back toward the United States. Consequently, the Soviet leadership took an increasingly unfavorable view of Bani-Sadr, who appeared to favor a speedy solution of the hostage conflict, while the Russians became far more supportive of both the militant students, who wanted to hold onto the hostages to keep the revolution going, and such clerical leaders as Ayatollah Beheshti, who supported them.[30] Khomeini, who sided with the students, was praised not only by the Tudeh, which was now one of his most fervent supporters, but also by Moscow as *Pravda* on February 24 cited Khomeini's statement that the students holding the hostages had given a "crippling blow to the American imperialists."

As Moscow began to side increasingly with the clerical leaders of Iran, articles began to appear in Soviet journals and newspapers emphasizing the "progressive" nature of Islam, with Leonid Medvenko going so far as to assert in a *New Times* article that while Islam could be either progressive or reactionary depending upon the circumstances:

> What distinguishes the present stage of the national liberation move-
> ment, which often raises the banner of Islam, is that this movement
> is not spearheaded only against imperialism, but gradually turns
> against the very foundations of capitalism. The conflict between the
> capitalist West and Moslem East, which has latterly become sharper
> still, is a vivid reflection of the ideological crisis of neo-colonialism,
> for it is in effect evidence of loss of faith in capitalism, which not so
> long ago regarded Islam as its ally. This evidently explains the West's
> fear of the process sometimes called the "regeneration of Islam."[31]

Interestingly enough, however, while Soviet observers tended to wax eloquent about the positive trends in Islam, Middle Eastern Communists remained considerably more skeptical about the clergy and a symposium appearing in the *World Marxist Review* spoke openly of the "limits of the clergy's progressive impulses."[32] The Middle Eastern Communists' caution was well taken because on March 20 Khomeini issued his strongest denunciation of the USSR to date, although he coupled it with strong criticism of the United States:

> We are fighting against international communism to the same degree
> that we are fighting against the Western world devourers led by

America, Israel and Zionism. My dear friends, you should know that the danger from the communist powers is not less than America. . . .

Once again I strongly condemn the dastardly occupation of Afghanistan by the plunderers and occupiers of the aggressive East. I hope that the Muslim and noble people of Afghanistan will as soon as possible achieve true victory and independence and be released from the grip of these so-called supporters of the working class.[33]

Then, in an attack on the Islamic Marxists and the Tudeh, Khomeini appeared to repudiate those Soviet writers who saw an anti-imperialist blending of Islam and Marxism:

. . . Most regretably, at times it can be seen that due to the lack of the proper and precise understanding of Islamic issues *some people have mixed Islamic ideas with Marxist ideas and have created a concoction which is in no way in accordance with the progressive teachings of Islam*. . . .[34] [emphasis added]

Khomeini's attack, coupled with Iran's termination of natural gas deliveries to the USSR because of a dispute over price, seemed to signal a deterioration in relations with the Soviet Union.[35] Fortunately for Moscow, however, by this time the Carter administration had lost patience on the hostage issue and in early April the United States expelled the Iranian diplomats from the United States, announced the imposition of economic sanctions while urging its NATO allies to do likewise, and warned it had "other means" available to free the hostages if the sanctions did not work. Seizing the opportunity presented by the American actions, Moscow offered Iran land transit facilities to circumvent a potential American naval blockade, and many of Moscow's East European allies, concerned about the USSR's future inability to supply them with sufficient fuel, journeyed to Tehran to try to arrange barter deals where they would obtain Iranian oil for the food and manufactured goods that might be embargoed by the West. As U.S.-Iranian tension again rose, Afghan leader Babrak Karmal, almost certainly acting on Soviet instructions, made another démarche to Tehran, this time to normalize relations with Iran (a similar note was sent to Pakistan).[36]

In sum, therefore, at the time of the abortive American hostage rescue on April 25, 1980, Moscow may have seen the Iranian government once again swinging back toward the USSR as the American threats took precedence over the Soviet invasion of Afghanistan.

SOVIET POLICY FROM THE ABORTIVE HOSTAGE RESCUE MISSION TO THE IRAN-IRAQ WAR

The ill-fated American rescue mission provided a golden opportunity for Moscow to reinforce its ties with Iran while at the same time enabling the USSR to demonstrate to the nations of the Middle East the dangers posed to them by the American military buildup in the Indian Ocean. It also aided Moscow in its efforts to divert Muslim attention from the Soviet invasion of Afghanistan, and Moscow lost little time in attacking the United States for the rescue attempt, comparing it to the raid by the Tel-Aviv "cutthroats" at Entebbe,[37] and claiming that the raid was part of a larger plot to overthrow the government of Ayatollah Khomeini.[38] The USSR also thrust itself forth again as the protector of Iran—and other Muslim countries—with *Izvestia* on May 1 asserting:

> It is not for nothing that influential commentators in the U.S. are admitting that the existence of the Soviet Union is the main factor that U.S. hawks are forced to take into account in their plans concerning Iran—and that's not all. It is also indicative that these same commentators admit that bellicose circles in the U.S. would long since have decided on extreme measures in their anti-Iranian schemes had they not taken into account certain indisputable facts of present day reality. Thus practical experience graphically shows whom the Islamic countries that are striving to consolidate their sovereignty and that want to be full masters in their own houses can rely upon.[39]

Writing in a similar vein, *New Times* Middle Eastern specialist Dmitry Volsky asserted that the rescue mission "showed how little respect imperialist policy makers have for the sovereignty of Muslim countries." Volsky, after then discussing NATO efforts to exploit the Afghan situation to build an anti-Soviet Muslim bloc, also asserted, rather optimistically, "it may already be said that the Muslim world as a whole refuses to join in Washington's anti-Soviet strategy."[40] Unfortunately for Volsky, the Islamic Conference which met several weeks after his article appeared was to prove his assertion premature, and despite the Soviet attempt to act as Iran's champion, it was to be Iran that was to lead the Islamic Conference in its denunciation of the USSR's invasion and occupation of Afghanistan.

The Islamic Conference meeting in mid-May was its second of 1980. After the diplomatic battering the Muslim nations administered to the USSR in January, Moscow may have expected better treatment in the May meeting because of both the abortive U.S. rescue mission and the Begin government's decision, announced just before the start of the session, to consider the formal annexation of East Jerusalem. Indeed, Israel was strongly denounced by the Muslim nations, while the United States also came in for a large share of criticism both for its support of Israel and for its "recent military aggression" against Iran.[41]

Nonetheless, while there was widespread condemnation of the United States, the Soviet Union also had its share of difficulties at the conference. In the first place, despite efforts of the PLO and other Steadfastness Front members, Afghanistan, which had been suspended from the conference in

January, was not readmitted. Secondly, despite a gesture by the Karmal government just before the meeting where the Soviet-installed Afghan president invited Iran and Pakistan to participate in talks aimed at arranging the withdrawal of Soviet troops from Afghanistan, Iran severely denounced the USSR at the conference and went so far as to include, as official members of its own delegation, eight Afghan rebel leaders.[42] Foreign Minister Ghotbzadeh led the Iranian delegation and denounced the USSR and the United States in equally harsh terms, condemning the Soviet Union's invasion of Afghanistan as "a flagrant violation of international law carried out in total disrespect for the sovereignty and territorial integrity of Afghanistan."[43] He also stated, in an obvious effort to prevent the conference from being diverted to the Palestine-Israel conflict, "For us, the liberation of Afghanistan is not less important than the liberation of Palestine." Ghotbzadeh was successful in his quest, as the Islamic Conference, despite the efforts of the Steadfastness Front, again called for the "immediate, total and unconditional withdrawal of all Soviet troops stationed on the territory of Afghanistan." It also set up a three-man committee, composed of Ghotbzadeh, the Foreign Minister of Pakistan, and the Islamic Conference secretary general to seek a solution of the Afghan problem.[44]

Despite the Islamic Conference's numerous criticisms of the United States, the May meeting must be considered another diplomatic defeat for the USSR which rejected the conference's Afghan Committee plan, and denounced the "representatives of reactionary Muslim quarters" who "succeeded in pushing through a resolution on the Afghan question couched in terms hostile to the people and government of Afghanistan."[45]

Once again, as in the case following the Islamic Conference in January, Moscow and its Arab allies sought to deflect Muslim criticism by concentrating their attention on Israeli actions in the West Bank and Gaza Strip and purported American support for them. Fortunately for Moscow, Israel was again to give the USSR ammunition for its propaganda efforts. Thus, following a terrorist attack against Jews in the West Bank city of Hebron who were returning from Sabbath services, Israel expelled the mayor and religious leader of that city and the mayor of a nearby city, who were accused of creating the atmosphere for the attack. A month later two West Bank Arab mayors were maimed by bombs and, at the same time, the Begin government began to push a bill for the formal annexation of East Jerusalem through the Israeli Parliament. Moscow seized on these events to claim that Egypt had capitulated to Israel and to demonstrate that by backing these actions, the United States was, in fact, an enemy of Islam. The USSR also proclaimed its willingness to vote sanctions in the Security Council against Israel "by virtue of its solidarity with the Arab and other Islamic countries that considered it necessary for the Security Council to take some steps in connection with the Israeli occupier's defiant action."[46] Indeed, Moscow was to use the numerous condemnations of Israel by the U.N. in the spring and summer of 1980—condemnations that were spearheaded by its Arab allies—to try to divert attention from Afghanistan where, despite a massive troop commitment, the USSR was facing serious difficulties in suppressing the rebels.[47]

Arab condemnation of Israeli actions in the West Bank, the passage of the May 26 deadline for the establishment of Palestinian autonomy, and the deterioration of Saudi-American relations led Moscow to float another trial balloon in July for the improvement of relations between Moscow and Riyadh. Writing in *Literaturnaia Gazeta* Igor Belyayev, citing the statement of Saudi Defense Minister Prince Sultan that "in the end, it turns out that the U.S. is only a colossus with feet of clay," noted that "certain members of the ruling family think it is time to resume diplomatic relations with the Soviet Union as well as with other Socialist countries." Belyayev also noted that the Soviet position on Camp David "coincides completely, for all practical purposes, with the position of the Wahabi Kingdom," and he also stated, a bit prematurely, that Saudi Arabia was making a "fundamental change" in its security doctrine. Belyayev asserted that because of U.S.-spread rumors about the Saudi ruling family, American support for Camp David, and Saudi unhappiness about the abortive Iran rescue mission, the "special relationship" between the United States and Saudi Arabia was coming to an end.[48]

While Saudi Arabia was to respond negatively to the Soviet trial balloon,[49] Saudi-American relations remained troubled and, in August, Saudi Arabia moved closer to Iraq as Saddam Hussein and King Khalid, in the first visit of an Iraqi leader to Saudi Arabia since 1958, jointly threatened to cut off aid to any nation that recognized Jerusalem as Israel's capital. Moscow could only welcome this development, as it further focused attention on Israeli actions in the West Bank while also appearing to pull Saudi Arabia farther away from the United States.

If the United States was encountering difficulty in rallying many Arab states in support of Camp David, it was having more success in improving its military position in the region. Thus, the United States and Turkey signed a major defense agreement in January, and the military coup that took place in Turkey in September seemed to arrest, at least temporarily, that country's slide into anarchy. The U.S. position was also bolstered by Greece's decision to return to NATO.[50] In the cases of both Greece and Turkey, the decisions of the national leadership to establish a closer military relationship with the United States seem to have been, at least in part, a consequence of the Soviet invasion of Afghanistan.

In addition to strengthening military relations with Turkey and Greece, the United States was also successful in obtaining base rights in Somalia, Oman and Kenya. In addition, while not formally having a base in Egypt, the United States began to develop a major military relationship with that country as by the spring and early summer of 1980 Egyptian and American forces began to carry out joint maneuvers. Needless to say, Moscow was very unhappy with these developments and used the joint U.S.-Egyptian maneuvers to castigate Sadat as a traitor to the Arab cause.

An *Izvestia* article on July 15 summarized Moscow's concerns with the growth of American power in the Middle East and its efforts to portray this development as a threat to Middle Eastern states:

> . . . The U.S. is speeding the implementation of its plans to create Middle Eastern "base states" where it could station large contingents of American military personnel, and the question is not one of deploying individual units, but, as observers point out—entire divisions together with the American fleet and the "rapid deployment force." Their purpose is to be the American militarists' "strike force" in the Middle East.
>
> Whom will the American bayonets be aimed against? First and foremost against the National liberation processes that are taking place in the region and against those countries that oppose the dictate of the American oil companies. It is also no secret that the American forces could be used at any moment to seize the petroleum resources of that very rich area of the world.[51]

As Soviet concern grew over the rise in U.S. military power in the Middle East, increasing Soviet concern over internal developments in Iran was also evident. While Moscow remained supportive of the Islamic fundamentalists who insisted on holding onto the hostages, the Soviet leadership was less happy with other actions of this group which included the purge and closing of Iran's universities, and their growing emphasis on the Islamization of Iranian society which seemed to give little chance for left-wing groups to operate openly. Meanwhile, the second stage of the Iranian parliamentary elections had brought about a victory for the representatives of the Islamic Republican Party, a development that, when combined with the revision of the new constitution giving Khomeini almost total power, seemed to ensure the further Islamization of Iranian life.[52]

While Moscow has always been willing to tolerate suppression of local Communists and left-wing forces so long as a country had good relations with the USSR and was following an "anti-imperialist" foreign policy line, its patience appeared to wear thin with Iran at the end of June when Foreign Minister Ghotbzadeh expelled the First Secretary of the Soviet Embassy in Iran, Vladimir Golvanov, on charges of espionage and followed this up two days later by again sharply criticizing the USSR and ordering Moscow to reduce the size of its diplomatic personnel in Iran to nine—the number of Iranian diplomats in the USSR.[53] Ghotbzadeh also stated that the Tudeh Party was taking advantage of Iran's preoccupation with the U.S. hostages to conduct activities benefiting the USSR. Two days later an estimated 500,000 Iranians marched in Tehran demanding the dissolution of the Fedayeen, Mujahadeen, and other left-wing groups.[54] Perhaps reacting to the rise in anti-leftist spirit as well as the denunciations by Ghotbzadeh, Moscow demanded more security at its embassy in

Tehran, claiming that it had information that "elements hostile to the USSR" planned to seize the embassy.[55] While the Soviet Embassy was not seized at that time, the Tudeh Party, which had been denounced by Ghotbzadeh, had its offices stormed on July 22 by a mob of Islamic militants.[56]

As the government of Iran took an increasingly hostile position toward the USSR, despite its continuing confrontation with the United States, Moscow continued to seek to convince the Iranians that they needed a good relationship with the USSR for protection against the United States. Thus *Pravda* on July 26 noted that the base agreement that the United States had just signed with Oman "unquestionably threatens the independence and national sovereignty of the Persian Gulf states, above all Iran." In addition, Moscow claimed that the United States was behind the major coup attempt against the Khomeini regime in July.[57] A *New Times* commentary on the abortive coup also noted that Iran suffered from the attempts of "some influential forces within the country to isolate it from its friends, the Soviet Union included." The commentary went on to say that these forces were "systematically conducting propaganda hostile to the USSR, slandering Soviet foreign policy, and distorting its character and aims so as to dull the vigilence of the Iranian people and distract their attention from the insidious acts of U.S. imperialism." The *New Times* article also implicitly criticized Iran's Muslim fundamentalists by attacking "counter-revolutionaries who were inciting groups of religious fanatics to action against the democratic and other leftist forces, in particular against the Tudeh party, which backs Ayatollah Khomeini's anti-imperialist line."[58] While seeking to demonstrate the USSR's "true friendship" with Iran, Moscow also undertook a series of very sharp criticisms of Foreign Minister Ghotbzadeh,[59] culminating with a major attack in *Pravda* on August 27 which called him a man of "pro-American orientation" who "hopes to undermine relations" between Iran and the USSR and "weaken Iran's efforts to achieve independence." The *Pravda* article also warned Iran, "It is common knowledge that when Soviet-Iranian ties weakened, the aggressors stepped up their intrigues and subversive activity against Iran."

Neither Ghotbzadeh, nor Bani-Sadr, who also was subjected to Soviet criticism, seemed cowed by the Soviet threats. Thus, on August 14, Ghotbzadeh strongly attacked the USSR in a letter to Soviet Foreign Minister Gromyko that was also broadcast on Tehran radio. In it Ghotbzadeh asserted that the USSR was no less "Satanic" than the United States, and accused Moscow of giving arms and satellite intelligence photos to Kurdish rebels fighting for autonomy and having its embassy and consulates spy on Iran. Ghotbzadeh also told Gromyko that Iran "shall not forget how the Soviet government treated our people during the past half century," in particular "the occupation of part of our sacred land and the emergence of a party which, since its founding has served as a fifth column for your country in our beloved land."[60]

While Moscow's relations with Bani Sadr and Ghotbzadeh deteriorated, the Soviet leadership evidently held out hope for the new prime minister, Islamic fundamentalist Ali Rajai,[61] who took office in August, as well as the Ayatollah Beheshti, head of the Islamic Republican Party, whom *New Times* Middle East specialist Dmitry Volsky cited as saying that Soviet-Iranian relations "are of a constructive nature and have good chances of developing."[62] Apparently, Moscow reasoned that while Bani Sadr wanted the hostages released so that Iran could get on with its economic development, the hard line Islamic Republicans, for whom Islamic purity took priority over economic development, would continue to drag out the hostage confinement, thereby preventing any Iranian-American reconciliation. While the Soviet leaders were far from happy with the suppression of Iran's leftist groups and ethnic minorities, particularly the Kurds, who again began to receive favorable Soviet press coverage, at the very least Moscow seemed hopeful that the continued holding of the hostages would keep Iran out of the American camp and on the "anti-imperialist" path. Unfortunately for the USSR, however, the outbreak of war between Iran and Iraq appeared to change the hostage equation in Iranian politics and once again held out the possibility of a rapprochement between Iran and the United States.

THE IRAN-IRAQ WAR

Tension had been building between Iran and Iraq almost from the time that Ayatollah Khomeini took power. Khomeini, who had been expelled from his place of exile in Iraq at the request of the Shah, was seen by the Iraqi leadership as a threat to the loyalty of its Shiite population, among whom Khomeini had lived for 15 years. At the same time, Iran saw Iraq as a cause of the unrest in the Arab-populated province of Kuzistan. Behind these concerns were two very different conceptions of the future. Iraq, which was seeking to become the leader of the Arab world, emphasized Arabism as its main propaganda theme and in February 1980 issued a Pan-Arab charter in an effort to rally the Arab states behind its leadership. By contrast, the central theme for Iran was Islam, and Ayatollah Khomeini and his entourage, who made no secret of their desire to export Iran's Islamic revolution, sought to rally the Muslim world, both Arab and non-Arab, behind the banner of Islam. Superimposed on this conflict was the historic Gulf rivalry between Arab and Persian, and by April 1980, when a serious border conflict broke out between Iran and Iraq, it seemed clear that each was trying to undermine the other's government. Indeed, Iraq President Saddam Hussein blamed Iran for the grenade attack against Deputy Premier Tariq Aziz, and, in retaliation, expelled thousands of Iraqi Shiites of Iranian parentage and demanded the renegotiation of the 1975 Iran-Iraq Treaty.[63] For their part, Ghotbzadeh and Khomeini pledged to overthrow the Iraqi regime which they depicted as the agent of the United States, and Bani-Sadr delivered the ultimate insult to Iraq by claiming that Arab nationalism—Ba'athist or otherwise—was anti-Islamic and equivalent to Zionism.[64] Iran also claimed that Iraq was behind the assassination attempt against Ghotbzadeh when the Iranian Foreign Minister was visiting Kuwait.

For its part, Moscow was very uncomforatable as the Iran-Iraq conflict heated up in April, as it appeared that the USSR might have to choose sides. While Soviet reporting of the conflict reflected a relatively neutral position, Radio Moscow seemed a bit more sympathetic to Iran[65] although the overall theme of Soviet propaganda was that it was a most unfortunate conflict from which only "imperialism" could benefit. From the Soviet point of view a war would only serve to divide the anti-American forces in the Middle East,[66] and Moscow naturally encouraged mediation attempts such as the one undertaken by PLO leader Yasser Arafat in early May. Unfortunately for Moscow, the mediation effort was a failure with Radio Tehran in an Arabic broadcast on May 7 repudiating Arafat's mission:

> The PLO, headed by Arafat, should lead an Arab campaign of con-
> frontation against the terrorist puppet regime in Baghdad, such as the
> one waged against the As Sadat regime in Egypt. As a matter of fact,
> the confrontation against the Baghdad regime must be even more
> severe, because the terrorist puppet regime in Baghdad is just as
> dangerous to the Muslim Iraqi people and the Palestine question as
> the As Sadat regime is to the Arab cause. Moreover, the Baghdad
> regime's alliance with Israel and the United States is as strong as
> that of Anwar Sadat.[67]

The Iran-Iraqi conflict continued to simmer during the summer and began to affect Soviet-Iranian relations directly in August when the Iranian Ambassador to the Soviet Union, Mohammed Mokri, told an embassy press conference that if Soviet military assistance to Iraq did not end, he doubted that Iran would keep its ambassador in Moscow.[68] The USSR then apparently sought to assuage the Iranians by offering to sell them arms (along with Iraq), albeit unsuccessfully, because two weeks later, Mokri announced at an embassy press conference that Iran had turned down the offer because it did not want to be a "regional gendarme or waste money on weapons."[69]

When the border skirmishing erupted into a full-scale war in mid-September, the Soviet Union was in a very awkward position as a good argument could have been made in the Kremlin to aid either side. On the one hand, Moscow was linked to Baghdad by a Treaty of Friendship and Cooperation and had long been Iraq's main supplier of military weaponry. In addition, Iraq had been a leading foe of the U.S.-sponsored Camp David agreements and, as a nation with pretensions to leadership in the Arab world, could one day become the focus of the "anti-imperialist" Arab unity that Moscow had sought for so long. Indeed, by its leadership at the two Baghdad conferences, Iraq demonstrated a potential for just such a role, and the growing relationship between Iraq and Saudi Arabia that was in evidence before the Iran-Iraq war erupted may have been seen by Moscow as a development that would further move the Saudis out of the American camp. Yet another argument that could have been made in the Kremlin for aiding Iraq was the fact that such aid would be a demonstration to the Arab world that Moscow was indeed a reliable ally (some Arab states had questioned this, despite Soviet aid to the Arab cause in the 1973 war). From the point of view of the Soviet economy, aid to Iraq would help assure the continued flow of Iraqi oil to the USSR and its East European allies.

Soviet opponents of aid to Iraq could point to the continued persecution of Iraqi Communists,[70] Iraq's clear move away from the USSR since the treaty was signed in 1972, as typified by its condemnation of Moscow because of its invasion of Afghanistan,[71] its February 1980 Pan-Arab charter which called for the elimination of both superpowers from the Arab world,[71] and the growth of its economic and even military ties with France and other West Euorpean nations. On balance, however, since the Russians saw Iraq as "objectively" a major anti-Western force, a very good argument could have been made to aid the Iraqis in the war.

On the other hand, however, a very good case could also have been made for aiding Iran. First and foremost, the Khomeini revolution detached Iran from its close alignment with the United States, thereby striking a major blow to the U.S. position in both the Persian Gulf and the Middle East as a whole. In addition, by holding onto the American hostages, the Khomeini regime carried on a daily humiliation of the United States, a factor that further lowered American prestige in the region. Consequently, any major Soviet aid effort to Iraq contained the possibility of ending the hostage impasse (indeed, as the war heated up, the Islamic fundamentalists in Iran suddenly seemed more responsive on the hostage issue, and on November 2 the fundamentalist-dominated Parliament voted to release the hostages, albeit conditionally) and even moving Iran back toward the American camp because of Iran's dependence on U.S. military equipment. Given Iran's large population (three times that of Iraq) and its strategic position along the Persian Gulf and at the Strait of Hormuz, such a development would clearly not be in Moscow's interest. Another strategic factor that the Soviet leadership had to take into consideration was that Iran, unlike Iraq, had a common border with the USSR, as well as with Soviet-occupied Afghanistan. While Iranian efforts on behalf of the Afghan rebels had so far been limited, one could not rule out a major increase in Iranian aid to the Afghan rebels, should Moscow side with Iraq, as well as a more pronounced effort on the part of Khomeini to infect the USSR's own Muslims with his brand of Islamic fundamentalism.[73] Finally, as in the case of Iraq, there was an important economic argument. While Iran had cut off gas exports to the USSR, the signing of a major transit agreement between the two countries just before the war erupted[74] may well have seemed to Moscow as the first step toward the resumption of natural gas exports, and given Iran's large available reserves of this fuel,

Moscow may wish to encourage the supply relationship, particularly if—as some experts predict—the USSR might run short of oil in the mid-1980s.

Soviet opponents of aid to Iran could have pointed to the Islamic fundamentalists' treatment of the Tudeh, although it was not as brutal as Iraq's treatment of its Communists, as well as its treatment of Iranian minorities with whom the USSR hoped to cultivate a good relationship. Here again, however, Iran's treatment of its Kurds seemed no worse than Iraq's. Finally, opponents of aid to Iran could have pointed to Iran's leading anti-Soviet role in Islamic conferences, although again there may not have been too much to choose between Iran's and Iraq's anti-Sovietism. The main factor in the Soviet evaluation of both countries was that they seemed far more anti-American than anti-Soviet, and both contributed to the weakening of the American position in the Middle East. For this reason, Moscow needed a good relationship with both and could not afford to alienate either.

Given this situation, it is not surprising that, at least to the time of this writing (February 1, 1982), Moscow has remained neutral while urging a speedy settlement of the war lest the "imperialists" benefit. Indeed, the outbreak and prolongation of the war has brought with it a number of rather serious problems for Moscow. In the first place, there was a major split in the anti-Sadat forces in the Arab world as Libya and Syria came out for Iran, while Jordan openly backed Iraq. In addition to Iraq breaking diplomatic relations with Syria and Libya, Saudi Arabia broke diplomatic relations with Libya,[75] although the Saudis did not formally associate themselves with Iraq. The end result of the war to date has been a major disruption of the "anti-imperialist" Arab unity that Moscow had wanted for so long. As New Times commentator Alexander Usvatov lamented,

> Fought between two non-aligned countries pursuing anti-imperialist policies, the war is bound to weaken them in the face of intensified imperialist scheming, and sows divisions and disarray in the world's anti-imperialist front, creating a serious threat to peace and international security.[76]

In addition to the split in the anti-Sadat front, Moscow feared a major American gain in the conflict. The emplacement of American AWACS aircraft and ground radar personnel in Saudi Arabia (following Iranian threats against Saudi Arabia) seemed to demonstrate American willingness to help defend Saudi Arabia and other Arab states in time of need and helped refute Moscow's charge that the U.S. military buildup in the Indian Ocean was a threat to the Arab world. Indeed, the AWACS move appeared to reverse the decline in Saudi-American relations and held out the possibility of a further improvement in relations.[77]

A related problem for the USSR was the formation of the Gulf Cooperation Council, an organization composed of Saudi Arabia, the United Arab

Emirates, Oman, Bahrein, Qatar and Kuwait. Precipitated both by the Soviet invasion of Afghanistan and the Iran-Iraq war, the organization was composed of conservative and basically pro-Western monarchies, three of whose members (Oman, Saudi Arabia and Bahrein) had military ties to the United States while only one, Kuwait, had diplomatic relations with the Soviet Union. As the organization took shape,[78] Moscow feared that it would provide both a military and political backdrop for increased American activity in the Persian Gulf, especially since Oman had already agreed to provide a base for the American Rapid Deployment Force.

Finally, as Iraq and Iran continued to bomb each other's oil installations, Moscow became concerned that, once the war was over, both countries might turn to the United States and Western Europe for aid in reconstruction. A Tass commentary on October 10 made clear this Soviet concern:

> It is easy to see in these conditions the imperialist powers are quite willing to turn the conflict to their advantage, to capitalize on the economic weakening of Iran and Iraq, so as to grant them imperialist economic aid on their own terms, whose aim will undoubtedly be to restore in those countries the positions of Western oil monopolies, to entangle them in the web of predatory financial agreements, in short to restore their economic domination.[79]

As the war continued, Moscow appeared to be able to do little but urge its immediate end, proclaim Soviet neutrality, and warn both Iran and Iraq, along with the other countries of the Middle East, that the United States was exploiting the war for its own benefit. The Soviet media also highlighted American efforts to create an international armada to patrol the Persian Gulf and emphasized the threat to the region posed by the visit of General David Jones, chairman of the U.S. Joint Chiefs of Staff, to Oman, Egypt, Saudi Arabia, and Israel.[80] In addition to denouncing American efforts to exploit the war, Moscow seemed to try to maintain some ties with both belligerents by allowing a limited amount of Soviet weaponry to be transhipped to both Iran and Iraq although the USSR publicly denied any such shipments.[81] As its frustration mounted over being unable to affect an end to the conflict which seemed to be greatly strengthening the Middle East position of the United States (and thereby weakening that of the USSR in the zero-sum game view of the Middle East held by Moscow),[82] the Soviet leadership made two moves: The first was to utilize the signing of a Friendship and Cooperation Treaty with Syria as a demonstration of the continued importance of Moscow to the Arab world; a second major Soviet effort was an open appeal for the neutralization of the Persian Gulf—a rather transparent device to reverse the gains made by the United States as a result of the war—in a speech made by Brezhnev during the Soviet leader's visit to India in December.

Assad's visit to Moscow in October 1980, three weeks after the outbreak of the Iran-Iraq war, was highlighted by the signing of a Friendship and Cooperation Treaty between Syria and the Soviet Union. This document seemed to give the USSR a stronger foothold in Syria at a time when that country, as well as the entire Middle East, was wracked by the Iran-Iraq war. Given the fact that the USSR had long been pressing Assad to sign such a document, the treaty must be considered a victory for Soviet policy although Assad's growing domestic and foreign isolation appear to be the prime cause for his willingness to sign it. The Israeli-Egyptian peace treaty and the growing normalization between the two countries left Syria in a weakened position vis-à-vis Israel, while at the same time Syria's growing conflict with Iraq had left it even more exposed. In addition, besides being bogged down in Lebanon, Assad faced a growing internal threat from the Muslim Brotherhood, which had been assassinating a number of prominent Alawi figures.[83] Adding to Syria's sense of isolation was a further cooling of its relationship with Jordan, which had become increasingly friendly with Iraq, who was granting it a large amount of economic aid.[84] These developments had increased Assad's dependence on the USSR and lay at the root not only of his endorsement of the Soviet invasion of Afghanistan but also of his decision to agree finally to a Friendship and Cooperation Treaty with Moscow, an action he had been resisting for almost a decade.[85]

Interestingly enough, however, despite the treaty, Assad continued to seek to keep a certain amount of flexibility in his relationship with the USSR. Thus, before signing the treaty with Moscow, he signed a unity agreement with Libya, thereby demonstrating that Syria was not as isolated as either its friends or foes may have thought. In addition, despite the outward harmony of the visit, there were clearly continuing disagreements as the final communiqué noted "a thorough and fruitful exchange of opinions" had taken place in an "atmosphere of mutual understanding"[86]—code words for disagreement. Part of the problem may have lain in open Syrian support for Iran in the war while, as mentioned above, the USSR wanted to remain neutral, although Moscow may have leaned a bit in the direction of Syria on this point by warmly praising the Iranian revolution in the joint communiqué. For its part Syria endorsed the Soviet position on Afghanistan, stressed the need for Soviet participation in all stages of a Middle Eastern settlement, and proclaimed Syria's willingness to "continue to repulse any attempts to undermine Soviet-Arab friendship." As far as Soviet military assistance was concerned, the joint communiqué merely stated that "questions of the USSR providing further assistance to Syria in strengthening her defense capability were discussed during the talks and relevant decisions adopted."

The treaty itself was a fairly standard Soviet Friendship and Cooperation Treaty, unique only in its denunciation of "Zionism as a form of racism" both in the preamble and in article 3.[87] Moscow, perhaps to maintain Syria's independent image, stated that it would "respect the policy of non-alignment pursued

by Syria" (similar language had been used in the Soviet-Afghan Treaty of Friendship and Cooperation of December 1978).[88] As in other treaties, both sides
promised to consult regularly, and to consult immediately in the case of situations jeopardizing the peace and security of one of the parties. In the area of
military cooperation, Article 10 of the treaty stated that "the parties shall
continue to develop cooperation in the military field on the basis of appropriate
agreements concluded between them in the interest of strengthening their
defense capability." Essentially, the treaty codified the existing relationship between the USSR and Syria, and in the absence of any secret military clauses,[89]
served to provide a formal foundation for the improved Syrian-Soviet relationship. Thus Moscow was assured of a formal presence in the very heart of the
Arab world (the other Soviet Friendship and Cooperation Treaties still in effect
with Arab states were with peripheral Iraq and South Yemen), while also
formally demonstrating Soviet support for Syria in the face of its conflicts with
surrounding Arab states and Israel.

Yet, for Moscow, the signing of the treaty with Assad and the provision of
additional military aid posed a number of problems. In the first place, beset
by internal and external difficulties Assad might provoke an international crisis,
either with Israel or with one of his Arab enemies, and then drag in the USSR.
Secondly, Assad, who had demonstrated his independence of Moscow on a
number of occasions in the past, might do so again, thus complicating Soviet
Middle Eastern policy at a time when, because of the Iran-Iraq war, Soviet policy
was already in a state of disarray. Indeed, in the crisis with Jordan in late
November 1980, and in the Lebanese "missile crisis" with Israel which began in
April 1981,[90] Assad was to demonstrate just such an independent turn.

The war between Iran and Iraq continued through November and directly
affected the Arab summit conference scheduled for the end of the month in
Amman, Jordan. Fearing that the Arab states would condemn it for aiding non-
Arab Iran in the war, Syria boycotted the conference and pressured Lebanon and
the PLO to do so as well, while Libya (which was also aiding Iran), Algeria, and
South Yemen, the other members of the Steadfastness Front also boycotted the
meeting. The Syrian-led boycott of the Arab summit was a blow to Moscow's
efforts to help rebuild "anti-imperialist" unity in the Arab world. An even
more serious problem for Moscow took place in the aftermath of the summit
when Syrian forces mobilized on Jordan's border in an effort to pressure King
Hussein. Syria claimed that it was mobilizing because King Hussein was
providing a base for the Muslim Brotherhood for its attacks on his regime, but
it seems more likely that Assad was trying to punish Hussein for hosting the
Arab summit which came out in support of Iraq in the Iran-Iraq war. In any
case Moscow was pulled into the situation because Assad chose the time of the
visit by Soviet Politburo member Vasili Kuznetsov, who had come to Damascus
to transmit the Soviet-Syrian treaty ratification papers, to stage the crisis. In
doing this, Assad clearly tried to demonstrate that Moscow backed him in the
crisis. For his part, perhaps to dispel this impression, Kuznetsov in his Damascus

speech at the height of the crisis, stressed the Soviet-Syrian treaty's importance in "eliminating hotbeds of dangerous tension in the Near East," and called for the peaceful solution of problems between Arab countries.[91] In any case, while Saudi Arabia was ultimately to mediate the crisis, the confrontation between Syria and Jordan helped to halt the slow rapprochement between Moscow and Amman (Hussein postponed a planned visit to Moscow) while once again reinforcing American-Jordanian ties which had been strained since Camp David. Indeed, Hussein turned to Washington with a request for arms to counter what he called a Soviet-backed threat to the security of his country.[92] Furthermore, as a result of the Syrian move, Moscow may well have felt that Jordan was more susceptible to American pressure to join the Camp David peace process.[93]

If the signing of the treaty with Syria was to cause Moscow more trouble than it expected, the Brezhnev visit to India and the proclamation of the Brezhnev plan for the neutralization of the Persian Gulf was not to prove much more efficacious. In many ways, India was an almost ideal place for Brezhnev to launch his Persian Gulf plan, which, like the Soviet Middle East peace plan launched at the height of the Lebanese civil war of 1976, seemed aimed at regaining the initiative for the Soviet Union at a time when Middle Eastern developments seemed out of Moscow's control.[94] The Indian government of Indira Gandhi was concerned about the growing military ties between the United States and China and by Chinese military aid to Pakistan. Indeed, these developments, coupled with the U.S. military deployment in the Indian Ocean and the victory of Republican presidential candidate Ronald Reagan, may have brought back memories of an earlier Republican administration's "tilt" to Pakistan in 1971. As a consequence, Indira Gandhi clearly felt the need for a close tie with Moscow, and the Russians, who had signed a major arms deal with India only a few months earlier, moved to reinforce the relationship further by agreeing to increase significantly Soviet shipments of oil and oil products to India to help compensate for the petroleum imports lost because of the outbreak of the Iran-Iraq war.[95] In return for Soviet military, political and economic support, India provided an important service to Moscow. As the largest nonaligned state, and as both one of the founders of the movement and the host of the February 1981 Nonaligned Conference, Indian political support for Moscow could be expected to assuage some of the nonaligned nations' unhappiness with Moscow because of its invasion of Afghanistan. Indeed, the final communiqué issued after the Brezhnev visit did not even mention Afghanistan and stated only that a "negotiated political solution alone can guarantee a durable settlement of the existing problems of the region," thereby echoing Moscow's call for Iran and Pakistan to begin negotiations with the pro-Soviet Afghan government. In addition, the communiqué also called for the dismantling of all foreign military and naval bases in the area "such as Diego Garcia" and the prevention of the creation of new bases, along with the return of Diego Garcia to Mauritius—a clear anti-American position.[96]

In addition to reaching agreement with India on these issues, Brezhnev also utilized his visit to call for the neutralization of the Persian Gulf. Given the importance of the Brezhnev plan, which received extensive publicity in the Soviet press, the five-point proposal, which was included in Brezhnev's speech to the Indian Parliament, is printed in its entirety below:

> We propose to the United States, other Western powers, China, Japan, all of the states which will show interest in this, to agree on the following mutual obligations:
>
> Not to establish foreign military bases in the area of the Persian Gulf and adjacent islands; not to deploy nuclear or any other weapons of mass destruction there;
>
> Not to use and not to threaten with the use of force against the countries of the Persian Gulf area, not to interfere in their internal affairs;
>
> To respect the status of non-alignment, chosen by Persian Gulf states; not to draw them into military groupings with the participation of nuclear powers;
>
> To respect the soverign right of the states of the region to their natural resources;
>
> Not to raise any obstacles or threats to normal trade exchange and the use of sea lanes that link the states of that region with other countries of the world.[97]

It seems clear that the Brezhnev plan had three main goals: (1) reversing the diplomatic and military gains that had accrued to the United States as a result of the war and the U.S. naval buildup in the region, by the call for the elimination of all "foreign" military bases; (2) preventing the formation of a Western-linked Persian Gulf security pact based on a U.S.-armed and supported Saudi Arabia, by the prohibition of military groupings of Persian Gulf states linked to nuclear powers; and (3) championing Iranian interests against the United States through the call for free use of the sea lanes and normal trade exchange (the United States had been considering a naval blockade against Iran as a step toward freeing the hostages).[98]

While the Brezhnev plan was warmly received in India, it was rejected by the United States and received only a mixed welcome in the Middle East. If one of the goals of the Brezhnev plan was to win support in Iran for Soviet policies, the Soviet plan did not meet with success. Indeed, as the Iranian-American negotiations toward release of the hostages moved into high gear, Soviet-Iranian relations appeared to deteriorate as Afghan refugees stormed the Soviet Embassy in Tehran on the anniversary of the Soviet invasion of Afghanistan and burned the Soviet flag. While Moscow strongly protested the action of "the unruly mob" and called for the punishment of the attackers and their organizers,[99] the official Iranian reply, while somewhat apologetic, said the attackers were justified in their actions.[100] It is doubtful whether the Soviet leaders noted the irony inherent in the Iranian statement since only a year before the Soviet press had used similar terms in justifying the Iranian seizure of the American Embassy in Tehran.

Nonetheless, the USSR apparently swallowed its anger, and Soviet broadcasts to Iran continued to emphasize that the USSR wanted friendly relations with Iran.[101] One cause of the Soviet effort to continue to seek close ties to Iran despite the embassy incident was the speed-up of the Iranian-American talks on freeing the hostages. Indeed as the date for the Carter administration's departure from office neared, the pace of the talks intensified and it appeared that an agreement might well be reached before Ronald Reagan took office. In an effort to prevent such a development, the Soviet media began to print and broadcast to Iran reports of an imminent American attack on that country,[102] and brushed aside American complaints that the Soviet broadcasts were harming the negotiations.[103] The Soviet ploy was ultimately to fail, however, and on January 20, 1981, the day Ronald Reagan was inaugurated, the hostages were finally released, thanks, in part, to the aid of Steadfastness Front member Algeria, which played an important mediating role.

MOSCOW'S RESPONSE TO THE REAGAN ADMINISTRATION'S MIDDLE EAST POLICY

In surveying their Middle Eastern position at the time that the Reagan administration took office, the Soviet leaders may well have felt that their position was a mixed one. In the first place, despite the divisions in the Arab world, Sadat remained isolated because of Camp David, which no other Arab state had endorsed. In addition, Moscow had close relations with the Front of Steadfastness and Confrontation (Syria, Libya, Algeria, South Yemen, and the PLO), who were the most vocal of the anti-Sadat nations in the Arab world and who dutifully echoed the Soviet policy line on such issues as Afghanistan in return for Soviet military aid and diplomatic support (Algeria was a partial exception to this pattern). In addition, Moscow had good relations with non-Arab and non-Muslim Ethiopia, a key African, as well as Middle Eastern state, although at the cost of alienating Somalia, which had gone over to the United States and which had granted the United States port facilities as well as a base for the American Rapid Deployment Force. While benefiting from its increasingly close ties to Ethiopia and the Steadfastness Front, Moscow also faced a number of problems. In the first place, while the Steadfastness Front Arab states and Ethiopia were willing to overlook the Soviet invasion of Afghanistan, both Iran and the Centrist,* or so-called moderate Arab states denounced the Soviet

---

*Saudi Arabia, Kuwait, Jordan, the United Arab Emirates, North Yemen, Somalia, Bahrein, Qatar, the Sudan, Morocco, and Tunisia. Iraq, which shared the Steadfastness stated goal of destroying Israel, but which was not a member of the Steadfastness Front because of its enmity toward Syria, also denounced the invasion while opposing Camp David.

action, and Moscow's efforts to demonstrate its fidelity to the Muslim cause by championing Iran in its conflict with the United States over the hostages and by diverting Muslim attention from the situation in Afghanistan to the Arab-Israeli conflict had met with only limited success. The other negative developments Moscow had to be concerned about as Reagan took office included a possible reconciliation between Iran and the United States, the increasing diplomatic acceptability of the U.S. military forces in the Persian Gulf, a very severe split in the anti-Sadat grouping of Arab states, and the possibility that Centrist Arab states like Jordan and Saudi Arabia might yet be drawn into the American-sponsored Camp David peace process. Moscow was soon to try to reverse these negative trends.

By the time the CPSU convened its 26th Congress on February 23, 1981, the outline of the Reagan administration's Middle East policy was already clear. The United States was seeking to build an anti-Soviet alliance of Middle East states, irrespective of their mutual conflicts, thereby pursuing a policy that was the mirror image of Soviet efforts to build an anti-imperialist bloc in the region. In his speech to the CPSU Congress, Brezhnev outlined the thrust of the Soviet response to the Reagan policy and to the negative trends in the Middle East that had hampered Moscow in its quest for influence in the region.[104] In the first place, to counterbalance the growing military power of the United States in the Persian Gulf and Indian Ocean region and the growing diplomatic accept-ability of that presence because of both the Soviet invasion of Afghanistan and the Iran-Iraq war, the Soviet leader reiterated his call, first made in India in mid-December 1980, for an international agreement to neutralize the Persian Gulf. The Soviet leader also offered, for the first time, to combine discussions of the Afghanistan situation with that of the Persian Gulf although he made it clear that Afghanistan's internal situation (that is, its Communist government) was not a matter for discussion, and that the USSR would not withdraw its forces from Afghanistan until the "infiltration of counterrevolutionary bands" was completely stopped and treaties were signed between Afghanistan and its neighbors to ensure that no further infiltration would take place.

As far as the Iran-Iraq war was concerned, the Soviet leader once again called for its immediate termination, and stated that the Soviet Union was taking "practical steps" to achieve that goal. In discussing the Arab-Israeli conflict Brezhnev denounced the Camp David peace process and again enumerated the tripartite Soviet solution for the conflict: (1) Israeli withdrawal from all terri-tories captured in 1967; (2) the right of the Palestinians to create their own state; and (3) the ensuring of the security of all states in the region, including Israel. Brezhnev also repeated the Soviet call for an international conference on the Arab-Israeli conflict, with the participation of the Arabs, including the PLO, and Israel, along with the United States and some European states. All in all,

---

The Centrist Arab states seemed willing to entertain the idea of peace with Israel; the Stead-fastness Front members did not.

the Soviet proposals on Afghanistan, the Persian Gulf, and the Arab-Israeli conflict, together with the announced efforts to end the Iran-Iraq war, seemed aimed at placing Moscow at the center stage of Middle Eastern diplomacy, a diplomatic position not enjoyed by the Soviet Union since the 1973 Arab-Israeli war.

Interestingly enough, the Soviet leader also made note in his speech of two related Middle Eastern phenomena to which the USSR was having difficulty in adjusting its policies: the Khomeini revolution in Iran and the rise of fundamentalist Islam. As far as Iran was concerned, Brezhnev noted that "despite its complex and contradictory nature, it is basically an anti-imperialist revolution, although domestic and foreign reaction is seeking to alter this character." Brezhnev also offered Soviet cooperation with Iran (no mention was made of Soviet-Iraqi relations in his speech), but only on the grounds of "reciprocity," perhaps a reference to continuing anti-Soviet speeches and activities in Iran. In discussing Islam, Brezhnev acknowledged that "the liberation struggle could develop under the banner of Islam," but also noted that "experience also indicates that reaction uses Islamic slogans to start counterrevolutionary insurrections."

In the aftermath of the 26th Party Congress, Moscow pursued two diplomatic policies. First, it sought to strengthen its ties with two of its Steadfastness Front allies—Libya and Algeria—with whom there had been some recent difficulties, and it also sought to cultivate two Centrist Arab states—Kuwait and Jordan—to prevent them from moving toward the United States.

Libyan leader Muammar Kaddafi arrived in Moscow on April 27 at a time when he was isolated in the Arab world (the alliance with Syria, signed in September 1970 was inoperative)[105] and was also in difficulty with many of his African neighbors because of the Libyan intervention in Chad. Moscow appeared rather ambivalent about Libya's efforts at unity with Chad, in part because of its negative effects on other African states (especially the Sudan and Nigeria), while Kaddafi's ideological pretensions also continued to bother the Soviet leadership. Nonetheless, Kaddafi's vehement anti-Americanism was on balance an asset for Soviet diplomacy while his political isolation and increasing conflict with the United States (the United States was to close Libya's diplomatic mission in Washington a week after Kaddafi's visit to Moscow, in part because of Libya's role in supporting international terrorism) made Libya increasingly dependent on the USSR.[106] For his part, Kaddafi, who made no secret of his desire to destroy Israel, continually requested more Soviet aid than Moscow was willing to offer and his request on behalf of the Steadfastness Front for more aid against Israel was made again during this visit to Moscow, his first since 1976.[107] Nonetheless, the final communiqué, which referred to the talks as having taken place in "an atmosphere of broad mutual understanding" (code words for disagreement over several issues), merely praised the Steadfastness Front (no specific promises of aid were announced), and in his welcoming speech, Brezhnev pointedly noted the differences—including ideological differences—between the USSR and Libya. Still, the USSR did go a long way toward legitimizing the Libyan role in Chad, as the final communiqué noted the "positive role that has been played by Libya's aid to Chad."[108] Moscow also denounced U.S. efforts to brand Libya as a terrorist state and also supported the Libyan position in the dispute over the former Spanish Sahara by endorsing the call for the right of self-determination for the Western Saharan people. While Moscow got Libya's support for the Soviet call to make the Persian Gulf and Indian Ocean areas "zones of peace," Moscow evidently was unable to get Kaddafi's agreement for an international conference on the Arab-Israeli conflict as there was no mention of the conference—long a major Soviet goal—in the final communiqué.[109]

The second Steadfastness state leader to come to Moscow for talks with the Soviet leadership in 1981 was Algerian President Chadli Ben Jedid, who came to the Kremlin on June 8. While the USSR and Algeria had maintained close ties since Algerian independence in 1962, the death of Houari Boumadienne in 1979 had raised questions about the future course of Algerian foreign policy. In addition, despite U.S. military aid to Morocco, the United States and Algeria had developed close economic ties. (Interestingly enough, despite Soviet military aid to Algeria, Morocco and the USSR had also developed close economic ties.) Finally, Algeria's role in the freeing of the U.S. hostages in Iran could not have been to Moscow's liking, although the Algerians were to deem it a "debt of honor" in repayment of John F. Kennedy's support of their drive for independence.[110] Nonetheless, the onset of the Reagan administration was to cause a chilling of U.S.-Algerian ties. In the first place the United States began to step up its military aid to Morocco and stated that it would no longer link arms sales to Morocco with Moroccan progress in achieving a negotiated settlement of the Spanish Sahara conflict.[111] Secondly, the long negotiations between Algeria and El Paso Natural Gas on a major U.S.-Algerian natural gas agreement fell through, leaving Algeria with an infrastructure expense of $2.5 billion for natural gas wells, pipelines, and liquification plants.[112] Finally, Reagan's general "tough-line" toward the Third World on such issues as the Law of the Sea served to alienate the Algerians. Thus when Ben Jedid came to Moscow, Algerian-U.S. relations had cooled considerably and Moscow may have looked forward to a further consolidation of Soviet-Algerian relations.

Nonetheless, all was not complete harmony during Ben-Jedid's visit as evidenced by the joint communiqué's assertion that the talks had taken place in an atmosphere of "frankness," and, as in the case of Libya, there was no mention of Algerian support for Brezhnev's call for an international conference on the Middle East.[113] For its part, however, Moscow endorsed Algeria's position on the Sahara conflict, as the communiqué noted that both sides agreed that the people of the Western Sahara had the right of self-determination, and both Algeria and the USSR condemned foreign bases in the Persian Gulf,[114] while Moscow also used the Algerian leader's visit to call for the transformation of the Mediterranean into a zone of peace, a maneuver that, if successful, would have meant the ejection of the U.S. Sixth Fleet from the Mediterranean.[115]

In sum, it would appear that in the case of the visits of both Algerian President Chadli Ben Jedid and Libyan leader Mu'ammar Kaddafi, Moscow gave somewhat more in diplomatic support than it got in return. Nonetheless, at a time when the Middle East was in a great state of flux, with many trends moving in a negative direction as far as the USSR was concerned, the Soviet leadership seemed willing to pay the diplomatic price to reinforce ties with both states. Interestingly enough, however, Moscow was to meet with greater diplomatic success during the visits of representatives of the Centrist wing in Arab politics, Kuwait and Jordan.

Even before Sheik Sabah al Ahmad al Sabah of Kuwait and King Hussein of Jordan visited Moscow, a number of the Centrist Arabs seemed to be pulling back from the close tie with the United States which had been precipitated by the Iran-Iraq war.[116] Thus, when the new American Secretary of State Alexander Haig toured the Middle East in early April, in an effort to rally support for the U.S. plan to create an anti-Soviet alignment while putting the Arab-Israeli dispute on the diplomatic "back burner," he met with little success as two of the Arab states he visited, Jordan and Saudi Arabia, indicated that they were more concerned with what they perceived as the threat from Israel (Saudi Arabia said this explicitly) than the threat from the Soviet Union.[117] In addition, fighting had once again escalated in Lebanon, and Haig took the opportunity to strongly condemn Syria for its "brutal" actions in that country, a move not calculated to drive a wedge between Damascus and Moscow. The lack of success of the Haig visit arrested the momentum of American policy in the region and set the stage for some diplomatic successes by the Soviet Union during the visits of Sheik Sabah and King Hussein.

Kuwait, whose deputy Premier Sheik Sabah visited Moscow on April 23, was a key target of Soviet diplomacy. As the only state in the Gulf Cooperation Council (GCC) with diplomatic relations with Moscow, it was also the most "nonaligned" and the Soviet leaders evidently hoped to use Kuwait's influence within the GCC (it is the second most important country after Saudi Arabia) to prevent that organization from committing itself too closely to the American side. For its part Kuwait had been carefully cultivating a relationship with the USSR since 1975, the last time Sheik Sabah had journeyed to Moscow. Then, as in April 1981, Kuwait's regional problems made it seek protection.[118] In 1975 Kuwait was confronted with territorial demands by Iraq; in 1981, while relations had improved with Iraq, a far more serious problem lay on its border with Iran whose warplanes were occasionally bombing and strafing Kuwaiti territory because of Kuwaiti aid to the Iraqi war effort. Under these circumstances (and also under pressure from the powerful Palestinian community in Kuwait), the Kuwaitis evidently felt they needed support not only from the United States, whose ability to aid Kuwait was increasingly in doubt since the fall of the Shah, but from the Soviet Union as well, and the Kuwaiti deputy premier, who was also his country's foreign minister, went a long way toward meeting his hosts' diplomatic needs during his visit to Moscow.[119] Thus not only did he denounce Camp David, he also came out in favor of an international conference on the Middle East, thereby supporting a cardinal Soviet goal, something neither Libya nor Algeria was willing to do. In addition he also announced Kuwait's opposition to the creation of foreign military bases in the Persian Gulf, thus supporting yet another central Soviet foreign policy goal. Finally, he joined Moscow in calling for an international conference on the Indian Ocean aimed at turning it into a "zone of peace" thereby supporting another Soviet diplomatic ploy to eliminate the U.S. military presence from the region.[120]

To be sure, there were areas of disagreement during the talks in which *Pravda* reported a "detailed exchange of views on the situation in the Persian Gulf."[121] Probably the most important issue of disagreement was Afghanistan (Kuwait continued to oppose the Soviet presence in Afghanistan) of which no mention was made in the formal communiqué. Nonetheless, on balance it was a most successful visit as far as Moscow was concerned since it was able to obtain Kuwaiti support for a number of major Soviet Middle East policies.

The visit of Jordan's King Hussein in late May could also be considered a diplomatic success for Moscow. The USSR had been seriously concerned that because of Syrian military pressure, Hussein might be pushed back into the American camp and into support of Camp David (Jordan had distanced itself from the United States in 1978 because of Camp David). Perhaps heightening Soviet concern was the so-called "Jordanian option" which was being promoted by Israeli Labor Party leader Shimon Peres. Until May, Peres's Labor Party was leading all the Israeli public opinion polls for the election scheduled for June 30, and Moscow may have seen a Peres victory as yet another enticement for Jordan to become involved in Camp David. For its part, however, since the 1978 Baghdad Conference, Jordan was very much a Centrist Arab state and saw far more benefit in maintaining close ties with Iraq and Saudi Arabia (which subsidized a considerable portion of the Jordanian economy) than in joining Israel and Egypt in the highly ambiguous autonomy negotiations.[122] By 1981, the once-isolated Jordanian monarch was now part of the general Arab consensus against Camp David, although Jordan's bitter dispute with Syria continued to simmer. The Syrian-Jordanian conflict (along with the Syrian-Israeli crisis over the emplacement of Syrian missiles in Lebanon)[123] was undoubtedly one of the topics of discussion between Brezhnev and Hussein, and *Pravda*'s reference to the talks having taken place in a "business-like atmosphere" may very well have referred to disagreements over Syria.[124] It is, in fact, possible that Hussein may have asked the USSR to use its influence with Syria to ease its pressure against Jordan, in return for Jordanian willingness to endorse Moscow's views on a number of key Middle Eastern issues. First and foremost was the convening of an international conference on the Middle East. Both in his speech at the welcoming banquet[125] and in the final communiqué Hussein supported this Soviet goal, thereby also demonstrating his opposition to the Camp David process. In addition Hussein also joined Moscow in opposing foreign bases in the Persian Gulf, thus supporting another key Soviet goal. Given the fact that the Jordanian defense minister accompanied Hussein, the groundwork may have also been laid during this visit for the subsequent Soviet-Jordanian SAM arms deal, as the joint communiqué noted that the two sides had agreed to work on further increasing trade, economic, cultural, and other (that is, military related) matters. All in all, Moscow was quite pleased by Hussein's visit and *New Times* correspondent Alexander Usvatov summarized Moscow's satisfaction:

> It is no secret that Tel Aviv and Washington have always regarded Jordan as a "weak link" in the Arab world, counting on drawing it by hook or by crook into the separate Camp David process and into their anti-Arab and anti-Soviet plans.
>
> The results of King Hussein's talks with Leonid Brezhnev and other Soviet leaders were a disappointment for those who entertained such hopes.[126]

While Moscow had gained considerable diplomatic mileage from the visits of Jordan's King Hussein and Kuwait's Sheik Sabah, the diplomatic shift by Sudanese President Jaafar Nimeri ran counter to the Soviet goal of keeping Egypt isolated in the Arab world. Under pressure from Libyan forces in Chad (again, Moscow must have wondered if the Libyan move into Chad was of benefit to the USSR), Nimeri decided to come out in support of Sadat's Camp David policy by restoring full diplomatic relations with Egypt at the end of March and urging the other Arabs to do so as well. Further angering Moscow was the Sudanese offer of military bases to the United States—if the United States would upgrade them first.[127] Moscow's unhappiness was reflected in an *Izvestia* commentary on April 14, two days after the Sudanese ambassador returned to Cairo:

> Egypt is doing everything in its power to try to break out of its political isolation without renouncing Camp David and its commitments to the U.S. and Israel. It sees its rapprochement with the Sudan as a way out. But does Sudan need to come to Sadat's aid, especially on an anti-Libyan basis? Wouldn't it be better to remain with Libya in a single Arab family that resolutely condemns Egypt's capitulatory policy and shameful deal with Israel?
>
> Cairo is suffocating in its isolation. It is playing up to Khartoum and trying to take on the role of intermediary in relations between Sudan and the U.S., promising Sudan bags of dollars and piles of American weapons.[128]

Despite the Sudanese shift back toward Egypt, on balance Moscow's Middle Eastern diplomatic position had clearly improved by the spring of 1981, and the USSR was to try to exploit a series of Middle Eastern crises in the spring and summer to improve its position still further.

MOSCOW AND THE MIDDLE EAST CRISES OF 1981

The Syrian Missile Crisis

The first major crisis which the USSR sought to exploit, albeit very carefully, was the crisis over the emplacement of Syrian anti-aircraft missiles in Lebanon, a crisis that was also of considerable benefit to Syria.

At the outbreak of the April fighting in Lebanon, in which Syria attacked Phalangist positions in Beirut and near Zahle, a Christian Lebanese city which lay astride a major Syrian communication route into Lebanon (the Phalange was seeking to consolidate a communications link between Zahle and the Christian positions in Northern Lebanon), Syria remained in a state of isolation in the Arab world, primarily because of its support for Iran in the Iran-Iraq war. In addition, because Saudi Arabia and Kuwait had cut off funds for the Syrian force in Lebanon, Syria's economic position had weakened, a development exacerbated by the continuing domestic unrest in Syria. When Syrian attacks against the Christians near Zahle escalated, Israel responded by shooting down two Syrian helicopters involved in the operation. Syria responded by moving surface-to-air missiles across the border into Lebanon opposite Zahle, thus breaking the tacit agreement with Israel made in 1976 whereby Israel did not interfere with the Syrian invasion of Lebanon, so long as no SAM missiles were moved into Lebanon and no Syrian forces were sent to South Lebanon. Israeli Prime Minister Begin responded by saying that if the missiles were not moved back into Syria, Israel would destroy them. The crisis was on.

While the exact nature of the Soviet role in the missile crisis is not yet known, several things do appear clear. In the first place, Assad's decision to move the missiles seems to have caught the USSR by surprise (as in the November 1980 crisis with Jordan, Assad apparently took action without consulting Moscow—despite the Soviet-Syrian treaty),[129] and it was not until more than a week after the crisis began that Moscow made any public comment about it. Indeed, Moscow did not make any public comments about the crisis until after it became clear that other Arab countries, particularly such Centrist states as Saudi Arabia and Kuwait, were rallying to Syria's side.[130] Such a development benefited the USSR by moving its client out of isolation in the Arab world and held out the possibility of rebuilding the anti-imperialist Arab unity that Moscow continued to hope for. An additional benefit flowing to the Soviet Union from the missile crisis was that it served to further weaken the American effort to build an anti-Soviet bloc of Arab states and further complicated relations between Saudi Arabia, which promised to aid Syria, and the United States, Israel's main supporter, at a time when relations had already become strained over congressional opposition to the AWACS sale to Saudi Arabia.[131] Yet another benefit of the crisis for Soviet diplomacy, albeit a fleeting one, lay in the fact that in the initial stages of the conflict the United States sought Soviet assistance in defusing it,[132] thereby once again demonstrating the importance of the Soviet Union to Middle East peacemaking. Although the United States was not pleased by the subsequent lack of Soviet assistance during the crisis, Brezhnev was also to exploit it to repeat Moscow's call for an international conference to solve the crisis.

While Moscow sought to exploit the missile crisis for its own benefit, once that crisis was underway, the USSR faced a number of dangers as well. First and foremost was the possibility that a full-scale war between Syria and Israel might erupt, into which Moscow could be drawn. For Moscow this was not an opportune time for such a war. With Reagan now willing to allow grain sales to the USSR and considering the resumption of the stalled SALT talks (a key Soviet priority), any major Middle Eastern war in which Moscow got involved might well reinforce the basically anti-Soviet tendency of the Reagan administration, doom the SALT talks, and possibly reverse Reagan's decision on grain sales. While Moscow, as well as Damascus, would profit from the extension of the radar-SAM network to Lebanon,[133] it would be far better for Moscow if this could be done without war. So long as war threatened, but did not break out, the Arabs would rally around Syria, and attention would be focused on the Arab-Israeli conflict—and away from the continuing Soviet occupation of Afghanistan. In addition, Moscow may have feared that a Syrian-Israeli war would bring the collapse of the Syrian regime, one of Moscow's closest allies in the Arab world.[134]

A second problem facing Moscow lay in the fact that President Reagan had sent an experienced trouble shooter, Philip Habib, to the Middle East in early May to try to prevent war. While Moscow and Damascus utilized the respite granted by the Habib mission to strengthen the missile position in Lebanon (Israel was unlikely to strike a blow at the missiles with Habib in the Middle East lest U.S.-Israeli relations be severely damaged), the Soviet leadership had to be concerned that Habib, in his shuttle diplomacy, might succeed in drawing Damascus away from Moscow, much as Kissinger had done in 1974.[135] For this reason Moscow bitterly attacked the Habib mission, claiming it was a device to impose Israel's will on Syria and the other Arabs.[136]

In the face of these dangers, Moscow adopted the dual policy of discrediting U.S. mediation efforts while also playing down the possibility of war. This strategy became evident in mid-May as the Soviet ambassador to Lebanon, Aleksander Soldatov, on May 16, stated that the developments in Lebanon "are unrelated to the Soviet-Syrian treaty."[137] Soldatov's comments may well have been a response to the article which appeared several days earlier in the Syrian journal *al-Ba'ath* which stated that if Israel attacked the SAM batteries, it would risk confronting not only Syria and its Arab supporters, but also "the strategic world of Syrian-Soviet Friendship and Cooperation."[138] Then *Pravda*, in a commentary by Soviet Middle East specialist Pavel Demchenko, on May 17, praised Syria as the main bastion of Arab forces opposed to Camp David and denounced Israel's demand for the removal of the Syrian missiles, which were there for "defensive" purposes, as a maneuver worked out by the United States and Israel.[139] Brezhnev himself entered the Middle East commentary with a speech in Tibilisi on May 22 in which he warned of the dangerous situation in the region and blamed Israel and the United States and also called for international talks to solve the crisis in a peaceful manner.[140] This was also the theme of his speech at the dinner honoring the visit of King Hussein on May 27 in which he also noted that the USSR wanted good relations with Israel.[141] Significantly, in neither speech did he mention the Soviet-Syrian Treaty.

As the crisis continued, Syria obtained increasing support for its position from the other Arabs: an Arab Foreign Ministers conference, called on the initiative of Algeria and the PLO in late May, pledged financial support to Syria (Saudi Arabia and Kuwait, which had cut off funds for the Syrian forces in Lebanon, resumed their contributions), and the Arab states pledged "total" military assistance to Syria in case of an Israeli attack on Syrian forces in Lebanon or Syria.[142] Much to Moscow's satisfaction the Arab states also warned the United States that continuation of its "unconditional" support to Israel "would lead to a serious confrontation between the Arab nation and the U.S."[143] Soon after this meeting, however, both Jordan and Iraq qualified their support to Syria, while for its part Syria did not even send a delegation to the Baghdad meeting of Islamic foreign ministers called to deal with the Lebanese crisis at the start of June.

The Destruction of the Iraqi Nuclear Reactor

On June 9, however, the missile crisis seemed to pale in importance as another Middle Eastern crisis replaced it in the headlines.[144] On that date Israeli aircraft destroyed an Iraqi nuclear reactor which the vast majority of Israelis feared was being constructed to develop a nuclear weapon for use against Israel. The Israeli action inflamed the Arab world far more than did the Syrian-Israeli confrontation over the Syrian missiles in Lebanon as many Arabs felt humiliated by the fact that the Israeli aircraft, which flew over Jordanian and Saudi airspace on the way to and from Iraq, were able to come and go unscathed while eliminating the most advanced nuclear installation of any Arab country. As might be expected Moscow moved quickly to try to exploit this situation, not only condemning the Israeli raid but also pointing to the fact that the Israeli action was carried out with American-supplied aircraft and that it took place despite—or indeed because of—the U.S. AWACS radar planes operating in Saudi Arabia.[145] Reagan's decision to postpone shipment of additional F-16 fighter-bombers to Israel because of the attack was deprecated by Moscow, which sought to exploit the Israeli action by utilizing it to focus Arab attention on the "Israeli threat" to the Arab world (rather than the "Soviet threat") and to undermine the American position in the region as Israel's chief supporter, while at the same time improving Soviet-Iraqi relations. In addition, Moscow evidently hoped that the Israeli attack would help to rebuild the "anti-imperialist" Arab unity that had been so badly dissipated by the Iran-Iraq war. As a commentary by *Pravda*, commentator Yuri Glukhov noted on June 16:

> (The Israeli raid) had again demonstrated the extent of the imperialist and Zionist threat hanging over the Arab countries, forcing them to set aside their differences, *which have become more pronounced of late.* . . .
>
> In order to carry out their schemes, the Israeli leaders and their patrons have also taken advantage of the situation that has come about in the Persian Gulf zone and the protracted and bloody conflict between Iraq and Iran. In recent months, Baghdad has virtually withdrawn from the Arabs' common front for the struggle to eliminate the consequences of Israeli aggression. . . .
>
> The criminal actions of Tel Aviv and its sponsors have demonstrated once again that the only enemy of the Arab peoples is imperialism and its henchmen, and that no task is more important than closing ranks in the face of the danger threatening their vital interests.[146] [emphasis added]

Moscow may have also seen the Israeli raid as undercutting Egyptian efforts to reenter the Arab mainstream, since it took place only four days after a Begin-Sadat summit. In addition to reestablishing full diplomatic relations with the Sudan, Egypt had sold Iraq thousands of tons of Soviet ammunition and spare parts to aid it in its war with Iran[147]—something noted with displeasure in Moscow, which was concerned about Sadat's lessening isolation.[148] Fortunately for Moscow, the Israeli raid did serve to abort any Iraqi-Egyptian rapprochement, despite Sadat's denunciation of the Israeli action.

Moscow, however, was to be less successful in its goal of exploiting the Israeli raid to undermine the U.S. position in the Arab world, and in particular to improve Soviet ties with Iraq. While there had been calls in the Arab world to embargo oil to the United States because of the raid, the Reagan administration's decision to join with Iraq in a U.N. Security Council vote condemning Israel seemed to deflate any such Arab pressures.[149] Indeed, the Iraqi-American cooperation at the U.N. seemed to set the stage for improved Iraqi-American relations, as Iraqi President Saddam Hussein, on the ABC television program "Issues and Answers," stated his interest in expanding diplomatic contacts with the United States and announced that he would treat the head of the American interests section in the Belgian Embassy in Baghdad as the head of a diplomatic mission.[150]

In taking this posture, the Iraqi leader appeared to be trying to drive a wedge between the United States and Israel, which was very unahppy with the U.S. vote in the U.N. On the other hand, Moscow may have seen that the United States was seeking to drive a diplomatic wedge between the USSR and Iraq. In any case, Soviet-Iraqi relations had been declining for a number of years and they were not helped by Moscow's position of neutrality in the Iran-Iraq war. A further deterioration in Soviet-Iraqi relations came in February 1981 at the 26th CPSU Congress (which the Iraqi Ba'athists had not attended) when the head of the Iraqi Communist Party (ICP) Aziz Mohammed denounced the Iraqi government for its acts of repression against the ICP and the Iraqi Kurds, and also condemned the Iran-Iraqi war and demanded the immediate withdrawal of Iraqi troops from Iran.[151] As Soviet-Iraqi relations were deteriorating, the United States moved to improve relations with the regime in Baghdad. Secretary of State Haig noted the possibility of improved Iraqi-American relations in testimony to the Senate Foreign Relations Committee in mid-March (Iraq was seen as concerned with "the behavior of Soviet imperialism in the Middle Eastern area")[152] and followed this up by sending Deputy Assistant Secretary of State Morris Draper to Iraq in early April.[153] To improve the climate for the visit, the United States approved the sale to Iraq of five Boeing jetliners.[154] While nothing specific came out of Draper's talks, Washington continued to hope that because of Iraq's close ties with Jordan and Saudi Arabia, the regime in Baghdad might abandon its quasi-Steadfastness-Front position and move toward a more Centrist position in the Arab world on the issue of making peace with Israel. Indeed, Saddam Hussein himself, in his ABC interview, gave some hints about just such a move. Nonetheless, the future direction of Iraqi policy remained to be determined, especially since as the Iran-Iraq war dragged on, the possibility existed that Iraq might have to turn back to Moscow to get sufficient arms to score a major victory. Indeed, the report of a large shipment of Soviet tanks to Iraq in the late fall seemed to signal a Soviet desire to improve relations.[155]

The Bombing of Beirut

While the furor of the Israeli attack on the Iraqi reactor slowly died, Middle East tensions were kept alive by a number of other events during the summer which Moscow sought to exploit. In the first place, following the re-election of Menahem Begin's Likud Party, Israel launched a series of attacks against Palestinian positions in Lebanon in an effort to keep the PLO off balance and keep it from launching terrorist attacks against Israel. The fighting quickly escalated with the PLO shelling towns in Northern Israel and the Israelis bombing PLO headquarters in Beirut, causing a number of civilian casualties in the process. While the United States condemned the bombing of Beirut and again delayed the shipment of F-16s to Israel—at the same time sending Habib back to the Middle East to work out a ceasefire (something that he accomplished in late July)—Moscow seized the opportunity once again to link the Israeli actions to the United States, and called for sanctions against Israel.[156] The bombing of Beirut also served to further inflame Arab tempers both against Israel and against the United States (there were once again calls for an oil boycott of the United States and heavy criticism of American support of Israel not only from the Steadfastness Front but also from such Centrist states as Jordan and Kuwait). All this activity, of course, served to further divert Arab attention from the continued Soviet occupation of Afghanistan while underlining the Soviet claim that it was U.S.-supported Israel, not the Soviet Union, that was the main threat to the Arab world.

The Libyan-American Clash over the Gulf of Sidra

The fourth in the series of Middle East crises occurring in 1981 took place in mid-August, and for the first time it was the United States, not Israel, which was directly involved. A number of questions remain about this incident, which involved the shooting down of two Libyan interceptor aircraft (SU-22) that had initially fired upon two American aircraft protecting U.S. maneuvers in the Gulf of Sidra, a region Kaddafi claimed as Libyan territorial waters but that the United States (and most of the international community, including the USSR) claimed was international waters.[157] In the first place, was the matter merely an accident in which an overeager Libyan pilot decided to fire his missiles (Libya had been challenging U.S. maneuvers in the Gulf of Sidra for several years and there had already been a number of incidents), or was it deliberately staged by Kaddafi? Secondly, was Moscow involved in the planning of the event, or was it caught by surprise? As far as Libya's planning of the incident is concerned, there are two factors to consider. On the one hand, Kaddafi was out of the country negotiating a treaty in South Yemen at the time of the incident. On the other hand, however, there were a number of coincidences that, when taken together, lead one to believe that there is a good possibility that Libya may indeed have planned the incident. In the first place, Libya was striving to emerge from its position of isolation in the Arab world, and had restored diplomatic relations with Morocco while also seeking to mend fences with Iraq and Saudi Arabia. Kaddafi may well have noted how Syria moved out of its position of isolation vis-à-vis the mainstream Arabs by means of its confrontation with Israel over the missiles in Lebanon, and since Israel did not border Libya, Kaddafi may have wished to utilize a military confrontation with the United States—whose reputation among Centrist Arabs had suffered as a result of the Israeli bombings of Beirut and the Iraqi reactor—for a similar purpose. Secondly, since he was in the process of negotiating a tripartite alliance with Ethiopia and the PDRY, he may have wished to use the incident to demonstrate that the alliance was needed against "U.S. imperialism" and was not directed at such Arab states as Saudi Arabia or North Yemen which otherwise might have been concerned about it. Third, an OPEC meeting was beginning in Geneva, and Kaddafi may have wished to use the incident as a backdrop for his demand for higher oil prices.[158] Finally, with a Soviet foreign office delegation led by Aleksei Shzezdoz visiting the country, and under increasing pressure from the United States, Kaddafi may have wished to utilize the incident as a justification for turning to Moscow for a Treaty of Friendship and Cooperation while ensuring that the United States would not escalate its retaliation against Libya. (It remained to be seen, of course, if Moscow would want to sign a treaty with such a mercurial Arab leader; yet if the USSR were to get base rights in return, the possibility could not be excluded.)

Whether or not Libya actually planned the incident, it did not take long for Moscow to try to exploit the battle over the Gulf of Sidra for its own benefit. Based on the initial Soviet reaction to the Gulf battle, it appears as if Moscow was caught by surprise. Nonetheless, after a day of reporting the events without commentary, once Moscow appeared certain that there would be no escalation, it began to try to show the Arabs that the incident demonstrated how dangerous it was for them to have an American fleet operating off their shores. Thus in a political commentary broadcast by Tass international service, Sergei Kulik set a tone for later Soviet treatment of the event:

> In commenting on the reports of the attacks by U.S. fighter planes on Libyan aircraft, many foreign observers agree that this dangerous incident has once again demonstrated the great threat which is created by the constant presence of American naval and air forces on the territories and waters belonging to other states thousands of kilometers away from the U.S. . . . off Africa's eastern coastline, in the Indian Ocean and the Persian Gulf a whole armada of American vessels continues to parade while keeping the oil producing countries of the Near East in their sights.[159]

A French language Soviet broadcast to North Africa on August 26 made this point even more explicit:

> Until now, when Washington concentrated an armada of warships in the Mediterranean and the Persian Gulf, when it created a network of military bases in the vicinity of Arab countries, everybody understood it was a dangerous thing but not everybody, *far from it*, realized to what extent this was dangerous.
>
> The U.S. provocation in the Gulf of Sidra has made a great many people look at the American military presence in quite a different light.[160] [emphasis added]

In addition to using the Gulf of Sidra incident to try to lessen the diplomatic acceptability of the U.S. military presence in the Persian Gulf, and also noting the highly negative Arab response to the American role in the incident, Moscow also cited it as justification for the signing of the Tripartite Treaty by Ethiopia, Libya, and South Yemen. The USSR also praised the treaty as "an important stage in strengthening the national liberation movement's solidarity and in stepping up their struggle against imperialism and reaction and for peace and progress."[161]

Moscow also maintained, however (in an apparent effort to reassure Saudi Arabia and North Yemen), that the treaty was "not directed against any other country or people."[162] Nonetheless, the text of the Tripartite Treaty which noted that one of its goals was the struggle against "reaction"—a commonly used term for the conservative Arab states of the Persian Gulf along with Egypt and the Sudan—may, in the long run, prove counterproductive to Soviet efforts to improve relations with the conservative Gulf states, given the close tie between the Tripartite Treaty nations and Moscow.[163]

The Upheaval in Iran

While Moscow was seeking to exploit the Libyan-American clash in the Gulf of Sidra to weaken the U.S. position in the Middle East, it was trying to follow the same policy during the upheavals in Iran that witnessed the ouster and escape to Europe of Iranian President Bani-Sadr, the assassination of his successor Mohammed Ali Rajai along with a number of key Iranian Islamic Republican Party leaders such as Ayatollah Beheshti, and a series of additional bombings and other attacks directed against the fundamentalist Khomeini government by the opposition Mujahadeen.

The central Soviet concern in its policy toward Iran was a fear that after the hostage release, the United States and Iran might move toward a rapprochement, particularly because of Iranian military requirements due to the Iran-Iraq war. Fortunately for Moscow, anti-Americanism remained the central foreign policy theme of the Khomeini regime during 1981 as it had been the previous year, and the regime's enemies were usually branded American or Zionist agents. Given Moscow's previous displeasure with Bani-Sadr, his departure was no loss, but the Soviet leadership was quite unhappy with the assassination of Beheshti whom *Pravda* characterized on July 3 as being "one of the most consistent proponents of an anti-imperialist, anti-American policy."[164] The bombings at the end of June and at the end of August, while eliminating a number of top Iranian leaders, gave Moscow the opportunity to reinforce Tehran's suspicions that the CIA was behind the incidents. Thus, in a Persian language broadcast immediately after the August bombings, Moscow radio commentator Igor Sheftunov stated:

> It is impossible to deny Washington's role in the terrorist activities against the Islamic Republic of Iran and its leaders. Since the fall of the monarchy and the installation of the Islamic Republic, U.S. imperialists have been doing their utmost to topple the republican regime and replace it with the old one. . . .

Washington has shown its sympathy toward Baktiar, the last Prime Minister of the Shah, and Bani Sadr the former President of Iran who is now a refugee. Both of these men are engaged in extensive terrorist activities against the Islamic Republic of Iran and its leaders.[165]

Moscow also sought to link U.S. aid to the Afghan rebels (early in 1981 Reagan had announced publicly that the United States was aiding the Afghani resistance) with U.S. aid to the opposition in Iran in an effort both to discredit the Afghan resistance in Iran and to drive a further wedge between Tehran and Washington.

Yet while Iranian-American relations remained highly strained, it did not appear as if Moscow was making a great deal of headway in improving its own position in Iran. Iranian leaders continued to be suspicious of Moscow both for its centuries-long record of hostility toward Iran and because of suspected ties between Moscow and Iranian ethnic minorities fighting for independence such as the Kurds. Indeed, Moscow may well have been placed in a difficult position when in late October the Kurdish Democratic Party of Iran, led by Abder-Rahman Ghassemlou, joined the opposition front headed by Bani Sadr and Mujahadeen leader Massoud Rajavi.[166] Moscow and Ghassemlou had long maintained friendly ties and the formation of the opposition front once again posed a difficult problem of choice for the USSR.

Yet another irritant in the Soviet-Iranian relationship has been Tehran's unhappiness that Moscow has taken only a neutral position on the Iran-Iraq war in the face of "flagrant Iraqi aggression" as the late Iranian Prime Minister Ali Rajai told Soviet Ambassador Vladimir Vinogradov on February 15,[167] a message repeated in October by the Iranian Ambassador Mohammed Mokri, during an Iranian delegation's visit to Moscow.[168] A third area of conflict has been Iranian unhappiness with the Soviet intervention in Afghanistan, despite Soviet efforts to tie the CIA to the resistance movements in both Iran and Afghanistan. Finally, while the Islamic fundamentalist regime has so far tolerated the Communist (Tudeh) Party and its ally, the majority faction of the Fedayeen guerrillas, it clearly remains suspicious of them as shown by Iranian Prime Minister Hussein Moussavi's declaration that members of the Tudeh and majority Fedayeen would be executed if, upon joining the revolutionary guards or other fundamentalist organizations, they failed to state their (Communist) party affiliation.[169]

For its part Moscow was clearly not happy with a number of Iranian policies, including frequent anti-Soviet comments by Iranian leaders,[170] the continued war with Iraq, and Iran's continuing controversy with Saudi Arabia (Iranian pilgrims had been arrested for demonstrating in Mecca), which helped reinforce the tie between Saudi Arabia and the United States. While Iran's growing international isolation (in 1981 Iran quarrelled with France over a hijacked gunboat and French asylum for Bani Sadr, while Japan decided to end its $3 billion investment in a huge Iranian petrochemical plant) may appear to Moscow as the factor that will ultimately push Iran over to the Soviet camp, by the end of 1981 no such movement had taken place.

The U.S.-Israel Strategic Cooperation Agreement

If Moscow sought to exploit the domestic upheavals in Iran to reinforce anti-American feelings there, it was also to move to exploit the Israeli-American agreement in principle on strategic cooperation reached during Israeli Prime Minister Begin's visit to Washington in early September. Moscow had already deplored the reelection of Begin and the appointment of the "superhawk" Arik Sharon as Israel's defense minister and sought also to exploit Reagan's decision in mid-August to finally allow the F-16s to go to Israel. Indeed, several Soviet commentators actually linked the release of the F-16s to the American-Libyan air clash which took place several days later.[171]

It was the strategic cooperation agreement (later to be formally signed when Sharon visited the United States in early December), however, which came in for the most criticism[172] as Moscow, which tends to have a military view of world events, may well have felt that the combination of the Israeli airforce and army with the American Sixth Fleet would militarily dominate the Middle East, while the American use of Israeli air bases in the Negev and the stockpiling of equipment in Israel for the U.S. Rapid Deployment Force would greatly enhance the ability of the United States to deploy its ground forces in the Middle East.[173]

While Moscow sought to show that the Israeli-American agreement, coming after the Israeli bombings of Beirut and the Iraqi reactor and the Libyan-U.S. clash over the Gulf of Sidra was a policy aimed at threatening the entire Arab world, the Soviet leaders themselves may have felt some need to make a gesture toward Israel before that country moved even further into the American camp. Thus, during Gromyko's visit to the United Nations in late September, he agreed to meet Israeli Foreign Minister Yitzhak Shamir.[174] It appears as if Moscow's willingness to meet with the Israeli foreign minister, the first such official meeting in six years, was a Soviet effort, as in the past, at a time of flux in Middle Eastern politics both to maintain some contact with the Israelis and to seek Israeli support for Moscow's idea of an international conference on the Arab-Israeli conflict.[175] While no such Israeli support for Moscow's position was to emerge from the conference, it appears that the meeting was seen as useful by both sides.[176] In any case, the Soviet-Israeli meeting was soon superseded in the thrust of Middle Eastern events by the assassination of Anwar Sadat, a development that once again put the region in an upheaval.

THE ASSASSINATION OF SADAT AND ITS AFTERMATH

Relations between Sadat and the USSR had been worsening steadily since the 1973 war, but in 1981 the deterioration accelerated. Not only was Sadat openly proclaiming himself to be the leading anti-Soviet force in the Middle East, but he had also announced that Egypt was sending aid to the Afghan rebels and he had agreed to both the stationing of U.S. troops in the Sinai (as part of the multinational force to separate Egypt and Israel after the April 1982 Israeli withdrawal) and to American use and development of the Egyptian base at Ras Banas for its Rapid Deployment Force.[177] In sum, Egypt under Sadat had become a centerpiece of the anti-Soviet Middle Eastern bloc which the United States was seeking to create, and Soviet-Egyptian relations plummeted to a new low as a result.

Three weeks before Sadat's assassination, the Egyptian leader had expelled seven Soviet diplomats, including the Soviet ambassador and about 1,000 Soviet technicians, on grounds that they were fomenting sedition in Egypt.[178] In addition, he dissolved the Egyptian-Soviet Friendship Society and arrested its President Abd As-Salam Az-Zayyat as part of a major crackdown on Egyptians opposed to his policies from both the Egyptian left and from the fundamentalist Muslim right.[179]

The assassination of Sadat by Muslim fundamentalists was greeted with considerable relief in Moscow, although there was a difference of opinion on the part of Soviet commentators on the future policies of the new regime. *Pravda* on October 14 cited the statement of the National Progressive Party, which opposed the referendum for the election of Hosni Mubarak to Egypt's presidency on the grounds that he intended to pursue Sadat's policies, "in particular to continue the Camp David policy and strengthen the alliance with the U.S." On the other hand *Izvestia* commentator Alexander Bovin, a senior Soviet analyst on the Middle East, said that he thought Egypt's policies might change after Israel completed its scheduled withdrawal from the Sinai in April 1982.[180] In any case, while Moscow saw the possibility of an improvement in relations with Egypt and, both before and after the assassination, was giving propaganda support to General Shazli, the exiled leader of the Egyptian "Patriotic Front" based in Libya (Shazli was urging Egypt to return to the Arab fold and improve ties with Moscow),[181] it expressed considerable irritation with the U.S. response to Sadat's assassination. Perhaps hoping for a repeat of the uncertain American reaction to the collapse of the Shah's regime in Iran, Moscow seemed particularly upset by Reagan's strong response to Sadat's assassination, which included the alerting of U.S. forces in the Mediterranean along with elements of the Rapid Deployment Force in the United States, the movement of ships of the Sixth Fleet toward Egypt, and the dispatch of former U.S. Presidents Carter, Ford, and Nixon to Egypt for Sadat's funeral.[182] On October 12 Moscow issued a warning to the United States against what it termed a "gross interference" in the internal affairs of Egypt, stating that "what is going on around Egypt cannot help but affect the security interests of the Soviet Union," which will "keep a close watch on the development of events."[183]

Unlike the situation in Iran in 1978-79, however, the United States did not appear deterred by the Kremlin warning. Indeed, in addition to pledging support to Mubarak, it dispatched several AWACS radar planes to patrol the border between Eygpt and Libya while also announcing that it would expand the planned U.S. Middle East military exercise "Bright Star" scheduled for November 1981. The United States also promised to step up arms shipments to both Egypt and the Sudan, both of whom were seen as being threatened by Libya.[184]

In the face of both the U.S. pledge of support for Mubarak and the new Egyptian president's initial consolidation of power (he overwhelmingly won the referendum on October 13 and was sworn in on October 14), Moscow appeared to change course somewhat on October 15 as Brezhnev sent Mubarak a congratulatory telegram on his election, pledging that Moscow would reciprocate any Egyptian readiness to improve Soviet-Egyptian relations.[185] In making this move, Moscow may have realized that there would be no immediate change in Egyptian foreign policy despite Sadat's assassination, and the most that could be hoped for was a "change in the direction of the wind" as Bovin had stated,[186] after the Israeli withdrawal in April. Nonetheless, the announcement on October 20 that the United States would replace cracked Soviet-made turbines for the Soviet-built Aswan Dam—the major symbol of Soviet-Egyptian cooperation— seemed to underline the fact that U.S. influence was to remain predominant in Egypt, at least in the short term, although Mubarak's subsequent decision to invite some of the expelled Soviet technicians back to Egypt may have raised some hope in Moscow.[187]

The assassination of Sadat, as a major turning point in the Middle East, also gave Moscow the opportunity again to call for an international conference to settle the Arab-Israeli conflict. This was one of the themes of the visit by PLO leader Yasser Arafat to Moscow two weeks after the Sadat assassination, as the PLO leader gave strong support to Moscow's call for the conference.[188] For its part Moscow granted the PLO mission in Moscow full diplomatic status, thus conferring increased diplomatic legitimacy on the Palestinian organization. While the Soviet move was the culmination of an increasingly close Soviet-PLO relationship, and the USSR may have wished to consolidate the relationship further in the period of uncertainty following the death of Sadat, Moscow nonetheless may also have wished to counter the possibility of the development of a formal relationship between Washington and the PLO. During his mediation of the fighting in Lebanon in July, U.S. special representative Philip Habib had, de facto, negotiated with the PLO (albeit via intermediaries), and in August both Anwar Sadat and former American National Security Adviser Zbigniew Brzezinski had advocated an American dialogue with the PLO.[189] Then, following Sadat's funeral, former presidents Carter and Ford stated that at some point the United States would have to begin to talk to members of the PLO, if not to Arafat himself.[190]

Less than week after Arafat's visit came a trip to Moscow by North Yemeni (YAR) President Ali Abdullah Salah. Like Jordan and Kuwait, North Yemen was a key Centrist Arab state which Moscow wished to keep from going over to the American camp, something Moscow feared might happen after the PDRY invasion of North Yemen in February 1979 had led to a major American military supply effort to the YAR.[191] Nonetheless, a lack of coordination between the United States, which was supplying the equipment, and Saudi Arabia, which was paying for it and which was concerned that North Yemen might become too strong if it obtained the weapons too quickly, led the North Yemeni president to turn to Moscow for arms later that year. Complicating the North Yemeni political situation still further was the South Yemeni-supported National Democratic front that posed both a political and military challenge to the regime in Sana. The end result was that the North Yemen government had to walk a delicate tight-rope between Saudi Arabia (which financed and influenced a number of North Yemeni tribes) and South Yemen (which supported the National Democratic Front and alternately invaded and advocated union with North Yemen) as well as between the United States, Saudi Arabia's main supporter, and the Soviet Union, the primary backer of South Yemen.[192] President Salah's primary aim in the talks in Moscow, therefore, appeared to be the acquisition of additional weaponry to deal with his internal and external problems, and he was successful in his quest as the final communiqué issued at the close of his visit stated that the two countries expressed the desire to continue "broadening and perfecting their advantageous cooperation" in the military field.[193] In return Salah thanked the USSR for its aid in strengthening North Yemen's "national independence and sovereignty," supported Moscow's call for an international conference on the Middle East, and condemned the establishment of foreign military bases in the Persian Gulf, while also supporting Moscow's peace plan for the Persian Gulf and Indian Ocean.[194] In sum, like the visits by the leaders of Kuwait and Jordan, the trip of North Yemeni President Salah can be considered a clear plus for Moscow, although Salah was to immediately visit Saudi Arabia following his visit to Moscow in an apparent effort to secure his position with that country.

Although the North Yemeni leader's visit to Moscow was greeted with satisfaction by Moscow, as was the election of the anti-NATO Andreas Papandreou to the premiership of Greece in late October, and the failure of President Reagan either to convince Jordanian King Hussein to join Camp David or get the King to reject a major surface-to-air missile deal with Moscow in favor of an American system during Hussein's visit to Washington in early November,[195] a number of other Middle Eastern developments took place during the fall of 1981 that were not to Moscow's satisfaction. In the first place, after a long and bitter debate the United States Senate agreed to the sale of AWACS aircraft to Saudi Arabia in late October, a development that appeared to cement U.S.-Saudi ties. Second, in a major policy change, a number of European states agreed to provide troops for the Sinai multinational force, thereby at least tacitly supporting Camp David. Third, the United States successfully mounted a major military exercise in the Middle East (Bright Star), thus demonstrating that it was developing the capability of a quick intervention there to aid its friends.

The debate over the AWACS highlighted the ambivalent Soviet position toward Saudi Arabia. On the one hand, as the leading Centrist Arab state opposed to Camp David, and as a major financial and political backer of the PLO, Saudi Arabia pursued two key Middle Eastern policies that Moscow also strongly supported. On the other hand, however, as a leading opponent of Soviet policy in Afghanistan and as a nation with increasingly close military ties to the United States, as evidenced by the emplacement of U.S.-controlled AWACS in Saudi Arabia soon after the start of the Iran-Iraq war, and as a nation that had sought to use its financial power to pry several Arab states out of the Soviet camp, Saudi Arabia was also a leading anti-Soviet force in the Arab world. Moscow's ambivalent position toward Saudi Arabia was especially apparent in 1981. In April Moscow warmly welcomed both Saudi Arabia's rebuttal of U.S. Secretary of State Haig's call for an anti-Soviet alliance during Haig's visit to the Middle East and Saudi Foreign Minister Saud al-Faisal's statement that Israel, not Moscow, was the main threat to the Arabs.[196] One month later, a key article in *Literaturnaia Gazeta*, written by Soviet commentator Igor Belyayev, noted, in discussing the failure of Haig's visit:

> Arab politicians, even the conservative ones, have never refused Soviet assistance in the struggle against their real enemy—the Israeli expansionists. The Arabs will hardly become accomplices in an anti-Soviet crusade under the aegis of the U.S.[197]

On the other hand, in late August, Moscow's chief oil analyst, Reuben Andreasian, bitterly noted Saudi Arabia's unwillingness to act against U.S. interests during an OPEC meeting to set oil prices, as he complained that despite the Israeli raid on the Iraqi nuclear reactor and the recent attack by U.S. airforce planes on Libyan aircraft, "on the very day the OPEC meeting opened," there was no agreement on prices.[198]

Moscow's central fear in the AWACS debate was that congressional approval for AWACS would cement the Saudi-American relationship to the point that Saudi Arabia might be persuaded both to support the Camp David agreements and also provide facilities for the American Rapid Deployment Force "in direct proximity to the extremely rich Persian Gulf oil fields"[199] — a fear that was even more openly expressed after the Senate approved (by failing to vote down) the AWACS agreement. *Pravda* on October 30 noted:

> The AWACS system will be effectively under direct U.S. control, not to mention the innumerable advisers who will now be sent to Saudi Arabia. All indications are that the U.S. would now prepare Saudi Arabia for the role of bridgehead.[200]

Moscow Radio Peace and Progress on October 30 went even further in its criticism, asserting that the AWACS deal was "aimed at transforming the Wahhabi Kingdom into a source of threat to the entire Islamic world."[201]

While the AWACS approval was a blow to the Soviet Middle East position since it strengthened Saudi-American ties, so too was the decision of several key European states to provide troops for the multinational force that the United States was organizing for the Sinai. The rapid evolution of the multinational force during the course of 1981 was of clear concern to Moscow, which saw it as a cover for the American RDF.[202] Ironically, it was because of Moscow's July 1979 veto of the UNEF force to patrol the Sinai (which, most likely, would have remained composed primarily of Third World states and thus was not a possible military threat against Soviet positions in the region) that the United States worked to create the multinational force.

The commitment of American troops for the force, a goal long pursued by Israel, which saw the United States as a far more reliable barrier to a future Eygptian attack than the U.N., was not approved by the U.S. Congress or Sadat until well into 1981, and, for most of the year, Western Europe had held aloof from participation in the multinational force. The election of François Mitterand to the presidency of France, however, together with the assassination of Sadat galvanized the Europeans to take a more active role and by the end of November the participation of France, England, Holland, and Italy in the Sinai force, despite some initial objections by Israel on the terms of their participation, was set. As might be expected, Moscow strongly opposed both U.S. and especially Western European participation in the multinational force. In the case of Western Europe, Moscow had long seen the Middle East as an area where, because of a much greater European oil dependency, a wedge could be driven between the United States and its NATO allies.[203] Consequently, Moscow condemned what it saw as a Western European "knuckling under" to Washington's "diktat" on the multinational force.[204] In addition because the multinational force was tied to the Camp David agreements, Moscow saw European participation in the Sinai force as a de facto legitimatization of Camp David, a development that ended American isolation as the sole Western state supporting the agreements.[205]

The Bright Star military exercise, which also involved some British and French participation, may be considered another gain for Washington—and concomitantly a loss for Moscow. The exercises took place in Egypt (with the participation of units of the Egyptian army and airforce), the Sudan, Somalia and Oman. While Moscow denounced "Bright Star" as a rehearsal for the invasion of both Libya and the Middle East oil fields (the Bright Star exercise was commanded by the head of the RDF), as a device for intimidating "progressive" governments in the Middle East such as Libya, Ethiopia, and South Yemen, and as a technique for strengthening pro-U.S. regimes in the region,[206] it had to be concerned about the rather impressive showing of the U.S. military, including a bombing run by B-52 bombers on a direct flight from the United States. This stood in sharp contrast to the difficulties encountered by the United States in its abortive hostage rescue mission in Iran in April 1980. Indeed, Moscow may well have been concerned that the successful U.S. Rapid Deployment Force exercise might have a positive influence on such Arab countries as Kuwait which had turned to Moscow, in part, because it could not be sure that the United States had either the capability or will to help it in case of a conflict with an unfriendly neighbor like Iran, which had again bombed Kuwaiti territory in early October.[207] The conclusion of a major U.S.-Pakistani military agreement, which held out the possibility of U.S. use of the Pakistani naval base at Gwandar and air base at Peshewar, seemed to further enhance U.S. capabilities for military intervention in the Persian Gulf.[208] Finally, the Egyptian component of Bright Star, in which 4,000 American and Egyptian troops participated, also served to improve relations between the United States and Egyptian military and between the Mubarak and Reagan governments, and Egyptian Defense Minister Abdel Halim Abu Ghazala stated that the exercises were a "rehearsal for a possible joint operation" to protect the oilfields of the Persian Gulf.[209]

As Bright Star was concluding its Egyptian phase on November 24, the Arab states, except for Egypt, were preparing for a major Arab summit conference in Fez, Morocco, one that was closely watched by Moscow. The central issue at the conference was the so-called Fahd Plan, a Saudi peace initiative first put forth in August, which held out, albeit somewhat vaguely, the possibility of Arab recognition and peace with Israel in return for a total Israeli withdrawal from all territories captured in 1967, including East Jerusalem, and the establishment of a Palestinian state. The assassination of Sadat, which seemed to make possible a rapprochement between Egypt and Saudi Arabia,[210] along with the U.S. Senate approval of AWACS, gave a new momentum to the Fahd Plan, which received little attention when it was first broached in August.

The Soviet reaction to the Fahd Plan was an interesting one. On August 12, Moscow Radio praised the plan, noting that it conformed in many ways to the Soviet Middle East peace plan (that is, total Israeli withdrawal; the establishment of a Palestinian state; and the right to exist of all states in the region).[211] Five days later, however, Moscow Radio Peace and Progress, in Arabic, attacked the plan because of its tie to American policy,[212] and *Izvestia* further criticized the plan on August 23 as an effort to undermine the PLO and decide the Palestinian peoples' fate "behind their backs." Moscow's criticism of Saudi Arabia and the Fahd Plan grew even harsher at the time when the AWACS deal was approved by the United States Senate as it was portrayed as a device to split the Arabs and spread Camp David,[213] but Moscow shifted its position again when Saudi Prince Faisal called for Soviet participation in the search for peace in the Middle East and sought to get Soviet support for the Saudi peace plan.[214] From Moscow's point of view, cooperation on the Fahd Plan, particularly when the Reagan administration was at best lukewarm about it, could be a means of driving a wedge between Saudi Arabia and Washington, despite the AWACS deal. From the Saudi perspective, Soviet support for the Fahd Plan may have been seen as necessary for rallying the Steadfastness Front Arab states to the support of the Fahd Plan at the Fez Summit. Indeed, Riyadh made a further gesture to Moscow —possibly for the same purpose—at a meeting of the Gulf Cooperation Council in mid-November when it supported the Kuwaiti view in the final communiqué which "confirmed the need to keep the region as a whole away from international conflicts, especially the presence of military fleets and foreign bases."[215] If this was indeed Riyadh's purpose in giving strong support to the principles of nonalignment at the GCC meeting (Riyadh may also have been embarrassed by a November 1, 1981 article in the Washington *Post* describing U.S. plans to make Saudi Arabia a major military and air command base for the U.S. RDF[216] and by Reagan's press conference statement on October 1 that the United States would not let Saudi Arabia be an Iran),[217] it did not work since the Steadfastness Front states, and particularly Syria and Libya, were strongly to oppose the Fahd Plan at the Fez Summit. Indeed, the Steadfastness Front had its own agenda at Fez—one endorsed by Moscow—which called for sanctions against Arab states making available military facilities to the United States and against European states providing troops for the Sinai force; the use of all Arab resources, including oil and petrodollars, to "resist the U.S.-Israeli strategic alliance"; and strengthening of relations with the USSR.[218] Neither the Fahd Plan nor the Steadfastness Front agenda, however, was to receive support at the Fez Summit which was to collapse less than six hours after it had begun because of the Steadfastness Front's hostility to the Fahd Plan, leaving the Arab world in a state of major disarray. In an attempt to put a positive light on the events at Fez, a Moscow Radio Arabic language broadcast rather plaintively urged the Arabs to rebuild their unity on an anti-imperialist basis,[219] something that even the most optimistic observers in Moscow must have realized was a very distant goal. Indeed, Dmitry Volsky, one of Moscow's most frank analysts of Middle Eastern affairs, in his analysis of the Fez Conference, summed up Soviet frustration with developments in the Arab world:

> The Arab world is living through difficult, troubled times full of contradictions. If additional proof of this were needed, it was provided by the sudden discontinuation of the summit conference that had just got under way in the Moroccan city of Fez. After a five-hour discussion, the decision to break it off was announced by King Hassan II of Morocco. In the opinion of the press, the pretext was disagreement over some points of the plan for a Middle East settlement submitted by Saudi Arabi—a pretext but hardly the real reason. For it is obvious that the disagreements over this question were indicative of different and at times opposite views on the strategy to apply in the struggle of the Arab peoples for a just peace in the Middle East.
>
> And on a broader plane, too, it would be putting it mildly to say that the Arab leaders are far from taking the same view of the development of their countries and of the region as a whole. To some the ideal is a sort of "America in the desert," where free enterprise would coexist with the life-style of the Bedouin tribes;

others think that the prototype of the future can be found only in the remote past, in "pure Islam"; still others—who are quite numerous—envision a socialist perspective. All this, naturally, affects the internal and foreign policies of the Arab countries; they differ in social content, and this is inevitable in the present conditions.

What is by no means inevitable are the internecine conflicts by which, alas, the entire Arab and, indeed, the whole Moslem world is rent. Take the war Morocco has been waging for several years now against the Polisario Front in Western Sahara, the continuing hostilities between Iran and Iraq, the tension on the Sudanese-Libyan border. There are smouldering embers also in other places. Understandably, all this prevents the Arab peoples from jointly tackling the acute problems, common to all of them, connected with the elimination of the consequences of Israeli aggression and the organization of a joint rebuff to the new bellicose moves of Tel Aviv and its overseas patrons. To uphold the independence of the Arab countries and the rights of their peoples—that is now the main concern to which, in the opinion of patriotic-minded people in the Arab world, both personal and all other ambitions should be subordinated.

But this is, evidently, easier said than done, all the more so since the enemies of the Arabs are extremely adept at inciting internecine strife, speculating on the narrow class aspirations of the privileged strata, and scaring the Arabs with the old "Soviet threat" bogey. Three years ago this insidious policy found embodiment in the Camp David deal. Now Camp David has been demonstrably deadlocked. But attempts to break the deadlock not by displaying common sense but by trying doggedly to blunder ahead in the same direction can prove very dangerous. Yet that is precisely what the current Washington Administration has been doing, especially since the death of Sadat. Now that this figure, odious literally to all Arabs, has gone, Washington is in a hurry in some way or other to go "beyond the Camp David framework." Not only the Somali regime and the small Arabian sultanate of Oman are already being tacked on to it factually if not formally, but also such a large Arab state as Sudan. Saudi Arabia, with its oil and petrodollars, is being assiduously courted. Attempts are being made to knock together a new bloc with a military spearhead on the coasts of the Persian Gulf and the Red Sea.

And the military spearhead is to be American. The decision on the sale to Saudi Arabia of an AWACS system which will be controlled by the Americans, the new steps to set up U.S. bases in Oman and Somalia, the planned weapons deliveries to Sudan, the agreement on the stationing in Sinai of the notorious "multinational force" the backbone of which will be largely American, and finally the Bright Star exercise—all these are only the most recent facts.[220]

Volsky's rather pessimistic analysis serves as a useful point of departure for evaluating the course of Soviet policy in the Middle East since 1970.

NOTES

1. For an excellent background history of Afghanistan, see Louis Dupree, *Afghanistan* (Princeton, Princeton University Press, 1978). For analyses of the Communist coup and the ultimate Soviet decision to invade Afghanistan, see John C. Griffiths, *Afghanistan: Key to a Continent* (Boulder, Colorado: Westview Press, 1981); Selig Harrison, "Dateline Afghanistan: Exit Through Finland?" *Foreign Policy* no. 41 (Winter 1980-81) pp. 163-82; Zalmay Khalilzad, "Soviet Occupied Afghanistan," *Problems of Communism* Vol. 29 no. 6 (November-December 1980) pp. 23-40; and Shirin Tahir-Kheli, "The Soviet Union in Afghanistan: Benefits and Costs," in *The Soviet Union in the Third World: Successes and Failures*, ed. Robert H. Donaldson (Boulder, Colorado: Westview Press, 1981) pp. 217-31

2. Brezhnev made this assertion during a dinner speech honoring the visit of Taraki for the signing of the Soviet-Afghan Treaty of Friendship and Cooperation. (*Pravda*, December 6, 1978).

3. Compare AP report in New York *Times*, May 4, 1979 citing United States intelligence sources.

4. Compare reports by Richard Burt, New York *Times*, April 13, 1979, and Jonathan C. Randal, Washington *Post*, May 10, 1979. It should be noted that the United States protested ineffectually as the Soviet military involvement in Afghanistan deepened.

5. *Pravda*, March 29, 1979.

6. Compare report by Don Oberdorfer, Washington *Post*, April 3, 1979.

7. Cited in Dmitry Volsky, "The Target: Afghanistan's Revolution," *New Times* no. 24, 1979, p. 13.

8. Compare Harrison, loc.cit., pp. 170-71.

9. For a description of the growing Soviet involvement in Afghanistan, see Griffiths, op.cit., Chapters 6-8.

10. For the Soviet reaction to Carter's moves, see *Pravda*, January 7, 1980.

11. Compare Baltimore *Sun*, January 16, 1980, for a list of the states supporting Moscow or abstaining in the U.N. vote.

12. Cited in report by Douglas Watson in the Baltimore *Sun*, January 21, 1980.

13. Cited in report by Michael Weisskopf, Washington *Post*, January 2, 1980. Afghanis and Iranians stormed the Soviet Embassy in Tehran but were driven off by Iranian police. One year later, however, the Iranian authorities were much slower to come to the defense of the embassy (see p. 398).

14. For the text of the Steadfastness Front declaration, see Radio Damascus Domestic Service, January 16, 1980 (translated in *Foreign Broadcast Information Service* [hereafter *FBIS*]: Middle East, January 17, 1980, pp. A2-6).

15. *Pravda*, January 30, 1980 (translated in *Current Digest of the Soviet Press* [hereafter *CDSP*] Vol. 32 no. 4, pp. 19-20).

16. Cited in report by Drew Middleton, New York *Times*, March 14, 1980.

17. Cited in report in Washington *Post*, February 10, 1980.

18. See Chapter 8, p. 331.

19. For a description of the actions taken at the Steadfastness Front Conference, see the report by Edward Cody in the April 16, 1980 issue of the Washington *Post*.

20. Editorial comment, *New Times* no. 17, 1980, p. 15.

21. See the report by Richard Burt in the December 19, 1979 issue of the New York *Times* and the report by Edward Cody in the June 5, 1980 issue of the Washington *Post*. For a good analysis of this development, see Nimrod Novik, *Between Two Yemens* (Tel Aviv University Center for Strategic Studies, Paper no. 11 (December 1980).

22. India also called for the United States to leave Diego Garcia and return it to Mauritius. For an analysis of Soviet-Indian relations, see Robert H. Donaldson, "The Soviet Union in South Asia: A Friend to Rely On?" *Journal of International Affairs* Vol. 34 no. 2, pp. 235-58.

23. Compare report by William Branigin, Washington *Post*, January 17, 1980.

24. Cited in New York *Times*, January 17, 1980.

25. Cited in report by Dusko Doder, Washington *Post*, January 18, 1980.

26. Cited in Baltimore *Evening Sun* Wire Service Report, January 28, 1980.

27. The text of the Islamic Conference declaration is found in the New York *Times*, January 30, 1980.

28. Cited in Reuters Report, New York *Times*, February 5, 1978.

29. Ibid.

30. Compare *Pravda*, February 12, 1980; *Izvestia*, March 26, 1980.

31. Leonid Medvenko, "Islam: Two Trends," *New Times* no. 13, 1980, pp. 23-25.

32. "Political Shifts in the Middle East: Roots, Factors, Trends," *World Marxist Review*, February 1980, pp. 58-64. The failure of the Soviet-sponsored Islamic Conference in Tashkent in September 1980 probably reinforced this view. *Izvestia*, on October 2, 1980, complained that the meeting had been boycotted by certain Muslim countries "because of excessive dependence on U.S. imperialism or a certain political myopia." It also asserted that the Tashkent meeting "facilitated the further consolidation of the Moslem anti-imperialist forces."

33. Translated in *FBIS* Daily Report: Middle East Iran Supplement no. 070, March 24, 1980, p. 7.

34. Ibid.

35. AP report in Baltimore *Sun*, March 18, 1980.

36. Cited in report by Kevin Klose, Washington *Post*, April 18, 1980.

37. *Pravda*, April 26, 1980.

38. *Pravda*, May 1, 1980.

39. Translated in *CDSP* Vol. 32, no. 17, p. 9.

40. Dmitry Volsky, "Turban or Helmet," *New Times* no. 20, 1980, p. 18.

41. Cited in report by Marvine Howe, New York *Times*, May 22, 1980.

42. Cited in report by Marvine Howe, New York *Times*, May 19, 1980.

43. Cited in report by Marvine Howe, New York *Times*, May 20, 1980.

44. The text of the resolution is found in the New York *Times*, May 23, 1980.

45. Compare editorial comment, *New Times* no. 22, 1980, p. 15.

46. *Pravda*, August 22, 1980 (translated in *CDSP* Vol. 32, no. 34, p. 13).

47. Compare Khalilzad, loc.cit., pp. 35-39.

48. *Literaturnaia Gazeta*, July 9, 1980 (translated in *CDSP* Vol. 32 no. 28, pp. 1-3, 19). There was one important difference between the Middle East positions of Moscow and Riyadh. The USSR already formally recognized Israel's existence; Saudi Arabia was not yet willing to do so although it made some hints to that effect in the summer of 1980. For a recent scholarly Soviet view of Saudi policy, see L. V. Valkova, *Saudovskaia Aravia v Mezhdunarodnykh Otnosheniiakh* (Moscow: Nauka, 1979).

49. On Soviet-Saudi ties, see Karen Dawisha, "Moscow's Moves in the Direction of the Gulf—So Near and Yet So Far," *Journal of International Affairs* Vol. 34 no. 2, p. 224.

50. The election of Andreas Papandreou as Greece's premier the following year, however, once again raised questions as to Greece's participation in NATO (see p. 418).

51. Translated in *CDSP* Vol. 32 no. 28, p. 13.

52. For a discussion of Iranian politics during this period, see Eric Rouleau, "Khomeini's Iran," *Foreign Affairs* Vol. 59 no. 1 (Fall 1980), pp. 12-17.

53. Cited in reports by Jay Ross in the Washington *Post*, July 1 and 3, 1980.

54. Cited in Reuters report in New York *Times*, July 5, 1980.

55. *New Times* no. 28, 1980, p. 3.

56. Cited in Baltimore *Sun*, July 22, 1980. The embassy was, however, to be tempo rarily seized at the end of December (see p. 398).

57. L. Skuratov, "Iran: Where the Threads of the Plot Lead," *New Times* no. 30, 1980, p. 8.

58. Ibid.

59. Compare *Pravda*, June 19, 1980.

60. Cited in Washington *Post*, August 15, 1980 and AP report Baltimore *Sun*, August 14, 1980.

61. Pavel Mezentsev, "USA-Iran: Threats and Blackmail," *New Times* no. 38, 1980, pp. 10-11.

62. Dmitry Volsky, "Iran: Sidetracking Attention," *New Times* no. 35, 1980, p. 21.

63. Cited in *Middle East Intelligence Service*, April 1-15, 1980.

64. Ibid.

65. Tass report April 19, 1980; and *Izvestia*, April 12, 1980, which cited foreign news services that Iraq had allowed Iranian emigrés to form armed groups on Iraqi soil to overthrow Khomeini.

66. Compare Dmitry Volsky, "Middle East: Turban or Helmet," *New Times* no. 20, 1980, p. 19.

67. Translated in *FBIS* Daily Report: South Asia, May 8, 1980, pp. 1-5.

68. Cited in report in Washington *Post*, August 9, 1980.

69. Cited in report in Baltimore *Sun*, August 23, 1980.

70. Compare Zakhar Kuznetsov, "In Unison with Imperialism," *New Times* no. 52, 1979, pp. 21-22.

71. Iraq, perhaps seeing a war on the horizon with Iran, appears to have backed off of its severe criticism of Moscow by April when the Afghan Foreign Minister Shah Mohammed Dost visited Baghdad. See Robert Rand, *Radio Liberty Report* no. 346/80, September 22, 1980.

72. The text of the Pan-Arab Charter may be found in *The Middle East*, April 1980, p. 20.

73. See Alexandre Benningsen, "Soviet Muslims and the World of Islam," *Problems of Communism* Vol. 29 no. 2 (March/April 1980), pp. 38-51. It should also be noted that the Afghans, except for the Shiite Hazara minority, are Sunni Moslems, and Afghans are not popular in Iran.

74. Compare Tass report, September 16, 1970.

75. Libya had criticized Saudi Arabia's decision to allow the stationing of U.S. AWACS aircraft on Saudi soil where they could be used against Iran (see p. 393).

76. Alexander Usvatov, "Put Out the Fire," *New Times* no. 40, 1980, p. 12.

77. Compare *Izvestia*, October 3, 1980.

78. For an analysis of the Gulf Cooperation Council, see Judith Perea, "Caution: Building in Progress," *The Middle East*, April 1981, p. 8-12.

79. Translated in *FBIS: USSR*, October 14, 1980, p. H-3.

80. Compare Tass report, in English, October 3, 1980 (*FBIS: USSR*, October 6, 1980, p. H-4).

81. Compare report by David K. Willis, *Christian Science Monitor*, October 14, 1980 and *Middle East Intelligence Survey*, October 1-15, 1980. See also Tass report in English, October 10, 1980; and Radio Moscow, in Persian, October 10, 1980 (*FBIS: USSR*, October 14, 1980, p. H-1).

82. For Western analyses of the impact of the Iran-Iraq war, see Claudia Wright, "Implications of the Iran-Iraq War," *Foreign Affairs* Vol. 59 no. 2 (Winter, 1980/81), 275-303; and Adeed I. Dawisha, "Iraq: The West's Opportunity," *Foreign Policy* no. 41 (Winter 1980/81), pp. 134-53. For Soviet analyses, see L. Medvenko, "The Persian Gulf: A Revival of Gunboat Diplomacy," *International Affairs* (Moscow) no. 12, 1980, pp. 23-29; A. K. Kislov, "Vashington i Irako-Iranskii Konflikt" ("Washington and the Iran-Iraq Conflict") *Ssha* no. 1, 1981, pp. 51-56; and N. Poliakov, "Put' K. Bezopasnosti v Indiiskom Okeane i Persidskom Zalive" ("The Way to Security in the Indian Ocean and Persian Gulf"), *Mirovaia Ekonomika i Mezhdunarodnie Otnosheniia*, no. 1, 1981, pp. 62-73.

83. Compare Reed, "Dateline Syria: Fin De Regime," loc.cit., pp. 177-85.

84. For an analysis of the changing alliances of King Hussein, see Adam M. Garfinkle, "Negotiating by Proxy: Jordanian Foreign Policy and U.S. Options in the Middle East," *Orbis* Vol. 24 no. 24 (Winter 1981), pp. 847-80. For the earlier Syrian-Jordanian alignment, see Chapter 6, pp. 208-09.

85. For the text of the treaty, see *Pravda*, October 9, 1980. For a discussion of Soviet-Syrian relations from 1970-78, see Freedman, *Soviet Policy Toward the Middle East Since 1970*, op.cit.; and Galia Golan, "Syria and the Soviet Union since the Yom Kippur War," *Orbis* Vol. 21 no. 4 (Winter 1978), pp. 777-801. See also Robert O. Freedman, "Soviet Policy Toward Syria Since Camp David," *Middle East Review*, forthcoming.

86. *Pravda*, October 11, 1980.

87. *Pravda*, October 9, 1980.

88. *Pravda*, December 6, 1978.

89. There were numerous rumors of such secret clauses. Compare report by Anan Safadi, Jerusalem *Post*, October 10, 1980.

90. See p. 406.

91. *Pravda*, December 3, 1980.

92. Cited in report of an interview with King Hussein by Pranay B. Gupte, New York *Times*, December 2, 1980. Hussein also stated that he had put aside plans to explore arms purchases from Moscow.

93. Compare Moscow Radio Arabic Broadcast, December 5, 1980.

94. For an analysis of the events surrounding the proclamation of the Soviet peace plan of April 1976, see Chapter 7, p. 264.

95. Press Trust of India News Agency, December 11, 1980, cited in report by Carol Honsa, *Christian Science Monitor*, December 12, 1980. Moscow increased shipments of oil by 1 million metric tons.

96. For the text of the final communiqué, see *Pravda*, December 12, 1980.

97. The text of the declaration is found in *FBIS: USSR*, December 11, 1980, p. D-7.

98. For a Soviet analysis of the significance of Brezhnev's plan, see the commentary by Igor Pavlovich, Moscow Radio Domestic Service (International Round Table), December 21, 1980 (*FBIS: USSR*, December 22, 1980, pp. CC-2).

99. For the text of the note, which was broadcast by Tass in English on December 28, 1980, see *FBIS: USSR*, December 29, 1980, p. H-1.

100. For the reports of the comments of Behzad Nabavi, Iranian government spokesman, on Radio Tehran Domestic Service, December 30, 1980, see *FBIS: South Asia*, December 30, 1980, pp. 1-5 -6.

101. Compare Tass report, January 12, 1981 in *FBIS: USSR*, January 13, 1981, p. H-1.

102. Compare *Pravda*, January 17, 1981 and Moscow Radio Persian Language Broadcast, January 17, 1981 (*FBIS: USSR*, January 19, 1981, pp. A-2 -3). Former Secretary of State Henry Kissinger's trip to the Middle East in early January was linked by Moscow to the invasion plan.

103. Compare Reuters report, New York *Times*, January 18, 1981.

104. For the text of Brezhnev's speech to the 26th Party Congress, see *Pravda* February 24, 1981 (translated in *CDSP* Vol. 33 no. 8, pp. 7-13).

105. For an analysis of the development of inter-Arab politics to early 1981, see Bruce Maddy-Weitzman, "The Fragmentation of Arab Politics: Inter-Arab Affairs Since the Afghanistan Invasion," *Orbis* Vol. 25, no. 2 (Summer 1981), pp. 389-407.

106. For a recent analysis of Libyan policy, see Ronald Bruce St.John, "Libya's Foreign and Domestic Policies," *Current History*, December 1981, pp. 426-29, 434-35.

107. See *Pravda*, April 28, 1981, for Kaddafi's banquet speech in which he portrayed himself as the representative of the Steadfastness Front. See *Al-Watan* (Kuwait) April 29, 1981, for his frank interview about areas of agreement and disagreement with Moscow (*FBIS: Middle East and Africa*, May 4, 1981, pp. Q-4-5).

108. Compare *Pravda*, April 28, 1981 and *Pravda*, April 30, 1981. A Libyan Arabic broadcast made a major point of this (compare Radio Tripoli Voice of the Arab Homeland, April 29, 1981) (*FBIS: Middle East and Africa*, April 30, 1981, p. Q-1).

109. During his banquet speech Kaddafi had stated that the Steadfastness Front considered it necessary "to obtain information" about the Soviet proposal for an international conference on the Palestinian problem.

110. For a recent analysis of Algerian policy under Chadli Ben-Jedid, see Robert Mortimer, "Algeria's New Sultan," *Current History*, December 1981, pp. 418-21, 433-34.

111. Statement by Morris Draper, deputy assistant secretary of State for Near Eastern and South Asian Affairs, as cited in the report by Bernard Gwertzman, New York *Times*, March 26, 1981.

112. For an analysis of the natural gas situation and other problems of U.S.-Algerian relations, see the report by Jonathan C. Randal, Washington *Post*, March 25, 1981.

113. *Pravda*, June 11, 1981.

114. Soon after Ben-Jedid's visit to Moscow, Morocco was to agree to a ceasefire and a referendum to determine the future of the former Spanish Sahara (compare report by Jay Ross, Washington *Post*, June 27, 1981), but the modalities of the proposed referendum led a number of observers to believe that this was just a Moroccan ploy. For an analysis of the Saharan problem, see William H. Lewis, "Western Sahara: Compromise or Conflict?"*Current History*, December 1981, pp. 410-13, 431.

115. For a description of Moscow's Mediterranean plan, see A. Usvatov, "USSR-Algeria: Common Approach," *New Times* no. 25, 1981, p. 7. Moscow through the U.N. was making a similar effort for the Indian Ocean, but without success.

116. At the Islamic summit in Taif, Saudi Arabia in late January for example, the emphasis was on Islamic opposition to Israel and the "Soviet threat" was played down, as was the Soviet invasion of Afghanistan (compare Claudia Wright, "Islamic Summit," *The Middle East*, March 1981, pp. 6-10). The absence of Iran, which had played a militantly anti-Soviet role in the previous Islamic conference in May 1981, however, may have been a factor in the downplaying of the Soviet threat along with Saudi Arabian efforts to achieve an Islamic consensus, which meant it had to have the support of Moscow's Steadfastness Front allies.

117. UPI report in Jerusalem *Post*, April 9, 1981. As a gesture to the United States, however, Saudi Arabia broke diplomatic relations with Afghanistan on the eve of the Haig visit (compare Reuters report, New York *Times*, April 8, 1981).

118. For an analysis of the 1975 visit, see Chapter 6, pp. 220-21.

119. For an interview with Sheik Sabah, see *The Middle East*, March 1981, p. 18. For an analysis of the domestic situation in Kuwait at the time of Sheik Sabah's visit to the USSR, see Helena Cobban, "Kuwait's Elections," *The Middle East*, April 1981, pp. 14-15. Kuwait's foreign policy problems and strategy are discussed in Claudia Wright, "India and Pakistan Join in Gulf Game," *The Middle East*, June 1981, pp. 31-32. According to Wright, Sheik Sabah also went to Moscow to get a nonaggression treaty negotiated between the PDRY and Oman so as to lessen Omani dependence on the United States. On this point,

see also *Al-Hadaf* (Kuwait), May 7, 1981 (translated in *FBIS: Middle East and Africa*, May 13, 1981, p. C-5).

120. *Pravda*, April 26, 1981.

121. Ibid.

122. For an analysis of the changing alliances of King Hussein, see Adam M. Garfinkle, "Negotiating by Proxy: Jordanian Foreign Policy and U.S. Options in the Middle East," *Orbis* Vol. 24, no. 24 (Winter 1981), pp. 847-80.

123. See p. 418.

124. The joint communiqué was printed in *Pravda*, May 30, 1981.

125. *Pravda*, May 27, 1981.

126. Alexander Usvatov, "King Hussein's Visit," *New Times* no. 23, 1981, p. 10. One additional issue on which Jordan and the USSR obviously did not agree, however, was the Iran-Iraq war, where Jordan continued strongly to back Iraq while Moscow continued to profess a neutral position.

127. Compare the report by Jonathan Randal, Washington *Post*, April 13, 1981.

128. Translated in *CDSP* Vol. 33, no. 15, p. 18.

129. See p. 408.

130. By the end of the first week in May, Arab army chiefs, meeting in Tunis, had pledged to aid Syria as had Kuwait and Saudi Arabia (compare report by Pranay Gupte, New York *Times*, May 8, 1981 and AP report, Baltimore *Sun*, May 3, 1981). Tass on May 8 and *Pravda* and Moscow Radio (Arabic language broadcast) on May 9 carried stories about the missiles, referring to them as a defensive measure. The stories coincided with the end of a visit to Damascus by Soviet First Deputy Foreign Minister Georgii Kornienko.

131. The Reagan administration had decided to reinforce U.S.-Saudi relations by selling Saudi Arabia five AWACS aircraft, advanced air-to-air missiles, and other sophisticated military equipment.

132. Compare report by Don Oberdorfer, Washington *Post*, April 30, 1981.

133. Soviet radar on Lebanese mountain peaks would aid Moscow's air deployments in the eastern Mediterranean.

134. To at least one Soviet commentator, the situation was somewhat reminiscent of June 1967. See Dmitry Volsky, "May 1981 is not June 1967," *New Times* no. 21, 1981, pp. 5-6.

135. See Chapter 5, pp. 167-70.

136. Compare Moscow Radio in Arabic, May 13, 1981 (*FBIS: USSR*, May 14, 1981, p. H-1).

137. Cited in Robert Rand, "The USSR and the Crisis over Syrian Missiles in Lebanon: An Analysis and Chronological Survey," Radio Liberty Report no. 227/81 (June 3, 1981), p. 6. Rand's study is an excellent analysis of the missile crisis from April 28, 1981 to May 29, 1981. (Note: Tass of May 5 denied that Soldatov had said the USSR regarded the Al Bekaa Valley [where Zahle is located] as a sector of substantial importance to the security of Syria.)

138. Cited in report in New York *Times*, May 13, 1981.

139. *Pravda*, May 17, 1981.

140. *Pravda*, May 23, 1981.

141. *Pravda*, May 27, 1981.

142. Cited in Jerusalem *Post*, May 24, 1981.

143. Cited in *Pravda*, May 26, 1981.

144. Moscow, however, had not forgotten the missile crisis and in early July carried out a joint military exercise with Syria including, for the first time, naval landings. For a report on the exercise which could be seen as a Soviet show of support for Syria after Begin's reelection, see the UPI report in the New York *Times*, July 10, 1981.

145. Compare *Pravda*, June 10, 11, and 16, 1981.

146. Translated in *CDSP* Vol. 33, no. 24, p. 17.

147. Compare the report by Nathaniel Harrison, *Christian Science Monitor*, April 1, 1981.

148. Compare Andrei Stepanov, "Taking Up a Point" (Soviet Neutrality in the Iran-Iraq War), *New Times* no. 17, 1981, p. 31.

149. Compare the report by Michael J. Berlin, Washington *Post*, June 19, 1981.

150. Cited in report by Edward Cody, Washington *Post*, June 19, 1981.

151. Aziz Mohammed's speech was also printed in *Pravda*, March 3, 1981.

152. Cited in report by Bernard Gwertzman, New York *Times*, March 20, 1981.

153. Compare report by Don Oberdorfer, Washington *Post*, April 11, 1981.

154. Ibid. Permission for the sale of the planes had been previously refused.

155. In early November, the London *Daily Telegraph* reported the shipment of 650 tanks from Poland (Baltimore *Sun*, November 12, 1981).

156. Compare the Tass statement in *Pravda*, July 22, 1981.

157. For an analysis of the background to this incident, see the report by Bernard Gwertzman, New York *Times*, August 21, 1981. For an examination of Kaddafi's attempt to improve his diplomatic position, see Claudia Wright, "Libya Comes in From the Cold," *The Middle East*, August 1981, pp. 18-25.

158. If this was one of his goals, he was unsuccessful as Saudi Arabia, despite the aircraft incident, stood firm on its price demands, something which Moscow also complained about (see p. 419).

159. Tass International Service, in Russian, August 20, 1981 (translated in *FBIS: USSR*, August 20, 1981, p. H-2).

160. Translated in *FBIS: USSR*, August 28, 1981, p. H-6.

161. *Pravda*, August 23, 1981. Criticism of the U.S. action came from such Centrist Arab states as Jordan, Kuwait, Bahrein and the United Arab Emirates and from the secretary of the Gulf Cooperation Council, and the Organization of African Unity (compare *FBIS: Middle East and Africa*, August 20 and 21, 1981).

162. Compare Moscow Radio in Turkish to Turkey, August 20, 1981 (*FBIS: USSR*, August 21, 1981, p. H-2).

163. Oman denounced the treaty in very strong terms (compare Muscat Domestic Service, August 26, 1981 and Salalah Domestic Service, August 27, 1981 (*FBIS: Middle East and Africa*, August 27, 1981, pp. C-1 -2) and strongly criticized the decision by the secretary of the Gulf Cooperation Council to denounce the U.S. attack on the Libyan aircraft without consulting the membership (compare *FBIS: Middle East and Africa*, August 31, 1981, p. C-3). For an interview with the GCC's Secretary General, Abdullah Bishara, who is trying to push the organization toward nonalignment, see *The Middle East*, September 1981, pp. 35-36. At its August ministerial meeting, however, several days after the Tripartite Treaty, the GCC decided "to strengthen political and security coordination between the member states" (see Nadia Hijab, "Gulf Council Shifts Into Second Gear," *The Middle East*, October 1981, pp. 25-26).

164. For Soviet attitudes toward the Iranian leadership, see Robert O. Freedman, "Soviet Policy Toward the Middle East Since the Invasion of Afghanistan," *Journal of International Affairs* Vol. 34 no. 2, pp. 290-91, 295-97.

165. Translated in *FBIS: USSR*, September 3, 1981, p. H-1.

166. Cited in AP report, New York *Times*, November 7, 1981. Syrian Communist leader Khaled Bagdash, however, was critical of Ghassemlou (compare *World Marxist Review*, November 1981, p. 33).

167. Cited in report in Washington *Post*, February 16, 1981.

168. Tehran Domestic Service, October 20, 1981 (*FBIS: USSR*, October 22, 1981, p. H-7).

169. Cited in Reuters report, New York *Times*, November 23, 1981.

170. Compare A. Ulansky, "Presidential Election in a Tense Atmosphere," *New Times* no. 40, 1981, p. 10. A statement by the Tudeh Party was even more critical (compare "For

a Return to Peace in a Society Based on Legality and Social Justice," Information Bulletin (*World Marxist Review*, November 1981, p. 21).

171. Compare Radio Moscow, in English, August 29, 1981 (*FBIS: USSR*, August 31, 1981, p. H-4).

172. Compare *Pravda*, September 8, 12, 14, 25, 1981.

173. The actual agreement, signed in December, was far more modest but Moscow sought to extract the maximum in propaganda value from it both when Begin came to the United States in September to negotiate the general principles of the agreement and when Sharon came in December to sign the detailed agreement.

174. The meeting was at Shamir's initiative.

175. Compare Tass International Service in Russian, September 25, 1981 (*FBIS: USSR*, September 25, 1981, p. CC-3) and Radio Moscow in English to North America, October 5, 1981 (*FBIS: USSR*, October 6, 1981, p. H-4).

176. Compare report by William Clayborn, Washington *Post*, September 26, 1981.

177. For articles summarizing Moscow's displeasure with Sadat at the time of the Egyptian president's visit to Washington in early August, see *Izvestia*, August 9, 1981 and August 28, 1981.

178. *Pravda*, September 18, 1981.

179. Moscow Radio announced, however, on October 1, 1981 that the Soviet branch of the Friendship Society would continue to operate (*FBIS: USSR*, October 2, 1981, p. H-1).

180. Bovin's comments came on Moscow television on October 25 (*FBIS: USSR*, October 26, 1981, p. H-1).

181. Compare Moscow Radio Peace and Progress in Arabic, September 7, 1981 (*FBIS: USSR*, September 10, 1981, p. H-1); Tass, in English, October 8, 1981 (*FBIS: USSR*, October 9, 1981, p. H-1); and Moscow Radio in Arabic, October 26, 1981 (*FBIS: USSR*, October 27, 1981, p. H-6).

182. For an analysis of Soviet and U.S. policy during the fall of the Shah, see Chapter 9, pp. 349-50.

183. *Pravda*, October 12, 1981.

184. Compare report by Don Oberdorfer, Washington *Post*, October 15, 1981.

185. *Pravda*, October 16, 1981.

186. Compare n. 180. In a speech on November 8, however, Mubarak hinted at nonalignment, stating "Egypt will not rotate in the orbit of any state" [Radio Cairo, November 8, 1981], cited in Robert Rand "Mubarak on the USSR," Radio Liberty Report No. 462/81, November 17, 1981.

187. Cited in report by Don Oberdorfer, Washington *Post*, October 21, 1981. For a good analysis of Moscow's initial approaches to Mubarak and his attitude toward the USSR, see Rand, ibid.

188. Moscow Radio Domestic Service, October 20, 1981 (*FBIS: USSR*, October 21, 1981, p. H-1). Arafat was quoted as saying at a press conference "We fully endorse the Soviet proposals advanced at the 26th CPSU Congress and we view them as the basis for a just settlement of the Palestinian problem." *Pravda*, on October 21, 1981, reported the joint Soviet-PLO support for the international conference and the granting of official diplomatic status to the PLO mission in Moscow.

189. Cited in report by Bernard Gwertzman, New York *Times*, August 13, 1981.

190. The text of the former presidents' comments is in the New York *Times*, October 12, 1981.

191. For an analysis of this event, see Chapter 9, pp. 352-54.

192. On the developments in North Yemen, see Novik, op.cit.

193. *Pravda*, October 29, 1981.

194. Saleh may have also wished to have Moscow's support in controlling the South Yemeni drive for the unification of the Yemens, following the strengthening of the PDRY by its alliance with Ethiopia and Libya.

195. Compare reports by Bernard Gwertzman, New York *Times*, November 3, 1981; Don Oberdorfer, Washington *Post*, November 6, 1981; and Reuters, Washington *Post*, November 9, 1981.

196. *Pravda*, April 12, 1981.

197. *Literaturnaia Gazeta*, May 27, 1981 (translated in *CDSP* Vol. 33, no. 21, p. 11).

198. Ruben Andreasian, "Disagreement in OPEC," *New Times* no. 35, 1981, p. 13. See also Ruben Andreasian, *Opek v Mire Nefti* (OPEC in the World of Oil) (Moscow: Nauka, 1978).

199. *Pravda*, August 26, 1981.

200. Translated in *FBIS: USSR*, November 3, 1981, p. A-3.

201. *FBIS: USSR*, November 2, 1981, p. H-2.

202. *Pravda*, March 29, 1981.

203. This, of course, had happened during the 1973 Arab-Israeli war. Compare *Izvestia*, January 8, 1981.

204. Tass, November 1, 1981 (*FBIS: USSR*, November 2, 1981, p. H-3).

205. Compare *Izvestia*, October 31, 1981.

206. Compare Moscow Radio in Arabic, November 8, 1981 (*FBIS: USSR*, November 9, 1981, pp. H-1 -2).

207. It may have also had a favorable impact on North Yemen.

208. As might be expected, Moscow was highly critical of Pakistan's increasingly close military tie to the United States (compare *Pravda*, September 27, 1981).

209. Cited in AP report, Baltimore *Sun*, November 24, 1981.

210. Unlike Sadat, who by 1981 was on very poor personal terms with the Saudi ruling family, Mubarak had kept up good personal relationships.

211. Radio Moscow in Arabic, August 12, 1981 (*FBIS: USSR*, August 13, 1981, p. H-1).

212. Compare *FBIS: USSR*, August 20, 1981, p. A-3.

213. *Izvestia*, November 5, 1981.

214. Compare Moscow Radio in Arabic, November 5 and 6, 1981 (*FBIS: USSR*, November 6, 1981, p. H-1, -4).

215. The text of the communiqué is found in *FBIS: Middle East and Africa*, November 12, 1981, p. C-4. Moscow, however, at least as reflected in a Moscow Radio Peace and Progress Arabic broadcast on November 12, 1981, was critical of the GCC meeting (*FBIS: USSR*, November 13, 1981, p. H-4). One of the key issues not settled in the GCC meeting was Oman's proposal regarding Gulf security. If adopted, the proposal would move the GCC closer to the United States.

216. Compare article by Scott Armstrong, Washington *Post*, November 1, 1981.

217. Compare New York *Times*, October 2, 1981.

218. Compare *Pravda*, September 20, 1981 and Moscow Radio Peace and Progress in Arabic, October 20, 1981 (*FBIS: USSR*, October 21, 1981, p. H-7).

219. Moscow Radio, in Arabic, November 27, 1981 (*FBIS: USSR*, December 1, 1981, pp. H-5, -6).

220. Dmitry Volsky, "There is Light at the End of the Tunnel," *New Times* no. 49, 1981, pp. 12-13.

11
Conclusions

In assessing Soviet policy toward the Middle East from the death of Nasser in September 1970 until the collapse of the Arab Summit at Fez in November 1981, one may conclude that Soviet policy toward the region has been primarily a reaction to a series of regional developments that Moscow not only had not caused, but that it was increasingly unable to shape to fit Soviet goals in the region, and that the Soviet position in the Middle East was weaker in 1981 than it was in 1970.

The Russians suffered a major loss to their Middle Eastern position in July 1971, when an abortive Communist-supported coup d'état in the Sudan triggered a wave of anti-Communism and anti-Sovietism throughout the Arab world. A year later Moscow suffered another blow when it lost control over a number of air and naval bases in Egypt, thus weakening the Soviet strategic position in the eastern Mediterranean. While the Soviet leaders were quick to exploit such events as the Munich massacre in September 1972 and the October 1973 Arab-Israeli war, they were outrun by events and found themselves in a worse position in the region following the war than before it. The United States took the diplomatic initiative in working out a series of disengagement agreements between Israel and its Arab neighbors in 1974; two of the Soviet Union's closest Middle Eastern allies, Syria and the PLO, fought each other in Lebanon in 1976; and Somali leader Siad Barre expelled the USSR from its bases in his country in 1977.

In 1979, following the Camp David agreements and the fall of the Shah, it appeared as if Moscow had recovered some of its lost ground, but the improvement was to be only a temporary one. To be sure, the Arab reaction to the Camp David agreements was very negative and a large anti-Sadat coalition of Arab states came into existence. Moscow clearly hoped that this coalition could be transformed into the "anti-imperialist" Arab unity it had so long desired.

A second Middle East development working to the advantage of the Soviet Union at this time was the fall of the Shah and the rise to power of Ayatollah Khomeini. As a result of the Shah's fall, not only did the United States lose its "policeman" of the Persian Gulf, but Moscow began to entertain the hope that the anti-American, anti-Israeli, and anti-Egyptian Khomeini might join the "anti-imperialist" grouping of Arab states formed as a result of Camp David, and that a large "anti-imperialist" Middle East bloc might thereby emerge—a hope that seemed closer to realization after the seizure of the U.S. hostages.

While the anti-Sadat Arab reaction to Camp David and the fall of the Shah were Middle Eastern developments working to the advantage of Moscow, the disruption of the anti-Sadat alignment caused by the renewal of hostility between Iraq and Syria and the outbreak of the Iran-Iraq war were developments that clearly worked to Moscow's disadvantage in its quest for Middle East influence, but that the USSR proved powerless to either prevent or control. As a result of these events and the Soviet invasion of Afghanistan, Moscow's hopes for the establishment of an "anti-imperialist" Middle Eastern bloc were dashed, and even the assassination of Sadat, who had become the Kremlin's primary enemy in the Middle East, proved of little immediate benefit to the USSR. Indeed, throughout the entire period, the Arab leaders of the Middle East, whom the Soviet leadership was diligently trying to court, were only too happy to accept Soviet aid but insisted on pursuing their own policies, even when these policies conflicted with those of the Soviet Union.

It is clear from these events that Soviet influence in the Middle East is very limited indeed. Despite massive outlays of military assistance and considerable economic aid to a number of states in the region, the Soviet leadership has been unable to persuade the elites of the area to adopt policies consistent with Soviet positions in many key situations. This has been most apparent in Egypt, where at the time of Nasser's death the USSR had control over a number of air and naval bases while also playing an active, albeit not dominant, role in Egypt's political and economic life. When Sadat took over from Nasser, however, he soon clashed with the Soviet Union, and by September 1981 the Egyptian leader had undermined the Soviet position in Egypt—which, because of its population, geographical location, and military power, is the most important state in the Arab world.

Sadat's first conflict with the Russians erupted in the summer of 1971, when he helped Sudanese leader Jaafar Nimeri regain power during the Communist-supported coup d'état against his regime. Following this event the Sudanese premier proceeded to execute a number of major Sudanese Communist leaders. When the Soviet Union appealed to Sadat to use his influence with Nimeri to save the lives of the Sudanese Communists, Sadat not only failed to help the Soviet leaders but also came out strongly in support of Nimeri's anti-Communist actions. In doing so Sadat came into direct conflict with the Soviet leadership, which had mounted a major propaganda campaign to save the lives of the Sudanese Communists.

The second serious Egyptian-Soviet clash came a year later when Sadat, dissatisfied with a perceived lack of Soviet support for his confrontation with Israel, expelled the Soviet military advisers from his country, ended Soviet control over Egypt's military bases, and turned to the United States. Thus, the Russians suffered a double loss: they were deprived of strategically important bases in Egypt, and their erstwhile ally had turned to their main opponent for assistance. Soviet-Egyptian relations improved following the Israeli retaliatory raids on Lebanon and Syria after the massacre of the Israeli athletes at Munich and the failure of the United States to bring the desired pressure on Israel, and the USSR proved willing to supply Egypt with both weapons and diplomatic support during the October 1973 Arab-Israeli war. Nonetheless, Soviet-Egyptian relations again deteriorated sharply after the war when Sadat, perceiving a chance to advance the Egyptian objective of securing an Israeli withdrawal from the occupied Sinai Desert, while also obtaining economic assistance for his lagging economy, turned again to the United States for support and signed the Sinai Agreement with Israel under U.S. mediation. Sadat then helped persuade the oil-producing Arab countries to lift their embargo against the United States, a policy that was in direct conflict with the Soviet effort to maintain the embargo, which was causing economic dislocations within the United States and political conflict within the NATO alliance.

Soviet-Egyptian relations continued to deteriorate after the end of the embargo as Sadat signed the Sinai II agreement with Israel, despite strong Soviet opposition, in September 1975 and abrogated the Soviet-Egyptian treaty of friendship in April 1976. His November 1977 trip to Jerusalem was also bitterly denounced by the USSR, as were the Camp David agreements, the Egyptian-Israeli peace agreement of March 1979, and Sadat's decision to develop an increasingly close military relationship with the United States which involved not only the provision of American military equipment to Egypt but also joint Egyptian-American military maneuvers and permission for the United States to use Egyptian military facilities for its Rapid Deployment Force. Meanwhile, during the entire period of his presidency, Sadat was also encouraging Western investment in Egypt and expanding Egypt's private sector—policies the Soviet leadership found highly objectionable because they seemed to reinforce economically the political turn Egypt was making toward the West. When Sadat was assassinated by Muslim extremists in October 1981, therefore, Moscow could only rejoice because its primary Arab enemy had left the Middle Eastern scene. Nonetheless, while Sadat's successor, Hosni Mubarak, made a number of small gestures to the USSR, American influence remained high in Egypt and it was an open question as to whether Moscow would be able to rebuild its once paramount position in that key Arab country.

While the Soviet leadership experienced its greatest difficulty in influencing the foreign and domestic policies of the Sadat regime in Egypt, its record was a more mixed one in countries like Syria, Iraq, Somalia, Libya, and South Yemen, the other major recipients of Soviet economic and military aid in the

Arab world. On the surface, it would appear that Soviet influence was highest in Syria, as witnessed by the Assad regime's decision in October 1980 to agree to a Treaty of Friendship and Cooperation with Moscow which it had been resisting for almost a decade. Nonetheless, serious disagreements pervaded the Soviet-Syrian relationship in the aftermath of the signing of the treaty as they had before that event. Relations between the USSR and Syria had become close for the first time in 1966 when a very left-wing, Alawite-dominated, Ba'athist government seized power in Damascus. Relations remained close until 1970, although there was a disagreement within the Syrian regime between strongman Salah Jedid and then Defense Minister Hafiz Assad on how close to draw to Moscow. When Assad, who favored a more limited relationship, overthrew Jedid in November 1970, a marked cooling of Soviet-Syrian relations took place. Soviet support to Syria during the 1973 war helped to warm relations again, but the Syrian refusal to attend the Soviet co-sponsored Geneva Peace Conference in December 1973 and the successful shuttle diplomacy of Henry Kissinger, which led both to a separation of forces agreement on the Golan Heights between Israel and Syria and the re-establishment of Syrian-American diplomatic relations, again chilled Soviet-Syrian ties. Yet another change in relations occurred in 1975 when Syria turned again to the USSR after the Sinai II agreement, only to clash violently with Moscow the following year when the USSR both criticized Syria's military intervention in Lebanon and delayed promised shipments of arms. Soviet-Syrian relations warmed again, however, in 1977 and Moscow was able to profit from the regional isolation of Syria following the Egyptian-Israeli peace agreement, the renewal of the feud between Damascus and Baghdad, and the eruption of a feud between Jordan and Syria, as well as by the growing instability within Syria to extract from the Syrians the long-desired Treaty of Friendship and Cooperation which Moscow saw as giving it a formal presence in the strategically located Arab state. Yet one can raise some questions about the ultimate value of such a treaty to the USSR. Both Egypt and Somalia have already abrogated similar treaties, and the Soviet-Iraqi treaty seems to have greatly diminished in importance due to the neutrality of the USSR in the Iran-Iraq war and the general cooling of Soviet-Iraqi relations.

Indeed, despite the treaty, Soviet influence in Syria would still appear to be limited. While Syria came out in support of the Soviet invasion of Afghanistan (an action taken *before* the signing of the treaty), Assad's staging of the crisis with Jordan in late November 1980 and the missile crisis in Lebanon in late April 1981 seemed to catch Moscow by surprise. Although the latter crisis worked out to Moscow's advantage, the former did not and complicated Soviet relations with both Jordan and its ally Iraq.

If Soviet-Syrian relations have been seen to have improved since 1977, the reverse has been true in the case of Iraq, once a primary Soviet ally in the Arab world. Even before 1977, the Iraqi regime opposed a number of major Soviet policies, including U.N. Resolution 242, the Soviet-American cease-fire resolution that ended the October 1973 war, and Soviet proposals for an Arab-Israeli peace settlement. While it had welcomed Soviet economic and political support for its oil nationalization in 1972 and Soviet military aid for its war against the Kurds in 1974 and to deter Iran, by 1975, thanks to its improved financial situation due to the rise in oil prices and its military/political position due both to its suppression of the Kurds and the 1975 treaty with Iran, Iraq began to move away from the USSR. Thus while Moscow had looked to Iraq to be a center of anti-Western activity in the Arab world, the regime in Baghdad, pursuing a major economic development strategy, turned to Western Europe and the United States for aid in industrialization and increasingly to France for military equipment. At the same time, in an effort to move out of its position of isolation in the Arab world and toward a position of leadership, the Ba'athist leaders of Iraq sought a rapprochement with Saudi Arabia, using an increasingly severe policy of repression of the Iraqi Communist Party as a demonstration of good faith to the anti-Communist Saudis.

Raising Moscow's ire further was the resumption of the Iraqi-Syrian quarrel, increasing tension between Iraq and both the PDRY and the PLO, and especially Iraq's attack on Iran in September 1980—all of which seemed to destroy any hopes Moscow might have had for the rebuilding of an "anti-imperialist" Arab unity. As these events occurred, Moscow grew increasingly critical of Baghdad and even permitted an Iraqi Communist Party leader to publicly criticize Iraq at the 26th CPSU Congress in March 1981. Even Israel's strike at the Iraqi nuclear reactor in June 1981 did not serve to restore Soviet-Iraqi relations to the 1972-74 level although, as the Iran-Iraq war went into its second year, Moscow may have entertained the hope that Baghdad might be forced to come back to the USSR as its military supplies were exhausted.

As Soviet-Iraqi relations declined, so did ties between the USSR and Somalia. At one time a close ally of Moscow, Somali leader Siad Barre rejected the Soviet plan for a Marxist federation on the Horn of Africa, and both abrogated Somalia's treaty of friendship with the USSR and expelled the Soviet Union from its bases in Somalia when Moscow backed Ethiopia in her conflict with his country. A further blow to Moscow was the Somali decision to grant the United States military facilities for the use of its Rapid Deployment Force—the same facilities that Moscow had invested its time, effort and rubles to develop.

If Moscow's ties with Egypt, Iraq and Somalia had deteriorated since the mid-1970s, and while relations with Syria remained tense, despite the 1980 treaty, Moscow did make progress in improving ties with Libya, Ethiopia and the PDRY. In the cases of Libya and Ethiopia, conflict with a neighbor prompted closer ties with Moscow while in the case of the PDRY, it was a combination of ideology (the South Yemeni leaders are professed Marxists) and difficulty with neighboring North Yemen and Oman. Nonetheless, all three countries are rather peripheral in the Middle East, and all three are also seen as threats to their neighbors. Indeed, Moscow's close ties with these regimes, especially since the formation of a formal alignment among them in August 1981, may prove, on balance, a liability for Moscow in that it may serve to push such Centrist Arab states as Saudi Arabia back toward Egypt (and toward the United States) much as Libyan activity in Chad and pressure against the Sudan were the key factors in prompting Sudanese President Jaafar Nimeri to reestablish full diplomatic relations with Egypt and offer the United States military bases in his country. To be sure, Moscow may hope to use such influence as it has in Libya, Ethiopia and South Yemen—and in Libya and Ethiopia, at least, Soviet influence remains limited—as a device to pressure the Centrist Arab states into concessions. Nonetheless, up until this time at least, it appears that Moscow's ties to Ethiopia, Libya and South Yemen, while productive for Moscow in the military sense, may well prove to be counterproductive politically. All in all, the Soviet shift from Egypt, the most prestigious Middle Eastern state, to Libya, South Yemen, Ethiopia and Syria, the most politically isolated, would appear to be yet another indication of the overall weakening of the Soviet position in the Middle East since 1970.

While Moscow has declined politically in the Middle East, its military position has improved since 1970. Although the USSR lost its extensive base arrangements in Egypt, it has gained the use of military facilities in South Yemen and Ethiopia, and to a lesser degree in Syria, while its invasion of Afghanistan has brought it to within fighter-bomber range of the Strait of Hormuz. In addition, Soviet military advisers are active in Algeria, Libya, Ethiopia, South Yemen, North Yemen, and Syria, and one cannot rule out the possibility that some Soviet advisers will be sent to Jordan to implement the recent SAM deal with that country. Indeed, Moscow's ability to deliver large amounts of high quality military equipment gives it a key means of influence in the conflict-ridden Middle East, although, as mentioned above, Soviet unwillingness to provide as much high quality equipment as a client state may want can also be a cause of conflict as shown in the cases of both Egypt and Syria. Perhaps even more important than Moscow's acquisition of military facilities, its use of advisers, and its willingness to sell or otherwise provide large quantities of military equipment, has been the increase in its interventionist capability in the Middle East. The Soviet ability to quickly move troops and equipment to the Middle East was first demonstrated in Ethiopia in 1977-78 and then on a far larger scale in Afghanistan in 1979, and Moscow has been expanding its already large airlift capability since then. It should be added, however, that both military moves were unopposed by the West and it could be expected that Moscow would have a much more difficult time engaging in a military operation that faced counteraction. In addition, the Soviet invasion of Afghanistan in 1979, while improving Moscow's overall military position in the Middle East, has had both military and especially political drawbacks. On the military side, while Soviet troops are gaining combat and counter-insurgency experience, increasing numbers of Soviet soldiers are also being killed. The Soviet invasion of Afghanistan has also rekindled suspicions about Soviet motives not only in such conservative Gulf states as Saudi Arabia (the Gulf Cooperation Council

was one outgrowth of the invasion) but also in the anti-American Islamic fundamentalist regime of Iran's Ayatollah Khomeini. While the Afghan guerrillas
remain divided, the very fact that they have been able to withstand Soviet
attacks for more than two years, and that Moscow has been unable to bring
about a "political" solution in Afghanistan, cannot but diminish Moscow's
prestige in the region.

While the Soviet Union's military power along the periphery of the Middle
East has grown—although Moscow has not yet been able to transform its military
power into political gain—the United States has also begun to rebuild its military
power in the region, although it, too, has had trouble translating its growing
military power into political influence. In addition, while Moscow appeared
decisive in going to the aid of its client regime in Ethiopia and in invading
Afghanistan—whatever the negative political ramifications of these moves—
U.S. policy, particularly in the late 1970s, appeared indecisive, a development
Moscow tried hard to exploit. Thus the United States was uncertain how to
react to the Soviet intervention to aid Ethiopia against Somalia; it seemed
unsure how to react to the weakening and subsequent fall of the Shah; and the
abortive U.S. hostage rescue mission in Iran was a disaster in terms both of planning and execution—a fact not lost on such weak states in the region as Kuwait.
Nonetheless the United States has moved to build up its fleet in the Indian
Ocean as a counter to Soviet military power; it has acquired facilities (not bases)
for its newly created Rapid Deployment Force in Egypt, the Sudan, Somalia,
and Oman; its AWACS arrangement with Saudi Arabia gives the United States
command and control capability in the air space in the Persian/Arab Gulf at
least until 1985 and probably thereafter; and its now annual military maneuvers
in the Middle East have given U.S. forces much needed training under simulated
Middle East combat conditions. While the United States has not obtained formal
base rights in such strategically located states as Saudi Arabia, the strengthened
American military presence in the region has, at the minimum, provided regional
elites with a counterweight to growing Soviet military power, thus limiting the
amount of military/political pressure the USSR can use against them.

Another example of the limited degree of Soviet influence in the Middle
East has been the unwillingness or inability of the Soviet leaders to effect
changes among the elites in the Arab states so as to bring to power leaders more
sympathetic to Soviet policies. Thus, in Egypt, Sadat succeeded in eliminating
from power the more pro-Soviet of the Egyptian hierarchy such as Aly Sabri,
while in Syria, Assad was able to oust the pro-Russian Salah Jedid clique from
power. In both major regime changes the Soviet leadership proved unable to
affect events. Similarly, as both the Sudan and Somalia moved from pro-Soviet
to pro-Western positions, Moscow seemed unable to take an effective action, nor
was Moscow able to replace the increasingly anti-Communist Saddam Hussein of
Iraq. In Afghanistan, Moscow's inability to use its political influence to alter
regime policy even in a Communist-dominated party closely tied to Moscow led
to the Soviet Union's being forced to invade that country in December 1979.

Given the Soviet leaders' lack of success in trying to modify the behavior of Middle Eastern cities and their inability to replace the elites with others more favorably inclined to Soviet policies, how can one explain the continued Soviet aid to these states and the Soviet leadership's willingness to support the Arabs to the point of confrontation with the United States during the October 1973 war? In seeking an answer to this question one must keep in mind the overall Soviet goal in the Middle East—the elimination of Western influence—and view Soviet activity as directed in support of that goal. The Soviet leadership, taking a long-term view of Middle Eastern politics, has been willing to pay a substantial price in economic and military aid to often recalcitrant Arab regimes in the hope of stimulating or reinforcing anti-Western trends in the Middle East or, at the very least, reversing anti-Soviet trends such as the one that occurred following the abortive coup d'état in the Sudan and the invasion of Afghanistan.

In particular, the Soviet leadership has utilized its economic and military aid on a number of occasions to reinforce anti-Western behavior that the leaders of an Arab state were already contemplating, behavior also beneficial to the Soviet Union. A case in point is Iraq's nationalization of the Iraqi Petroleum Company's oil fields at Kirkuk in June 1972; the Russians promised developmental aid to support the nationalization. While the Russians were undoubtedly happy to see the weakening of the Western-owned oil consortium, the impetus for the nationalization decision lay not in the Soviet Union but in the Iraqi regime, which wanted to gain control over the major source of hard currency, on which its economic development plans depended. Similarly, the Soviet leaders strongly encouraged the Arab nations to impose and maintain the oil embargo against the United States, and the Arab states did in fact do so. Nonetheless, the Arabs were clearly acting on their own initiative, as was demonstrated when the embargo was lifted despite Soviet efforts to maintain it. In addition, the USSR provided the weaponry for Egypt to go to war in October 1973, but the decision for war was an Egyptian one, not a Soviet one. Finally, while the USSR provided military support for Assad's opposition to the Sinai II accord, the ultimate decision was Assad's, not Brezhnev's, and while the anti-U.S. tirades of Kaddafi are useful to Soviet policy, their origin may be found in Kaddafi's frustrations, not Moscow.

In their efforts to foster and reinforce anti-Western trends in the Middle East, the Soviet leadership changed its policy toward the Communist parties of the Arab world following the debacle in the Sudan in July 1971. Before then, the Brezhnev regime had shown its preference for good relations with the one-party regimes of the Arab world and had tried to convince the Arab Communists that they should be satisfied with the basically educational and propagandistic role of teachers of "scientific socialism" to the leaders and masses of Arab states. Indeed, in an effort to remove the suspicion and hostility with which the Arab leaders viewed the Communist parties of their state, the Soviet leadership encouraged the Communist Party of the Sudan to dissolve and join Nimeri's one-party regime. However, this request was refused by an important faction of the Sudanese Communist Party, which then supported a coup d'état against Nimeri in July 1971—an event that was to have a very negative effect on Soviet policy toward the Arab world and result in the decimation of the leadership of the Sudanese Communist Party.

Following this event, it became apparent to the Soviet leaders that the policy of urging dissolution of Arab Communist parties had failed, and the Brezhnev regime then began to actively encourage "national fronts" in the Arab world in which the Communists would participate as partners, although clearly as junior partners. By stressing the fact that the Communists recognized that the Arab nationalist parties were the dominant force in each national front, the CPSU hoped to allay the fears of the Arab nationalists that the Communists would use their positions to overthrow the nationalist regimes.

At the same time, however, it was clearly the wish of the Soviet leadership that the presence of Communists within the national front would help steer the Arab nationalist leaders away from the West and counter the wave of anti-Communism and anti-Sovietism that swept through the Middle East after the failure of the Communist-supported coup attempt in the Sudan. Interestingly enough, throughout the entire period after the dissolution of the Egyptian Communist Party in early 1965, the CPSU also sought to influence the one-party regimes of the Arab states directly through relations on a party level, and by 1981 the CPSU had established party relations with the Algerian FLN, the Egyptian ASU, the Ba'ath parties of Iraq and Syria, and the UPONF (National Front United Political Organization) of South Yemen.

These policies, however, were not particularly successful from the point of view of Soviet foreign policy aims in the Arab world—at least not in the short run. For example, while the coup-weakened Iraqi Ba'athist regime, after much Soviet urging, finally established a national front in July 1973, its subsequent behavior, including its rejection of the Soviet-sponsored cease-fire in the October war, clearly did not indicate that the establishment of the national front made the Iraqi regime any more amenable to Soviet demands on issues the Iraqis deemed important. Similarly, the presence of Communists in Syria's national front did not prevent Assad from sending Syrian troops to fight the PLO in Lebanon when he determined it was necessary to do so. All in all, it appears that Arab regimes had established party-to-party relations with the CPSU, established national fronts, and allowed Communists into their governments—in nominal positions—primarily to extract more economic and military assistance from the USSR. It also seems that Yasir Arafat of the PLO, by occasionally taking a Palestinian Communist with him on visits to Moscow, has also followed a similar policy.

While a number of Arab regimes thus appear to be exploiting Soviet desires to establish national fronts, the Arab Communists have not shown much enthusiasm for the new Soviet policy. Indeed, this is one of the issues on which the Syrian Communist Party split, and Arab Communists writing in the *World*

Marxist Review have openly criticized Soviet policies toward the so-called Revolutionary Democratic regimes of the Arab world. While the Soviet decision to print these articles may have been merely an attempt to assuage the Arab Communists' anger by giving them a public forum to air their grievances, the articles also would seem to point to an underlying mood among some Arab Communists that might indicate that future Communist-supported coup d'état attempts, on the models of the events in the Sudan in July 1971, are not to be ruled out.

Indeed, the Iraqi government's crackdown on the Iraqi Communist Party appeared to be based on the fact that the ICP, unhappy at the course of the government's economic and foreign policies, had sought to infiltrate the Iraqi army and Ba'athist Party. This development led not only to the execution of a number of Iraqi Communists, but also to a sharp deterioration of Soviet-Iraqi relations. Nonetheless, given the unstable politics of the Middle East and the narrow bases of such Arab regimes as the Iraqi and Syrian Ba'ath, the Arab Communists may well be tempted to ally with a faction in the nation's army, carry out the coup, and then present the Soviet Union with a fait acompli. This would confront the Soviet leadership with the unpleasant choice of either assisting the new Communist regime (and alienating the Arab nationalists) or watching such a regime turn to China or even be ousted by neighboring Arab states, as occurred in the Sudan in 1971.

It is no doubt because of these very unpleasant alternatives that the Soviet leadership has been urging the Arab Communists to bide their time and to realize that the evolution of the Revolutionary Democratic regimes to socialism is a very long process. The current turn of some Arab nationalist leaders toward the West may, however, convince the Arab Communists that time is not on their side. It is quite possible that some members of the Soviet political leadership, dismayed by the course of events in the Middle East since Nasser's death, and particularly since the October 1973 Arab-Israeli war, may wish to work more actively for a change in some of the ruling Arab regimes. In any case, as in Iraq, the Soviet Union is likely to be blamed for the activities of the Arab Communist parties whether or not it instigates them, and in the near future, at least, the Arab Communists are more likely to cause problems for Soviet policy makers in the Middle East than to be of help to them.

Another characteristic of Soviet policy in the Middle East in the 1970-1981 period has been its stark opportunism in seeking to reinforce anti-Western trends, and nowhere has this been more evident than in Iran following the fall of the Shah. Thus when the Islamic fundamentalists were persecuting the Tudeh and other left-wing forces, as well as the Kurds, in the period before the hostage seizure, Moscow did not hesitate to criticize them, albeit somewhat gently. Following the hostage seizure, however, the fundamentalists were warmly praised as being a major anti-imperialist force in Iran. Indeed, while Moscow has shifted its position markedly on such individuals as Bani Sadr, depending on whether or not they supported policies favorable to the USSR, the Islamic fundamentalists and Khomeini himself were warmly praised by the USSR after the hostage taking. They were seen by Moscow to be more interested in Islamic purity than economic development and could be expected therefore to hold onto the hostages, irrespective of the economic problems that the holding of the hostages caused Iran, thereby prolonging the conflict between Iran and the United States, humiliating the United States on a daily basis, and weakening the overall position of the United States in the Middle East.

Given the major blow to the American Middle Eastern position caused by the loss of Iran as the American policeman of the Persian Gulf, Moscow's primary goal with respect to Iran has been to prevent its return to the American camp. For this reason it has been willing to aid any individual or group within Iran that appeared to work against such a rapprochement, whether it be left-wing Kurds in the summer of 1979 when it appeared Iran was slipping back toward the United States, or the most fundamentalist of the Islamic religious leaders such as the Ayatollah Beheshti after the hostage seizure. The Soviet leaders' reasoning seemed to be that if the USSR could not, at least in the short run, win Iran over to its own side, then it would do everything it could to prevent Iran from shifting back to the United States. Thus, Moscow has supported the hostage taking, vetoed the U.S. sanctions proposal in the U.N. Security Council, offered land transit routes for Iran to overcome the effects of an American blockade, and even offered Iran arms, while repeatedly emphasizing that it was Iran's protector against the United States. While these acts may have won little gratitutde from Iran's leaders, from the Soviet perspective they were warranted so long as they strengthened Iran's position against the United States. Nonetheless, the release of the hostages, despite Soviet attempts to prevent it, must be seen as a defeat for Soviet policy, particularly as it removed a major obstacle to a possible Iranian-American rapprochement.

Interestingly enough, however, just as in the time of the Shah, Iran has caused problems in the Soviet Union's overall Middle East policy. While in the Shah's day Iran was a key element of the American anti-Soviet alliance grouping, today it is a major factor preventing the formation of the "anti-imperialist" Arab unity which Moscow has been seeking. Thus its conflict with Iraq has split the Arab world and has been a factor preventing the pro-Soviet "Steadfast-ness and Confrontation Front" from attracting other Arab countries such as Saudi Arabia, Jordan and Kuwait to its side, while also adding another element to the conflict between Iraq and Syria. In addition, despite Soviet efforts to appear as the champion of Iran (and Islam) against the United States, the Iranian leaders have caused Moscow problems in the Islamic world, where Iran has been one of the leading forces condemning the Soviet invasion of Afghanistan and where Iran has worked to prevent the pro-Moscow Arabs from diverting Islamic attention from Afghanistan to the Palestine-Israel conflict. To be sure, Moscow is far better off with a neutral Iran, despite its occasional anti-Soviet diatribes, than an Iran closely aligned with the United States. Yet, so long as Iran is a factor creating disorder in the Arab world while promoting anti-Sovietism in the Islamic movement, and it would appear to play such a role so long as the Islamic fundamentalist regime remains in power, Moscow will have a difficult time increasing its influence in the Middle East.

One of the problems that continues to beset the USSR in its Middle East policies is the factor of Marxism. As an avowedly Marxist country, the USSR has no choice but to promote Marxism, but the ideology is viewed with deep suspicion in many parts of the Middle East, particularly the antireligious component of the doctrine. While the USSR has attempted to demonstrate that Marxism and Islam are not antithetical doctrines, it has not had particular success in making its case in Iran where Marxist guerrillas have clashed with the Islamic regime and where Khomeini has personally attacked efforts to reconcile Marxism and Islam. Suspicion of Soviet doctrine continues in Wahhabi Saudi Arabia as well, despite several Soviet efforts to improve relations with that oil-rich country. Compounding this problem for the Soviet leadership have been the Marxist policies of the Afghani regime which seized power in April 1978, policies that took on clearly antireligious overtones. This exacerbated Afghanistan's relations with Iran and Pakistan and seriously disturbed Soviet-Iranian and Soviet-Pakistani relations as well, a problem for Moscow which was compounded when the Soviet Union invaded Afghanistan in December 1979. Despite the efforts of the Soviet-installed Karmal regime to demonstrate that it was a supporter of Islam, neither Iran nor Pakistan has been persuaded, and their suspicions of Moscow deepened.

In addition to its opportunistic efforts to influence Middle East states so as to foster anti-Western trends in the Middle East, the Soviet leadership also strengthened its ties to the two main Arab guerrilla organizations, the PLO and the PFLOAG (later called the PFLO) in the period following Nasser's death. Interestingly enough, just as in the cases of Iraq and Libya, the two organizations welcomed Soviet support at a time when they were encountering serious difficulties—the PLO after being mauled by Hussein's troops in September 1970 and July 1971, and the PFLOAG after encountering increasing resistance from the new, Sandhurst-trained Sultan of Oman and his British and Iranian troops. Espousing anti-Western slogans, the leaders of both guerrilla organizations became frequent visitors to Moscow after the Soviet debacle in the Sudan. They were rewarded with economic, military, and medical support in return for advocating the Soviet line on Middle Eastern issues. Yet, in following the example set by the leaders of Egypt, Syria, Iraq, and Libya, who espoused anti-Western slogans in return for Soviet support, the guerrilla organizations joined the long list of Arab leaders who were exploiting the Soviet drive for influence in the Middle East while giving little more than lip service to Soviet policies in return. Indeed, the PLO's unwillingness to recognize Israel, a development that would aid Soviet diplomatic efforts in the Middle East, demonstrates the limited Soviet influence within that organization.

One of the central techniques used by Moscow to try to increase its influence in the Middle East and reduce that of the United States has been to capitalize on the Arab-Israeli conflict. The Israeli attacks on Palestinian guerrilla bases in Lebanon and Syria in September 1972, following the massacre of Israeli athletes at the Olympic Games in Munich, gave the Soviet Union an opportunity to underline its support of the Arab cause while simultaneously undermining the position of the United States, which the Soviet leadership sought to link to Israel's policies. Indeed, the events at Munich set off a wave of terrorism and counterterrorism that inflamed the Arab-Israeli conflict to a fever pitch, a development that helped Sadat in his efforts to rally the other Arabs behind his military plans. Consequently, the USSR again became important to the Arab leaders, given the U.S. support of Israel.

Meanwhile, a shortage of oil had become a serious problem in the United States, which for the first time had become vulnerable to Arab oil pressure. Consequently, throughout 1973, with Arab-Israeli tensions rising, the Soviet leaders began to urge the Arabs to use their "oil weapon" against the United States. This dual policy of linking the United States to Israeli actions (such as the killing of three PLO leaders in Beirut) and urging the use of the Arab oil weapon against the United States, was also followed during the 1973 Arab-Israeli war, which the Soviet leadership saw not only as an opportunity to regain its lost ground in the Middle East but also as a chance to strike a potentially decisive blow against U.S. interests in the region through the establishment of the long-coveted Arab unity on an "anti-imperialist" basis.

In turning to an evaluation of Soviet behavior during the October war, one is struck by the fact that in many ways its opportunism is analogous to the behavior of American oil companies during the American energy crisis. Thus, while the oil companies may not have deliberately planned the energy crisis, they were certainly quick to exploit it for their own benefit—so quick, in fact, that many observers accused them of deliberately plotting the crisis. The situation with regard to the Soviet role in the October war would appear to be similar. While the Russians may not have actively supported Egypt's decision to go to war against Israel—at least until the coup in Chile—and while the Soviet leaders were very hesitant in both their reporting of the war and their support of the Arabs in the first few days of the conflict when they sought a cease-fire, they were quick to try to exploit the Arab military success against Israel and the strains in NATO and the EEC caused by the war and the oil embargo. Unfortunately for the Russians, however, their gains from the war were essentially transient ones.

Thus, the "anti-imperialist" unity of the Arabs soon dissolved, and the United States emerged several months after the war with a better Middle Eastern position than it possessed before it began—despite the massive Soviet military support for the Arabs during the war and U.S. support for Israel. In addition, the war strengthened the domestic position of Egyptian President Anwar Sadat, who soon reverted to his earlier policy of moving to improve economic and political relations with the West. This, when coupled with his increasingly close ties with oil-rich Saudi Arabia, another nation that moved to restore its relations with the United States after the war, created an Egyptian-Saudi axis in the Middle East that was potentially much more favorably inclined toward the United States than toward the USSR. This alignment possessed the potential of attracting even such a country as Syria, and a great deal of Soviet effort in the 1973-1977 period was directed toward preventing Syria's adhesion to the Saudi-Egyptian axis. In addition, as oil-hungry Western Europe and Japan hurried to make long-range economic and military deals with the oil-producing Arab states (and Iran), further difficulties were created for Soviet policy makers because the USSR now had to cope with Western European and Japanese competition in the region, as well as American. The Arab states were able to play off all the major powers against each other, thus limiting the amount of influence any one power, including the USSR, could wield.

The disruption of the Saudi-Egyptian axis because of the September 1978 U.S.-sponsored Camp David agreements gave Moscow yet another opportunity to exploit the Arab-Israeli conflict, as Egypt proved to be the only Arab state willing to make peace with Israel, and Moscow sought to build its policy on reinforcing the anti-Camp David and anti-Sadat unity that appeared to take shape in the Arab world in the aftermath of Camp David. The rebirth of the Syrian-Iraqi conflict, however, together with the Soviet invasion of Afghanistan put an end to the anti-Sadat unity in the Arab world. Nonetheless, the USSR was to try to exploit the Arab-Israeli conflict to deflect the criticism of Muslim nations following its invasion of Afghanistan. Thus Moscow, in addition to highlighting American pressure against Muslim Iran, seized upon the actions of Israeli Prime Minister Begin in expanding West Bank settlements and formally annexing East Jerusalem to divert Muslim attention from Afghanistan. Together with its Steadfastness Front allies, it strongly supported a number of United Nations resolutions condemning Israel in the period following the Afghan invasion, often isolating the United States as the sole supporter of Israel in the process. Yet while both Israel and the United States came in for heavy Muslim criticism, Moscow was not very successful in diverting Muslim wrath. Thus the Islamic conferences of January and May 1980 condemned the USSR as well as the United States, with Iran taking the lead in the latter conference in preventing the diversion of Islamic attention from Afghanistan to Israel. Then, when the outbreak of the war between Iran and Iraq was to further disrupt the anti-Sadat coalition of Arab states while simultaneously strengthening the position of the United States in the Middle East, Moscow again tried to use the Arab-Israeli conflict to rally the Arabs into the long-desired "anti-imperialist" unity. Thus it exploited the Israeli-Syrian "missile crisis," the Israeli attack on the Iraqi nuclear reactor, and the brief Israel-PLO war in South Lebanon in 1981 in an effort to help rebuild the "anti-imperialist" Arab unity—albeit with very limited success.

While Moscow has sought to exploit the tension inherent in the Arab-Israeli conflict to enhance its own position in the Middle East, it has also sought to regain the diplomatic initiative that has been in the hands of the United States almost continuously since the 1973 war. Thus, Moscow has called for the resumption of the Geneva conference to establish a Model I Arab-Israeli settlement in which Israel would withdraw from all the territory it captured in 1967, but would have its sovereignty within its June 4, 1967 borders acknowledged by the Arabs and possibly guaranteed by the USSR and the United States. In addition, the USSR called for a Palestinian state to be created on territory to be evacuated by Israel on the West Bank and Gaza Strip. To make such a plan more agreeable to Israel, the USSR also suggested a staged withdrawal—albeit over a short period of time—and the establishment of demilitarized zones on both sides of the border with U.N. forces stationed in these zones for a specified period of time and a "normalization" of Soviet-Israeli relations.

Such a plan, should it be accepted, would be very much in the Soviet Union's interest for a number of reasons. In the first place, it would preserve the state of Israel, whose existence has become an important part of Soviet strategy in the Middle East. For a number of years the USSR has sought to consolidate "anti-imperialist Arab unity" around Arab enmity toward Israel, which the USSR portrays as the linchpin of Western imperialism in the Middle East. The mere fact of an Israeli withdrawal to the prewar 1967 lines would not remove the potential threat of a future Israeli attack on the Arabs, or the memories of the generations-long Arab-Israeli conflict. Indeed, by supporting the concept of a Model I peace plan (and opposing the concept of a Model II peace, in which Israel would have trade, cultural, and diplomatic relations with its neighbors), the USSR would apparently hope to keep at least a certain amount of latent hostility alive in the Arab-Israeli relationship, thereby forcing the Arabs to retain at least a modicum of unity to confront the putative Israeli threat. The Soviet leaders evidently hope they could then exploit that unity to enhance their own position in the Middle East and weaken the position of the United States.

A second benefit for the USSR of such a plan would be the termination of the American role as mediator in limited Arab-Israeli disengagement agreements. This role has brought the United States a great deal of prestige in the Arab world since the 1973 war, for it demonstrated to the Arabs that it was the United States, and not the Soviet Union, that was able to secure Israeli territorial withdrawals. In addition, the fact that it was the United States that mediated an end to the Israeli-PLO wars in South Lebanon in both 1978 and 1981 further reinforced the importance of the United States in Middle East peacemaking to the Arab leaders. Once a final, as opposed to another partial, agreement would be reached, the necessity for American mediation would be ended, and the Soviet leaders may reason that this would lead to a drop in U.S. prestige and influence in the Arab world, as well as an end to the quarrels between the Arab states over the disengagement agreements that have impeded the Soviet drive to help create the "anti-imperialist" Arab unity they have sought.

Yet another benefit of such a plan would be that, by preserving Israel, the United States would not be alienated. Given the strong emotional and political ties between Israel and the United States, which have been reiterated by the new U.S. President, Ronald Reagan, on a number of occasions, despite several U.S.-Israeli clashes, the USSR would clearly jeopardize even the remnants of détente that still exist, and the chances for a Senate ratification of another SALT agreement, by working for Israel's destruction. It is for this reason, if no other, that the Soviet leadership, in speeches to Arab leaders as well as in its peace plans, has endorsed Israel's right to exist as an independent state. Indeed, the Soviet leaders may well recall the sharp deterioration in Soviet-American relations following Soviet aid to the Arabs during the 1973 war; and, particularly at a time when both Soviet-American and Sino-Soviet relations are strained, the Soviet leadership would obviously not like to witness the further deterioration of Soviet-American relations that would be caused by any Soviet support for a plan to destroy Israel. Concomitantly, the establishment of a Model I Arab-Israeli peace would also lessen the possibility of a superpower conflict over an Arab-Israeli war that could lead to a nuclear confrontation, yet another consequence of a peace agreement most welcome to the Soviet leadership.

A fourth benefit for the Soviet Union from her peace plan, if it were accepted, would be the establishment of a Palestinian state. Given current trends in Arab politics, the Soviet leadership obviously hopes that such a state, whose creation they began to advocate in late 1973, would be an ally of Soviet policy in the Arab world and would help combat American influence in the region. Given the fact that South Yemen, Syria, and Libya, currently the Soviet Union's most important Arab allies, are mistrusted by their fellow Arabs, the USSR would clearly benefit from having another close ally in the very center of the Middle East. In addition, the Russians obviously believe that such a state, sandwiched between a hostile Israel and an equally hostile Hussein regime that has not forgotten PLO attempts to overthrow it, and under probable pressure from Syria as well, would be dependent on Soviet support and hence would have an interest in maintaining close relations with the USSR. Under a Model I peace plan, it would also serve to keep alive Arab-Israeli tensions, thus aiding the USSR in its quest for an "anti-imperialist" Arab unity.

Yet, the very fact that Israel and Egypt have reached a Model II peace agreement presents a major obstacle to Soviet peacemaking schemes. Having obtained a Model II peace from Egypt, it is doubtful that Israel would accept anything less from Syria, Jordan, or any Palestinian entity that might one day emerge from negotiations. Indeed, Israel already has a quasi Model II economic relationship with Jordan, given its "open bridges" policy which has been in existence since soon after the June 1967 war. To be sure, Moscow may hope that the post-Sadat/Mubarak regime (or its successor) will scale down its peace arrangement with Israel from a Model II to a Model I or abandon it altogether. Such a maneuver, however, would cost Egypt heavily both in terms of its economic and military ties to the United States and in terms of risking a war with Israel—a development that would jeopardize some of the gains reached since 1973 including regaining the Sinai, reopening the Suez Canal, the major spurt in oil exports, and the major burst in tourism—the latter three items earning Egypt more than $4 billion in hard currency annually.

Whatever the final nature of an Arab-Israeli peace settlement, it is clear that Moscow wants an international conference to be the means for obtaining it—not U.S. shuttle diplomacy. Soviet leaders have most often pointed to the Geneva conference as a vehicle to reach a settlement, although they have differed among themselves somewhat as to the urgency of convening the conference. An examination of the course of Soviet policy since the 1973 war indicates that Soviet calls for the resumption of the Geneva conference were usually at their strongest when it appeared that the United States was going to secure a diplomatic success in its mediation efforts and the USSR faced the possibility of being frozen out, or when Middle Eastern events were moving out of Soviet control. This was particularly evident in the period from February 1974 to August 1975, when Kissinger was first negotiating an Israeli-Syrian disengagement agreement and then working to reach a second Egyptian-Israeli disengagement agreement, and in the period from April to October 1976, during the escalating civil war in Lebanon, when the USSR saw developments there moving in a direction inimical to its interests. Moscow was to again call for such a conference at the height of the Iran-Iraq war in December 1980 when Middle Eastern developments were once again moving contrary to Soviet hopes. In such a situation, the call for reconvening of the Geneva conference was a Soviet effort to regain some diplomatic momentum by participating as an equal with the United States in a major meeting dealing with the Middle East. The reasoning behind the timing of the issuance of Soviet peace plans in April and October 1976 seems to have been the same, for the Soviet leadership presented its plans at times when the Soviet position in the Middle East was in serious trouble because of the fighting in Lebanon.

The Soviet leaders may also feel that the dynamics of a reconvened Geneva conference would give the USSR the opportunity to champion the Arab cause while isolating the United States as the supporter of Israel, thus enabling the USSR to regain some of the influence she has lost to the United States in the Arab world since 1973. While the USSR has also, on occasion (such as Brezhnev's Trade Unions Congress speech in March 1977), played down the urgency of reconvening Geneva, this would appear to be more a tactical than a strategic policy. The very reversal of Brezhnev's statement on the urgency of Geneva, first by Moscow Radio and then by Brezhnev himself (all within the space of one month), as well as the joint Soviet-American statement of October 1, 1977, indicates that the USSR would much prefer to reconvene a Geneva conference, even if the Arab states were not united in their policies, and even if the conference were to encounter "difficulties" (to use Kosygin's term), rather than wait for the United States to work out yet another settlement—and obtain Arab appreciation for her efforts.

One of the obstacles facing the reconvening of the Geneva conference, however, has been the refusal of the PLO to agree to live in peace with Israel and the refusal of both Israel and the United States to meet with the PLO until it takes such a position. It was for this reason, perhaps, that the USSR sought to use the Security Council debate on the Middle East of January 1976, at which the PLO was invited to participate, as a device to facilitate the reconvening of Geneva and possibly even to serve as a partial substitute for it. This ploy proved unsuccessful, however, for Israel boycotted the session because of the PLO presence and the United States maintained its support of Israel, to the point of vetoing an anti-Israeli resolution. The Soviet interpretation of the joint Soviet-American statement of October 1, 1977, seems to have been a similar maneuver, although it, too, did not meet with much success. It would appear that unless the USSR or the Arabs can persuade the United States to allow the PLO to participate at Geneva without a change in its position toward Israel, or the Palestine National Council reverses its March 1977 decision and agrees to live in peace with Israel, it is unlikely that the Geneva conference will be reconvened. All in all, since the Russians are now on record as demanding the participation of the PLO from the beginning and on an equal basis in any Geneva discussions, the prospect of an early convening of a Geneva peace conference is not bright, unless some sort of diplomatic device for the mutual recognition of Israel and a Palestine government in exile can be arranged just prior to the opening of the conference—a rather doubtful prospect, given the stated position of the PLO.

In this situation, what are the Soviet leaders likely to do in the future? In the absence of any forward movement toward Geneva due to PLO opposition to Israel's existence, the United States will, most likely, continue to work for an expansion of the Camp David accords. Especially since the collapse of the Fez Summit indicated that the Arab world was not yet ready to come to a general agreement on peace with Israel, the United States will probably seek to win over the Centrist Arab states to peace with Israel, a policy that, if successful, would isolate the Soviet Union in the camp of the rejectionist "Front of Steadfastness and Confrontation." Such a development may hinge, however, on whether an adequate autonomy arrangement can be achieved for the Palestinians. In any case, if the United States were to gain the acceptance of key Centrist states to peace with Israel, there would be little the USSR could do to avert it since, as mentioned above, Soviet influence over the Arab states is very limited. Consequently, should the elites of the Arab Centrist states decide to enter into a peace agreement with Israel, as Egypt has already done, it is unlikely that the USSR could exercise influence over any one of them to prevent such an agreement from being signed. In such a situation, the USSR might, of course, seek to bring to power other elites who would be more favorably inclined to Soviet policy. Nonetheless, when one examines the elite changes that have occurred in the Middle East from 1970 to 1981, it becomes clear that Soviet ability to affect elite change is very limited.

The USSR can be expected to utilize its extensive propaganda apparatus, as well as the Arab Communist parties that it controls, to denounce a U.S.-mediated peace agreement—much as it did when the Sinai II agreement and Camp David peace agreements were concluded. It is doubtful, however, whether such propaganda attacks would have any strong effect if the majority of the

Arab world (Egypt, Jordan, Saudi Arabia, Kuwait, and possibly a post-Assad Sunni-ruled Syria) would endorse the agreement. Indeed, even when Egypt was isolated in its decision to accept the Sinai II agreement and Camp David, the Soviet propaganda campaign proved unable either to prevent the agreement or to overturn it (or Sadat) once it had been signed.

Faced with the unwelcome possibility of an American-orchestrated peace agreement that she is unlikely to be able to prevent, the USSR may try to pressure the leaders of the PLO to change their position vis-à-vis Israel in order to go to Geneva, where, the Russians could argue, with the backing of the USSR, the PLO would get a better deal than it would get from a peace settlement worked out under American auspices. Unfortunately for the Russians, they have very limited leverage over the constituent elements of the PLO, and such pressure might well be ineffective, unless the Palestinians see it in their own interest to change their program.

One should also consider the possibility that the USSR might choose to acquiesce in U.S. peacemaking efforts for a limited period of time, hoping that they might fail. Admittedly, the Soviets are not likely to be quiet, given the nature of their opposition to the first Syrian-Israeli disengagement agreement (support for Syria's war of attrition), to the Sinai II agreement, and to Sadat's trip to Jerusalem and Camp David. Nonetheless, if the Israeli coalition government led by Menahem Begin continues to adhere to the hardline policies he enunciated during the 1981 election campaign and immediately afterwards, this could lessen the chances for peace and push such states as Saudi Arabia and Jordan over to the side of the rejectionists—a development that the USSR would clearly welcome, since it would keep Egypt isolated and help create the "anti-imperialist" Arab unity Moscow has wanted for so long.

Even if an American-arranged peace agreement should be reached, the Soviet leaders may still be relatively acquiescent. They may assume that given their close ties to the PLO in the past, they may be able to influence any Palestinian or Palestinian-Jordanian entity that is created by a peace settlement. Similarly, since the Soviet leadership takes, to use its terminology, a "strategic" (long-term) view of Middle Eastern developments, they may reason that the conservative monarchies of Saudi Arabia, Kuwait, and the United Arab Emirates may soon be replaced by radical regimes of the Syrian type, which would appeal to the USSR for support, and that the Mubarak regime, beset by domestic economic problems, may yet fall, to be replaced by a more radical regime. In addition, the Soviet leadership may reason that conflict over the high price of oil may split the conservative oil-producing Arab states away from their alignment with the United States, a development that could spur them to turn to the Soviet Union for support and protection.

Such a policy of "watchful waiting" and exploiting regional developments rather than opposing a U.S.-mediated peace agreement, is also less damaging to Soviet-American relations, particularly in the early 1980s, when the USSR will be intent on securing a strategic arms agreement and possibly economic agreements as well. Yet one could question the value of this type of "watchful waiting" policy, since in the past both Syria and Iraq have exploited their relationship with the USSR to pursue goals not particularly to the liking of the Soviet leadership. It is also possible that the oil price problem can be solved without causing a rupture in Arab-American relations, and that pro-American trends will continue—particularly if an Arab-Israeli peace agreement is achieved.

Nonetheless, given the overall Soviet goal of expelling Western influence from the Middle East, a region rich in oil on which the West depends, and one with a number of strategic communication routes, the Soviet leadership seems willing to continue to provide large amounts of military and economic aid and diplomatic support to Arab regimes that often oppose the USSR, in the hope of spurring anti-Western trends in the region. While the ultimate success of this strategy remains very much in doubt—the Russians were further from their goal in January 1982 than they were at the time of Nasser's death in 1970—there is as yet no indication that the Soviet leadership has given up its efforts to increase Soviet influence in the Middle East while diminishing and ultimately eliminating that of the United States and her Western allies.

Indeed, the Soviet leaders seem willing to pay the costs involved in pursuing such a policy because they have made the basic decision that the Middle East is a region of major importance to the Soviet Union.

BIBLIOGRAPHY

DOCUMENTARY COLLECTIONS AND STATISTICAL STUDIES

The Camp David Summit. Washington: United States Department of State Publication No. 8954, September 1978.

Documents and Resolutions of the 25th Congress of the Communist Party of the Soviet Union. Moscow: Novosti Press Agency Publishing House, 1976.

Documents of the 24th Congress of the Communist Party of the Soviet Union. Moscow: Novosti Press Agency Publishing House, 1971.

From Encroachment to Involvement: A Documentary Study of Soviet Policy in the Middle East 1945-1973. Edited by Yaacov Ro'i. Jerusalem: Israel Universities Press, 1974.

The Israel-Arab Reader: A Documentary History of the Middle East Conflict. Edited by Walter Laqueur. New York: Bantam Books, 1975.

The Policy of the Soviet Union in the Arab World: A Short Collection of Foreign Policy Documents. Moscow: Progress Publishers, 1975.

SSSR i arabskie strany 1917-1960. Moscow: Government Printing Office of Political Literature, 1960.

Vneshniaia torgovlia SSSR 1918-1966. Moscow: Mezhdunarodnye Otnosheniia, 1967.

Vneshniaia torgovlia SSSR za 1967; 1968; 1969; 1970; 1971; 1972; 1973; 1974; 1975; 1976; 1977; 1978; 1979. (Soviet Foreign Trade Annual). Moscow: Mezhdunarodnye Otnosheniia, 1968-80.

BOOKS

Abu-Lughod, Ibrahim, ed. *The Arab-Israeli Confrontation of June 1967: An Arab Perspective*. Evanston, Ill.: Northwestern University Press, 1970.

Agwani, M. S. *Communism in the Arab East*. Bombay: Asia Publishing House, 1969.

Alexander, Yonah, ed. *International Terrorism: National, Regional and Global Perspectives*. New York: Praeger, 1976.

Alla, Malamud Ata. *Arab Struggle for Economic Independence*. Moscow: Progress Publishers, 1974.

Al-Marayati, Abid A., ed. *The Middle East: Its Governments and Politics*. Belmont, Calif.: Duxbury Press, 1972.

Andreasian, Ruben. *Opek v Mire Nefti*. Moscow: Nauka, 1978.

Anthony, John Duke, ed. *The Middle East: Oil, Politics and Development.* Washington, D.C.: American Enterprise Institute, 1975.

Avakov, R. M., E. A. Bragina, and K. L. Maidanik, eds. *Razvivaiushchiesia strany: Zakonomernosti, tendentsii, perspectivy.* Moscow: Mysl', 1974.

Badeau, John. *An American Approach to the Arab World.* New York: Harper & Row, 1968.

Baker, William. *Egypt's Uncertain Revolution under Nasser and Sadat.* Cambridge: Harvard University Press, 1978.

Becker, A. S., Bent Hansen, and Malcolm Kerr. *The Economics and Politics of the Middle East.* New York: American Elsevier, 1975.

Becker, A. S., and A. L. Horelick. *Soviet Policy in the Middle East.* Rand Publication R-504-FF. Santa Monica, Calif.: Rand Corporation, 1970.

Be'eri, Eliezer. *Army Officers in Arab Politics and Society.* New York: Praeger, 1970.

Bodianskii, V. L. *Sovremennyi kuveit.* Moscow: Nauka, 1971.

Brandon, Henry. *The Retreat of American Power.* New York: Delta, 1973.

Chubin, Sharam. *Soviet Policy Toward Iran and the Gulf.* London: I.S.S. Adelphi Paper no. 157.

Cottam, Richard W. *Competitive Interference and Twentieth Century Diplomacy.* Pittsburgh: University of Pittsburgh Press, 1967.

Dagan, Avigdor. *Moscow and Jerusalem.* New York: Abelard-Schuman, 1970.

Dann, Uriel. *Iraq under Kassem.* New York: Praeger, 1969.

Dayan, Moshe. *Breakthrough: A Personal Account of the Egypt-Israel Peace Negotiations.* New York: Knopf, 1981.

Dolidze, D. I. *Problemy edinstva antiimperialisticheskoi borby.* Moscow: Nauka, 1973.

Donaldson, Robert, ed. *The Soviet Union in the Third World.* Boulder, Colorado: Westview, 1981.

Duncan, W. Raymond, ed. *Soviet Policy in the Third World.* New York: Pergamon, 1980.

Dupree, Louis. *Afghanistan.* Princeton: Princeton University Press, 1978.

Evron, Yair. *The Middle East.* New York: Praeger, 1973.

Fairhall, David. *Russian Sea Power.* Boston: Gambit, 1971.

Farer, Tom J. *War Clouds on the Horn of Africa.* Washington, D.C.: Carnegie Endowment, 1976.

Fedchenko, A. F. *Irak v borbe za nezavisimost'.* Moscow: Nauka, 1970.

Freedman, Robert O. *Economic Warfare in the Communist Bloc: A Study of Soviet Economic Pressure against Yugoslavia, Albania and Communist China.* New York: Praeger, 1970.

Freedman, Robert O., ed. *World Politics and the Arab-Israeli Conflict.* New York: Pergamon, 1979.

Gafurov, B. G., and G. F. Kim. *Zarybezhnyi vostok i sovremennost'.* Moscow: Nauka, 1974.

Gafurov, B., ed. *Religiia i obshchestvennaia misl'narodov vostoka.* Moscow: Nauka, 1971.

Gerasimov, O. *Irakskaia neft'.* Moscow: Nauka, 1969.

Gilison, Jerome M., ed. *The Soviet Jewish Emigre.* Baltimore: Baltimore Hebrew College, 1977.

Glassman, Jon D. *Arms for the Arabs: The Soviet Union and War in the Middle East.* Baltimore: Johns Hopkins, 1975.

Golan, Galia. *The Soviet Union and the PLO.* Jerusalem: Hebrew University, Soviet and East European Research Center, 1976. Also published as Adelphi Paper no. 131 (London: Institute for Strategic Studies, 1976).

——. *Yom Kippur and After: The Soviet Union and the Middle East Crisis.* New York: Cambridge University Press, 1977.

——. *The Soviet Union and the Palestine Liberation Organization.* New York: Praeger, 1980.

Golan, Matti. *The Secret Conversations of Henry Kissinger.* New York: Quadrangle, 1976.

Goldman, Marshall. *Soviet Foreign Aid.* New York: Praeger, 1967.

——. *Detente and Dollars: Doing Business with the Soviets.* New York: Basic Books, 1975.

——. *The Enigma of Soviet Petroleum: Half Empty or Half Full.* London: Allen and Unwin, 1980.

Gorbatov, O. M., and L. I. Cherkasskii. *Sotrudnichestvo SSSR so stranami arabskogo vostoka i Afriki.* Moscow: Nauka, 1973.

Griffiths, John C. *Afghanistan: Key to a Continent.* Boulder, Colorado: Westview Press, 1981.

Hammond, Paul, and Sidney Alexander, eds. *Political Dynamics in the Middle East.* New York: Elsevier, 1972.

Harrison, Selig. *In Afghanistan's Shadow: Baluch Nationalism and Soviet Temptations.* Washington: Carnegie Endowment, 1981.

Hazan, Baruch. *Soviet Propaganda: A Case Study of the Middle East Conflict.* Jerusalem: Israel Universities Press, 1976.

Heikal, Mohammed. *The Cairo Documents.* New York: Doubleday, 1973.

——. *The Road to Ramadan.* New York: Quadrangle, 1975.

——. *The Sphinx and the Commissar.* New York: Harper & Row, 1978.

Hudson, Michael C. *Arab Politics: The Search for Legitimacy.* New Haven: Yale University Press, 1977.

Hurewitz, J. C. *Middle East Politics: The Military Dimension.* New York: Praeger, 1969.

——, ed. *Oil, the Arab-Israeli Dispute, and the Industrial World.* Boulder, Colo.: Westview Press, 1976.

Ivanov, M. S., ed. *Natsional'nye protsessy v stranakh blizhnego i srednego vostoka.* Moscow: Nauka, 1970.

Kalb, Marvin, and Bernard Kalb. *Kissinger.* New York: Dell, 1975.

Kanet, Roger, and Donna Bahry, eds. *Soviet Economic and Political Relations with the Developing World.* New York: Praeger, 1975.

Kerr, Malcolm. *Regional Arab Politics and the Conflict with Israel.* Rand Publication RM-5966-FF. Santa Monica, Calif.: Rand Corporation, 1969.

——. *The Arab Cold War.* New York: Oxford University Press, 1970.

Khadduri, Majid. *Republican Iraq.* New York: Oxford University Press, 1969.

——. *Political Trends in the Arab World.* Baltimore: Johns Hopkins Press, 1970.

Khouri, Fred J. *The Arab-Israeli Dilemma.* Syracuse, N.Y.: Syracuse University Press, 1968.

Kim, G. F., and F. I. Shabshina. *Proletarskii internatsionalizm i revoliutsii v stranakh vostoka.* Moscow: Nauka, 1967.

Kimhe, David, and Dan Bawly. *The Six-Day War: Prologue and Aftermath.* New York: Stein and Day, 1971.

Klieman, Aaron S. *Soviet Russia and the Middle East.* Baltimore: Johns Hopkins Press, 1970.

Klinghoffer, Arthur J. *The Soviet Union and International Oil Politics.* New York: Columbia University Press, 1977.

Kohler, Foy D., Leon Goure, and Mose L. Harvey. *The Soviet Union and the October 1973 Middle East War.* Miami: Center for Advanced International Studies, University of Miami, 1974.

Kotlov, L. I. *Iemenskaia arabskaia respublika.* Moscow: Nauka, 1971.

Koury, Enver M. *The Balance of Military Power: The Arab-Israeli Conflict.* Washington, D.C.: Institute of Middle Eastern and African Affairs, 1976.

——. *The Crisis in the Lebanese System*. Washington, D.C.: American Enterprise Institute, 1976.

Krammer, Arnold. *The Forgotten Friendship: Israel and the Soviet Bloc 1947-1953*. Urbana: University of Illinois Press, 1974.

Kutsenkov, A. A., ed. *Rabochii klass i antiimperialisticheskaia revoliutsiia v Azii, Afrike, i Latinskoi Amerike*. Moscow: Nauka, 1969.

Kylagina, L. M., ed. *Arabskie strany: Turtsia; Iran; Afganistan*. Moscow: Nauka, 1973.

Landis, Lincoln. *Politics and Oil: Moscow in the Middle East*. New York: Dunellen, 1973.

Laqueur, Walter. *The Soviet Union and the Middle East*. New York: Praeger, 1959.

——. *The Road to Jerusalem*. New York: Macmillan, 1968.

——. *The Struggle for the Middle East*. New York: Macmillan, 1969.

——. *Confrontation: The Middle East in World Politics*. New York: Bantam Books, 1974.

Laron, Ram. *Hamaatzamot v'hamizrah hatikon*. Tel Aviv: Bronfman, 1970.

Lederer, Ivo J., and Wayne S. Vucinich, eds. *The Soviet Union and the Middle East*. Stanford, Calif.: Hoover Institution Press, 1973.

Lenczowski, George. *Russia and the West in Iran, 1918-1948*. Ithaca: Cornell University Press, 1949.

——. *Soviet Advances in the Middle East*. Washington, D.C.: American Enterprise Institute, 1971.

Levkovskii, A. I. *Ekonomicheskaia politika i gosudarstvennyi kapitalizm v stranakh vostoka*. Moscow: Nauka, 1972.

Linden, Carl. *Khrushchev and the Soviet Leadership 1957-1964*. Baltimore: Johns Hopkins Press, 1966.

Long, David, and Bernard Reich, eds. *The Government and Politics of the Middle East and North Africa*. Boulder, Colorado: Westview, 1980.

Lutskia, N. S., ed. *Arabskie strany: Istoriia; ekonomika*. Moscow: Nauka, 1974.

Lutsky, V. *Modern History of the Arab Countries*. Moscow: Progress Publishers, 1969.

Mackintosh, J. M. *Strategy and Tactics of Soviet Foreign Policy*. London: Oxford University Press, 1963.

Mansfield, Peter. *The Middle East: A Political and Economic Survey*. 4th ed. London: Oxford University Press, 1973.

McCagg, William O., Jr., and Brian D. Silver, eds. *Soviet Asian Ethnic Frontiers*. New York: Pergamon, 1979.

McGwire, Michael, Ken Booth, and John McDonnell, eds. *Soviet Naval Policy Objectives and Constraints.* New York: Praeger, 1975.

McLaurin, R. D. *The Middle East in Soviet Policy.* Lexington, Mass.: D. C. Heath, 1975.

——, Mohammed Mughisuddin, and Abraham Wagner. *Foreign Policy Making in the Middle East.* New York: Praeger, 1977.

Mirskii, G. I. *Tretii mir: Obshchestvo, vlast', armiia.* Moscow: Nauka, 1976.

Monroe, Elizabeth, ed. *The Changing Balance of Power in the Persian Gulf.* New York: American Universities Field Staff, 1972.

Mueller, Kurt. *The Foreign Aid Programs of the Soviet Bloc and Communist China.* New York: Walker, 1967.

Namir, Mordecai. *Shlihoot b'Moskva.* Tel Aviv: Am Oved, 1971.

Nielsen, Waldemar A. *The Great Powers and Africa.* New York: Praeger, 1969.

Novick, Nimrod. *Between Two Yemens: Regional Dynamics and Superpower Conduct in Riyadh's "Backyard."* Tel Aviv: Center for Strategic Studies, paper No. 11, 1980.

Nukhovich, E. S. *Ekonomicheskoe sotrudnichestvo i manevry antikommunistov.* Moscow: Mezhdunarodnye Otnosheniia, 1969.

Nutting, Anthony. *Nasser.* New York: Dutton, 1972.

O'Neil, Bard E. *Armed Struggle in Palestine.* Boulder, Colorado: Westview Press, 1978.

Ottaway, David, and Marina Ottaway. *Algeria: The Politics of a Socialist Revolution.* Berkeley: University of California Press, 1970.

Pennar, Jaan. *The USSR and the Arabs: The Ideological Dimension.* New York: Crane Russak, 1973.

The Persian Gulf, 1975: The Continuing Debate on Arms Sales. Hearings before the Special Subcommittee on Investigations of the Committee on International Relations, House of Representatives. Washington, D.C.: U.S. Government Printing Office, 1976.

Polk, William. *The United States and the Arab World.* 3d rev. ed. Cambridge, Mass.: Harvard University Press, 1975.

Ponomaryov, B., et al. *History of Soviet Foreign Policy 1917-1945.* Moscow: Progress Publishers, 1969.

Potskhveriia, B. M., and E. A. Orlov, eds. *Mezhdunarodnye otnosheniia na blizhnem i srednem vostoke posle vtoroi mirovoi voiny.* Moscow: Nauka, 1974.

Pranger, Robert J. *American Policy for Peace in the Middle East 1969-1971.* Washington, D.C.: American Enterprise Institute, 1971.

Primakov, E. M. *Anatomiia Blizhnevostochnogo Konfliicta.* Moscow: Mysl', 1978.

Quandt, William B. *Decade of Decisions: American Policy toward the Arab-Israeli Conflict 1967-1976.* Berkeley: University of California Press, 1977.

———, Fuad Jabbar, and Ann Lesch. *The Politics of Palestinian Nationalism.* Berkeley: University of California Press, 1973.

Ra'anan, Uri. *The USSR Arms the Third World.* Cambridge, Mass.: M.I.T. Press, 1969.

Rabinowich, Itamar. *Syria under the Ba'ath 1963-1966.* Jerusalem: Israel Universities Press, 1972.

Ramazani, Rouhollah K. *Iran's Foreign Policy 1941-1973.* Charlottesville: University Press of Virginia, 1975.

Ro'i, Yaacov, and Ilana Dimant-Kass. *The Soviet Military Involvement in Egypt, January 1970-July 1972.* Soviet and East European Research Center Research Paper no. 6. Jerusalem: Hebrew University, 1974.

Ro'i, Yaacov, ed. *The Limits to Power: Soviet Policy in the Middle East.* London: Croom Helm, 1979.

Romaniecki, Leon. *The Arab Terrorists in the Middle East and the Soviet Union.* Soviet and East European Research Center Paper no. 4. Jerusalem: Hebrew University, 1973.

Rubin, Barry. *Paved with Good Intentions: The American Experience and Iran.* New York: Oxford, 1970.

Rubinstein, Alvin Z. *Red Star on the Nile: The Soviet-Egyptian Influence Relationship since the June War.* Princeton: Princeton University Press, 1977.

———, ed. *Soviet and Chinese Influence in the Third World.* New York: Praeger, 1975.

Sachar, Howard M. *Europe Leaves the Middle East 1936-1954.* New York: Alfred A. Knopf, 1972.

Safran, Nadav. *From War to War.* New York: Pegasus, 1969.

Saikal, Amin. *The Rise and Fall of the Shah.* Princeton: Princeton University Press, 1980.

Sakharov, Vladimir. *High Treason.* New York: Putnam, 1980.

Seale, Patrick. *The Struggle for Syria.* London: Oxford University Press, 1965.

Semin, N. S. *Strany SEV i Afrika.* Moscow: Mezhdunarodnye Otnosheniia, 1968.

Sevortian, R. E. *Armiia v politicheskom rezhime stran sovremennogo vostoka.* Moscow: Nauka, 1973.

Shafir, Michael. *Rumanian Policy in the Middle East 1967-1972.* Soviet and East European Research Center Paper no. 7. Jerusalem: Hebrew University, 1974.

Shaked, Haim, and Itamar Rabinowitch, eds. *The Middle East and the United States.* New Brunswick: Transaction Books, 1981.

Shakhbazian, G. S. *Gosudarstvennyi sektor v ekonomike Iraka*. Moscow: Nauka, 1974.

Sharabi, Hisham. *Palestine and Israel*. New York: Pegasus, 1969.

Sheehan, Edward R. F. *The Arabs, Israelis and Kissinger: A Secret History of American Diplomacy in the Middle East*. New York: Reader's Digest Press, 1976.

Sheldon, Della, ed. *Dimensions of Detente*. New York: Praeger, 1978.

Sherbiny, Naiem, and Mark Tessler, eds. *Arab Oil: Impact on the Arab Countries and Global Implications*. New York: Praeger, 1976.

Shiff, Zeev, and Raphael Rothstein. *Fedayeen*. New York: David McKay, 1972.

Singer, Marshall R. *Weak States in a World of Powers*. New York: Free Press, 1972.

Smirnov, S. R., ed. *A History of Africa 1918-1967*. Moscow: Nauka, 1968.

Smolansky, Oles M. *The Soviet Union and the Arab East under Khrushchev*. Lewisburg, Pa.: Bucknell University Press, 1974.

Spechler, Dina. *Internal Influences on Soviet Foreign Policy: Elite Opinion and the Middle East*. Soviet and East European Research Center Paper no. 18. Jerusalem: Hebrew University, 1976.

Spector, Ivan. *The Soviet Union and the Muslim World*. Seattle: University of Washington Press, 1956.

Stephens, Robert. *Nasser: A Political Biography*. New York: Simon and Schuster, 1971.

Stookey, Robert W. *Yemen: The Politics of the Yemen Arab Republic*. Boulder, Colo.: Westview Press, 1978.

Talbott, Strobe, ed. *Khrushchev Remembers*. Boston: Little, Brown, 1970.

Trevelyan, Humphrey. *The Middle East in Revolution*. Boston: Gambit, 1970.

Ulam, Adam. *Expansion and Coexistence: A History of Soviet Foreign Policy 1917-1967*. New York: Praeger, 1968.

Ulianovsky, R. *Sotsialism i osvobodivshikhsia strany*. Moscow: Nauka, 1972.

Ushakova, N. A. *Arabskaia respublica Egipet*. Moscow: Nauka, 1974.

Valkova, L. V. *Saudovskaia Aravia v Mezhdunarodnykh Otnosheniiakh*. Moscow: Nauka, 1979.

Weizman, Ezer. *The Battle for Peace*. New York: Bantam Books, 1981.

Whetten, Lawrence L. *The Canal War: Four Power Conflict in the Middle East*. Cambridge, Mass.: M.I.T. Press, 1974.

Wolfe, Thomas W. *Soviet Power and Europe*. Baltimore: Johns Hopkins Press, 1970.

World Communism 1967-1969: Soviet Efforts to Re-Establish Control. Washington, D.C.: U.S. Government Printing Office, 1971.

Yaari, Ehud. *Fatah*. Tel Aviv: Levin-Epstein, 1970.

Yodfat, Aryeh. *Arab Politics in the Soviet Mirror*. Jerusalem: Israel Universities Press, 1973.

Zabih, Sepehr. *The Communist Movement in Iran*. Berkeley: University of California Press, 1966.

Zhurkin, V. V., and E. Primakov, eds. *Mezhdunarodnye konflikty*. Moscow: Mezhdunarodnye Otnosheniia, 1972.

ARTICLES

Adie, W. A. C. "Peking's Revised Line." *Problems of Communism* 21, no. 5 (September-October 1972): 54-68.

Agaryshev, A. "Beirut: Days of Trial." *New Times* (Moscow), no. 51 (1975): 24-25.

Akopian, G. "Ob antiimperialisticheskoi napravlennosti natsionalizma razvivaiushchikhsia stran." *Mirovaia ekonomika i mezhdunarodnye otnosheniia*, no. 9 (September 1975): 77-87.

Albright, David E. "Soviet Policy in Africa." *Problems of Communism* 27, no. 1 (January-February 1978): 20-39.

Alexandrov, V. "Dynamic Progress." *New Times* (Moscow), no. 42 (1976): 14-15.

Alov, Oleg. "Wanted: A Genuine Mid-East Settlement." *New Times* (Moscow), no. 14 (1975): 8-9.

——. "The Settlement Issue." *New Times* (Moscow), no. 12 (1977): 4-5.

Andreasian, Ruben. "Disagreement in OPEC." *New Times* (Moscow), no. 35 (1981): 13.

Andronov, Iona. "The Change-over in the White House." *New Times* (Moscow), no. 33 (1974): 6-7.

Apalin, G. "Peking Provocations." *New Times* (Moscow), nos. 45-46 (1973): 28-30.

Ashhab, Naim. "To Overcome the Crisis of the Palestine Resistance Movement." *World Marxist Review* 15, no. 5 (May 1972): 71-78.

——. "The Balance of World Forces and the Middle East Crisis." *World Marxist Review* 19, no. 3 (March 1976): 116-23.

Bakdash, Khalid. "International Policy and the National Struggle of the Communists." *World Marxist Review* 18, no. 10 (October 1975): 10-22.

Barnds, William. "China and America: Limited Partners in the Indian Subcontinent." In *Sino-American Detente and Its Policy Implications*, edited by Gene T. Hsiao, pp. 226-48. New York: Praeger, 1974.

Bechtold, Peter K. "New Attempts at Arab Cooperation: The Federation of Arab Republics 1971-?" *Middle East Journal* 27, no. 2 (Spring 1973): 152-72.

Becker, Abraham S. "Oil and the Persian Gulf." In *The USSR and the Middle East*, edited by Michael Confino and Shimon Shamir, pp. 173-214. Jerusalem: Israel Universities Press, 1973.

Beliaev, I. P. "Ssha i blizhnevostochnyi krizis." *Ssha*, no. 3 (March 1976): 16-27.

Bennigsen, Alexandre. "Soviet Muslims and the World of Islam." *Problems of Communism* 29, no. 2 (March/April 1980): 38-51.

Bronin, I. "Arabskaia neft—Ssha—zapadnaia Evropa." *Mirovaia ekonomika i mezhdunarodnye otnosheniia*, no. 2 (February 1972): 31-42.

Bukharov, Victor. "Palestinian National Council Session." *New Times* (Moscow), no. 25 (1974): 12-13.

Campbell, John. "The Soviet Union in the Middle East." *Middle East Journal* 32, no. 1 (Winter 1978): 1-12.

Campbell, Robert W. "Some Issues in Soviet Energy Policy for the Seventies." *Middle East Information Series*, nos. 26-27 (Spring-Summer 1974): 92-100.

Carlson, Sevinc. "China, the Soviet Union and the Middle East." *New Middle East* (London), no. 27 (December 1970): 32-40.

Cherniavina, V. "Energeticheskie problemy stran EEC." *Mirovaia ekonomika i mezhdunarodnye otnosheniia*, no. 4 (April 1974): 56-65.

Cooley, John. "Moscow Faces a Palestinian Dilemma." *Mid East* 11, no. 3 (June 1970): 32-35.

——. "The Shifting Sands of Arab Communism." *Problems of Communism* 24, no. 2 (March-April 1975): 22-42.

Dann, Uriel. "The Communist Movement in Iraq since 1963." In *The USSR and the Middle East*, edited by Michael Confino and Shimon Shamir, pp. 377-98. Jerusalem: Israel Universities Press, 1972.

Dawisha, Adeed I. "Iraq: The West's Opportunity." *Foreign Policy* 41 (Winter 1980/81): 134-53.

Dawisha, Karen. "Moscow's Moves in the Direction of the Gulf—So Near and Yet so Far." *Journal of International Affairs* 34, no. 2: 219-33.

Demchenko, Pavel. "Arab Oil for the Arabs." *New Times* (Moscow), no. 25 (1972): 10-11.

Field, Michael. "Iraq—Growing Realism among the Revolutionaries." *New Middle East* (London), no. 29 (February 1971): 27-29.

"Foundation of Soviet-Egyptian Relations." *New Times* (Moscow), no. 22 (1974): 17.

Freedman, Robert O. "The Partition of Palestine: Conflicting Nationalism and Power Politics." In *Partition: Peril to World Peace,* edited by Thomas Hachey, pp. 175-212. New York: Rand McNally, 1972.

———. "Soviet Dilemmas in the Middle East." *Problems of Communism* 23, no. 3 (May-June 1972): 71-73.

———. "The Soviet Union and the Communist Parties of the Arab World: An Uncertain Relationship." In *Soviet Economic and Political Relations with the Developing World*, edited by Roger E. Kanet and Donna Bahry, pp. 100-34. New York: Praeger, 1975.

———. "The Lingering Impact of the Soviet System on the Soviet Jewish Immigrant to the United States." In *The Soviet Jewish Emigre*, edited by Jerome M. Gilison, pp. 32-58. Baltimore: Baltimore Hebrew College, 1977.

———. "Detente and U.S. Soviet Relations in the Nixon Years." In *Dimensions of Detente*, edited by Della W. Sheldon. New York: Praeger, 1978, pp. 84-121.

———. "The Soviet Image of the Carter Administration's Policy Toward the USSR: From the Inauguration to the Invasion of Afghanistan." *Korea and World Affairs* 4, no. 2 (Summer 1980): 224-67.

———. "Soviet Policy Toward the Middle East Since the Invasion of Afghanistan." *Journal of International Affairs* 34, no. 2 (Fall/Winter 1980-1981): 283-310.

———. "Moscow and the Gulf in 1981." *Middle East Insight* 2, no. 2, (1981): 13-20.

———. "Soviet Policy Toward Ba'athist Iraq." In *The Soviet Union in the Third World*, edited by Robert H. Donaldson. Boulder, Colorado: Westview Press, 1981, pp. 161-91.

———. "Soviet Policy Toward Syria Since Camp David." *Middle East Review* (Fall/Winter 1981-82): 31-42.

Gal'perin, G. "Efiopiia: Protsess obnovleniia." *Mirovaia ekonomika i mezhdunarodnye otnosheniia*, no. 1 (January 1975): 118-24.

Garfinkle, Adam M. "Negotiating by Proxy: Jordanian Foreign Policy and U.S. Options in the Middle East." *Orbis* 4, no. 24 (Winter 1981): 847-80.

Gaspard, J. "Damascus after the Coup." *New Middle East* (London), no. 28 (January 1971): 9-11.

Gasteyger, Kurt. "Moscow and the Mediterranean." *Foreign Affairs* 46, no. 4 (July 1968): 676-87.

Gavrilov, I. "Arab Press on the Middle East Situation." *New Times* (Moscow), no. 36 (1972): 8-9.

Ginsburgs, George. "Moscow's Reaction to Nixon's Jaunt to Peking." In *Sino-American Detente and Its Policy Implications*, edited by Gene T. Hsiao, pp. 137-59. New York: Praeger, 1974.

Golan, Galia. "Syria and the Soviet Union Since the Yom Kippur War." *Orbis* 21, no. 4 (Winter 1978): 777-801.

Gvozdev, Yuri. "Democratic Yemen: Problems and Aims," *New Times* (Moscow), no. 48 (1972): 14-15.

Hardt, John P. "West Siberia: The Quest for Energy." *Problems of Communism* 22, no. 3 (May-June 1973): 25-36.

Harris, Mervyn. "From Nile to Euphrates: The Evolution of a Myth." *New Middle East* (London), nos. 42-43 (March-April 1972): 46-48.

Harrison, Selig. "Dateline Afghanistan: Exit Through Finland." *Foreign Policy*, no. 41, pp. 163-87.

Henze, Paul B. "Communism and Ethiopia." *Problems of Communism* 30, no. 3 (May-June 1981): 55-74.

Hottinger, Arnold. "Arab Communism at a Low Ebb." *Problems of Communism* 30, no. 4 (July-August 1981): 17-32.

Iashin, B. D. "O nekotorykh amerikanskikh podkhodakh k problemam mira i bezopasnosti v Indiiskom Okeane." *Ssha*, no. 1 (January 1978): 49-58.

Ibrahim, Baqir. "The Masses, the Party and the National Front." *World Marxist Review* 19, no. 8 (August 1976): 49-56.

Ignatov, Alexander. "Iraq Today." *New Times* (Moscow), no. 21 (1974): 22-25.

———. "This Spring in Damascus." *New Times* (Moscow), no. 24 (1974): 26-28.

"Iraq: Left out in the Cold." *The Middle East* (London), no. 26 (December 1976): 71-72.

Ismail, Abdel Fattah. "On Socialist Orientation." *World Marxist Review* 20, no. 10 (October 1977): 36-41.

Ivanov, A. "Soviet Imports from Developing Countries." *Foreign Trade* (Moscow), no. 9 (September 1974): 38-43.

Kaisi, Imad. "Lebanon: Once Again 'No Victor and No Vanquished'." *The Middle East* (London), no. 26 (December 1976): 16-20.

Katin, V. "Tel-Aviv's Atrocious Crime." *New Times* (Moscow), no. 9 (1973): 20-21.

Kerr, Malcolm. "The Middle East and China." In *Policies toward China: Views from Six Continents*, edited by A. M. Halpern, pp. 437-56. New York: McGraw-Hill, 1965.

———. "The Convenient Marriage of Egypt and Libya." *New Middle East* (London), no. 48 (September 1972): 4-7.

Khalilzad, Zalmay. "Soviet Occupied Afghanistan." *Problems of Communism* 29, no. 6 (November-December 1980): 23-40.

Kimhe, Jon. "The Soviet-Arab Scenario." *Midstream* 30, no. 10 (December 1973): 9-22.

Kislov, A. K. "Nasushchnye problemy blizhnevostochnogo uregulirovaniia." *Ssha*, no. 7 (July 1977): 22-33.

——. "Vashington i Irako-Iranskii Konflikt." *Ssha* no. 1 (1981): 51-56.

Kiva, A. "Sotsialisticheskaia orientatsiia: Nekotorie problemy teorii i praktiki." *Mirovaia ekonomika i mezhdunarodnye otnosheniia*, no. 10 (October 1976): 19-32.

Klekovsky, R. "Fruitful Co-operation between CMEA States and the Arab Countries." *Foreign Trade* (Moscow), no. 8 (August 1974): 16-19.

Klimov, Alexander. "Ancient Syria Today." *New Times* (Moscow), no. 16 (1976): 24-25.

Kornilov, Y. "Meetings with the Fedayeen." *New Times* (Moscow), no. 42 (1972): 23-25.

Krutikin, Mikhail. "Iran: Uphill Road of Change." *New Times* (Moscow), no. 19 (1979): 12-13.

Kudryavtsev, Viktor. "The Political Consolidation in the UAR." *New Times* (Moscow), no. 43 (1970): 6-7.

——. "On the Arab Diplomatic Front." *New Times* (Moscow), no. 4 (1973): 12-13.

——. "Ssha i palestinskaia problema." *Ssha*, no. 2 (February 1975): 69-73.

Landau, Jacob. "Lebanon in Some Soviet Publications." *Middle Eastern Studies* 12, no. 2 (May 1976): 209-12.

Laqueur, Walter, and Edward Luttwak. "Kissinger and the Yom Kippur War." *Commentary* 58, no. 3 (September 1974): 33-40.

Larin, Vladimir. "Ethiopia: Who Gains from the Tension?" *New Times* (Moscow), no. 19 (1977): 10.

Legum, Colin. "The USSR and Africa: The African Environment." *Problems of Communism* 27, no. 1 (January-February 1978): 1-19.

Levesque, Jacques. "L'Intervention Sovietique en Afghanistan." *L"URSS dans les relations internationales*. Bordeaux: University of Bordeaux (forthcoming).

Levgold, Robert. "The Soviet Union's Changing View of Sub-Saharan Africa." In *Soviet Policy in Developing Countries*, edited by W. Raymond Duncan, pp. 62-82. Waltham, Mass.: Ginn-Blaisdell, 1970.

Levy, Avigdor. "The Syrian Communists and the Ba'ath Power Struggle 1966-1970." In *The USSR and the Middle East*, edited by Michael Confino and Shimon Shamir, pp. 395-417. Jerusalem: Israel Universities Press, 1973.

Levy, Walter J. "World Oil Cooperation or International Chaos." *Foreign Affairs* 52, no. 4 (July 1974): 690-713.

Lowenthal, Richard. "Russia, the One-Party System and the Third World." *Survey*, no. 58 (January 1966): 43-58.

Maddy-Weitzman, Bruce. "The Fragmentation of Arab Politics: Inter-Arab Affairs Since the Afghanistan Invasion." *Orbis* 25, no. 2 (Summer 1981): 389-407.

Mansfield, Peter. "After the Purge." *New Middle East* (London), no. 33 (June 1971): 12-15.

"Marching Together: The Role of the Communists in Building a Broad Alliance of Democratic Forces." *World Marxist Review* 16, no. 2 (February 1973): 111-18.

Medvenko, Leonid. "Islam and Liberation Revolutions." *New Times* (Moscow), 43 (1979): 18-23.

———. "Islam: Two Trends," *New Times* (Moscow), 13 (1980): 23-25.

Medzini, R. "China and the Palestinians." *New Middle East* (London), no. 32 (May 1971): 34-40.

Mezentsev, Pavel. "USA-Iran: Threats and Blackmail." *New Times* (Moscow), 38 (1980); 10-11.

Mirsky, Georgi. "Israeli Aggression and Arab Unity." *New Times* (Moscow), no. 28 (1967): 6-8.

———. "The Middle East: New Factors." *New Times* (Moscow), no. 48 (1973): 18-19.

———. "The Path of the Egyptian Revolution." *New Times* (Moscow), no. 30 (1972): 21-24.

Mishlawi, Tewfik. "Crackdown on Communists in Iraq." *The Middle East*, no. 45 (July 1978): 29-30.

Mohammed, Aziz. "The Socialist Community Is Our Dependable Ally." *World Marxist Review* 18, no. 1 (January 1975): 53-61.

———. "Tasks of the Revolutionary Forces of Iraq." *World Marxist Review* 19, no. 9 (September 1976): 10-18.

Mortimer, Robert. "Algeria's New Sultan." *Current History* (December 1981): 418-21, 433-34.

Mosley, Phillip. "The Kremlin and the Third World." *Foreign Affairs* 46, no. 1 (October 1967): 64-77.

Mroue, Kerim. "Use the Opportunities of the New Situation in the Middle East." *World Marxist Review* 17, no. 3 (March 1974): 90-97.

Naumov, Pavel. "In Egypt Today." *New Times* (Moscow), no. 12 (1974): 24-26.

"New Stage in the National Liberation Movement." *World Marxist Review* 15, no. 11 (November 1972): 58-82.

Newsom, David. "America Engulfed." *Foreign Policy*, no. 43 (Summer 1981): 17-32.

Nikolayev, V. "Trying Days for Lebanon." *New Times* (Moscow), no. 16 (1976): 10-11.

Ojha, Ishwer C. "The Kremlin and Third World Leadership: Closing the Circle?" In *Soviet Policy toward Developing Countries*, edited by W. Raymond Duncan, pp. 9-28. Waltham, Mass.: Ginn-Blaisdell, 1970.

Osipov, A. I. "Evoliutsiia amerikano-egipetskikh ekonomicheskikh sviazei." *Ssha*, no. 8 (August 1977): 33-45.

Pennar, Jaan. "The Arabs, Marxism and Moscow: A Historical Survey." *Middle East Journal* 22, no. 3 (September 1968): 433-47.

Perlmutter, Amos. "Big Power Games, Small Power Wars." *Transaction* 7, nos. 9-10 (July-August 1970): 79-83.

Petrov, R. "Steps toward Arab Unity." *New Times* (Moscow), no. 35 (1971): 20-22.

"PLO Mends Fences with Egypt." *The Middle East* (London), no. 20 (June 1976): 86-87.

Ploss, Sidney. "Politics in the Kremlin." *Problems of Communism* 19, no. 3 (May-June 1970): 1-14.

Poliakov, N. "Put' K. Bezopasnosti v Indiiskom Okeane i Persidskom Zalive." *Mirovaia ekonomika i mezhdunarodnye otnosheniia*, no. 1, 1981, pp. 62-73.

"Political Shifts in the Middle East: Roots, Factors, Trends." *World Marxist Review* (February 1980): 58-64.

Ponamarev, Boris. "Under the Banner of Marxism-Leninism and Proletarian Internationalism: The 24th Congress of the CPSU." *World Marxist Review* 14, no. 6 (June 1971): 3-19.

Portniagin, A. D. "Politika Ssha v zone persidskogo zaliva." *Ssha*, no. 6 (June 1977): 17-26.

Potemkin, Iu. "Alzhir: Problemy dal'neishego sotsial'no-ekonomichekogo progressa." *Mirovaia ekonomika i mezhdunarodnye otnosheniia*, no. 9 (September 1976): 92-98.

Potomov, Y. "A Just Peace for the Middle East." *New Times* (Moscow), no. 24 (1972): 15-16.

——. "Middle East Alliance against Progress." *New Times* (Moscow), no. 34 (1972): 4-5.

——. "The Egypt-Libya Merger Project." *New Times* (Moscow), no. 36 (1973): 10-11.

——. "Middle East Settlement: Urgent Task." *New Times* (Moscow), no. 31 (1974): 21-22.

——. "The Lebanon Crisis: Who Stands to Gain." *New Times* (Moscow), no. 26 (1976): 8-9.

Povey, Terry. "Iran's Autonomy Seekers." *The Middle East* (August 1979): 41-43.

Price, David Lynn. "Moscow and the Persian Gulf." *Problems of Communism* 28, no. 2 (March-April 1979): 1-13.

Prignetov, Alexei. "Lebanon: First Steps toward Settlement." *New Times* (Moscow), no. 44 (1976): 14-15.

Primakov, Y. "Energeticheskii krizis v kapitalisticheskikh stranakh." *Mirovaia ekonomika i mezhdunarodnye otnosheniia*, no. 2 (February 1974): 65-72.

———. "Pruzhiny blizhnevostochnoi politiki Ssha." *Ssha*, no. 11 (November 1976): 3-15.

———. "Sbalansirovanii kurs' na Blizhnem Vostoke ili staraia politika inimi sredstvami." *Mirovaia ekonomika i mezhdunarodnye otnosheniia*, no. 12 (December 1976): 33-51, and no. 1 (January 1977): 51-60.

Quandt, William. "Riadh Between the Superpowers." *Foreign Policy*, no. 44 (Fall 1981): 37-56.

———. "Saudi Arabian Security and Foreign Policy in the 1980s." *Middle East Insight* 2, no. 2, pp. 25-30.

Ra'anan, Uri. "Soviet Policy in the Middle East 1960-1973." *Midstream* 30, no. 10 (December 1973): 23-45.

Rachkov, B. V. "Energeticheskie problemy Soedinenykh Shtatov." *Ssha*, no. 3 (March (1974): 29-43.

Ramazani, R. K. "Iran and the Arab-Israeli Conflict." *World Politics and the Arab-Israeli Conflict*, edited by Robert O. Freedman. New York: Pergamon, 1979), pp. 129-46..

———. "America and the Gulf—Beyond Security and Peace." *Middle East Insight* 2, no. 2, pp. 2-9.

Rand, Robert. "Mubarak on the USSR." Radio Liberty Report no. 462/81, November 17, 1981.

———. "The USSR and the Crisis over Syrian Missiles in Lebanon: An Analysis and Chronological Survey." Radio Liberty Report no. 227/81, June 3, 1981.

Reed, Stanley. "Dateline Syria: Fin De Regime?" *Foreign Policy* no. 39 (Summer 1980): 176-90.

Remnek, Richard. "Soviet Policy in the Horn of Africa: The Decision to Intervene." In *The Soviet Union and the Third World: Successes and Failures*, edited by Robert H. Donaldson, pp. 125-49. Boulder Colorado: Westview Press, 1981.

Repin, Anatoly. "Jordan Today." *New Times* (Moscow), no. 25 (1976): 12-13.

Rouleau, Eric. "Khomeini's Iran." *Foreign Affairs* 59, no. 1 (Fall 1980): 1-20.

Rumyanstev, V. "Syria on the Alert." *New Times* (Moscow), no. 40 (1972): 8-9.

Safran, Nadav. "The Soviet-Egyptian Treaty." *New Middle East* (London), no. 34 (July 1971): 10-13.

Schreiber, J. "Growth of Peace Sentiment in Israel." *New Times* (Moscow), no. 26 (1975): 10-11.

Shaked, Haim, Esther Souery, and Gabriel Warburg. "The Communist Party in the Sudan 1946-1971." In *The USSR and the Middle East*, edited by Michael Confino and Shimon Shamir, pp. 335-74. Jerusalem: Israel Universities Press, 1973.

Shamir, Shimon. "The Marxists in Egypt: The 'Licensed Infiltration' Doctrine in Practice." In *The USSR and the Middle East*, edited by Michael Confino and Shimon Shamir, pp. 293-319. Jerusalem: Israel Universities Press, 1973.

Shaoui, Nicholas. "The Middle East Crisis and the Arab Liberation Movement." *World Marxist Review* 14, no. 9 (September 1971): 28-34.

———. "The Anti-Imperialist Front and the Arab Liberation Movement." *World Marxist Review* 17, no. 8 (August 1974): 30-37.

Shatilov, A. B. "Bezopasnoct' Indiiskogo Okeana: Dva podkhoda." *Ssha*, no. 1 (January 1977): 54-61.

Shmarov, Vladimir. "The Baghdad Dialogue." *New Times* (Moscow), no. 5 (1974): 10-11.

———. "Turkey: Control over Bases." *New Times* (Moscow), no. 32 (1975): 12-13.

Shmelyov, Georgi. "Solidarity the Keynote." *New Times* (Moscow), no. 28 (1974): 10.

Shumilin, Boris. "Zionist Fabrications and the Reality." *New Times* (Moscow), no. 16 (1972): 12-13.

Singer, J. David. "International Influence: A Formal Model." In *International Politics and Foreign Policy*, edited by James N. Rosenau, pp. 380-91. New York: Macmillan, 1969.

Skuratov, L. "Iran: Where the Threads of the Plot Lead." *New Times* (Moscow), no. 30 (1980): 8.

Smirnov, V., and I. Matyukhin. "USSR and the Arab East: Economic Contacts." *International Affairs* (Moscow), no. 9 (September 1972): 83-87.

Spichkin, V. "Energeticheskii kriziz v Ssha." *Mirovaia ekonomika i mezhdunarodnye otnosheniia*, no. 3 (March 1974): 85-98.

Spiegel, Stephen. "The United States and the Middle East Crisis." *Middle East Review* 9, no. 3 (Spring 1977): 25-33.

St.John, Ronald Bruce. "Libya's Foreign and Domestic Policies." *Current History* (December 1981): 426-29, 434-35.

Stepanov, A. "Hour of Trial for the Palestinians." *New Times* (Moscow), no. 42 (1978): 6-7.

———. "Syria: On Guard." *New Times* (Moscow), no. 16 (1978): 14-15.

———. "Taking Up a Point." *New Times* (Moscow), no. 17 (1981): 31.

"Sudan: Invasion or Coup?" *The Middle East* (London), no. 22 (August 1976): 92-94.

Sylvester, Anthony. "Mohammed vs. Lenin in Revolutionary Sudan." *New Middle East* (London), no. 34 (July 1971): 26-28.

Tahir-Kheli, Shirin. "The Soviet Union in Afghanistan: Benefits and Costs." In *The Soviet Union in the Third World: Successes and Failures*, edited by Robert H. Donaldson, pp. 217-31. Boulder, Colorado: Westview Press, 1981.

Thompson, W. Scott. "Parameters on Soviet Policy in Africa: Personal Diplomacy and Economic Interests in Ghana." In *Soviet Policy in Developing Countries*, edited by W. Raymond Duncan, pp. 83-106. Waltham, Mass.: Ginn-Blaisdell, 1970.

Tsaplin, Y. "USSR-Somalia—Road of Friendship." *New Times* (Moscow), no. 28 (1977): 14-15.

——. "Miniblocks in Africa." *New Times* (Moscow), no. 22 (1978): 20-21.

Ulianovsky, R. "Nekotorie voprosy nikapitalisticheskogo razvitiia." *Kommunist*, no. 4 (1971): 103-12.

——. "Marxist and Non-Marxist Socialism." *World Marxist Review* 14, no. 9 (September 1971): 119-27.

——. "O edinom anti-imperialisticheskom fronte progressivnikh sil v osvobodivshikhsia stranakh." *Mirovaia ekonomika i mezhdunarodnye otnosheniia*, no. 9 (September 1972): 76-86.

Usvatov, Alexander. "Iran's Troubled August." *New Times* (Moscow), no. 36 (1979): 10-11.

VanHollen, Christopher. "Don't Engulf the Gulf." *Foreign Affairs* (Summer 1981): 1064-78.

Vatikiotis, P. J. "Egypt's Politics of Conspiracy." *Survey* 18, no. 2 (Spring 1972): 83-99.

——. "Two Years after Nasser: The Chance of a New Beginning." *New Middle East* (London), no. 48 (September 1972): 7-9.

Volsky, Dmitry. "Changes in the Sudan." *New Times* (Moscow), no. 30 (1971): 10-11.

——. "A Frank Talk with Some Arab Colleagues." *New Times* (Moscow), no. 37 (1972): 4-5.

——. "The Middle East Situation." *New Times* (Moscow), no. 39 (1972): 6-7.

——. "King Faisal's Holy War." *New Times* (Moscow), no. 5 (1973): 26-27.

——. "The Beirut Crime." *New Times* (Moscow), no. 16 (1973): 12-13.

——. "New Opportunities and Old Obstacles." *New Times* (Moscow), no. 32 (1973): 14-15.

——. "Soviet-American Relations and the Third World." *New Times* (Moscow), no. 36 (1973): 4-6.

——. "Step Toward Settlement." *New Times* (Moscow), no. 23 (1974): 8-9.

——. "Arab East: Miracles and Realities." *New Times* (Moscow), no. 24 (1974): 12-13.

——. "Behind the Conflicts." *New Times* (Moscow), no. 34 (1977): 8-9.

——. "Blackmailing the Arabs." *New Times* (Moscow), no. 2 (1975): 10-11.

——. "Security or Confrontation." *New Times* (Moscow), no. 2 (1976): 8-9.

——. "The Lebanese Drama and the Middle East." *New Times* (Moscow), no. 29 (1976): 10-11.

——. "Flop or Maneuver." *New Times* (Moscow), no. 52 (1978): 16-17.

——. "Vicious Circle." *New Times* (Moscow), no. 5 (1979): 8-9.

——. "The Target: Afghanistan's Revolution." *New Times* (Moscow), no. 24 (1979): 12-13.

——. "Turban or Helmet." *New Times* (Moscow), no. 20 (1980): 18-20.

——. "Iran: Sidetracking Attention." *New Times* (Moscow), no. 35 (1980): 20-21.

——. "May 1981 is not June 1967." *New Times* (Moscow), no. 21 (1981): 5-6.

——. "There is Light at the End of the Tunnel." *New Times* (Moscow), no. 49 (1981): 12-13.

——, and A. Usvatov. "Israeli Expansionists Miscalculate." *New Times* (Moscow), no. 42 (1973): 10-11.

Whetten, Lawrence J. "Changing Soviet Attitudes toward Arab Radical Movements." *New Middle East* (London), no. 18 (March 1970): 20-27.

Wright, Claudia. "Implications of the Iran-Iraq War." *Foreign Affairs* 59, no. 2 (Winter 1980/81): 275-303.

——. "Islamic Summit." *The Middle East* (March 1981): 6-10.

Yellon, R. A. "Shifts in Soviet Policies toward Developing Areas." In *Soviet Policy in Developing Countries*, edited by W. Raymond Duncan, pp. 225-86. Waltham, Mass.: Ginn-Blaisdell, 1970.

Yodfat, A. "Unpredictable Iraq Poses a Russian Problem." *New Middle East* (London), no.

——. "Moscow Reconsiders Fatah." *New Middle East* (London), no. 13 (December 1969): 15-18.

——. "The USSR and the Arab Communist Parties." *New Middle East* (London), no. 32 (May 1971): 29-33.

——. "Russia's Other Middle East Pasture—Iraq." *New Middle East* (London), no. 38 (November 1971): 26-29.

Yost, Charles. "The Arab-Israeli War: How It Began." *Foreign Affairs* 46, no. 2 (January 1968): 304-20.

Zakaria, Ibrahim. "The Struggle of the Sudanese Communists." *World Marxist Review* 20, no. 4 (April 1977): 55-62.

Zlatorunsky, Aleksei. "Libya and Its Problems." *New Times* (Moscow), nos. 18-19 (1974): 35-36.

PERIODICALS

Arab Report and Record, 1969-77.

Baltimore *Sun*, 1975-82.

Christian Science Monitor, 1969-82.

Current Digest of the Soviet Press, 1969-72.

Foreign Affairs, 1969-82.

Foreign Broadcast Information Service Daily Reports (USSR; Middle East and Africa; South Asia), 1969-82.

Foreign Policy, 1972-82.

Foreign Trade (Moscow), 1969-82.

International Affairs (Moscow), 1967-82.

Kommunist (Moscow), 1969-82.

Middle East (London), 1974-82.

Middle East Journal, 1964-82.

Middle East Review, 1973-82.

Mirovaia ekonomika i mezhdunarodnye otnosheniia (Moscow), 1969-82.

New Middle East (London), 1968-73.

New Times (Moscow), 1964-82.

New York *Times*, 1969-82.

Peking Review, 1969-82.

Pravda, 1969-82.

Problems of Communism, 1969-82.

Radio Liberty Reports, 1969-82.

Ssha, 1970-82.

Washington *Post*, 1970-82.

World Marxist Review, 1960-82.

INDEX

475

ABOUT THE AUTHOR

Robert Owen Freedman is Dean of the Peggy Meyerhoff Pearlstone School of Graduate Studies and Professor of Political Science at the Baltimore Hebrew College. He is the author of *Soviet Policy Toward the Middle East Since 1970* (New York: Praeger, 1975, 1978), (here in its third edition) and *Economic Warfare in the Communist Bloc: A Study of Soviet Economic Pressure Against Yugoslavia, Albania, and Communist China* (New York: Praeger, 1970). He is also editor of *World Politics and the Arab-Israeli Conflict* (New York: Pergamon, 1979). Dr. Freedman has written extensively on questions of Soviet foreign policy and Middle East politics and has served as a consultant to the State Department.

Dr. Freedman received his B.A. from the University of Pennsylvania and his M.A., Russian Institute Certificate, and Ph.D. from Columbia University. Prior to coming to serve as the Dean of Graduate Studies of the Baltimore Hebrew College, Dr. Freedman was Associate Professor of Political Science and Soviet and Middle East area specialist at Marquette University and Assistant Professor of Social Sciences at the United States Military Academy. Dr. Freedman also served as an infantry officer in the United States Army.